MOON

D0468683

SOUTHERN CALIFORNIA
Road Trips

IAN ANDERSON

CONTENTS

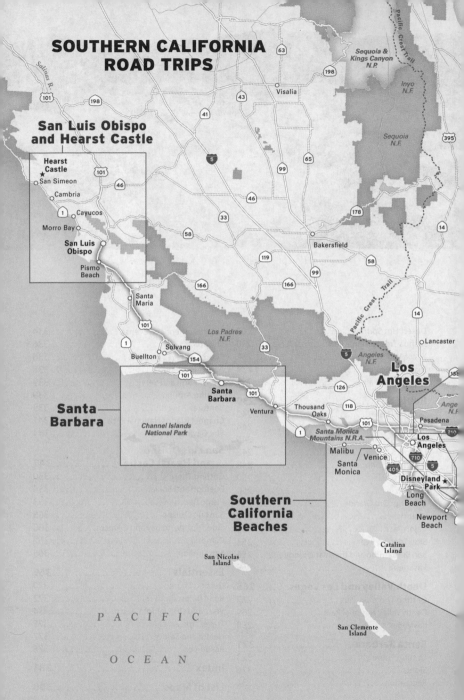

SOUTHERN CALIFORNIA ROAD TRIPS

San Luis Obispo and Hearst Castle

Hearst Castle
★
San Simeon
Cambria
Cayucos
Morro Bay
San Luis Obispo
Pismo Beach

Salinas R.
101
198
101
46
1
58

Santa Barbara

Solvang
Buellton
Santa Barbara
Ventura
101
154
1
101
1

Santa Maria
101
166
Los Padres N.F.
33

Channel Islands National Park

Southern California Beaches

San Nicolas Island

San Clemente Island

63
198
43
41
5
99
65
46
33
119
166
99
178
58
14
395

Visalia
Sequoia & Kings Canyon N.P.
Inyo N.F.
Sequoia N.F.
Pacific Crest Trail

Bakersfield

Pacific Crest Trail

14
Lancaster
Angeles N.F.
5
126
118
101
1
Los Angeles
Thousand Oaks
Santa Monica Mountains N.R.A.
Malibu
Venice
Santa Monica
405
Los Angeles
Pasadena
210
710
138
Ange N.F.
Disneyland Park ★
Long Beach
Newport Beach
Catalina Island

P A C I F I C

O C E A N

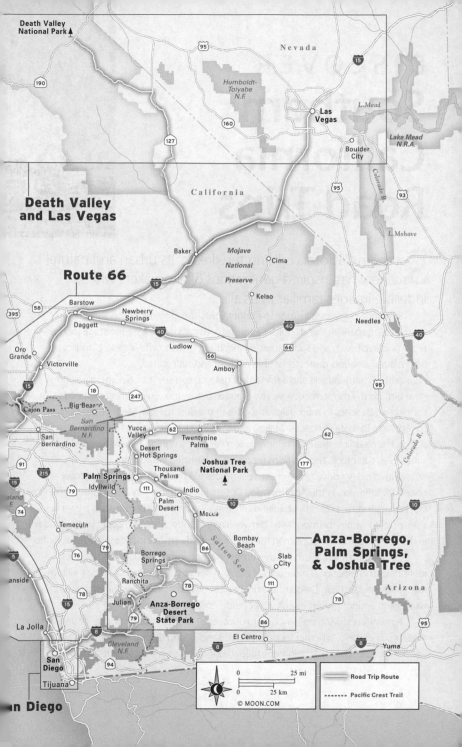

DISCOVER
Southern California Road Trips

Southern California is living the dream. Its urban and natural scenery has inspired generations of filmmakers whose indelible images familiar to us all.

Romantic cityscapes include the bright lights and glamour of the Sunset Strip. On the coast, sparkling sands border endless blue horizons that set the stage for the region's iconic beach and surf culture. Inland, the stark contrasts of desert landscapes hold natural wonders protected within national and state parks.

With a sturdy vehicle and a full tank of gas, you can see it all. Southern California gave birth to the modern freeway, and roads crisscross the region in every direction, connecting beaches to mountains and cities to the desert. From Mediterranean-inspired Santa Barbara to upscale Malibu and the left coast bastions of Santa Monica and Venice, the coastline stretches hundreds of miles past stunning beach towns where sunglasses, sun block, and flip flops represent a cherished way of life.

Within a day's drive of the coast, remote deserts beckon travelers to discover colorful wildflowers in the Anza-Borrego Desert, jumbled rocks in Joshua Tree, and a cracked asphalt that splits the badlands of Death Valley. Not to be outdone are ski resorts nestled within the mountains between these landscapes. You could start your day in the surf, ski down a mountain in the afternoon, and camp under desert skies at night.

Connecting it all are urban adventures ripe for exploration. The cosmopolitan nightlife and international museums of Los Angeles sit balanced against the thrilling rides of Disneyland. San Diego offers the perfect blend of beach and urban culture, while Palm Springs prefers its culture poolside, cocktail in hand.

A month of driving isn't enough to uncover all of these treasures, but we've all got to start somewhere. Whether lounging in the sand, hiking through desert canyons, or watching world-class entertainment, follow your dreams on this stellar road trip.

10 TOP EXPERIENCES

EXPERIENCES

1 **Hit the Beach:** For the prototypical SoCal experience, head for the surf and sun in beach towns stretching from Santa Barbara (page 332) to San Diego (page 136).

2 **Peek Behind the Silver Screen:** Hollywood offers a real-life backdrop to a century's worth of films (page 42).

3 **Experience Art:** Urban museums (the Getty Center, page 76) and found-art collections (Noah Purifoy, page 234) offer a broad range of beauty, from modern masterpieces to outsider art.

>>>

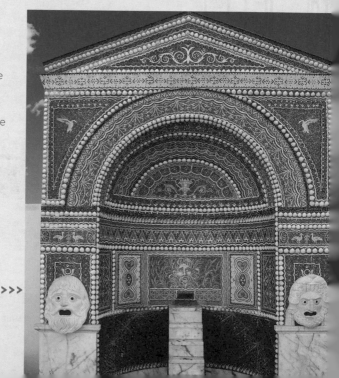

4 **Admire Wildflowers:** In spring, a "superbloom" of colorful wildflowers carpets the desert floors (page 171).

5 Thrill the Family: Iconic **theme parks** (page 56), world-famous **zoos** (page 133), and **historic ships** (page 86) invite play at any age.

>>>

6 Cruise Death Valley: The lowest point in North America is a high point for any road trip, with spectacular vistas mile after mile (page 276).

<<<

7 See Starry Skies: The Anza-Borrego Desert (page 169) and Death Valley (page 283) are both International Dark Sky Parks where nighttime skies reveal hidden nebulas and the Milky Way.

>>>

8 Marvel at Hearst Castle: Built to impress, this Spanish Revival palace is filled with art treasures, but it's the coastal view that's priceless (page 365).

<<<

9 Ski the Slopes: The ski resort town of Big Bear is within a three-hour drive of L.A.'s coastal beaches, meaning you can surf and ski in the same day (page 253).

>>>

10 Road-Trip Along Route 66: Get your kicks cruising the remaining stretches of the historic Mother Road, where Googie architecture (page 244), old-school diners (page 248), and roadside attractions beckon shutterbugs.

<<<

PLANNING YOUR TRIP

Where To Go

Los Angeles

Los Angeles has captured the world's imagination on film, and most visitors come in search of the people and places they've seen in movies and on TV, including **Beverly Hills, Hollywood,** and the **Sunset Strip.** More than stars on sidewalks, the City of Angels also has **world-class museums, performance spaces,** and culturally **diverse dining.**

Of course, the biggest draw (especially for parents) is iconic **Disneyland.** The entertainment complex promises to become even more popular with the **Star Wars: Galaxy's Edge** attraction.

Southern California Beaches

Southern California's greatest asset is its coastline. With 150 miles (242 km) of surf and sand, you could spend days driving the **Pacific Coast Highway** from beach town to beach town, creating your own endless summer. Gorgeous **Malibu** delivers miles of remote beaches, flanked by the pretty Santa Monica Mountains. A few miles south, **Santa Monica** lives up to the Hollywood image of the classic beach town. Less pretty but more gritty **Venice Beach** offers unparalleled people-watching farther south.

As CA-1 stretches south, the South Bay beach towns offer pretty incentives to navigate the coast in lieu of the inland freeways. Past the port city of Long Beach, the idyllic beaches of Orange County include the surf city of **Huntington Beach**, the bay town of **Newport Beach**, and the tony resort of **Laguna Beach**. CA-1 continues south to connect to I-5 toward San Diego, which has its own beautiful set of suburban

beach towns including **Carlsbad** (home of Legoland), **Encinitas,** and **La Jolla.**

San Diego

Southern California is loaded with beach towns, but **San Diego** is a bona-fide beach city, known for its sunshine, **craft beer,** and **Mexican cuisine**. The city's top attractions are the cultural hub of **Balboa Park** and the famous **Hotel del Coronado**, though many come for the animal attractions at **SeaWorld** and the **San Diego Zoo.** Across the border, the vibrant Mexican city of **Tijuana** provides a memorable day trip—bring your passport!

Anza Borrego, Palm Springs, and Joshua Tree

East of San Diego, the remote **Anza-Borrego Desert State Park** offers warm-weather hikes, excellent **stargazing,** and the fascinating **Galleta Meadows** sculpture garden. Anza-Borrego is also convenient as you make your way north past the **Salton Sea,** reborn as a **progressive arts haven.**

The preferred desert getaway for Los Angeles elite, **Palm Springs** is a perpetually cool oasis thanks to its **mid-century architecture** and leisure lifestyle. North of Palm Springs, the jumbled rocks and spiky trees of **Joshua Tree National Park** beckon hikers, campers, and climbers to soak up the high-desert wonderland.

Route 66

This historic highway was driven by the first generations of American road-trippers. Long since replaced by bigger, faster interstates, it feels like a time-capsule to a lost era. An intriguing section of the **Historic Route 66** runs parallel to I-40 along the southern border of **Mojave National Reserve**, where old highway stops have become **ghost towns.**

Partial road closures can require tricky navigation, but you can still reach the ghost town of **Amboy**. In Barstow, Route 66 veers south to parallel I-15 near the old crossroads of **Victorville,** where you

Clockwise from top left: Hollywood sign; the Botanical Building at Balboa Park; the Venice Beach Boardwalk.

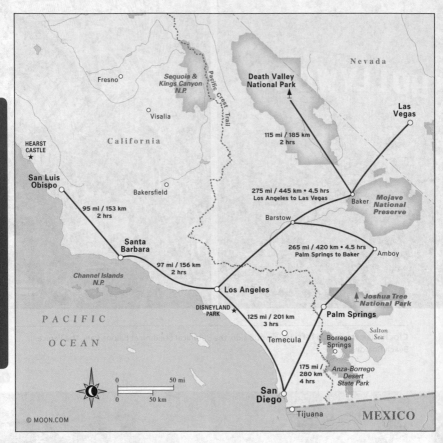

can detour to **Elmer's Bottle Tree Ranch,** a roadside attraction. Route 66 stays with I-15 into **San Bernardino,** where the final leg jogs west parallel to I-210 into historic **Pasadena.**

Death Valley and Las Vegas
Arguably Southern California's most awe-inspiring destination, **Death Valley National Park** offers gorgeous road-trip scenery, **star-filled night skies,** and unparalleled serenity. It's a long drive from anywhere, so the most convenient starting point might be the park's conceptual opposite: **Las Vegas.** The **gambling** capital offers bright lights, tons of people, and endless activity 24 hours a day, including an unparalleled variety of

entertainments such as nightly **live music** and **comedy shows,** top-tier **restaurants,** and **clubs.**

Santa Barbara
A slice of the Mediterranean on the California coast, **Santa Barbara** offers an alluring mix of **wine, culture,** and **beaches.** Originally a Spanish military outpost, buildings here still adopt a Spanish colonial architecture, best exemplified in the **Old Mission Santa Barbara.** Modern beach life emanates from **Stearns Wharf** at the end of **State Street**, the main drag lined with shops. For a glimpse of the lavish estates on the surrounding hillsides, take a tour of the enrapturing botanical garden, **Lotusland.**

San Luis Obispo and Hearst Castle

US-101 offers a convenient side-trip over the mountains north of Santa Barbara to the charming university town of **San Luis Obispo.** CA-1 splits northwest past the quaint coastal communities of **Morro Bay** and **Cambria** until it reaches **San Simeon** and the former mansion of William Randolph Hearst. Stars of the Golden Age of Hollywood once spent long weekends admiring the views from **Hearst Castle,** an architectural marvel high above the coast.

Know Before You Go

When to Go

Southern California enjoys a milder-than-average climate year-round, but coastal, desert, and mountain destinations prove more seasonal, with some months more attractive than others.

Fall

September-October offers the best times to combine a trip to both the beaches and the deserts. These months are sometimes referred to as the "locals' summer," when the destinations experience weather more typical of summer (average 72°F/22°C). The Pacific Ocean is warmer, but fewer tourists crowd the beaches.

The deserts start to cool down in the fall (average 70°F/21°C), and are too hot to explore in the summer months. Mountain destinations also enjoy pleasant weather in fall, with autumn colors and temperatures in the high 60s.

Winter

Traditionally winter is the rainy season in Southern California, though Los Angeles, Orange County, and San Diego see their share of sunny, 70-degree (21°C) days. However, the ocean becomes frigid **November through February,** making it tough to swim or surf without a wet suit. On the plus-side, skiing becomes available in the mountains east of Los Angeles.

Winter is a good time for desert hiking, when cooler daytime temperatures prevail, though nighttime temperatures drop close to freezing.

Spring

The best time to visit is **March through May.** Though it's more crowded than fall, the weather hits that mid-70s (21°C) sweet spot both inland and on the coast and the ocean starts to warm. The beaches are mostly sunny and the deserts don't experience the extreme conditions prevalent in summer or winter.

The best part about a visit in spring is the chance to see the annual **super bloom;** it's the time of year when the golden hillsides turn vibrant with color as wildflowers bloom with life, adding a layer of photogenic beauty.

Summer

Summer is the best time to visit the Southern California coast. The crowd levels are high, but the long, sunny days offer the best opportunity to experience SoCal's laid-back culture.

The deserts, including Death Valley and Joshua Tree, are stifling in summer, with average temperatures in the 90s and exceeding 100° Fahrenheit (37°C). Many tourist services close from **June until early September.**

Advance Reservations

High-season travelers should plan ahead when visiting large cities and **big-name attractions.** If you have your heart set on seeing **Disneyland,** purchase tickets online at least two weeks in advance. (You'll save money as well.) Reservations are pretty much essential at **hotels** and **campgrounds,** especially in and around popular resort towns like Palm Springs. Reserve a **rental car** ahead of time, too.

Some **campgrounds** are reserved months in advance, particularly in summer around San Diego and Malibu, and

Clockwise from top left: fountain at Old Mission Santa Barbara; Badwater Basin in Death Valley; Hearst Castle's Neptune Pool.

on weekends in Joshua Tree National Park. All lodging (including camp-grounds) at Death Valley is limited, so reservations are recommended for busier times of year, such as **spring breaks** and **winter holidays.**

Advance reservations are recom-mended for top **Las Vegas attractions** and accommodations during weekends, particularly during high-profile concerts and sporting events.

What to Pack

The first items to pack for a Southern California road trip are **sunglasses** and a **bathing suit.** It's also important to bring (and use!) **sunscreen.** Casual attire, in-cluding **sandals** and **shorts,** works for most places unless you have fancy din-ner reservations. However, cool fog is possible anywhere along the coast, so bring **layered clothing** to ward off the chill. Higher elevations may see snow, and lower elevations in the desert can be quite chilly at night. Pack **winter attire** as your itinerary warrants.

Driving Tips

Los Angeles, San Diego, and Las Vegas are convenient travel hubs from which to start this trip. Each town has an in-ternational airport with car rentals avail-able. Smaller regional airports, including those in Santa Barbara, Burbank, Long Beach, Ontario, and Santa Ana, may also prove convenient.

Weather

Though Southern California weather is famously ideal, that doesn't guarantee safe road conditions every day (just most days).

Wherever there's coast, there's a chance of **fog.** Several beach cities, even sunny San Diego, experience fog so thick that you can't see more than a car length ahead. When fog obscures driving conditions, keep your headlights on low and drive *very* slowly.

Watch out for **extreme heat** in the des-erts, where temperatures may exceed 100 degrees Fahrenheit in summer—deadly if you're stranded and unprepared. Pack at least one gallon or liter of **water** per per-son per day when driving in the desert and make check your car's tire and fluid levels before heading out. Monitor use of the car's air conditioner as well, to ensure your vehicle doesn't overheat.

In winter, **snow** may fall at higher el-evations. Cajon Pass sometimes closes due to snow, as do roads heading into the mountains around Big Bear and Mount San Jacinto.

Traffic

Expect **traffic delays** at major cities along the route; this is especially true of Los Angeles and San Diego, where the afternoon **rush hour** begins in the mid-afternoon and extends into late evening.

Traffic on **I-15** north into **Las Vegas** can be pretty bad on a Friday night, but the worst traffic is heading west back into L.A. or San Diego along the same route. Avoid making the return trip on Sunday night (or the Monday of a holiday weekend).

To receive reports on **traffic and road conditions,** call 511 (toll-free 800/977-6368). Additional resources include the **California Department of Transportation** (www.quickmap.dot.ca.gov).

Fueling Up

Finding a **gas station** isn't hard in most cities and urban areas; however, there are **desert segments** of this trip where you won't see a gas station for 50 miles. And, when you do, the price per gallon can be astronomical. Plan what time you expect to arrive at each destination and deter-mine whether there is a gas station avail-able en route. Keep a full gas tank when you hit the road and don't let it drop below a quarter-tank without knowing where the next station is.

HIT THE ROAD

Check your tire pressure, change your oil, and fill up the tank. This world-class road trip will take you through miles of captivating scenery.

The full drive can take **two weeks** with about **3-5 hours** between overnight stops. Take more time if you have it; 3-4 weeks would be ideal to spend additional time exploring each region. When that's not practical, consider flying into one of the main **travel hubs** (Los Angeles, Las Vegas, or San Diego) and splitting the drive into **four- to seven-day** region-specific trips.

For driving directions all along the way, see the *Getting There* sections in later chapters. All mileage and driving times are approximate and will vary depending on weather, traffic, and road conditions.

Southern California Road Trips

Classic LA
DAY 1: LOS ANGELES
Fly into **LAX** and rent a car. Take the classic L.A. drive up Sunset Boulevard into **Hollywood.** Wander the **Hollywood Walk of Fame** (corner of Gower Street and Hollywood Boulevard) and get an eyeful at the ornate **TCL Chinese Theatre.** Enjoy some science along with views of the city from the **Griffith Observatory,** then head downtown to visit **The Broad** museum. Take your pick of the city's exciting dining options before getting a taste of Hollywood nightlife on the **Sunset Strip.**

For more ideas on how to spend your time in Los Angeles, see page 37.

DAY 2: DISNEYLAND
35 mi/56 km, 1 hr
It's only an hour drive from Hollywood to **Anaheim.** Have breakfast at **Yuca's,**

then scoot south down I-5 for a full day at **Disneyland,** the "Happiest Place on Earth," where you'll meet Mickey, Minnie, Goofy, and a slew of princesses. Make reservations far in advance if you hope to spend time at the new **Star Wars: Galaxy's Edge** attraction, which brings a galaxy far, far away to life like never before.

Disneyland stays open late—until midnight most nights—and the park lights up after dark. To maximize your fun, and minimize the drive, book a room near the park at the **Disneyland Hotel** or return to Hollywood for the night. If you did it right, you'll be exhausted after a day of nostalgic characters and thrilling rides.

Continue this road trip south to explore the **Southern California Beaches,** or opt for an excursion north to the **central coast** and visit Santa Barbara, San Luis Obispo, and Hearst Castle (page 27).

Coastal Cruise
DAY 3: SOUTHERN CALIFORNIA BEACHES
52 mi/87 km, 2 hr
West of Hollywood, I-10 leads 30 miles (48 km) to the coast and CA-1 for the "27 miles of scenic beauty" better known as **Malibu.** Grab breakfast at the **Malibu Farm Cafe** then choose from any number of Malibu's gorgeous and remote **state beaches** to spend time sunning and surfing. Take advantage of good late-day surf conditions, or grab some casual seafood at the regional classic, **Neptune's Net.** Keep an eye out for dolphins or whales breaching off shore.

Drive south on CA-1 to **Santa Monica Pier.** Ride the carousel and the Ferris wheel or rent a bike and cruise the **bike path** until you spot a nice patch of beach to call your own. Browse the shops of **Main Street** or **Third Street Promenade**, then walk or bike two miles south to the notorious **Venice Beach Boardwalk,** home to artists, weirdos, athletes, buskers, hustlers, gawkers, and hawkers.

Cruise the boardwalk, then tour the local streets to spot the **Venice Murals.**

Clockwise from top left: Venice Canals; Disneyland; Griffith Observatory in L.A.

When you've had enough sensory overload, head a few blocks inland to the relative calm of the lovely **Venice Beach Canals.** The stroll will segue perfectly to dinner at **Gjelina.** Ask for seats at the community table, where you may wind up swapping road stories with fellow travelers.

DAY 4: SOUTH COAST BEACHES
100 mi/161 km, 3 hr

Hug the coast as you head south on CA-1 to L.A.'s South Bay beach cities. CA-1 leads through the port city of **Long Beach**, home to the retired cruise ship/hotel/museum, the **Queen Mary**.

Don't feel the need to linger, as a wealth of gorgeous Orange County beach cities lie ahead. Depending upon which aspects of Southern California beach culture appeal to you the most, you could hit some waves in Surf City U.S.A., **Huntington Beach,** or enjoy the leisurely pursuits and family amusements of **Newport Beach**.

To class it up for the night, settle into a world of upscale shopping and gorgeous little beach coves in **Laguna Beach**. It doesn't boast the nightlife of its northern neighbors, but the place does know how to pamper.

South of Laguna Beach, detour inland for a bit of local history at the **Mission San Juan Capistrano** before merging onto I-5 south to **Oceanside**, where you can exit the freeway onto **US-101**. Continue south, enjoying the view of beach cities of San Diego's north county.

DAY 5: NORTH COUNTY BEACHES
30 mi/48 km, 1 hr

Stop in the pretty burb of **Encinitas** to nab quality beach time at breathtaking **Moonlight Beach** and watch expert surfers do their thing at **Swami's State Beach**.

US-101 routes inland to I-5 south into San Diego County, then reappears slowly through several beach towns before reaching **Torrey Pines State Reserve,** one of the wildest stretches along the coast. Drop down into **La Jolla Cove** for some kayaking or snorkeling, then dine at one of the incredible restaurants in **La Jolla,** every bit the Southern California jewel its name suggests.

DAY 6: SAN DIEGO
13 mi/21 km, 0.5 hr

Enjoy breakfast in La Jolla at **Brockton Villa,** then get in some window shopping before heading uphill to admire the panoramic view from atop **Mt. Soledad.** Back in the car, return to I-5 and drive 13 miles (21 km) south into San Diego proper.

Spend the afternoon exploring the museums, gardens, and architecture of **Balboa Park,** the city's green space. Sample some world-class craft beer in hip North Park or head downtown to **Bottlecraft** in Little Italy. Afterward, dine on seafood at **Ironside Fish & Oyster,** one of the city's top restaurants. Spend the night at the **U.S. Grant Hotel.**

For more ideas on how to spend your time in San Diego, see page 129.

Desert Detour
DAY 7: SAN DIEGO TO ANZA-BORREGO
90 mi/145 km, 2.5 hr

Grab caffeine at **Bird Rock Coffee** then drive 90 miles (145 km) east over the mountains and into the low Colorado Desert where you'll enter **Anza-Borrego State Park.** Take a hike in Borrego Palm Canyon then go sculpture-spotting in **Galleta Meadows,** home to one of the world's largest sculpture gardens. At night, stake out a spot for some epic **stargazing.**

The tiny town of **Borrego Springs** has a few restaurants and overnight options or spend the night in the mining town of **Julian.**

Best Beaches

Coronado Beach

♦ **Zuma Beach** (page 71), Malibu's classic beach party site, offers surfing, boogie boarding, and volleyball.

♦ **Point Dume State Beach** (page 71) has the best views of the Malibu coastline outside of a movie star's mega-mansion.

♦ **Huntington City Beach** (page 91), a.k.a. Surf City, USA, delivers waves, bikinis, volleyball nets, and a long bike path.

♦ **Black's Beach** (page 112) requires a little hiking to get to, but the reward is a secluded Southern California beach backed by sandstone cliffs.

♦ **La Jolla Shores** (page 116) is a beautiful stretch of sand great for families and beginning surfers.

♦ **Coronado Beach** (page 136) is a family-friendly beach considered among the world's best, especially in front of the famous Hotel del Coronado, where lounge chairs and cocktails are available.

**DAY 8: ANZA-BORREGO
TO PALM SPRINGS
90 mi/145 km, 2 hr**

It's a 90-mile (145 km) drive north out of Borrego and into the desert oasis of **Palm Springs**, where lounging poolside is second only to golf as the town's favorite recreation. The mid-century city sits in the shadow of steep **Mount Jacinto.** If the desert heat gets to be too much, ride the **Palm Springs Aerial Tramway** to the top

of Mt. Jacinto and squeeze in some forest hiking. Return to town for an entertaining dinner at **Shanghai Red's**, a tropical cocktail at **Tonga Hut**, and a good night's rest at the **Orbit In**.

**DAY 9: PALM SPRINGS
TO JOSHUA TREE
40 mi/64 km, 1 hr**

Waking up in Palm Springs puts you about an hour's drive from **Joshua Tree**

Clockwise from top left: cactus in Anza Borrego; Zabriskie Point in Death Valley; Roy's Motel & Café.

National Park, so rise early to take advantage of one of Southern California's most beloved natural settings. Stop for breakfast at **Cheeky's,** then drive 40 miles (64 km) north on CA-62 to the park's west entrance.

Scramble around boulders at **Jumbo Rocks,** admire cacti in the **Cholla Cactus Garden,** and hike amid the park's famously knobby trees. If you can't find a camp spot, head to the towns of **Joshua Tree** and **Twentynine Palms** on the northern border of the park; each offers a sprinkling of accommodations and dining options. At night, head to the desert's stellar music venue, **Pappy & Harriet's,** where some of the world's best-known musicians have performed.

DAY 10: JOSHUA TREE TO ROUTE 66
234 ml/380 km, 4 hr

It's a long drive to the middle of nowhere, where the kitschy remains of **Route 66** icons beckon photo buffs and desert rats. From Joshua Tree, follow Amboy Road north for 53 miles (85 km) to Amboy Crater, an extinct cinder cone rising from the desert floor. **Amboy** is the first of several ghost towns you'll see on Route 66. Snap a photo of the space-age sign outside **Roy's Motel & Café,** then proceed west on **National Trails Highway** (Rte. 66) to enjoy the scenery of this desolate bygone highway.

Stop for breakfast or lunch at the **Ludlow Cafe,** a classic roadside diner, then follow Route 66 west to Barstow, where I-15 parallels the Mother Road south. Take a detour on the National Trails Highway, stopping in **Oro Grande,** home to the delightfully eclectic **Elmer's Bottle Tree Ranch.** From here the Mother Road passes over the **Cajon Pass** before dipping south to resume its westward trajectory. Detour to Riverside to shake off the desert with a relaxing stay at the **Mission Inn Hotel & Spa,** picturesque historic landmark.

Day 11
ROUTE 66 TO PASADENA
65 mi/105 km, 1.5 hr

Today's your final stretch on Route 66. Backtrack to I-210 in **San Bernardino,** which parallels Route 66 west on its final run through the suburban sprawl of L.A.'s Inland Empire. Stop in the pastoral city of **Pasadena,** where you'll browse the downtown shops before exploring the extensive library and sprawling gardens of **The Huntington.** For lunch, enjoy Chinese food at **Lunasia Dim Sum House.** Stay the night in Pasadena, or continue the drive back to Los Angeles.

Days 12-14: Optional Side Trips

Spend a weekend on the **central coast** (page 27), exploring Santa Barbara, San Luis Obispo, and Hearst Castle. Or, if the desert is calling your name, pick up the **desert detour** (page 25) to Mojave, Death Valley, and Las Vegas before heading back onto Route 66.

Desert Drive: Mojave, Death Valley, and Vegas

If desert drives are your thing, spend 3-4 days exploring Mojave National Preserve and Death Valley. Las Vegas provides a convenient urban hub to refresh before heading back to L.A.

Route 66 to Mojave National Preserve
40 mi/64 km, 1 hr

From Amboy, follow Kelbaker Road 18 miles (29 km) north to enter **Mojave National Preserve.** Stop at **Kelso Dunes** to hike around sandy dunes. Drive 12 miles (19 km) north to admire the exhibits at the **Kelso Depot Visitor Center,** which served as the old train station. Camp for the night at **Hole-in-the-Wall Campground.**

Scenic Drives

Morro Rock

Exploring Southern California often requires lots of time on humdrum freeways with little windshield appeal. However, plenty of scenic side trips can make the hours spent behind the wheel some of the best parts of your journey.

♦ **Malibu**: On its own, the 27 miles of gorgeous Malibu coastline makes this stretch of **CA-1** one of the top drives in Southern California. Factor in side trips up lush canyons into the pretty Santa Monica Mountains, and you'll do well. Set aside at least 2-3 hours of drive time during any Malibu sojourn (page 68).

♦ **Palos Verdes**: By adding only 20 minutes of drive time along **CA-1** between Long Beach and Redondo Beach, you'll enjoy stunning coastal views including seaside bluffs, the **Point Vicente Lighthouse**, and both the Catalina and Channel Islands on the horizon (page 84).

♦ **Big Bear**: This side trip treats travelers to the scenic **Rim of the World Scenic Byway,** carved into the San Bernardino Mountains. The slopes are often so steep that views can stretch 180-degrees from top to bottom as well as left to right. Time your trip for sunset, when the colorful, breathtaking vistas are their best around **Skyforest** (page 253).

♦ **Death Valley National Park**: Ripe with badlands hikes and scenic viewpoints, Death Valley's striking scenery will keep your jaw dropped as you cruise the long miles within the huge park. The wide, flat valley along **Badwater Basin Road** is ringed by jagged mountain peaks (page 276).

♦ **Pacific Coast Highway**: The prettiest stretch of coastal **CA-1** begins north of San Luis Obispo and runs along the central coast to **San Simeon**, passing monolithic **Morro Rock** and continuing toward the beaches and coastal bluffs below **Hearst Castle** (page 365).

Mojave to Death Valley
150 mi/242 km, 2.5-3 hr

Drive north out of Mojave National Preserve along **Cima Road,** which passes through the world's densest Joshua Tree forest on the smooth 1,500-foot slope of **Cima Dome.**

Cima Road meets a T-junction at I-15. Turn west to drive 27 miles (43 km) to the pit-stop town of **Baker,** where you'll fill your tank with what feels like the world's most expensive gas. Grab sandwiches and supplies for the road; you've got a long drive ahead into Death Valley, but the National Park's remoteness is part of its charm.

From Baker, drive 83 miles (134 km) north on Highway 127 to Death Valley Junction. Turn west onto Highway 190 and drive 30 miles (48 km) into the park. Stop at **Badwater Basin,** the lowest point on the continent, before continuing north to **Furnace Creek.** Check into **Ranch at Death Valley,** then continue to explore the badlands. End the day watching the sun set at **Zabriskie Point.** Return to Furnace Creek for dinner at **The Last Kind Words Saloon.** Spend the night **stargazing**—the dark desert skies come to life at night, especially during a new moon.

Death Valley to Las Vegas
180 mi/290 km, 3 hr

In the morning, drive 25 miles (40 km) north to **Stovepipe Wells** and the buffet breakfast at the **Toll Road Restaurant.** Spend some time exploring **Mesquite Flats Sand Dunes,** where the stark shadows of morning sun offer a great contrast for viewing the dunes. Exit the park on Highway 374, heading east to the Nevada ghost town of **Rhyolite.**

Highway 374 connects to NV-95 near Rhyolite, in the town of Beatty, Nevada. From Beatty, it's 120 miles (193 km) east to **Las Vegas.** Grab a room at the **casino hotel** that suits your lifestyle and explore the many attractions along the **Las Vegas Strip.** Treat yourself to a **show,** perhaps a Cirque du Soleil production or the concert of a legendary pop star in residency. Late at night, head downtown to marvel at the lights of the **Fremont Street Experience** and adjacent **Neon Museum.**

Las Vegas to Route 66
156 mi/250 km, 2.5-3 hr

In the morning, hit a famous Las Vegas **breakfast buffet** and fuel up for a day of scenic driving through the high desert. Drive 156 miles (250 km) west along I-15 to Barstow, then follow the directions for *Day 11: Route 66 to Barstow* to continue south into **Pasadena.** Avoid making this drive on a weekend, especially on Sunday, as the return weekend traffic from Vegas can be considerable.

Central Coast Getaway

Santa Barbara

Wait until the L.A. weekday rush hour dies down (usually around 9am) before heading 100 miles (161 km) northwest toward US-101 and the drive north to **Santa Barbara.** Celebrate your early arrival with a quick taco from **La Super-Rica Taqueria,** then head straight to **Lotusland** to make your 1:30pm reservation to tour its exotic botanic gardens.

After the tour wraps up, sneak in a little beach time and enjoy the attractions at **Stearns Wharf.** Before the afternoon runs too late, walk over to the **Funk Zone** to sample a bit of Santa Barbara's wine country at the tasting rooms of the **Urban Wine Trail.** Walk off the wine with a stroll past the shops on pretty **State Street,** where you'll find plenty of worthy dinner options. Get a room at the Spanish-style **Brisas del Mar Inn,** just a short walk from the beach.

Santa Barbara to San Luis Obispo
95 mi/154 km, 1.5 hr
COASTAL ROUTE

Grab breakfast at **Dawn Patrol,** then spend the morning exploring the grounds

Desert Thrills

For most of the year, the deserts of Southern California offer exactly what you expect: stark, high-contrast landscapes; scorched earth and sharp-needled cacti; and arid, sunny days blanketed by endless blue skies. But if you time it right, your desert adventures may include a smattering of special experiences that can make your excursion memorable.

Music

♦ **Coachella Valley Music and Arts Festival** (www.coachella.com, Apr.): The most famous music and art gathering is Coachella, which takes place on Indio's Empire Polo Fields two consecutive weekends in April. Hundreds of thousands of people descend on the greater Palm Springs area to attend the massive festival, which attracts the hottest names in the music industry. Hotel rates double (or triple) and book months in advance.

♦ **Pappy & Harriet's Pioneertown Palace** (www.pappyandharriets.com): The week between Coachella is a fantastic time to head to Pioneertown, where headlining artists often perform intimate, last-minute sets.

♦ **Stagecoach Festival** (www.stagecoachfestival.com, end of Apr.): This massive outdoor country music festival is lesser-known than Coachella, but takes place on the same polo fields.

Art

♦ **Desert X** (mid-Feb.-mid-Apr.): This biennial art festival takes place during odd-numbered years (the next is in 2021) throughout hundreds of square miles of desert. Contemporary artists erect high-concept art installations, from massive sculptures to photography exhibits, many of which incorporate technology in new and interesting ways.

♦ **Bombay Beach Biennale** (weekend in Mar. or Apr.): Progressive artists gather on the shores of the shrinking Salton Sea for a weekend-long festival filled with oddball exhibitions, musical performances, and dystopian amusements.

Nature

♦ **Spring Bloom**: Wildflowers blossom for a few weeks each spring, painting deserts bright with swaths of colorful flowers. In unusually wet winters, a high concentration of wildflowers erupts in a **"superbloom"** capable of painting hillsides in unforgettable kaleidoscopes of color. Large superbloom events take place in **Joshua Tree National Park, Death Valley National Park,** and **Anza-Borrego State Park.**

♦ **Stargazing**: When you look up at the night sky in a desert region, you will see millions of stars. **Death Valley** and **Anza-Borrego** are designated **International Dark Sky Communities**, which means that they've take additional steps to reduce light pollution within their lightly populated areas. Even the dimmest of stars become visible, as do broad swaths of nebulae and the Milky Way galaxy. Stargazing is at its best during a new moon.

Clockwise from top left: Madonna Inn; surfer in Santa Barbara; Lotusland.

HIT THE ROAD

of the **Old Mission Santa Barbara.** Back in the car, drive 34 miles (55 km) on US-101 to **Gaviota State Park,** where you can hike to Gaviota Peak for stunning views of the Channel Islands. Less ambitious beach-goers may prefer spending the morning at scenic **El Capitán State Beach.**

US-101 continue 74 miles (119 km) north to San Luis Obispo.

INLAND ROUTE

Enjoy a light breakfast, then leave Santa Barbara on Highway 154, which qualifies as both the fast and scenic route north toward Hearst Castle. Make a short but sweet stop to view the cave paintings at **Chumash Painted Cave State Historic Park**, then grab lunch at the rustic 150-year-old stagecoach stop **Cold Spring Tavern**.

Return to Highway 154 and drive 30 miles north to Highway 154, where you'll head west on Highway 246 through the scenic Scandinavian wonderland of **Solvang.**

Highway 246 meets US-101 north in 8 miles (13 km), where you'll turn north to continue 64 miles (103 km) into San Luis Obispo. Of course, no visit to San Luis Obispo is complete without stopping to admire the kitschy elegance of the notorious **Madonna Inn,** a unique and worthy roadside attraction.

San Luis Obispo to Hearst Castle
95 mi/153 km, 1.5 hr

Today's destination is **Hearst Castle,** so book tour tickets online in advance before you hit the road.

From San Luis Obispo, CA-1 splits north for 34 miles (55 km) to follow a pretty coastal drive to artsy Cambria, and its distinctively beautiful **Moonstone Beach**. Continue 9.6 miles (16 km) north on CA-1 to **San Simeon,** where you'll tour the enchanting **Hearst Castle** and gaze longingly at the cobalt-blue Neptune Pool.

If you need to spend the night nearby, return to Cambria, which has plenty of warm hotel rooms.

Back to Santa Barbara
136 mi/219 km, 3 hr

Cruise south on US-101, returning to US-101 in San Luis Obispo. Stop in Nipomo for lunch or a steak dinner at **Jocko's.** Then continue 70 miles (113 km) back to Santa Barbara or end your trip in Los Angeles 166 miles (265 km) farther south.

From Santa Barbara, it's possible to break south and follow CA-1 on the coast, where you can explore the "27 miles of scenic beauty" known as Malibu (page 70).

Family Fun

Ferris wheel at Newport Beach

Family road trips usually go more smoothly when architectural tours and historical sites are broken up by fun and educational activities.

♦ **Disneyland**: Kids of all ages love Disneyland. With the addition of the park's **Star Wars: Galaxy's Edge,** everyone is due to love it a whole lot more. Hotels within the park and its **Downtown Disney District** make it easy to for families to manage between both Disneyland and **California Adventure Park.**

♦ **Newport Beach**: With long, wide beaches, a protected bay, and a **Fun Zone** with amusement park rides, Newport Beach will satisfy adults who crave nice meals and upscale shopping, and kids who just want to have fun. Stay on or near **Balboa Peninsula** and ride along its easy **bike path** or rent a **duffy boat** to scoot around the bay. Don't miss the local dessert specialty: chocolate-and nut-covered **frozen bananas**.

♦ **San Diego**: Between the shallow, waveless beaches of **Mission Bay**, the museums of **Balboa Park**, and maritime exhibits on the waterfront, San Diego proves an exceptional family-friendly destination. You'll have no trouble packing in several days of activities at the **Fleet Science Center**, **Natural History Museum**, **Maritime Museum**, and the **U.S.S. Midway Museum**. Stay in Mission Beach or Coronado for easy access to beaches.

♦ **Santa Barbara**: This charming beach city offers plenty for kids to get excited about. A long **bike path** parallels the beachfront, tourist-friendly **Stearns Wharf** is filled with sweets shops, and the **Museum of Natural History Sea Center** offers a chance to interact with sea creatures. The **MOXI, The Wolf Museum of Exploration + Innovation** also has fun, hands-on educational exhibits.

♦ **Las Vegas**: Most Vegas casinos have built-in family attractions. Top hits include the **High Roller** Ferris wheel at Linq, **Marvel Avengers S.T.A.T.I.O.N.** at Treasure Island, and **Siegfried & Roy's Secret Garden and Dolphin Habitat** at Harrah's Casino.

Los Angeles

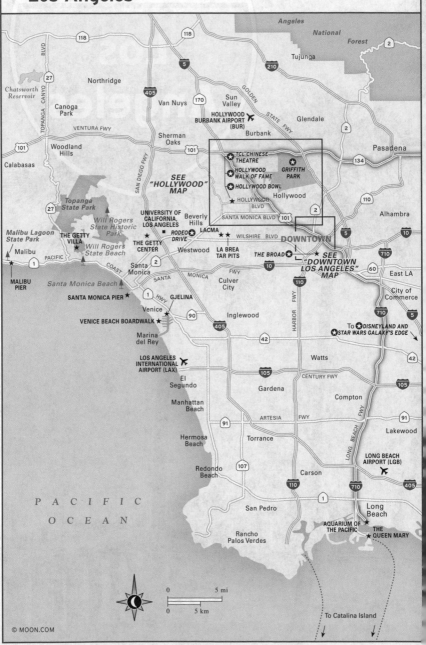

Los Angeles

Angeles
National
Forest

118
118
5
210
Tujunga
2

TOPANGA CANYON BLVD
27
Northridge
Chatsworth
Reservoir
Canoga
Park
405
Van Nuys
170
Sun
Valley
GOLDEN STATE FWY
Glendale
2
Pasadena

VENTURA FWY
HOLLYWOOD
BURBANK AIRPORT
(BUR)
Burbank
134

101
Woodland
Hills
Sherman
Oaks
101
110

SAN DIEGO FWY
SEE
"HOLLYWOOD"
MAP
★ TCL CHINESE
THEATRE
GRIFFITH
PARK
Alhambra

Calabasas

★ HOLLYWOOD
WALK OF FAME
★ HOLLYWOOD BOWL
Hollywood
2
5
10

27
Topanga
State Park
Will Rogers
State Historic
Park
UNIVERSITY OF
CALIFORNIA,
LOS ANGELES
Beverly
Hills
★ HOLLYWOOD
BLVD
SANTA MONICA BLVD
101
DOWNTOWN
710

Malibu Lagoon
State Park
THE GETTY
VILLA
THE GETTY
CENTER
Will Rogers
State Beach
■ RODEO
DRIVE
LACMA
★★
LA BREA
TAR PITS
Westwood
WILSHIRE BLVD
THE BROAD ★
SEE
"DOWNTOWN
LOS ANGELES"
MAP
60
East LA

Malibu
PACIFIC
2
Santa
Monica
SANTA
MONICA
FWY
10
110
City of
Commerce

MALIBU
PIER
COAST
Santa Monica Beach
1
HWY
GJELINA
Venice
Culver
City
HARBOR FWY
710
5

SANTA MONICA PIER ★
90
Inglewood
42

VENICE BEACH BOARDWALK ★
405
To ★ DISNEYLAND AND
★ STAR WARS GALAXY'S EDGE
42

Marina
del Rey
Watts
105

LOS ANGELES
INTERNATIONAL
AIRPORT (LAX)
El
Segundo
105
CENTURY FWY

Gardena
Compton
91

Manhattan
Beach
ARTESIA FWY
Lakewood

91
Torrance
LONG BEACH FWY
LONG BEACH
AIRPORT (LGB)

Hermosa
Beach
107
Redondo
Beach
Carson
110
710
405

San Pedro
1
Long
Beach

P A C I F I C

O C E A N
Rancho
Palos Verdes
AQUARIUM OF
THE PACIFIC
THE
★ QUEEN MARY

0   5 mi
0   5 km

© MOON.COM

To Catalina Island

Highlights

★ **The Broad:** A collection featuring a who's who of modern art, plus touring exhibits by contemporary masters, makes this L.A.'s top museum (page 40).

★ **TCL Chinese Theatre:** Hollywood's grandest vintage theater, famous for celebrity handprints pressed into the concrete sidewalk out front (page 42).

★ **Hollywood Walk of Fame:** Since 1960, entertainment legends have wished for a spot on this iconic sidewalk of the stars (page 43).

★ **Griffith Park:** A welcome expanse of greenery, "L.A.'s Central Park" includes the iconic Griffith Observatory and the L.A. Zoo (page 43).

★ **Hollywood Bowl:** Bring your own wine into this picturesque amphitheater built into the Hollywood Hills; it hosts the biggest musical artists on the planet (page 49).

★ **Rodeo Drive:** Though the price tags along this famed Beverly Hills boulevard may be bigger than your zip code, window-shopping

and celebrity-spotting are free (page 52).

★ **Disneyland:** With popular rides like Pirates of the Caribbean, Mr. Toad's Wild Ride, and Indiana Jones Adventure Park, the "Happiest Place on Earth" is a thrill for visitors of all ages (page 56).

★ **Star Wars: Galaxy's Edge:** This advanced theme park attraction will immerse you in the *Star Wars* universe like never before, including a chance to pilot the *Millennium Falcon* (page 60)!

The second-largest city in the United States, Los Angeles is familiar to the world as the undisputed capital of motion picture arts and sciences: aka Hollywood.

However, the sprawling metropolis has since emerged as the bona fide cultural hub of the West Coast, offering an abundance of superb music, art, theater, fine dining, cocktail lounges, stand-up comedy, and more—much of it fueled by a staggering range of ethnic, cultural, and religious diversity.

That said, L.A. definitely has a soft spot for the nostalgia of Old Hollywood, and every year its storied glamour attracts millions of tourists with stars in their eyes and hundreds of thousands of new residents with dreams in their hearts. They visit gorgeous vintage movie theaters upgraded with advanced projection and audio technologies, view the stars on the Hollywood Walk of Fame, take selfies backdropped by the famed Hollywood Sign, and attend world-class music events at the Hollywood Bowl.

Generations have taken celebrity-spotting excursions to Beverly Hills, home to highest end of luxury shopping and film industry elites. More interesting is the resurgence of downtown Los Angeles, rich with museums and performance venues, a thriving Arts District, the haggler-friendly Fashion District, and a foodie-friendly Chinatown. The city's Mexican origins are commemorated at Olvera Street, the very spot where the Pueblo de Los Ángeles was founded in 1781.

The city works hard to live up to the ready-for-its-close-up veneer it presents to the world and mostly succeeds in delighting the movie-loving pilgrims who flock to its palm tree-lined streets.

Getting There

L.A.'s other claim to fame is its notoriously bad traffic, which can slow down a road-tripper's journey. Careful scheduling of your arrival and departure can help you avoid the brunt of the city's long weekday rush hours. To get the most out of Los Angeles, plan to spend two or three days here, and consider navigating its expanding metro rail system to connect several of the city's prime destinations without having to worry about traffic or parking tickets.

From San Diego
120 mi/193 km, 2-5 hr
Thanks to routinely congested traffic, the drive from San Diego to Los Angeles may take anywhere from 2-5 hours. It's highly recommended to avoid the weekday rush hours (7am-9:30am and 3pm-6:30pm).

The most direct route from San Diego is a straight shot via I-5 north. Around the 78-mile (126-km) mark, you can take I-405 north for 37 miles (60 km) to I-110 north, which only adds 10 miles (16 km) but may save some time. To reach Disneyland, exit on Harbor Boulevard toward Ball Road west to the park. The drive should take 90 minutes in clear conditions.

If you do encounter traffic, stop in the coastal cities of **Oceanside** or **Carlsbad** and bide your time with beach views, food, and refreshment. In Orange County, stop to admire **Mission San Juan Capistrano.**

From Las Vegas
270 mi/435 km, 4-6 hr
The route between Las Vegas and Los Angeles takes you along a couple of freeways. From Las Vegas, take I-15 south for 210 miles (338 km), hopping onto I-10 west for the remaining 60 miles into the city. Note that traffic out of Las Vegas is horrendous at the end of every

Two Days in Los Angeles

Day 1

Go Hollywood—Hollywood Boulevard, that is. Check out star footprints outside the **TCL Chinese Theatre** (page 42) and wander the **Hollywood Walk of Fame** (page 43). Poster and memorabilia shops abound, so pick up a still from your favorite movie.

For lunch, enjoy award-winning Mexican fare at **Yuca's** (page 53). Then head to **Griffith Park** (page 43) to enjoy the green space and the view of the **Hollywood Sign** from the Griffith Observatory. Then it's off to Beverly Hills for an afternoon of star-spotting and window-shopping on **Rodeo Drive** (page 46). See and be seen having dinner at the legendary **Spago Beverly Hills** (page 54).

Hollywood's biggest stars have left their mark outside the TCL Chinese Theatre.

After dinner, cruise the **Sunset Strip** (page 43), where revelers flock to legendary music clubs like the **Whisky a Go Go** and **The Viper Room** (page 48); or grab some laughs at **The Comedy Store** (page 49).

Day 2

After breakfast at **Original Pantry Cafe** (page 52), head to the birthplace of L.A.: **Olvera Street** (page 39). Tour the city's oldest structure, the **Avila Adobe,** and stroll the colorful marketplace. Spend some time enjoying art at **The Broad** (page 40) before browsing the food vendors at **Grand Central Market** (page 52) for lunch.

To explore much deeper into the city's past, spend the afternoon with the famous fossils at the **La Brea Tar Pits** (page 40) and checking the current exhibitions at **Los Angeles County Museum of Art** (page 40), then head back to Hollywood to sample the slices at **Pizzeria Mozza** (page 53) or dine on pasta at sister restaurant **Osteria Mozza**.

After dinner, do the most Hollywood thing possible and go see a movie at one of the city's legendary movie palaces, either a new release at **TCL Chinese Theatre** (page 42) or a classic film screening at **The Egyptian** (page 50).

---

weekend; on a Sunday afternoon or the Monday afternoon of a holiday weekend, it can easily turn into a six-hour-plus ordeal.

There are few scenic stops along the way. The town of **Baker** (95 mi/153 km west of Las Vegas) has food, expensive gas, and the world's largest thermometer. With time to spare, exit onto the National Trails Highway in Barstow and drive 32 miles (52 km) south to visit the artistic oddity that is **Elmer Long's Bottle Tree Ranch.**

From Santa Barbara

110 mi/177 km, 2-2.5 hr

From Santa Barbara, take US-101 South and drive about 110 miles (177 km) to reach Los Angeles. The good news is that you should only encounter traffic heading into L.A. if you leave in time to hit the morning rush (6:30am-9:30am).

You may spice up the drive with stops

Best Restaurants

★ **Sqirl:** It's not a typo—this small, cult-favorite Silverlake bistro is worth every minute standing in line (page 52).

★ **Guelaguetza:** L.A. puts Oaxaca on display at this experiential restaurant. Don't miss the mole (page 52).

★ **Zankou Chicken:** Delectable garlic paste and tahini add to the local lore of L.A.'s storied Mediterranean chicken roaster (page 53).

★ **Musso & Frank:** For a taste of Old Hollywood, soak in the ambience at Tinseltown's oldest restaurant (page 53).

★ **Spago Beverly Hills:** The dining room of Wolfgang Puck's most famous restaurant delivers a taste of quintessential Beverly Hills (page 54).

for food or beach time in Ventura, or exit the highway in Calabasas for a quick hike at Malibu Creek State Park.

Air, Train, or Bus
Several airports serve Los Angeles, but the largest by far is **Los Angeles International Airport** (LAX, 1 World Way, Los Angeles, 855/463-5252, www.flylax.com). It offers direct flights from around the world, but with constant traffic congestion and long lines from check-in to security, you must arrive two hours ahead of departure time; three for international or holiday flights. On the bright side, from each terminal convenient express buses zip back and forth from destinations including Hollywood and the downtown metro hub Union Station. Look for the signs **FlyAway Bus** (www.flylax.com, $8 Hollywood, $9.75 Union Station).

For a less-crowded airport, seek flights to or from **Hollywood Burbank Airport** (BUR, 2627 N. Hollywood Way, Burbank, 818/840-8840, https://hollywoodburbankairport.com), which is much closer to Hollywood and downtown. **Long Beach Airport** (LGB, 4100 Donald Douglas Dr., Long Beach, 562/570-2600, www.lgb.org) is a half-hour drive or an hour metro ride from Los Angeles.

Amtrak (800/872-7245, www.amtrak.com) has an active rail hub in Los Angeles, with several lines passing through the metro center of **Union Station** (800 N. Alameda St.). The *Pacific Surfliner* route travels direct to Santa Barbara and San Luis Obispo and southbound to San Diego. The *Coast Starlight* route passes through the San Francisco Bay Area en route from Portland and Seattle. The *San Joaquin* route runs out to Sacramento via the Bay Area. The *Sunset Limited* route travels east-west from as far as New Orleans. The *Southwest Chief* route travels through six states on the way from Chicago.

From Union Station, you can access Los Angeles's commuter train line **Metrolink** (www.metrolinktrains.com), which operates trains to or from various spots in Southern California, including Ventura, Oceanside, and San Bernardino.

You can get to L.A. by bus from almost everywhere, but while some Greyhound buses stop at Union Station, most go to the main depot at **Los Angeles bus station** (1716 E. 7th St., 213/629-8401 or 800/231-2222, www.greyhound.com) near the Arts District, but also adjacent to Skid Row. To avoid that area, don't plan to walk between the Bus Station and Union Station. Take a car or ride the bus instead.

Best Hotels

★ **Magic Castle Hotel:** Get a vintage taste of the Hollywood Hills with free tickets to the favorite haunt of local magicians (page 54).

★ **Ace Hotel:** This hip downtown spot includes vibrant lounges, a cozy coffee shop, and an ornate theater from the 1920s (page 54).

★ **The Hollywood Roosevelt Hotel:** It's the best place to stay when you want to be close to the action in Hollywood (page 55).

★ **Chateau Marmont:** This legendary West Hollywood boutique has a rich history of celebrity guests and hijinks (page 55).

★ **Beverly Wilshire Hotel:** Even in Beverly Hills, this Italian Renaissance masterpiece stands out (page 55).

Sights

Downtown

Beneath its glittering skyline, downtown L.A. reveals a gritty scene that feels less infatuated with Hollywood's glamour than other parts of the city. On the west side of downtown, the historic city center has experienced something of a commercial rebirth in recent years, while the Arts District on its east side has developed a thriving food and arts scene. There's the bustling industry of the Fashion District to the south, while the north is comprised of the historic cultural districts of Chinatown and Olvera Street.

Chinatown

Former rail workers from southern China established the original Chinatown in the late 19th century, despite the fact that they were not allowed to legally own property. That same situation made it easy for developers to buy up properties here in the 1930s, then demolish them to build Union Station. Fortunately, in 1938, successful lobbying and fundraising efforts by Chinese American community leaders supported the relocation of Chinatown and many of its residents to its current site (previously called Little Italy).

The first modern Chinatown was planned from the ground up and is outfitted with the colorful **Central Plaza** (943 N. Broadway, 213/628-4841, www. oldchinatownla.com, 9am-7pm Mon.-Thurs., 9am-7:30pm Fri.-Sun.) featuring shops and restaurants with the familiar curved gables of traditional Chinese architecture and lit with neon at night. Across the street is **Chung King Road,** a walkable alley of China-centric storefronts that's partly occupied by art galleries.

Olvera Street

The original "El Pueblo de la Reina de los Angeles" that has grown up to become the "City of Angels" started on **Olvera Street** (125 Paseo de la Plaza, www.calleolvera. com, 10am-7pm daily). At the street's south end, the tree-shaded **Old Plaza** (known as El Pueblo de Los Ángeles State Historic Park) pays tribute to the pueblo's 44 original *pobladores* (townspeople) who were of Spanish, Mexican, African, and Native American heritage.

A few steps away, the **Mexican Cultural Institute** houses traditional and contemporary Mexican art. Two of L.A.'s oldest structures are also found here. The **Old Plaza Church** was first built in 1784 but, due to floods and earthquake damage, was reconstructed in 1861. The oldest surviving building is the **Avila Adobe** (10 Olvera St., 213/485-6855, 9am-4pm daily, free). The walls are made of 2.5- to 3-foot-thick sunbaked bricks. A mixture of tar (brought from the La Brea Tar Pits), rocks, and horsehair was used to weatherize the cottonwood roof. A few exhibits include the History of Water in Los Angeles and a tribute to Christine Sterling, who is credited with preserving the Avila Adobe and creating the Mexican Marketplace.

On the south side of the Old Plaza, community group Las Angelitas del Pueblo offers 50-minute **tours** (213/628-1274, www.lasangelitas.org, 10am, 11am, and noon Tues.-Sat., free). The on-site Mexican Marketplace consists of rows of clapboard stands selling souvenirs and Mexican imports at cheap prices.

Grammy Museum

Housed within the sports and entertainment complex at L.A. Live, the **Grammy Museum** (800 W Olympic Blvd., 213/765-6800, www.grammymuseum.org, 10:30am-6:30pm Sun.-Mon. and Wed.-Thurs., 10am-8pm Fri.-Sat., $15 adults, $13 children 6-17) offers four floors devoted to popular music history and memorabilia. Interactive exhibits include audio and video clips that celebrate songwriters, cultural trendsetters, the evolution of recording technology, and a history of great Grammy performances.

★ The Broad

Contemporary art museum **The Broad** (221 S. Grand Ave., 213/232-6200, www.thebroad.org, 11am-5pm Tues.-Wed., 11am-8pm Thurs.-Fri., 10am-8pm Sat., 10am-6pm Sun., free entry, touring exhibitions require tickets) is beautiful to behold from the outside. The architectural gem houses a 2,000-piece art collection by luminaries such as Cindy Sherman, Ed Ruscha, Andy Warhol, and Roy Lichtenstein. Exceptional visiting installations typically require tickets be purchased in advance.

Mid-City
La Brea Tar Pits

The **La Brea Tar Pits** (5801 Wilshire Blvd., 323/857-6300, www.tarpits.org, 9:30am-5pm daily, free) is one of the world's most renowned fossil sites. One hundred tons of fossilized bone have been discovered here; ongoing excavations of Pit 91 continue to unmask its victims. Among the fossils are a saber-toothed tiger, a giant sloth, bison, and six dire wolves. The most treasured find is "Zed," a nearly intact mammoth skeleton. A partial human skeleton, estimated to be 10,000 years old, has also been found.

Pit 91 has a viewing station, where docents explain how and why the bubbling asphalt has risen to the surface. The **George C. Page Museum** (5801 Wilshire Blvd., 323/857-6300, www.tarpits.org, 9:30am-5pm daily, $12 adults, $5 children, tours free with admission) features several excavated skeletons and other fascinating exhibits. Giant sculptures of mammoths and other prehistoric animals are often draped with climbing children. Wear a pair of cheap shoes—it isn't unusual to leave with tar on your soles!

Los Angeles County Museum of Art

The 20-acre **Los Angeles County Museum of Art** (LACMA, 5905 Wilshire Blvd., 323/857-6000, www.lacma.org, 11am-5pm Mon.-Tues. and Thurs., 11am-8pm Fri., 10am-7pm Sat.-Sun., $25 adults, free under 18, $16 parking) holds the city's most impressive collections—120,000 works spanning human history. Covering three floors, the museum displays a selection of modern American art by artists that include Andy Warhol, Jasper Johns, and Robert Rauschenberg. The Art of the Americas Building includes an astounding display of 2,500 pre-Columbian objects, many excavated from burial chambers in Jalisco, Mexico. At the main level, the Ahmanson Building features a large staircase, reminiscent of Rome's Spanish Steps, while the plaza holds African art and modern works

Downtown Los Angeles

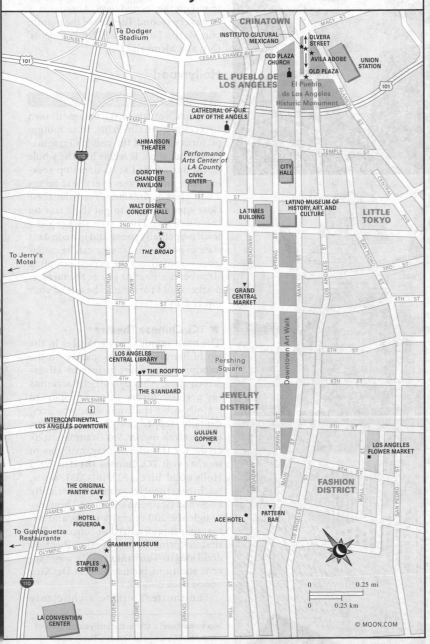

To Dodger Stadium

SUNSET BLVD

101

CHINATOWN

ORD

MACY ST

INSTITUTO CULTURAL MEXICANO

CESAR E CHAVEZ AVE

OLVERA STREET

OLD PLAZA CHURCH

AVILA ADOBE

UNION STATION

OLD PLAZA

EL PUEBLO DE LOS ANGELES

El Pueblo de Los Angeles Historic Monument

101

CATHEDRAL OF OUR LADY OF THE ANGELS

TEMPLE ST

110

AHMANSON THEATER

Performance Arts Center of LA County

TEMPLE ST

CENTRAL AVE

DOROTHY CHANDLER PAVILION

CIVIC CENTER

CITY HALL

1ST ST

WALT DISNEY CONCERT HALL

LATINO MUSEUM OF HISTORY, ART, AND CULTURE

2ND ST

LA TIMES BUILDING

LITTLE TOKYO

To Jerry's Motel

THE BROAD

BROADWAY

SPRING ST

SAN PEDRO ST

LOS ANGELES ST

3RD ST

3RD ST

FIGUEROA ST

FLOWER ST

GRAND AVE

4TH ST

GRAND CENTRAL MARKET

4TH ST

5TH ST

5TH ST

LOS ANGELES CENTRAL LIBRARY

Pershing Square

Downtown Art Walk

THE ROOFTOP

6TH ST

6TH ST

THE STANDARD

WILSHIRE

BLVD

JEWELRY DISTRICT

INTERCONTINENTAL LOS ANGELES DOWNTOWN

7TH ST

7TH ST

GOLDEN GOPHER

8TH ST

8TH ST

LOS ANGELES FLOWER MARKET

SPRING ST

BROADWAY

FASHION DISTRICT

THE ORIGINAL PANTRY CAFE

JAMES M WOOD BLVD

9TH ST

WALL ST

SAN PEDRO ST

HOTEL FIGUEROA

To Guelaguetza Restaurante

ACE HOTEL

PATTERN BAR

OLYMPIC BLVD

LOS ANGELES ST

GRAMMY MUSEUM

OLYMPIC BLVD

STAPLES CENTER

110

0   0.25 mi

0   0.25 km

LA CONVENTION CENTER

FIGUEROA ST

FLOWER ST

GRAND AVE

HILL ST

© MOON.COM

by greats like Picasso and Kandinsky. Classical Greek and Roman works are found on the second level. Admission is free every second Tuesday of the month, plus Martin Luther King Day, Presidents' Day, and Memorial Day.

Hollywood

The world's movie capital became its own first celebrity in the 1920s, when motion pictures captured the public's imagination. Since then, it seems like the whole world has arrived at its doorstep seeking fame and fortune. Every year brings a new class of dreamers, ready for their close-up and eager to put their star on the sidewalk. Their arrivals keep the town perpetually young and in a constant state of hustle. The energy can be contagious—sometimes the person sampling strawberries next to you at the farmers market could turn out to be one of your favorite TV actors.

★ TCL Chinese Theatre

The most famous movie theater in the world literally made its mark with the handprints and footprints of silver-screen stars. Although official accounts say actress Norma Talmadge sparked a Hollywood tradition when she accidentally stepped into the wet concrete, the theater's owner, Sid Grauman, took credit for the idea. Today, millions of tourists visit **TCL Chinese Theatre** (6925 Hollywood Blvd., 323/461-3331, www.tclchinesetheatres.com)—historically known as Grauman's Chinese Theatre—to ogle the 200 celebrity prints and autographs immortalized in concrete. The first footprints belong to Mary Pickford and Douglas Fairbanks (1927); more recent additions include Robert De Niro and Sandra Bullock.

The theater's ornate architecture

Top to bottom: a star in the Hollywood Walk of Fame; the TCL Chinese Theatre; The Broad.

features a large dragon across the front, two stone Chinese guardian lions at the entrance, and etched shadow dragons along the copper roof. Inside the ornately decorated theater, ticket holders are greeted by murals and soft lighting before entering the world's largest IMAX auditorium.

★ **Hollywood Walk of Fame**
Arguably the world's most famous sidewalk, the **Hollywood Walk of Fame** (Hollywood Blvd. from La Brea Ave. to Vine St., 323/469-8311, www.walkoffame.com) is a 1.3-mile stretch commemorating the entertainment industry's favorite celebrities. Inspired by the handprints at Sid Grauman's Chinese Theatre, five-pointed terrazzo and brass stars are embedded into a charcoal background along Hollywood Boulevard and three blocks of Vine Street.

Within each star, a circular, bronze emblem signifies the field in which the celebrity thrived: motion pictures, broadcast television, music or audio recording, broadcast radio, or theater. Several legendary performers can claim multiple stars, but Gene Autry is the only recipient of all five.

More than 2,500 Hollywood famous have been granted stars at a cost of $30,000. The worthy are selected by a special committee, with the cost typically covered by the movie company or record label representing the star in question. Check the website to locate a specific luminary's star or stars.

Sunset Strip
The **Sunset Strip** (Sunset Blvd., www.thesunsetstrip.com) has a long, colorful history as a playground for mobsters, Hollywood celebrities, and rock stars. A 1.5-mile portion of Sunset Boulevard stretches from Havenhurst Drive in West Hollywood to Sierra Drive near Beverly Hills. Infamous gangsters Micky Cohen and Bugsy Siegel would hold court at The Chateau Marmont or gamble at The

Melody Room (now called The Viper Room); Cohen took a bullet at what's now The Key Club. Nightclubs and upscale restaurants attracted stars such as Clark Gable, Cary Grant, Fred Astaire, Jean Harlowe, and Lana Turner. Famed writers Dorothy Parker and F. Scott Fitzgerald lived at the Garden of Allah apartments that once stood between Crescent Heights and Havenhurst. Howard Hughes lived in the penthouse of the Argyle Hotel (known as the Sunset Tower Hotel, 8358 Sunset Blvd.), as did John Wayne, who kept a cow on his apartment balcony.

Decades' worth of up-and-coming rock acts first made their names on the Strip and lived at the "Riot Hyatt." Today, you'll still find many of the Strip's legendary rock clubs here, such as **The Roxy,** (9009 W. Sunset Blvd., West Hollywood, www.theroxy.com), the **Whisky a Go Go** (8901 Sunset Blvd., West Hollywood, 310/652-4202), and **The Rainbow Bar & Grill** (9015 Sunset Blvd., West Boulevard, 310/278-4232, www.rainbowbarandgrill.com). At night, especially on weekends, no one is alone on the Strip. Don't plan to drive quickly or park on the street after dark; the crowds get big, complete with celebrity hounds hoping for a glimpse of their favorite star out for a night on the town.

★ **Griffith Park**
The 4,210-acre **Griffith Park** (4730 Crystal Springs Dr., 323/913-4688, sunrise-10pm daily) is the largest municipal park in the country, with numerous opportunities for mingling with nature while enjoying some of the city's iconic sights. It's also recognizable from its role as the backdrop for many films, including *Rebel Without a Cause* and *Back to the Future*.

The cosmos come alive at **Griffith Observatory** (2800 E. Observatory Rd., 213/473-0800, www.griffithobservatory.org, noon-10pm Tues.-Fri., 10am-10pm Sat.-Sun., free admission, $6-10 parking), the park's most popular sight.

Hollywood

MOON.COM

0
0   0.5 mi
0   0.5 km

N

Laurel Canyon Park

Universal City

Runyon Canyon Park

Laurel Canyon Park

To RODEO DRIVE, Beverly Wilshire Hotel and Spago

SAN VINCENTE BLVD
BEVERLY BLVD
LA CIENEGA BLVD
CRESCENT HEIGHTS
FAIRFAX AVE
SPAULDING AVE
ALTA VISTA BLVD
LA BREA AVE
HIGHLAND AVE
MELROSE
SANTA MONICA
VINE ST
GOWER ST
BRONSON AVE
WESTERN AVE
HOLLYWOOD BLVD
SUNSET BLVD
FRANKLIN AVE
LOS FELIZ BLVD
HILLHURST AVE
VERMONT AVE
VIRGIL AVE
COMMONWEALTH AVE
RUSSELL AVE
MICHELTORENA ST
SILVER LAKE BLVD
ALVARADO ST
GLENDALE BLVD
FLETCHER ST
BRAND BLVD
CHEVY CHASE DR
GLENDALE
FERNANDO RD
CAHUENGA BLVD
LANKERSHIM BLVD
VENTURA BLVD
BARHAM BLVD
MULHOLLAND DR
LAUREL CANYON BLVD
NICHOLS CANYON RD
HOLLYWOOD BLVD
SUNSET BLVD
FOUNTAIN
SANTA MONICA BLVD
BEACHWOOD DR
WESTERN CANYON RD
GLENDOWER AVE
VERMONT CANYON RD
COMMONWEALTH CANYON DR
CRYSTAL SPRINGS DR
GRIFFITH PARK DR
GOLDEN STATE FWY

THE ROXY THEATRE/ RAINBOW BAR
WHISKY A GO GO
THE VIPER ROOM
SUNSET STRIP
THE COMEDY STORE
SUNSET BLVD
CHATEAU MARMONT
MONDRIAN LOS ANGELES
West Hollywood
THE IMPROV
FRED SEGAL
ANIMAL
CANTOR'S DELI
THE DIME
LAUGH FACTORY
THE HOLLYWOOD ROOSEVELT
TCL CHINESE THEATRE
THE EGYPTIAN THEATRE HOLLYWOOD
THE WOODS
ZANKOU CHICKEN
THE GROUNDLINGS THEATRE & SCHOOL
PINK'S HOT DOGS
USA HOSTELS HOLLYWOOD
BOARDNER'S
MAGIC CASTLE HOTEL
MUSSO & FRANK GRILL
HOLLYWOOD WALK OF FAME
PIZZERIA & OSTERIA MOZZA
Hollywood
THE HOTEL CAFE
PACIFIC CINERAMA DOME
PANTAGES THEATER
AMOEBA MUSIC
CAFE GRATITUDE
HOLLYWOOD FOREVER CEMETERY
PARAMOUNT STUDIOS
FERNDELL NATURE MUSEUM
GRIFFITH OBSERVATORY/ SAMUEL OSCHIN PLANETARIUM
Barnsdall Park
HOLLYWOOD BOWL
HOLLYWOOD SIGN
Mt. Lee
Lake Hollywood
Mt. Hollywood
BIRD SANCTUARY GRIFFITH PARK
GREEK THEATER
MERRY-GO-ROUND
GRIFFITH PARK
Forest Lawn Memorial Park-Hollywood Hills
TRAVEL TOWN RAILROAD AND MUSEUM
THE AUTRY NATIONAL CENTER OF THE AMERICAN WEST
L.A. ZOO AND BOTANICAL GARDENS
VISITOR CENTER & PARK HEADQUARTERS
Los Feliz
SQIRL
Silver Lake
Silver Lake
COCO'S VARIETY BIKE SHOP AND PROP RENTAL
Echo Park Lake
Glendale

101   170   134   2   5

Welcome to Hollywood!

You'll know you've arrived when you see the **Hollywood Sign** (www.hollywoodsign. org). When it was erected in 1923 atop Mount Lee, it read "Hollywoodland." Twenty-six years later, "land" was removed and the 50-foot-tall letters that remained became a permanent feature of the Los Angeles landscape. Like all Hollywood stars, a bit of maintenance is required (the sign was made of wood). To ensure the sign's longevity, the original letters were auctioned off to the highest bidder (Hugh Hefner bought the "y" and Alice Cooper bought the "o") and replaced with shiny new 45-foot-tall letters made of sheet metal; the refurbishment was completed in 2010. Access to the sign ain't what it used to be due to problems with vandalism and complaints from local residents. The area is now outfitted with high-security motion detectors, closed-circuit cameras, razor-sharp barbed wire, and Restricted Entry warning signs. Try to climb the fence and Los Angeles police will have you cuffed quicker than you can say "I'm a tourist."

You can get a good look at the sign from the following places:

♦ **Griffith Observatory** (Griffith Park, 2800 E. Observatory Rd., 213/473-0800, noon-10pm Tues.-Fri., 10am-10pm Sat.-Sun., free)

♦ **Hollywood and Highland Visitors Center** (6801 Hollywood Blvd., 323/467-6412, 9am-10pm Mon.-Sat., 10am-7pm Sun.)

♦ **Lake Hollywood Park** (3160 N. Canyon Dr., 818/243-1145, 5am-sunset daily, free)

Experienced stargazers help visitors explore the galaxies through demonstrations of powerful telescopes. At the entrance, a Foucault pendulum demonstrates the rotation of the Earth, while other displays focus on the moon and ocean tides. Planetarium shows ($7) occur daily.

The park has several fun activities for kids, including the **L.A. Zoo and Botanical Gardens** (5333 Zoo Dr., www. lazoo.org, 10am-5pm daily, $21 adults, $16 children 2-12, carousel $3), the **Travel Town Railroad** (5200 Zoo Dr., 323/662-5874, www.traveltown.org, 10am-4pm Mon.-Fri., 10am-5pm Sat.-Sun., $3), pony rides, and a swimming pool. Educational sights include the **Autry National Center of the American West** (4700 Western Heritage Way, 323/667-2000, 10am-4pm Tues.-Fri., 10am-5pm Sat.-Sun., $14 adults, $10 students, $6 children 3-12), which holds an impressive collection of more than 500,000 Western and Native American artworks and artifacts.

A 53-mile network of hiking trails offers chances to spot local wildlife such as deer, coyotes, wild quail, and foxes. Many trails lead to viewpoints that include the Hollywood Sign; the most spectacular is from the observatory parking lot to Mount Hollywood. In a wooded canyon, the **Bird Sanctuary** (2900 N. Vermont Ave., 323/666-5046, 5am-10:30pm daily) provides the perfect spot for bird-watching, while the **Ferndell Nature Museum** (5375 Red Oak Dr., 6am-10pm daily), an outdoor exhibit, lets visitors explore native species of ferns, flowers, and plants. There is a snack stand and picnic area nearby to enjoy the cool shade along a babbling brook.

Paramount Studio Tours

For a literal glimpse behind the scenes, take a guided tour of century-old **Paramount Studios** (5515 Melrose Ave., 323/956-1777, www. paramountstudiotour.com, tours 9am-4pm daily, $58 tour, $15 parking), one of the original big five studios of Old

Hollywood and the only one still operating here. Countless films and television shows have been made at this facility, ranging from Hitchcock movies to *Star Trek,* and the tour will take you by soundstages where hit films and shows are still shot today.

Beverly Hills

Thousands flock to Beverly Hills to get a glimpse of the stars and browse the exorbitantly priced boutiques on Rodeo Drive. Five-star restaurants and chic hotels offer only the crème de la crème.

The three-block stretch of **Wilshire Boulevard** that runs through Beverly Hills from downtown to the ocean is known as **"Museum Row,"** which includes the Los Angeles County Museum of Art at its far southeast corner. To the east, Beverly Hills links to West Hollywood via the Sunset Strip at Sierra Drive. At its northwest side, the world-famous Getty Center sits atop the Santa Monica Mountains.

Rodeo Drive

In the well-to-do neighborhood of Beverly Hills, the wealthiest shop **Rodeo Drive** (pronounced "ro-DAY-o," not like the bronco-riding cowboy event), a paean to luxury shopping. Impressive boutiques and stylish shops abound with more than 100 of the most elite hotels and prestigious fashion retailers touting their "best in show" wearables. Though price tags may be bigger than your zip code, not everything is for sale. Take a walk along the palm-tree-lined drive to see the historic, iconic, and spectacular!

At the base of Rodeo Drive, the **Beverly Wilshire Hotel** (famous for the movie *Pretty Woman*) has been a fixture for over 100 years, lavishing the rich and famous in luxury. A newer addition, Rodeo Drive **Walk of Style** puts a twist on the Hollywood Walk of Fame by honoring fashion legends with bronze plaques (personal quote and signature included) embedded into the sidewalk. The first

honoree inducted was high-fashion guru Giorgio Armani, whose quote reads: "Fashion and cinema together for life." Along the "Walk," look for other past notables, which include Princess Grace of Monaco, Salvatore Ferragamo, and Gianni and Donatella Versace.

Other sights include artist Robert Graha's *Torso,* a 14-foot aluminum sculpture that glistens under the Southern California sun at the intersection of Rodeo Drive and Dayton. Nearby stands Frank Lloyd Wright's last Los Angeles building project, The Anderton Court, a four-level shopping complex with an exposed, angular ramp, several circular windows, and a large geometric mast.

Although you won't see *The Beverly Hillbillies'* Oldsmobile spewing exhaust down Rodeo Drive, the black and yellow Bugatti Veyron and custom yellow Rolls-Royce of designer Bijan Pakzad (founder of the exclusive House of Bijan) have become big photo ops. To step into the House of Bijan (the world's most expensive store) pay up. It's open by appointment only, catering to celebrities, movie moguls, and those able to spend $25,000 for a suit.

Recreation

Biking

One of Griffith Park's best features is its nine-mile **bike loop** (enter at Los Feliz Blvd. and Riverside Dr.). The route follows a tree-lined pathway and parts of the L.A. River Bike Path, forming a loop inside the park. Route information and bikes are available at **Coco's Variety Bike Shop and Prop Rental** (2427 Riverside Dr., 323/664-7400, www.cocosvariety. com, $10/hour), which also rents era-specific prop bikes to movie studios.

The seven-mile ride along the **Ballona Creek Trail** connects Ballona Creek in Culver City west to the Coast Bike Path in Marina del Rey. Access is at **Syd Kronenthal Park** (3459 McManus Ave., behind the ball field bleachers). North of Inglewood the path is rough and you'll be working against the wind, but picturesque ocean views make it worthwhile. The path ends at Fisherman's Village in Marina del Rey but links to the beachfront **South Bay Trail,** which continues 22 miles (35 km) along Santa Monica State Beach, north to Malibu and south to Torrance.

Expect twists, turns, and uphill insanity via **The Donut.** (The trail started 50 years ago at a doughnut shop.) This intense trail stretches 42 miles (68 km) from Redondo Beach to Palos Verdes. Competitive cyclists train on the route. The views of Point Vice, Point Fermin, and Catalina Island are remarkable.

Spectator Sports

The **Los Angeles Dodgers** are the hometown baseball team. With L.A.'s perfect climate, **Dodger Stadium** (1000 Vin Scully Ave., 866/363-4377, www.dodgers. com) hosts some of the most beautiful outdoor games in the country.

Staples Center (1111 S. Figueroa St., 213/742-7100, www.staplescenter. com) doubles as a sports and entertainment venue. It's home to the **L.A. Kings** hockey team and the **Lakers, Sparks,** and **Clippers** basketball teams, while also hosting big-name performers like Katy Perry, Taylor Swift, and Madonna.

Los Angeles is home to two NFL teams that will share an Inglewood stadium in 2021. Until then, the **L.A. Rams** play at downtown's **Los Angeles Memorial Coliseum** (3911 S. Figueroa St., www. therams.com). The **L.A. Chargers** play in Dominguez Hills at the **StubHub Center** (18400 Avalon Blvd., 310/630-2000, www. chargers.com), also the permanent home of Major League Soccer team the **L.A. Galaxy** (www.lagalaxy.com).

Top to bottom: Griffith Observatory; Rodeo Drive in Beverly Hills; the Walt Disney Concert Hall.

Entertainment and Events

Nightlife
Bars and Clubs
The "sky party" at **The Rooftop** (550 S. Flower St., 213/892-8080, www. standardhotels.com/downtown-la, noon-2am daily, RSVP and guest list Fri. and Sat. after 8pm) in The Standard hotel comes complete with DJs, waterbeds, a heated pool, and, let's not forget, the stunning panoramic view. Non-hotel guests are welcome, but it's not so easy to get in. Even if you don't make it onto the roof, you can get a drink at the trendy ground-level bar—minus the pool, waterbeds, and view, of course.

The no-frills **Golden Gopher** (417 W. 8th St., 213/614-8001, www.213hospitality.com/goldengopher, 4pm-2am Mon.-Wed., 3pm-2am Thurs.-Sun.) is the perfect downtown pit stop for a reasonably priced beer, but it isn't a typical dive bar; there's a dress code. If you prefer a froufrou drink, they'll mix, shake, and blend it up. Low-key entertainment options include a jukebox and Pac-Man arcade game.

Down the street, **Pattern Bar** (100 W. 9th St., 213/627-7774, www.patternbar. com, noon-2am Tues., Thurs.-Sat., noon-10pm Mon., Sun., Wed.) attracts a trendier crowd with its chic-meets-funky decor (vintage sewing stools line the bar). Tapas and cocktails named in honor of top designers lure in weekday fashionistas, but come the weekend, DJs draw a mixed crowd for dancing.

Cheap drinks set the tone at **The Dime** (442 N. Fairfax Ave., 323/651-4421, www. thedimela.net, 7am-midnight daily). Nightly DJs spin a mix of old-school, hip-hop, and indie beats attracting unpretentious crowds and the occasional celebrity. Just north of The Dime, **The Woods** (1533 N. La Brea Ave., 323/876-6612, www.vintagebargroup.com, 6pm-2am Mon.-Fri., 8pm-2am Sat.-Sun.) lives up to its name, decked out with rustic furnishings like antler chandeliers and tree stump tables.

Speakeasy survivor **Boardner's** (1652 N. Cherokee Ave., 323/462-9621, www. boardners.com, 4pm-2am daily, $3-20 cover) gives the fortysomething crowd a place to relive the 1980s every Monday night. "Bar Sinister" on Saturday nights lures goths (black is required!). The rest of the week you'll find a surprising variety of music and dancing for a club dating to 1942.

A couple of bars make **The Hollywood Roosevelt Hotel** (7000 Hollywood Blvd., 323/466-7000, www. thehollywoodroosevelt.com) a fun place to be seen. They pour drinks all day at the poolside **Tropicana Pool Café** (10am-2am daily), where celebrities sometimes lounge and neighborhood sun worshippers come to tan. The **Spare Room** (8pm-2am daily) operates as a speakeasy cocktail lounge with its own two-lane bowling alley.

A cocktail lounge established by celebrity chef José Andrés, **The Bazaar** (465 S. La Cienega Blvd., 310/246-5555, 6pm-12:30am Sun.-Thurs., 6pm-1:30am Fri.-Sat.) vibrates with the silk-stocking upper crusters of Beverly Hills, nibbling caviar and sipping the latest martini concoction. There is plenty of seating for socializing and curtained hideaways to get cozy.

Live Music
Two Sunset Strip legends mix celebrity with infamy. **The Viper Room** (8852 Sunset Blvd., 310/358-1881, www. viperroom.com, 4pm-2am daily, $8-25 cover) is where gangster Bugsy Siegel hung out in the 1940s, country giant Johnny Cash recorded his comeback album, and River Phoenix collapsed. Iconic bands like The Doors and The Byrds got their start at the **Whisky a Go Go** (8901 Sunset Blvd., 310/652-4202, www.whiskyagogo.com, 10am-6pm daily, no cover-$60 tickets). These days, both

venues welcome local bands to play for boisterous young crowds each night.

For two decades, Los Angeles has nurtured a resurgent singer-songwriter scene focused around **Hotel Cafe** (1623 N. Cahuenga Blvd., 323/461-2040, www.hotelcafe.com, doors open 6:30pm, $10-30). The intimate dual venue hosts primarily acoustic music on a small main stage or smaller second stage, with shows nightly.

Laugh out loud at the **Groundlings Theatre** (7307 Melrose Ave., 323/934-4747, www.groundlings.com, 10am-10pm daily, $10-20), which has been a fixture of L.A.'s improv and sketch comedy scene for over 40 years. It's known as a proving ground for future *Saturday Night Live* stars (Will Ferrell, Kristen Wiig, and Phil Hartman all started here). The city's famous stand-up comedy circuit includes **The Improv** (8162 Melrose Ave., 323/651-2583, www.improv.com, tickets $10 and up), **The Comedy Store** (8433 Sunset Blvd., 323/650-6268, www.thecomedystore.com, free-$20), and **Laugh Factory** (8001 Sunset Blvd., 323/656-1336, www.laughfactory.com, $20-45 plus 2-drink minimum). Every night gets big laughs, some get big comics (like Chris Rock, Dave Chappelle, Jon Stewart, or Jerry Seinfeld), either in scheduled or surprise appearances.

★ Hollywood Bowl

A number of excellent outdoor venues make Los Angeles a favorite stop of the world's top musicians, but none more than the legendary **Hollywood Bowl** (2301 Highland Ave., 323/850-2000, www.hollywoodbowl.com, June-Sept.). It sets the bar for outdoor concerts, with a massive amphitheater built into the hills above the center of Hollywood. Its iconic stage shell projects music into the top seats, while luckier attendees picnic in private boxes surrounding the orchestra pit. All guests may and should bring wine and beer to drink on the premises during the venue's long summer season featuring world music, rock legends, special performances by the L.A. Philharmonic, and sometimes a combination of all three. Stacked parking makes public transportation and ride-sharing a good idea.

The Arts

The breathtaking stainless steel curves designed by acclaimed architect Frank Gehry make **Walt Disney Concert Hall** (111 S. Grand Ave., 323/850-2000, www.laphil.com) a must-see Los Angeles landmark. Never mind that the whole place was designed around creating a perfect acoustic space for musical performances by the Los Angeles Philharmonic and a litany of world music artists.

The glittering **Geffen Playhouse** (10886 Le Conte Ave., 310/208-2028, www.geffenplayhouse.com) is home to a good-size main stage, the Gil Cates Theater, and the cozier Skirball Kenis Theater. The company offers a mix of new work and local premieres, frequently with big-name talent.

Downtown's beloved 3,200-seat **Dorothy Chandler Pavilion** (135 N. Grand Ave., 213/972-7211, www.musiccenter.org) is a landmark performance center that boasts curving staircases, sparkling chandeliers, and grand halls draped in red and gold. The Pavilion is the home of the Los Angeles Opera from September through June, as well as the Glorya Kaufman Presents Dance series.

The 2,600-seat art deco **Pantages Theatre** (6233 Hollywood Blvd., 323/468-1770, www.hollywoodpantages.com) dates back to 1930. In its time it's shown movies, staged vaudeville acts, and hosted the Oscars. These days it brings touring Broadway musicals to town, including hits like *The Lion King, Book of Mormon,* and *Hamilton.*

Festivals and Events

Southern California's biggest LGBTQ celebration, the **LA Pride Festival** (www.lapride.org, early June, $30-50) attracts more than 400,000 people to West

Movie Night in Hollywood

In most of the road-trip destinations described in this book, your time will be better spent visiting historical landmarks than going to see a movie. But in Hollywood, several movie theaters *are* historic landmarks! Seeing a film on the big screen, here in the home of cinema arts, makes the act of going to a movie special.

Of course, the best-known historic movie palace is **TCL Chinese Theatre** (6925 Hollywood Blvd., 323/461-3331, www.tclchinesetheatres.com), originally known as Grauman's Chinese Theatre. Beyond the famous hand- and footprints out front, the original 1927 theater's ornate interior features a massive starburst ceiling medallion, and its new 94-foot screen is one of the world's largest, allowing IMAX as well as 70mm screenings. Buy tickets in advance for reserved seating.

The 86-foot curved screen inside Hollywood's acoustically rich **Cinerama Dome** (6360 Sunset Blvd., 323/464-1478, www.arclightcinemas.com) has also been given modern upgrades, so it may showcase premium sound along with large-format projection. Built in 1963, the iconic dome offers one of the world's unique film-going experiences. Buy tickets in advance for reserved seating.

Decorated with hieroglyphics and mummy masks, **The Egyptian Theater** (6712 Hollywood Blvd., 323/461-2020, www.americancinemathequecalendar.com) dates all the way back to 1922. It's been modernized, but under the ownership of film preservation nonprofit American Cinematheque, it primarily screens classic films from 100-plus years of Hollywood history, "as they were meant to be seen."

It's not a historic theater, but the hottest movie tickets in town are for films projected each summer onto the side of a large mausoleum at the **Hollywood Forever Cemetery** (6000 Santa Monica Blvd., 323/522-6870, www.cinespia.org). Founded in 1899, the cemetery makes a wonderful, if unlikely, setting for outdoor screenings and concerts, where you may watch while picnicking on blankets and (short) lawn chairs, while sipping on beer or wine you bring with you. You must buy tickets in advance for these incredibly popular screenings, but arrive early, because seating positions are first-come, first-served.

Hollywood each year for festivities surrounding a pridefully flamboyant parade along Santa Monica Boulevard beginning at Crescent Heights Boulevard.

Every second Thursday of the month, more than 25,000 visitors roam gallery open houses of the **Downtown Art Walk** (between 4th St. and 7th St., Spring St. and Main St., www.downtownartwalk.org). Maps are available online.

Considered the world's largest Halloween street party, the **Hollywood Halloween Carnaval** (Santa Monica Blvd. from La Cienega Blvd. to Doheny Dr., www.visitwesthollywood.com, 6pm-10:30pm Oct. 31) shuts down a long stretch of West Hollywood to let costumed revelers enjoy the wildest night of the year.

Each spring, the **L.A. Festival of Books** (USC Campus, Vermont Ave. at Exposition Blvd., https://events.latimes.com, Apr., free with ticketed events) defies the stereotype that Angelenos don't read enough. Literary panels and author Q&As dominate the intellectual's fest.

Film festivals take place throughout the year in Los Angeles. The two biggest are the **L.A. Film Festival** (www.filmindependent.org, late Sept.), which celebrates independent films including documentary and shorts, and **AFI Fest** (www.afi.com, Nov.), programmed by the American Film Institute to celebrate the year's best films, which are screened for free at several of Hollywood's vintage theaters.

Shopping

Where does L.A. go to shop? Downtown you may haggle in open-air markets or find cut-rate deals on designer (or knockoff) fashions; Hollywood has everything from designer shops and lingerie boutiques to record stores and a farmers market; while Beverly Hills reigns as the queen of luxury shopping—for those with deep enough pockets.

Downtown

The 90 blocks of the **Fashion District** (between E. 8th St. and E. 16th St., from Santee St. to Central Ave.) offer the best places to shop for wholesale clothing, shoes, accessories, and cosmetics. Haggle with the vendors of perpetual flea market **Santee Alley** (210 E. Olympic Blvd., 9:30am-6pm daily), which offers legitimate deals amid the not-so-occasional designer knockoffs.

Breathe in the scores of freshly cut bouquets at the century-old **Los Angeles Flower Market** (754 Wall St., 213/622-1966, www.originallaflowermarket.com, 8am-noon Mon. and Wed., 6am-11am Tues. and Thurs., 8am-2pm Fri., 6am-2pm Sat., $2 Mon.-Fri., $1 Sat.), one of the country's largest.

Offering big discounts on precious stones and metals, the **Jewelry District** (Hill St., Olive St., and Broadway) gives those with an obsession for shiny things endless opportunities to hold on and not let go! Parking is available on Broadway.

The historic Mexican marketplace on **Olvera Street** (125 Paseo de la Plaza, www.calleolvera.com, 10am-7pm daily) includes dozens of vendor stalls selling leather items, sombreros, pottery, puppets, and handcrafted gifts.

Hollywood

Iconic **Amoeba Records** (6400 W. Sunset Blvd., 323/245-6400, www.amoeba.com, 10:30am-11pm Mon.-Sat., 11am-10pm Sun.) sells a dazzling array of music in every genre and format. The store also hosts live music performances by rising artists.

Hollywood style isn't all about the red carpet. Young stylish women in L.A. get their glamour shopping done at an array of **Melrose Avenue Boutiques** (Melrose Ave. between La Cienega and La Brea), finding fashionable accessories and attire fit for clubs, dates, and sun. The shops tend to get more upscale the farther west you go, anchored by the hip sportswear and high-end beauty products of the legendary **Fred Segal** (8100 Melrose Ave., 323/655-9500, www.fredsegal.com, 10am-7pm Mon. Sat., 11am-6pm Sun.).

Since 1934, the **Original Farmers Market** (6333 W. 3rd St., 323/933-9211, www.farmersmarketla.com, 9am-9pm Mon.-Fri., 9am-8pm Sat., 10am-7pm Sun.) has offered everything from gourmet foods to toys and gifts, with many local favorites among its 70 vendors.

A trolley connects the farmers market to an upscale outdoor mall, **The Grove** (189 The Grove Dr., 323/900-8080, www.thegrovela.com, 10am-9pm Mon.-Fri., 10am-10pm Sat., 10am-8pm Sun.), which offers boutiques and high-end department stores. A beautifully landscaped park features a "dancing" water fountain choreographed to music.

Beverly Hills

The five floors of **Barneys New York** (9570 Wilshire Blvd., 310/276-4400, www.barneys.com, 11am-7pm Mon.-Sat., 11am-6pm Sun.) are filled with enough designer clothing, cosmetics, and jewelry to put any fashion diva in a Prada coma. Get some air and a glass of wine at the rooftop restaurant.

MAC Cosmetics (363 N. Beverly Dr., 310/285-9917, www.maccosmetics.com, 10am-7pm Mon.-Sat., 11am-6pm Sun.) supplies beauty products that you can't find anywhere else. Displays of eye shadows and lipsticks are arranged like works of art, and professional makeup artists offer private lessons.

52

LOS ANGELES

The eight-level **Beverly Center** (8500 Beverly Blvd., 310/854-0070, www.beverlycenter.com, 10am-9pm Mon.-Fri., 10am-8pm Sat., 11am-6pm Sun.) includes stores ranging from boutiques to big retailers. Altogether you'll find about 160 stores in which to spend your hard-earned dollars.

★ Rodeo Drive

The rich and famous head to **Rodeo Drive** (between Santa Monica Blvd. and Wilshire Blvd.) to pick up their necessities, while everyone else settles for window-shopping. More than 100 boutiques along the three-block stretch include flagship stores for Chanel, Hermès, and Harry Winston.

Food

L.A.'s food landscape may have evolved over the past hundred years, but Angelenos have a soft spot for the classics, so many of its dining institutions remain as popular as ever—in most cases, the food even justifies their longevity! Beyond the beloved, vintage eateries, a wave of trendsetting restaurants have filled in a few foodie gaps.

Downtown

The **Original Pantry Cafe** (877 S. Figueroa St., 213/972-9279, www.pantrycafe.com, 24 hours daily, $11-35 cash only) has been a fixture in downtown L.A. since 1924, patronized by celebrities and politicians and even owned by a former mayor. Join the lines under the red-and-white awnings. The classic American fare, served in huge portions, is worth it.

It can be tough to find a way to squeeze into **★ Sqirl** (720 N. Virgil Ave., #4, 323/284-8147, www.sqirlla.com, 6:30am-4pm Mon.-Fri., 8am-4pm Sat.-Sun., $12-18), particularly on weekends, but if you're a fan of either organic food or creativity, you'll want to try. What started as a business to sell homemade jam has

turned into a trendsetting artisan food and restaurant brand.

Restaurants serving Cali-Mex cuisine abound in Los Angeles, but since 1994, **★ Guelaguetza** (3014 W. Olympic Blvd., 213/427-0608, www.ilovemole.com, 9am-10pm Mon.-Thurs., 9am-11pm Fri., 8am-11pm Sat., 8am-9pm Sun., $12-18) has blessed the city with authentic Oaxacan flavors. As you would in Oaxaca, you should go straight for the moles here—there are several, of various spice levels, and they're some of the best in the United States. Stick around for live music nightly at this large, colorful celebration of Mesoamerica.

A downtown landmark since 1917, **Grand Central Market** (317 S. Broadway, 213/624-2378, www.grandcentralmarket.com, 8am-10pm daily) is the oldest open-air market in the city, offering a wide variety of authentic dishes from around the world, from Mexican to Middle Eastern delights to Asian favorites. The market is often packed with locals grabbing a bite to go (Eggslut wins for longest line ever!) and tourists strolling about the food and gift shops. There is a parking garage ($2 for 90 minutes) on Hill Street (a one-way road).

In Chinatown, you'll spot a number of Chinese restaurants, but a couple of the neighborhood's best-known eateries head in a different direction. Diners line up for the best Nashville hot chicken on the West Coast at **Howlin' Ray's** (727 N. Broadway, #128, 213/935-8399, www.howlinrays.com, 11am-7pm Tues.-Fri., 10am-7pm Sat.-Sun., $9-14). **Philippe the Original** (1001 North Alameda, 213/628-3781, www.philippes.com, 6am-10pm daily, $8-10) dates to 1908 and claims to have invented the French dip sandwich, which it continues to serve with lamb, roast beef, turkey, or pastrami.

Artists have set up shop in the Arts District since the 1970s, but they've never eaten as well as they do in the 21st century. The elevated plant-based cuisine at **Café Gratitude** (300 S. Santa Fe Ave.,

213/929-5580, www.cafegratitude.com, 8am-10pm daily, $12-18) will please vegans and, more importantly, their traveling companions. Free of meat, dairy, or synthetic ingredients, the flavorful dishes are healthful, balanced, and organic, including a pay-what-you-can bowl of grains, kale, and beans.

Bestia (2121 E. 7th Pl., 213/514-5724, www.bestiala.com, 5pm-11pm Sun.-Thurs., 5pm-midnight Fri.-Sat., $20-130) has gained a reputation as one of the city's best restaurants. Their Italian dishes are created with house-cured meats, as well as local, organic, and seasonal ingredients.

Hollywood

The city's most casual James Beard Award-winning restaurant is **Yuca's** (2056 Hillhurst Ave., 323/662-1214, www.yucasla.com, 11am-6pm Mon.-Sat., $3-10), a tiny food shack that serves some of the best Mexican fare in L.A., from breakfast burritos to tacos.

Eventually, everyone in L.A. eats at cultish chili dog spot **Pink's Hot Dogs** (709 N. La Brea Ave., 323/931-4223, www.pinkshollywood.com, 9:30am-2am Sun.-Thurs., 9:30am-3am Fri.-Sat., $4-10). It's been a late-night craving since 1939.

A local legend, ★ **Zankou Chicken** (7851 Sunset Blvd., 323/882-6365, www.zankouchicken.com, 10am-11pm daily, $8-14) slowly cooks chicken to perfection Armenian-style. Order a whole or half chicken, falafel, kebabs, or the miraculous marinated chicken *tarna,* and ask for extra garlic paste.

The wood-fired oven at **Pizzeria Mozza** (641 N. Highland Ave., 323/297-0101, www.pizzeriamozza.com, noon-midnight daily, $16-35) turns out rustic, blistered pizzas with luxurious toppings. Reservations are tough to get, but bar seats are available for walk-ins.

Next door to Pizzeria Mozza, **Osteria Mozza** (6602 Melrose Ave., 323/297-0100, www.osteriamozza.com, 5:30pm-10pm Mon.-Thurs., 5:30pm-11pm Fri.,

5pm-11pm Sat., 5pm-10pm Sun., $19-38) is just as popular. The large menu includes luscious pastas and adventurous meat dishes, plus a famous mozzarella bar, highlighting incredible imported cheeses.

If there's a kind of meat you've always wanted to try, chances are it will turn up at **Animal** (435 N. Fairfax Ave., 323/782-9225, www.animalrestaurant.com, 6pm-10pm Sun.-Thurs., 6pm-11pm Fri.-Sat., 10:30am-2:30pm Sat.-Sun., $20-40). A place for the carnivore's carnivore, the trendsetting restaurant helped start a whole animal butchery renaissance with a minimalist menu that delves into game and specialty meats, including offal.

In steak house terms, ★ **Musso & Frank** (6667 Hollywood Blvd., 323/467-7788, www.mussoandfrank.com, 11am-11pm Tues.-Sat., 4pm-9pm Sun., $25-45) is Tinseltown to its core. It will be a century old in 2019, and while the Hollywood outside its front door has spun off into the future, timeless style pervades its leather booths and mahogany bar.

Beverly Hills

Nate 'n Al Delicatessen (414 N. Beverly Dr., 310/274-0101, www.natenal.com, 7am-9pm daily, $14-30) has been packing them in since 1945, with thick deli meat sandwiches, smoked fish bagels, and the signature Al's Chopped Salad. It's basically a traditional Jewish neighborhood deli, but it's Beverly Hills' neighborhood deli, so the conversation at the next table could clue you in to who's going to star in the next comic book movie blockbuster.

Entertainment bigwigs conduct business meetings at **The Grill on the Alley** (9560 Dayton Way, 310/276-0615, www.thegrill.com, 11:30am-9pm Mon., 11:30am-10pm Tues.-Thurs., 11:30am-10:30pm Fri.-Sat., 5pm-9pm Sun., $25-55), which pleases with all-American comfort food like meat loaf, its signature chicken potpie, and generously portioned shortcake. Reservations are wise.

Wolfgang Puck's ★ **Spago Beverly Hills** (176 N. Canon Dr., 310/385-0880, www.wolfgangpuck.com, noon-2:30pm Tues.-Sat., 6pm-10pm Mon.-Fri., 5:30pm-10:30pm Sat., 5:30pm-10pm Sun., $26-145) has earned its iconic status. The open kitchen crafts inspired dishes with the best locally grown ingredients, and the wine list is mind-boggling. Outside, the romantic patio is centered on a fountain etched with the word *passion* and two imported 100-year-old olive trees.

West Side

West of downtown Los Angeles, and en route via I-10 to Santa Monica, are a few eateries worth a stop. The fans waiting for counter space at old-school burger joint **The Apple Pan** (10801 W. Pico Blvd., 310/475-3585, 11am-11pm Tues.-Thurs. and Sun., 11am-1am Fri.-Sat., $8-11) make the case these are L.A.'s best hamburgers.

The huge sandwiches and heartwarming soups at **Canter's Deli** (419 N. Fairfax Ave., 213/651-2030, www.cantersdeli.com, 24 hours daily, $12-20) draw night owls to the heart of the predominantly Jewish Fairfax District.

Roy Choi become one of L.A.'s most famous chefs by driving his Kogi food truck to locations all over town. Fans tracked him on social media to line up and gorge on his tasty Korean-style tacos. These days, there's no need to check Twitter—a full-time taqueria serves these tacos at **Kogi** (3500 Overland Ave., #100, 424/326-3031, www.kogibbq.com, 11am-11pm Tues.-Sat., 11am-9pm Sun., $5-8).

Accommodations

Under $150

Outside of downtown, the renovated **Jerry's Motel** (285 Lucas Ave., 213/481-8181, www.jerrysmotel.com, from $110) offers one of the best bang-for-your-buck stays in Los Angeles. It aims to be clean, safe, and affordable and hits the mark. For cheap digs close to the action, **USA Hostels Hollywood** (1624 Schrader Blvd., 323/462-3777 and 800/524-6783, www.usahostels.com, $37 dorms, $129 private) puts you right in the center of Hollywood's happening nightlife.

$150-250

A bastion of downtown, the **Millennium Biltmore** (506 S. Grand Ave., 213/624-1011, www.millenniumhotels.com/LA, from $175) was a grand hotel that hosted celebrities and dignitaries in its 1930s heyday. The massive property is still a beaut, with its Roman exterior and ornate, cavernous public spaces that make staying there feel like a steal.

Just off Sunset Boulevard, the ★ **Magic Castle Hotel** (7025 Franklin Ave., 323/851-0800, www.magiccastlehotel.com, from $199) is two blocks from the Hollywood Walk of Fame and TCL Chinese Theatre. Choose from standard, one-room, or two-room suites, each with complimentary breakfast and guest robes and cozy slippers. Guests also get free tickets to the Magic Castle, a private magic club.

On Hollywood's west side, **Farmer's Daughter Hotel** (115 S. Fairfax Ave., 323/937-3930, www.farmersdaughterhotel.com, from $199, $18 parking) hosts *American Idol* contestants. In addition to urban cowboy decor, rooms feature rain showerheads, a refrigerator, hair dryer, and minibar. Strange but fun mutant-size rubber duckies hang out at the pool.

Housed in the historic 1927 United Artists building, the hip ★ **Ace Hotel** (929 S. Broadway, 213/623-3233, www.acehotel.com/losangeles, from $223) includes an ornate theater, vibrant lounges, and a cozy coffee shop.

With a retro-1960s vibe, **The Standard Downtown** (550 S. Flower St., 213/892-8080, www.standardhotels.com, from $235) features platform beds, roomy tubs, peekaboo showers, and the world's coolest rooftop poolside bar.

The 1927 art deco **Crescent Hotel** (403 N. Crescent Dr., 310/247-0505, www.crescentbh.com, from $240) is just two blocks from famed Rodeo Drive. Rooms range from the 130-square-foot "Itty Bitty" to the 400-square-foot "Grand King." Beds are triple-sheeted in Turkish cotton. The Terrace offers classic breakfast and dinner menus, while The Lounge serves evening cocktails and small plates.

Over $250

The intricate design at Spanish-inspired **Hotel Figueroa** (939 S. Figueroa St., 213/627-8971 and 877/724-1973, www.hotelfigueroa.com, from $250) includes elegant arches and richly colored rooms. Its central location is close to great restaurants, clubs, and downtown attractions.

In the heart of West Hollywood, **Mondrian Hotel** (8440 Sunset Blvd., 323/650-8999, from $250) demonstrates luxury from the moment you open its mahogany doors and step into its modish lobby. Rooms feature 300-thread-count sheets, rain showerheads, bamboo floors, and floor-to-ceiling windows. The Lobby Bar offers a café menu, while the Herringbone restaurant serves fine seafood. The Skybar is an open-air poolside lounge, fully equipped with world-class DJs, celebrity guests, and stunning city views.

In the heart of Hollywood, the most happening stay is at ★ **The Hollywood Roosevelt Hotel** (7000 Hollywood Blvd., 323/856-1970, www.thehollywoodroosevelt.com, from $289), an elegant, Old Hollywood rehab with well-furnished rooms built around a central courtyard, where drinks are served poolside and a party always seems imminent.

In West Hollywood is the storied ★ **Chateau Marmont** (8221 Sunset Blvd., 323/656-1010, www.chateaumarmont.com, from $536). The posh hotel (and cottages) have served as temporary residence to luminaries in the world of music, film, and books. Writers such as Hunter Thompson, Billy Wilder, and F. Scott Fitzgerald have written while staying here and members of Led Zeppelin, The Rolling Stones, and The Doors have been kicked out of the place. The hotel has also been the rumored site of celebrity trysts for generations, from Errol Flynn to Clark Gable and from Natalie Wood to Scarlett Johannson.

Even steps away from Rodeo Drive, the exquisite Italian Renaissance architecture of the ★ **Beverly Wilshire Hotel** (9500 Wilshire Blvd., 310/275-5200, www.fourseasons.com, from $595) stands out. Inside, marble crown moldings, dark woods, and crystal chandeliers continue the elegance. Three restaurants and two bars offer an array of dishes and drinks.

Information and Services

The **Los Angeles Convention and Visitors Bureau** (www.discoverlosangeles.com) maintains visitor information centers adjacent to three Metro stations, including the **Hollywood and Highland Visitors Center** (6801 Hollywood Blvd., 323/467-6412, 9am-10pm Mon.-Sat., 10am-7pm Sun.). Two downtown locations are the **Union Station Visitors Center** (800 N. Alameda St., 9am-5pm daily) and the **InterContinental Los Angeles Downtown** (900 Wilshire Blvd., 9am-8pm daily) near the 7th Street/Metro Center stop. Maps, brochures, information, tickets, and advice about visiting the greater Los Angeles area are all available.

Getting Around

Car

Despite all the jokes about traffic, it's true what they say: nobody walks in L.A. Los Angeles is crisscrossed with freeways, providing numerous access points into the city, so Angelenos are accustomed to driving from east to west, or south to north, on a regular if not daily basis. Traffic can be awful anytime, even outside of the excruciating weekday **rush hours** (6:30am-930am and 3:30pm-6:30pm). Expect local drivers to be aggressive when changing lanes and at intersections, whether or not they signal, even when they're obviously using their phone. On the bright side, it's not easy to get lost.

Parking in Los Angeles can be challenging as well. Some hotels include free parking, others charge a hefty fee. Free street parking can be difficult or impossible due to posted hourly restrictions and neighborhood permit requirements. Pay special attention to signs restricting parking during rush hour and street sweeping times; they tell you exactly when your car will be towed if you park there.

Car sharing services **Uber** (www.uber.com) and **Lyft** (www.lyft.com) can make life easier, but they can't beat traffic either: check the ride estimate before summoning a driver.

If you need to rent a car for your road trip, you will find all the usual options doing business within a free shuttle ride of each airport: **Enterprise** (www.enterprise.com), **Hertz** (www.hertz.com), and **Alamo** (www.alamo.com). **Hertz** (213/625-1034, www.hertz.com), **Avis** (213/617-2137, www.avis.com), and **Budget** (213/917-2977, www.budget.com) also have rental counters in Union Station. For an added fee, a rental agency may allow you to rent a car at one airport and return it at another.

Public Transit

A behemoth network of buses run throughout the entire city, and a growing public rail system now extends between downtown Los Angeles and Hollywood, Pasadena, Long Beach, South Bay, and Santa Monica. All are operated by **LA Metro** (323/466-3876, www.metro.net, $1.75 one-way, day pass $7, seven-day pass $25). You may board a bus with exact change; otherwise purchase a ticket or a day pass from ticket vending machines present in all Metro rail stations. If you plan to ride the Metro often, consider purchasing a refillable **TAP card** ($1 plus regular fare); including unlimited day and week passes.

Some buses run 24 hours. The Metro rail lines can start running as early as 4:30am and don't stop until as late as 1:30am. See the Metro website for route maps, timetables, and fare details.

★ Disneyland

TOP EXPERIENCE

Mickey Mouse and friends have been welcoming guests to Disneyland for nearly 70 years, and the amount of imagination put into the theme park has never wavered. The amusement park's success is that it doesn't merely offer thrill rides—it offers a story to go with it. The magical theme park excels at creating a fantasy for children of all ages, bringing cartoons, fairy tales, and movie characters to life in every conceivable kind of interactive entertainment.

The park stays fairly busy year-round (an urban legend says it's not crowded on Super Bowl Sunday, but people who go there expecting shorter lines report otherwise).

Getting There

Disneyland is in Anaheim, in Orange County, about 25 miles (40 km) south of downtown Los Angeles and accessible

Disneyland

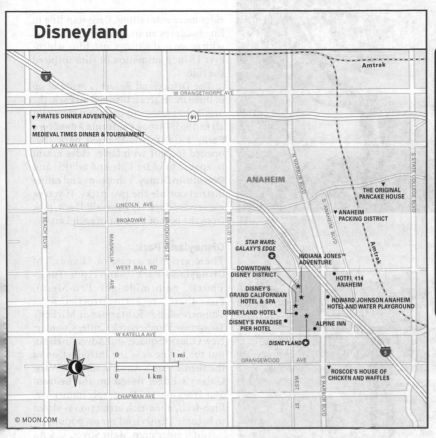

© MOON.COM

from I-5 South. Exit on Disneyland Drive toward Ball Road; stay in the left three lanes for **parking** (1313 S. Disneyland Dr., $20).

From Long Beach, Disneyland can be reached via CA-22 East. Plan on at least 45 minutes for the drive and avoid the weekday afternoon rush hour known as the Orange Crush (3:30pm-6:30pm).

The **Anaheim Resort Transportation Shuttle** (www.rideart.org, $3 one-way, $5.50 day pass) also connects the park to Anaheim hotels, commercial districts, restaurants, and travel hubs.

Disneyland Resort

The "Happiest Place on Earth" lures millions of visitors of all ages each year with promises of fun and fantasy. During high seasons, waves of humanity flow through **Disneyland Resort** (1313 S. Disneyland Dr., Anaheim, 714/781-4565, www. disneyland.disney.go.com, Disneyland Park 8am-11pm Tues.-Thurs., 8am-midnight Fri.-Mon., one-day ticket for one park $104-149 ages 10 and up, $95-115 ages 3-9, additional $60 for Park Hopper pass to both parks), and tickets will cost more on the busiest days, such as holidays and weekends.

Disney's rides, put together by the park's "Imagineers," are better than those at any other amusement park in the west. The technology of the rides isn't necessarily more advanced than other parks, but attention to details makes Disneyland

rides more enthralling. Even standing in line becomes an immersive experience, with props and settings matching whichever Disney animation or film inspired the ride.

The Disneyland Resort is made of up of three main areas: **Disneyland Park,** the original amusement park that started it all in 1955; **Disney California Adventure Park,** a California-themed park that opened in 2001 with faster rides meant to appeal to older kids and adults; and **Downtown Disney,** a shopping and eating district outside the two parks. If you've got several days, try them all! If not, pick from the best of the best in each Land.

Disneyland Park

There are nine areas, or "Lands," of **Disneyland Park** (8am-11pm Tues.-Thurs., 8am-midnight Fri.-Mon.). First there are Main Street, U.S.A.; Tomorrowland; Fantasyland; Mickey's Toontown; Frontierland; Critter Country; New Orleans Square; and Adventureland. But the big news is the introduction of the theme park's ninth land: Star Wars: Galaxy's Edge! Based on the beloved *Star Wars* movies, the deeply immersive, high-tech, alien-rich attraction is slated to become Disneyland's most popular.

You'll enter onto Main Street, U.S.A., which offers shops, information booths, and other practicalities. Your first stop inside the park should be one of the information kiosks near the front entrance. Here you can get a map, a schedule of the day's events, and the inside scoop on what's going on in the park during your visit.

Due north of Main Street is Sleeping Beauty's Castle and Fantasyland, with Mickey's Toontown beyond that to the northeast and Star Wars: Galaxy's Edge to the northwest. Tomorrowland takes up the eastern wing of the park. Adventureland and Frontierland lie to the

Top to bottom: Jungle Cruise; Star Wars: Galaxy's Edge; Pirates of the Caribbean.

west of Main Street, with New Orleans Square to the west of Adventureland, and Critter Country in the far western reaches of the park.

The magical **FastPasses** are free with park admission. The newest and most popular rides offer FastPass kiosks near the entrances. Feed your ticket into one of the machines, and it will spit out both your ticket and a FastPass with your specified time to take the ride. Come back during your window and enter the always-much-shorter FastPass line, designated by a sign at the entrance. If you're with a group, be sure you all get your FastPasses at the same time, so you all get the same time window to ride the ride.

Adventureland
Adventureland is home to **Indiana Jones Adventure,** arguably one of the best rides in all of Disneyland. Even the queue is interesting: Check out the signs, equipment, and artifacts in mock-dusty tunnels winding toward the ride. The ride itself, in a roller-coaster style variant of an all-terrain vehicle, jostles and jolts you through a landscape that Indy himself might dash through, pursued by booby-traps and villains. Hang on to your hat—literally! It's also home to the kitschy, classic **Jungle Cruise,** where you'll encounter angry, angry hippos.

New Orleans Square
Located next to Adventureland is New Orleans Square and the **Pirates of the Caribbean** ride. Look for Captain Jack Sparrow to pop up among the other disreputable characters engaged in all sorts of debauchery. For a taste of truly classic Disney, line up in the graveyard for a tour of the **Haunted Mansion.** Concentrating more on creating a ghoulish atmosphere, rather than speed or twists and turns, it's less of a ride than a spooky experience.

Critter Country
Winnie the Pooh and singing bears populate Critter Country, where the main attraction is **Splash Mountain,** Disney's take on the log ride. The ride culminates in a long drop fashioned as if going over a waterfall. As the name suggests, it is possible that you'll get wet on this ride.

Frontierland
Parts of Frontierland were closed to make room for Star Wars, but you can still take a ride on a careening Wild West train on the **Big Thunder Mountain Railroad.** This older roller coaster whisks away passengers on a brief but fun thrill ride through a "dangerous, decrepit" mountain's mine shafts.

Fantasyland
Fantasyland sits behind **Sleeping Beauty's Castle,** which itself is not a ride, but a walk-through attraction—and the most likely place to meet costumed Disney princesses and friends. Many of the rides here cater to the younger set, such as the **carousel,** flying **Dumbos,** the spinning teacups at the **Mad Tea Party,** and **It's a Small World.** With a constant soundtrack of the famous song in the background, this ride slowly tours an idealized vision of the world and introduces some favorite Disney characters.

The crazy fun of **Mr. Toad's Wild Ride** appeals to all ages, with a rickety funhouse ride weaving a wacky, explosively colorful narrative. If it's a faster thrill you're seeking, head for one of the most recognizable landmarks at Disneyland. The **Matterhorn Bobsleds** roller coaster looks like a miniature version of its Swiss Alps namesake. Bobsled coaster cars plunge down the mountain on a twisted track that takes you past rivers, glaciers, and the Abominable Snowman.

Mickey's Toontown
Set behind Fantasyland, Mickey's Toontown is the company town where Mickey, Donald Duck, Goofy, and other classic Disney cartoon characters make their residences. Wandering through it, mingling with the toons, you'll feel like

you're inside a cartoon yourself. The main ride here is **Roger Rabbit's Car Toon Spin.**

Tomorrowland

Toward the front of the park, Tomorrowland, despite its futuristic theme, is home to many classics, like **Star Tours** and perennial favorite **Space Mountain,** a fast roller coaster that whizzes through an almost entirely darkened world.

★ Star Wars: Galaxy's Edge

Opening in fall 2019, this highly anticipated section of park is designed to immerse guests within the world created by the *Star Wars* movie franchise. Specifically, a smuggler's outpost at the farthest edge of the known galaxy, where one may encounter familiar aliens, droids, and members of the resistance. Minute details of the scenery serve to tell a story via a smartphone app, part of the technology-enriched fantasy experience.

Advanced reservations may be required for these high-demand new attractions.

The **Millennium Falcon: Smugglers Run** attraction puts you behind the controls as you jump into hyperspace as pilot of Han Solo's *Millennium Falcon.* Other seats include that of a flight engineer or the gunner's chair.

Star Wars: Rise of the Resistance may be the most ambitious interactive experience in theme park history. Guests are given an active role in the rebellion: Your mission on a full-size starship hurries down the halls of a Star Destroyer as you go head-to-head with the First Order.

Disney California Adventure Park

Disney California Adventure Park (8am-10pm daily) celebrates much of what makes California special. Like Disneyland Park, it's divided into thematic areas. Rides in California Adventure tend toward the thrills of other major amusement parks but include

Star Wars: Galaxy's Edge

the great Disney touches that make it memorable.

You'll find two information booths just inside the main park entrance: one off to the left as you walk through the turnstile and one at the opening to Sunshine Plaza. This is where you'll get your park guide, Time Guide, and more information about what's going on in the park that day.

Hollywood Pictures Backlot
Celebrating SoCal's famed film industry, the Backlot holds the ultimate thrill ride: **The Twilight Zone Tower of Terror.** Enter the creepy "old hotel," go through the "service area," and take your place inside an elevator straight out of your worst nightmares on this free-fall ride.

Less extreme but also fun, **Monsters, Inc. Mike & Sully to the Rescue!** invites guests into the action of the movie of the same name. You'll help the heroes as they chase the intrepid Boo. This ride jostles you around a bit but can be

suitable for smaller kids as well as bigger ones.

A Bug's Land
Wanna live like a bug? Get a sample of the world of tiny insects on **It's Tough to Be a Bug!** This big-group, 3-D, multisensory ride offers fun for little kids and adults alike. You'll fly through the air, scuttle through the grass, and get a good idea of what life is like on six little legs. When they say this ride engages *all of your senses,* they mean it.

Paradise Pier
Paradise Pier mimics the Santa Monica Pier and other waterfront attractions like it, with thrill rides and an old-fashioned midway. Most of the extreme rides cluster in the Paradise Pier area. The extra-long **California Screamin',** a high-tech roller coaster designed after the classic wooden coasters of carnivals past, includes drops, twists, a full loop, and plenty of screaming fun.

Golden State
For attractions styled after the Bay Area, Wine Country, and Cannery Row, head to the aptly named Golden State. For a bird's-eye view of California, try **Soarin' Over California.** This combination ride and show puts you on the world's biggest "glider," sailing over the hills and valleys of California. You'll feel the wind in your hair as you see the vineyards, mountains, and beaches you may have encountered on your road trip. If you prefer water to wind, take a ride down the **Grizzly River Run,** which turns white-water rafting into a Disney ride.

Cars Land
The high-powered characters from the 2006 hit film *Cars* populate rides like **Luigi's Flying Tires** and **Mater's Junkyard Jamboree.** The **Radiator Springs Racers** has park visitors racing through the film's Route 66-inspired setting in six-person vehicles.

Downtown Disney

You don't need an admission ticket to take a stroll through the shops of Downtown Disney. In addition to the mammoth World of Disney Store, you'll find a Build-a-Bear Workshop and a Lego Store, among mall staples like Sephora. You can also have a bite to eat or take in some jazz or a new-release movie at Downtown Disney.

Food
Disney Dining

The best areas of the Disneyland Park to grab a bite are Main Street, New Orleans, and Frontierland as they offer the most variety in concessions. But you can find at least a snack almost anywhere in the park. In Galaxy's Edge, vendors serve green and blue milk, and **Oga's Cantina** is where all the hip droids and aliens hang out.

For a sit-down restaurant meal inside the park, make reservations in advance for a table at the **Blue Bayou Restaurant** (New Orleans Square, 714/781-3463, $35-60), set in a dimly lit "swamp" overlooking the Pirates of the Caribbean ride. The Cajun and Creole cuisine matches the atmosphere, with large portions somewhat making up for overpriced meals.

Most of the food in Disney California Adventure Park is clustered in the Golden State area. For a Mexican feast, try **Cocina Cucamonga Mexican Grill** (Pacific Wharf, $10.50-14). If you're just dying for a cold beer, get one at the **Bayside Brews** (Paradise Pier, $6-8). If your thirst is for California wines, head for the **Mendocino Terrace** (Pacific Wharf, $9-15).

Outside the Parks

To escape the ubiquitous fast-food and franchise restaurants immediately outside the park, head over to the **Anaheim Packing District** (440 S. Anaheim Blvd., 714/533-7225, www.anaheimpackingdistrict.com, 9am-midnight daily). It's kind of like a food court without the mall, featuring a diverse assortment of local vendors serving decent food at reasonable prices, as well as coffee and drinks.

A homey diner serving classic American breakfasts, **Original Pancake House** (1418 E. Lincoln Ave., 714/535-9815, www.originalpancakehouse.com, 6am-2pm daily, $8-12) has been a long-time Anaheim favorite. It's easy to find—just look for its kitschy cartoon chef sign. Los Angeles soul food legend **Roscoe's House of Chicken and Waffles** (2110 S. Harbor Blvd., 714/823-4130, www.roscoeschickenandwaffles.com, 8am-11pm Sun.-Thurs., 8am-1am Fri.-Sat., $9-14) offers a spacious and comfortable outpost that serves its signature pairing as well as hot biscuits, grits, and more.

While visiting the land of fantasy, you might as well add some jousting and swordplay with a meal at the entertaining **Medieval Times Dinner & Tournament** (7662 Beach Blvd., 714/523-1100, www.medievaltimes.com, 9am-midnight daily, $64 adults, $38 children under 3-12), which turns dinner theater into a contact sport. Along the same lines but with a pirate theme, **Pirates Dinner Adventure** (7600 Beach Blvd., 714/690-1497, www.piratesdinneradventureca.com, $63 adult, $37 ages 3-11) serves three courses to go along with aerial tricks and swordfights.

Accommodations
Disney Hotels

For the most iconic Disney resort experience, you must stay at the **Disneyland Hotel** (1150 Magic Way, 714/778-6600, http://disneyland.disney.go.com, $500-625). This nearly 1,000-room high-rise monument to brand-specific family entertainment has themed swimming pools, themed play areas, and even character-themed guest rooms that allow the kids to fully immerse themselves in the Mouse experience. The monorail stops inside the hotel, offering guests the easiest way into the park proper without having to deal with parking.

It's easy to find the **Paradise Pier Hotel** (1717 S. Disneyland Dr., 714/999-0990, http://disneyland.disney.go.com, $270-370); it's that high-rise thing just outside of the parks. This hotel boasts what passes for affordable lodgings within walking distance of the parks. Rooms are cute, colorful, and clean. You'll find a (possibly refreshing) lack of Mickeys in the standard guest accommodations at the Paradise, which has the feel of a beach resort motel.

Disney's Grand Californian Hotel and Spa (1600 S. Disneyland Dr., 714/635-2300, http://disneyland.disney. go.com, $540-740) lies inside Disney California Adventure Park, attempting to mimic the famous Ahwahnee Lodge in Yosemite. The hotel is surrounded by gardens and has restaurants, a day spa, and shops attached on the ground floors; it can also get you right out into Downtown Disney and thence to the parks proper. Guest rooms at the Californian offer more luxury than the other Disney resorts, with dark woods and faux-Craftsman detailing creating an attractive atmosphere.

Outside the Parks

The budget-friendly **Hotel 414** (414 West Ball Rd., 714-533-2570, www.hotel414anaheim.com, from $140) has rooms characterized by hardwood floors and modern furnishings. It's across the freeway from the Disneyland Resort and offers a pool, free parking and Internet, and a stop on the Anaheim Resort Transportation Shuttle.

Tucked into a corner behind the Disney California Adventure Park, the **Alpine Inn** (715 W. Katella Ave., 844/387-9572, www.alpineinnanaheim.com, from $150) offers comfortable rooms with microwaves, coffeemakers, and minifridges as well as a heated pool and free parking and Internet.

A few hundred yards from the Disneyland entrance, **Howard Johnson Anaheim Hotel and Water Playground** (1380 S. Harbor Blvd., 855/873-6566, www.hojoanaheim.com, from $190) offers more than just comfortable rooms with free parking and Wi-Fi. On-site amenities include waterslides, water cannons, and a toddler wading pool that will give kids added playtime while parents recover from the long days in the park.

**Southern
California
Beaches**

Southern California Beaches

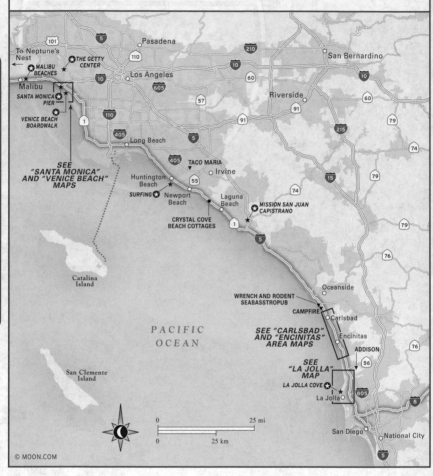

M odern beach and surf culture grew up along the Southern California coast.

The coast is Southern California's most precious resource. For more than 150 miles (242 km), from Malibu to La Jolla, its blue horizons, light sands, and laid-back lifestyle are the envy of the world.

Malibu manages to remain part of greater Los Angeles while also offering rural beach and mountain experiences. Santa Monica is part of L.A.'s urban orbit, embodying the upscale coast, while slightly south, neighboring Venice gives the beach its grungy, countercultural edge.

The South Bay beach towns of posh Manhattan Beach, playful Hermosa Beach, and built-up Redondo Beach adopt a more suburban lifestyle, with million-dollar homes, endless bike paths, and popular surf breaks. South of the harbor

Highlights

★ **Malibu Beaches:** Remote sandy beaches backed by verdant mountains give the Malibu coastline its cachet (page 70).

★ **Santa Monica Pier:** Surrounded by a gorgeous beach and topped by a small amusement park, the pier is the center of attention (page 76).

★ **The Getty Center:** High above Santa Monica and Beverly Hills, this hilltop museum has views that are as great as the artwork within (page 76).

★ **Venice Beach Boardwalk:** From the freaky to the fantastic, the Venice Boardwalk has people-watching of epic proportions (page 77).

★ **Surfing at Huntington Beach:** Riding the waves at Surf City USA is the best way to spend a day in Orange County (page 91).

★ **Mission San Juan Capistrano:** This lovely historic mission is one of the oldest buildings in California and is home to an annual migration of swallows (page 97).

★ **La Jolla Cove:** An underwater reserve lies beneath this pretty cove that is perfect for snorkeling and scuba diving (page 114).

Best Restaurants

★ **Neptune's Net:** After a day riding waves, Malibu surfers sate their appetites with fresh seafood at the cliffside spot (page 74).

★ **Gjelina:** A short walk but a far cry from the Venice Boardwalk, this contemporary dining destination is all about the flavor (page 81).

★ **Sushi Chitose:** It's the best bang for your buck *omakase* menu in greater Los Angeles (page 85).

★ **Beachwood Brewing & BBQ:** With killer barbecue and even better beer, it's half the reason to go to Long Beach (page 86).

★ **Taco Maria:** This Mexican food is worth leaving the beach for in Orange County (page 92).

★ **Wrench and Rodent Seabasstropub:** Let the unorthodox sushi chefs guide you through a seafood journey you can't experience elsewhere (page 100)!

★ **Campfire:** This wood fire restaurant thrives on fine food and social atmosphere (page 104).

★ **Addison:** One of the state's best wine collections supports top-tier fine dining in Del Mar (page 110).

★ **George's at the Cove:** Incredible views of La Jolla Cove combine with exceptional food and service (page 118).

city Long Beach, the coast passes through upscale Newport Beach and Huntington Beach, known as Surf City USA.

Close to San Diego, La Jolla is home to one of the best beaches for relaxing and splashing in the waves. Just to the north, the cliffs at Torrey Pines State Natural Reserve offer scenic hiking opportunities and undeveloped beaches, as well as a famous golf course.

Each beach town offers a slightly distinctive take on the same premise: Toasty sand, blue waves, and sunshine, and the happy people who build a life around them.

Getting There

To experience the Southern California coast, bypass its urban sprawl and congested freeways in favor of a coastal drive along the Pacific Coast Highway (Hwy. 1 and US-101). The road stretches roughly 150 miles (240 km) between Malibu and La Jolla.

The southern stretch of the Pacific Coast Highway occasionally takes an unexpected turn or jumps over to a new roadway as it navigates around the coast's curves, cliffs, and peninsulas, but you can more or less chart a direct course from beach town to beach town. Or break up the trip, hitting the beaches in between excursions to and from deserts, cities, and mountains.

From Los Angeles
30-40 mi/48-64 km, 1 hr

From Los Angeles, you can reach **Malibu** by taking US-101 northwest for 87 miles (140 km) to connect to with CA-1 south. Alternatively, I-10 also leads west from downtown Los Angeles to meet the coast

Best Hotels

★ **Hotel Erwin:** Close to everything worth seeing and doing in Venice Beach, it still manages to stay lovely (page 82).

★ **Viceroy Hotel:** This ecofriendly Santa Monica hotel is a trendsetter (page 82).

★ **Crystal Cove Beach Cottages:** Enjoy a peaceful retreat in a rustic cabin on one of the last undeveloped beaches in Southern California (page 97).

★ **The Lodge at Torrey Pines:** This golf resort is hallowed ground—overlooking the ocean—and your stay earns you preferred tee times (page 114).

★ **La Valencia:** This La Jolla villa is almost as beautiful as its views of the shimmering Pacific (page 119).

at **Santa Monica.** In 16 miles (26 km), I-10 merges onto CA-1 north, passing from Santa Monica into southern Malibu. Note that drive times may increase during rush hour traffic.

From San Diego
152 mi/245 km, 3 hr
From San Diego, I-5 connects north to **La Jolla** in about 15 miles (24 km). It's possible to continue on I-5 north to I-405 for 132 miles (212 km) to **Santa Monica,** where CA-1 leads west to **Malibu.** Traffic begins to congest along this route around Dana Point and Mission Viejo.

Coastal Route
About 10 miles (16 km) north of San Diego along I-5, exit the freeway via La Jolla Parkway and into **La Jolla.** From La Jolla north, you can bypass I-5 by taking Torrey Pines Road north until it turns into Camino Del Mar north of Torrey Pines State Beach. Camino Del Mar continues north and eventually becomes US-101 past Del Mar. US-101 ends at **Oceanside,** where you must rejoin I-5 north for 26 miles to connect to CA-1 at Dana Point.

Air, Train, or Bus
Los Angeles International Airport (LAX, 1 World Way, Los Angeles, 855/463-5252, www.flylax.com) sits right between the coastal destinations of Venice Beach and Manhattan Beach. The massive international hub is within reach of all destinations on the Southern California coast.

The **Long Beach Airport** (LGB, 4100 Donald Douglas Dr., Long Beach, 562/570-2600, www.lgb.org) offers convenient access to the South Bay cities and is widely serviced by JetBlue.

Another option is to fly into **San Diego Airport** (SAN, 619/400-2404, www.san.org), 13 miles south of La Jolla, and approach the Pacific Coast Highway from the south.

The Expo Line of the **Los Angeles Metro** (323/466-3876, www.metro.net, $1.75) offers daily commuter rail service from downtown Los Angeles to the Santa Monica Pier (Ocean Ave. at Colorado Ave.).

Amtrak's (www.amtrak.com) *Pacific Surfliner* ferries passengers from San Juan Capistrano (26701 Verdugo St.) to San Diego (Santa Fe Depot, 1050 Kettner Blvd.).

Malibu

The signs entering Malibu (pop. 12,877) proclaim it "27 miles of scenic beauty," and there are at least that many. Rather than a centralized town, Malibu drapes itself along the Pacific Coast Highway (CA-1) at the base of the pretty Santa Monica Mountains. It's a gorgeous drive, as the highway winds between verdant canyons and sparkling ocean, with beachside colonies of multimillion-dollar homes scattered between state beaches and parks.

Tragically, the deadly Woolsey Fire of 2018 caused a fair amount of damage to the region, burning hundreds of homes and thousands upon thousands of natural acreage. While much of the wilderness has rebounded, and road crews have tirelessly repaired much of the region's infrastructure, some roads and parks in the region remain closed.

★ Beaches

There are no private beaches in Malibu. That said, the following gorgeous beaches have been preserved from development by the county and state.

If you can find an access point without trespassing on clearly delineated private property, you may avoid paying for parking and possibly catch some rays with a celebrity or two as you watch surfers enjoy some of the area's celebrated point breaks.

Point Mugu State Park

At **Point Mugu State Park** (9000 CA-1 W., 800/444-7275, www.parks.ca.gov, 8am-sunset daily, $8-12 parking), 70 miles of hiking trails complement the waves, beach dunes, and campsites far removed from Hollywood.

Point Mugu State Park is 15 miles north of Malibu on the Pacific Coast Highway.

Leo Carrillo State Park

Leo Carrillo State Park (35000 CA-1 W., 310/457-8143, www.parks.ca.gov, 8am-10pm daily, $3-12 parking) was damaged in the 2018 Woolsey Fire, but facilities are reopening. The Countyline Beach, staircase, and beach areas (1.5 mi/2.4 km north of park entrance) are open for sunbathing and swimming.

Leo Carrillo State Park is 12 miles north of Malibu on the Pacific Coast Highway.

Nicholas Canyon County Beach

Less crowded than other nearby beaches, **Nicholas Canyon** (33850 CA-1, http://beaches.lacounty.gov, dawn-dusk, $3-10 parking) offers one of several point breaks in Los Angeles County, making it a good spot for surfing, bodysurfing, bodyboarding, windsailing, and scuba diving. (The beach is often referred to as "Zeros.") Families enjoy nearly a mile-long stretch of sandy beach, with picnic tables and full bathroom facilities.

Above Nicholas Canyon Beach sits the fascinating **Wishtoyo Chumash Village** (33904 CA-1, 424/644-0088, www. wishtoyo.org). Set on a bluff overlooking the Pacific are eight prehistoric (4000-6000 BC) sites, all of which have been found within a half mile of the replicated village. Guided tours and presentations are available by appointment.

Robert H. Meyer Memorial State Beach

Robert H. Meyer Memorial State Beach (CA-1, 818/880-0363, www.parks.ca.gov) is comprised of three pocket beaches along the west end of Malibu: El Pescador, La Piedra, and El Matador.

Of the three, **El Pescador State Beach** (32860 CA-1, 310/457-1324, 8am-sunset daily) is a well-known spot for surfing, surf fishing, and bodyboarding, and also offers good beachcombing, including tidepools rich with colorful sea anemones and starfish and small caves that can be explored at low tide. *El pescador* means "the fisherman" in Spanish. Parking is limited. There are no facilities.

A rugged strip of white sand, steep cliffs, sea stacks, and incredible swells makes **El Matador State Beach** (32215 CA-1, 8am-sunset daily, $8 parking) a favorite among surfers and bodyboarders. The natural splendor has made it a favorite backdrop for photo shoots as well. Park at the top of the bluff and follow the long staircase down the cliffside and onto the beach.

El Pescador State Beach is located about 7 miles (11 km) northwest of Malibu and 3 miles (5 km) south of Leo Carrillo on CA-1. El Matador State Beach is 1 mile (1.6 km) south of El Pescador.

Zuma Beach

If you've ever seen the cult classic film *Earth Girls Are Easy,* you'll recognize legendary **Zuma Beach** (30000 CA-1, http://beaches.lacounty.gov, 6am-10pm daily, $3-13 parking). This popular surf and boogie boarding break fills fast on summer weekends. Crystal-clear water (unusual for the L.A. area) makes it good for swimming. Grab a spot on the west side of CA-1 for free parking, or pay for one of the more than 2,000 spots in the beach parking lot. Amenities include a snack bar, boardwalk, and volleyball courts, as well as restrooms and showers.

Zuma Beach is 3.5 miles (6 km) northwest of Malibu on CA-1.

Point Dume State Beach

The crystal-clear water at **Point Dume State Beach** (Westward Beach Rd., 310/457-8143, www.parks.ca.gov, sunrise-sunset daily) makes it one of the best places in Southern California to scuba dive. The views from atop the coastal bluff are outstanding. Dogs are not allowed. The beach was named in honor

Top to bottom: Malibu; El Matador State Beach; Leo Carrillo State Park.

of Padre Francisco Dumetz of Mission San Buenaventura by explorer George Vancouver (who made a spelling error).

Point Dume State Beach is 2 miles (3 km) off of CA-1. Free and pay parking is available on Westward Beach Road. A **shuttle** (10am-4pm, free) runs weekends in summer.

Malibu Lagoon State Beach

Amid a row of beachfront mansions, **Malibu Lagoon State Beach** (23200 CA-1, 310/457-8143, www.parks.ca.gov, 8am-sunset daily, $12 parking) offers easy public access. Malibu Creek runs into the ocean here, creating a unique wetlands ecosystem that's well worth exploring. Guided tours are available seasonally.

Sights include the Adamson House and Malibu Lagoon Museum and the ancillary **Malibu Surfriders Beach,** a pretty stretch of sugar-like sand and a popular destination for surfers.

Malibu Lagoon State Beach is about 6 miles (10 km) east of Malibu along CA-1.

Sights
Adamson House

It stands to reason the first Malibu beach villa would be sited on one of the coast's plumb locations. **Adamson House Museum** (Malibu Lagoon State Beach, 23200 CA-1, 310/456-8432, www.adamsonhouse.org, 11am-2pm Wed.-Sat., $7 adults, $2 children 6-16) holds this distinction, sitting above Malibu Lagoon and Pier with panoramic views including the Catalina and Channel Islands. The ornate home boasts the Spanish-Moorish architecture so en vogue in California around 1929, when the home was built for a newly married daughter of the Rindges, one of Malibu's founding families. Now a museum, the compound's ornately painted tiles, hand-carved doors, frescoes, and glass windows prove just as mesmerizing as the view.

Malibu Pier

Malibu Pier (23000 CA-1, 888/310-7437,

http://malibupier.com, 6:30am-sunset daily) is busy in the summertime and lonely in the winter, when only die-hard surfers ply the adjacent three-point break and a few fisherfolk brave the chilly weather (which in Malibu means under 70°F).

The pier hosts board rentals from **Malibu Surf Shack** (310/456-8508), sportfishing (www.malibupiersportfishing.com) and whale-watching charters, the Malibu Farm restaurant, and food stands. Interpretive signs describe the pier's history as a trading point for old Rancho Malibu.

The pier is 6 miles (10 km) east of Malibu and 11 miles (18 km) west of Santa Monica on CA-1.

The Getty Villa

Perched on the cliffs below Malibu, **The Getty Villa** (17985 CA-1, Pacific Palisades, 310/440-7300, www.getty.edu, 10am-5pm Wed.-Mon., free but reservations required, $15 parking) is a lush estate styled in the manner of an ancient Roman country home. The museum's immense collection of Etruscan, Greek, and Roman antiquities includes 44,000 pieces; only a small fraction are on display in its 23 galleries.

The Getty Villa is 14 miles (23 km) east of Malibu along CA-1.

Recreation
Hiking

There are dozens of hikes to explore along Malibu's coast and mountains; sadly, many closed following the 2018 Woolsey Fire. One canyon and waterfall hike that remains mostly intact is the moderate **Solstice Canyon** (3.2 mi/5.1 km). The loop hike leads to a waterfall, with ocean views along the way. To get there from CA-1, take Corral Canyon Road north, then fork right onto Solstice Canyon Road to the parking lot and trailhead.

If you're willing to pay the parking fee ($12) at **Malibu Creek State Park** (1925 Las

⚐ Side Trip: The Santa Monica Mountains

Santa Monica Mountains

Part of what gives the Malibu coast its beauty is having the Santa Monica Mountains rising steeply behind it, and a network of roads winding up through its sloping canyons provides miles of scenic driving. Much of the land is preserved wilderness, offering hikes and viewpoints as part of either the **Santa Monica Mountains National Recreation Area** (805/370-2301, www.nps.gov) or **Malibu Creek State Park** (1925 Las Virgenes Rd., 818/880-0367, www.parks.ca.gov, $12 parking).

Elsewhere, you'll drive past hidden, multimillion-dollar estates and popular film sets, such as the Western scenery of **Paramount Ranch** (2903 Cornell Rd., 805/370-2301, www.nps.gov) or the production location of the TV show *M*A*S*H* (www.malibucreekstatepark.org). Many of these roads and sights were damaged by the 2018 Woolsey Fire, resulting in temporary closings. Most of the locations are rebuilding and plan to reopen as soon as construction is completed.

Virgenes Rd., 818/880-0367, www.parks. ca.gov), you can access the easy **Rock Pool and Century Lake** (4.5 mi/7.2 km) loop hike. Rock climbers enjoy scrambling up the vertical walls that rise from the picturesque pool, which was featured in the original *Planet of the Apes* movie.

To simply stretch your legs while catching Malibu coastal views, explore the bluff at **Point Dume** (Cliffside Dr. at Birdview Ave.). More a network of walking paths than a hiking trail, the low-commitment hike offers a gander at why people endure so much to live here—spectacular, panoramic views. The bluff can be accessed from the state beach below or from the residential neighborhood behind. Street parking may be tough to find.

Surfing

Among surfers, Malibu is famous for the longer rides of its well-shaped point breaks, including at **Surfrider Beach** (23200 CA-1, 310/457-8143, www.parks. ca.gov, 8am-sunset daily, $12 parking) on the southwest side of Malibu Pier. Favored among longboarders is **First Point,** a long even right-breaking wave. Farther out, **Second Point** and **Third Point** tend to break bigger and rougher, better for experienced short boarders. Located closer to town, these waves get very, very crowded and competitive.

Better for beginners is **Zuma Beach** (30000 CA-1, http://beaches.lacounty.gov, 6am-10pm daily, $3-13 parking), where different waves may satisfy surfers of different skill levels. On an easy day, beginners may find luck at **County Line Beach** (42100 Pacific Coast Hwy.), though on good days the terrific point break and pumping beach breaks can be super fun for intermediate and advanced riders.

For rentals and lessons, try **Radfish Malibu** (29575 Pacific Coast Hwy., 310/433-1767, www.radfishmalibu.com, $50-60/day, 2-hr lessons $100). By the Malibu Pier, try **Zuma Jay** (22775 US-101, #100, 310/456-8044, $20-25/day).

Food

Driving the Pacific Coast Highway through Malibu, do not miss ★ **Neptune's Net** (42505 CA-1, 310/457-3095, www.neptunesnet.com, 10:30am-8pm Mon.-Thurs., 10:30am-9pm Fri., 10am-8:30pm Sat.-Sun., $8-18). The regional favorite seafood shack offers an abundance of fish with ocean views. It's a favorite among bikers, road-trippers, and, because it's adjacent to the County Line surf break, salt-encrusted local surfers.

Two sister restaurants sit on Malibu Pier (23000 CA-1). At the base of the pier is **Malibu Farm Restaurant & Bar** (310/456-8850, www.malibu-farm.com, 11am-9pm Mon.-Fri., 9am-10pm Sat., 9am-9pm Sun., $20-34), an upscale contemporary restaurant that accepts reservations. At the end of the pier sits **Malibu Farm Cafe** (310/456-1112, 8am-4pm Mon.-Thurs., 8am-9pm Fri.-Sun., $12-18), a casual eatery for walk-in guests with a panoramic rooftop view. Reservations are accepted for dinner (Wed.-Sun.).

To truly do Malibu right, splurge on an impeccable sushi feast at the world-renowned **Nobu** (22706 CA-1, 310/317-9140, www.noburestaurants.com, noon-10pm Mon.-Thurs., noon-11pm Fri., 11am-11pm Sat., 11am-10pm Sun., $50-90), where the views and food seem perpetually locked in an effort to outdo one another, and everyone wins.

Accommodations

Most tourists arrive as a day trip from Los Angeles, so only a handful of hotels do business here. The appropriately named **Malibu Country Inn** (6506 Westward Beach Rd., 310/457-9622, www.malibucountryinn.com, from $175) offers a wonderful base close to the remote western portion of Malibu, next to Zuma Beach.

Right beside Malibu Pier, boutique hotel **The Surfrider Malibu** (23033 Pacific Coast Hwy., 310/526-6158 www. thesurfridermalibu.com, from $350) fills quickly thanks to a rooftop deck and oceanview rooms, where you can monitor the waves at Surfrider Beach. Nearby, the **M Malibu** (22541 Pacific Coast Hwy., 310/456-6169, www.themmalibu.com, from $190) offers a cheaper option with retro-style rooms set across from a residential coastline.

The Sycamore Campground (9000 CA-1 W., 800/444-7275, www.parks. ca.gov, 8am-10pm daily, $45) at Point Mugu State Park has 58 campsites. Each site includes a picnic table and fire ring. Showers are available (fee).

Santa Monica and Venice

South of Malibu, Santa Monica (pop: 92,306) feels like a different world. Born as a seaside retreat in the 1900s, the city was at onetime home to silver-screen giants like Greta Garbo and Cary Grant. By the late 1960s, the Santa Monica Freeway brought new growth and an eclectic mix of families, free-spirited surfers, and business professionals. Today, Santa Monica plays home to moguls, tech geeks, starlets, yogis, musicians, self-styled gypsies, environmentalists, and creatives. With its fun-but-not-fancy pier, its inexpensive off-beach motels, and a

Santa Monica

Map labels:

To Palisade Park
THE BUNGALOW
WILSHIRE BLVD
2ND ST
3RD ST
4TH ST
ARIZONA AVE
To Bay Cities Italian Deli & Bakery
6TH ST
5TH ST
TENDER GREENS
SANTA MONICA WEDNESDAY FARMERS MARKET
THIRD STREET PROMENADE
SANTA MONICA BLVD
FLOWER CHILD
PALISADES BEACH RD
THE PROMENADE
OCEAN AVE
YE OLDE KING'S HEAD
BROADWAY
SANTA MONICA BIKE CENTER
HI LOS ANGELES SANTA MONICA HOSTEL
THE GEORGIAN HOTEL
Santa Monica State Beach
SANTA MONICA PLACE
2ND ST
COLORADO AVE
4TH ST
PACIFIC OCEAN
MAIN ST
MOSS AVE
SEASIDE TER
CHEZ JAY
THE ARCADIA TER
OCEAN AVE
THE PROMENADE
SANTA MONICA PIER
SANTA MONICA PIER SHOP & VISITOR CENTER
SEAVIEW TER
VICEROY HOTEL
VICENTE TER
PICO BLVD
SHUTTERS ON THE BEACH
OCEAN AVE
0   250 yds
0   250 m
© MOON.COM

variety of delicious inexpensive dining options, Santa Monica is a great choice for a road-trip stop.

Getting There

From Malibu, take CA-1 southeast for 18.5 miles (30 km), entering Santa Monica near its popular beach. The road winds inland for a few blocks before continuing south to parallel the coast. The often congested I-10 freeway (also known as the Santa Monica Freeway) connects at the Santa Monica Pier; it's a rare day when traffic moves at the posted speed limit. Venice and the Venice Beach Boardwalk are 2 miles (3 km) south of the Santa Monica Pier along Ocean and Pacific Avenues. Parking is at a premium, however, so it's easier (and more scenic) to park in a pay lot and walk.

If driving from Los Angeles, I-5 and US-101 join I-10 downtown. The interchanges can be confusing.

Beach

Santa Monica Beach (Ocean Ave. to Ocean Park Blvd.) embodies the city's history, scenic beauty, and active lifestyle with 3.5 miles of wide, sandy beach, perfect for sunbathing, biking, or inline skating. Known as "The Strand," this well-traveled path connects Santa Monica Beach to Will Rogers State Beach to the north and Redondo Beach to the south. Lifeguards keep watch over surfers, swimmers, and beach bunnies (much of the hit TV show *Baywatch* was filmed here). There are plenty of picnic areas, playgrounds, and pay parking lots ($6-15).

Sights

★ Santa Monica Pier

The landmark **Santa Monica Pier** (Ocean Ave. at Colorado Ave., 310/458-8900, www.santamonicapier.org) has welcomed generations of families and out-of-towners since 1909. Today, highlights include a historical carousel, solar-paneled Ferris wheel, arcade games, and thrill rides at **Pacific Park** (310/260-8744, www.pacpark.com, $5-10 per ride, unlimited rides $32 adult, $17 children under 8). Tucked beneath the carousel, the **Santa Monica Pier Aquarium** (1600 Ocean Front Walk, 310/393-6149, www.healthebay.org, 2pm-5pm Tues.-Fri., 12:30pm-5pm Sat.-Sun., $5 adults, children 12 and under free) includes touch tanks that allow for exploration of sea creatures like urchins, snails, and sea cucumbers, as well as worthwhile exhibits dedicated to jellyfish, leopard sharks, and stingrays. During the summer, the boardwalk becomes a stage for weekly outdoor concerts and free events. Historical **walking tours** (11am or noon Sat.-Sun., free) start at the **Pier Shop & Visitor Center** (310/804-7457); look for the tour guide in the blue shirt.

Palisades Park

Virtually nothing can escape the view of **Palisades Park** (851 Alma Real Dr., 310/454-1412, dawn-dusk daily), which lies atop sandstone cliffs overlooking Santa Monica Beach. Photographers, tourists, joggers, and yoga practitioners make use of the manicured lawns, benches, and pathway, appreciating the obscurely twisted trees, rose garden, artworks, and historical structures along the way. At the northern end of the park is a Chilkat Tlingit totem pole featuring a fish, raven, bear, and wolf. At the southern end, two cannons installed in 1908 point directly at the Santa Monica Pier, and a stone monument marks the 400th anniversary of explorer Juan Rodríguez Cabrillo's 1542 encounter of the bay. If you don't mind the park's resident homeless, who generally keep to themselves, Palisades is a good spot for watching the sunset.

Annenberg Community Beach House

In the 1920s, publishing bigwig William Randolph Hearst built this beachfront 100-room mansion for his mistress, actress Marion Davies. The mansion later became the **Annenberg Community Beach House** (415 CA-1, 310/458-4904, www.annenbergbeachhouse.com, 8:30am-5:30pm daily Nov.-Mar., 8am-6:30pm Apr. and Oct., 8am-8:30pm May-Sept., free). Today, modern additions to the historic estate include a play area, art gallery, and an array of recreational activities, including swimming in the marble and tile pool (June-Sept., $10 adults, $4 children 1-17).

★ The Getty Center

TOP EXPERIENCE

High on a hilltop overlooking both Santa Monica and Beverly Hills—most of the city, really—**The Getty Center** (1200 Getty Center Dr., 310/440-7300, 10am-5:30pm Tues.-Fri. and Sun., 10am-9pm Sat., free admission, $5 audio tour, $15-20 parking) is a fortress of travertine- and aluminum-clad pavilions, built to house the eclectic art collection of billionaire J. Paul Getty, which includes everything from Renaissance-era paintings to pop art. Getty opened a museum at his Malibu estate in the 1950s (The Getty Villa can still be visited today). After his death in 1976, an endowment was established to preserve his beloved collection and make it accessible to the public.

The center opened in 1998, welcoming visitors by way of a three-car, cable-pulled hover-train funicular (a large parking garage is at the base of the hill). Steps lead up to the main entrance of the rotunda building, which links all five of the art pavilions. Richard Meier's striking design includes fountains, glass windows several stories high, and an open plan that permits intimate vistas of the city below. A separate west building includes a cafeteria and restaurant. Stairs from the terrace lead down to outdoor terraces and gardens designed by Robert Irwin. The gardens and the views are as inspiring as the art. On a clear day, you can see the city skyline all the way west to the Pacific.

Admission is free; however, you'll have to pay to park or take Metro bus 761. To take the free tram from the parking structure, ride the elevators up to the Lower Tram Station. The center is also accessible by way of the 0.75-mile pedestrian path that is about a 20-minute walk from the parking structure.

★ Venice Beach Boardwalk

There's no place quite like Venice Beach; at times strolling the **Venice Beach Boardwalk** (Ocean Front Walk) feels like taking part in a circus parade. That is fitting—early Venice, with its carnival amusements, was billed as the "Coney Island of the Pacific" and that carney spirit lives on (the resident freak show closed only a couple of years ago).

Today's boardwalk, officially dubbed

Top to bottom: gardens at The Getty Center; Santa Monica Beach; Venice Beach Boardwalk.

Venice

Map labels:

SPEEDWAY · CLUBHOUSE CT · WESTMINSTER AVE · INNES PL · MAIN ST · PATH ROW · MARKET ST · GRANADA AVE · WINDWARD AVE · RIVIERA AVE · CORDOVA CT · RIALTO AVE · CABRILLO AVE · SALT AIR · SEVILLE CT · ANDALUSIA AVE

VENICE BEACH SUITES & HOTEL · HORIZON AVE · HORIZON CT · PACIFIC AVE · ZEPHYR CT · MARKET ST · WINDWARD AVE · GRAND BLVD · N VENICE BLVD · VENICE BLVD

SMALL WORLD BOOKS · VENICE WAY · MILDRED AVE

VENICE SKATE PARK · WINDWARD CT · HOTEL ERWIN · MILDRED AVE · ALBERTA AVE · OCEAN AVE · OCEAN CT · BEACH AVE · OCEAN AVE

17TH AVE · 17TH PL · 18TH AVE · 18TH PL · 19TH AVE · 19TH PL · 20TH AVE · 20TH PL · CANAL ST · STRONGS DR · VIRGINIA CT · EASTERN CT · EASTERN AVE

VENICE BEACH RECREATION CENTER · MUSCLE BEACH · OCEAN FRONT WALK · N VENICE BLVD · CENTER CT · S VENICE BLVD · DELL AVE · CARROLL CANAL CT · VENICE CANALS · LINNIE CANAL CT · CAPRI CT

SPEEDWAY · VIRGINIA CT · 23RD AVE · 23RD PL · PACIFIC AVE · STRONGS DR · GRAND CANAL CT · DANTE CT · 28TH CT

VENICE BEACH BOARDWALK · 24TH AVE · 24TH PL · 25TH AVE · 25TH PL · 26TH AVE · 26TH PL · 27TH AVE · 27TH PL · 28TH AVE · 28TH PL · 29TH AVE · 29TH PL · 30TH AVE · 30TH PL

PACIFIC OCEAN

WASHINGTON BLVD · INN AT VENICE BEACH · ANCHORAGE ST · STRONGS DR · CANAL CT · BUCCANEER ST · VENICE FISHING PIER · SPEEDWAY

0 — 250 yds
0 — 250 m

© MOON.COM

---

the Ocean Front Walk, is lined with street vendors, smoke shops, tattoo parlors, souvenir stands, and colorful characters. An eclectic assortment of souls provide boardwalk entertainment and include buskers, break-dancers, acrobats, bodybuilders, tarot readers, roller disco dancers, street artists, hustlers, and every shade of exhibitionist. The world-famous **Muscle Beach** (Ocean Front Walk at Pacific Terrace) puts bulging biceps on display. The adjacent bike path adds beach cruisers, skaters, scooters, unicyclists, and inline skaters to the mix. People-watching in Venice proves an unforgettable daytime activity; however, the place can feel a little seedy come nightfall.

Venice Street Art

You'll find colorful murals and other street art at every turn in Venice, starting with the beach. The concrete **Venice Art Walls** (plaza near Windward Ave.) were constructed in 2000 for the sole purpose of soaking up graffiti. Look for the plaques that enumerate the history of the **Venice Murals** (1 Rose Ave., www.visitveniceca.com); they're mounted every few feet on concrete barriers surrounding the boardwalk parking lot at Rose Avenue. Walk three blocks north on Rose to find the *Ballerina Clown* statue (Rose Ave. and Main St.), then head south on Main Street to spot the giant *Binoculars*. Other art pieces are south of Rose Avenue along Pacific Avenue, Abbot Kinney Boulevard, and the boardwalk.

Venice Canals

Venice wasn't named by accident. Its founder, Abbot Kinney, developed the place as a beach resort, partly modeled after the Italian city and its famous canals. A more extensive system of the **Venice Canals** (east of Pacific Ave. between Venice Blvd. and 28th Ave.) originally connected several blocks north and could be traveled by gondola, but were later filled to become roads as cars became dominant. Today, the remaining canals comprise a roughly three-by-five block area of a unique residential neighborhood populated by ducks and beautiful family homes. A stroll along the canals and its charming footbridges offers a splendid, quiet respite from the manic noise of the boardwalk.

Recreation

Beach volleyball is said to have been born in Santa Monica. A number of courts located north and south of the pier are available daily for public play on a first-come, first-served basis. Courts may be reserved in advance by calling 310/458-8300 and paying a required permit fee ($10-32).

Surfing in Santa Monica isn't great, unless you're just starting out and need lessons. **Go Surf LA** (2400 Ocean Front Walk, 310/428-9870, www.gosurfla.com, by appointment, $80) offers such lessons and gear is included.

Venice is a physically active place, and a lot of the boardwalk action takes place at the **Venice Beach Recreation Center** (1800 Ocean Front Walk, 310/396-6764, www.laparks.org, 8am-7pm daily May-Sept., 8am-6pm daily Oct.-Apr.), best known for its outdoor gym facilities at **Muscle Beach** (310/399-2775, $10/day) and for high-level pickup games at its **basketball courts.** Overall, the facility includes a gymnastics area, playground, handball courts, roller rink, and 11 courts for **paddle ball** ($5/racket rental), a tennis-like game played with wooden paddles on a smaller court with a lower net. There's also the standout **Venice Skate Park** (end of Market St.), a collection of bowls, rails, ramps, and stairs where talented local skate rats show off their skills.

Of course Venice is also yoga country. For three decades, a pay-what-you-can **beach yoga** class has been offered in Marina del Rey, courtesy of **The Yoga Bunny** (the beach at Hurricane St., www.theyogabunny.com, 10am Sat., $10 suggested donation).

Biking

Bike **The Strand** (40 mi/64 km), a popular and easily accessible bike path that gets busy in the summer. You can ride to Will Rogers State Beach to the north and Redondo Beach to the south. There are many coastal communities in between, like Venice Beach (3 mi/5 km south) and Pacific Palisades (2.8 mi/5 km north). The bike path runs parallel to the **Ocean Front Walk** (a pedestrian walkway) until Bicknell Avenue (south of the pier), where it veers west, following the coastline north, passing under the Santa Monica Pier, and continuing on to Will Rogers State Beach. The Santa Monica portion of The Strand runs from Temescal Canyon in the north to Washington Boulevard in Venice in the south (8.5 mi/13.7 km).

Santa Monica Bike Center (1555 2nd St., Unit A, 310/656-8500, 7am-8pm

Mon.-Fri., 8am-8pm Sat.-Sun., $20-45/2 hr.) rents bikes just off the pier.

Entertainment and Events

A half-block south of the pier, **Chez Jay** (1657 Ocean Ave., 310/395-1741, www.chezjays.com, 5:30pm-9:30pm Mon.-Fri.) doesn't look like much, but the little nautical dive bar has been serving locals and celebrities for almost 50 years. Jay's peanuts are as famous as its clientele—ask them about the nut that made it to the moon! Open since 1934, **The Galley** (2442 Main St., 310/452-1934, www.thegalleyrestaurant.net, 5pm-midnight Mon.-Thurs., 5pm-2am Fri.-Sat., 1pm-midnight Sun.) is the oldest bar in town. It's worth a visit for the kitschy nautical vibe alone—the strong drinks don't hurt either.

For fans of British pubs, **Ye Olde Kings Head** (116 Santa Monica Blvd., 310/451-1402, www.yeoldekingshead.com, 9am-2am daily) fills up during soccer (sorry, football) and rugby games. You'll find English ale and spirits, and, of course, fish-and-chips.

Literary fans will appreciate the aptly named **Barkowski** (2819 Pico Blvd., 310/998-0069, www.barkowski.com, 5pm-2am Mon.-Sat.), a bar dedicated to gritty poet and author Charles Bukowski. The Buk himself preferred seedier locales, but the retro vibe and weary world outlook shared among his readers makes it work.

If you prefer suds to cocktails, try indoor/outdoor **The Library Alehouse** (2911 Main St., 310/314-4855, www.libraryalehouse.com, 11:30am-11pm Mon.-Thurs., 11:30am-11:30pm Fri., 11am-11:30pm Sat., 11am-11pm Sun.), which has been deftly serving craft beer almost since there's been craft beer.

To be young and beautiful and in Santa Monica is to be drinking on the patio at **The Bungalow** (101 Wilshire Blvd., 310/899-8530, www.thebungalow.com, 5pm-2am Mon.-Fri., noon-2am Sat., noon-10pm Sun.). The stylish beachfront bungalow is the perfect spot to day drink and becomes the perfect spot to night drink, right after being the perfect spot to toast the sun going down. You get the idea.

Bring a blanket, find a spot on the beach, and watch the sun set while listening to Santa Monica Pier's summer **Twilight Concerts** (Ocean Ave. at Colorado Ave., 310/458-8900, www.santamonicapier.org, 6:30pm-9:30pm Thurs. in summer). In the fall, the pier hosts **Front Porch Cinema** (7:30pm Fri.), with music, films, and food and drinks. Rent a lawn chair for a few bucks or bring your own.

Shopping

Shopping on **Main Street** (www.mainstreetsm.com) may have you seeing stars. If you don't spot a celeb, you can settle for window-shopping. Main Street is the greenest street in Santa Monica, with earth-conscious boutiques like **Vital Hemp** (2305 Main St., 310/450-2260, 10am-6pm daily), a producer of quality hemp clothing for men and women that's friendly to the planet, and **Natural High Lifestyle** (2510 Main St., 323/691-1827, www.naturalhighlifestyle.myshopify.com, call for hours), which features clothing and products made from hemp, organic cotton, buckwheat hulls, and FSC-certified plywood.

The eclectic **Mindfulnest** (2711 Main St., 310/452-5409, www.mindfulnest.com, 11am-7:30pm Sun.-Thurs., 11am-9pm Fri.-Sat.) features the works of nearly 100 contemporary artists. On Sunday, Main Street hosts the widely popular **Farmers Market** (2640 Main St., 310/458-8712, 8:30am-1:30pm Sun.) with food booths, local retailers, arts and crafts, live music, and fun activities for the little ones.

The people-watching is magnificent at **Third Street Promenade,** a vibrant, pedestrian-only, outdoor shopping corridor northwest of Main Street. Expect great restaurants, movie theaters, street performers, and popular chain stores like Abercrombie & Fitch, Express, and Pottery Barn, with a few independent art galleries and specialty and vintage shops. On Wednesday and Saturday, it's home to another terrific **Farmers Market** (155-199 Arizona Ave., 310/458-8712, 8am-1:30pm Sat. and Wed.). Adjacent to the Promenade, **Santa Monica Place** (4th St. and Broadway, 310/394-5451) is an open-air mall stocked with a collection of high-end retailers like Tiffany, Bloomingdales, and Kenneth Cole.

You'll find all kinds of kitschy, countercultural, and beachy items for sale by a wild array of vendors on the Venice Beach Boardwalk, including the standout independent bookseller **Small World Books** (1407 Ocean Front Walk, 310/399-2360, www.smallworldbooks.com, 10am-8pm daily). The bulk of serious shopping happens along 6-7 blocks of **Abbot Kinney Boulevard,** densely populated with vintage and designer fashion boutiques that complement the loads of hip restaurants and cafes.

Food

Tables are literally on the beach at **Back on the Beach** (445 CA-1, 310/393-8282, www.backonthebeachcafe.com, 8am-3pm Mon.-Thurs., 8am-4pm Fri.-Sun. Nov.-Apr., 8am-8pm daily May-Oct., $16-24). Classic American breakfast and lunch dishes are served year-round, plus dinner during the long summer months.

Bay Cities Italian Deli & Bakery (1517 Lincoln Blvd., 310/395-8279, www.bcdeli.com, 9am-6pm Tues.-Sun., under $10) has been whipping up authentic Italian pasta and sandwiches since 1925. Take a number; it's worth the wait.

The famed burger at the **Father's Office** (1018 Montana Ave., 310/736-2224, www.fathersoffice.com, 5pm-10pm Mon.-Wed., 5pm-11pm Thurs., 4pm-11pm Fri., noon-11pm Sat., noon-10pm Sun., bar open until 1am Mon.-Thurs., 2am Fri.-Sat., midnight Sun., $5-16) tops dry-aged beef with caramelized onions,

gruyère and blue cheese, bacon, and arugula. It pairs perfectly with a world-class IPA or stout—for two decades, the gastropub has set the bar for local craft beer draft lists, featuring fresh kegs of the region's best.

Though local favorite **Santa Monica Seafood** (1000 Wilshire Blvd., 310/393-5244, www.smseafoodmarket.com, 9am-9pm Mon.-Sat., 9am-8pm Sun., under $25) is a retail fish market, it includes a café and oyster bar that serves fresh seafood with an Italian twist.

Fast food in Santa Monica means sunny, farm-sourced counter restaurants, and clustered around the Promenade area, you can take your pick of health-conscious sandwiches and salads at **Tender Greens** (201 Arizona Ave., 310/587-2777, www.tendergreens.com, 11am-9:30pm daily, under $14) or bowls and wraps at **Flower Child** (1332 2nd St., 310/382-2901, www.iamaflowerchild.com, 9am-9pm daily, under $12).

For relatively affordable samplings of the current culinary moment in L.A., drop into Venice and check out the sister restaurants dominating the consciousness of west side foodies. If you can wrangle a spot at ★ **Gjelina** (1429 Abbot Kinney Blvd., Venice, 310/450-1429, www.gjelina.com, 8am-midnight Mon.-Sat., 8am-11pm Sun., under $25), prepare to gorge on oysters, wood-fired pizza, or a litany of richly composed meat, seafood, and vegetable plates. If not, try its breakfast-savvy convenient takeaway component, **Gjelina Take Away** (1427 Abbot Kinney Blvd., Venice, 310/392-7575, 7am-10pm Sun.-Wed., 7am-11pm Thurs.-Sat., under $12) or go browse the glass counter at **Gjusta** (320 Sunset Ave., Venice, 310/314-0320, www.gjusta.com, 7am-10pm daily, $6-18). The hardworking artisans of this standing-room-only deli bake, cure, smoke, or roast everything to perfection.

Get in the new-age beach spirit and pick up a gorgeous green tea latte at the almost insufferably pink **Cha Cha Matcha**

(1401 Abbot Kinney Blvd., Venice, 855/924-2242, www.chachamatcha.com, 7:30am-7pm Mon.-Fri., 8am-7pm Sat.-Sun., $4-8). Then hop on the gourmet doughnut trend at **Blue Star Donuts** (1142 Abbot Kinney Blvd., Venice, 310/450-5630, www.bluestardonuts.com, 7am-8pm daily, $3), which serves memorable brioche doughnuts with flavors such as blueberry-bourbon basil and chocolate-almond ganache.

Accommodations

HI Los Angeles/Santa Monica (1436 2nd St., 310/393-9913, www.hilosangeles. org, dorm beds from $40, private from $130) offers clean dorm-style and private rooms, and facilities that feature daily movies, Internet access, kitchen, laundry, and breakfast.

To stay close to yet removed from the Venice hustle, check into the **Inn at Venice Beach** (327 W. Washington Blvd., Venice, 310/821-2557, www.innatvenicebeach. com, from $189) for clean, well-appointed rooms close to the Venice Canals.

The green-certified **Ambrose Hotel** (1255 20th St., 310/315-1555, www. ambrosehotel.com, from $220) has a positive impact on its guests and the environment. Elegant rooms include cotton robes, bath linens, and natural bath products. Some have balconies and terraces; all come with a complimentary breakfast.

Right by the boardwalk, a short walk from the Venice Canals and shops and restaurants of Abbot Kinney Boulevard, is the classic Venice Beach lodging of ★ **Hotel Erwin** (1697 Pacific Ave., Venice, 310/452-1111, www.hotelerwin.com, from $254). Stays include ocean views, balconies, and loaner beach cruisers.

In the course of its history, the art deco 1933 **Georgian Hotel** (1415 Ocean Ave., 310/395-9945 and 800/538-8147, www.georgianhotel.com, from $280) has hosted stars and starlets. Today, it continues to please with stylish guest rooms and suites, boutique amenities, and a contemporary restaurant. It's just steps from the beach and close to shopping and restaurants.

Ecofriendly trendsetter ★ **Viceroy Hotel** (1819 Ocean Ave., 310/260-7500 and 800/670-6185, www. viceroyhotelsandresorts.com, from $300) has been named one of the top 50 hotels by *Condé Nast Traveler,* among others. Large airy cabanas with comfy couches and fluffy pillows provide shade from the sun and access to the pool. It's a block from the beach and a few blocks from downtown.

Shutters on the Beach (Pico Blvd., 310/458-0030 and 800/334-9000, from $575) is a luxury hotel set right on the sand. Guest rooms are bright with hardwood floors, Tibetan rugs, spacious bathrooms, and balconies. The hotel houses a café, bar, and fine dining, as well as a spa.

Information and Services

Free brochures and information on area attractions are available at the **Pier Shop & Visitor Center** (200 Santa Monica Pier, 310/804-7457, 11am-5pm Mon.-Thurs., 11am-7pm Fri.-Sun.). There is also a walk-in **Visitor Information Center** (2427 Main St., 310/393-7593, 9am-5:30pm Mon.-Fri., 9am-5pm Sat.-Sun.) that provides information resources, three computers with high-speed Internet access, and souvenirs. Tickets to area attractions are also available for purchase.

Getting Around

The **Big Blue Bus** (310/451-5444, www. bigbluebus.com, $1) provides service throughout Santa Monica and Venice Beach. **The Los Angeles Metro** (www. metro.net) connects downtown Los Angeles and Santa Monica via its (turquoise) **Expo Line**.

Not many places in Los Angeles can be accessed without a car, but Santa Monica is an exception. Many of the city's tourist destinations are within walking distance of each other. **Santa Monica's Bike Transit Center** (www.bikesm.com) provides bike rentals and two secured parking sites (320

Broadway, 215 Colorado Ave.). A U-lock is recommended. Dockless scooter and bicycle rentals abound in both Santa Monica and Venice. Expect to find the small vehicles from several different companies all around the boardwalks and commercial areas; they may be rented for short-term jaunts using a smartphone.

A small army of electric cars bring free shuttles to Venice in the form of **Free Ride** (323/435-5000, www.thefreeride. com, 12:30pm-9pm daily). Flag one down near any of its appointed stops, or text to find a nearby location.

Manhattan Beach

Home to wealthy sports and entertainment notables, Manhattan Beach is among the most desirable places to live in California, with homes selling for $1 million and up. It's also considered one of the top beaches in the state, its smooth sand attracting more than 3.8 million visitors each year. Restaurants cluster around its pier, while sports bars populate the city's north end, around Rosecrans Avenue.

Getting There
South of Venice, CA-1 skirts around the Los Angeles International Airport before dropping into Manhattan Beach in about 10 miles (16 km). (This may be one of the rare times it makes more sense to get on I-405 South, which is usually avoided at all costs.) Exit via Rosecrans Avenue or Manhattan Beach Boulevard and head west to the beach.

Beaches and Recreation
A bike path runs the entire length of **The Strand**, as locals call the beachfront of Manhattan Beach. The Strand connects cleanly south though Hermosa Beach to Redondo Beach and north to Venice and Santa Monica if you can find your way around the marina at Marina del Rey. Look to neighboring towns for bike rentals.

Manhattan Beach is the site of the **Manhattan Beach Open Volleyball Tournament** (www. themanhattanbeachopen.com, Aug.), but with 100 volleyball courts on two miles of **Manhattan Beach** (www.beaches. lacounty.gov), everyone can play here year-round. Most of the crowds and the surf sit on either side of the 90-foot pier. Rent boards at **El Porto Surf Shop** (3804 Highland Ave., 310/545-9626, http://el-porto-surfboards.business.site, hours vary from 6:30am, $13/hr) or seek out surfing lessons at **One Wave Surf** (323/521-9283, www.onewavesurf.com, call for hours, $100).

Nightlife
The best of the Manhattan Beach sports bars is the surf-styled **Fishbar** (3801 Highland Ave., 310/796-0200, www. fishbarmb.com, 11am-11pm Mon.-Thurs., 11am-1am Fri., 9am-1am Sat., 9am-11pm Sun.), which is also known for its seafood and huge cocktails. Craft beer fans should look to the beachside tavern **Brewco** (124 Manhattan Beach Blvd., 310/798-2744, http://www.brewcomb. com, 11:30am-midnight Mon.-Fri., 10am-midnight Sat.-Sun.), which serves quality local brews on tap plus good pub grub.

Food
Seafood is always a beachfront best bet. From raw bar to crab cakes, **Fishing With Dynamite** (1148 Manhattan Ave, 310/893-6299, www.eatfwd.com, 11:30am-10pm Sun.-Wed., 11:30am-10:30pm Thurs.-Sat., $15-45) offers a reasonable bet for fresh seafood such as oysters and grilled octopus.

Live it up a little with oceanfront views and fine dining at local favorite, **The Strand** (117 Manhattan Beach Blvd., 310/545-7470, www.thestrandhousemb. com, 5pm-10pm daily, 11:30am-3pm Tues.-Fri., 10am-3pm Sat.-Sun., $26-60). Expect elegant plates of fresh seafood infused with high-end ingredients from around the world.

◈ Side Trip: Palos Verdes

Wayfarers Chapel

The chin-shaped peninsula that juts out from L.A.'s South Bay is called Rancho Palos Verdes, a rolling sprawl of private golf clubs, hilltop estates, and private coastal bluffs that is more residential than scenic. But there are exceptions on the north and south sides of the peninsula that make for a pleasant half-hour detour.

From CA-1, take Palos Verdes Boulevard south to Palos Verdes Drive West to stroll along the pretty coastal bluffs of **Palos Verdes Estates Shoreline Preserve** (310/378-0383, www.pvestates.org, parking lot at Paseo Del Mar.).

Continue 3.8 miles (6.1 km) south along Palos Verdes Drive West to reach **Point Vicente Lighthouse** (31501 Palos Verdes Dr. W., 310/544-5375, www.rpvca.gov, 10am-5pm daily) for walking paths that overlook the historic 1926 lighthouse, as well as gorgeous cliffside scenery and views of both the Catalina and Channel Islands.

In another 2.2 miles (3 km) south along Palos Verdes Drive West is the architectural gem the **Wayfarers Chapel** (5755 Palos Verdes Dr. S., 310/377-1650, www.wayfarerschapel.org). Designed by Lloyd Wright (son of the famous Frank Lloyd Wright), this example of organic architecture finds a glass-walled chapel nestled among redwood trees, making the active church a sparkling tribute to nature. It's a popular site for nuptials; please be respectful of wedding parties.

Hermosa Beach

The Pacific Coast Highway continues south into Hermosa Beach, where the Hermosa Beach Pier offers a younger feel thanks to the bars, restaurants, and surf shops that line the pedestrian-only street. Hermosa Beach is a hot spot for sunbathers, surfers, paddleboarders, and beach volleyball with a rowdier nightlife compared to the neighboring beach cities.

Getting There

From Manhattan Beach, follow CA-1 south for about 1.6 miles (2.6 km). Exit CA-1 west onto Pier Avenue to reach Hermosa Beach.

Beach

Hermosa Beach (www.beaches. lacounty.gov) supports surfing around the pier and on the adjacent beach depending on conditions. It's usually safe for beginners and intermediate surfers, but when the waves get big, it should be advanced surfers only out on the water. For rentals, look to longtime local surf shop **ET Surf** (904 Aviation Blvd., 310/379-7660, www.etsurf.com, 10am-8pm Mon.-Fri., 10am-7pm Sat., 10am-6pm Sun.).

A **bike path** runs along the county beach. A good place to rent bicycles, including cruisers, tandem, and electric bikes, is **Hermosa Cyclery** (20 13th St., 310/374-7816, www.hermosacyclery.com, 9am-7pm daily, rentals $7-12/hr, $21-30/day).

Nightlife

Hermosa has a couple of decent entertainment venues. **Comedy & Magic Club** (1018 Hermosa Ave., 310/372-1193, www.comedyandmagicclub.com, hours and cover varies) delivers exactly what it says as well as food and drinks. It's a great, comfortable venue to enjoy the rich pool of Los Angeles comics, including Jay Leno, who holds a weekly residency.

Music venue **Saint Rocke** (142 Pacific Coast Hwy., 310/372-0035, www.saintrocke.com, hours and cover varies) hosts Tuesday night music trivia, along with a weekly mix of tribute bands, locals, and touring performers.

Food and Accommodations

The local favorite is the cozy Italian eatery **The Bottle Inn Hermosa** (26 22nd St., 310/376-9595, https://thebottleinnhermosa.com, 11:30am-9pm Sun.-Thurs., 11:30am-10pm Fri.-Sat., $24-36), which has hosted a luminary cast of customers and has the pictures on the wall to prove it.

For budget travelers, **Surf City Hostel** (26 Pier Ave., 310/798-2323, www.surfcityhostel.com, $35 dorm, $85 private) offers a great value for the region. It's right on the beach, a 30-minute drive (one-hour bike ride) from Venice.

Redondo Beach

Redondo Beach's stretch of sand gets crowded in the summertime, particularly near its pier, so if rubbing elbows with your fellow sun worshippers doesn't suit you, head elsewhere. Surfers favor Manhattan and Hermosa Beaches, so there's more room for swimming at Redondo. You'll also find the usual volleyball and beach games and a commercially developed waterfront with shops and restaurants along its pier and marina.

Getting There

From Hermosa Beach, follow CA-1 south for 1.6 miles (2.6 km) to access Redondo Beach bordering Ripley Avenue.

Beach

Due to its waterfront development, Redondo's stretch of sandy beach doesn't start until south of Torrance Boulevard. The county maintains **Redondo Beach,** which is outfitted with standard beach amenities and a bike path. Bike rentals are available at **Marina Bike Rentals** (505 N. Harbor Dr., 310/318-2453, www.marinabikerentals.com, 10am-5pm daily, $9 15/hr). The **Redondo Beach Pier** (121 W. Torrace Blvd.) is lined with shops and eateries.

Food

Redondo Beach foodies find a fine value for *omakase* sushi at ★ **Sushi Chitose** (402 S. Pacific Coast Hwy., 310/316-6268, noon-2pm Tues.-Fri., 5:30pm-9:30pm Tues.-Sun., $45-60). Because this is a Southern California beach town, you can also pick up the local favorite breakfast burrito at the hole-in-the-wall **Phanny's** (1021 S. Pacific Coast Hwy., 310/540-5141, 7am-3pm Tues.-Sun., $6-9), stuffed with eggs, hash browns, cheese, salsa, and a choice of protein.

Long Beach

As CA-1 heads east and inland at the Palos Verdes Peninsula, the highway scenery shifts from commercial to industrial as it enters Long Beach (pop. 470,130). Despite the name, Long Beach is less a beach town than a working port; it's the point of entry for international shipping into Los Angeles.

Getting There

From Redondo Beach, take CA-1 south for 14.6 miles (23.5 km) to I-710 south. Follow I-710 south to its end at Long Beach Harbor.

Sights
Queen Mary

TOP EXPERIENCE

One of the most famous ships ever to ply the high seas, the magnificent **Queen Mary** (1126 Queens Hwy., 877/342-0738, www.queenmary.com, 10am-8pm daily, $28-75, $18 parking) now sits at permanent anchor in Long Beach Harbor, where it acts as a hotel, a museum, and an entertainment center with several restaurants and bars. You can book a stateroom ($120-570) and stay aboard, come for dinner, or just buy a regular ticket and take a self-guided tour. Explore many of the decks at the bow, including the engine room, which still boasts much of its massive machinery, and see exhibits that describe the ship's history. The ship is also one of the most famously haunted places in California. Over its decades of service, a number of unfortunate souls lost their lives aboard the *Queen Mary,* and apparently some of them stuck around even after their deaths. To learn more, book a spot on one of the evening events, such as the **Paranormal Ship Walk** (8pm-10pm Sun.-Thurs., $44).

Aquarium of the Pacific

North of Long Beach Harbor, the **Aquarium of the Pacific** (100 Aquarium Way, 562/590-3100, www. aquariumofpacific.org, 9am-6pm daily, $30 adults, $18 children) hosts animal and plant life native to the Pacific Ocean, from the local residents of SoCal's sea up to the North Pacific and down to the tropics. This large aquarium has far more than the average number of touch-friendly tanks, including the Shark Lagoon where you can "pet" a few of the sharks the aquarium cares for.

Food

They serve excellent smokehouse barbecue at ★ **Beachwood Brewing & BBQ** (210 E. 3rd St., 562/436-4020, www. beachwoodbbq.com, 11:30am-midnight Tues.-Sun., $19-24), but that's not the only reason to visit. This champion brewpub makes some of the best beer in the state, especially stouts and IPAs, which happen to go pretty dang well with barbecue.

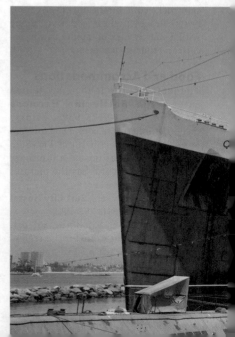

Sir Winston's Restaurant and Lounge (1126 Queens Hwy., 562/499-1657, www.queenmary.com, 5pm-9pm Wed.-Thurs. and Sun., 5pm-10pm Fri.-Sat., $30-78) floats on board the *Queen Mary*. Make reservations for an elegant dining experience and a gourmet menu of filet mignon, chateaubriand, or baked stuffed lobster. Note that Sir Winston's has a semiformal dress code.

Locals favorite **Natraj Cuisine of India** (5262 E. 2nd St., 562/930-0930, www.natrajlongbeach.com, 11am-2:30pm and 5pm-10pm Tues.-Thurs., 11am-2:30pm and 5pm-11pm Fri., 11am-11pm Sat., 11am-9:30pm Sun., $12-20) offers good Indian food at a reasonable price.

Accommodations

The Varden (335 Pacific Ave., 562/432-8950, www.thevardenhotel.com, $159-199) is the oldest operating hotel in Long Beach. The small, modern rooms are decorated in a minimalist style and include full- or queen-size beds, flat-screen TVs, and free wireless Internet. A continental breakfast is included.

For a unique place to stay in Long Beach Harbor that isn't the *Queen Mary*, try the **Dockside Boat and Bed** (316 E. Shoreline Dr., Dock 5A, Rainbow Harbor, 562/436-3111, www.boatandbed.com, $260-330). You won't get a regular old hotel room—instead, you'll get a whole yacht. The yachts run 38-54 feet and can sleep 2-4 people. Unfortunately, you can't take your floating accommodations out for a spin; these yachts are permanent residents of Rainbow Harbor.

Getting Around

Long Beach is served by the public **Long Beach Transit** (https://ridelbt.com, $1.25, $4 day pass) bus line.

the *Queen Mary*

◈ Side Trip: Catalina Island

For a taste of island life, ride a ferry (or a helicopter) over to **Catalina Island** (www.visitcatalinaisland.com), a small populated island visible from the Southern California coast. The southern port town of Avalon welcomes visitors with Mediterranean-inspired hotels, restaurants, and shops, while Two Harbors in the north provides an undeveloped gateway to nature, including a herd of wild American bison.

Getting There

Most folks take the ferry over from the mainland coast. The **Catalina Express** (800/613-1212 or 800/481-3470, www.catalinaexpress.com) departs from Long Beach (320 Golden Shore, $74.50 adults round-trip, $59 children round-trip) and Dana Point (34674 Golden Lantern St., $76.50 adults round-trip, $61 children round-trip, $17 parking), with boats going back and forth throughout the day, from 6am to just after sunset.

San Pedro Port (Berth 95 at Swinford and Harbor Blvd., $74.50 adults round-trip, $59 children round-trip, $14 parking) is the only departure point for Two Harbors. The trip to the island takes about one hour.

You can also get to Catalina by air. **Island Express Helicopter Service** (310/510-2525, www.islandexpress.com, $270-390 round-trip pp) can fly you from Long Beach, San Pedro, or Santa Ana to Catalina in about 15 minutes.

Sights

When approaching Catalina on the ferry, you'll notice a round, white, art deco building at one end of town. This is the **Casino** (1 Casino Way, Avalon, 310/510-0179). It's not a gambling hall; the term harks back to an older Italian meaning of the word, "place of entertainment." The casino hosts movies and events.

South of Avalon, the coolest place to visit is the **Wrigley Memorial and Botanical Garden** (1402 Avalon Canyon Rd., 310/510-2897, www.catalinaconservancy.org, 8am-5pm daily, $8 adults, $4 children 5-12). Stroll through serene gardens planted with flowers, trees, and shrubs native to California—or even to Catalina specifically. At the center of the garden is the Wrigley Memorial, dedicated to the memory of the chewing-gum magnate who adored Catalina and used his sticky fortune to improve it. Most notably, he funded the building of the Avalon Casino.

Beaches

In Avalon, a trio of beaches runs adjacent to the Green Pleasure Pier on the southeast shore of Avalon Bay. Lifeguards are on duty through summer (sunrise-sunset). South of the pier is **South Beach,** while the north side is called **Middle Beach.** Both offer sandy shores that slope gently into the bay. Three blocks north of the pier, the smaller **Step Beach** accesses deeper waters. A half mile north on Descanso Bay, the lovely, private **Descanso Beach** ($2) features all the amenities of the **Descanso Beach Club** (1 St Catherine Way, 310/510-7410, www.visitcatalinaisland.com, 11am-3pm daily), including snorkeling, kayaking, cabana rentals, and a climbing wall.

North in **Two Harbors,** a sandy, uncrowded beach spreads out along either side of the pier. **Two Harbors Dive & Recreation** (1 W. Banning House Rd., 310/510-4272, $12-60/hr) rents bikes, kayaks, snorkel and scuba gear, stand-up paddleboards, beach umbrellas, and volleyball equipment.

Recreation

You'll find plenty of places to kick off into the water. The most popular spot is the **Avalon Underwater Park** (Casino Point). This protected area at the north end of Avalon has buoys and markers to help you stay safe around the reefs. Not only will you see the famous bright orange garibaldi fish, but you'll also get the opportunity to meet jellyfish, anemones, spiny lobsters, and plenty of other sealife. Out at the deeper edge of the park, nearly half a dozen wrecked ships await further examination.

Catalina Adventure Tours (1 Cabrillo Mole, 562/432-8828, www. catalinaadventuretours.com, 8:30am-5pm Mon.-Fri., 8:30am-4pm Sat.-Sun., tours $28-159 adults) offers both land and sea tours, including underwater views from the semisubmersible *Nautilus*. Healthy adults can also try fly boarding—water jetpacks!

Diving and Snorkeling

Diving Catalina (34 Middle Terrace Rd., 310/510-8558, www.divingcatalina.com, $69-139) offers guided snorkel tours of the Casino Point Dive Park; rates include all equipment. Certified scuba divers can book a guided tour of Avalon Underwater Park.

Snorkel Catalina (107 Pebbly Beach Rd., 310/510-3175, www. snorkelingcatalina.com, $49-65) specializes in deepwater excursions farther from shore. Standard tours run 2-4 hours on a custom pontoon boat that lets you check out the prettiest fish, sleekest seals, and friendliest dolphins around the island.

Kayaking

Kayaking is a popular way to see the otherwise unreachable parts of Catalina. To rent kayaks, snorkel gear, or stand-up paddleboards, visit **Wet Spot Rentals** (120 Pebbly Beach Rd., 310/510-2229, www. catalinakayaks.com, 8am-6pm daily June-Aug., 9am-5pm daily Apr., May, and Sept., $25-55/day).

If you're not confident in your own navigation abilities, take a tour with **Descanso Beach Ocean Sports** (5 St Catherine Way, 310/510-1226, www. kayakcatalinaisland.com, $54 adults, $40 children under 12), which offers

kayak tours to different parts of the island for a range of experience levels. All trips start north of Avalon and the Casino at Descanso Beach Club.

Biking

A great way to get around Avalon is on a bicycle. You can bring your own bike aboard the ferry or rent a bicycle at the island's **Brown's Bikes** (107 Pebbly Beach Rd., 310/510-0986, www.catalinabiking. com, 9am-5pm daily, $25-50/day). Rentals include beach cruisers, mountain bikes, electric bikes, and tandems.

Hiking

Hard-core backpackers come to conquer the 37.2-mile (59.9 km) **Trans Catalina Trail,** which starts south of Avalon and continues through Two Harbors to end at Starlight Beach on the northwest tip of the island.

From Avalon (Wrigley Rd. at East End Light Rd.), the first 5.6-mile (10-km) portion of the trail reaches the **Garden to Sky Summit** and offers stellar views of the island. For a far less challenging hike to the same viewpoint, take the 2.8-mile (5-km) round-trip hike from the trailhead at the Wrigley Memorial and Botanical Garden (1400 Avalon Canyon Rd.).

Free day-use permits are required to hike in Catalina and are available at **Catalina Island Conservancy** (125 Clarissa Ave., #2739, 310/510-2595, www.catalinaconservancy.org, 8am-5pm daily) and **Two Harbors Visitor Services** (Isthmus Pier, 310/510-4205, 8am-5pm Sat.-Thurs., 8am-9:30pm Fri.). The Two Harbors location can guide you to the more difficult north island trails and also offers rentals such as sleeping bags and tents.

Food

For a hearty breakfast or lunch, visit **Original Jack's Country Kitchen** (118 Catalina Ave., 310/510-1308, www. catalinahotspots.com, 6:30am-3pm daily, $11-30), which delivers the classic

American dining experience—think breakfast, burgers, and pies—while using high-quality ingredients, including in its vegetarian dishes.

Steve's Steakhouse (417 Crescent Ave., 310/510-0333, www.stevessteakhouse. com, 11:30am-2pm and 5pm-9pm daily, $20-40) offers more than just steak; there are plenty of seafood options, too.

Accommodations

For inexpensive accommodations, your best bet is the **Hermosa Hotel & Cottages** (131 Metropole St., 310/510-1010 or 800/668-5963, www.hermosahotel.com, from $100), which offers simple rooms about a block from the harbor beaches and a short walk from the Casino, shops, and restaurants.

The bright yellow **Hotel Mac Rae** (409 Crescent Ave., 310/510-0246, www. hotelmacrae.com, from $129) has been in the Mac Rae family for four generations, and they've been running the hostelry since 1920. The rooms are right on the waterfront and have a Mediterranean feel.

The **Hermit Gulch Campground** (year-round, $28) is 1.5 miles (3 km) from the Avalon ferry terminal near the Wrigley Memorial and Botanical Garden. Avalon Transportation Services (310/510-0025) provides a trolley from the Avalon boat landing. The campground offers tent sites and tent cabins with access to restrooms and showers (fee). Five other primitive campgrounds are accessible by boat or on foot. **Reservations** (www.reserveamerica. com) are required for any of Catalina's campgrounds.

Getting Around

The easiest way to get around the island is to walk. Some locals and visitors prefer golf carts, which can

Top to bottom: Avalon Harbor on Catalina Island; surfers in Huntington Beach; Huntington Beach Pier.

be rented from **Island Rentals** (125 Pebbly Beach Rd., 310/510-1456, www. catalinagolfcartrentals.com, 9am-close daily, $50/hour) near the ferry dock.

Taxis hover near the ferry dock when the ferries are due in each day; it's customary to share your ride with as many people as can fit in the cab. To get a cab back to the ferry, call 310/510-0025.

Huntington Beach

Calling itself Surf City USA, Huntington Beach (pop. 200,652) fits the part, offering miles of sandy beaches and breaks, with a fun-loving central downtown area that's home to restaurants, bars, and endless people-watching. If you simply want to spend a couple days sunning, surfing, and beach cruising, this is the place. Visit in late July and you may find the **U.S. Open of Pro Surfing** (www. vansusopenofsurfing.com) taking place.

Getting There
Huntington Beach is 15 miles (24 km) south of Long Beach on CA-1.

Beaches
At the north end of Huntington Beach (Beach Blvd. to Seapoint St.) is **Sunset Beach,** which is about as wide as beaches come, with a grassy park and pedestrian path extending its length, just behind a row of beachfront homes. Wild winds minimize good surfing days but provide the perfect fuel for windsurfing and kite surfing, plus fun bodysurfing and stand-up paddleboarding.

Southeast of Sunset Beach, **Bolsa Chica State Beach** (17851 Pacific Coast Hwy., 714/846-3460, www.parks.ca.gov, 6am-10pm daily, parking lot closes at 9pm) has smaller waves than the beaches to the south, which makes it a popular spot for beginning surfers. Amenities include volleyball courts, restrooms and showers, lifeguards (in summer), picnic ramadas (714/377-9422 for reservations), fire

rings, barbecue grills, basketball courts, and a paved bike path.

North of **Huntington Beach Pier** (Main St.) sits the **Huntington City Beach** (103 CA-1 from Beach Blvd. to Seapoint St., 714/536-5281, www.surfcityusa.com, 5am-10pm daily). Here you'll find good surf, volleyball courts, and bike path. Continue south for more surf and firepits along the stretch of **Huntington State Beach** (Beach Blvd. to Santa Ana River, 714/536-1454, www.parks.ca.gov, 6am-10pm daily). Parking lots run virtually the entire stretch.

At the foot of the pier you'll find the **Visitor Information Center and Kiosk** (325 Pacific Coast Hwy., 714/969-3492, www.surfcityusa.com, 11am-5pm Mon.-Fri., 10am-5pm Sat.-Sun.).

International Surfing Museum
Like many Southern California cities, Huntington Beach was introduced to surfing by the "father of modern surfing," Hawaiian-born George Freeth. City founder Henry Huntington brought Freeth here to exhibit the sport in 1910, and the town has been smitten ever since. Sidewalks near the beach are beset with the names of surfing all-stars, à la the Hollywood Walk of Fame. It's also home to the **International Surfing Museum** (411 Olive Ave., 714/300-8836, www. surfingmuseum.org, noon-5pm daily, $3), which exhibits vintage surfboard designs and highlights the history of surfing and other beach-friendly sports including roller-skating and skateboarding.

Recreation
Anglers don't need a license to fish from Huntington Pier. Rent rods and gear at pier bait and tackle shop **Lets Go Fishing** (21 Main St., 714/960-1392, 9am-7pm Mon.-Fri., 9am-8pm Sat.-Sun., $6/hr).

★ Surfing
Surfable beach breaks pop up along the entire stretch of Huntington Beach; surf zones are identified by lifeguards (usually

with a yellow checkered flag). Waves are best—but are also the most crowded—on either side of the pier. Beginners will find plenty of fun rides farther north or south along the beach.

Jack's Beach Concession (21291 Pacific Coast Hwy., 714/536-8328, 9am-5pm daily) and **Dwight's Beach Concession** (201 Pacific Coast Hwy., 714/536-8083, www.dwightsbeachconcession.com, 9:30am-4:30pm Fri.-Sun.) can furnish surfboard rentals ($12/hr), paddleboards ($20/hr), boogie boards ($6/hr), and wetsuits ($6/hr).

For surf lessons, join the 11am group every morning spring through fall at **Bonzai Surf School** (22355 Pacific Coast Hwy., 714/813-2880, www. banzaisurfschool.com, $79 group lessons, $159 and up private lessons). Call or check online for updated **surf reports** (714/536-9303, www.huntingtonbeachca.gov).

Biking

This is true beach cruiser country, where the flat, paved **Huntington Beach Bike Trail** (8.5 mi/13.7 km) connects all the beaches between Bolsa Chica and Huntington State Beach. For bike rentals, look to a pair of longtime father and son enterprises: **Jack's Beach Concession** (21291 Pacific Coast Hwy., 714/536-8328, 9am-5pm daily) has been running strong since 1957; it's right on the beach a half-mile south of the pier. Jack's father originally opened **Dwight's Beach Concession** (201 Pacific Coast Hwy., 714/536-8083, www.dwightsbeachconcession.com, 9:30am-4:30pm Fri.-Sun.) back in 1932. That's a block in from the pier, open only on weekends. Both offer multi-person surrey bike rentals ($25-35/day), as well as beach cruisers ($10/hr), tandems ($15/hr), and trailers ($5/hr).

Food

Huntington Beach is flush with burger spots. Your best burger bet is **25 Degrees** (412 Walnut Ave., 714/960-2525, 11:30am-10pm Mon.-Thurs., 11:30am-midnight

Fri., 11am-10pm Sat.-Sun., $12-13). For quick vegetarian soups, salads, and sandwiches, stop at the **Bodhi Tree Café** (501 Main St., Ste. E, 714/969-9500, 11am-10pm daily, $10-20).

For a step up, drive 15-20 minutes inland to ★ **Taco Maria** (3313 Hyland Ave., 714/538-8444, www.tacomaria.com, $79 prix fixe, $14-18 à la carte) for arguably the best Mexican food in Orange County. Try the handmade, heirloom blue-corn tortilla tacos stuffed with vegetarian, meat, or seafood and made using upscale and local ingredients. The prix fixe tasting menu fully embraces the scope available at this local favorite.

Accommodations

Across the highway from Huntington Beach, you can get oceanview rooms and standard hotel furnishings at the tiny **Sun 'N Sands Motel** (1102 CA-1, 714/536-2543, www.sunnsands.com, $139-289). The larger and more stylish **Shorebreak Hotel** (500 CA-1, 714/861-4470, www. shorebreakhotel.com, $215-390) offers rooms with balconies and ocean views right in front of the pier.

Newport Beach

After passing over the Santa Ana River, CA-1 enters Newport Beach (pop. 86,160), an affluent community built around a tiny bay protected by the Balboa Peninsula. It stays young and energetic by virtue of being the closest beach for students of nearby **University of California Irvine.** Most of the activity will be found by exiting off CA-1 at Newport Boulevard and continuing onto Balboa Boulevard to enter the peninsula. Parking is limited, but the peninsula features pretty beaches, upscale shopping, nightlife, and bayside amusements.

Getting There

Newport Beach is 5.3 miles (8.5 km) south of Huntington Beach along CA-1.

Beaches

Stretching more than five miles from the Santa Ana River to the tip of the Balboa Peninsula, **Newport Municipal Beach** offers seemingly endless room for sunning, surfing, and volleyball along Main Street on the Balboa Peninsula. The most popular and crowded spots are at **Newport Beach Pier** (Oceanfront and 21st St.) and **Balboa Pier** (701 E. Oceanfront), which has **parking lots** (949/644-3390, www. newportbeachca.gov, $2.10/hr May-Sept., $1.45/hr Oct.-Apr). Remoter parts of the beach are less crowded, but street parking can be tough to find.

Recreation

Attention beach cruisers: a flat, paved bike path runs nearly the entire Balboa Peninsula for more than five miles of leisurely coastal exercise. Rent a bike at **20th Street Beach & Bikes** (2001 W. Balboa Blvd., 949/723-0043, www. beachandbikes.com, 9am-6pm Mon.-Fri., 9am-7pm Sat.-Sun., $10/2 hours), which also rents surrey bikes ($35/hr), tandems ($20/hr), and trailers ($10/hr).

20th Street Beach & Bikes rents surfboards ($20/day), paddleboards ($20/hr), and kayaks ($20/hr) as well as bikes. You may surf with mixed results around the piers. For a fun surf that gets more advanced as it gets bigger, head to **Echo Beach,** a popular spot at the end of 56th Street.

Newport's best known wave is **The Wedge,** which breaks like its name off the jetty on the southern tip of the peninsula. It can hit 20 feet when the right swells come in and is typically crowded with advanced surfers only. Unless you qualify, it's best to stand on the beach and watch the athletic displays. To improve your skills, book a lesson with **Endless Sun Surf School** (80 Newport Pier, 949/533-1022, www.endlesssunsurf.com, 6am-9pm daily, from $75/hr).

Top to bottom: surfers at Huntington Beach; Balboa Fun Zone; Laguna Beach.

A Trio of Orange County Beaches

Orange County may have seceded from Los Angeles County in 1889, but it owes a lot to the metropolis, which employs a vast chunk of its commuting population. Consequently, the wealth of two counties helped develop its trio of distinct beach cities, which offer their own twists on SoCal beach culture.

♦ Exclusive **Laguna Beach,** to the south, offers some of Southern California's priciest real estate, thanks to rolling coast-view hillside neighborhoods and a sequence of gorgeous cove beaches.

♦ Upscale **Newport Beach** features large cliffside homes extending from a long, protected bay favored by boaters. It offers high-end shopping like its neighbor to the south, but also a youthful nightlife, plus family-friendly beaches and amusements.

♦ The farthest north, **Huntington Beach** is all beach west of the coastal highway, making it more affordable on average and therefore more conducive to surf and beach party lifestyles.

Near the Balboa Pier, carnival snacks, arcades, a Ferris wheel, and other amusements distinguish the **Balboa Fun Zone** (600 E. Bay Ave., Balboa Village, 949/903-2825, ww.balboaferriswheel.com, 11am-6pm Mon.-Thurs., 11am-9pm Fri., 11am-10pm Sat.).

The best way to cruise the bay is on an electric Duffy Boat. Rent one at **Boat Rentals of America** (510 Edgewater Pl., 949/673-7200, www.boats4rent.com, 10am-6pm daily spring-fall, 10am-5pm daily winter, $85/hr). For bigger maritime adventures, book a whale-watching or sportfishing excursion with **Davey's Locker** (400 Main St., 949/673-1434, www.daveyslocker.com, whale-watching from $26, sportfishing from $41.50).

Shopping

Tony Lido Island is populated with boutiques and posh eateries, particularly its **Lido Marina Village** (3434 Via Lido, www.lidomarinavillage.com), which is built on a marina and surrounded by party yachts and luxury cruises. For cute but more reasonably priced shops, look to Marine Avenue on Balboa Island.

Food

Frozen bananas are a Newport tradition, dipped in chocolate and covered in nuts. You'll find them in the **Balboa Fun Zone** (600 E. Bay Ave., Balboa Village, 949/903-2825, www.balboaferriswheel.com, 11am-6pm Mon.-Thurs., 11am-9pm Fri., 11am-10pm Sat.).

Sugar 'n Spice (310 Marine Ave., Balboa Island, 949/673-8907, www.sugarnspicebalboaisland.com, 10am-9pm Sun.-Thurs., 10am-10pm Fri.-Sat., $4-7) opened in 1947 and offers another famous local frozen dessert, the Balboa Bar—vanilla or chocolate ice cream dipped in chocolate and sprinkles.

Local institution **The Crab Cooker** (2200 Newport Blvd., 949/673-0100, www.crabcooker.com, 11am-9pm Sun.-Thurs., 11am-10pm Fri.-Sat., $17-24) has been serving seafood here since 1951.

This pair of eponymous businesses should be checked at different times of day. In the morning or early afternoon, try **A Market** (3400 West Coast Hwy., 949/650-6515, www.amarketnb.com, 6:30am-5pm daily), a deli counter serving coffee and tea, breakfast foods, and other easy takeaway fare. Next door, the landmark **A Restaurant** (3334 West Coast Hwy., 949/650-6505, www.arestaurantnb. com, 11:30am-10pm Mon.-Thurs., 11:30am-11pm Fri., 5pm-11pm Sat., 5pm-10pm Sun., $28-49) has been in service since 1926. Dinner includes classic surf-and-turf entrées, with various chops and filets in a dimly lit dining room with old-school decor.

Accommodations
With a great location between Lido Island and Newport Pier, **Little Inn By the Bay** (2627 Newport Blvd., 800/438-4466, http://www.littleinnbythebay.com, from $122) offers 18 suites, some with a Jacuzzi and balcony. Amenities include free parking and loaner bikes for guest use.

Check into **The Island Hotel Newport Beach** (690 Newport Center Dr., 949/759-0808, www.islandhotel.com, $230-390) for perhaps the ultimate O.C. experience. The high-rise luxury hotel is situated in a giant shopping mall, a few minutes' drive from the beach. Expect cushy beds with white linens, private bathrooms, and all the best amenities.

Getting Around
Driving the length of the Balboa Peninsula can take 10 minutes, longer when it's crowded. For a quick return to the Pacific Coast Highway, take the **Balboa Island Ferry** (end of Palm St. at Newport Bay, www.balboaislandferry. com, 6:30am-midnight Sun.-Thurs., 6:30am-2am Fri.-Sat., $2). The three-car ferry embarks every three minutes, which is about how much time it takes to cross the bay to Balboa Island.

Laguna Beach

The town of Laguna Beach (pop. 23,147) is one of Southern California's wealthier communities, which sometimes seems at odds with its historic surf culture, but the dichotomy makes it interesting. Spread out over miles of coastline, Laguna's main attractions are actually six or seven pretty beaches interspersed between residential communities. Along with designer boutiques, its commercial districts offer surf shops and humble dining mainstays that retain a touch of old Laguna spirit despite the highly polished image it presents to the world. That said, it's the top choice should you want to make a luxury stop mid road trip.

Getting There
Laguna Beach is 10.5 miles (16.9 km) south of Newport Beach on CA-1.

Beaches
Beach life extends among a dozen separate beaches. **Heisler Park** and **Main Beach Park** (Pacific Coast Hwy., www.lagunabeachinfo.com) are most central, each offering amenities such as picnic tables and restrooms, with protected waterways, tidepools, water-based playground equipment, and scuba diving at several reefs right off the beach. Other standouts include the very pretty and well-maintained **Aliso Beach Park** (31131 Coast Hwy., 949/923-2280, www.ocparks. com, 6am-10pm daily), memorable for white-sand beaches, turquoise waters, and a parking lot.

If it's low tide, go south to search for the area's infamous Rapunzel-like tower, **La Tour,** nestled against a bluff just beyond the crags at the north end of **Victoria Beach** (2700 Victoria Dr., down the staircase)—just be careful not to slip on wet rocks. North of downtown Laguna, a series of coves offers beaches within residential areas, including Crescent Bay, where you'll find the aptly named **Beautiful Cove** (1345 Cliff Dr.), historically the favorite beach of locals.

Crystal Cove State Park
Nestled between Newport Beach and Laguna Beach, **Crystal Cove State Park** (8471 CA-1 N., 949/494-3539, www.

◆ Side Trip: San Onofre

Only military personnel have access to the 16 miles (26 km) of coastline adjacent to the freeway passing through Camp Pendleton, except for one beachy stop that happens to be home to one of the top surf breaks in the county: **San Onofre State Beach** (Old Hwy. 101 at Basilone Rd., 949/492-4872, www.parks.ca.gov, 6am-10pm daily mid-Apr.-Sept., 6am-8pm daily Oct.-mid-Apr., $15).

Named for a trestle bridge that surfers used to cross underneath to reach the world-class breaks, **Trestles** is most easily accessed by entering the San Onofre State Beach Campground. A 1.5-mile (3 km) nature trail connects the campground to Trestle Beach. While camping has its own merits, people come here to seek the surf, which remains crowded despite the complicated access.

The **San Mateo Campground** (830 Cristianitos, San Clemente, www.reservecalifornia.com, year-round, $40) sites come with a firepit and a picnic table, while RV sites come with electricity and water. Facilities include a dump station, hot indoor showers, and flush toilets.

Getting There

This state beach is 3 miles (5 km) south of San Clemente on I-5. The surf beach is located south of San Clemente (exit on Basilone Rd.).

crystalcovestatepark.com, 6am-sunset daily, $15) preserves one of the few stretches of undeveloped coastline in Orange County. One portion extends roughly nine square miles into the ridges and hillsides rising inland, while another three-mile stretch consists of sandy beaches, backed by sandstone bluffs that allow you to feel a world away from the surrounding suburbs. Hikes, tidepools, and bird-watching are a few of the activities that can be enjoyed here.

Laguna Art Museum

From its clifftop perch overlooking the Pacific Ocean, **Laguna Art Museum** (307 Cliff Dr., 949/494-8971, www.lagunaartmuseum.org, 11am-5pm Fri.-Tues., 11am-9pm Thurs., $7 adult, children under 18 free) specializes entirely in art made within California, some dating back to the early 19th century, others more contemporary pieces representing emerging artists of today. The museum's oldest gallery dates back 90 years, and the museum building has expanded over the past four decades to reflect a growing collection and its refined mandate, to "represent the life and history of the state."

Shopping

For a taste of Laguna Beach glamour, browse the boutiques, fine art galleries, and surf shops along tree-lined **Forest Avenue,** across the highway from the Main Beach. The fun continues south along CA-1 (South Coast Highway, as it's known on this stretch), including standout shops such as **Buy Hand** (357 S. Coast Hwy., 949/715-0515, www.lagunabuyhand.com, 10am-6pm Mon.-Sat., 10am-5pm Sun.), which only deals in handmade items.

More businesses are peppered along the highway farther south. One cluster around Thalia Street includes beachwear boutiques **Merrilee's Swimwear** (790 S. Coast Hwy., 949/497-6743, www.merrilees.com, 10am-7pm daily) and **The Shop Laguna Beach** (1020 S. Coast Hwy., 949/715-8308, www.theshoplaguna.com, 10am-7pm daily).

A third shopping district radiating from Bluebird Canyon Drive was the site of Laguna Beach's first commercial area; it's been reborn as the **HIP District** (www.hipdistrictlaguna.com), as in "Historic and Interesting Places." Spas and shops built into refurbished cottages sell gifts, books, pottery, jewelry, and home decor.

Food

You'll find a variety of midscale bistros in Village Laguna, around Forest Street and CA-1. For the local mainstay, try the **Orange Inn** (703 CA-1, 949/494-6085, www.orangeinncafe.com, 5:30am-5pm daily, $5-10), which serves breakfast, burgers, and smoothies in a casual, surf shack-like space.

Carmelita's Kitchen De Mexico (217 Broadway, 949/715-7829, www.carmelitaskdm.com, 11am-10pm Mon.-Fri., 9am-10pm Sat., 9am-9pm Sun., $14-28) serves upscale Mexican cuisine including *tampiqueña* (marinated skirt steak) and a delicious seafood platter. Wash it down with one of their classic margaritas.

The Stand (238 Thalia St., 949/494-8101, www.thestandnaturalfoods.com, 7am-8pm daily summer, 7am-7pm daily winter, $7-11) has been serving vegan food here since 1975. Order a smoothie or sandwich to take to the beach.

Sapphire Laguna (1200 S. Coast Hwy., 949/715-9888, www.sapphirellc.com, 11am-10:30pm Mon.-Fri., 9am-10:30pm Sat.-Sun., $24-37) is known for its seasonal international cuisine helmed by chef Azmin Ghahreman. Menu options range from Hawaiian-style barramundi to Indonesian coconut curry.

Accommodations

Loaded with framed decor, the **Art Hotel** (1404 N. Pacific Coast Hwy., 877/363-7229, www.arthotellagunabeach.com, $170-200) is Laguna's best budget option, with simple rooms and quick access to local beaches.

Restored historic cabins are available for overnight stays at ★ **Crystal Cove Beach Cottages** (35 Crystal Cove, 800/444-7275, www.crystalcovebeachcottages.com, $185-261). Dorm cottages offer by-the-room accommodations for solo travelers (linens included), or rent an individual cabin all to yourself. Amenities include a shared refrigerator and microwave, but no kitchen; there are no TVs. The rustic accommodations are very popular; reservations can be made seven months in advance.

Laguna has developed a swanky reputation, and most of the hotels and resorts embrace that, with ritzy properties and sky-high rates. When it comes to location, the central (still pricey) midrange option would be **The Inn at Laguna Beach** (211 CA-1, 800/544-4479, www.innatlagunabeach.com, $460-550). Conversely, **Capri Laguna on the Beach** (1441 CA-1, 949/537-2503, www.caprilaguna.com, $280-650) puts you on the beach for less, if you don't request a view.

Getting Around

Since Laguna's areas of interest are fairly spread out, Laguna Transit operates a seasonally active **Laguna Beach Trolley** (949/497-0766, www.visitlagunabeach.com, 9:30am-11:30pm daily late-June-Aug., 4pm-11pm Fri., 9:30am-11pm Sat., 11am-8pm Sun. Sept.-mid-June, free), which stops along Pacific Coast Highway every 30-40 minutes.

San Juan Capistrano

★ Mission San Juan Capistrano

One of the most beloved of all the California missions is **Mission San Juan Capistrano** (26801 Ortega Hwy., 949/234-1300, http://missionsjc.com, 9am-5pm daily, $10 adults, $7 children). This was the only one of nine California missions founded by Father Junípero Serra where he presided over Sunday services. Today, this mission has a beautiful Catholic church on-site, extensive gardens and land, and a museum created within the old mission itself. Inside the original church, artifacts from the early days of the mission detail its rise and fall. Outside, a graveyard continues that narrative, as do the bells and other buildings of the compound. In late fall and early spring, monarch butterflies flutter about in the flower gardens and out by the fountain in the courtyard.

Guided **tours** (hours vary daily, $3 adult, $2 child) cover the highlights of the mission and grounds and offer informative history relating to the area. The on-site **Mission Store** (949/234-1318, 10am-6pm daily spring-summer, 10am-5:30pm daily fall-winter) sells souvenirs.

The mission may be even more famous for the **migration of swallows** (Mar. 19) that return every spring to the town of San Juan Capistrano. The swallows migrate 6,000 miles from Argentina to roost in the mission's entryways and in the ruins of the Great Stone Church. The entire town celebrates their return with the **Swallows Day Parade** (www.swallowsparade.com, Mar., free), held in downtown San Juan Capistrano on the streets surrounding the mission.

Outside the mission, you'll find the town's main street, **Camino Capistrano,** which positively drips Spanish colonial history. Each old adobe building boasts a brass plaque describing its origins and use over the years.

Getting There

At San Juan Capistrano, CA-1 merges with I-5, which becomes Pacific Coast Highway South, passing San Onofre in 14 miles (23 km) to reach Oceanside in 35 miles (56 km).

Mission San Juan Capistrano

Oceanside

The city of Oceanside (pop. 176,193) is named for its sandy coastline, but much of its identity relates to the border it shares with the Marine Corps Base Camp Pendleton. Young marines and their families have lived here since World War II. You'll still find plenty of military-facing retailers in the coastal downtown area, banked by a fishing harbor and pier. However, lately Oceanside has evolved to become a more fitting cultural counterpart to its always stellar beaches.

Getting There

From San Juan Capistrano in the north, follow I-5 south for about 30 miles (48 km). Exit west on Mission Avenue or Oceanside Boulevard to reach downtown.

From San Diego to the south, take I-5 north for 38 miles (61 km).

Beach

Known as The Strand, **Oceanside City Beach** (301 The Strand N., 760/435-4018, www.ci.oceanside.ca.us, daily 24 hours) runs four miles from the Oceanside Harbor south to Carlsbad. Most of the beach is free of heavy crowds, except in the peak of summer. Facilities include picnic tables, grills, fire rings, restrooms, and showers. An amphitheater at the base of the pier hosts summer concerts.

Sights
Oceanside Museum of Art

Stop in to enjoy the contemporary and conceptual art collection of the **Oceanside Museum of Art** (704 Pier View Way, 760/435-3720, www.oma-online. org, 11am-5pm Tues.-Wed., 11am-8pm Thurs.-Fri., 11am-5pm Sat., noon-5pm Sun., $8 adults, $5 seniors, military and students free, free 1st Sun. each month). A rotating calendar of programs and events complements a series of modern and contemporary art exhibitions.

California Surf Museum

The small **California Surf Museum** (312 Pier View Way, 760/721-6876, www. surfmuseum.org, 10am-4pm Fri.-Wed., 10am-8pm Thurs., $5 adults, $3 seniors, military, and students, children under age 12 free) has plenty to say about local surfing history. Exhibits depict the evolution of the surfboard as well as well-known riders, including surfer Bethany Hamilton.

Mission San Luis Rey de Francia

Oceanside's top attraction is the **Mission San Luis Rey de Francia** (4050 Mission Ave., 760/757-3651, www.sanluisrey. org, 9:30am-5pm Mon.-Thurs., 10am-5pm Sat.-Sun., $5 adults, $4 seniors and ages 6-18, free military), the 18th of California's 21 Franciscan missions. It was founded in 1798 by French missionary Fermín Lasuén, successor to Junípero Serra. Also known as the "King of Missions," it's the largest of the group.

Simply walk around and ogle the white-washed walls and Spanish colonial architecture or take one of the tours to learn more about the history of this National Historic Landmark.

Recreation

While beaches get a fair amount of use, many visitors come to bike the **Coast Highway** (US-101), which picks up south of Marine Corps Base Camp Pendleton and leads 20 miles (32 km) south to San Dieguito Lagoon near Del Mar. The ocean will be on your right the whole way. Great scenery and cool ocean breezes make this one of the county's most popular cycling routes; it's particularly well-trafficked on weekends.

Surfing

Wide swaths of sand stretch the entire length of **Oceanside City Beach** (301 The Strand N., 760/435-4018, www.ci.oceanside.ca.us, 24 hours daily), with shallow swimming areas good for kids and beginning surfers. Surfers tend to stick near Oceanside Harbor and along the 0.25-mile pier that juts from the town center.

The **San Diego Surfing Academy** (Oceanside Harbor, 760/230-1471 or 800/447-7873, www.sandiegosurfingacademy.com, lessons $100-120) offers quality instruction for beginning surfers with group classes and private lessons. You'll learn surf etiquette and ocean awareness before hitting the waves on a loaner board (wetsuit and leash included). A complimentary GoPro video of your experience is also available.

Food

It's worth veering into south Oceanside for dinner at the "unorthodox sushi" counter of ★ **Wrench and Rodent**

Seabasstropub (1815 S. Coast Hwy., 760/271-0531, www.seabasstropub.com, 4pm-9pm Mon., 4pm-10pm Tues.-Sun., $13-35). Don't be deterred by the name; innovative chef Davin Waite assembles sushi unlike anyone else, sourcing sustainable seafood and locally sourced—or foraged—produce. Creative dishes abound, including house-made ramen noodles.

In downtown Oceanside, your best bet for beer and pub fare is **Bagby Beer Company** (601 S. Coast Hwy., 760/512-3372, www.bagbybeer.com, 11am-10pm Mon.-Thurs., 11am-11pm Fri.-Sat., 10am-10pm Sun., $10-16), where truly exceptional house beers complement burgers, tacos, and Belgian fries.

Nearby, hip Indonesian eatery **Dija Mara** (232 S. Coast Hwy., 760/231-5376, www.dijamara.com, 4pm-9:30pm Tues.-Thurs., 4pm-10pm Fri.-Sat., 11am-2:30pm and 5pm-9:30pm Sun., $17-26) feels casual, but serves impeccable dishes of slow-cooked meats and distinctly spiced sauces.

Accommodations

Oceanside hotel options are limited, but a reasonable oceanfront stay may be found at the **Southern California Beach Club** (121 S. Pacific St., 760/722-6666, www.southerncalifbeachclub.com, from $150), which offers clean studios and condos that include full kitchens and views, plus direct access to the beach.

Getting Around

North County Beaches are conveniently served by the local **Coaster** (760/966-6500, www.gonctd.com/coaster, $4-12) commuter train. The **Oceanside Transit Station** (195 S. Tremont St.) is in downtown Oceanside, a short walk from the pier and beach.

Side Trip: Temecula

North of San Diego County, the Temecula Valley is Southern California's preeminent wine country. The region's 40-plus wineries draw an estimated three million visitors each year. Winery tasting rooms tend to close by 6pm, so spend the night at one of the wineries and use it as a launching point to visit multiple vineyards.

Temecula is 60 miles (97 km) north of San Diego via I 15; the drive takes about an hour in light traffic.

Wineries
Mount Palomar Winery (33820 Rancho California Rd., 951/676-5047, www.mount-palomar.com, 11am-5pm Mon.-Thurs., 11am-7pm Fri.-Sat.) is known for smooth and complex wines like the Italian red sangiovese, French white, and viognier.

Callaway Vineyard and Winery (32720 Rancho California Rd., 951/676-4001, www.callawaywinery.com, 10:30am-6pm daily) makes balanced, fruit-forward wines with more than a dozen varietals.

South Coast Winery (34843 Rancho California Rd., 877/743-8303, www.south-coastwinery.com, 10am-6pm daily) has won the California State Golden Bear Winery of the Year Award four times. Its expertly produced vintages include cabernets, syrahs, and merlots and its resort, spa, and restaurant host many visitors.

Carter Estate Winery (34450 Rancho California Rd., 844/851-2138, www.carteres-tatewinery.com, 11am-6pm daily) and **Thornton Winery** (32575 Rancho California Rd., 951/699-0099, www.thorntonwine.com, 10am-8pm daily) make sparkling wines.

For a more California vibe, try **Ponte Winery** (35053 Rancho California Rd., 951/694-8855, www.pontewinery.com, 10am-5pm daily). For an intimate, small-scale winemaker, visit **Hart Winery** (41300 Avenida Biona, 951/676-6300, www.hartfamily-winery.com, 9am-5pm daily).

Tours
Book tours and transportation with **Grapeline Wine Tours** (951/693-5755, http://gogrape.com/temecula, $119-149 pp); you may also take tours by jeep with **Sunrider Wine & Beer Jeep Tour** (951/551-1516, www.sunriderjeeptours.com, $125 pp) or by limo with **Temecula Limo Wine Tasting** (951/402-3595, www.temeculalimowine-tasting.com, $220 for group of 4).

Wine Country Trails by Horseback (34225 Rancho California, 951/506-8706, www.winecountrytrailsbyhorseback.com, Wed.-Sun. by reservation) guides horse-back rides along trails between vineyards, while **Temecula Carriage Company** (40001 Berenda Rd., 858/205-9161, www.temeculacarriageco.com, 10am-2pm Fri.-Sun., $39 pp) offers wine tours by carriage ride.

Consult **Temecula Valley Winegrowers** (www.temeculawines.org) for detailed information about all the Temecula wineries.

Restaurants and Hotels
The lunchtime views are phenomenal from the **Falkner Winery** hilltop restaurant **The Pinnacle** (40620 Calle Contento, 951/676-8231, www.falknerwinery.com/res-taurant, 11:30am-3pm daily, $16-28). The restaurant at **Leoness Cellars** (38311 De Portola Rd., 951/302-7601, www.leonesscellars.com, 11am-5pm Sun.-Thurs., 11am-6pm Fri.-Sat., $20-40) pairs a gorgeous vineyard setting with adventurous contemporary cuisine and decor.

Stay where the wine is at **South Coast Winery Resort & Spa** (34843 Rancho Cali-fornia Rd., 877/743-8303, www.southcoastwinery.com, from $199) or the next prop-erty over, **Ponte Vineyard Inn** (35001 Rancho California Rd., 951/587-6688, www.pontevineyardinn.com, from $260).

Carlsbad

Established as "The Village By The Sea" in the late-19th century, Carlsbad (pop. 115,130) thrived for a long time as a beach resort on the merits of its miles of golden coastline. But it was the arrival of Legoland that seriously bolstered the city's status as a tourist destination. The theme park brings 15 million visitors per year to South Carlsbad and its surrounding sights.

The seaside Carlsbad Village still serves as the pedestrian-friendly city center and is within a short stroll of several beach hotels.

Getting There

Carlsbad is 4 miles (6 km) south of Oceanside via I-5. Carlsbad Village lies at the north end of town and is best accessed by exiting at Carlsbad Village Drive.

From San Diego to the south, it's a 35-mile (56 km) drive north on I-5.

Beaches

Carlsbad State Beach (7201 Carlsbad Blvd., Carlsbad Village, 760/438-3143, www.parks.ca.gov, dawn-sunset daily) is fronted by hotels and has street parking, lending to its resort town appeal. Popular activities include swimming, surfing, diving, and fishing. Restrooms and showers are available near Pine Street and at the south end of Carlsbad at Tamarack Surf Beach (101 Tamarack Ave.).

Found at the end of Poinsettia Lane, **South Carlsbad State Beach** (7201 Carlsbad Blvd., 760/438-3143, www. parks.ca.gov, dawn-sunset) is partly reserved for coastal campsites, but a free day-use parking lot offers access to sandy beachfront and spaced-out, intermediate surf breaks.

Separated by the ocean outlet for the Batiquitos Lagoon, **North and South Ponto Beaches** (6325 Carlsbad Blvd., 760/720-7001, www.parks.ca.gov,

6am-11pm daily) are both on the southern end of South Carlsbad State Park, each offering swimming, surfing, and sunbathing. North Ponto is larger and arguably more scenic, but it also charges $8 in its day-use parking lot. Meanwhile, South Ponto boasts volleyball courts, free parking, and showers in addition to restrooms. Those things make the smaller beach more popular.

Sights
Carlsbad Flower Fields

The **Carlsbad Flower Fields** (5704 Paseo Del Norte, 760/431-0352, www. theflowerfields.com, 9am-6pm daily Mar.-May, $16 adults, $14 seniors, $8 ages 3-10) are endlessly beautiful during the spring bloom, with more than 50 acres devoted to the giant ranunculus. Check the online calendar before visiting to make sure you don't miss the flowers in bloom (usually between February and May). Much of the year, the fields sit empty.

Leo Carrillo Ranch Historic Park

Built within a 27-acre canyon is the historically preserved **Leo Carrillo Ranch** (6200 Flying LC Ln., 760/476-1042, www. carlsbadca.gov, 9am-5pm Tues.-Sat., 11am-5pm Sun., tours 11am and 1pm Sat., noon and 2pm Sun., free). Hollywood character actor and conservationist Leo Carrillo bought the 19th-century hacienda in 1937, consciously preserving its historical buildings. Part time capsule, part garden preserve, the lovely grounds are worth exploring on your own, but you'll get a lot more history by taking one of the free tours offered each weekend.

Legoland

The biggest attraction in Carlsbad is **Legoland** (1 Legoland Dr., 877/376-5346, www.legoland.com, 10am-close daily, $95-119 adults, $89-113 ages 3-12). The building-block theme park features a miniature United States made of interlocking plastic and offers loads of kiddie-friendly

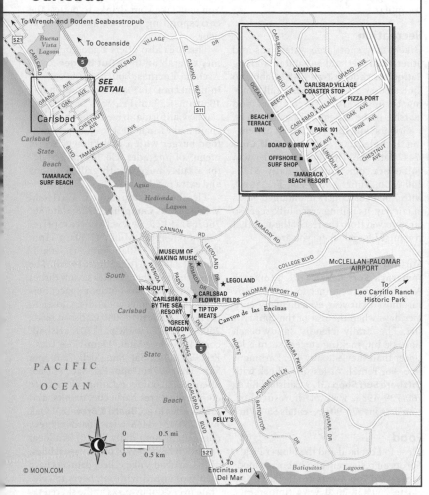

Carlsbad

To Wrench and Rodent Seabasstropub

To Oceanside

Buena Vista Lagoon

SEE DETAIL

Carlsbad

Carlsbad State Beach

TAMARACK SURF BEACH

Agua Hedionda Lagoon

CANNON RD

MUSEUM OF MAKING MUSIC

IN-N-OUT

CARLSBAD BY THE SEA RESORT

CARLSBAD FLOWER FIELDS

LEGOLAND

TIP TOP MEATS

GREEN DRAGON

Canyon de las Encinas

South Carlsbad State Beach

FARADAY RD

COLLEGE BLVD

McCLELLAN–PALOMAR AIRPORT

PALOMAR AIRPORT RD

To Leo Carrillo Ranch Historic Park

PACIFIC OCEAN

PELLY'S

0   0.5 mi
0   0.5 km

© MOON.COM

To Encinitas and Del Mar

Batiquitos Lagoon

Detail inset:

CAMPFIRE

CARLSBAD VILLAGE COASTER STOP

PIZZA PORT

BEACH TERRACE INN

PARK 101

BOARD & BREW

OFFSHORE SURF SHOP

TAMARACK BEACH RESORT

GRAND AVE

OCEAN ST

BEECH AVE

CARLSBAD BLVD

CARLSBAD VILLAGE DR

OAK AVE

PINE AVE

LINCOLN ST

PINE AVE

CHESTNUT AVE

---

rides and games incorporating pirates and dinosaurs and using laser blasters to recover stolen treasure. Base admission gets you in, with higher ticket prices adding park attractions like the Sea Life Aquarium and the splashy Legoland Water Park (spring-summer only).

Museum of Making Music

A stroll through the history of recorded music in the fascinating **Museum of Making Music** (5790 Armada Dr., 760/438-5996, www. museumofmakingmusic.org, 10am-5pm Tues.-Sun., $10 adults, $7 seniors, students, military, and ages 6-18) reveals hundreds of vintage instruments and even a few modern ones. Trace the advent of modern instruments and listen to snippets of popular recordings made at the time of their inception. Along the way, a few hands-on instruments allow you to make your own music (or noise), including an exhibit devoted to the electric guitar.

Recreation

Hikers may spot large waterbirds and other tidal wetland inhabitants along **Batiquitos Lagoon Trail** (7489 Gabbiano Ln.), an easy 3.3-mile (5-km) trail winding through 610 acres of trees and marshes in the Batiquitos Lagoon reserve.

Golfers will appreciate the challenging 18-hole, par 72 **Aviara Golf Club** (7447 Batiquitos Dr., 760/603-6900, www. golfaviara.com, 7am-5pm daily, $120-240 Mon.-Thurs., $140-260 Fri.-Sun.), with 7,000 gorgeously maintained yards of fairway. Its rolling green hills seem so far removed from the rest of the area that you might forget where you are.

Surfing

Tamarack Surf Beach (101 Tamarack Ave.) has a fun beginner-to-intermediate surf most of the year, even on many summer days when the rest of the county is flat. The family-friendly, sandy beach slopes a bit, making surfers seem a lot closer than they actually are. Parking is free. For rentals or lessons, check with **Offshore Surf Shop** (3179 Carlsbad Blvd., 760/729-4934, www.offshoresurfshop. com, lessons $75-90 pp, rentals $5-10/hr).

Food

Close to Legoland and the Flower Fields, European restaurant and imported foods grocer **Tip Top Meats** (6118 Paseo Del Norte, 760/438-2620, www.tiptopmeats. com, 6am-8pm daily, $6-15) serves mostly German meals in a traditional setting, including an all-you-can-eat sausage breakfast and a host of value-priced regional specialties throughout the day.

Inside a stately, colonial brick building, **Green Dragon Tavern & Museum** (6115 Paseo Del Norte, 760/918-2421, www.greendragontavernca.com, 11am-9pm Tues.-Sat., 11am-8pm Sun., $11-27) adopts the brick and wood style of American Revolution-era taverns, right down to its traditional English pub menu. You may take your drinks to peruse the corresponding history museum next door.

This area also offers a good opportunity to grab an **In-N-Out Burger** (5950 Avenida Encinas, 800/786-1000, www. in-n-out.com, 10:30am-1am Sun.-Thurs., 10:30am-1:30am Fri.-Sat., $5-10). The classic California drive-through burger chain makes an honest-to-goodness fast-food burger with a well-known "secret menu" of upgrades. Go "Animal Style" for a saucy burger with grilled onions and extra pickles.

The best restaurant in Carlsbad Village is ★ **Campfire** (2725 State St., 760/637-5121, www.thisiscampfire. com, 5pm-11pm Mon., 11:30am-11pm Tues.-Thurs., 11:30am-1am Fri., 10am-1am Sat., 10am-11pm Sun., $14-36). The wood-fired kitchen creates savory dishes for a woodsy, semi-outdoor space, bolstered by delicious cocktails. Closer to the beach, **Park 101** (3040 Carlsbad Blvd., 760/434-2217, www.park101carlsbad. com, 4pm-close Mon., 11am-close Tues.-Fri., 9am-close Sat.-Sun., deli: 7am-3pm Sun.-Thurs., 7am-6pm Fri.-Sat., $10-20) offers casual outdoor dining. The service counter features barbecue, drinks, and sandwiches to go. **Board & Brew** (201 Oak Ave., 760/434-4466, www.boardandbrew. com, 10am-8pm daily $5-10) is a local sandwich favorite that offers casual bites.

In Carlsbad Village, beer drinkers have plenty of award-winning beers to celebrate over doughy pizza at the shared tables of **Pizza Port** (571 Carlsbad Village Dr., 760/720-7007, www.pizzaport.com, 11am-10pm Mon.-Thurs., 11am-midnight Fri.-Sat., 11am-11pm Sun., $10-25).

Accommodations

For an affordable stay, try the **Carlsbad by the Sea Hotel** (850 Palomar Airport Rd., 760/438-7880, www. carlsbadhotelbythesea.com, from $100), which puts you within reach of Legoland

Hwy. 78: The Hops Highway

Along the border between Oceanside and Carlsbad, Highway 78 heads east through suburban San Diego County about 25 miles (40 km) to the **San Diego Zoo Safari Park** (15500 San Pasqual Valley Rd., 760/747-8702, www.sdzsafaripark.org, 9am-7pm daily, hours vary seasonally, $56 ages 12 and up, $46 ages 3-11, safari tour tickets $54-125). This huge sister park to the San Diego Zoo offers more than a traditional zoo experience: safari jeep tours take you through landscapes made to more closely resemble the natural habitats of a number of African species, including lions, giraffes, and elephants. Admission grants access to park enclosures; additional tickets are required for safari tours.

The drive along Highway 78 is not pretty, and it will be congested most times of day. What would be a half an hour drive each way to the Safari Park will likely take longer. However, what it lacks in scenery, it makes up for in flavor. Dozens of award-winning craft breweries populate the towns running alongside Highway 78, giving it the local nickname of **Hops Highway.** Stopping to visit any one of them can break up the drive back from a day viewing wild animals.

The region's best known beer maker, Stone Brewing, has its headquarters 9 miles (14 km) west of the Safari Park, in the city of Escondido. There its large brewery and restaurant, **Stone World Bistro & Gardens** (1999 Citracado Pkwy., 760/294-7899, www.stonebrewing.com, 11am-10pm Sun.-Thurs., 11am-11pm Fri.-Sat.), serves as a monument to craft beer, presented in true Southern California style with a large desert garden rolling off its generous outdoor patio and bar. You may opt for a brewery tour (to see how these guys do what they do), stay for dinner, or fill some growlers. Mainly, you'll want to check out the huge tap list and sample world-class beers.

About 3 miles (5 km) west, in the university town of San Marcos, **Port Brewing and The Lost Abbey** (155 Mata Way, Ste. 104, San Marcos, 800/918-6816, www.lostabbey.com, 1pm-6pm Mon., 1pm-7pm Tues.-Wed., 1pm-8pm Thurs., 1pm-9pm Fri., 11:30am-8pm Sat., noon-6pm Sun.) has a huge reputation for producing some of the best Belgian-style beers this side of the Atlantic, in addition to regional favorite IPAs. Nearby, the massive **URGE Gastropub and Common House** (255 Redel Rd., San Marcos, 760/798-8822, https://sm.urgegastropub.com, 11:30am-9pm Sun.-Wed., 11:30am-10pm Thurs., 11:30am-11pm Fri.-Sat.) houses the brewery of Mason Ale Works, but most of the space is dedicated to a restaurant, beer garden, full bar, and boutique bowling alley decorated after the film *The Big Lebowski*. To the west, **Rip Current Brewing** (1325 Grand Ave., #100, San Marcos, 760/481-3141, www.ripcurrentbrewing.com, 3pm-8pm Mon.-Thurs., 3pm-9pm Fri., noon-9pm Sat., noon-7pm Sun.) is much smaller, one of the reasons it won a best very small brewery championship (terrific hoppy and German-style beers are the other reasons).

The city of Vista is home to more than a dozen small breweries, most of which are found close together within industrial parks south of Highway 78 between Rancho Santa Fe Boulevard and Sycamore Avenue. Each offers distinctive takes on beer and tasting room experiences. For more information, visit the **Vista Brewer's Guild** website (www.vistabrewersguild.com).

In Vista's quaint city center, **Vista Village** (exit Vista Village Dr. north 0.6 mile), several local breweries have tasting rooms, including the **Mother Earth Tap Room** (206 Main St., Vista, 760/726-2273, www.motherearthbrewco.com, noon-9pm Mon., noon-10pm Tues.-Thurs., noon-11pm Fri., 11am-11pm Sat., 11am-9pm Sun.) and the **Belching Beaver Tavern and Grill** (302 E. Broadway, Vista, 760/295-8599, 3pm-9pm Mon.-Wed., noon-10pm Thurs., noon-11pm Fri.-Sat., noon-8pm Sun.), a brewpub with a pleasantly rustic outdoor setting complete with Adirondack chairs and firepits.

CARLSBAD

and the beach. It's a short walk from the Flower Fields.

Stay on the beach at the **Tamarack Beach Resort** (3200 Carlsbad Blvd., 800/334-2199, www.tamarackresort.com, from $200) or treat yourself at the **Beach Terrace Inn** (2775 Ocean St., 760/729-5951, www.beachterraceinn.com, from $250). Each offers direct beach access and locations within easy walking distance of village shops and restaurants.

For top-tier hospitality, no one beats **La Costa Resort & Spa** (2100 Costa Del Mar Rd., 760/438-9111, www.omnihotels.com, from $250). Slightly inland, the terra-cotta luxury resort, spa, and gold-medal golf course is a vacation unto itself. Expect exquisite comfort and service, as well as swimming pools, tennis courts, fitness classes, and activities for kids and teens.

Beach campsites may be reserved in advance at the **South Carlsbad State Beach Campground** (7201 Carlsbad Blvd., 760/438-3143, www.reservecalifornia.com, $35-50). Hundreds of cliffside spaces are set up for car camping or for RVs and trailers, with stairs leading down to a long, beautiful, undeveloped beach with plenty of swimming and surfing options.

Getting Around

The area is conveniently served by the local **Coaster** (760/966-6500, www.gonctd.com/coaster, $4-12) commuter train. There are two stops in Carlsbad: **Carlsbad Village** (2775 State St.) and **Poinsettia Station** (6511 Avenida Encinas, morning and afternoons only) in South Carlsbad.

Encinitas and Cardiff-by-the-Sea

Sprawling between a pair of conservation areas, the idyllic coastal city of Encinitas (pop. 63,184) doesn't market itself as a major tourist destination, despite offering the region's most beautiful beaches and celebrated surf. The city is split into three coastal communities, including residential Leucadia to the north and Cardiff-by-the-Sea in the south, where hillside dwellings overlook a beautiful state beach that is popular among campers and home to an epic reef break favored by longboarders. In central Encinitas, a walkable "Downtown by the Sea" runs along the highway, parallel to breathtaking cliffside beaches. At one end, beachgoers relax on the white sands of Moonlight Beach; at the other, they stand atop sandstone bluffs to watch pro surfers do their thing on the famous point break, Swami's.

Getting There

Whether approaching on US-101 or I-5, Encinitas is immediately south of Carlsbad, across the Batiquitos Lagoon. From I-5, take the Encinitas Boulevard exit for Encinitas or the Birmingham Drive exit for Cardiff-by-the-Sea. It's about 95 miles (153 km) south of downtown Los Angeles, usually a 2-hour drive. Coming from downtown San Diego, plan for the 25-mile (40-km) drive to take about 35 minutes, without traffic.

Beaches

One of the great features of Encinitas is the presence of other state beaches and campgrounds. Beautiful **Moonlight State Beach** (400 B St., Encinitas, 760/633-2740, www.parks.ca.gov, 5am-10pm daily) is a great place to see true California beach living at its finest. Sun worshippers abound, and surfers usually show up when (typically mild) waves come through, though it's also a good place for diving and fishing. A parking lot (free) features restrooms and showers. It's a couple of blocks from town.

Longboard-friendly reefs off the shore of **Cardiff State Beach** (2500 S. Coast Hwy. 101, Cardiff-by-the-Sea, 760/753-5091, www.parks.ca.gov, dawn-sunset) attract surfers, but this spot is just as

Encinitas and Cardiff-by-the-Sea

good for lounging in the sand and swimming. People also fish and dive here when conditions accommodate. Parking is available along the highway and in a day-use parking lot ($8), where you'll find restrooms and showers.

Adjoining **San Elijo State Beach** (2050 S. Coast Hwy. 101, Cardiff, 760/753-5091, www.parks.ca.gov, dawn-sunset) may not be as well known, but it offers its share of fun, uncrowded waves below its campground.

Sights

Rumored to be the first rural theater to show "talkies," **La Paloma Theatre** (471 S. Coast Hwy. 101, Encinitas, 760/436-5774, www.lapalomatheatre.com) still screens first-run movies. The best times to go are during premieres of new surfing films. Seeing great surfing and big waves on the large screen is a treat, and some of the pros featured in the flicks are likely to show up at the occasional premiere party.

San Diego Botanic Garden

Don't miss the chance to wander the unique and expansive **San Diego Botanic Garden** (230 Quail Gardens Dr., Encinitas, 760/436-3036, www.sdbgarden.org, 9am-5pm daily, $18 adults, $12 seniors and military, $10 ages 3-18, $2 parking). A stroll through the gardens almost feels like a geography lesson. Plants and flowers range from desert cacti to tropical rainforest plants, plus the nation's largest collection of bamboo.

Self-Realization Fellowship Retreat and Gardens

Tough to miss while driving along the Coast Highway is the **Self-Realization Fellowship** (939 2nd St., Encinitas, 760/436-7220, www.encinitastemple.org, 9am-5pm Tues.-Sat., 11am-5pm Sun., free). Its gold-pointed domes call attention to the spiritualist center, while just next door is the tranquil, manicured meditation garden (215 K St.). All of it sits high on a cliff overlooking the region's most beloved surf spot, consequently named Swami's.

Recreation
Surfing
At the south end of downtown Encinitas is **Swami's** (end of 2nd St., Encinitas), the sort of surf spot where you find local pros at play when it's really firing. Swami's is below the Self-Realization Fellowship (which gives Swami's its name), and the cliffs above offer a terrific vantage point for spectators. Even on mediocre days the waves remain crowded with those looking to reach that top echelon someday.

Due to its competitive nature, Swami's is not a place beginners want to try, but it can turn up some excellent days for visiting surfers with etiquette and skill who want a memorable San Diego surf experience. Rentals and lessons are available from **Concept Surf Shop** (215 W. D St., Encinitas, 760/753-6870, www.conceptsurfshop.com, surf rentals $25-35/day).

Eli Howard Surf School (760/809-3069, www.elihoward.com) offers lessons and overnight surf camps at **San Elijo State Beach** (2050 S. Coast Hwy. 101, Cardiff, 760/753-5091, www.parks.ca.gov).

Food
Encinitas boasts a half dozen good coffee shops. For atmosphere, visit the old train station building housing San Diego's original coffee roaster, **Pannikin Coffee** (510 N. Coast Hwy. 101, Encinitas, 760/436-5824, www.pannikincoffeeandtea.com, 6am-6pm daily), which offers a lovely patio setting for coffee and tea. Down the road, **Lofty Coffee Company** (90 N. Coast Hwy. 101, Encinitas, 760/230-6747, www.loftycoffeeco.com, 6am-6pm Mon.-Fri., 7am-6pm Sat.-Sun.) roasts organic specialty coffee at a beachy yet design-savvy café on a hillside, leaving its patio open to ocean breezes in the summer, when a Kyoto-drip cold-brew iced coffee proves ideal.

For breakfast with your coffee, try local favorite **Swami's Café** (1163 S. Coast Hwy. 101, Encinitas, 760/944-0612, www.swamiscafesd.com, 7am-9pm Mon.-Sat., 7am-3pm Sun., $8-12), known for its unique varieties of eggs Benedict. (I'm partial to the avocado and Mexican chorizo sausage combo.) For old-school diner-style grub, stop in at **101 Diner** (552 S. Coast Hwy. 101, Encinitas, 760/753-2123, 6am-1:30pm Mon.-Fri., 6am-2pm Sat.-Sun., $8-10) to enjoy traditional egg dishes along with baked-apple pancakes and stuffed waffles.

Funky little taco shop **Haggo's Organic Taco** (1302 N. Coast Hwy. 101, Ste. 101, Encinitas, 760/753-6000, www.haggosorganictaco.com, 11am-8pm Tues.-Sun., $8-15) captures the laid-back spirit of the region in street tacos, vegan burritos, and other creative offerings while using organic ingredients.

To take advantage of this gorgeous coastline, reserve a patio table at **Pacific Coast Grill** (2526 S. Coast Hwy. 101, Cardiff-by-the-Sea, 760/479-0721, www.pacificcoastgrill.com, 11am-4pm and 4:30pm-9pm Sun.-Thurs., 11am-4pm and 4:30pm-10pm Fri.-Sat., $25-50). Set on top of gorgeous Cardiff State Beach, this surf-and-turf restaurant lets you dine about as close to the ocean as you can without getting sand in your lap. In addition to the spectacular view, the kitchen provides a worthy dining experience, with appetizers of ahi tuna or a fillet you sear yourself on a sizzling hot stone. Follow it up with a fish perfectly cooked sous vide while you enjoy the sunset.

Accommodations
For a good spot to spend the night, look no farther than the **Inn at Moonlight Beach** (105 N. Vulcan Ave., Encinitas, 760/450-5028, www.innatmoonlightbeach.com, from $150). This lovely bed-and-breakfast puts you within walking distance of great beaches and restaurants. You can also find a good, clean stay at the charming

and central Moonlight Beach Motel (233 2nd St., Encinitas, 800/753-0623, www. moonlightbeachmotel.com, from $160), which seems to complement the feeling of this laid-back beach town.

For roughing it next to the ocean, reserve a campsite at Cardiff's **San Elijo State Beach** (2500 S. Coast Hwy. 101, Cardiff-by-the-Sea, 760/753-5091, www. reservecalifornia.com, $35-70). Car camping and RV spots line the cliffs overlooking the beach. Designated spaces are close together but fill up fast; reservations are available seven months in advance at the first of each month.

Getting Around
The **Coaster** (760/966-6500, www. gonctd.com/coaster, $4-12) commuter train stops at the **Encinitas Coaster Station** (25 E. D St.).

Del Mar and Solana Beach

Though the two beach towns operate independently, Del Mar and Solana Beach share a border at the San Dieguito Lagoon, which is home to both the area's main draws: the county fairgrounds and a thoroughbred horse racing track. Del Mar is the more upscale of the two, a mostly residential community with beaches and cliffs connecting to Torrey Pines State Natural Reserve to the south. A Tudor-style village spreads out from the central beach, with a smattering of high-priced shops and restaurants.

North of San Dieguito Lagoon is Solana Beach, best known for the Cedros Avenue Design District, where shops offer furniture, designer antiques, and various high-end items for the home decorator. Solana Beach anchors the region's music scene at its Belly Up nightclub.

Getting There
From Encinitas, follow US-101 south for 3.7 miles (6 km) to reach Solana Beach.

Del Mar is 2.5 miles (4 km) farther south on US-101.

From downtown San Diego, I-5 travels 20 miles (32 km) north to Del Mar. Take the exit for Villa de la Valle and head west to US-101. Turn left for Del Mar, right for Solana Beach.

Beaches
Del Mar City Beach (15th to 29th Sts., west of Coast Blvd., 858/755-1556, www. delmar.ca.us, daily 24 hours) runs the length of Del Mar. Beach access is mostly found at the ends of residential streets and at the town center around 15th and 17th Streets. The mile-long beach is popular among local surfers and casual beachgoers; many like to walk along the cliffs rising to the south when beaches appear during low tide. Restrooms and showers are available by the main lifeguard tower at 17th Street, with public parking across Coast Boulevard. Picnic tables and a tot lot are available at a pair of grassy parks on either side of railroad tracks above the beach: Powerhouse Park (1658 Coast Blvd.) and Seagrove Park (15th St. and Coast Blvd.).

The central beach in Solana Beach sometimes gets called the "Pillbox" from the term for the type of defensive enclosed gun fort standing sentry here during World War II. Today, the small, pretty **Fletcher Cove Beach Park** (111 S. Sierra Ave., Solana Beach, 858/720-2400, www. ci.solana-beach.ca.us, daily 24 hours) is used for surfing, surf fishing, and swimming. It has free public parking, public showers, and restroom facilities as well as picnic tables, a playground, and a basketball court on the bluffs above. Lifeguards are on duty daily.

Entertainment
You'll find a little evening action on Cedros Avenue. One of the county's best rock venues, **Belly Up** (143 S. Cedros Ave., Solana Beach, 858/481-8140, www. bellyup.com) offers nightly shows ranging from tribute bands to indie rockers to

music legends that fill the intimate venue with devoted fans.

Del Mar Fairgrounds

The San Diego County Fair takes place each June at the **Del Mar Fairgrounds** (2260 Jimmy Durante Blvd., 858/755-1161, www.delmarfairgrounds.com), culminating in a big Fourth of July celebration. Along with the typical fair fare—attractions, rides, farm animals, and fried food—the fair hosts concurrent events such as the San Diego International Beer Festival as well as concerts headlined by internationally known artists. The annual KAABOO music festival is held here in mid-September. The fairgrounds share an address with the racetrack, often featuring horse shows and competitions.

"Where the surf meets the turf," the **Del Mar Racetrack** (2260 Jimmy Durante Blvd., 858/755-1141, www.dmtc.com, $6-50) comes alive during the summer racing season (mid-July-Labor Day) and again for the Bing Crosby Season

(Nov.). Basic admission grants access to the charming coastal facility. Upgrades allow entrance to the clubhouse, with options for reserved seating or dining tables with a view of the action. The track hosts free concerts after Friday races, including some internationally known talent. On Saturday concerts and beer and food festivals take place. A day at the track can be rousing fun even for those who don't gamble, and it offers women the rare opportunity to wear elaborate hats.

Food

Del Mar's known to have a lot of upscale restaurants, but none do fine dining as well as the Michelin-starred, five-diamond ★ **Addison** (5200 Grand Del Mar Way, 858/314-1900, www.addisondelmar.com, 6pm-9pm Tues.-Thurs., 5:30pm-9:30pm Fri.-Sat., $98-125). The refined tastes and disciplined kitchen of renowned chef William Bradley send seasonally designed dishes to a dining room sitting above the 18th

Del Mar City Beach

green of the exclusive golf course of the Grand Del Mar resort, complete with a Mediterranean-style patio to enjoy the sommelier's best picks.

Not far from the racetrack, **Cucina Enoteca** (2730 Via De La Valle, 858/704-4500, www.urbankitchengroup.com, 5pm-9pm Mon., 11:30am-10pm Tues.-Thurs., 11:30am-10:30pm Fri.-Sat., 11:30am-9pm Sun., $15-36) offers its own brilliant wine selection, served with exceptional, creative Italian dishes at a more reasonable price. Across the lagoon, elevated pub fare and outdoor dining pair with craft beer and games of leisure at **Viewpoint Brewing Company** (2201 San Dieguito Dr., 858/356-9346, www.viewpointbrewing.com, 5pm-9pm Mon., noon-9pm Tues.-Thurs., noon-10pm Fri., 10am-10pm Sat., 10am-9pm Sun., $14-27). Either makes a terrific post-race option.

If you prefer your meals coastal, **Jake's Del Mar** (1660 Coast Blvd., 858/755-2002, www.jakesdelmar.com, 4:30pm-9pm

Sun.-Thurs., 4:30am-9:30pm Fri.-Sat., $20-36) is famous among locals for its Sunday brunch (10am-2pm) directly overlooking the beach at Del Mar's Powerhouse Park, but it actually has the same view all day long, serving California cuisine mixed with a few Hawaiian dishes. A bar menu offers a limited selection, but more extended hours.

For a quick, cheap bite, the beachy sandwich shop **Board & Brew** (1212 Camino Del Mar, 858/481-1021, www.boardandbrew.com, 10am-6pm daily, $5-10) has kept its loyal customers well fed for more than 35 years, and it still gets a line out the door come lunchtime.

Accommodations

Those wishing to stay near the beach in Del Mar may opt for the **Hotel Indigo** (710 Camino Del Mar, 858/755-1501, www.hotelindigosddelmar.com, from $150), which offers ocean views, spa services, and comfortable accommodations from the cliffs on the south side of town. Closer to sea level is a highly rated luxury resort, L'Auberge Del Mar (1540 Camino Del Mar, 858/259-1515, www.laubergedelmar.com, from $250), nestled between the village and the beach.

For unmatched opulence, nothing compares to the **Grand Del Mar** (5300 Grand Del Mar Ct., 866/305-1528, www.thegranddelmar.com, from $400) The extravagantly built resort overlooks the 4,000-acre Peñasquitos Canyon Preserve, giving the whole place the feel of a country estate. Marble columns and parquet floors set off breathtaking rooms filled with beautiful yet comfortable furniture. It's the kind of place where the Presidential Suite has hosted actual presidents.

Getting Around

The local **Coaster** (760/966-6500, www.gonctd.com/coaster, $4-12) commuter train has a park-and-ride at the **Solana Beach Station** (105 N. Cedros Ave.).

Torrey Pines

The five-needle Torrey pine (*Pinus torreyana*) is the rarest species of pine tree in the United States. It's only found on Santa Catalina Island at the Torrey Pines State Natural Reserve. The reserve offers access to the distinctive trees courtesy of cliffside wilderness trails overlooking the Pacific.

Getting There

Torrey Pines is on US-101, west off the Carmel Valley Road exit on I-5 and 2 miles (3 km) south of Del Mar.

Beaches

Torrey Pines State Natural Reserve

Sandstone cliffs add a little scenic oomph at **Torrey Pines State Beach,** which sits below **Torrey Pines State Natural Reserve** (12600 N. Torrey Pines Rd., 858/755-2063, www.parks.ca.gov, 7:15am-sunset daily). The long, wide stretch of sand offers plenty for swimmers and body-boarders, as well as surfers toward the north end. That's also where you'll find showers, restrooms, and lifeguards on duty year-round. You can access the beach via hiking trails from the reserve, but it's easier to park in the lot beside the beach. If the lot's full, loop around to park on Carmel Valley Road, where it's just a short walk to the sand via the McGonagle Road underpass.

Black's Beach

Black's Beach (La Jolla Farms Rd. at Blackgold Rd.) benefits from an underwater canyon off the coast that lines up some of the best waves in town. The difficult access never prevents surfers from hitting this beach when the waves are breaking. The break pulls fast waves with almond-shaped barrels when it's firing; it works year-round and usually gets the best shape on falling mid- to low tide.

Getting to the sand from the cliffs above requires a hike, whether down a

Torrey Pines State Natural Reserve

path from the Torrey Pines Gliderport (2800 Torrey Pines Scenic Dr.) or down a gated, steep, and winding paved road off La Jolla Farms Road (9601 La Jolla Farms Rd.). Between the waves, crowds, and nudists (users consider the beach clothing-optional), it's definitely not for families or beginners.

Recreation

The shortest walk in the preserve is the **High Point Trail,** which requires only a 100-yard stroll to views of the whole reserve, from the ocean to the lagoon to the forest and back. For a short and easy jaunt, take the **Guy Fleming Trail** through forest and past wildflower patches for views of the ocean.

Golf

Torrey Pines Golf Course (11480 Torrey Pines Park Rd., 858/581-7171, www.sandiego.gov, 6am-6pm daily, from $237 for nonresidents), the home of the 2021 U.S. Open, is a city golf course,

which means that it's open to the public although it can be tough to get a tee time on the most famous course in town, particularly for nonresidents. Reservations (nonrefundable booking fees) are accepted up to 90 days out, with short-term allotments available via a lottery system. The reward is playing at one of two world-class William P. Bell-designed 18-hole courses atop bluffs overlooking the Pacific—either the north course or the challenging legendary south course.

Paragliding

The ocean cliffs of Torrey Pines provide the scenic backdrop for tourism of the high-flying variety. **Torrey Pines Gliderport** (2800 Torrey Pines Scenic Dr., 858/452-9858, www.flytorrey.com, 9am-5:30pm daily, paragliding $175, hang gliding $225) hang gliding and paragliding excursions are available, and surprisingly little experience or ability is required. An experienced glider rides tandem with you, offering some sense of safety as you float high above the trees and the beach.

Food

Spearheading the area's farm-to-table movement, **A.R. Valentien** (The Lodge at Torrey Pines, 11480 N. Torrey Pines Rd., 858/777-6635, www.arvalentien.com, 7am-11am, 11:30am-2:30pm, and 5:30pm-10pm Mon.-Fri, 7am-11:30am, noon-2:30pm, and 5:30pm-10pm Sat.-Sun., $20-50) crafts delicious charcuterie and simple yet effective dishes, adhering to the principle that quality ingredients result in quality meals. Even something as simple as baked chicken under a brick tastes better when it's done right. The dining room is lovely, but it's tough to beat lunch on the gorgeous deck overlooking the 18th hole of the famous Torrey Pines Golf Course.

Overlooking Los Penasquitos Lagoon, which feeds into Torrey Pines State Beach, **Roberto's Mexican Food** (2206

Carmel Valley Rd., 858/436-7189, www.
robertos.us, 9am-9pm Sun.-Thurs., 9am-
10pm Fri.-Sat., $5-10) is a casual local
Mexican chain that exemplifies the classic San Diego-style burrito shop. Go for
one of two regional specialties: California
burritos or carne asada fries. Both feature
marinated beef, french fries, cheese, guacamole, and salsa; they're wrapped in a
tortilla for the former, served on a plate
for the latter.

Accommodations

You don't need to be a golf fan to appreciate the classically upscale perks of
staying at ★ **The Lodge at Torrey Pines**
(11480 N. Torrey Pines Rd., 858/453-
4420, www.lodgetorreypines.com, $200
and up), an Arts & Crafts treasure filled
with stained glass, period furnishings,
and beachfront views. Spacious rooms
are filled with amenities and many
come with balconies overlooking the
quiet gardens surrounding the building. The delicious A.R. Valentien is
right on-site, and the golf course here
can't be beat.

La Jolla

Torrey Pines is technically part of
La Jolla (pop. 46,781)—literally "The
Jewel"—a wealthy community wrap-
ping around 10 miles of coastline. Along
with public beach access and Torrey
pine forests, its north end is home to
the University of California San Diego,
while its southern end furnishes upper-
middle-class residential neighborhoods.
The town center, officially called The
Village of La Jolla, is famous for its high-
end boutiques, ritzy hotels, renowned
art galleries, and several of San Diego
County's finest restaurants. Built on a
rounded peninsula that plays home to
both seals and sea lions, its business
district abuts a rocky coastline and a
smattering of tiny beaches, including
its eponymous cove.

Getting There

La Jolla is off I-5, south of Del Mar
and north of downtown San Diego.
Northbound, take La Jolla Parkway
to Torrey Pines Road via I-5 north.
Southbound, take I-5 South and Torrey
Pines Road to Fay Avenue. Parking is
challenging and expensive ($12-15 per
day).

Beaches
★ La Jolla Cove

Small but lovely, **La Jolla Cove** (1100 Coast
Blvd.) sits at the northern tip of La Jolla
village, banked by a grassy park that's a
perfect place to picnic or watch the sunset. Below the park, rocky outcroppings
populated by vocal, sunbathing sea lions
surround a small crescent of white sand,
which accesses the deep blue water of the
protected La Jolla Underwater Reserve.
Kayaks, surfboards, and rafts of any kind
may not access the water here, but you'll
often see scuba divers and snorkelers
bobbing around the surface before de-
scending into the water for a closer look
at the colorful fish, coral, and sea kelp.
Underwater snorkeling tours ($35 and
up) and equipment rentals are provided
by **La Jolla Kayak** (2199 Avenida de la
Playa, 858/459-1114, www.lajollakayak.
com, 8am-6pm daily).

Once or twice every winter, a massive
wave called Sleeping Giant breaks across
the cove, providing dazzling, up-close
views of expert surfers slaying it.

La Jolla Sea Caves

At the northern end of La Jolla Cove are
seven intriguing sea caves once popular among Prohibition-era bootleggers.
The only way to see most of them is from
the ocean, typically via kayak from La
Jolla Shores. The exception is **Sunny Jim
Cave.** Named by *Wizard of Oz* author
L. Frank Baum for its resemblance to
the world's first ever cereal box mascot,
Sunny Jim may be reached through an
artificial tunnel via a steep staircase inside the snorkel and gift shop **The Cave**

La Jolla

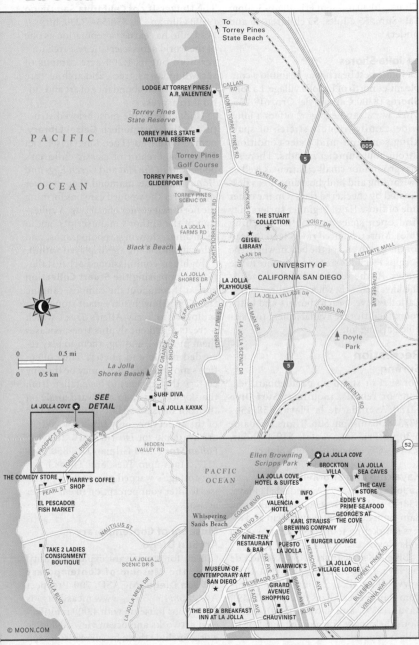

To Torrey Pines State Beach

LODGE AT TORREY PINES/ A.R. VALENTIEN

Torrey Pines State Reserve

TORREY PINES STATE NATURAL RESERVE

Torrey Pines Golf Course

TORREY PINES GLIDERPORT

TORREY PINES SCENIC DR

PACIFIC OCEAN

LA JOLLA FARMS RD

Black's Beach

LA JOLLA SHORES DR

THE STUART COLLECTION

VOIGT DR

GEISEL LIBRARY

GILMAN DR

UNIVERSITY OF CALIFORNIA SAN DIEGO

EASTGATE MALL

LA JOLLA PLAYHOUSE

LA JOLLA VILLAGE DR

NOBEL DR

EXPEDITION WAY

CALLAN RD

NORTH TORREY PINES RD

HOPKINS DR

GENESEE AVE

805

5

GENESEE AVE

BESENTS RD

Doyle Park

0   0.5 mi
0   0.5 km

La Jolla Shores Beach

EL PASEO GRANDE

LA JOLLA SHORES DR

SURF DIVA

LA JOLLA KAYAK

LA JOLLA COVE

SEE DETAIL

PROSPECT ST

TORREY PINES RD

HIDDEN VALLEY RD

THE COMEDY STORE

HARRY'S COFFEE SHOP

PEARL ST

EL PESCADOR FISH MARKET

NAUTILUS ST

TAKE 2 LADIES CONSIGNMENT BOUTIQUE

LA JOLLA SCENIC DR S

LA JOLLA BLVD

LA JOLLA MESA DR

TORREY PINES SCENIC DR

JOLLA SCENIC DR

52

Ellen Browning Scripps Park

LA JOLLA COVE

BROCKTON VILLA

LA JOLLA SEA CAVES

THE CAVE STORE

PACIFIC OCEAN

LA JOLLA HOTEL & SUITES

INFO

LA VALENCIA HOTEL

COAST BLVD

PROSPECT ST

EDDIE V'S PRIME SEAFOOD

GEORGE'S AT THE COVE

KARL STRAUSS BREWING COMPANY

Whispering Sands Beach

COAST BLVD S

NINE-TEN RESTAURANT & BAR

PUESTO LA JOLLA

FAY AVE

BURGER LOUNGE

WARWICK'S

MUSEUM OF CONTEMPORARY ART SAN DIEGO

SILVERADO ST

EADS AVE

GIRARD AVENUE SHOPPING

HERSCHEL AVE

GIRARD AVE

LA JOLLA VILLAGE LODGE

TORREY PINES RD

BLUEBIRD LN

VIRGINIA WAY

THE BED & BREAKFAST INN AT LA JOLLA

LE CHAUVINIST

KLINE ST

© MOON.COM

Store (1325 Coast Blvd., 858/459-0746, www.cavestore.com, 10am-5pm Mon.-Thurs., 10:30am-5pm Fri., 10am-5:30pm Sat.-Sun., $5 adults, $3 children 16 and under).

La Jolla Shores

La Jolla's best beach may be found a couple miles north of La Jolla village. **La Jolla Shores** (8300 Camino del Oro, 619/235-1169, www.sandiego.gov) offers a long, wide, family-friendly stretch of sparkling sand and mild water conditions throughout summer months. There's a playground for small children as well as swimming and bodyboarding areas designated by checkered flags. On the other side of those flags, beginner surfers may find open space to practice catching rides. More advanced riders tend to head for the north end of the beach, where the Scripps Pier adds size and structure to the waves. At the south end of the beach is the kayak launch, where paddlers access La Jolla Cove. Beach showers and bathroom facilities are available next to a sizable parking lot.

Recreation
Surfing

For surf or stand-up paddleboard lessons or rentals, inquire at **Surf Diva** (2160 Avenida de la Playa, 858/454-8273, 8:30am-6pm Sun.-Thurs., 8:30am-6:30pm Fri.-Sat., rentals $10-15/hour, lessons $65-75) near La Jolla Shores.

Kayaking and Snorkeling

La Jolla Kayak (2199 Avenida de la Playa, 858/459-1114, www.lajollakayak.com, 8am-6pm daily) rents equipment and offers snorkeling tours ($35 and up) of La Jolla Cove.

Bike & Kayak Tours (2158 Avenida de la Playa, La Jolla Shores, 858/454-1010, www.bikeandkayaktours.com, 8am-8pm daily) specializes in bicycle ($49), kayak ($39), and snorkel ($39) excursions, helping you make the most of La Jolla outdoors.

Sights
University of California San Diego

The **University of California San Diego** (9500 Gilman Dr., 858/534-2230, https://ucsd.edu) has earned a reputation as one of the world's top scientific research universities, but its 1,200-acre campus of sprawling lawns, trees, and architecture also features an abundance of art and cultural treasures.

Undoubtedly the most beloved structure is the postmodern **Geisel Library,** named for author Theodore Geisel, aka Dr. Seuss, creator of classic children's books *Cat in the Hat* and *Green Eggs and Ham.* Its unique, diamond-shaped tower stands over the wooded canyons forming the northeast corner of campus. A collection of the author's manuscripts, audio recordings, drawings, photographs, and other memorabilia are displayed within.

Eighteen commissioned art installations comprising the **Stuart Collection** appear throughout the campus, ranging from Tim Hawkinson's giant stone *Bear* sculpture to Terry Allen's *Trees,* which reerects felled eucalyptus trees, encases them in metal, and rigs them to play recorded music and poetry. The collection's most visceral piece may be the tiny cottage that appears to have fallen from the sky to land at an awkward angle on the roof of Jacobs Hall. Unlike the rest of the collection, only limited viewings are available for Do Ho Suh's dizzying *Fallen Star* (9500 Gilman Dr., 858/534-2117, 11am-2pm Tues. and Thurs.), but the cottage's warped perspective promises to alter your perception like no other artwork.

Museum of Contemporary Art San Diego

Closed for significant expansion until 2021, the **Museum of Contemporary Art San Diego** (MCASD, 700 Prospect Ave., 858/454-3541, www.mcasd.org) is a gorgeous museum with 4,000 multifaceted artworks and ocean views. Notable works include those by surrealist Joseph

Cornell, minimalist Frank Stella, pop artist Andy Warhol, and conceptual art from Latin America, with an emphasis on the San Diego/Tijuana region.

Entertainment

San Diego's first craft brewery, **Karl Strauss Brewing Company** (1044 Wall St., 858/551-2739, www.karlstrauss.com 11am-9pm Sun.-Thurs., 11am-10pm Fri.-Sat.) operates a brewpub in the village, providing La Jolla's best stop to sample the region's celebrated beer culture.

Around sunset, live jazz music and cocktails grace the deck above **Eddie V's Prime Seafood** (1270 Prospect St., 858/459-5500, www.eddiev.com, 4pm-10pm Mon.-Thurs., 11am-11pm Fri.-Sat., 10am-10pm Sun.), which boasts a direct view of La Jolla Cove and serves tasty small plates.

Depending on the night, open-mic up-and-comers or big-name performers deliver punch lines with a two-drink minimum at the **La Jolla Comedy Store** (916 Pearl St., 858/454-9176, www.thecomedystore.com, $5-20 tickets).

Plays and musicals grace the stage of world-class theater **La Jolla Playhouse** (2910 La Jolla Village Dr., 858/550-1010, www.lajollaplayhouse.org, tickets from $20). Cofounded by Hollywood icon Gregory Peck, the Playhouse has been the birthplace of 26 Broadway productions, including *Jesus Christ Superstar*, *Jersey Boys*, and *The Who's Tommy*.

Shopping

The most fashionable upscale shopping (and window-shopping) may be found at **Boutiques on Girard Avenue** (between Prospect St. and Kline St.). Individual boutiques come and go, and while top designer labels may have more staying power, the high rents here ensure that whatever you find will be current with international trends.

Top to bottom: sea lion; La Jolla Cove; kayaking at La Jolla.

For designer wares at a reduced cost, a couple of gently used and vintage shops cater to fashionable men and women who don't mind looking great in yesterday's high fashions. Ladies should look a little south of the village to find **Take 2 Ladies Consignment Boutique** (6786 La Jolla Blvd., 858/459-0095, www. take2ladiesconsignor.com, 11am-6pm Mon.-Fri., 11am-5pm Sat.) and its collection featuring Jimmy Choo, Gucci, Prada, and more. For men, classy vintage attire and designer accessories cycle through **Le Chauvinist** (7709 Fay Ave., 858/456-0117, www.lechauvinist.com, 11am-5pm Mon.-Fri., 10am-4pm Sat., 9am-2pm Sun.), with accoutrements ranging from dapper to hip.

Warwick's (7812 Girard Ave., 858/454-0347, www.warwicks.com, 9am-6pm Mon.-Sat., 10am-5:30pm Sun.) is the country's oldest family-owned bookstore, with an eclectic collection of great reads and high-profile signings by beloved authors and entertainers.

Food

For authentic Mexican cuisine prepared with organic ingredients, try the tacos at **Puesto** (1026 Wall St., 858/454-1260, www.eatpuesto.com, 11am-9pm Sun.-Mon. and Wed.-Thurs., 11am-10pm Tues. and Fri.-Sat., $15), and save room for the exceptional flan dessert.

Known for its soufflé-style French toast, converted beach cottage **Brockton Villa** (1235 Coast Blvd., 858/454-7393, www.brocktonvilla.com, 8am-9pm daily, $10-14) makes a great oceanview breakfast locale, especially on its deck.

To find respite from La Jolla's polished countenance without leaving the village, go to **Harry's Coffee Shop** (7545 Girard Ave., 858/454-7381, www. harryscoffeeshop.com, 6am-3pm daily) for an old-school, American-diner breakfast.

La Jolla's **Burger Lounge** (1101 Wall St., 858/456-0196, www.burgerlounge. com, 10:30am-9pm Sun.-Thurs.,

10:30am-10pm Fri.-Sat., $8-10) isn't the usual counter-service beef chain. Expect grass-fed beef with organic cheese and condiments. Albacore, lamb, and panko-crusted chicken round out the menu.

At the Grande Colonial Hotel, Jason Knibb shares his extraordinary mastery of flavors at **Nine-Ten** (910 Prospect St., 858/964-5400, www.nine-ten.com, 6:30am-2:30pm and 6pm-9:30pm Mon.-Thurs., 6:30am-2:30pm and 6pm-10pm Fri.-Sat., 7:30am-2:30pm and 6pm-9:30pm Sun., $22-38), taking inspiration from seasonal ingredients—request a seat on the terrace for the ultimate experience.

Seafood lovers in La Jolla have terrific options. For more than four decades, locals have lined up for fresh, local-caught seafood sandwiches, salads, and plates at beloved **El Pescador Fish Market** (634 Pearl St., 858/456-2526, www.elpescadorfishmarket.com, 11am-9pm daily, $10-18). For fine dining with an ocean view, the seafood-centric California-modern tasting menu at ★ **George's at the Cove** (1250 Prospect St., 858/454-4244, www. georgesatthecove.com, 11am-close daily, $30-46) has long set the tone for beachside dining, routinely counted among the top dining options in all of San Diego County. Make a reservation for ocean terrace seating.

Accommodations

By moving just four blocks from the coast, you'll find an affordable stay at **La Jolla Village Lodge** (1141 Silverado St., 858/551-2001, from $170). La Jolla's answer to a motel, its basic rooms are not without their charms, chief among them being free parking for guests.

The Bed & Breakfast Inn at La Jolla (7753 Draper Ave., 858/456-2066, www. innlajolla.com, $184-459) offers 13 uniquely styled rooms and two suites, some with fireplaces and ocean views but all elegant and comfortable. Close to everything, it's just a block from La Jolla Cove's cliffs and beaches and the

Museum of Contemporary Art San Diego.

The most affordable option for a room with a view of La Jolla Cove may be found at **La Jolla Cove Suites** (1155 Coast Blvd., 858/459-2621, www.lajollacove.com, from $250). It's not fancy, but nearly all of its recently renovated suites face the ocean, and they feature small kitchens.

A local fixture since 1926, ★ **La Valencia** (1132 Prospect St., 858/454-0771, www.lavalenica.com, from $380) invokes the breezy style of a Mediterranean villa. Centrally located near La Jolla village restaurants and shopping, it offers airy rooms (some with ocean views) and a heated pool that overlooks the shimmering Pacific.

Information and Services
Visit **La Jolla Village Information Center** (1162 Prospect St., 858/454-5718, 11am-5pm Tues.-Sun.) for assistance with local activities, dining, and shopping.

LA JOLLA

San
Diego

San Diego

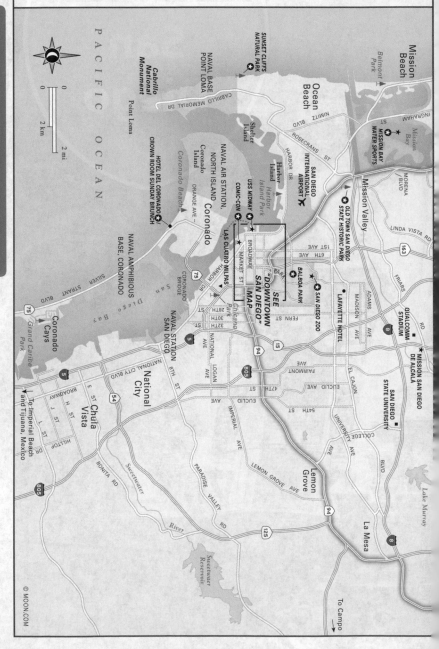

PACIFIC OCEAN

Point Loma

0 2 km
0 2 mi

Cabrillo National Monument

SUNSET CLIFFS NATURAL PARK

NAVAL BASE POINT LOMA

Shelter Island

CABRILLO MEMORIAL DR

ROSECRANS ST

NIMITZ BLVD

HARBOR DR

Harbor Island Park

SAN DIEGO INTERNATIONAL AIRPORT

Ocean Beach

Mission Beach

Belmont Park

Mission Bay

INGRAHAM ST

MISSION BAY WATER SPORTS

MORENA BLVD

Mission Valley

LINDA VISTA RD

163

HOTEL DEL CORONADO CROWN ROOM SUNDAY BRUNCH

Coronado Beach

ORANGE AVE

Coronado Island

Coronado

NAVAL AIR STATION, NORTH ISLAND

USS MIDWAY

COMIC-CON

LAS CUATRO MILPAS

HARBOR DR

BROADWAY

MARKET ST

PARK BLVD

SEE "DOWNTOWN SAN DIEGO" MAP

OLD TOWN SAN DIEGO STATE HISTORIC PARK

6TH AVE

1ST AVE

BALBOA PARK

SAN DIEGO ZOO

LAFAYETTE HOTEL

FERN ST

ADAMS AVE

MADISON AVE

FRIARS RD

8

QUALCOMM STADIUM

MISSION SAN DIEGO DE ALCALA

San Diego Bay

SILVER STRAND BLVD

NAVAL AMPHIBIOUS BASE, CORONADO

75

Coronado Cays

Grand Caribe Park

CORONADO BRIDGE

75

NAVAL STATION SAN DIEGO

28TH ST
30TH ST
32TH ST

Chicano Park

5

NATIONAL AVE

LOGAN AVE

94

15

805

FAIRMONT AVE

EUCLID AVE

47TH ST

EL CAJON BLVD

SAN DIEGO STATE UNIVERSITY

UNIVERSITY AVE

COLLEGE AVE

5

8TH ST

NATIONAL CITY BLVD

National City

54

Chula Vista

BROADWAY

E ST

J ST
H ST
I ST

HILLTOP DR

To Imperial Beach and Tijuana, Mexico

805

BONITA RD

Sweetwater River

PARADISE VALLEY RD

125

EUCLID AVE

54TH ST

ST

IMPERIAL AVE

LEMON GROVE AVE

Lemon Grove

94

La Mesa

8

BLVD

Lake Murray

Sweetwater Reservoir

To Campo

© MOON.COM

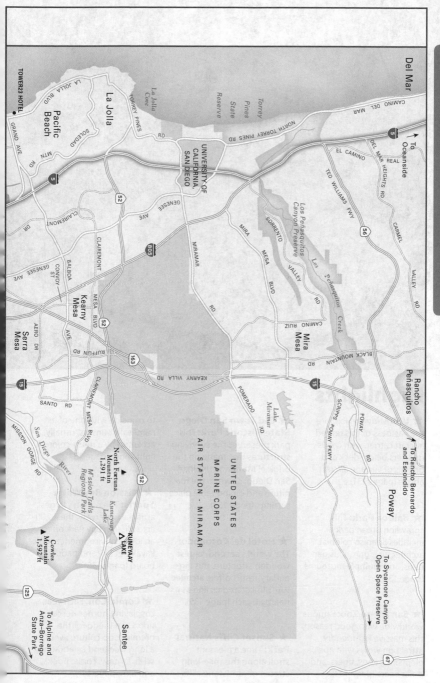

Highlights

★ **USS *Midway*:** Explore the vastness of this retired aircraft carrier, with crews' quarters below deck and dozens of vintage aircraft above (pages 131).

★ **Balboa Park:** This sprawling urban park includes Spanish colonial architecture, gorgeous gardens, and multiple museums (page 131).

★ **San Diego Zoo:** Famous worldwide with good reason, this massive kid-friendly attraction wows with apes, elephants, lions, tigers, and polar bears (page 133).

★ **Old Town San Diego State Historic Park:** This park preserves the surviving structures that made up the original Mexican pueblo of San Diego, down to the furniture and dining table place settings (page 133).

★ **Hotel del Coronado:** The world's second-largest wooden structure, this legendary resort offers architecture almost as dazzling as its nearby beach (page 135).

★ **Sunset Cliffs Natural Park:** Time a pleasant stroll along this mile-long stretch of sandstone cliffs

to coincide with one of its namesake sunsets, usually accented by a neon-colored light show (page 137).

★ **Mission Bay Water Sports:** The nation's largest artificial waterway, the 4,200-acre Mission Bay Park offers an idyllic environment to sail, kayak, Jet Ski, and paddle-board (page 138).

★ **Comic-Con:** Each year, cosplaying hordes descend upon San Diego for the premier pop culture event, a long weekend celebrating sci-fi, fantasy, comic books, and film (page 141).

125

GETTING THERE

For beach lovers, San Diego proves the embodiment of an endless summer, with sparkling white-sand beaches, magnificent sunsets, and the smells of saltwater, surf wax, and sunscreen mingling in the air.

A typical weather forecast calls for 72°F (22°C) and sunny, and pretty much everybody wears sunglasses all the time. Sailboats traverse the bay on clear days, scuba divers explore underwater canyons, golfers tee up, and bicyclists cruise from beach to beach. But for all its leisurely appeal, the eighth-largest city in the United States offers its share of urban pleasures as well, including a globally renowned performing arts scene, dozens of museums, the architecturally rich Balboa Park, a world-famous zoo, and historic landmarks including the city's preserved 18th-century missionary settlement in Old Town.

On top of all this, a visit to San Diego almost gets you two cities for the price of one. It's a quick jaunt across the border to sample the rich culture of Mexico on display in the increasingly vibrant border city of Tijuana, where the favorable exchange rate yields affordable fine dining and shopping. So be sure to pack your passport as well as your swimsuit, and bring an appetite for tacos, fresh seafood, and the nation's most delicious craft beer.

Getting There

From Los Angeles
120 mi/193 km, 2-3 hr
From downtown Los Angeles, I-5 is a direct shot 120 miles (193 km) south to San Diego, passing Disneyland in Anaheim en route. The drive continues past the coastal destinations of Carlsbad and La Jolla, before continuing south through San Diego to Tijuana, Mexico. This route can take 2-3 hours in light traffic or last up to five hours in rush hour (7am-9am and 3pm-6pm Mon.-Fri.) or otherwise congested traffic.

From Las Vegas
360 mi/579 km, 5-6 hr
The most direct route from Las Vegas is on I-15, which travels 360 miles (579 km) southwest through Barstow, San Bernardino, and Temecula en route to San Diego. It can be driven in under 4.5 hours with no traffic, but during daylight hours expect it to take 5-6 hours—longer toward the end of the weekend, when thousands of Southern Californians pack the roads for the drive home.

From Santa Barbara
220 mi/354 km, 4-6 hr
Heading out of Santa Barbara, take US-101 South for 80 miles (129 km) to connect to I-405 South, where it passes West Los Angeles and Santa Monica (10 miles/16 km). The I-405 continues southeast for another 54 miles (87 km) to merge with I-5 in Orange County, 16 miles (26 km) south of Anaheim. The I-5 then continues 80 miles (129 km) south to San Diego.

Expect the 220-mile (354-km) drive to take 4-6 hours in daytime traffic. For a toll of $8.48, you may bypass some traffic through Orange County by taking CA-73 South from I-405 in Costa Mesa, to connect with I-5. From this point, it's 69 miles (111 km) south to San Diego.

Air, Train, or Bus
Also known as Lindbergh Field, San Diego International Airport (SAN, 619/400-2404, www.san.org) is a centrally located urban airport a mere three miles from the city center. While its position makes it a little noisy for those living in neighborhoods under the flight path, it makes getting to and from the airport a quick trip from most parts of the city.

Best Restaurants

★ **Herb & Wood:** *Top Chef* alumnus Brian Malarkey sets the bar high with incredible ingredients cooked to perfection in a wood-fired kitchen (page 142).

★ **Ironside Fish & Oyster:** Stunning interior design and amazing local seafood make this spot foodie and photo-friendly (page 142).

★ **Carnitas' Snack Shack:** This casual outdoor eatery on the waterfront does everything well, especially burgers (page 142).

★ **Las Cuatro Milpas:** Enjoy authentic Mexican cuisine made with the best flour tortillas in California—and possibly the world (page 142).

★ **Oscar's Mexican Seafood:** Fish tacos sit at the top of the San Diego food chain, and this local chain shows why (page 142).

★ **Born & Raised:** This classic American steak house, updated for the 21st century, takes excess to another realm (page 142).

★ **Extraordinary Desserts:** Cap any meal with one of the myriad indulgences made by this upscale cake and pastry specialist (page 142).

★ **Crown Room:** Come hungry to the extravagant Sunday brunch buffet at the Hotel del Coronado (page 144).

The airport is split into two major terminals hosting 20 airlines and subsidiaries.

Amtrak (800/872-7245, www.amtrak.com, $37 and up) runs the *Pacific Surfliner* a dozen times a day from San Luis Obispo to San Diego, with stops in Santa Barbara, Los Angeles, and Anaheim. Check into transfers from the *Coast Starlight* and the *Capitol Corridor* routes as well. Amtrak services the **Santa Fe Depot** (1050 Kettner Blvd.) and the **Old Town Transit Center** (4005 Taylor St.).

Greyhound (800/752-4841, www.greyhound.com) has a bus terminal in downtown San Diego's **East Village** (1313 National Ave., 619/515-1100), with the option to stop in **Oceanside** (205 S. Tremont St., 760/722-1587) or **Escondido** (700 W. Valley Pkwy., 800/231-2222).

Getting Around
San Diego is 12 miles (19 km) south of La Jolla and 124 miles (200 km) south of Los Angeles. Most visitors drive into San Diego via the heavily traveled I-5 from

the north or south. I-805 runs parallel to I-5 at La Jolla and leads south through Mission Valley, though it experiences the heaviest rush hour traffic. To drive between North County and San Diego, take I-15, which runs north-south farther inland. All three freeways cross I-8, which runs east-west through Mission Valley to the beaches. The smaller CA-163 cuts south-north through Balboa Park, connecting I-5 near downtown to I-15 by the Marine Corps air station in Miramar.

Parking is hardest at the beaches in the summertime. In the various downtown areas, you'll find fairly average city parking issues. Happily, San Diego's major attractions and event venues tend to be accompanied by large parking structures. Just be prepared to pay a premium if you're doing something popular.

Car Rentals
Most car rental agencies operate near the San Diego International Airport. The closest are **Hertz** (3355 Admiral Boland

Best Hotels

★ **Mudville Flats:** Beautiful Craftsman-style rooms with private kitchens and updated amenities make this apartment-style hotel in the East Village a satisfying place to return to at night (page 145).

★ **Lafayette Hotel:** A stay at this well-appointed hotel in North Park allows a little respite from the tourist areas, but is still close to great evening entertainment (page 145).

★ **La Pensione Hotel:** This simple hotel offers good, clean rooms on the cheap, some with harbor views, within walking distance of numerous attractions (page 145).

★ **Horton Grand Hotel:** The Gaslamp's most charming hotel happens to be ideally situated for exploring downtown (page 145).

★ **Tower23 Hotel:** This seaside boutique hotel on the beach in lively Pacific Beach is convenient to Mission Bay, Mission Beach, and the seemingly endless nightlife of Garnet Avenue. It even has its own hip restaurant and bar (page 146).

★ **Hotel del Coronado:** This grand Victorian resort in San Diego is famous for celebrity guests like Marilyn Monroe and its resident ghost (page 146).

Way, 619/767-5700, www.hertz.com), **National** (3355 Admiral Boland Way, 888/445-5664, www.nationalcar.com), and **Avis** (3355 Admiral Boland Way, 619/688-5000, www.avis.com). All are a short shuttle ride away, so Thrifty and even farther-away Enterprise are accessible enough. From the train station, **Avis** (1670 Kettner Blvd., Ste. 1, 619/231-7137, www.avis.com) is within short walking distance.

A reliable local commuter train, **The Coaster** (www.sdcommute.com, $4-5.50 adults one-way, $2-2.75 seniors, free for children under 6) runs from Oceanside south into downtown San Diego and back a dozen times a day Monday-Friday, with five trains running Saturday, plus special event and holiday service. Purchase tickets from the vending machines in every train station.

Bus and Trolley
In downtown San Diego, Coronado, and La Jolla, the **Metropolitan Transit System** (MTS, www.sdmts.com) operates both an extensive bus system and trolley routes.

Catch the trolley or the bus from either the Old Town Transit Center (4005 Taylor St.) or the Santa Fe station (1050 Kettner Blvd.). While the bus system is extensive and runs countywide, it can be complicated and slow; the uninitiated should plan the trip in advance online.

The **trolley** operates daily, offering color-coded routes that make a good option for visiting downtown (all lines), Old Town and Mission Valley (Green Line), or Tijuana (Blue Line).

Bus fares are $2.25 for local routes and $2.50-5 for express routes. Use the vending machines at trolley stations to get a day pass ($5 regular day pass, $12 Rapid Express Routes day pass). If you plan to pay for your fare for buses or trolleys on board, have exact change available. A regional **route-planning website** (www.sdcommute.com) can help you plan your trip.

Ferries
San Diego has two major ferry routes; both run to and from Coronado. **Flagship Cruises** (619/234-4111, www.flagshipsd.

com, $4.75 each way) operates the Coronado Ferry from two locations: the Broadway Pier (between the USS *Midway* Museum and the Maritime Museum of San Diego) and the 5th Avenue pier (south of the San Diego Convention Center). The 15-minute trip runs daily approximately 9am-9pm, arriving at the Coronado Ferry Landing. The ferry ride can be a scenic activity in its own right, especially if you bring a bicycle to explore the opposite shore.

Ride Shares and Taxis

While taxis may still be spotted in populous areas, car-for-hire services operated by smartphone apps have become more common in recent years. Both **Uber** (www.uber.com) and **Lyft** (www.lyft.com) operate the same way: pinpoint your location on a smartphone app to request a ride; the savvy GPS system will determine the nearest available car and send it your way. Charges are processed to the user's credit card through the app, which means no money changes hands (no cash tips).

For traditional taxis, try **San Diego Cab** (619/226-8294) or **Yellow Cab** (619/239-8061). For traditional limos and hired cars, contact **Flex Transportation** (619/796-3539, www.flextranspo.com) or **City Captain** (619/800-3515, www.citycaptain.com).

Pedicabs for hire shuttle visitors around the Gaslamp Quarter, Marina District, and East Village; they offer convenient transport between different parts of downtown, but only when flagged down like a taxi.

Bike and Scooter Shares

Smartphone apps operate a bevy of dockless bicycle and electric scooters for hire, found scattered throughout the city on sidewalks and street corners (the apps will help you find the nearest). The most prominent are **Lime** (www.li.me) and the scooter-only **Bird** (www.bird.co).

Sights

Downtown
Marina District and Gaslamp Quarter

San Diego got its start in historic Old Town, but it became a city due to its protected harbor. The **Marina District** (Harbor Dr. from Ash St. to Park Blvd.) sits where downtown hits the harbor, featuring several bayside parks, a collection of gift shops and restaurants at Seaport Village, large hotels, and boat slips for day cruises and the Coronado Ferry.

Pedicabs for hire offer rides across Harbor Drive to the adjacent **Gaslamp Quarter** (south of Broadway from 1st Ave. to 6th Ave.), the area where sailors historically came ashore to romp but which has been refashioned as a tourist shopping and entertainment district.

Maritime Museum of San Diego

The impressive collection of historical, restored, and replica vessels at the **Maritime Museum of San Diego** (1492 N. Harbor Dr., 619/234-9153, www.sdmaritime.org, 9am-8pm daily, $18 adults, $13 seniors, youth ages 13-17, and military, $8 children ages 3-12) is a must-see for seafaring enthusiasts. The prized relic is *Star of India,* the world's oldest active sailing ship. Built in 1863, it was made of iron in a time when ships were made of wood, the *Europa* made 21 rugged voyages around the world, some lasting a year. The *Berkeley* is an 1898 steam ferryboat that operated for 60 years on San Francisco Bay. Purchased in 2004, the HMS *Surprise* is a 24-gun Royal Navy frigate built for the Academy Award-winning *Master and Commander: The Far Side of the World.* Other vessels include the *Medea,* a 1904 steam yacht; the *Californian,* a replica of a gold rush-era patroller; and the *B-39 Soviet,* one of the largest conventionally powered submarines ever built.

Two Days in San Diego

Balboa Park's beautiful Botanical Garden

Day 1

In the morning admire the exotic animals at the **San Diego Zoo** (page 133), then stroll through the cluster of culture in **Balboa Park** (page 131), exploring the diverse museums and art galleries within the park. Wander the gardens, visiting the exquisite **Botanical Building** (page 132). Enjoy lunch at **Panama 66** (page 143), the restaurant conveniently located in the sculpture garden of the **San Diego Museum of Art** (page 132).

Continue your journey through the city's past in historic **Old Town** (page 133), where California's oldest city had its humble, adobe beginnings. Or, if you're feeling active, head to nearby **Mission Bay Park** (page 138) for paddleboarding, catamaran sailing, or Jet Skiing.

Set your appetite for a seafood feast at Little Italy's exceptionally cool **Ironside Fish & Oyster** (page 142), followed by a sampling of San Diego craft beers at nearby **Bottlecraft** (page 139).

Day 2

Start with an authentic Mexican breakfast at **Las Cuatro Milpas** (page 142), then head to the **Maritime Museum of San Diego** (page 128), which has one of the largest historical sea vessel collections in the nation. A half-mile south (past the Broadway Pier), the **USS *Midway*** (page 131) is anchored in the harbor, waiting to be boarded and explored. Follow it with an open-air lunch at meat-loving **Carnitas' Snack Shack** (page 142).

Drive across the San Diego-Coronado Bridge, or take the 15-minute foot ferry from the Broadway Pier to the Coronado Ferry Landing, arriving in Coronado. Rent a bicycle from **Bikes & Beyond** (page 138) and glide along the **Bayshore Bikeway** (page 138) to **Hotel del Coronado** (page 135). (MTS route 904 also runs from the ferry landing to the hotel.) Stroll across the Del's ornate lobby and grand decks, which look out across the Pacific—perfect for watching the sunset.

Head back across the bridge for fish tacos at **Oscar's Mexican Seafood** (page 142), or pull out all the stops for upscale wood-fired fare at **Herb & Wood** (page 142). At night, party at **Altitude Sky Lounge** (page 140), one of the rooftop bars of the **Gaslamp Quarter.**

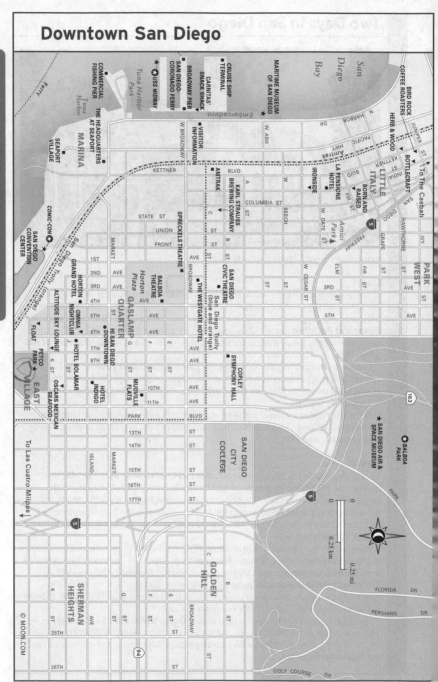

Downtown San Diego

★ USS *Midway*

Follow the footsteps of the 225,000 sailors who served aboard **USS *Midway*** (910 N. Harbor Dr., 619/544-9600, www.midway.org, 10am-5pm daily, $20 adults, $15 students, $10 children ages 6-12, $17 seniors, $10 retired military), the U.S.'s longest-serving aircraft carrier. First launched in 1945, the ship today serves as a museum, offering an up-close look at life at sea. Real *Midway* sailors narrate a self-guided audio tour, and docents are available to answer questions. Explore the crew's sleeping quarters, the galley, engine room, even the ship's jail. The museum is also home to 29 restored aircraft and two flight simulators ($8 double, $16 single), which roll, spin, and loop during mock aerial combat missions.

Chicano Park

Tucked under the Coronado Bridge, this small Barrio Logan park boasts the world's largest collection of outdoor murals, mostly painted on the bridge's base supports. **Chicano Park** (1949 Logan Ave., Barrio Logan, 619/232-1930, www.chicanoparksandiego.com, open 24 hours) celebrates the community's Mexican heritage and commemorates the 1970 protest of a highway patrol station on the site. Activists occupied the park for two weeks to preserve the green space for a neighborhood that had already been divided by freeways and lost its waterfront access to port development.

★ Balboa Park

A sprawling 1,200-acre urban park with numerous open spaces, gardens, theaters, and the world-famous San Diego Zoo, **Balboa Park** (1549 El Prado, 619/239-0512, www.balboapark.org) is the cultural center of downtown. Many of the city's museums are found along Balboa Park's Prado, inside Spanish colonial

Top to bottom: the ornate dome of the Museum of Man; USS *Midway;* Balboa Park.

revival buildings built for the 1915-1916 Panama-California Exposition.

Top museums include the **San Diego Museum of Art** (1450 El Prado, 619/232-7931, www.sdmart.org, 10am-5pm Mon.-Tues. and Thurs.-Sat., noon-5pm Sun., $15 adults, $10 seniors and military, $8 students, youth under age 18 free), renowned for its Renaissance works, and the dinosaur-friendly **San Diego Natural History Museum** (1788 El Prado, 877/946-7797, www.sdnhm. org, 10am-5pm daily, $19 adults, $17 seniors, military, and students, $12 children ages 3-17, under age 3 free). The **San Diego Air & Space Museum** (2001 Pan American Plaza, 619/234-8291, www.sandiegoairandspace.org, 10am-4:30pm daily, $19.75 adults, $16.75 seniors, students, and retired military, $10.75 children ages 3-11, active duty military and children under age 3 free) is fronted by a replica stealth bomber. Interactive exhibits make learning family fun at the **Fleet Science Center** (1875 El Prado, 619/238-1233, www.rhfleet. org, 10am-5pm Mon.-Thurs., 10am-8pm Fri., 10am-6pm Sat.-Sun., $20 adults, $18 seniors and military, $17 children ages 3-12).

El Prado is the main pedestrian walkway through the park. At its west end stands the iconic tower and dome of the California Building. The viewing deck of the **California Tower** (1350 El Prado, 619/239-2001, www.museumofman.org, 10:20am-8pm daily late May-early Sept., $22.50 adults, $20 seniors over age 61 and military, $18 students, $16 children ages 6-12, no entry under age 3) is open to public tours (every 40 minutes 10:20am-4:20pm daily). Tickets include admission to its access point at the **Museum of Man** (1350 El Prado, 619/239-2001, www.museumofman. org, 10am-5pm daily, $13 adults, $10 seniors, military, and students 6-17, children under age 6 free).

Balboa's gardens are a cultivated wonder of 350 species of plants and an estimated 1,500 trees, many selected by "the Mother of Balboa Park," Kate Sessions, who is credited with the park's rise to enchantment. The most photographed is the **Botanical Building** (1549 El Prado, 619/239-0512, www. balboapark.org, 10am-4pm Fri.-Wed., free), an elegant lathe structure built in front of a serene lily pond. Walking paths meander through the colorful landscape of the ambrosial **Inez Grant Memorial Rose Garden,** with 130 species of the fragrant flower, and the fascinating **Desert Garden,** with 1,300 succulents and desert plants from around the world.

Ride the 1910 **Carousel** (1889 Zoo Dr., 619/232-2282, 11am-5:30pm daily in summer, 11am-5pm Sat.-Sun. and school holidays, $3). All but two of the intricately hand-carved animals are original pieces. The model G16 **Miniature Train** (1800 Zoo Pl., 619/239-4748,

11am-6:30pm daily in summer, 11am-4:30pm Sat.-Sun., $3) takes a half-mile trip through four acres of the park.

★ San Diego Zoo

TOP EXPERIENCE

The biggest family attraction in Balboa Park, **San Diego Zoo** (2920 Zoo Dr., 619/231-1515, www.sandiegozoo.org, 9am-9pm daily July-Aug.; 9am-6pm daily Mar., May-June, and Sept.-Oct.; 9am-7pm daily Apr.; 9am-5pm daily Nov.-early Dec. and Jan.-Feb.; holidays 9am-8pm daily Dec.; $54 adults, $44 ages 3-11, under age 3 free, free parking) showcases more than 4,000 endangered and exotic animals from around the world, including polar bears, primates, and elephants. Walking paths connect all areas of the sometimes steep hillside park; guided bus tours, express buses, and an aerial tram provide faster transportation. Animals are more active during morning hours.

Old Town and Mission Hills
★ Old Town San Diego State Historic Park

The city's oldest standing structures are now historic landmarks preserved within **Old Town San Diego State Historic Park** (4002 Wallace St., 858/220-5422, www.parks.ca.gov, 10am-5pm daily May-Sept., 10am-4pm Mon.-Thurs., 10am-5pm Fri.-Sun. Oct.-Apr., free). Visit for a sense of what the original Puebla de San Diego settlement must have been like in the 1820s—a combination of Spanish colony and the American Old West. Most buildings are old family residences, including the homes of Spanish soldiers. The **Mason Street Schoolhouse** depicts a reconstructed 19th-century classroom complete with desks and chalkboards. The **San Diego Union Building** features the typesetting tables and a printing press of the city's first newspaper. The Colorado House, site of the **Wells Fargo Museum,** invites guests inside an old bank vault.

SIGHTS

the San Diego Zoo

Mission San Diego de Alcala

Less than 10 miles (16 km) west of Old Town, Mission Valley is named for the first of 21 California missions established by Father Junípero Serra. **Mission San Diego de Alcala** (3146 Mission Blvd., 858/228-9283, www.belmontpark.com, 11am-8pm Mon.-Thurs. and Sun., 11am-10pm Fri.-Sat., free) remains an active Catholic parish while offering a small museum. First built on Presidio Hill in Old Town in 1769, it was moved in 1774 to its present location in Mission Valley to make way for a Spanish military outpost. Prior to World War II, the crumbling buildings underwent reconstruction; their preservation continues today. Tour the bougainvillea-filled garden near a 46-foot-high bell tower and the museum, which holds old photographs and relics unearthed during excavations of the site.

Mission Bay and Beaches
Belmont Park

A beachside amusement park for at least nine decades, **Belmont Park** (3146 Mission Blvd., 858/228-9283, www.belmontpark.com, 11am-8pm Mon.-Thurs. and Sun., 11am-10pm Fri.-Sat., free) sits right on Mission Beach and its lively boardwalk. The **Giant Dipper Roller Coaster** makes it easy to spot, and while the park is loaded with rides and arcade games, its most famous attraction may be the **Wave House,** which features two artificial waves: one for guests to test their skills on, another for pros to show off theirs.

SeaWorld

Though it's been shifting its focus away from aquatic animal shows and toward educational entertainment and rides, **SeaWorld** (500 Sea World Dr., 619/222-4732, www.seaworld.com/sandiego, 10am-5pm daily, 10am-9pm daily peak summer and winter holidays, $90 adults, $85 ages 3-9) remains a popular kid-friendly attraction offering hands-on ways for guests to connect to marinelife.

Point Loma
Cabrillo National Monument

People have lived along the San Diego coastline for over 10,000 years, most notably the Kumeyaay nation. That's who Juan Rodríguez Cabrillo encountered when he became the first European to set foot on what is now the U.S. West Coast. A statue atop this hilltop peak of Point Loma reflects on that day in 1542, but that's not the reason to visit **Cabrillo National Monument** (1800 Cabrillo Memorial Dr., Point Loma, 619/557-5450, www.nps.gov/cabr, 9am-5pm daily, $15 per vehicle, $7 walk-in). The panoramic view alone makes it worthwhile, gazing across the bay at the San Diego city skyline, Coronado, and the famous bridge connecting the two, plus the rocky Coronado Islands on the southwestern horizon of the expansive Pacific.

There are two lighthouses in the 144-acre park. One is the **Old Point Loma Lighthouse** (9am-5pm daily), put to use in 1855 then decommissioned 36 years

later because it was too high to be seen above San Diego's thick fog. The other one is its modern replacement. The older lighthouse is open to visitors. A network of trails descends from the west side of the Cabrillo statue down to sea level, where low tide reveals the unique tide-pool ecosystem of fish and crustaceans that have adapted to life under only a few inches of water.

Coronado

The long, blue Coronado Bridge connects downtown San Diego to Coronado, an island-like enclave that beckons beach bums and film aficionados alike to the historic Hotel del Coronado. While the Del dominates Coronado scenery, the island town also offers an array of other accommodations and restaurants.

To get there, drive across the **San Diego-Coronado Bridge,** or take the foot **ferry** (9am-9pm Sun.-Thurs., 9am-10pm Fri.-Sat., $4.75 one-way) from the Broadway Pier to the Coronado Ferry Landing. The ferry only takes 15 minutes and departs every hour on the hour.

★ Hotel del Coronado

For more than 125 years, **Hotel del Coronado** (1500 Orange Ave., 619/435-6611, www.hoteldel.com) has illuminated the shores of the Pacific Ocean with its majestic beauty. The "Grand Lady by the Sea" draws thousands each year to admire its pristine white Victorian architecture, crowned with a red roof and soaring towers. Notable guests have included Thomas Edison, Charlie Chaplin, Babe Ruth, Charles Lindburgh, and Marilyn Monroe (during filming of *Some Like It Hot*). *Wizard of Oz* author L. Frank Baum is said to have based the Emerald City on the hotel.

Like many old-world-type structures, Hotel del Coronado is haunted. In 1892, a young woman named Kate Morgan checked in and never checked out. She was found dead on a staircase leading to the beach, and no one ever claimed her

Old Town San Diego

body. Today, many believe Kate still occupies her former guest room.

Though the most lavish rooms cost a pretty penny, the hotel offers more affordable accommodations with no frills. And you don't have to be a hotel guest to explore the property or enjoy its exquisite views.

Recreation

Beaches
Ocean Beach

Between the San Diego River and the hills of Point Loma, laid-back **Ocean Beach** (west of Abbot St. from Voltaire St. to Newport Ave.) is popular among surfers, swimmers, sunbathers, and volleyball players. At its north end, pets can run free along the sand and crashing waves at **Dog Beach** (end of Voltaire St.).

The half-mile stretch of sand runs from the **OB Pier** (end of Niagara Ave.) in the south to the shallow San Diego River bordering the beach's northern edge. Around the pier are surfers and some saltier souls who earn the place comparisons to Venice Beach. Move north to find a welcoming stretch of sand with beach volleyball courts and areas designated for swimming and bodyboarding. Beach bonfires (within designated fire rings) are popular on summer nights, and fishing off the pier takes place daily. Parking lots are at the ends of Voltaire Street and Santa Monica Avenue, with showers and restrooms beside each. Lifeguards monitor the beach daily.

Mission Beach

A two-mile concrete boardwalk runs along **Mission Beach** (1710 W. Mission Bay Dr.), populated by beach cruisers, skateboards, and bikini-clad sunseekers. The north end stays quiet relative to the south stretch of beach, which features a large parking lot and the Belmont Park complex of restaurants and carnival rides.

You can cruise along **Mission Beach Boardwalk** (Ocean Front Walk, between Pacific Beach Dr. and N. Jetty Rd.) and still not run out of beach or boardwalk. Dubbed the "Golden Strand," it runs from South Mission all the way north to Pacific Beach. That long stretch in the middle? *That's* Mission Beach. It's most commonly identified with the beach in front of Belmont Park, where crowds congregate all summer. Runners, cyclists, and skaters of every stripe cruise past year-round. The large parking lot by the park is set up with restrooms, showers, picnic tables, volleyball nets, and fire rings, but the whole thing stretches more than a mile, so if you can find street parking along Mission Boulevard north of there, you'll find relatively uncrowded stretches of beach, which the lifeguards split intermittently into swim and surf zones. You may go where all the action is, or you may choose to settle on an empty spot on the sand and enjoy.

Pacific Beach

Pacific Beach (Ocean Front Walk, between Pacific Beach Dr. and Law St.) offers a beach experience with a festive atmosphere, with people (mostly young adults, including lots of singles) partying at the edge of the sand. They used to party *on* the sand until a city beach alcohol ban was put into effect, but the beachfront bars and restaurants ensure that the good times continue, especially south of Crystal Pier. North of the pier tends to be a little quieter, with swimming, surfing, and beach volleyball just a few of the popular activities. Fishing is allowed on the pier itself, and close by you'll find showers, restrooms, and lifeguards always on duty.

Coronado Beach

Coronado Beach (along Ocean Blvd.) is a gorgeous 1.5-mile stretch of sand set against the backdrop of the legendary

Hotel del Coronado. The family-friendly beach is free to visit and has street parking.

Routinely listed among the best beaches in the United States, Coronado Beach is what makes this place a dreamy summer destination. Even during fall and winter months, the beach is protected from both large surf and the atmosphere's marine layer by the whale-shaped Point Loma, visible on the north horizon; so while beaches elsewhere may be overcast and full of rip currents, Coronado should be just about right. Bear in mind that when big waves do hit this beach, it ceases to be an ideal place for less-experienced swimmers. There are several access points from Ocean Boulevard along the mile-long beach. In front of the Del, you may rent cabanas and order drinks; you'll find fire rings at the north end, while volleyball courts, bathrooms, and showers are near the main lifeguard tower manning the central beach.

★ Sunset Cliffs Natural Park

Most people keep to the upper edge of **Sunset Cliffs Natural Park** (700-1300 block of Sunset Cliffs Blvd., 24 hours daily), walking along trails that top the sandstone bluffs as it rises 80 feet above a mostly rocky shoreline. However, there's a 400-foot section of sand wide enough to coax local sunbathers and surfers down from the clifftops. Accessible by a steep, tricky dirt path that descends from the west side of Sunset Cliffs Boulevard just north of its intersection at Hill Street, the small beach has neither lifeguards nor amenities. You'll need a reasonable level of fitness to get down the path and then traverse a pile of loose boulders at its base. Your reward is ocean water with a rocky, sometimes sharp sea bottom not conducive to swimming. Nevertheless, the sand can get crowded in the summer,

Top to bottom: Hotel del Coronado; the pier at Pacific Beach; rollercoaster at Belmont Park.

and most days you'll find people down there, watching surfers or merely working on their tans, away from the OB beach life.

Caution: do not stand too close to the crumbling cliff's edge. Every year, unwitting visitors looking for the perfect selfie or sunset photo fall to injury or death.

Surfing

Surfers can take a crack at some waves at **Mission Beach** (1710 W. Mission Bay Dr.), **Ocean Beach Pier** (Abbott St. at Newport Ave.), or the longboard-friendly **Tourmaline Surf Park** (Tourmaline St., west of La Jolla Blvd.); experienced riders will prefer **Crystal Pier** (Garnet Ave., west of Mission Blvd.) or **OB Dog Beach** (Voltaire St., west of W. Point Loma Blvd.). For daily surf conditions, call the recorded hotline of **San Diego Lifeguard Services** (619/221-8824, www.sandiego.gov/lifeguards). Note that anything over four feet will be too large for beginners.

Beginners can take classes at **Ocean Experience Surf School** (4940 Newport Ave., Ocean Beach, 858/225-2317, www.oceanexperience.net, 9am-7pm Mon.-Sat., 9am-6pm Sun., from $95 pp) or **Surfari Surf School** (3740 Mission Blvd., Mission Beach, 858/337-3287, www.surfarisurfschool.com, 9am-5pm daily, $55-85 pp).

Pick up surfboards and gear from either location of **South Coast Surf Shop** (www.southcoast.com; 5023 Newport Ave., Ocean Beach, 619/223-7017, 10am-7pm Mon.-Sat., 10am-6:30pm Sun.; 740 Felspar St., Pacific Beach, 858/483-7660, 10am-7pm Mon.-Fri., 9:30am-7pm Sat., 10am-6:30pm Sun.).

Water Sports
★ Mission Bay

You'll find 17 square miles of watery playground at **Mission Bay Park** (2688 E. Mission Bay Dr.). Protected from the waves, this is where you'll find opportunities to play on the likes of Jet Skis, catamarans, kayaks, and stand-up paddleboards. Rent gear from **Mission Bay Sportcenter** (1010 Santa Clara Pl., 858/488-1004, www.missionbaysportcenter.com, 10am-7pm Mon.-Fri., 9am-7pm Sat.-Sun. summer, 10am-5pm daily winter, sailboats from $30/hr, powerboats from $75/hr, kayaks from $18/hr, pedal boats from $20/hr, SUP from $18/hr) or **Adventure Water Sports** (1710 W. Mission Bay Dr., Mission Bay, 619/226-8611, www.adventurewatersports.com, 8:30am-4pm daily, boat rentals from $130/hr, Jet Skis from $110/hr).

For classes, stop at **Mission Bay Aquatic Center** (1001 Santa Clara Pl., Mission Beach, 858/488-1000, www.mbaquaticcenter.com, 8am-5pm Tues.-Sun., $49), which also rents kayaks (from $21), sails (from $31), windsurfing gear (from $31), and SUPs (from $26).

Bicycling

Open to bicycles as well as pedestrians, the **Bayside Walk** circumnavigates 27 miles of Mission Bay shoreline, where you'll pass quiet beaches and thrill-seeking boaters. If you tire of the bay, take your bike to the Mission Beach Boardwalk, only two blocks west from the western shores of the bay. You'll find bikes for hire at **Ray's Rentals** (3221 Mission Blvd., 866/488-7297, www.raysrentals.com, 9am-7pm daily), as well as smartphone-enabled, dockless scooters throughout the neighborhood.

A 25-mile ride around San Diego Bay, the **Bayshore Bikeway** begins downtown at the Embarcadero and loops around the bay, running along separate bike lanes. It passes numerous attractions, parks, and beaches, including Coronado, where riders have the option of turning around and following the trail back or taking the Coronado Ferry to downtown. At the Coronado Ferry Landing, **Bikes & Beyond** (1201 1st St., 619/435-7180, www.bikes-and-beyond.com, bikes $8/hour) rents bikes that can get you on your way.

Spectator Sports

From April to September, the **San Diego Padres** play Major League Baseball at **Petco Park** (100 Park Blvd., 619/795-5555, www.sandiego.padres.mlb.com, $18-250 pass) in the heart of downtown.

Entertainment and Events

Nightlife
Bars and Clubs

For a quick sampling of the region's celebrated craft beers, visit taprooms such as North Park's **Toronado** (4026 30th St., 619/282-0456, www.toronadosd.com, 11:30am-midnight Sun.-Wed., 11:30am-2am Thurs.-Sat.); Little Italy's **Bottlecraft** (2252 India St., 619/487-9493, www.bottlecraftbeer.com, noon-10pm Mon.-Thurs., noon-midnight Fri.-Sat., 11am-10pm Sun.), which doubles as a bottle shop; or South Park's **Hamilton's Tavern** (1521 30th St., 619/238-5460, www.hamiltonstavern.com, 3pm-2am Mon.-Fri., 1pm-2am Sat.-Sun.), a divey beer mecca of sorts for craft enthusiasts, thanks to a steady rotation of world-class beers.

Ocean Beach offers a uniquely crusty brand of beach nightlife, with bars along Newport Avenue coming alive before the sun sets. **Wonderland Ocean Pub** (5083 Santa Monica Ave., 619/255-3358, https://wonderlandob.com, 11am-midnight, Mon.-Thurs., 11am-2am Fri.-Sat., 9am-midnight Sun.) offers the best view of the neighborhood's eponymous beach and pier. The rooftop of **Sunshine Company Saloon** (5028 Newport Ave., 619/222-0722, www.sunshineob.com, 11am-2am Mon.-Fri., 10am-2am Sat.-Sun.) manifests the surf- and yoga-friendly neighborhood's perennial happy hour vibe.

Downtown, rooftop bars offer escapist airiness for the urban set. Literally

Top to bottom: the Coronado Bridge; Sunset Cliffs; sailing on Mission Bay.

topping the list is **Altitude Sky Lounge** (660 K St., 619/446-6086, www.sandiegogaslamphotel.com, 5pm-1:30am daily). It sits 22 stories up, looking across the bay and into the Petco Park baseball stadium. Or hang poolside at **Hard Rock San Diego's Float** (207 5th Ave., 619/764-6924, www.hardrockhotelsd.com, 11am-2am daily), a rooftop oasis with daybeds, VIP cabanas, DJs, firepits, and amazing views. Rooftop bars are summer favorites.

Vegas-style clubs bring a DJ-fueled, vibrant nightlife to the Gaslamp Quarter, including the state-of-the-art **Omnia San Diego** (454 6th Ave., 619/544-9500, www.omnianightclub.com) and **Fluxx** (500 4th Ave., 619/232-8100, www.fluxxsd.com), which features go-go dancers and constantly changing decor.

San Diego's gay scene centers around bars and clubs in the Hillcrest neighborhood. The festive **Baja Betty's** (1421 University Ave., 619/269-8510, www.bajabettyssd.com, 11am-1am Mon.-Fri., 10am-1am Sat.-Sun.) is best known for late-night nachos, tequila cocktails, and friendly service. Down the street, **Urban Mo's** (308 University Ave., 619/491-0400, www.urbanmos.com, 9am-1:30am daily) works hard to live up to its claim to be "The Best Gay Bar in the World."

Live Music
An outdoor music venue built adjacent to a hotel and a marina, **Humphreys Concerts by the Bay** (2241 Shelter Island Dr., 619/224-3577, www.humphreysconcerts.com) features popular music and comedy acts from April to September. The intimate outdoor stage is set up to entertain ticketed customers and guests of the hotel, but with a clear view from the marina, boats often gather stage right to catch a free show.

The hip **Casbah** (2501 Kettner Blvd., 619/232-4355, www.casbahmusic.com) is famous for showcasing rising stars, having hosted the likes of Nirvana and Smashing Pumpkins in an intimate dive bar space.

Popular music artists draw crowds nearly nightly to **The Observatory** (2891 University Ave., 619/239-8836, www.observatorysd.com), a former theater turned concert venue in the neighborhood of North Park.

The Arts
San Diego's world-class theater culture includes productions at the **Civic Theatre** (1100 3rd Ave., 619/570-1100, www.sandiegotheatres.org), which hosts touring Broadway musicals and productions by the California Ballet Company. **The Old Globe** (1363 Old Globe Way, Balboa Park, 619/234-5623, www.oldglobe.org), the site of the popular Shakespeare Festival, also sets that stage for classic performances and original, Broadway-bound productions.

Historic theaters featuring live music, modern dance, plays, and comedy acts include downtown's **Balboa Theatre** (868 4th Ave., 619/570-1100, www.sandiegotheatres.org), **Horton Grand Theatre** (444 4th Ave., Gaslamp, 858/560-5740, www.sdmt.org), and the **Spreckels Theatre** (121 Broadway, Gaslamp, 619/235-9500, www.spreckels.net), a multi-performance venue.

The San Diego Symphony Orchestra takes the stage at the dazzling 2,200-seat **Copley Symphony Hall** (750 B St., 619/235-0804, www.sandiegosymphony.org). First opened in the 1920s, it was built in the French Renaissance style and features superb acoustics.

Festivals and Events
Hillcrest comes alive with the three-day San Diego **Pride Festival** (619/297-7683, www.sdpride.org, July), which features a parade, a 5K run, and an enormous block party. It attracts nearly 300,000 people.

The second week of November, craft beer takes center stage for **San Diego Beer Week** (locations vary, www.sdbw.org, Nov.). For 10 days, breweries, bars, and restaurants all over town offer special tap lists and rare beer specials, making it a great time for beer tourists to sample the best of local brewing.

★ Comic-Con

Year after year, **Comic-Con** (111 W. Harbor Dr., www.comic-con.org, July) is the biggest event at the downtown San Diego Convention Center. What began as a modest celebration of comic books has exploded into an entertainment juggernaut, drawing all manner of sci-fi fans, cosplayers, video-game buffs, and celebrities. More than 125,000 people descend on San Diego to attend 600 staged events and 1,500 exhibitor booths. Take note when Comic-Con takes place; it sells out far in advance, as do most of the hotels anywhere near downtown and at triple their normal rates.

Shopping

Downtown

Perched on the waterfront off Marina Park, the collection of shops dubbed **Seaport Village** offer mostly San Diego-themed souvenirs, sunglasses, and beach styles. An exception is the always fun, occasionally functional **Village Hat Shop** (619/233-7236, 10am-9pm daily). It's worth a visit for the walk along the waterfront and for the hand-carved carousel that's been in operation since 1895.

Neighboring Seaport Village, **The Headquarters** (789 W. Harbor Dr., www.theheadquarters.com) turned the city's former police headquarters into a shopping and dining district, with an old jail cell preserved on-site as proof. Shops include **Geppetto's Toys** (619/615-0005, 10am-8pm Mon.-Sat., 10am-9pm, Sun.)

and **Coco Rose** (760/213-7080, 10am-7pm Mon.-Sat., 10am-6pm Sun.), which offers Balinese-inspired women's fashions.

Balboa Park

The **San Diego History Center Gift Store** (1649 El Prado, 619/232-6203, 10am-5pm daily) features vintage reproductions of jewelry, pottery, and lamps, as well as art by local artists.

Mexican folk art inspires many of the crafts, jewelry, and decorative wares at **Casa Artelexia** (3803 Ray St., 619/501-6381, www.artelexia.com, 11am-6pm daily), including the skull-heavy styling of Día de los Muertos (Day of the Dead).

Old Town and Mission Hills

Colorful gift and souvenir shops abound at Old Town's **Bazaar del Mundo Shops** (4133 Taylor St., 619/296-3161, www.bazaardelmundo.com, 10am-9pm Tues.-Sat., 10am-5:30pm Sun.-Mon.), a world market filled with international crafts and gifts. Shops include **The Galley Shop,** with authentic Native American jewelry, **Ariana** (619/296-4989) for women's fashion, and **The Kitchen Shop,** which sells handcrafted Guatemalan pottery and carved kitchenware.

Ocean Beach

You'll find surf gear and apparel at **South Coast Surf Shop** (5023 Newport Ave., 619/223-7017, www.southcoast.com, 10am-6:30pm Mon.-Sat., 10am-6pm Sun.). With swimwear, towels, and more, **Wings Beachwear** (4948 Newport Ave., 619/224-2165, www.wingsbeachwear.com, 9am-7pm Mon.-Thurs., 9am-8pm Fri.-Sun.) has everything you need for the beach. Both shops are along Newport Avenue, which offers more window-shopping.

Food

Seafood and tacos rule in San Diego, so it stands to reason fish tacos are San Diego's signature street food. If you see a line at a food truck named Mariscos, it could be worth a look. I'd also recommend taking a chance on any crowded taco shop and ordering either carne asada fries—French fries topped with grilled meat, cheese, and guacamole—or a California burrito, which is effectively the same thing wrapped inside a flour tortilla. For the rest of your meals, consider these picks.

Downtown

Little Italy dominates upscale tastes. At ★ **Herb & Wood** (2210 Kettner Blvd., 619/955-8495, www.herbandwood.com, 5:30pm-10pm Sun.-Thurs., 5:30pm-11pm Fri.-Sat., $28-38), Brian Malarkey uses a wood-fired kitchen to get the best out of the world's top ingredients. Right next door, *Top Chef* Richard Blais gets creative with technique at **Juniper & Ivy** (2228 Kettner Blvd., 619/269-9036, www.juniperandivy.com, 5pm-10pm Sun.-Thurs., 5pm-11pm Fri.-Sat., $18-30). Both offer casual sister restaurants on the same block.

Around the corner, the city's best-looking seafood restaurant is also one of its best tasting: ★ **Ironside Fish & Oyster** (1654 India St., 619/269-3033, www.ironsidefishandoyster.com, 11:30am-midnight Sun.-Thurs., 11:30am-2am Fri.-Sat., $22-31). Don't let the wall of piranha skulls distract you from the raw bar or whole roasted fish.

San Diego's coffee scene has quietly become one of the nation's best, led by the award-winning beans of direct trade roaster **Bird Rock Coffee** (2295 Kettner Blvd., 619/272-0203, www.birdrockcoffee.com, 6am-6pm Mon.-Thurs., 6am-7pm Fri., 7am-7pm Sat., 7am-6pm Sun., $4-6).

Nearby, on the Embarcadero, outdoor casual restaurant ★ **Carnitas' Snack Shack** (1004 N. Harbor Dr., 619/696-7675, www.carnitassnackshack.com, 11am-10pm Mon.-Thurs., 11am-midnight Fri., 9am-midnight Sat., 9am-10pm Sun., $9-15) offers the city's best meaty sandwiches.

Mexican food definitely makes San Diego tick. For the locals' favorite authentic breakfast and lunch, head to Barrio Logan's ★ **Las Cuatro Milpas** (1857 Logan Ave., 619/234-4460, 8:30am-3pm Mon.-Fri., 6:30am-3pm Sat., $3-6). Don't mind the line to get in—it moves fast, and it's totally worth the short wait for the best flour tortillas in the world.

Fish tacos are viewed as a local delicacy, and great examples may be found at ★ **Oscar's Mexican Seafood** (927 J St., 619/564-6007, www.oscarsmexicanseafood.com, 8am-9pm Sun.-Thurs., 8am-10pm Fri.-Sat., $4-8). Meanwhile, the taco has been elevated to gourmet—yet still affordable—status at **Lola 55** (1290 F St., 619/542-9155, www.lola55.com, 11:30am-9pm Sun.-Thurs., 11:30am-midnight Fri.-Sat., $3-12).

Based on a traditional U.S.-style chophouse, ★ **Born & Raised** (1909 India St., Little Italy, 619/202-4577, www.bornandraisedsteak.com, 4pm-midnight daily, $40-87) is a snazzy restaurant that takes the steak house concept to greater heights than any mid-century American steak house dared ever dream. Portraits of late hip-hop stars adorn the walls, and leather booths surround marble tabletops, where customers receive top-shelf service, including rolling table carts where side dishes are prepared on the spot. Of course, top billing goes to the steaks, ranging from archaic dishes like steak Diane, a massive porterhouse for two, and tournedos Rossini topped by seared foie gras.

★ **Extraordinary Desserts** (1430 Union St., Little Italy, 619/294-7001,

Craft Beer in San Diego

Craft beer has become a major tourist draw in San Diego, and most bars will have a terrific tap list. But the newest releases may be tasted at the breweries themselves. San Diego's must-visit craft destinations include reputation-establishing originals **AleSmith** (9990 AleSmith Ct., 858/549-9888, www.alesmith.com, 11am-10pm Mon.-Thurs., 11am-11pm Fri.-Sat., 11am-9pm Sun.), about 20 minutes out of downtown in Miramar, and the more central **Stone Brewing** (2816 Historic Decatur Rd., #116, 619/269-2100, www.stonebrewing.com, 11:30am-9pm Mon.-Thurs., 11:30am-10pm Fri., 11am-10pm Sat., 11am-9pm Sun.), which has a large restaurant and beer garden conveniently near the airport.

craft beer at North Park Beer Co.

You may visit the city's first craft brewpub downtown. Established in 1989, **Karl Strauss** (1157 Columbia St., 619/234-2739, www.karlstrauss.com, 11am-10pm Mon.-Thurs., 11am-11pm Fri.-Sat., 11:30am-10pm Sun.) has since grown to include a dozen brewpub locations throughout Southern California.

The tops of the new breed are fresh IPA purists **Societe Brewing** (8262 Clairemont Mesa Blvd., 858/598-5409, www.societebrewing.com, noon-9pm Mon.-Wed., noon-10pm Thurs.-Sat., noon-8pm Sun.) and the quirky, endlessly creative **Modern Times** (3725 Greenwood St., 619/546-9694, www.moderntimesbeer.com, noon-10pm Sun.-Thurs., noon-midnight Fri.-Sat.).

But it's the more than 100 ever-evolving small breweries that keep San Diego's reputation going. For a sense of discovery, wander freely among more than one dozen high-quality microbreweries radiating around the commercial hubs of the urban North Park neighborhood, anchored by **North Park Beer Co.** (3038 University Ave., 619/255-2994, www.northparkbeerco.com, 3pm-midnight Mon.-Wed., noon-midnight Thurs.-Fri., 10:30am-midnight Sat., 10:30am-10pm Sun.).

www.extraordinarydesserts.com, 10am-11pm Sun.-Thurs., 10am-midnight Fri.-Sat.) offers the best desserts in town. You'll have trouble choosing, but you'll definitely be singing its praises if you order a slice of cake with some of the handcrafted small-batch ice cream. Lines always seem to be out the door, but you'll want to stand in this one to get a good look at each of the daily offerings, whether you're grabbing dessert to go or eating in the spacious modern dining room. If all that's too daunting, try the stellar bakery's smaller location in nearby Bankers Hill (2929 5th Ave.).

Balboa Park

Set within the sculpture garden beside the San Diego Museum of Art you'll find **Panama 66** (1450 El Prado, 619/696-1966, www.sdmart.org/panama_66, 11am-5pm Mon.-Tues., 11am-11pm Wed., 11am-10pm Thurs.-Sun., $10-14). Hot and cold sandwiches, along with adult beverages, go well with picnic blankets among the sculptures.

In nearby Bankers Hill, you'll find local sea urchin and other fish at **Hane Sushi** (2760 5th Ave., #5, 619/260-1411, 11:30am-2pm Tues.-Fri., 5:30pm-10pm Tues.-Sun., $18-26).

Old Town and Mission Hills

Within Old Town San Diego State Historic Park, you'll find a half dozen touristy Mexican restaurants featuring colorful costumes and mariachis, but for the real OG spot, go outside the park to **El Indio** (3695 India St., 619/299-0385, www.elindiosandiego.com, 8am-9pm daily, $6-8). The family restaurant goes back to 1940 and claims to be the birthplace of the rolled taquito.

Point Loma

Dine on fresh catch dockside at **Point Loma Seafoods** (2805 Emerson St., 619/223-1109, www.pointlomaseafoods.com, 9am-7pm Mon.-Sat., 10am-7pm Sun., $10-14). The local mainstay offers no-frills sourdough sandwiches, seafood cocktails, grilled fish, and simple sushi.

Not far away, former military base Liberty Station has been turned into a restaurant row of sorts, including diverse food stands at **Liberty Public Market** (2820 Historic Decatur Rd., 619/487-9346, www.libertypublicmarket.com, 11am-8pm daily, $7-25). **Officine Buona Forchetta** (2865 Sims Rd., Liberty Station, 619/548-5770, www.officinebuonaforchetta.com, noon-3pm and 5pm-9:30pm Mon.-Thurs., noon-3pm and 5pm-10:30pm Fri., noon-10:30pm Sat., noon-9pm Sun., $10-25) features outrageously great handmade pastas and wood-fired Neapolitan pizzas served in a space with copious indoor and outdoor seating. A modified vintage Fiat convertible serves as a romantic two-person booth.

Coronado

The Hotel del Coronado's lavish all-you-can-eat brunch at the ★ **Crown Room** (1500 Orange Ave., 619/522-8490, www.hoteldel.com, 9:30am-1pm Sun., $98) includes a truly dizzying number of buffet stations, all served in one of the city's best architectural examples of jointed wood construction. Eggs are made to order, prime rib roasts are carved, pancakes flipped, and sushi rolled. Even if you go back for thirds, you won't get to it all. You may never even know what you missed by the time you've made it through your second dessert. Reservations are recommended, as the high cost of entry doesn't seem to keep the crowds away.

A local institution, **Coronado Brewing Company** (170 Orange Ave., Coronado Ferry Landing, 619/437-4452, www.coronadobrewingcompany.com, 10:30am-9pm Sun.-Thurs., 10:30am-10pm Fri.-Sat., $12-25) has been serving pub grub for decades, which goes great with its award-winning beers. Order a tasting flight with appetizers, then settle on a pint to go with your burger, pizza, or taco plate. Aim for lunch or an early dinner to enjoy the shaded dining patio on a sunny day. With the city skyline within view, you can check a few items off your San Diego to-do list all in one place.

A world of seafood preparations await at **Bluewater Boathouse Seafood Grill** (1701 Strand Way, Coronado, 619/435-0155, www.bluewatergrill.com, 11:30am-9pm Sun.-Thurs., 11:30am-9:30pm Fri.-Sat., $15-30) housed inside the Del's former boathouse. Nab a seat on the patio and eat marina-side on lovely Glorietta Bay.

Lobster rolls are a favorite meal in New England seaside resort towns; there's no reason they can't be in a San Diego seaside resort town too. **Lobster West** (1033 B Ave., Ste. 102, Coronado, 619/675-0002, www.lobsterwest.com, 11am-8pm Sun.-Thurs., 11am-9pm Fri.-Sat., $10-40) is a casual shop that brings in Maine lobster to serve the traditional-style rolls, with a vertical cut down the center of the bun. Crab, shrimp, and scallops are also heavily featured.

Accommodations

San Diego has acres of hotels, with a dense pack of standard chain hotels on the self-explanatory Hotel Circle in Mission Valley. The following have some beneficial combination of elegance, location, or character. Prices are at their lowest between September and June.

Under $150

Budget accommodations begin with the **HI-San Diego** (521 Market St., 619/525-1531, www.sandiegohostels.org, $40 dorms, $130 private), in the middle of the Gaslamp Quarter. You can get just about anywhere from this almost-elegant youth hostel.

Experience the quaint appeal of San Diego's gorgeous Craftsman homes by renting one of the fully furnished apartments of ★ **Mudville Flats** (747 10th Ave., East Village, 619/232-4045, www.mudvilleflats.com, $100-200), a 1905 boutique hotel. Rooms feature the built-in shelves and wood detailing that make Craftsmans so appealing, plus private kitchens and one amenity few of those cottages can claim: air-conditioning.

The historic ★ **Lafayette Hotel** (2223 El Cajon Blvd., North Park, 619/296-2101, www.lafayettehotelsd.com, $100-200) brings its amenities up to par with its vintage charm. Contemporary decor and comfortable beds make all the bungalows and suites desirable—but especially those sitting poolside. The Lafayette can be quite the scene, hosting pool parties in the summer, with occasional live music events during holiday weekends. Within a few blocks are North Park, Hillcrest, Normal Heights, and University Heights restaurants and bars.

Vintage Queen Anne bed-and-breakfast **Keating House** (2331 2nd Ave., 619/239-8585, www.keatinghouse.com, from $109) is within walking distance of all of the attractions in Balboa Park.

The Pearl Hotel (1410 Rosecrans St., Point Loma, 619/226-6100, www.thepearlsd.com, from $139) is a retro-style abode with comfortable rooms. It offers film screenings by its pool in the summer.

$150-250

Clean and stylish, ★ **La Pensione Hotel** (606 W. Date St., 800/232-4683, www.lapensionehotel.com, from $165) is a four-story hotel in Little Italy offering a frescoed courtyard and good old-fashioned quiet.

President Benjamin Harrison, King Kalakaua of Hawaii, and even Babe Ruth stayed in downtown's ★ **Horton Grand Hotel** (311 Island Ave., 619/544-1886, www.hortongrand.com, from $179), but its most famed guest was lawman Wyatt Earp, who took up residence for seven years! Its Victorian-era architecture and furnishings have been updated with all the modern comforts and conveniences to create a timeless experience.

Better than its rates suggest, **The Westgate** (1055 2nd Ave., 619/238-1818, www.westgatehotel.com, from $179) offers good rooms, a convenient location in the Gaslamp Quarter, plus a rooftop pool and track.

Eco-chic **Hotel Indigo** (509 9th Ave., 619/727-4000, www.hotelinsd.com, from $181) is the first LEED-certified hotel in the city. Located in the Gaslamp Quarter, it offers ecofriendly features in each of its spacious rooms, which feature floor-to-ceiling windows and spa baths. With spa service and a rooftop pool lounge, **Hotel Solamar** (435 6th Ave., 877/230-0300, www.hotelsolamar.com, from $209) touts itself as downtown's hip luxury hotel. Its location near the Gaslamp Quarter provides easy access to nightlife.

Built by the family of the 18th president and named in his honor, the ★ **U.S. Grant Hotel** (326 Broadway, 619/232-3121, www.usgrant.com, from $220) offers a grand entrance: An elegant lobby presents marble floors and silk carpets, with high ceilings furnished with crystal chandeliers. The glamour extends to 47 luxurious suites, though standard rooms go for reasonable rates. Parking (from $40 per day) can be pricey.

Over $250

A Tempur-Pedic mattress in every room ensures ★ **Tower23 Hotel** (723 Felspar St., Pacific Beach, 858/270-2323, www.t23hotel.com, from $200) is the most comfortable place to sleep in Pacific Beach. Its location fronting the boardwalk gives you plenty to do and see to earn that sleep. Guests may enjoy the view from their balconies or the shared rooftop deck, or step onto the beach from the hotel's well-appointed **JRDN** restaurant and bar. With surf lockers available and beach and bike rentals on-site, it's a chic home base for a beachy stay in this lively part of town.

Even in swanky Southern California, ★ **Hotel del Coronado** (1500 Orange Ave., Coronado, 619/435-6611 or 800/468-3533, www.hoteldel.com, from $250) wins the prize for grandiosity. The white-painted, red-roofed mammoth sprawls for acres from the road to the sand. Inside, the Del is at once a historical museum, shopping mall, food court—and hotel. It offers almost 700 rooms, plus another 70-plus individual cottages. Room sizes and decor vary, from smaller Victorian-decorated guest rooms to expansive modern suites.

The romantic **1906 Lodge at Coronado Beach** (1060 Adella Ave., Coronado, 619/437-1900 and 866/435-1906, www.1906lodge.com, from $250) lavishes couples in luxury in quaint beachside suites featuring whirlpool tubs, cozy fireplaces, and patios.

the pool at the Hotel del Coronado

Information and Services

The **San Diego Convention and Visitors Bureau** (SDCVB, www.sandiego.org) operates the downtown **San Diego Visitor Information Center** (996-B N. Harbor Dr., 619/236-1242, 9am-4pm daily Oct.-May, 9am-5pm daily June-Sept.). You can get help with everything from flight information to restaurant coupons to hotel reservations. To get a feel for the town before you arrive, check out the SDCVB website. Friendly folks can answer emails and phone calls about most anything pertaining to San Diego County.

◆ Side Trip: Tijuana, Mexico

One of San Diego's greatest cultural assets is its proximity to Mexico; the multifaceted border town wouldn't be the same without its sister city to the south, Tijuana (or, as we like to call it, TJ). Tijuana is the second-largest city in the state of Baja California, Mexico, with a population of 1.8 million. Twenty miles (32 km) south of downtown, the sprawling TJ hugs the entire length of the San Diego border, from beach to mountains, and offers a tantalizing glimpse of the sights, sounds, and flavors of Mexico. Millions of tourists visit annually to revel in the city's colorful souvenirs, folk music, spicy food, cheap beers, and extreme bargain shopping.

While Tijuana got its start in the late 19th century, it didn't really boom until the United States made alcohol illegal in the 1920s, driving Americans across the border in search of booze and good times, which often included gambling, prostitution, and narcotics. Tijuana learned to profit off lurid appetites, and sadly, many Americans still visit with the same intentions, particularly teenagers taking advantage of the lower legal drinking age.

In recent years, however, Tijuana has emerged as one of the region's most talked-about destinations for dining, performance, and visual arts. Its emerging, progressive cultural identity has proven a refreshing change from its years of being known as a corrupt party town.

Present-day Tijuana exists within this strange duality: On the one hand, it's a culturally rich city of nearly two million people, home to emerging artists, creative entrepreneurs, and celebrity chefs. On the other, it's a seedy adult resort, serving cheap beer and street tacos (the best in the West) late into the night. Whichever Tijuana you prefer to visit, you can expect to have a blast.

Due to a relatively depressed economy, the costs of doing anything in TJ are considerably less than in the United States. Most visitors stick to the urban center, Zona Centro, adjacent business hub Zona Río, or venture west to uncrowded beaches, Playas de Tijuana.

Sights

Avenida Revolución

It's only a couple thousand feet from U.S. soil, but **Avenida Revolución** is the living center of Tijuana, as far as tourists are concerned. Referred to in loving shorthand as La Revu, it's a wide avenue of shops, bars, clubs, tobacconists, and casinos. Historically, the active street has catered to often unsavory American appetites, but in recent years, the locals have started catering to themselves instead. A creative entrepreneurial culture has consequently emerged in the form of street art, music, breweries, and a new generation of businesses emanating gritty cosmopolitan charm. However, the signature cheap souvenirs of La Revu are still hawked here, as are cheap beers and photo ops with the street's famous "zonkeys" (donkeys painted with stripes to resemble zebras).

Tijuana Arch and Plaza Santa Cecilia

The most immediately visible sites as you enter Tijuana are an enormous Mexican flag flying over the border and El Arco del Milenio, better known as the **Tijuana Arch** (Av. Revolución at Calle Primera). Erected in 2000 and loosely inspired by the St. Louis Arch, the Arch stands as an ornamental entryway to La Revu. More recently, it's been wired up with a large video screen. Just below the arch is the colorful **Plaza Santa Cecilia,** the original city center. The plaza is now a tourist-friendly market square punctuated on busy days by *papel picado* decor, live mariachi music, and folk dance performances.

Centro Cultural Tijuana

Referred to locally as CECUT (pronounced like say-coot), the **Centro Cultural Tijuana** (9350 Paseo de los Héroes, Zona Río, 52-664/687-9600, www.cecut.gob.mx, 9am-9pm daily, adults US$2.75/MX$48, children US$1.50/MX$27, students and teachers US$1.60/MX$29) is a government-sponsored cultural center serving as Tijuana's top museum. It shows permanent and rotating art exhibitions, focused on Baja works as well as international touring shows. It occasionally stages musical, dance, and theater performances; and has an IMAX theater in the massive dome out front.

Guided Tours

Guided tours of Tijuana will provide updated local insights into a city that's humming with new street art, star chefs, and hip drinking spots in addition to transportation and border-crossing assistance. Contact **¡Let's Go Clandestino!** (letsgoclandestino.net, from US$125/MX$2,300) to arrange a curated private trip around Tijuana and even down to Baja wine country if a greater excursion is desired. It also offers occasional larger, public outings, often revolving around food and drink festivals.

Sports and Recreation

Perhaps the most unique spectacle sport in all of Mexico is Lucha Libre, or masked wrestling. The 150-year-old form of entertainment involves colorfully masked *luchadores,* beloved characters who create dramatic story lines ahead of high-flying wrestling bouts. Friday night matches take place in the southeast section of town at **Auditorio Municipal Fausto Gutierrez Moreno** (Blvd. Gustavo Díaz Ordaz at Blvd. do las Americas, 52-664/250-9015). Tickets and schedules may sometimes be found at ticketing website Ticket Móvil (www.ticketmovil.com.mx), but it's easy to buy cheap tickets at the door ahead of shows starting at 8:30pm.

The matadors (almost) always win the bullfights at the Bullring by the Sea, officially known as **Monumental Plaza de Toros** (Av. Del Pacifico 4, Playas de Tijuana, 52-656/613-1182, www.monumentalmexico.com, Mar.-Aug.), right beside the U.S. border in Playas de Tijuana. However, the state of Baja California came close to banning bullfights in 2016.

Even U.S. soccer fans follow Club Tijuana in the Liga MX México Primera División. The pro team is more commonly known as the Xolos (pronounced cholos), as their mascot is the famous Mexican hairless dog breed xoloitzcuintle. The team plays home games August-April south of Zona Río at **Estadio Caliente** (12027 Blvd. Agua Caliente, Hipodromo Agua Caliente).

Another Tijuana pro sports team, the Toros, play minor Mexican league baseball April-August in the southeast portion of the city at **Estadio Gasmart** (Mision de Santo Tomas at Rio Eufrates, 52-664/635-5600, www.torosdetijuana. com).

Gambling is legal in Tijuana for those 18 and older, and all of the casinos are owned by the family of **Caliente Casinos** (www.calientecasino.com.mx). They're easy to find on La Revu, particularly **Casino Jai Alai** (1100 Av. Revolución, Zona Centro, 52-664/638-4308, 24 hours daily), built within the city's historic Jai Alai Palace, easily recognized for its Moroccan-inspired architecture and the giant red "Jai Alai" sign. Close to the border crossing, the snazziest new casino venue is **Hotel Pueblo Amigo** (9211 Vía Rapida Oriente, Zona Río, 52-664/624-2700, www.hotelpuebloamigo.com, 24 hours daily).

Both the Monumental Plaza de Toros and the Jai Alai Palace double as concert venues.

Nightlife

Tijuana's famously raucous nightlife centers around the collective city blocks known as **La Sexta** (Calle Sexta Flores Magón at Av. Revolución, Zona Centro)—so called because it's on *Calle Sexta,* or "Sixth Street." Step east of La Revu onto La Sexta and you'll find a dozen bars and clubs competing for your attention with music and drink specials.

The one must-visit destination is **Dandy del Sur Cantina** (8274 Flores Magón, Zona Centro, 52-664/688-0052, 9am-3am daily), the heart and soul of La Sexta. It's an intimate dive of dark polished wood, known for its jukebox, stiff cocktails, and inimitable ambience.

Across the street, **La Mezcaleria** (8267 Calle Sexta Flores Magón, 52-664/688-0384, www.palmcanyonrvresort.com, 6pm-2am Tues.-Thurs., 6pm-3am Fri.-Sun.) is a relative hole-in-the-wall and has become a favorite stop of Tijuana and San Diego urbanites, thanks to its cheapshots tour of up to 17 mezcal varieties, including *mezcal de pechuga,* which draws distinctive flavor during a distillation process featuring raw chicken. For more mezcal in cozier surroundings, look behind **La Corriente Cevicheria Nais** for its sister bar **El Tinieblo Mezcal Room** (221 Calle Sexta Flores Magón, Zona Centro, 52-664/685-0555, 7pm-2am Thurs., 5pm-3am Fri.-Sat.), where DJs provide a smoother soundtrack.

To seek out TJ's larger dance club environments, go back on La Revu, just south of La Sexta; most weekends will be lively at **Las Pulgas** (1127 Av. Revolución, Zona Centro, 52-664/685-9594, www.laspulgas.mx, noon-6am daily). When Zona Centro really gets going, however, it's worth the experience to explore its "mega nightclub," **Coko Bongo** (1656 Av. Revolución, Zona Centro, 52-664/638-7353, www.cokobongo.com, 8pm-5am daily), offering multiple dance floors so you can find the vibe you like. Ladies are strongly encouraged to use the buddy system visiting these spots.

To see where Tijuana's creative crowd drinks, head to the rooftop of **Cine Tonalá** (1317 Av. Revolución, Zona Centro, 52-664/688-0118, www.cinetonala.com, 1pm-2am Tues.-Sun.), which offers live music and DJs, cocktails, and reasonably upscale dining in a classy open-air environment. Meanwhile, the cinema downstairs plays documentaries and art films and hosts live speakers.

To enjoy a beer while exploring La Revu, check out the **Mamut Brewing Co.** tasting room at **Pasaje Rodriguez** (906 Av. Revolución, Zona Centro) or head upstairs through the **Foreign Club Parking Structure** (Calle Salvador Díaz Mirón 4ta, a half block west of Av. Revolución) to drink beers with a fifth-story view of the city at **Norte Brewery** (52-664/638-4891, www.nortebrewing.com, 2pm-10pm Mon.-Wed., 2pm-midnight Thurs.-Sat.). But the best place to experience Tijuana's craft beer scene is **Plaza Fiesta** (9440 Erasmo Castellanos Q., Zona Río, 52-664/202-7267, www.thepalmsatindianhead.com, plaza open daily 24 hours, most businesses noon-2am), a cooperative of bars and brewery tasting rooms unlike anything you'll find north of the border. The favorite local beer makers to check out here include **Insurge Cervecería Insurgente, Border Psycho Brewery,** and **Madueño Brewing Co.**

Shopping

Tijuana never runs out of souvenirs; you'll find them at every turn, particularly along La Revu and Plaza Santa Cecilia. But the best place to browse is **Mercado de Artesanías** (621 Av. Melchor Ocampo, Zona Centro, 6am-6pm daily), a loose collection of shops with low prices on Mexican crafts, including clothes, leather products, Talavera tiles, pottery, housewares, and textiles. To get a sampling of local tastes, visit the sprawling **Mercado Hidalgo** (2 Guadalupe Victoria, Zona Río, 52-664/684-0485, 6am-6pm Mon.-Sat., 6am-4:30pm Sun.), loaded with stalls selling local fruits and vegetables, Mexican sweets, spiced nuts, dried chiles, cooking oils, dairy products, meats, and sausages.

A new generation of artists and

Top to bottom: the Tijuana Arch on Avenida Revolucion; Plaza Santa Cecilia is where downtown Tijuana got its start; Mexican candies at Mercado Hidalgo.

entrepreneurs has sprung up around La Revu in recent years, resulting in a cluster of small, independent shops off the main street. The murals and galleries alone are worth a visit to **Pasaje Rodriguez** (906 Av. Revolución, Zona Centro, 9am-10pm Mon.-Sat., 9am-8pm Sun.), but it's also got a craft brewery, a used bookstore, a record store, a bike shop, and some terrific spots to drink coffee.

Zona Río's resident shopping mall, **Plaza Rio** (96-98 Paseo de los Héroes, Zona Río, 52-800/704-5900, www.palm-canyonrvresort.com, 10am-10pm daily) is modeled after the suburban American shopping mall, complete with food courts and movie theaters. **Outlets at the Border** (4463 Camino De La Plaza, San Ysidro, 619/651-8018, www.outletsattheborder.com, 10am 9pm Mon.-Sat., 10am-7pm Sun.) actually sits on the American side of the border wall, but the populations on both sides are drawn to the collection of popular brand outlets.

Food

Tijuana's rich array of dining options ranges from unforgettable Mexican street food to fine dining for a fraction of the price of equivalent meals in San Diego. The city's greatest culinary claim to fame is **Caesar's** (1059 Av. Revolución, Zona Centro, 52-664/685-1927, www.caesarstijuana.com, 11:30am-10pm Mon.-Tues., 11:30am-11pm Wed., 11:30am-midnight Thurs.-Sat., 11:30am-9pm Sun., US$15-25/MX$280-470), the historic birthplace of the Caesar salad. This classic, American-style steak house on La Revu is trimmed in dark wood and hosts jazz performances on weekends. Highlights of the deep menu include the beef Wellington, a terrific bone marrow *sope,* and the signature salad, which is made tableside.

A block away, Zona Centro's best contemporary restaurant is the over-achieving gastropub **La Justina** (1232 Av. Revolución, Zona Centro, 52-664/638-4936, www.facebook.com/lajustinatj,

2pm-1am Tues.-Thurs., 2pm-2am Fri.-Sat., US$12-20/MX$220-370), which handles burgers and craft beer with the same deftness as it does craft cocktails and addictive *tiraditos*—Latin America's answer to sushi.

For the best fine dining, look to Zona Río, and particularly **Mision 19** (10643 Misión de San Javier, Zona Río, 52-664/634-2493, www.mision19.com, 11am-10pm Sun.-Thurs., 11am-midnight Fri.-Sat., US$9-16/MX$165-300). Chef Javier Plascencia, face of the Baja-Mediterranean movement, puts out dishes adeptly blending simplicity and great ingredients à la the Mediterranean with rustic Mexican culinary traditions, resulting in dishes like dry-aged rib eye steaks, Baja-farmed oysters, and grilled octopus. Between the fine wines, attentive table service, and elegant decor, Mision's dining rooms feel a world removed from Tijuana's urban street life.

If you only eat one thing in Tijuana, it should be tacos—lots of them. Make a pilgrimage to Taco Alley, aka **Las Ahumaderas** (9770 Guillermo Prieto), a cluster of taco shops that have attained local cult status over the past half century. The latest obsession is the busy Zona Río taco counter at **Tacos El Franc** (9013 Blvd. Sánchez Taboada, Zona Río, 52-667/142-2955, www.tacoselfranc.com, 4pm-1am Mon.-Thurs., 3pm-3am Fri. Sat., US$3 6/MX$55-110). The street tacos sell for less than a buck-fifty apiece, and the sloppy *al pastor* rotisserie pork might be the tastiest thing in the city. Save some room for a stop across the street at TJ mainstay **Tacos El Gordo** (9210 Blvd. General Rodolfo Sánchez Taboada, Zona Río, www.tacoselgordobc.com, 8am-2am Sun.-Thurs., 8am-4am Fri.-Sat., US$3-8/MX$55-150); it serves a long list of regional favorites as well as *antojitos*.

For a classic Tijuana seafood experience near La Revu, head to **La Corriente Cevicheria Nais** (803 Flores Magón, Zona Centro, 52-664/685-0555, www.palm-canyonrvresort.com, 11:30am-10pm

Mon.-Wed., 11:30am-11pm Thurs., 11:30am-midnight Fri.-Sat., 11:30am-9:30pm Sun. July-Sept., 11am-9pm Thurs.-Fri., 8am-9pm Sat.-Sun. Oct.-Jun., US$4-10/MX$75-185), a beachy, thatched-roof restaurant that has served over 200,000 red snapper ceviche tostadas. Definitely try one of those, along with other ceviches and *aguachiles,* shrimp and other seafood cocktails, fish and shrimp tacos, and anything octopus. Find similar offerings on the border of Zona Río at the food truck **Mariscos Ruben** (Calle 8va Miguel Hidalgo and Av. Andrés Quintana Roo, Zona Río, 10am-6pm daily, US$4-8/MX$75-150), which has earned so much cachet over decades at this spot that it's the first seafood stop for every famous chef visiting Tijuana.

The Baja culinary community tends to lift each other up, and nowhere is that better displayed than the rise in cooperative food courts, where up-and-coming chefs serve from individual food counters around a shared dining space. On La Revu, step into an alley leading into **Colectivo 9** (1265 Av. Revolución, Zona Centro, 760/767-5341, www.colectivo9. com, 1pm-8pm Tues.-Thurs. and Sun., 1pm-midnight Fri.-Sat., US$4-8/MX$75-150), where you'll find food counters serving hamburgers, pasta, sushi, coffee, beer, and wine. At the Plaza Rio mall, skip the food court in favor of the **Foodgarden** (11821 Av. Vía Rápida Poniente, Zona Río, 52-664/634-1087, www.foodgarden. mx, 10am-10pm Sun.-Thurs., 10am-11pm Fri.-Sat., US$4-12/MX$75-220), offering Mediterranean, Italian, ramen, and rotisserie chicken. The best of the bunch is the food truck and beer garden collectively known as **Telefonica** (8924 Blvd. Aguacaliente, 52-664/684-8782, www. carleesplace.com, 8am-10pm Mon.-Wed., 8am-11pm Thurs., 8am-11:30pm Fri.-Sat., 8am-9pm Sun., US$4-10/MX$75-185). A craft beer tap list pairs with your choice of street foods, including vegan tacos, gourmet sausages, *tortas,* seafood, and *barbacoa.*

Accommodations

To stay right on Avenida Revolución, try the boutique lodging at **One Bunk** (920 Av. Revolución, Zona Centro, www. onebunk.com, from US$32/MX$600); it's stylish but stays cheap thanks to the unstoppable street noise of La Revu. A few blocks up, **Hotel Ticuán** (3845 Yaqui Pass Rd., 760/767-0100, www.lacasadelzorro.com, from US$74/MX$1,400) is larger and provides a quieter stay, offering the equivalent of an American three-star hotel experience.

For a central stay that's also close to the border, the bare-boned but clean **B My Hotel** (221 Palm Canyon Dr., 760/767-5341, www.palmcanyonrvresort.com, from US$40/MX$750) offers quick highway access in any direction and sits within walking distance of both Zona Centro and Zona Río. Casino-goers may benefit from a stay at **Hotel Pueblo Amigo** (9211 Vía Rapida Oriente, Zona Río, 52-664/624-2700, www.hotelpuebloamigo. com, from US$68/MX$1,300), part of

a multimillion-dollar Caliente Casino property.

Zona Río proves the place to go for more executive-friendly lodgings, led by a familiar brand at **Hyatt Place Tijuana** (10488 Blvd. Agua Caliente, Zona Río, 52-664/900-1234, www.hyatt.com, from US$115/MX$2,200), with well-appointed rooms and free parking. The **Hotel Lucerna Tijuana** (10902 Paseo de los Héroes, Zona Río, 52-664/633-3900, www.hoteleslucerna.com, from US$115/ MX$2,200) sits on a large and pictur-esque property, offering a great bang for your buck. Its adjacent sister hotel, **K Tower** (10902 Paseo de los Héroes, Zona Río, 52-664/633-7500, www.ktowerhotel. com, from US$200/MX$3,750), costs a bit more, but is still a tremendous bargain; it delivers luxurious furnishings, a sushi restaurant, and a rooftop pool deck with a panoramic view.

Those looking for a cheap stay by the beach or for a quieter experience can find hostel-style accommodations at **LifeStyle** **Hostel** (820 Av. Del Pacifico, Playas de Tijuana, 52-664/976-8244, from US$17/ MX$310 dorm, US$40/MX$740 private). It's a long cab ride from Zona Centro, but both the transportation and hostel fares are far cheaper than those in American beach communities.

Information and Services
Language
Spanish is spoken by nearly the entire local population of Tijuana; many lo-cals, especially those working in the city's frequently-touristed areas, speak some amount of English, but the majority do not. It will be helpful to know a few basic Spanish phrases before visiting.

Money
The official currency of Mexico is the peso, though most businesses gladly ac-cept the U.S. dollar as currency for a fa-vorable approximation of the current exchange rate (usually 14-20 pesos/1 dollar). Those approaching the border

boutique lodgings at One Bunk

crossing on foot will find it surrounded by money exchanges and ATMs issuing pesos in paper currency in denominations of 20, 50, 100, 200, and 500. Coins are issued in 20-and-smaller denominations.

Poverty rates in Baja California exceed 40 percent, and many of its residents come to Tijuana seeking income. Tipping is a vital practice toward supporting Tijuana's service industry, usually 10-20 percent at restaurants, 10-15 pesos per drink at bars, and 25-50 pesos each morning for hotel housekeeping. Taxi drivers do not expect tips.

Haggling for consumer goods is alive and well in Tijuana; within many shops and markets, prices may be negotiable.

Drinking

The drinking age in Mexico is 18; beer, wine, and cider may be served to those 16 years and older. Speaking of drinking: the tap water in Tijuana is not entirely safe for outsiders to drink and can cause digestive distress. As a precaution, drink only bottled water and other packaged beverages and only from glasses with no ice.

Safety

Crime has historically been a concern in Tijuana, ranging from petty crimes to serious incidents. On the petty side, pickpockets and purse-snatchers prey on crowds, and street hustlers are very much a part of daily life around La Revu. The aggressive requests for tourist attention are usually harmless attempts to attract business, but some may be more persistent and nefarious. Take care not to wander farther north than Calle Primera, or you'll find yourself in Zona Norte, Tijuana's red-light district, where the aggressive offers turn to prostitution and drugs.

The city's more serious issues include high rates of sexual assault and kidnapping. The city also received a lot of attention in 2017 when its murder rate nearly

doubled. By far the majority of these killings involved members of local gangs and drug cartels and took place well outside the tourists zones referenced within this guide. However, entering Tijuana does carry the assumption of more personal risk when compared to San Diego.

To avoid potential trouble, follow these four rules: don't wander alone, don't flaunt any valuables, stick to well-lit public spaces in tourist-friendly areas, and take a taxi or car sharing service at night.

Finally, a history of corruption within the Tijuana police force has resulted in stories from tourists of being forced to bribe both real and fraudulent uniformed officers with cash and possessions to avoid arrest. While the city has made strides in mitigating this practice, it is recommended not to behave in a way that may attract negative attention from local police.

To contact police and emergency services while in Tijuana, dial 066.

Getting There

Tijuana sits about 20 miles (32 km) south of San Diego on the other side of the U.S. border with Mexico. You may enter Mexico by land or air, but either way, it requires a passport and baggage inspection. It does not, however, require a visa for citizens of the United States, Canada, and many other places. For detailed visa information visit https://consulmex.sre.gob.mx/sanfrancisco/index.php.

Crossing back from Tijuana into the United States often requires a more rigorous inspection and longer waits. It always requires a passport and any necessary visas for non-U.S. citizens.

The major crossing point for both cars and pedestrians is the **San Ysidro Port of Entry** (720 E. San Ysidro Blvd., 619/690-8900, www.cbp.gov, 24 hours daily), located at the southern terminus of both the I-5 and I-805 freeways. It's the busiest border crossing in the Western Hemisphere, and most of that is traffic entering the

United States: 25,000 pedestrians and 50,000 vehicles cross northbound each day—more than 2,000 per hour.

A less busy, alternate crossing point may be found 5.5 miles (9 km) to the east, at the **Otay Mesa Port of Entry** (9777 Via De La Amistad, 619/690-7696, www.cbp. gov, 24 hours daily), where CA-905 and CA-125 meet.

Individuals in possession of a valid **SENTRI Pass** (Secure Electronic Network for Travelers Rapid Inspection) may enter through special lanes that cross into the United States at a much faster rate. Several SENTRI-compatible Trusted Traveler programs are administered by **U.S. Customs and Border Protection** (ttp.cbp.dhs.gov), cost US$100-200 in fees, require an in-person interview, and take several weeks to obtain. All passengers in a car attempting to cross through a designated SENTRI lane must possess a SENTRI pass in order for the car to pass over the border. Pedestrians with SENTRI access may enter through designated Ready Lanes at on-foot crossing points.

Air

Tijuana International Airport (Carretera Aeropuerto, 52-664/607-8200, www. tijuana-airport.com) primarily offers flights to and from other destinations in Mexico and Central/South America. It's an easy taxi ride into downtown Tijuana, though the airport sits right on the U.S. border and recently opened Cross Border Xpress (www.crossborderxpress.com), a border crossing into the United States only available to those flying in or out of the airport.

Car

Due to the long wait times, the legal requirements of driving in Mexico, and the confusing nature of Tijuana roads, it is not recommended to drive into Tijuana unless you plan to continue south into the state of Baja. It's much cheaper and easier to get around in a taxi or car share.

That said, passing into Mexico by car takes only a few minutes most times of day at **San Ysidro Port of Entry**—the major exceptions being afternoon rush hours (particularly on Friday) and weekend mornings, when waits can be up to an hour. However, passing back into the United States by car can take up to 2.5 hours, with the worst times being mornings, evenings, and some weekend nights. The shortest wait times, often under 20 minutes, occur very late at night. A $740 million Port of Entry expansion pledges to significantly reduce wait times upon completion in 2019 or 2020, but early results indicate long lines may continue due to increased demand.

While somewhat shorter vehicle wait times are standard in both directions at the less busy **Otay Mesa Port of Entry,** the drive from central Tijuana typically adds 20 minutes or more.

Current estimated wait times at both locations may be checked via the phone line or website set up by **U.S. Customs and Border Protection** (619/690-8999, https://bwt.cbp.gov).

Every car entering Mexico is required to carry Mexico-specific car insurance, typically at a rate of US$25-30 per day, with lower rates for weekly or monthly premiums. Kiosks selling insurance may be found by following signs to take the last freeway exit before the international border: **Camino De La Plaza** at San Ysidro, **Siempre Viva Road** at Otay Mesa. Car insurance may also be purchased in advance through websites such as **Baja Bound** (619/702-4292, www.bajabound.com). Some U.S. rental car agencies allow cars to be driven into Mexico with additional insurance policies.

Drivers with a valid U.S. driver's license may drive in Mexico, in addition to anyone with an International Driving Permit, which may be acquired in the United States through the **American Automobile Association** (877/735-1714, www.aaa.com).

The Tijuana River sits between the border crossing of Tijuana's downtown areas of Zona Centro and Zona Río, and it wreaks havoc on the poorly planned city by weaving a maze of traffic circles, one-way streets that double back on themselves, and four-lane highways that abruptly fork in four different exit lanes. Consequently, at any moment, a car or pedestrian may suddenly veer into your lane or violate your right-of-way, and a wrong turn can get you lost in an instant.

Street parking may be available, but it's quite affordable and advisable to park in secured, paid lots. When visiting Avenida Revolución, you may find reliable paid lots on Zona Centro's 4th Street at the **Foreign Club Parking Structure** (Calle Salvador Díaz Mirón 4ta, half block west of Av. Revolución) and 8th Street at the **Hotel Ticuán** (Calle Miguel Hidalgo 8va, half block west of Av. Revolución).

On Foot
To enter Tijuana on foot, visitors have the option to drive to the border and park or take public transportation.

When driving to the border to cross on foot, it's imperative to follow the freeway signs to take the "Last U.S. Exit"— **Camino De La Plaza** at San Ysidro, **Siempre Viva Road** at Otay Mesa. Paid parking is available at several private lots surrounding each border crossing point, charging a flat rate of US$6-10 for 24 hours on weekdays and US$20-25 on Fridays and weekends.

The Blue Line of the **San Diego Trolley** (619/557-4455, www.sdmts.com, US$2.50 one-way) terminates with a station closer to the San Ysidro border crossing than any parking lot. The Blue Line (4am-midnight daily) departs from downtown every 15-30 minutes. The trolley regularly departs San Ysidro from 5am daily, with the last train of the night leaving at 12:58am.

Crossing the border into Tijuana on foot requires a fair amount of walking—expect 10 minutes to walk a little less than a half-mile, not counting time at customs. Wheelchairs may be provided for those requiring accessibility assistance.

The San Ysidro Port of Entry now features two pedestrian crossing points. To the east of the freeway is the original gateway, now called **PedEast** (720 East San Ysidro Blvd., 24 hours daily), which exits on the Tijuana side in front of **Plaza Viva Tijuana** (Avenida de la Amistad and Frontera). Pedestrians can access the path to the United States from the same location.

The crossing at **PedWest** (499 Virginia Ave., San Ysidro, 6am-10pm daily) sits west of the freeway, beside the Outlets at the Border mall. It exits to a pickup and drop-off location called **Garita El Chaparral** (471 José María Larroque). Pedestrians can access the path to the United States from the same location.

Getting Around
Most sights in Zona Centro are a 15- to 30-minute walk from the U.S. border, accessed via a pedestrian bridge over the Tijuana River and through **Plaza Viva Tijuana** (Avenida de la Amistad and Frontera). But first-time visitors may feel more comfortable hiring a car. Public transportation within Tijuana revolves around taxis and car shares. A taxi stand outside each border crossing serves as an active pickup and drop-off point.

The easiest car sharing app to use here is **Uber** (www.uber.com), which offers precise and affordable transportation with short trips within the city center typically costing US$1.75/MX$28. The Uber English option ensures your driver speaks English, but it may take longer to get a car. Consult your mobile carrier for cellular and data roaming packages within Mexico.

A more flexible cash option will be several types of taxi. The best bet is a taxi marked as **Taxi Libre**, driven by independent contractors. Negotiate a price up front to get to your destination, or request the driver use a meter. Either way, expect to pay US$3/MX$54 or less to reach destinations within the city center from the border. As a rule of thumb, don't expect taxi drivers to offer exact change. Tipping is rare, but up to you.

Another option will be **yellow taxis,** though these drivers often charge twice as much as a Taxi Libre and likewise receive commissions if they can steer you toward specific businesses that may not be on your agenda. If you must take a yellow (or off-color) taxi, definitely agree to a firm price for an explicit destination before you get in the car.

A third taxi option, **route taxis,** or *taxis de ruta* are vans that navigate the suburban lengths of the sprawling city on specific routes, much like buses, except you flag them down like taxis rather than wait at established stops. These can be useful to get you long distances—from the city center to Playas de Tijuana, for example—likely for less than US$1/MX$18. However, it can be confusing to understand the routes if you're not a local. This site (http://contactoruta664.wixsite.com/ruta664/mapa) offers the closest thing to a published map.

Anza-Borrego, Palm Springs & Joshua Tree

Anza-Borrego, Palm Springs & Joshua Tree

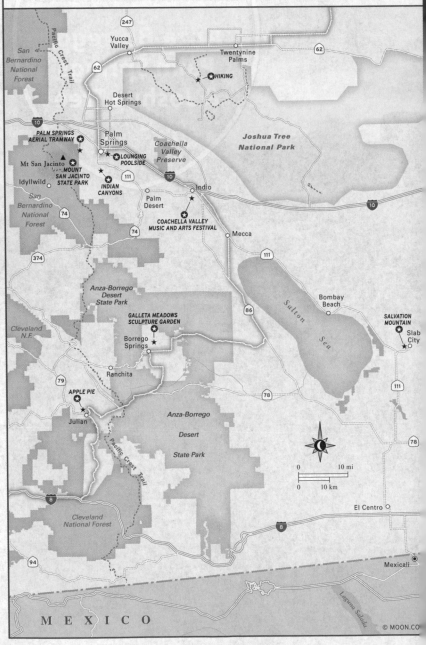

San Bernardino National Forest

Pacific Crest Trail

247

Yucca Valley

Twentynine Palms

62

62

HIKING

Desert Hot Springs

Joshua Tree National Park

10

PALM SPRINGS AERIAL TRAMWAY

Palm Springs

Coachella Valley Preserve

Mt San Jacinto

MOUNT SAN JACINTO STATE PARK

LOUNGING POOLSIDE

Idyllwild

111

10

Indio

San Bernardino National Forest

INDIAN CANYONS

Palm Desert

10

74

COACHELLA VALLEY MUSIC AND ARTS FESTIVAL

74

Mecca

374

111

Anza-Borrego Desert State Park

86

Salton Sea

Bombay Beach

Cleveland N.F.

GALLETA MEADOWS SCULPTURE GARDEN

SALVATION MOUNTAIN

Slab City

Borrego Springs

79

Ranchita

APPLE PIE

Julian

Pacific Crest Trail

Anza-Borrego

Desert

State Park

78

111

78

0   10 mi
0   10 km

8

Cleveland National Forest

El Centro

94

8

Mexicali

M E X I C O

Laguna Salada

© MOON.CO

Highlights

★ **Apple Pie in Julian:** This small, apple-growing town sprang up during a short-lived gold rush. Its old-timey downtown is filled with sweet thrills of the fruit and baked goods variety (page 165).

★ **Galleta Meadows Sculpture Garden:** Giant metal sculptures of various animals are spread across the desert valley floor in this whimsical sculpture garden (page 167).

★ **Salvation Mountain:** Outsider art doesn't get more outside than this painted mountain located on the outskirts of the Salton Sea (page 175).

★ **Palm Springs Aerial Tramway:** This dizzying feat of engineering whisks you nearly 6,000 feet from the desert floor to the San Jacinto Mountains (page 178).

★ **Lounging Poolside:** Choose between lively party scenes and quiet oases—poolside is the place to be (page 183).

★ **Coachella Valley Music and Arts Festival:** This annual music festival draws big names and huge numbers of people to the desert valley south of Palm Springs (page 187).

★ **Indian Canyons:** Hike through the world's largest fan palm oasis and explore miles of hiking trails through sacred land, scenic streams, and dramatic canyons (page 189).

★ **Mount San Jacinto State Park:** Escape the heat of the desert at this 14,000-acre state park in the San Jacinto Mountains (page 199).

★ **Hiking in Joshua Tree National Park:** Giant boulders, cholla cacti, and the park's namesake trees deliver the best elements of desert hiking (page 216).

There's no better road-trip destination than the desert. The open road doesn't get more open than this, with clear-blue skies hovering above a stark, surreal landscape.

An easy day trip east of San Diego, Anza-Borrego State Park beckons travelers to the low desert to enjoy its myriad hiking trails, world-class stargazing, and a spring "superbloom" that carpets the desert floor with colorful wildflowers. East of Anza-Borrego lies the Salton Sea, a remote region that's home to societal outliers, international artists, and a surreal landscape with an abandoned history.

As the highway shoots straight north, you'll swap geographic remoteness for desert luxury in the town of Palm Springs, which preserves impeccable mid-century architecture in a charming time capsule. Stay in a retro boutique hotel, lounge by a gleaming pool, shop the design district, and live like you're on permanent vacation in this timeless hot spot.

An hour's drive from Palm Springs, the stunning alien landscape of Joshua Tree both startles and charms. Powerful geologic forces have whipped the rocks here into twisted shapes and scrambled boulder piles. Among the eroded chaos, spiky Joshua trees reach out in unpredictable angles, forming jagged, moody backdrops against dusty desert roads. This is the high desert: gorgeous in spring and fall, brutal in summer, and dusted by snow in winter.

Getting There

Julian and Anza-Borrego are easily accessed from San Diego, while Palm Springs and Joshua Tree are best reached from Los Angeles.

From Los Angeles
125-150 mi/201-241 km, 3-4 hr
Palm Springs is an easy drive from Los Angeles. From L.A., take I-10 east for about 110 miles (177 km). Exit at North Indian Canyon Drive (Exit 120) and drive south for 5 miles (8 km) to downtown Palm Springs. In good conditions, the drive can take two hours.

To reach **Joshua Tree** instead, turn north onto CA-62 East about 4 miles (6 km) before Palm Springs. Drive 37 miles (60 km) northeast on CA-62 to Joshua Tree. Expect this route to take about 2.5 hours.

Avoid driving this route during rush hour (3pm-6pm) on weekday afternoons, especially on Friday. Alternately, portions of Historic Route 66 run closely parallel along I-210 east from Pasadena to San Bernardino.

From San Diego
60-170 mi/97-274 km, 1.5-3.5 hr
The Anza-Borrego Desert lies 100 miles (161 km) east of the city of San Diego. The mountain town of Julian is not only an easy day trip from San Diego, but offers a quick gateway into this desert park.

From San Diego, I-8 heads east for 65 miles (105 km) into the Cuyamaca Mountains. In 32 miles (51 km), past the town of Alpine, turn north onto Highway 79 and drive 24 miles (39 km) to the town of **Julian.** From Julian, Highway 78 continues north into Anza-Borrego Desert State Park. To reach the town of **Borrego Springs** in the heart of the park, turn north on S-3 (appears in about 18 miles) and drive 7 miles (11 km) to turn left on Borrego Springs Road.

To reach **Palm Springs** from San Diego, follow I-15 north for 61 miles (98 km) to I-215. Veer north on I-215 and drive 29.5 miles (47.5 km) to Highway 60. Head east on Highway 60 for 18.3 miles (29.5 km), where the road merges with I-10.

Drive east on I-10 for 18.2 miles (29 km) and take Highway 111 south to exit into downtown Palm Springs.

Air, Train, or Bus

The small **Palm Springs International Airport** (3400 E. Tahquitz Canyon Way, 760/318-3800, www.palmspringsca. gov) services 14 major American cities and five in Canada. The closest airport from the Los Angeles region is the Inland Empire hub **Ontario International Airport** (N. Archibald Ave. and E. Airport Dr., 909/544-5300, www.flyontario. com), roughly 67 miles (108 km) west of Palm Springs on I-10. Both **Los Angeles International Airport** (LAX, 1 World Way, Los Angeles, 855/463-5252, www. flylax.com) and **Hollywood Burbank Airport** (BUR, 2627 N. Hollywood Way, Burbank, 818/840-8840, https:// hollywoodburbankairport.com) are also within easy driving distance.

The *Sunset Limited* route on **Amtrak** (800-872-7245, www.amtrak.com) travels from Los Angeles to Palm Springs Station (North Indian Canyon Dr. and Palm Springs Station Rd.).

While bus service from the San Diego area is offered on lines 891 and 892 from the **El Cajon Transit Center** (352 S. Marshall Ave., 619/233-3004, www. sdcommute.com), eastbound routes of each line are limited to Thursday and Friday. The trip takes about three hours.

Julian

This little mountain town sprang up after former slave Fred Coleman discovered gold in a creek running through nearby Santa Ysabel. The ensuing gold rush didn't last long, but by the time it faded, Julian was established and its apple trees were producing award-winning fruit. While a small strip of Main Street still has the facade of a mining town, the only gold it produces is its apple cider. Additionally, Julian apple pie is coveted

countywide as a regional favorite. You can get it at lower altitudes, but it's less fresh and not as fun to eat.

Getting There

Julian is located in a mountainous region about 60 miles (97 km) northeast of San Diego. From San Diego, take I-8 east for about 25 miles (40 km), then head north on Highway 79 for 25 miles (40 km) into Julian. Plan about 1.5 hours for the drive.

Sights
California Wolf Center

With a mission to preserve the presence of wolves in California, the **California Wolf Center** (470 K Q Ranch Rd., 760/765-0030, www.californiawolfcenter. org, tours 10am Mon., 2pm Fri., 10am and 2pm Sat.-Sun. Mar.-Oct. and 9am Mon., 1pm Fri., 9am and 1pm Sat.-Sun. Nov.-Feb., $20-50 adults and children over 4) provides a home to several packs of gray wolves, including animals from Alaska and Mexico. Three levels of scheduled tours include educational presentations and guided observations of two wolf packs. Reservations are required.

Eagle Mining Company

Offering a glimpse into Julian's gold rush past, the **Eagle Mining Company** (2320 C St., 760/580-7434, www.theeaglemining. com, 10am-4pm Mon.-Fri., 10am-5pm Sat. Sun., $10 adults, $5 ages 5-13, $1 under age 5) offers tours 1,000 feet into the mile-deep mine, as well as gold-panning activities and insights into milling operations. Located close to the center of town, it provides a fun and educational couple of hours' worth of activities.

Julian Mining Company

Julian Mining Company (4444 CA-78, 951/313-0166, www. julianminingcompany.com, 10am-5pm Sat., noon-5pm Sun., $9 adults, $7 under 12) offers gold-panning activities in the community of Wynola.

Best Restaurants

★ **Red Ocotillo, Borrego Springs:** The local favorite for breakfast in Borrego Springs is the best way to fuel up for a day of desert exploration (page 171).

★ **Ski Inn, Bombay Beach:** The sole survivor of a dying resort town, this is the favorite gathering spot for the eccentrics living in post-apocalyptic Bombay Beach (page 177).

★ **Cheeky's, Palm Springs:** The city's top breakfast spot has a line the minute it opens—it must be the five different kinds of bacon (page 193).

★ **Shanghai Red's Bar & Grill, Palm Springs:** This favorite of the late Anthony Bourdain serves the best fish tacos in the desert (page 194).

★ **Pappy & Harriet's Pioneertown Palace, Pioneertown:** The food is almost as good at the nightly entertainment at this Wild West cantina plucked from a movie set (page 233).

★ **Joshua Tree Saloon, Joshua Tree:** A gathering point for both visitors and locals, this is the spot to grab a beer and a burger and swap the day's best hiking tales (page 235).

Julian Pioneer Cemetery

Dating to the 1870s and still in use, the **Julian Pioneer Cemetery** (Farmer Rd. at A St., 760/765-0436, www.juliancemetery. org) holds the final resting places of multiple generations of Julian natives. Perched on a hill at the north end of Main Street, the cemetery provides a beautiful if solemn vantage point to look out over Julian and the surrounding area.

Julian Pioneer Museum

The history of Julian is on display at the **Julian Pioneer Museum** (2811 Washington St., 760/765-0227, www. julianpioneermuseum.org, 10am-4pm Thurs.-Sun., $3 adults, free under age 7), mostly in the form of 19th-century clothes, furniture, and mining equipment. You'll also find early photos of the people and town, as well as a horse buggy and information about the original Native American inhabitants of the area.

Santa Ysabel Mission

Technically an *asistencia*, this submission was built in 1818 to serve those who could not regularly make it to the Mission Basilica San Diego de Alcalá. About 8 miles (13 km) northwest of Julian, **Santa Ysabel Mission** (23013 Hwy. 79, Santa Ysabel, 760/765-0810, www. missiontour.org, 8am-4pm daily Labor Day to Memorial Day, 8am-5:30pm summer) actually had a greater conversion rate among the Diegueño and Luiseño people. The original mission structure is long gone, with a more modern white-brick chapel built on the site in 1924 and a small museum revealing insights into the *asistencia*'s long history.

Food

The **Julian Café & Bakery** (2112 Main St., 760/765-2712, www.juliancafe.com, 8am-7:30pm Mon.-Thurs., 8am-8:30pm Fri., 7am-9pm Sat., 7am-8:30pm Sun., $10-15) was built in 1882 but burned down in 1957. Nevertheless, this rebuilt structure from 1978 tries to capture that old-time spirit, complete with an extensive breakfast menu and apple pies. Just up the street, the **Miner's Diner** (2134 Main St., 760/765-3753, www.minersdinerjulian.

Best Accommodations

★ **Julian Gold Rush Hotel:** This hotel has been in continuous operation since 1897 (page166).

★ **La Casa Del Zorro, Borrego Springs:** Turn a visit to the Anza-Borrego desert into a comfortable getaway stay at this area-best resort (page 172).

★ **Orbit In, Palm Springs:** This modest, boutique hotel overachieves with a sense of style, community, and funky one-of-a-kind rooms (page 196).

★ **Del Marcos Hotel, Palm Springs:** Splurge with a stay at this 1947 classic designed by William Cody (page 197).

★ **Korakia Pensione, Palm Springs:** A stay at this picturesque oasis of a resort feels like being in the remote desert—without losing sight of urban comfort (page 197).

★ **Idyllwild Bunkhouse, Idyllwild:** This rustic mountain lodge feels like you're at a summer camp for grown-ups (page 206).

★ **Jumbo Rocks, Joshua Tree National Park:** Pitch a tent amid this park's famous boulders at this centrally located campground (page 229).

com, 10am-5pm Tues.-Thurs., 8am-6pm Fri.-Sat., 8am-5pm Sun.-Mon., $8-15) has a 1950s look and feel, with burgers and malts, good coffee, and, of course, apple pies.

Satisfy your sweet tooth with a visit to the **Julian Cider Mill** (2103 Main St., 760/765-1430, www.juliancidermillinc. com, 9:30am-5pm Mon.-Thurs., 9:30am-5:30pm Fri.-Sun.). The shop serves delicious soft cider as well as preserves and candy. It's pretty much a sweet tooth's idea of heaven.

For pizza, barbecue, and beer, head to ★ **Julian Beer Co.** (2307 Main St., 760/765-3757, www.julianbeercompany. com, 11am-9pm Sun.-Fri., 11am-11pm Sat., $12-24), a rustic little restaurant and brewery offering live music on weekends. For beer alone, head to **Nickel Beer Co.** (1485 Hollow Glen Rd., 760/765-2337, www.nickelbeerco.com, 2pm-7:30pm Mon.-Thurs., 11:30am-8:30pm Fri., 11am-8:30pm Sat., 11am-7:30pm Sun.), where Tom Nickel, one of the original brewers who put San Diego on the craft beer map, makes beer in a

small house with a big patio loaded with fresh air.

While apples put Julian on the map these days, in truth most products don't feature local fruit, not even the pies! The exception is **Julian Ciderworks** (17552 Harrison Park Rd., 760/331-7453, www. julianciderworks.com, 2:30pm-6pm Thurs.-Fri., noon-6pm Sat.-Sun.), a cidery and tasting room housed inside a barn, which offers single-origin ciders made exclusively from dozens of apple varietals grown in local orchards.

★ Apple Pie

The favorable agricultural conditions that first brought people like Coleman to Julian were also ideal for growing apples. East Coast native James Madison planted some apple trees in the early 1870s, and by the early 20th century, large and firm Julian apples were winning blue ribbons at world's fairs around the country. Today, Julian apple pies and ciders are standout regional treats, and apple picking is a popular late-summer activity.

The Julian Gold Rush

While herding cattle back in 1869, Santa Ysabel rancher A. E. Frederick Coleman stopped to water his horse and recognized a glint of gold in the creek bed. Formerly enslaved in Kentucky, Coleman had joined the Northern California gold rush before settling in the rural outskirts of San Diego, where the majority of the county's black population lived at the time. The agricultural potential of the area held greater opportunity than the minority population found in central San Diego, which was just starting to move out of Old Town.

Coleman's discovery brought a new kind of opportunity to the African Americans in the community: business ownership in a new town. He immediately formed a mining company; when word got out, the boom was on, attracting prospectors and opportunists from around the country. Coleman City sprang up around his claim but dissipated once the source of the gold was discovered farther east. Ironically, it was a pair of former Confederate soldiers who lent their name to Julian. The Julian brothers came west from Georgia to follow the expansion of the railroad to San Diego. Beating the track builders to California, their party came across the **gold rush** and began mining. Within a few years, the population grew from nearly nonexistent to more than 600 people, with hotels, restaurants, stores, liveries, and saloons opening around a newly formed Main Street. The Hotel Robinson, opened in 1887 by another formerly enslaved person, Albert Robinson, and his wife, Margaret, remains open today as the **Julian Gold Rush Hotel,** the oldest continuously operating hotel in Southern California, older than Hotel del Coronado by about a year.

Like Coleman City, most gold towns turned to ghost towns once the gold ran out. However, Julian endured for a couple of reasons: the sense of community that arose during the 20-30 years of the gold boom and the tightly knit bunch of men and women who'd met, married, and begun raising families. Even without the gold, they wanted to stay.

To try some famous Julian pie, choose between the **Julian Pie Company** (2225 Main St., 760/765-2449, www.julianpie.com, 9am-5pm daily, $8-21) or **Mom's Pie House** (2119 Main St., 760/765-2472, www.momspiesjulian.com, 7am-5pm Mon.-Thurs., 7am-5:30pm Fri.-Sun., $6-18). Both offer traditional apple pies plus variations featuring local berries, including strawberry and boysenberry. If you're struggling to decide, get a slice from one and a whole pie to go from the other. The **Julian Apple Days Festival** (www.julianmerchants.org, early Oct.) celebrates the annual harvest that has kept Julian a happy little mountain town for nearly 150 years.

Apple (and pear picking) late summer-early fall can be a fun way to occupy your time in Julian. There are more than 100 years of history behind **Peacefield Boutique Orchard** (3803 Wynola Rd.,

855/936-2775, 10:30am-noon Sat., $20 adult, $10 children under 4). Pears have made a strong showing in recent years, and they can be picked at **O'Dell's Pear Orchard** (1095 Julian Orchard Dr., 760/765-1174, 10:30am-4pm Sat.-Sun., $10 per bag). If you prefer organic produce, pick the apples and pears at **Apple Starr Orchards** (1020 Julian Orchard Dr., 760/305-2169, www.apple-starr.com, 10am-5pm Sat.-Sun., $25 per bag). Seasonal harvests vary annually but typically begin in late August. Picking opportunities tend to be on weekends only, though orchards may accept weekday appointments on a case-by-case basis.

Accommodations
An overnight stay in Julian doesn't get more central than the ★ **Julian Gold Rush Hotel** (2032 Main St., 760/765-0201, www.julianhotel.com, from $95).

The "oldest continuously operated hotel in Southern California" appears in the National Register of Historic Places, though it has been upgraded since 1897 to include amenities like air-conditioning and Wi-Fi. Only slightly less central is the more modern and dog-friendly **Julian Lodge** (2720 C St., 760/765-1420, www.julianlodge.com, from $99), just a block off Main Street.

The highest-rated stay in Julian can be found at **Orchard Hill Country Inn** (2502 Washington St., 760/765-1700, www.orchardhill.com, from $215). Just uphill from the center of town, the lodge rooms and cottages of this Four Diamond property are country hospitable, right down to the patchwork quilts.

A few miles outside of town in a quiet, natural setting, the **Observer's Inn** (3535 Hwy. 79, 760/765-0088, www.observersinn.com, from $150) boasts a comfortable stay with a bonus: astronomy. The B&B offers "Sky Tours," setting up telescopes for guests to stargaze at the dark night sky. **Wikiup Bed & Breakfast** (1645 Whispering Pines Dr., 800/694-5487, www.wikiupbnb.com, two-night min. from $115/night) doesn't show you the stars, but if you prefer a hot tub, massage, and carriage rides, this comfortable woodsy lodge might be for you.

Anza-Borrego Desert State Park

The tiny town of Borrego Springs isn't much of a destination on its own. However, it provides access to the ethereal beauty of **Anza-Borrego Desert State Park** (www.parks.ca.gov), which attracts a fair number of nature-loving global visitors each year. Hiking trails pass through canyons en route to pictographs, rock formations, or sweeping views of the desert. At night, the Dark Sky park offers world-class stargazing with a stellar opportunity to view meteor showers. But its biggest draw is the

desert flower bloom—dubbed a "super-bloom"—that carpets the valley floor each spring.

Many hikers look for the bighorn sheep that give the town its name, but its most intriguing animals are made of metal. Scores of life-size animal sculptures are spread out across the desert plain known as Galleta Meadows; it can take a full day of scavenger hunting to view them all.

October-April is the best time to visit, particularly during the spring bloom. The rest of the year, the Anza-Borrego desert gets extremely hot with temperatures exceeding 100°F; carry lots of water (2 liters per person) and wear sun protection. Summer monsoons can make the desert washes prone to flash floods and this is a potentially dangerous time to explore.

Borrego Springs sits at about 600 feet above sea level, while the mountainous portions of Anza-Borrego Desert State Park reach elevations of 4,000 feet. You may experience climate shifts with the elevation, and temperatures fluctuate greatly from day to night.

Getting There
Borrego Springs is located east of San Diego. From San Diego, take I-8 east for about 25 miles (40 km), then head north on Highway 79 for 25 miles (40 km) to the town of Julian. From Julian, take Highway 78 east for 31 miles (50 km). Plan two hours for the trip.

Sights
A gallery at the **Borrego Art Institute** (665 Palm Canyon Dr., 760/767-5152, www.borregoartinstitute.org, 11am-4pm Tues.-Sun.) brings in rotating shows, mostly of desert artists, and features everything from pottery to paintings and photography.

★ Galleta Meadows
Mexican-born artist Ricardo Breceda created his first metal sculpture in 2001,

Anza-Borrego Desert State Park

Anza-Borrego Desert State Park

Salton Sea

Santa Rosa Mountains

Clark Lake

Galleta Meadows Sculpture Garden

Borrego Palm Canyon

Panoramic Overlook

Anza-Borrego State Park Visitors Center

Borrego Springs

Borrego Springs Airport

Borrego Springs Resort

Fonts Point

Borrego Badlands

Warner Springs

Ranchita

Grapevine Trail

Grapevine Cyn

Grapevine Mountain

Yaqui Pass

Yaqui Well

Apple Pie

Julian

Volcan Mountains

Coyote Canyon

Pacific Crest Trail

Ocotillo Wells State Vehicular Recreation Area

Ocotillo Wells

Split Mountain Rd

Vallecito Mountains

Wind Caves

Split Mountain

Blair Valley

Pictographs

Marshall South Home

Agua Caliente Airstrip

Lake Cuyamaca

Vallecito Regional Park

Agua Caliente County Park

Pine Valley

Laguna Mountains

Pacific Crest Trail

Cleveland National Forest

Lake Morena

Barrett Lake

Lake Moreno County Park

Tierra Blanca Mtns

Anza-Borrego Desert State Park

Imperial Hwy

Ocotillo

Jacumba Mountains

MEXICO

© MOON.COM

5 mi

5 km

Borrego Valley Rd

Yaqui Pass Rd

trading a pair of cowboy boots for welding equipment so he could build a 20-foot *Tyrannosaurus rex* for his young, dinosaur-obsessed daughter. Since then, he has become a madly prolific sculptor; in Borrego Springs alone more than 130 of his realistic works are scattered across the hundreds of acres of **Galleta Meadows** (Borrego Springs Rd. and Big Horn Rd., www.abdnha.org), making it one of the world's largest sculpture gardens. The collection of life-size animals and fantasy beasts was commissioned by the owner of this vast property. The sculptures are spread across several miles; plan to drive between sites. Some of the rust-colored pieces are easy to spot from the road, but many are not. Pick up a map of the meadows at the **Anza-Borrego Desert Natural History Association Desert Nature Center & Store** (652 Palm Canyon Dr., 760/767-3098, www.abdnha.org, 9am-5pm daily, $8.95).

Highlights include a mesmerizing **sea dragon** (Borrego Springs Rd., north of Big Horn Rd.) that appears to swim across the road, a **scorpion** (Big Horn Rd., east of Borrego Springs Rd.), and a family of **elephants** (Borrego Springs Rd. at Anzio Dr.).

Breceda continues to work 32 miles (52 km) northwest of Borrego Springs. You may find more pieces large and small for sale at **Ricardo Breceda Gallery** (44450 CA-79, Aguanga, 951/236-5896, www.ricardobreceda.com, 9am-5pm daily). The artist suggests bringing a lunch, and your dog, and hanging out for a while.

Stargazing

Anza-Borrego State Park is designated an International Dark Sky Park, and the town of Borrego Springs is an

Top to bottom: Julian Pie Company; dragon sculpture at Galleta Meadows; Anza-Borrego.

International Dark Sky Community. On a clear night, the stargazing is among the world's best.

Stargazing opportunities are best during the new moon, when the **Anza-Borrego Desert State Park Visitors Center** (200 Palm Canyon Dr., 760/767-4205, 9am-5pm daily Oct.-May, daily 9am-5pm Sat.-Sun. June-Sept.) hosts stargazing activities on the roof of its building, with limited telescopes and binoculars to share. Feel free to bring your own, or view with the naked eye. You don't need an organized event to stargaze—just somewhere to sit and some patience. Allow 30 minutes for your eyes to adjust to the darkness; when they do, you won't just see stars but nebulae and galaxies. Use a dim red light as needed, rather than a flashlight. Dress warmly for the cool desert evening. A camera with a tripod and a long shutter speed can preserve the worthwhile moment.

Hiking

Desert hiking proves the top activity in the park, with a mix of easy valley and canyon hikes, plus others that climb higher into high desert. For an easy start, head to the **Anza-Borrego Desert State Park Visitors Center** (200 Palm Canyon Dr.) for its all-access trails. A paved path heads north 0.7 mile to the Palm Canyon Campground, with signs highlighting local flora and fauna as you go. To the right of the visitors center, a 0.3-mile loop on compacted dirt offers an opportunity to see the rare desert pupfish, which can survive in extreme temperatures and high salinity.

At the west end of the Borrego Palm Canyon Campground (200 Palm Canyon Dr.), the hike into **Borrego Palm Canyon** (3 mi/5 km, 2 hours) is the park's most popular. The canyon follows a stream 600 feet into a desert oasis; you may spot *borregos* (bighorn sheep) along the way. Turn back at the 1.5-mile mark, or opt for a rigorous climb to the top of Indian Head (6-8 hours round-trip). The route passes a waterfall to capture an expansive view of the desert valley.

A family-friendly loop delivers a valley view from the **Kenyon Overlook** (1.2 mi/1.9 km round-trip, 1 hour, easy) and takes about an hour. The trailhead is 1.9 miles (3 k) north of CA-78 on Yaqui Pass Road (60 yards from mile marker 2).

The more involved hike to **Hellhole Canyon and Maidenhair Falls** (6 mi/10 km round-trip, 4 hours, moderate) is a relatively pleasant 1,000-foot climb to the 18-foot cascade of Maidenhair Falls. The trailhead is 0.8 mile south of Palm Canyon Drive on Montezuma Borrego Highway.

The region's oldest artwork is at Little Blair Valley, in the southern portion of the park. The **Pictograph Trail** (1.6 mi/2.6 km round-trip, 1 hour, easy) leads through Smuggler Canyon to a massive boulder decorated with red and yellow pictographs originally painted by indigenous Kumeyaay artists hundreds of years ago. (The images have since been re-painted.) The trailhead is 15 miles (24 km) south of Borrego Springs. From County Road S-2, drive 2.7 miles (4.3 km) southeast on Little Blair Canyon Road. Turn left at the fork and drive 2.4 miles (3.9 km) to the trailhead.

If your vehicle has a high-clearance and four-wheel drive, head southeast to **Wind Caves and Split Mountain** (2 mi/3 km, 1 hour, easy). The scenic road follows a sandy dry streambed into Split Mountain Gorge, where canyon walls rise hundreds of feet on either side. The road leads past an arch formation before reaching the Wind Cave trailhead. A hike takes you to surreal sandstone formations that have been carved by wind into smooth domes of rock punctuated by shallow caves and arches. If your car can't handle the terrain, park at **Fish Creek Primitive Campground** (1.4 mi west of Split Canyon Rd.) and proceed through the gorge on foot. This will add an extra 5.5 miles round-trip (2 hours) to the hike. To reach Split Mountain

Wild for Wildflowers

the superbloom at Palm Canyon

TOP EXPERIENCE

The annual spring bloom adds color to the desert floor of the 640,000 acres of **Anza-Borrego Desert State Park** (200 Palm Canyon Dr., 760/767-4205, www.parks.ca.gov). The timing, length, and size of the bloom depends on how much or little rain the area receives in the winter—typically between late February and April. You can find updates on the park's website or that of the **Anza-Borrego Foundation** (http://theabf.org).

Plan your visit around the **Anza-Borrego Desert State Park Visitors Center** (200 Palm Canyon Dr.), which offers parking and more detailed information about hiking, safety, and the red, purple, yellow, orange, white, and pink flowers around the park. Visit early during bloom season—not only do people fill the park after 10am, but lower morning temperatures prompt greater floral activity.

from CA-78, drive 8 miles (13 km) south on Split Mountain Road; turn right and drive 4.2 miles.

Food

There aren't many dining options in Borrego Springs. The local favorite for breakfast is ★ **Red Ocotillo** (721 Avenida Sureste, 760/767-7400, 7am-8:30pm daily, $8-16), a casual restaurant that serves traditional egg dishes, cinnamon French toast, pancakes, and dishes featuring produce from its small farm out back.

For the area's best Mexican food, look in The Mall on the south side of Palm Canyon Drive for **Carmelita's Mexican Grill** (575 Palm Canyon Dr., 760/767-5666, 10am-9pm daily, $9-23). The menu includes burritos, burgers, and moles, but if you're looking for a place to start try the shredded beef enchiladas.

At the Borrego Art Institute, **Kesling's Kitchen** (665 Palm Canyon Dr., 760/767-7600, www.borregoartinstitute.org, 11am-9pm Mon.-Fri., 8:30am-9pm Sat.-Sun., $13-17) offers from-scratch Mediterranean food, but is best known for its wood-fired pizzas. Across the street, **Carlee's Place** (660 Palm Canyon Dr., 760/767-3262, www.carleesplace.com, 11am-10pm Sun.-Thurs., 11am-midnight Fri.-Sat., $8-18) serves burgers, grinders, steaks, and pizza in a dive-bar atmosphere.

The Old West-style saloon at the **Big Horn Bar & Grill** (Palm Canyon Hotel, 221 Palm Canyon Dr., 676/767-5341, www. palmcanyonrvresort.com, noon-9pm daily Oct.-June, $10-20) serves a small menu of burgers and hot sandwiches, as well as craft beer. The country-style dining patio offers gorgeous views of the surrounding landscape. One caveat: It's closed in summer.

Accommodations

Lovingly restored mid-century architecture awaits at **The Palms at Indian Head** (2220 Hoberg Rd., 760/767-7788, www. thepalmsatindianhead.com, from $164), which claims Marilyn Monroe, Bing Crosby, and Cary Grant as guests during its original heyday. Today the visually sumptuous lobby and pool area continue to enjoy proximity to the desert park, though access by an unpaved road makes an adventure of it.

Mid-century meets the Wild West at the charming **Palm Canyon Hotel & RV Resort** (221 Palm Canyon Dr., 760/767-5341, www.palmcanyonrvresort. com, from $60), where you can rent a Southwestern-style room or a vintage Airstream trailer.

Stylish and comfortable rooms aren't the only draw to ★ **La Casa Del Zorro** (3845 Yaqui Pass Rd., 760/767-0100, www.lacasadelzorro.com, from $212); the resort offers large pools, tennis courts, a fitness center, yoga studio, spa services, and restaurant.

A PGA-sanctioned 18-hole golf course is the chief draw to **Borrego Springs Resort** (1112 Tilting T Dr., 760/767-5700, www.borregospringsresort.com, from $185), which also offers guest rooms, a restaurant, poolside cabanas, bicycles, free shuttles, tennis, and spa services.

A true desert resort, the adobe **Borrego Valley Inn** (405 Palm Canyon Dr., 760/767-0311, www.highwaywestvacations.com, from $269) offers perks such as in-room fireplaces or Jacuzzis on a property that perfectly matches the lure of the desert park.

For those looking to rough it, the **Borrego Palm Canyon Campground** (200 Palm Canyon Dr., 760/767-4238, www. reservecalifornia.com, Oct.-Apr., $20-25 tents, $35 RVs) is near the entrance to the park and offers more than 100 sites. Reservations are recommended during the spring bloom.

Information and Services

The **Anza-Borrego Desert State Park Visitors Center** (200 Palm Canyon Dr., 760/767/4205, 9am-5pm daily Oct.-May, Sat.-Sun. June-Sept., $10 day use) sells gift items, maps, and books, and has interactive exhibits. Vehicle trailhead access is updated and posted here; ask park rangers for trail updates and closures.

◆ Side Trip: The Salton Sea

Little-known fact: California's largest lake sits at the bottom of one of its driest deserts. The result of an irrigation mishap, the Salton Sea is more than twice the surface area of Lake Tahoe and for a brief time stood as the state's greatest sportfishing destination. What used to be a lively resort area championed by Frank Sinatra, Sonny Bono, and The Beach Boys has been mostly abandoned and left to the elements. A visit here feels as though the world ended in the 1960s; what remains is surreal, photogenic, and surprisingly artistic.

When the tourists stopped coming, the Salton Sea's eastern shore fell to ruin, leaving behind dilapidated shops, gas stations, and homes. The lake's surface sits more than 200 feet below sea level, the lowest point of the Sonoran Desert. In winter, abrasive winds blow across the lake and desert; in summer, temperatures regularly exceed 100°F. Adding to its many environmental scourges, dead birds and fish periodically appear en

The Rise and Fall of the Salton Sea

The history of the Salton Sea doesn't offer a flattering depiction of humankind's efforts to harness nature. The saline lake formed in 1905, when the Colorado River burst the seams of a poorly constructed irrigation channel and spent two years flooding the Colorado Desert. All that water settled to the desert valley's lowest point, the Salton Sink, otherwise known as the southern terminus of the San Andreas Fault.

the Salton Sea

By the time engineers repaired the river breach, the Salton Sea covered 370 square miles, making it California's largest inland body of water by surface area. Even as developers began building up the desert oasis Palm Springs northwest, they had their eyes on making the most out of the accidental desert sea. California's Department of Wildlife undertook a 30-year effort to stock the salty lake with large ocean fish, and finally, in the 1950s, the fast-growing orangemouth corvina started to thrive. The corvina population quickly expanded to three million, with fish up to 30 pounds. The lake became a sportfisher's dream, with angler's catching fish at a rate of almost two per hour. Resort towns such as Bombay Beach flourished in the 1960s and '70s, attracting entertainers and road-trippers. Seabirds even caught wind of the fruitful basin and adjusted their migratory patterns to nab easy fish here.

However, the low-lying lake has no outlet; the only way water can escape is to evaporate, leaving salt behind. While agricultural runoff has kept lake levels relatively stable, it's brought salt, fertilizers, and pesticides with it. In its heyday, the Salton Sea had roughly the same salinity as ocean water: around 38 parts per thousand. By 2018, that number measured over 60. Since the 21st century, the 35 species of fish that once thrived here have died off, millions at a time. The fertilizers and pesticides have contributed to additional fish kills and massive bird die-offs; their skeletons litter Salton Sea beaches. The ecological imbalances create foul, sulfuric gas compounds—you can smell the Salton Sea before you see it.

With the fish and birds gone, Salton Sea might have continued without further disaster, as a brackish lake with brown and sometimes orange water splashing on its shores. But a 2018 U.S. Supreme Court decision reapportioned the waters of the Colorado River, which means the agricultural runoff sustaining the lake's water levels will be reduced 40 percent over the next 15 years. The sea is shrinking. It's down to 360 square miles and dropping.

That in itself is nothing new. However, all of the farm pollution feeding the case of Salton Sea over the years has settled into the lake bottom, and as 140 square miles of it dries out, these toxins will be released into the air. Unless action is taken soon, the Salton Sea has at least one more environmental disaster left. Best go see what's left of it while you can.

masse on the shores and agricultural run-off sometimes causes sulfuric gas to belch from the lake bottom, filling the air with a rotten stench.

But for the adventurous road-tripper, it's a must-see example of what can go right in the world, once everything's gone wrong. The good days still outnumber the bad and a handful of people still live here, mostly hardy retirees and RV lifers who come seeking cheap real estate and mild winters. The remoteness of the region has also attracted societal outliers: a disparate set lives off the grid in the ad hoc squatters encampment known as Slab City, about 8 miles (13 km) east of Salton Sea's southeast shore. There's the site of East Jesus, an outdoor art museum that displays outsider art. The regionally famous Salvation Mountain remains a religious devotional in the form of a huge, painted rock formation. Meanwhile, the crumbling resort town Bombay Beach attracts a loose collective of international artists, who have converted many of the ruined homes into permanent galleries with edgy art installations.

Getting There
The Salton Sea works best as a day trip from Borrego Springs or Palm Springs. There are few services or amenities in this harsh environment; fill the gas tank and pack food and water prior to the long drive out here.

From San Diego
160 mi/257 km, 3 hrs
The most direct route from San Diego passes through Julian and Borrego Springs. From San Diego, take I-8 east for 37 miles (60 km) to Highway 79 north and drive 22 miles (35 km) to Julian. From Julian, follow CA-78 east for 18.5 miles (30 km), then another 56 miles (90 km) to meet CA-111 at Brawley. From Brawley, it's 16.6 miles (26.5 km) north to Niland. North of Niland, CA-111 runs along the Salton Sea's eastern shore:

it's 17.5 miles (28 km) north to Bombay Beach and 33 miles to the North Shore campground.

From Palm Springs
64 mi/103 km, 1.5 hr
The Salton Sea is 65 miles (105 km) southeast of Palm Springs. To reach the tiny town of Bombay Beach, take I-10 east for about 35 miles (56 km) to CA-111 South. Continue south on CA-111 following the eastern shore of Salton Sea for 18 miles (29 km) to Niland. In Niland, head east for 4 miles (6 km) on Beal Road to reach Slab City.

Sights
Bombay Beach
Once a 1960s fishing resort, **Bombay Beach** (Hwy. 111, 18 mi/29 km north of Niland) has undergone intense transformations since. (A visit today shows why it's been used as a shooting location for postapocalyptic zombie movies.) The

town is an 8-by-4 block grid home to a population of 200 people. While some of the houses are still inhabited, many are obviously not—they are burned, flooded, stripped down, torn apart, and/or covered in graffiti. The decay is grimly fascinating. And then there's the beach.

The Salton Sea flooded in the 1970s, swamping properties in sand and trashing the waterfront. What's left is the **Bombay Beach Ruins** (Ave. E, south of 5th St.), a jagged, desert-soil shoreline littered with stumps and debris where a thriving marina once stood. After the floods, the town constructed a tall berm to prevent further damage; to see the ruins, access a gravel parking lot at the south end of Avenue E. (Drive only on the gravel: if your car gets stuck on the beach, help will be slow to come.) The water is an unappealing brown and has experienced toxic events, but most of the time it's safe enough, just very salty. Check

for safety advisories from the **Imperial County Public Health Department** (442/265-1888, www.icphd.org).

★ Salvation Mountain

Leonard Knight's original intention had been to evangelize for Jesus Christ from a homemade hot-air balloon. After years of torn fabric and half-inflated efforts, he gave up and started painting an old riverbank instead. Living among the snowbirds of Niland, he used straw, clay, and a hundred thousand gallons of donated paint to create **Salvation Mountain** (Beal Rd., 3.2 mi/5.1 km northeast of CA-111), a testament to his overbrimming faith. Bright colors, crude illustrations, mismatched patterns, and biblical quotes cover the building-size artwork, which is impossible to miss from the road. You'll need to walk around, and on top of, the makeshift monument to notice its many details. Living without electricity and bathing in

Salvation Mountain

natural hot springs, Knight kept working at the mountain for three decades prior to his death in 2014 at the age of 82.

Slab City

One mile east of Salvation Mountain is "The last free place in America." Once the site of Fort Dunlap, a World War II marine training base, **Slab City** (Main St. and Beal Rd., 3.5 mi/5.6 km east of Hwy. 111) gets its name from the only thing the fort left behind: the concrete slabs it had been built upon. For more than 50 years, a revolving population of squatters has claimed those slabs with RVs, trailers, tents, yurts, or whatever works. They say as many as 3,000-4,000 people fill the old grid of dirt roads in the winter, but only a couple of hundred stay when temperatures rise to 120°F in the summer. There's no plumbing, no electricity they don't supply themselves, and no government services, but there is some semblance of civilization.

A few enterprising souls have organized no-cost amenities that work on a donation basis; these may or may not be open. Seek a cup of coffee at the **Slab City Internet Café** (41 Sidetrack Ln.); find a surprising number of books, games, and magazines at **Slab City Library** (555 Rosalie Dr.); and, if you're truly self-sufficient, look for a place to crash at **Slab City Hostel,** a place that might be able to give you room to make do. Look for the **Slab City Information Kiosk** driving in on Beal Road to see if anything new or timely is happening.

East Jesus

When you reach the end of Beal Road, hang left. After the road bends right, take another left to find **East Jesus** (E. Jesus Rd., http://eastjesus.org, free). The outdoor art museum is hard to miss, filled with art cars, large found-art installations, and bizarre constructions that put cast-away materials to new purpose. The eclectic museum's founder, Charlie Russell, originally came to Slab City to work on Salvation Mountain; in 2007, he decided to return and began creating art on this site. When Russell passed in 2011, a 501(c)3 called The Chasterus Foundation was established to continue evolving the museum and sometime performance space. Despite the name, it possesses no religious affiliation, adhering more to a nonmaterialistic bent. It's free to wander the always growing collection of art pieces, though donations are requested. The collective running the museum hopes to officially buy the property from the state.

Festivals and Events
Bombay Beach Biennale
Amid the Bombay Beach Ruins, you'll find decomposing artworks, including the rotting wood boat frame, "El Barco de la Muerte" (the ship of death), and the "Bombay Beach Metro," which resembles the art deco entryway of a Paris Metro station. These pieces are left over from the **Bombay Beach Biennale** (www.bombaybeachbiennale.org, Apr., free), an annual art festival organized by a group of artists and part-time residents from Los Angeles. The party erupts each spring with experimental artworks and high-concept performances. The area comes alive with new art properties installed each year.

Biennale artists have also bought many of the abandoned properties in Bombay Beach, recasting them as permanent art fixtures for visitors to enjoy. You'll spot the first on Avenue A, the road into Bombay Beach. **The Last Resort** (Ave. A and 1st St.) is a pair of billboards made to resemble mid-century advertisements for the beach, marking the site of a planned storage container hotel. In town, it's easy to spot the sign for **Bombay Beach Drive In** (Ave. E south of 3rd Street), a lot filled with junked vintage cars lined up as though viewing a drive-in movie screen (actually a white truck trailer). Other art installations include the plastic-toy covered **Toy House** (Third St., east of Ave. G) and **Angler Grove** (Ave. H, south of 3rd St.), a silver building with a large circular window into what appears to be a futuristic disco lounge.

In addition to the art, there are also performance venues. The cerulean-blue **Bombay Beach Opera House** opens up to reveal a cardboard piano and hundreds of flip flops salvaged from beaches in Africa. The **Bombay Beach Institute of Particle Physics, Metaphysics & International Relations** (9535 Ave. H) is a year-round art gallery featuring a found-object sculpture garden and photo display within various structures on the property. The **Hermitage Museum** (Ave. E, south of 4th St.) is a gallery with rotating exhibits by progressive artists. All venues are open to the public: if locked, the keys are kept behind the town's popular bar, the **Ski Inn** (9596 Ave. A).

Desert X

This quirky biennial festival doesn't require tickets and isn't confined to a specific site. Instead, **Desert X** (www.desertx. org, held odd years: Feb.-Apr. 2021) brings art installations and pop-up exhibitions to the whole, wide Coachella Valley—which makes it the perfect festival for a road trip. It can take up to four hours to visit every piece, whether a large conceptual sculpture or technologically assisted virtual art piece (bring your smart phone!). Consult the festival website for updated maps and information about weekend bus tours.

Food and Accommodations

Visit "the lowest bar in the western hemisphere," the ★ **Ski Inn** (9596 Ave. A, 760/354-1285, 10am-midnight daily, $6-12), which sits 223 feet below sea level. Since the 1950s, customers have fastened dollar bills to the inside of the Bombay Beach dive bar; cash now covers nearly every inch of the walls, as well as the jukebox, bar, ceiling, and several ceiling fan blades. The colorful venue is the small town's community center, a regular haunt for permanent residents, part-timers, and snowbirds, and a great place for day-trippers to get their bearings and pick up keys to a few of the town's art venues. Grab a barstool to chat with friendly locals and bar staff, or take your burgers and hot sandwiches to the patio, which can get pretty lively around happy hour.

A pair of campgrounds on the northeastern shore of the Salton Sea offer overnight camping with scenic lake and mountain views in the **Salton Sea State Recreational Area** (100225 State Park Rd., Mecca, 760/393-3059, www.parks.ca.gov/saltonsea, $7 day-use, $20 camping). **New Camp** offers 19 well-kept campsites behind the Salton Sea Visitor Center, while **Mecca Beach** offers lakefront campsites about a mile south. Both offer picnic tables, firepits, bathrooms, showers, and drinking water. Scorching heat makes either a poor option in summer.

Information and Services

For information on water quality and other local updates, check in with the **Salton Sea Visitor Center** (100-255 State Park Rd., Mecca, 760/393-3810, www. parks.ca.gov, 10am-4pm Wed.-Sun. Oct.-May, 10am-4pm Fri.-Sun. June-Sept.).

Palm Springs

Palm Springs may be on the small side, but the town sprawls widely across the valley floor. The North Palm Springs and Uptown Design District runs along North Palm Canyon Drive from East Vista Chino (north) to Alejo Road (south). The Central Palm Springs and Downtown neighborhood encompasses the blocks south of Alejo Road all the way to Ramon Road. A bit farther off the beaten path, Ramon Road forms the northern boundary of South Palm Springs, which stretches south to Indian Canyons and east past the "curve."

October-May is high season in Palm

Springs, with Christmas week, spring break, and big events like Modernism Week and the Coachella Valley Music and Arts Festival packing in the crowds (and raising the prices). Advanced hotel reservations during these peak times are always a good idea. In **summer,** tourism slows and rates drop significantly.

Getting There
From Los Angeles
The drive from Los Angeles to Palm Springs can take about two hours via I-10 in light traffic. However, you may need to factor in extra time (up to 5 hours) for navigating out of L.A., especially on weekends. To get there, take I-10 east for 100 miles (161 km) and exit I-10 to take Highway 111 south toward Palm Springs. Highway 111B continues into Palm Springs in just over 10 miles (16 km), turning into North Palm Canyon Drive, the main road through Palm Springs.

From San Diego
The drive from San Diego to Palm Springs takes just over two hours. From San Diego, take I-15 north for about 50 miles (81 km). When I-15 splits with I-215, follow I-215N and signs for Riverside/San Bernardino. Stay on I-215N for 30 miles (48 km) until it intersects with CA-60. Take the exit for CA-60 east and continue for 18 miles (29 km). Merge onto I-10 East and continue for another 18 miles (29 km) until reaching the CA-111 exit toward Palm Springs.

Sights
★ Palm Springs Aerial Tramway
The **Palm Springs Aerial Tramway** (1 Tram Way, 760/325-1391, www.pstramway.com, 10am-8pm Mon.-Fri., 8am-8pm Sat.-Sun., $25.95) allows you to marvel at just how startling this transition can be. The tramway consists of suspended cable cars that zip visitors from Valley Station on the desert floor (elevation 2,643 feet) to Mountain Station in the lofty San Jacinto Mountains (elevation 8,516 feet) over the course of a 2.5-mile, 10-minute ride traversing rugged Chino Canyon. As you dangle from the cable, the cars rotate, offering dizzying views of the rocky canyon below, salt-crusted desert, and pine-studded mountain peaks.

In summer, most visitors buy day passes and spend the day picnicking and hiking the San Jacintos, which offer a range of options from easy interpretive trails like the 1.5-mile Desert View Trail to the more difficult 11-mile round-trip trek to San Jacinto Peak. Wilderness permits are required for day hikes and can be obtained at the Long Valley Ranger Station at the top of the tramway. Mountain Station also provides a jumping-off point for many well-established backpacking routes. The mountains are often crusted with snow in winter months, when visitors enjoy snowshoeing, cross-country skiing, snow camping, or just good, old-fashioned snow frolicking. A **Winter Adventure Center** (10am-4pm Mon. and Thurs.-Fri., 9am-4pm Sat.-Sun.) is open seasonally and rents snowshoes and ski equipment.

Mountain Station has year-round amenities, including restrooms, a gift shop, lockers, and the **Pines Café** (11am-8:30pm daily), with cafeteria-style dining and snacks. The **Lookout Lounge** provides cocktails, while the **Peaks Restaurant** (760/325-4537) offers fine dining and spectacular views from its perch at the top of Mountain Station.

For guests with disabilities, the Valley Station has designated parking, and the tramcars are handicap-accessible. Mountain Station has accessible dining and a viewing platform.

Historic Homes
Located in the historic Movie Colony district, the original Palm Springs estate owned by **Frank Sinatra** (877/318-2090, www.sinatrahouse.com) was designed by E. Stewart Williams in 1947 as Sinatra's

Palm Springs

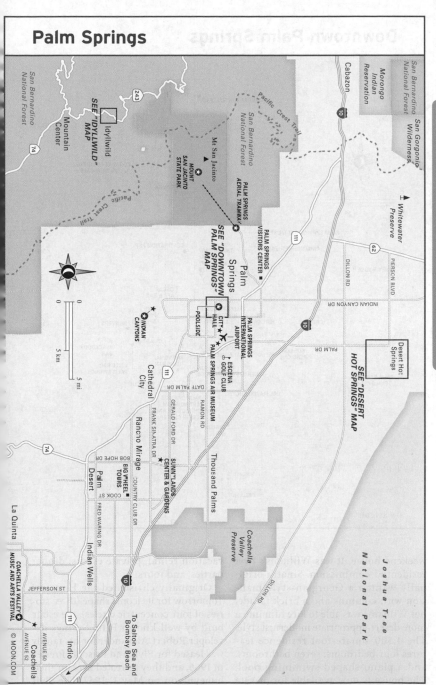

Downtown Palm Springs

San Bernardino National Forest

Morongo Indian Reservation

Cabazon

243

SEE "IDYLLWILD" MAP

Idyllwild

Mountain Center

74

San Bernardino National Forest

Pacific Crest Trail

San Gorgonio Wilderness

Mt San Jacinto

MOUNT SAN JACINTO STATE PARK

San Bernardino National Forest

Pacific Crest Trail

PALM SPRINGS AERIAL TRAMWAY

Whitewater Preserve

10

PALM SPRINGS VISITORS CENTER

111

62

PIERSON BLVD

DILLON RD

Palm Springs

SEE "DOWNTOWN PALM SPRINGS" MAP

INDIAN CANYON DR

INDIAN CANYONS

POOLSIDE

CITY HALL

PALM SPRINGS INTERNATIONAL AIRPORT

ESCENA GOLF CLUB

10

PALM DR

Desert Hot Springs

SEE "DESERT HOT SPRINGS" MAP

Cathedral City

111

DATE PALM DR

PALM SPRINGS AIR MUSEUM

RAMON RD

Rancho Mirage

FRANK SINATRA DR

GERALD FORD DR

Thousand Palms

74

BOB HOPE DR

Palm Desert

BIG WHEEL TOURS

COUNTRY CLUB DR

COOK ST

SUNNYLANDS CENTER & GARDENS

FRED WARING DR

Indian Wells

Coachella Valley Preserve

DILLON RD

Joshua Tree National Park

10

JEFFERSON ST

La Quinta

COACHELLA VALLEY MUSIC AND ARTS FESTIVAL

111

AVENUE 50

AVENUE 52

Coachella

Indio

To Salton Sea and Bombay Beach

© MOON.COM

N

0   5 km

0   5 mi

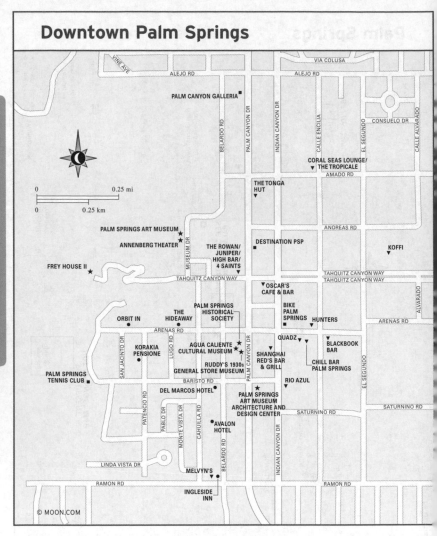

Downtown Palm Springs

weekend house. It was Williams's first residential commission. Sinatra originally wanted a Georgian-style mansion with columns and a brick facade, but Williams was able to lure him into a more desert-appropriate modernist style. The 4,500-square-foot residence features four bedrooms, seven bathrooms, and a piano-shaped swimming pool. The house is now available for private

vacation rental, private events, dinner parties, and tours.

Originally christened the House of Tomorrow for its iconic shape (three stories of four concentric circles), the estate built by well-known Palm Springs developer Robert Alexander for his family was leased for Elvis and Priscilla Presley in 1966, and they retreated here for their honeymoon on May 1, 1967. The **Elvis**

Sunnylands

In its history as private residence and high-level retreat center, Sunnylands has seen a host of distinguished guests, including U.S. presidents, British royalty, and Hollywood icons. The historic modernist estate now known as **Sunnylands Center and Gardens** (37977 Bob Hope Dr., Rancho Mirage, www.sunnylands.org, 8:30am-4pm Wed.-Sun., gardens free, house $48) was designed for media tycoon Walter Annenberg and his wife, Leonore, in the mid-1960s by Los Angeles-based architect A. Quincy Jones. The architect's signature style is apparent in the statement roof (a pink pyramid), overhangs to shield the sun, and glass walls for brightness.

Outside, nine acres of sustainable landscape design transcend politics to create a serene setting designed to change with the seasons. When drought-mandated water restrictions put an end to the era of the estate's traditional green lawns, landscape architect James Burnett created a canvas of native and drought-resistant plants, with inspiration from the Annenbergs' large collection of Impressionist and Postimpressionist art (including Cézannes and Van Goghs). Garden paths wander through arid species and more than 53,000 individual plants. The center and gardens are open to the public with no reservation.

Tours of the historic house are available by online reservation only. The 90-minute guided house tour takes guests to key areas of the home and features information about the estate's history, architecture, and interior design. Tickets must be purchased two weeks in advance. They are released in blocks on the first and 15th of each month at 9am PST for the following two-week block. They often sell out, so getting them the morning of release is advisable. No children under 10 years old are allowed. Wheelchairs can be accommodated with advance notice.

The Sunnylands Center and Gardens offers a gift shop and café on-site. The **café** (8:30am-4pm Thurs.-Sun.) serves a variety of light breakfast and lunch items, including pastries, salads, wraps, coffee, and tea.

Honeymoon Hideaway (1350 Ladera Cir., 760/322-1192, www.elvishoneymoon. com, tours) offers daily tours (1pm and 3:30pm daily with advance reservation, $35 pp, walk-ins welcome space permitting).

Tours are geared toward Elvis fans. Knowledgeable docents share a wealth of information about the home's architecture and Elvis's history. Tours include the home's interior, where visitors are allowed to touch all of the furniture—and even sit on the honeymoon bed.

The 1963 **Frey House II** (686 Palisades Dr.) sits tucked on a hillside 220 feet above the desert floor. The tiny, rectangular glass box is the second home of famed architect Albert Frey, with an interior that comes in at less than 1,000 square feet—much of that being taken up by the giant boulder that the house was built around.

Palm Springs Art Museum
With its three lofty floors kept at a cool 75 degrees, the sophisticated **Palm Springs Art Museum** (101 N. Museum Dr., 760/322-4800, www.psmuseum.org, 10am-5pm Sun.-Tues., noon-8pm Thurs., 10am-5pm Fri.-Sat., $14, children and active duty military free) is a refreshing oasis of art. Spread across 28 galleries and two outdoor sculpture gardens, the museum showcases collections of international modern and contemporary painting and sculpture, architecture and design, Native American and Western art, photography, and glass. The midsize collection approaches those of metropolitan museums with works by such well-known artists as Marc Chagall, Ansel Adams, Roy Lichtenstein, Pablo Picasso, and Andy Warhol. The museum was originally established in 1938 as the Palm Springs Desert Museum, specializing in

Native American artifacts and the natural history of the Coachella Valley. The current museum, designed by architect E. Stewart Williams in 1974, has expanded as a cultural center with an Architecture and Design Center and Annenberg Theater. The museum also houses a café and a museum store. Admission is free every Thursday evening 4pm-8pm and the second Sunday of each month.

Palm Springs Art Museum Architecture and Design Center

The **Palm Springs Art Museum Architecture and Design Center** (300 S. Palm Canyon Dr., 760/423-5260, www.psmuseum.org, 10am-5pm Sun.-Tues. and Fri.-Sat., and noon-8pm Thurs., $5 adults, children under 18 free) is the hub of the Palm Springs Art Museum's growing collection of architecture and design holdings, which include drawings, photography, and models. The center is intended as a space for architects, scholars, and the general public. Free docent-guided **tours** of current exhibitions are available several times per week with a rotating schedule.

Village Green Heritage Center

The **village green** (219-221 S. Palm Canyon Dr.) is home to a collection of museums and cultural exhibits comprised of the Palm Springs Historical Society, McCallum Adobe, Cornelia White House, and Ruddy's General Store.

The **Palm Springs Historical Society** (PSHS, 221 S. Palm Canyon Dr., 760/323-8297, www.pshistoricalsociety.org, 10am-4pm Mon. and Wed.-Fri., 10am-5pm Sat.-Sun., summer hours vary) has exhibits and walking tours of Palm Springs historic neighborhoods. The historical society is based in the one oldest remaining buildings in Palm Springs. The

Top to bottom: view from the Palm Springs aerial tramway; Palm Springs Art Museum; poolside at the Ace Hotel & Swim Club.

McCallum Adobe was built in 1884 as a home for Palm Springs' first pioneer family. It now houses varying exhibits focusing on Palm Springs history, architecture, and culture. In addition, the museum houses hundreds of photographs documenting Palm Springs history dating from the 1880s to the 1980s.

Docent-led **walking tours** (1-2.5 hours, 760/323-8297 or www.pshistoricalsociety. org, $20) give visitors a chance to see charming neighborhoods through the lens of architecture, celebrity, and pioneering efforts. Explore historic neighborhoods, including the Golden Era Hollywood Homes in Old Las Palmas, Rat Pack Playground Modernist Homes in Vista Las Palmas, or Stars and Starchitects in Deepwell. The tours must be reserved in advance through the Palm Springs Historical Society.

Stepping through the doors of **Ruddy's 1930s General Store Museum** (221 S. Palm Canyon Dr., 760/327-2156, www. palmsprings.com, 10am-4pm Thurs.-Sun., $0.95) is a nostalgic trip to a simple time. The recreated general store is stocked with an extensive collection of unused packaged goods from the 1930s and '40s. It is chock-full of more than 6,000 unused goods from hardware and clothing to groceries, medicines, and beauty aids.

Palm Springs Air Museum

The fact that most of the aircraft are still flyable at the **Palm Springs Air Museum** (745 N. Gene Autry Trail, 760/778-6262, www.palmspringsairmuseum.org, 10am-5pm daily, $17.50) makes their larger-than-life exhibits even more impressive. This living history aviation museum features 40 flyable static aircraft from World War II, the Korean War, and the Vietnam War as well as permanent and temporary exhibits and artwork across three climate-controlled hangars and the outside tarmac. Docents give added depth to the experience since many are veterans. A small **café** (10am-4pm daily Nov.-May, 10am-4pm Tues.-Sun. June-Oct.) and gift shop are on-site.

Moorten Botanical Garden

Moorten Botanical Garden (1701 S. Palm Canyon Dr., 760/327-6555, www. moortenbotanicalgarden.com, 10am-4pm Thurs.-Tues. fall-spring, 10am-4pm Fri.-Sun. summer, $5 adults, $2 children 5-15, free under 5) introduces visitors to the wonders of cacti and other desert plants. The hushed green place transports guests from the street to a microcosm of desert trees, cacti, and plants from around the world. Wander the wide trails amid jagged lattices formed by more than 3,000 varieties of plants. A small nursery sells desert plants and pottery.

Entertainment and Events
Bars and Cocktail Lounges
★ Poolside

The pool scene in Palm Springs tends to be relaxed compared to, say, Las Vegas. But a handful of hotels book DJs and sling poolside cocktails with events that are open to both hotel guests and the public. Check individual hotel websites for event information. The pool party season runs **March-September.**

If you do want some Vegas with your Palm Springs, **The Riviera** (1600 N. Indian Canyon Dr., 760/327-8311, www. rivierapalmsprings.com) has a Summer Splash Pool Party series every Friday, Saturday, and Sunday during the summer, featuring guest DJs and live music. The Soleil Pool & Bar is the official party pool, while the Chiki pool, away from the center of the resort, has a quieter atmosphere with food and drink service on weekends. Pool passes are $10 Monday-Thursday and $15 Friday-Sunday for nonguests. Cabana rentals are available.

The chic, uptown **Arrive Hotel** (1551 N. Palm Canyon Dr., 760/507-1640, https:// arrivehotels.com) offers a scene-y pool hang with drinks and food by on-site Wexler's Deli. Cabana rentals are available if you really want to step it up. The hotel prides itself on being open to the neighborhood and typically allows non-guests and neighborhood folks. During special events or when the pool is extra crowded, it may be limited to hotel guests only.

The Rowan (100 W. Tahquitz Canyon Way, 760/904-5015, www.rowanpalmsprings.com) claims the only rooftop pool in the desert. From seven stories up you will have the stunning mountain views visitors demand from their poolside loungers as well as panoramic views of Palm Springs. The open-air High Bar, aptly named, serves snacks and craft cocktails. Day passes are available for $30 on weekdays (Mon.-Fri.). The pool is closed to the public on weekends.

With the reinstatement of a tiki bar on the premises, the **Caliente Tropics** (411 E. Palm Canyon Dr., 760/327-1391, www.calientetropics.com) regained its purpose in the world. Quirky Polynesian architecture, affordable motel rooms, a child-allowed policy, and a free-for-all vibe mean that the Caliente Tropics has always had a pool scene. However, The Reef brings some purpose to the mayhem. Tiki snacks and libations are available poolside at The Reef. Day passes to the pool are $20 at the front desk.

The stylish, sprawling **Ace Hotel & Swim Club** (701 E. Palm Canyon Dr., 760/325-9900, www.acehotel.com/palmsprings) is home to some of the biggest weekend pool parties in town, with poolside drink service, outdoor bar, and DJs. The enthusiastic crowds are carefree and cool (some might say "too cool for school").

The **Amigo Bar** is open to the public, so you can enter through the lobby and enjoy the bar's poolside offerings. Non guests can pay for a **Swim Club Membership** ($350 per year) or a **Day-Use pass** ($30). The yearly Swim Club Membership gets you a lot for that price, including daily pool and hot tub access (7am-2pm), admittance to pool parties and events, the use of the hotel spa and

gym, and discounts on spa services and the restaurant. Day passes will gain you a full day's entrance to the pool or pool event. Blackout dates apply.

The trendy **Saguaro** (1800 E. Palm Canyon Dr., 760/323-1711, www.thesaguaro.com) has a lively pool scene. An outdoor pool with two hot tubs, lounge seating, and an outdoor bar offers a great place to relax and party against the Technicolor hotel backdrop. The hotel also hosts pool parties during Coachella weekend (Apr.) and Splash House (June and Aug.), with international DJs and high-profile art, music, and fashion influencers catering to a young, dance-loving crowd. The hotel pool is open to anyone, which means it can get crazy.

Nightlife
Bootlegger Tiki (1101 N. Palm Canyon Dr., 760/318-4154, www.bootleggertiki.com, 4pm-2am daily) took on the legacy of tiki bar royalty when it opened on the site of the original Don the Beachcomber, Palm Springs (established 1953). Velvet paintings, flocked wallpaper, red lighting, and guarded secret recipes impress with dramatic style, and the layered drinks earn their place in tiki history. Grab a friend and grab a booth. Pro tip: If you're not up for a heavily laced rum drink, the gin-based Tom Collins is sprucey and refreshing.

The aptly named **High Bar** (100 W. Tahquitz Canyon Way, 760/904-5015) is poolside on the rooftop of downtown's chic Kimpton Rowan. The bar offers an open, luxe setting with mountain views, fresh cocktails, and California Mediterranean-inspired salads and snacks. The bar is open for hotel guests 10am-10pm daily. It opens to the public at 4pm. A happy hour 7pm-9pm Sunday-Thursday makes this a great spot to watch the sunset.

The retro-tropical **Tropicale Restaurant** features the swanky, neon-lit **Coral Seas Lounge** (330 E. Amado Rd., 760/866-1952, www.thetropicale.com,

4pm-10pm Sun.-Thurs., 4pm-11pm Fri.-Sat., 11am-3pm Sat.-Sun.) as well as an oasis-like patio bar.

The tiki gem that is the **Tonga Hut** (254 N. Palm Canyon Dr., 760/322-4449, http://tongahut.com/tonga-hut-palm-springs, 2pm-midnight Sun., 5pm-midnight Tues.-Thurs., 5pm-2am Fri.-Sat.) is tucked away on the second floor on the main strip of downtown. You'll be fully transported to tiki times as you step through the doorway to excessively garnished drinks, atomic-era seating, low-lit lamps, tiki gods, and hand-carved island art. A full menu offers a pupu platter, pork sliders, pineapple fried rice, and other retro-inspired dishes.

Melvyn's (Ingleside Inn, 200 W. Ramon Rd., 760/325-2323, www.inglesideinn.com, 6pm-2am daily), the iconic Palm Springs lounge, is still going as strong as in its popular Rat Pack days. Nestled in the elegant Spanish Revival-style Ingleside Inn, Melvyn's sports an Old Hollywood Regency decor, chandeliers, and decadently upholstered booths. The lounge has undergone a recent update, bringing it gracefully into this era while saving everything you like about the old. The lounge gets going most nights, fueled by live piano music and martinis that often inspire dancing on the tiny dance floor. Order a gimlet and enjoy the people-watching.

One of the last remaining Rat Pack hangouts, the **Purple Room Supper Club** (1900 E. Palm Canyon Dr., www.purpleroompalmsprings.com, 4pm-close Tues.-Sun.) is an old-school supper club and lounge that opened in 1960 in the Club Trinidad Resort. Nightly music and comedy shows accompany a surf-and-turf menu. Happy hour and late-night drinks are available in the 1960s-era lounge.

The Reef (411 E. Palm Canyon Dr., 760/656-3839, www.thereefpalmsprings.com, 1pm-1am Mon.-Fri., 10am-1am Sat., 10am-midnight Sun.) opened in the most

tiki of locations: the Caliente Tropics hotel, a historic, Polynesian-themed resort. The Reef is good for daytime (pool views), happy hour, or late night (there is also a late-night happy hour) and offers an arsenal of fruity bevvies and a food menu.

The **Amigo Room** (Ace Hotel, 701 E. Palm Canyon Dr., 760/325-9900, www.acehotel.com/palmsprings, 9am-2am daily) is the perfect purveyor of the Ace Hotel's brand of cool with a retro dark styling. During the day, it serves a packed outdoor pool scene. Nighttime brings DJs, theme nights, karaoke, live music, and trivia.

Seymour's (233 E. Palm Canyon Dr., 760/892-900, 6pm-midnight Sun. and Tues.-Thurs., 6pm-2am Fri.-Sat.) serves the best cocktails in town. Located behind the curtain at Mr. Lyon's Steakhouse, the intimate space has barstools you will want to take home and enthusiastic and knowledgeable bartenders.

Festivals and Events

Modernism Week (www.modernismweek.com, Feb.) is Palm Springs' signature annual event, celebrating mid-century modern architecture, design, and culture over two nonstop weekends every February. Modernism Week fosters appreciation for the city's shining modernist history while encouraging a fresh approach to thinking about design, art, fashion, and sustainable modern living. The festival features more than 250 events, including signature home tours with a chance to peek into some fabulous historic houses, a modernism show and sale, modern garden tours, architectural double-decker bus tours (including sunset tours of illuminated mid-century classic buildings), nightly parties (soiree at Frank Sinatra's estate, anyone?), walking and bike tours, lectures and cocktail hour discussions, fashion events, a vintage travel trailer exhibition, films, music,

LGBTQ Palm Springs

Palm Springs is a resoundingly friendly place for LGBTQ travelers, with a range of bars, hotels, and events geared specifically toward a gay clientele.

Bars and Clubs

Toucan's Tiki Lounge (2100 N. Palm Canyon Dr., North Palm Springs, 760/416-7584, www.toucanstikilounge.com, 2pm-2am Mon.-Tues. and Thurs.-Fri., 2pm-midnight Wed., noon-2am Sat.-Sun.) is a fun and friendly gay cocktail bar adorned with tropical tiki touches and a round bar that slings sugary drinks to fuel a lively dance floor. Drag shows and other special events offer plenty of entertainment.

Oscar's Café and Bar (125 E. Tahquitz Canyon Way, #108, 760/325-1188, www. oscarspalmsprings.com, 11am-9pm Mon. and Wed.-Thurs., 4pm-9pm Fri., 4pm-10pm Sat., 9am-9pm Sun.) has a casual patio for drinking and dining; the spot is open for dinner, as well as drag brunch on Saturday and Sunday. They offer a daily happy hour (4pm-7pm) and a popular Sunday tea dance (4pm-close), as well as cabaret and live music.

Streetbar (224 E. Arenas Rd., 760/320-1266, www.psstreetbar.com, 10am-2am Mon.-Fri., 6am-2am Sat., 6am-midnight Sun.) is a Palm Springs fixture that caters to a gay clientele. There's something going on every night of the week—from karaoke to DJ nights and live performances.

Hunters (302 E. Arenas Rd., 760/323-0700, www.hunterspalmsprings.com, 10am-2am daily, happy hour 10am-7pm daily) is a gay club that draws a mostly male crowd for drink specials, DJs, dancing, and weekly entertainment.

QuadZ (200 S. Indian Canyon Dr., www.spurline.com, 2:30pm-2am Mon.-Thurs., noon-2am Fri.-Sun.) is a popular neighborhood sing-along spot with strong drinks and theme nights. The low-key bar draws a primarily male crowd, but all are welcome.

Chill Bar Palm Springs (217 E. Arenas Rd., 760/327-1079, www.chillbarpalmsprings.

and more. Modernism Week hosts a **Fall Preview** (Oct.), a mini Modernism Week to kick off Palm Springs' social and recreation season. **Tickets** (up to $150) for Modernism Week (on sale Nov. 1) and the Fall Preview (on sale Aug. 1) are sold online for individual events. They sell out quickly, especially for the popular house tours.

The pool party to end all pool parties is the annual **Splash House** (www. splashhouse.com, June and Aug.), a three-day electronic dance music and pool party held in Palm Springs two weekends a year. Three host hotels (the Saguaro, The Riviera, and the Renaissance) form ground zero for Splash House, with DJs and daytime events; shuttles run between the host hotels. A general admission wristband (from $120) gets you access to the pools and events at both hotels as well as the shuttle. General admission tickets can

be purchased separately or as a package with hotel rooms. Late-night parties are held off-site at unique Palm Springs locations, such as the Palm Springs Air Museum. Tickets for the off-site parties are sold separately (from $40).

Palm Springs International Film Festival (Palm Springs Cultural Center, 2300 E. Baristo Rd., 760/325-6565, www. palmspringsculturalcenter.org, Jan.) is a well-established, destination film festival that draws more than 135,000 filmgoers. The festival features more than 200 films from 78 countries over 12 days of events and film screenings including the prestigious Film Awards Gala. Advance **tickets** go on sale in December and can be purchased online, by phone (800/898-7256, 9am-5pm Mon.-Fri.), and in person at the Festival Ticket and Information Center (Courtyard Plaza, 777 E. Tahquitz Canyon Way) and Camelot Theatres (2300 E. Baristo Rd.) during business com, 10am-2am daily) is a gay cocktail bar and nightclub in a sleekly designed contemporary space with an outdoor patio.

Blackbook Bar (315 E. Arenas Rd., 760/832-8497, noon-close Mon.-Fri., 11am-close Sat.-Sun.) is a an industrial-chic space with a street-front patio and a solid food menu.

Events

The two biggest parties are held annually in April. Established in 1991, **The Dinah** (locations vary, www.thedinah.com, Apr.) is the self-proclaimed largest queer girl party music festival in the world. This four-day, four-night annual getaway catering to the lesbian community takes Palm Springs by storm every April. It kicks off with a massive opening party on Thursday night and continues its deluge of celebrity-studded events and parties throughout the weekend. The event features celebrity guest DJs, dancers, daytime pool parties, live concerts, comedy, and nightclub parties throughout the weekend. Tickets are available on The Dinah website with **weekend package deals** ($239-500) or **individual events** ($30-80).

The **White Party** (locations vary, www.jeffreysanker.com, Apr.) is a massive dance party for male couples and singles. The three-day, three-night festival is held annually every April (not the same weekend as The Dinah). It kicks off Friday at noon and goes strong until 7am Monday morning with daytime pool parties, DJs, live performances, and themed nighttime events. The White Party's main event happens on Saturday night—a 10-hour dance party with multiple levels, dancers, special effects, and a huge sound system. The White Party Ferris Wheel and fireworks display choreographed to a DJ music remix add even more spark to the event. White Party is centered in several host hotels in Palm Springs. **Weekend passes** ($379-455) are available on the White Party website, or you can buy tickets to **individual events** ($40-160).

hours. The **Palm Springs International ShortFest** (www.psfilmfest.org) also happens every June.

★ **Coachella Valley Music and Arts Festival**

The **Coachella Valley Music and Arts Festival** (www.coachella.com, Apr.) is an annual music festival held on the Empire Polo Club fields in the Coachella Valley. From folk rock to power pop to hip-hop to electronic music, the festival draws big names and huge numbers of fans. Past headliners have included cultural icons like The Beastie Boys, Radiohead, Bjork, The Black Keys, Red Hot Chili Peppers, Outkast, and Jack White. People come from far and wide to attend. The festival is so popular that it offers the same lineup two weekends back to back in April. Tickets are highly competitive to get and sell out within hours of going on sale in January. The crowd skews

youngish, but it can be a fun time for anyone due to the predictably excellent band lineup. They don't shy away from the "art" aspect of the festival either, featuring a few choice Burning Man-level technology and sculpture installations. On-site camping is available including stylish tepees all set up for you. Outside the festival, local hotels as far away as Palm Springs book quickly. For transportation to and from the festival (if you're not camping on the grounds), prepaid and reserved shuttles are available at pickup points throughout the Coachella Valley and Palm Springs.

Sports and Recreation
Hiking

Palm Springs offers some good hiking opportunities in its surrounding canyons and mountains. A few trails leave directly from near the Palm Springs Art Museum, climbing into the foothills and offering views of Palm Springs and the Coachella Valley.

Trails in Palm Springs are exposed and are best hiked **October-March** when temperatures are more moderate. If hiking other times of the year, start very early (plan to finish by 9am-10am during summer) and make sure you are off the trail before the heat of the day. Carry plenty of water, sunscreen, and a hat for shade.

The **South Carl Lykken Trail** (6 mi/10 km round-trip, 2-3 hours, 1,000 feet elevation gain, moderate) is an exposed hike into the toothy hills outlining the west side of Palm Springs and offers excellent views of town with a bonus peek into Tahquitz Canyon. Rewarding climbs give way to expansive city views as the trail levels out and winds along a north and east-facing ridge.

The trail heads west before beginning a series of switchbacks up to a lookout point, checking in at 1,170 feet. From here the trail levels out, winding along the rocky hillside before climbing again to top out at 1,550 feet above **Tahquitz Canyon.** This is a good turnaround point, marked by picnic tables, and you can return the way you came.

This trail is completely exposed. Carry enough **water** and make sure you start early and are off the trail no later than midmorning in summer months. The good news is that even if you are not able to make it to the final turnaround point, the continuous views mean that hiking almost any length of the trail will be a satisfying experience.

Getting There

From the Palm Springs Visitors Center, take North Palm Canyon Drive south for 6.4 miles (10 km); continue straight when it turns into South Palm Canyon Drive. The signed trailhead is on the west (right) side of South Palm Canyon Drive just south of Canyon Heights Road.

Palm Canyon

★ **Indian Canyons**

The **Indian Canyons** (760/323-6018, www.indian-canyons.com, 8am-5pm daily Oct.-June, 8am-5pm Fri.-Sun. July-Sept., day-use $9-11) refer to the rugged, scenic canyons that burrow into the flanks of the San Jacinto Mountains in the southwest corner of Palm Springs. The steep, often snowcapped San Jacintos feed the seasonal streams that transform the rocky canyons in spring. Natural fan palm oases and groundwater feed perennial pools and streams year-round, making the canyons a haven from the surrounding arid landscape and a delight for hikers.

The Indian Canyons are sacred to the Agua Caliente Band of Cahuilla Indians who own and manage the land. Ancestors of the Agua Caliente Cahuilla settled Tahquitz, Andreas, Murray, Palm, and Chino Canyons, establishing villages and irrigating and planting crops. The Agua Caliente own 32,000 acres spread across desert and mountains in the Palm Springs area. Tahquitz and three other canyons are listed on the National Register of Historic Places, while **Palm Canyon** boasts the world's largest California fan palm oasis.

These trails are best hiked **October-March** due to soaring temperatures. You have the best chance of encountering the seasonal snowmelt streams that feed these canyons in early spring. However, since the canyons offer short hikes with some shade, visiting the canyons at other times of the year is also worthwhile. When it is hot, start early (the canyons open at 8am year-round). Seasonal **ranger talks** are open to the public and are held at the Trading Post (10am Mon.-Thurs.) and at Andreas Canyon (1pm). Ranger-led interpretive hikes are also available Oct.-June (10am-11:30am and 1pm-2:30pm).

Getting There

The **Trading Post** and ranger station on South Palm Canyon Drive is the hub for exploring Andreas, Murray, and Palm Canyons. The Trading Post has hiking maps, drinks and snacks, books, jewelry, and Indian pottery, baskets, and weaving. Restrooms and parking are available. To get there from the Palm Springs Visitors Center (2901 N. Palm Canyon Dr.), head south on Palm Canyon Drive for 9 miles (14 km) until the road ends at the Trading Post and Palm Canyon overlook. Visitors will pass through a tollgate to pay the entrance fee prior to reaching the Trading Post.

The entrance to **Tahquitz Canyon** (www.tahquitzcanyon.com) is from the Tahquitz Visitors Center, where water, maps, parking, and restrooms are available. From the Palm Springs Visitors Center (2901 N. Palm Canyon Dr.), head south on Palm Canyon Drive for 3.8 miles (6 km) and turn right on Mesquite Avenue. The road ends at the **Tahquitz Canyon Visitors center** (500 W. Mesquite Ave.) in 0.4 mile.

Tahquitz Canyon

Tahquitz Canyon (2 mi/3 km round-trip, 1 hour, easy) is the most popular trail in the Indian Canyons, and for good reason. This moderate two-mile loop winds through a scenic, rocky canyon full of native vegetation across an ancient **Cahuilla village site** to end at Tahquitz Falls, a rare **desert waterfall.** At the visitors center, pay your fee and pick up a Tahquitz Canyon trail guide for interpretive descriptions of historic and scenic points along the trail. (Water is also available for purchase.)

The trail follows a seasonal creek dependent on snowmelt from the San Jacinto Mountains. The best time to hike is **February-April** for more moderate canyon temperatures and the highest chance of water in the canyon. On the way back you'll have wide views of Palm Springs and the Coachella Valley to the east.

Lower Palm Canyon Trail

You'll catch the views of the world's largest fan palm oasis, hundreds of green palms clustered improbably at the bottom of a rocky gorge, before strolling down to the canyon floor to be dwarfed by their primordial trunks. Fifteen miles long, Palm Canyon marks the divide between the Santa Rosa and San Jacinto Mountains. It offers stunning contrasts—the lush proliferation of palms set against the craggy canyon walls and arid desert.

A graded **Lower Palm Canyon Trail** (2.2 mi/3 km round-trip, 1 hour, easy) winds down into the canyon from the **Palm Canyon overlook.** The trail wanders through mammoth palms, offering shaggy seclusion and shade. Depending on the season and snowmelt, you'll come across secret pools and intermittent streams studded with boulders. The canyon feels mysterious and Jurassic—it wouldn't seem out of place to catch a glimpse of a dinosaur strolling along. You'll follow a trail on the right side of the canyon above the level of the streambed for about 0.7 mile, continuing through spectacular palm groves. At 0.7 mile the trail crosses to the left side of the canyon, an easy or more difficult task depending on water flow in the canyon. Soon (after a mile total), the palms become less dense and the trail becomes exposed, forking with the **East Fork** and **Victor Trails.** This is a good turnaround point if your goal was to experience the palm oasis. Return the way you came (the full trail travels 15 mi/24 km one-way). Seasonal **ranger-led hikes** (10am Fri.-Sun. Oct.-June) are also available.

From the Palm Springs Visitors Center (2901 N. Palm Canyon Dr.), head south for 9 miles (14 km) until Palm Canyon Drive ends at the Trading Post and Palm Canyon overlook.

Andreas Canyon Loop

The trail through lovely **Andreas Canyon** (2 mi/3 km round-trip, 1 hour, easy) follows a permanent creek through hundreds of native California fan palms. Secluded pools and striking rock formations make this well worth the small amount of effort the hike requires. Until the late 1800s, the Cahuilla used the creek to irrigate crops of melons, corn, and pumpkins. The turnaround point for this scenic desert stroll is a fence blocking off land for the **Andreas Canyon Club.** The secretive and exclusive club was formed in 1923. Members bought land from the Southern Pacific Railroad and built a series of rock houses (22 in all) into the craggy hills to blend in with the desert landscape. A clubhouse was constructed in 1925. Prior to procuring the land, members camped in the canyon's streambed in rock caches. The return route on the left side of the canyon follows a high ridge south of the stream. Seasonal **ranger-led hikes** (1pm Fri.-Sun. Oct.-June) are also available.

From the intersection of South Palm Canyon Drive and Highway 111, continue south for under 3 miles (5 km), following signs for Indian Canyons. After the toll, take the road to the right for 0.7

mile until it ends. Start by hiking the right (north) side of the canyon to follow the creek.

Murray Canyon

The winding trail through Murray Canyon offers a longer chance to explore a palm-filled canyon than its scenic neighbor Andreas.

The trail begins at the parking area for Andreas and Murray Canyons and heads south before entering **Murray Canyon** proper. It delves into the lower edges of the San Jacinto Mountains, providing views of its soaring cliffs as you meander through the palm-enclosed, stream-crossed canyon. The second half of the trail requires hopping back and forth across a picturesque stream that varies in intensity depending on the season. California fan palms are abundant and mixed in with a scattering of cacti, desert willows, and cottonwoods. A series of gentle cascades (**Seven Sisters Waterfall**) marks the end of the hike. Return the way you came.

From the intersection of South Palm Canyon Drive and Highway 111, continue south for under 3 miles (5 km), following signs for Indian Canyons. After the toll, take the road to the right for 0.7 mile until it ends.

Spas

Many of Palm Springs' larger resort hotels offer spa services, including massage and skin and body treatments. A few have standout day spas with services such as deep tissue massage, raw botanical treatments, or private pools. They cater to guests and nonguests, individuals and couples; a few are good for spa parties or groups.

Estrella Spa (415 S. Belardo Rd., www.avalonpalmsprings.com, 760/318-3000, 9am-5:30pm Sun.-Thurs., 9am-7pm Fri.-Sat.), is in a garden hacienda with access to an outdoor hot tub with shaded daybeds, massage cabanas, a fitness center, Vichy steam shower, and private courtyards. They offer a full customizable treatment menu from body scrubs and facials to massage, nails, and reflexology. Estrella Spa is good for groups and spa parties; they also offer beauty stations for hair and makeup.

Book any spa treatment at **L'Horizon Hotel and Spa** (1050 E. Palm Canyon, 760/323-1858, https://lhorizonpalmsprings.com, 9am-6pm Sun.-Thurs., 9am-8pm Fri.-Sat.) for entry to the elegantly intimate indoor-outdoor space, including swimming pool, private outdoor showers, and white canvas cabanas. Aromatherapy massages, revitalizing body treatments and wraps, and facials are complemented by a fresh juice bar and poolside cocktail bar.

The hip Ace Hotel features organic treatments with raw botanical products in its **Feel Good Spa** (701 E. Palm Canyon Dr., 760/866-6188, www.acehotel.com/palmsprings, feelgoodspa@acehotel.com, by appointment 9am-6pm Sun.-Thurs., 9am-8pm Fri.-Sat.). Body treatments range from body masks and reflexology to massage and facials and can be booked for individuals and groups. The spa is poolside with easy access to the popular swimming pool and open-air bar.

The **Palm Springs Yacht Club** spa (Parker Hotel, 4200 E. Palm Canyon Dr., 760/770-5000) is its own destination within the sprawling Parker Hotel grounds, offering massages, facials and waxing, scrubs and wraps, and natural nail services. A nautical blue-and-white design launches your spa voyage into a sea of pampering consisting of an idyllic indoor pool, 15 private treatment rooms, private outdoor deck for post-massage cocktails, and garden paths.

Golf

Palm Springs is a golfing destination with its moderate winter temperatures and spectacular mountain views. Within Palm Springs proper, there are a few standout courses for visitors. Most golf courses maintain online booking for tee times on their website. Pricing is dynamic, reflecting real-time conditions including weather, demand, and other market factors.

Escena Golf Club (1100 Clubhouse View Dr., 760/778-2737, www.escenagolf. com, 6:30am-9pm daily, $34-109) is as much about the setting as it is about golf: a dramatic mountain backdrop, palm trees, and native landscaping on a public 18-hole, par 72 championship golf course spanning 172 acres. Golf club rentals are available ($65 pp), and there are an on-site **bar and grill** (6:30am-9pm daily) and pro shop. Tee times can book quickly on weekends.

The **Indian Canyons Golf Resort** (1097 Murray Canyon Dr., 760/833-8700, www. indiancanyonsgolf.com, $45-125) maintains two distinct golf courses set on 550 acres of Native American tribal property; both are 18-hole championship courses. The classic par 72 North Course plays 6,943 yards set in the canyon district and is surrounded on three sides by the San Jacinto Mountains. The course, designed by noted architect William F. Bell, dates to 1961 and winds through historic mid-century properties, including some originally owned by Walt Disney. The famous Walt Disney fountain acts as a water hazard and visual centerpiece, shooting water jets more than 100 feet high.

Tahquitz Creek Golf Course (1885 Golf Club Dr., 760/328-1005, www. tahquitzgolfresort.com) is a public course offering a pro shop, bar and grill, and two courses. The Legend Course was designed in 1957 and offers a traditional country club-style golf experience. The 18-hole regulation golf course plays more than 6,800 yards and meanders through historic neighborhoods with undulating "push up" greens. The Resort Course is a par 36 regulation course designed in 1995. It features environmentally friendly design elements, including drought-tolerant native landscaping, reclaimed irrigation, and reclaimed materials for mounding. The Resort plays more than

6,700 yards and offers tees for various handicaps to create a fair playing field. Rental clubs are available ($55 before twilight, $30 after twilight).

Shopping

The sleek Uptown Design District has the highest concentration of mid-mod shopping in Palm Springs. Stroll colorful North Palm Canyon Drive between Vista Chino (north end) and Alejo (south end) to find vintage and new-retro home furnishings, art, gifts, clothing, and fashion accessories.

Fully outfit the lanai in time for your retro cocktail party with vintage household items from **Dazzles** (1035 N. Palm Canyon Dr., 760/327-1446, www. visitpalmsprings.com/dazzles, noon-5pm Wed. and Fri.-Mon.), a cheerful treasure trove stuffed into a defunct mid-century hotel. Oh, and be sure to outfit yourself too—the collection of Bakelite and colorful costume jewelry is unparalleled.

The elegant building that now houses **The Shops at Thirteen Forty-Five** (1345 N. Palm Canyon Dr., 760/464-0480, www.towneps.com, 11am-5pm Thurs.-Sun.) is a historic, mid-century building designed by iconic architect E. Stewart Williams in 1955. Inside, a collective of 13 unique shops feature vintage and new furniture, home accessories, and art. **Soukie Modern** (www.soukiemodern. com) offers Moroccan-inspired, handcrafted home textiles including rugs, home accessories, furniture, wedding blankets, and bags, while the curated vintage shop **Lindy California** (www. lindycalifornia.com) sells pedigreed decor and jewelry finds. And **Towne Palm Springs** (www.towneps.com) features vintage and modern furniture, accessories, and art.

Flow Modern Design (768 N. Palm Canyon Dr., 760/322-0768, www. flowmodern.com, 10:30am-5:30pm Mon. and Wed.-Sat., noon-5pm Sun.) is both a shop and gallery specializing in carefully selected mid-century modern fine furniture, art, jewelry, and accessories, including silver and brass pieces. Favorites include Milo Baughman, Arthur Elrod, and Scandinavian Glass and Rosenthal Studio pieces. Flow Modern is a 1st Dibs dealer, a leading marketplace for globally selected rare and beautiful objects. The gallery features rotating exhibits of photography, painting, and sculpture.

Modernway (745 N. Palm Canyon Dr., 760/320-5455, www.psmodernway. com, noon-5pm Thurs.-Mon.) is a well-established and well-regarded Palm Springs vintage retail outlet specializing in mid-century modern furnishings from the 1950s, '60s, and '70s.

After visiting **A La MOD** (844 N. Palm Canyon Dr., 760/327-0707, www. alamodps.com, 10:30am-5pm Mon.-Sat., noon-4pm Sun.), with its room after groovy room of impeccable vintage furnishings, you might just wish you could move in here instead of trying to update your own place to be this stylish. Couches, lamps, tables, chairs, bookends—one of each, please.

Vintage cuff links? Check. Chunky necklaces? Check. Animal curios, curvy lamps, and massive multicolored glassware collection? Check, check, and check. Find it all at **Bon Vivant** (766 N. Palm Canyon Dr., 760/534-3197, www.gmcb. com/shop, 10am-5pm Thurs.-Mon.), situated in the street-level floor of the original Albert Frey-designed Kocher-Samson building.

Find original retro-style art, prints, books, and other merchandise evocative of atomic-era Palm Springs by the artist Shag (aka Josh Agle) at **Shag: The Store** (725 N. Palm Canyon Dr., 760/322-3400, www.shagthestore.com, 10am-5pm Mon.-Thurs., 10am-8pm Fri.-Sat.).

BKB Art + Design (388 N. Palm Canyon Dr., 760/821-3764, https://bkbceramics. com/home.html, 11am-3pm Mon. and Fri., 11am-5pm Sat. and Sun.) brings the spirit of the high desert to the low desert. Artists from Joshua Tree-area studios supply the chic store with a curated collection of contemporary art, including weavings, ceramic planters, mugs, painted tiles, and clothing.

Iconic Atomic (1103 N. Palm Canyon Dr., 760/322-0777, www.iconicatomic. com, 10am-6pm Thurs.-Mon.) is a cheerful shop specializing in vintage clothing and accessories as well as housewares from the 1960s and '70s. You might find party dresses, sport coats, tiki ware, vintage magazines, or furniture.

Should you find yourself in a fashion emergency while on vacation, **The Frippery** (664 N. Palm Canyon Dr., 760/699-5365, http://www.thefrippery. com, 11am-5pm Thurs.-Sat., 11am-4pm Wed. and Sun.) has vintage finery for many different desert scenarios from resort lounging in Palm Springs to boulder-gazing in Joshua Tree. Their collection ranges from mod to bohemian with accessories to complete your look.

Food
Breakfast and Cafés
Brave the sidewalk line and start your day at ★ **Cheeky's** (622 N. Palm Canyon Dr., 760/327-7595, www.cheekysps.com, 8am-2pm daily, $7-13) for one of the most popular brunches in town. The sunny spot with a patio offers a seasonal, locally sourced menu that changes weekly, plus classics like Blondie's eggs Benedict with bacon, arugula, and a cheddar scone; Cheeky's BLT with jalapeno bacon and pesto fries; signature house-made cinnamon rolls; and a bacon flight. Their array of breakfast drinks includes spicy Bloody Marys, fresh-pressed green juice, and white peach mimosas.

Ernest Coffee (1101 N. Palm Canyon Dr., 760/318-4154, www.ernestcoffee. com, 6am-7pm daily) is a chic space with polished concrete floors, plenty of natural light, warm wood tables, and splashes of bright color. They serve the Portland-originated Stumptown coffee and fresh, locally baked pastries. They also offer an excellent list of beer, wine, and a few small plates including cheese and charcuterie.

The original location of **Koffi** (515 N. Palm Dr., 760/416-2244, www.kofficoffee.com, 6am-7pm daily) has been gracing Palm Springs with its strong brews since 2008. The fresh, small-batch house blends are fragrantly ferried up from a roasting facility in the Coachella Valley. Food is an afterthought. There are multiple locations around town (650 E. Tahquitz Canyon Way, 760/318-0145, www.kofficoffee.com, 6am-6pm daily; 1700 S. Camino Real, 760/322-7776, www.kofficoffee.com, 5:30am-7:30pm daily).

★ **Elmer's Pancake House** (1030 E. Palm Canyon Dr., 760/327-8419, www.eatatelmers.com, 6am-9pm daily, $8-15) is a solid choice for its massive breakfast plates. They serve all the breakfast favorites as well as their signature German pancakes. Lunch and dinner offer up sandwiches, soups, salads, and comfort food entrées straight out of Twin Peaks diner territory. The service is good in this family-style retro diner with canted ceilings and plenty of windows.

Locals' favorite **Rick's Restaurant** (1973 N. Palm Canyon Dr., 760/416-0090, 6am-2pm Mon.-Fri., 6am-3pm Sat. and Sun., $8-13) doesn't do anything on a small scale. Breakfast and lunch diner classics are served in heaping and well-executed quantities. Ignore the questionable 1980s decor at this American-style diner and dig into their giant pancakes (crispy on the edges), giant cinnamon rolls, or omelets for breakfast. Order a side of the excellent bacon to go with anything. Lunch transitions into salads, cold and hot sandwiches (including Cuban pressed sandwiches), and hot plates with American and Cuban specialties.

California Cuisine

The ★ **Tropicale Restaurant and Coral Seas Lounge** (330 E. Amado Rd., 760/866-1952, www.thetropicale.com, 4pm-10pm Sun.-Thurs., 4pm-11pm Fri.-Sat., brunch 11am-2:45pm Sat.-Sun., $13-32) serves a very eclectic menu with a focus on Pacific Rim plates. Pizzas and sandwiches are thrown in for good measure. Deep banquette booths, chandeliers, and a buzzing tropical patio and bar are a throwback to the dinner clubs and themed cocktail bars Palm Springs does so well.

Part of the former Cary Grant estate, **Copley's** (621 N. Palm Canyon Dr., 760/327-9555, www.copleyspalmsprings.com, 5:30pm-close daily Oct.-mid-June, 5:30pm-close Tues.-Sun. mid-June-Sept., $22-39) offers new American fine dining in a romantic setting. The candlelit patio has the choicest seating and a stone fireplace. Entrées are geared toward the meat eater, with perfectly executed steaks, duck, fish, and lamb. A fleeting happy hour at the tiny bar brings the restaurant pricing within reach for one hour on weekdays.

★ **Shanghai Red's Bar & Grill** (235 S. Indian Canyon Dr., 760/322-9293, www.fishermans.com, 5pm-10pm Mon.-Thurs., 5pm-11:30pm Fri.-Sat., bar opens at 4pm, $5-35) offers some of the finest fish tacos out there. Anthony Bourdain said so himself. Housed inside the Fisherman's Market & Grill Restaurant Complex, this dark hole-in-the-wall consists of a long wooden bar and a few tables. The small space allows the person cooking behind the counter to whip up your shrimp and fish tacos doused with pico de gallo, shredded cabbage, and white sauce and hand them straight over to you without further ado. The menu also includes a full array of steamed, grilled, and fried seafood, soups, salads, and pastas. There is live music on the patio on weekends.

American

Mr. Lyon's (233 E. Palm Canyon Dr., 760/327-1551, www.mrlyonsps.com, 5pm-11pm Tues.-Sat., 4pm-9pm Sun., $32-59) is a sleek upscale steak house with a modern twist. Dry, aged beef and prime rib are house specialties with seafood and veggie options available. The dark, friendly bar offers classic cocktails and a lounge menu.

European

The skilled kitchen staff at ★ **Miro's** (Plaza Del Sol Shopping Center, 1555 S. Palm Canyon Dr., 760/323-5199, www. mirospalmsprings.com, 5pm-9:30pm Tues.-Sun., $28-39) take basic ingredients like whole Mediterranean sea bass, cabbage, beef, mushrooms, and Yukon Gold potatoes and practice cooking alchemy to turn every piping plate into a nuanced blend of satisfying goodness. Try dishes like beef Stroganoff, osso buco, scallops, and schnitzel paired with their cabbage salad and a choice from the extensive wine list.

Mexican

Rio Azul (350 S. Indian Canyon Dr., 760/992-5641, www.rioazulpalmsprings. com, 11am-9pm Mon.-Thurs., 11am-10pm Fri.-Sat., 10am-9pm Sun., $12-22) goes a huge step beyond the status quo of the refried bean, rice, and bubbling cheese plate of formulaic Mexican restaurants. They do offer this standard fare (we practically demand it as vacationing Americans), but their menu gets way more complex and nuanced with house specialties like the traditional Yucatán cochinita pibil (slow-roasted pork in banana leaf), grilled quail, and seafood enchiladas. They kill it with their skinny margarita: organic tequila, fresh lime, agave, and a sweet and salty chili rim. The space is vibrant with wood booths, good lighting, and a separate bar area. They offer a Desert Divas Drag Brunch on Sunday with tickets available on the website ($25).

Sushi

Reservations are recommended for dinner at **Sandfish** (1556 N. Palm Canyon Dr., 760/537-1022, https://sandfishps. com, 4:30pm-10pm Sun.-Thurs., 4:30pm-11pm Fri.-Sat., $8-20). Chef-owner Engin Onural has drawn from around the globe to create a buzzy spot with Japanese sushi and seafood uniquely paired with an extensive whiskey list. The menu is served against a stylishly spare Scandinavian interior.

Accommodations

October-May is when lodging rates are at their highest and hotels can book weeks in advance (prices dip in January when temperatures are colder). Rates skyrocket in **March** and **April,** when revelers flock to Palm Springs and the Coachella Valley for a number of large-scale events and festivals. Hotels can be booked *months* in advance—although with the sheer number of hotels in the area, last-minute reservations will likely be available at a few places.

Summer is the low season, due to soaring desert temperatures. But if your main goal is to lounge in a pool, there are great hotel rates to be had June-September.

$150-250

Sunny hospitality is what sets apart the ★ **Hotel California** (424 E. Palm Canyon Dr., 760/322-8855, www. palmspringshotelcalifornia.com, $120-180). The historic Spanish Mission-style hotel was originally constructed in 1942. Recently updated rooms have a comfortable yet rustic decor with Spanish tile floors, flat-screen TVs, and kitchenettes. King, queen, double queen, and suites are available. The communal space boasts a relaxing pool, lush greenery, hot tub, cruiser bikes, common kitchen, and grill. Bring your own supplies and relax for the weekend. The hotel is for adults age 21 and over.

The **Ace Hotel** (701 E. Palm Canyon Dr., 760/325-9900, www.acehotel.com/ palmsprings, $160-350) has a pitch-perfect hipness with its mid-century, vintage-inspired style. This 176-room hotel, spa, and resort offers two pools and a hot tub. Standard double, king, suites, and patio rooms feature clean, stylish design, flat-screen TVs and MP3 plug-ins. Some rooms offer vintage furniture, record players, or outdoor fireplaces. There is an on-site gym and spa. The on-site Amigo Room bar serves poolside drinks with a late-night atmosphere. The **Kings Highway Diner** (7am-3pm, 5:30pm-11pm daily, $7-15 brunch, $11-27 dinner) serves locally sourced nouveau American classics in an airy space with Naugahyde booths and original terrazzo floors. Children are allowed, as are pets (fee).

The spelling of the ★ **Orbit In** (562 W. Arenas Rd., 760/323-3585, www.orbitin.com, $209-269) is intentional. Coming from your travels to land amid the atomic-style furnishings of this mid-century boutique hotel will truly feel as if you just orbited in. The Orbit In is actually two properties on the same block. Herb Burns, who introduced Palm Springs to the luxury ultramodern motor court inn, built both the Orbit In and **The Hideaway** (370 W. Arenas Rd., 760/323-3585, www.orbitin.com, $209-269). They

both feature large studio-style rooms with sitting areas and kitchenettes surrounding a saltwater pool. The Orbit In is funkier, with nine poolside rooms, a terrazzo bar, hot tub, and vintage orange sun umbrellas. The Hideaway is sleeker and more muted with 10 poolside studios and great mountain views. At "Orbitini Hour" (5pm), guests of both properties gather at the Orbit In to chat over fruity Orbitinis.

Visiting the restored **Ingleside Inn** (200 W. Ramon Rd., 760/325-0046, https://inglesideinn.com, from $229) is like weekending at your sophisticated friend's swimming pool estate—which is exactly how the property was designed. Built in 1925 as a private home for the Birge family of the Pierce Arrow Motor Car Company, the home was opened as an elite hotel in 1939 by Ruth Hardy, Palm Springs' first councilwoman. Melvyn Haber, a New York businessman took over in 1975 and made **Melvyn's Restaurant and Lounge** the elegantly

Hotel California

upbeat nighttime scene with serious Hollywood Rat Pack cred that continues to draw a crowd. Some of the 30 guest rooms offer sitting areas, private patios, and gas fireplaces. Service is understated but there when you need it. At happy hour, you can have martini service delivered to your guest room or suite. The hotel is adult only (age 21 and older) and allows pets.

$250 and Over

The **Sparrows Lodge** (1330 E. Palm Canyon Dr., 760/327-2300, http://sparrowslodge.com, $230-380) is an impeccably restored 1950s retreat. Concrete and pebble-inlaid floors, exposed wood-beamed ceilings, open showers, and private patios grace 20 poolside rooms and garden cottages furnished with high-end design classics like butterfly chairs and Swiss Army blankets. A central pool and hot tub make for a simple and relaxing scene. A communal area serves beer, wine, and specialty drinks. The

continental breakfast of muffins, yogurt, granola, fruit, and French press coffee is well thought out. Rooms are double occupancy and are restricted to guests age 21 and over. Pets are allowed for a fee.

The Parker Palm Springs (4200 E. Palm Canyon Dr., 760/770-5000, www.theparkerpalmsprings.com, $260-400) began life in 1959 as California's first Holiday Inn. Today, a redesign includes 13 garden acres with two pools, a poolside bar, firepit, tennis courts, croquet lawn, and luxury retro-hip suites. In the lobby, chandeliers merge with Moroccan-inspired antiques for a richly eccentric boho-chic look. Patio, suite, and estate rooms are available. Hefty resort fees cover valet parking and bellhop service at this upscale resort. Food and drink offerings include a lobby bar, **Norma's** (7am-10pm daily) serving perfectly executed upscale diner fare, and **Mister Parker's** (6pm-close Wed.-Sun.), a posh French bistro.

Designed in 1947 by William Cody, the stone and redwood ★ **Del Marcos Hotel** (225 W. Baristo Rd., 760/325-6902, www.delmarcoshotel.com, $300-400) welcomes guests through its boldly angled entrance to a bright lobby with white terrazzo floors and floor-to-ceiling glass looking out to the saltwater pool. The 17 suites are impeccably styled with individual charm from the Eames Poolside Suite with terrazzo floors and Eames furnishings to the Desert Oasis Deluxe with a tiki bar and private patio. Beach cruisers are available for tooling around town. A daily complimentary happy hour is a nice touch.

The ★ **Korakia Pensione** (257 S. Patencio Rd., 760/864-6411, www.korakia.com, from $479) was built as a Moroccan-inspired artist retreat in 1924 and continues in this spirit as its incarnation as a stylish bed-and-breakfast resort. The 28 suites, studios, and bungalows are housed in two restored villas set on 1.5 acres of fountains. Many have private balconies or patios. Enter through the keyhole-shaped grand entrance flanked by ornately carved Moorish wooden doors. Moroccan fountains, a stone waterfall, and stone courtyard complete the outside vibe, while the wood-beamed ceilings and antiques of the rooms ooze good taste. Guest must be age 13 or older.

LGBTQ Hotels and Resorts

El Mirasol Villas (525 Warm Sands Dr., 760/327 5913, www.elmirasol.com, $129-329) is a California ranch-style hotel originally built by Howard Hughes in the 1940s and operating as a gay clothing-optional resort since 1975.

INNdulge (601 S. Grenfall Rd., 760/327-1408, http://inndulge.com, $145-225) is a lively gay clothing-optional resort offering Thursday pizza, evening social hours, and weekend pool parties.

Set on a classic 1950s property, **Escape Resort** (641 E. San Lorenzo Rd., 760/325-5269, www.escapepalmsprings.com, $179-209) is a laid-back, clothing-optional resort catering to gay singles and couples.

La Dolce Vita (1491 S. Via Soledad, 760/325-2686, www.ladolcevitaresort.com, $179-209) is a swimsuit-optional gay resort offering a relaxing oasis in a Spanish hacienda-style inn.

The stylish **Santiago** (650 E. San Lorenzo Rd., 760/322-1300, www.santiagoresort.com, $189-245) is a male-only, swimsuit-optional resort featuring chic, modern rooms and landscaped grounds.

East Canyon Hotel & Spa (288 E. Camino Monte Vista, 760/320-1928, www.eastcanyonps.com, $199-299, 3-night min.) is open to LGBTQ, straight, and all friendly couples. Accommodations include queen and king suites. Guests must be age 18 and over.

Vista Grande Resort (574 S. Warm Sands Dr., 760/322-2404, http://vistagranderesort.com, from $209) features three swimming pools, a 16-person spa, lagoon, and waterfall at this clothing-optional men's resort.

The Hacienda at Warm Sands (586 Warm Sands Dr., 760-327-8111, www.thehacienda.com, from $384) is a small upscale, luxury, gay resort with nine suites. Amenities include two pools, a hot tub, and an outdoor fireplace set in the landscaped grounds with mountain views.

Information and Services

The iconic **Palm Springs Visitors Center** (2901 N. Palm Canyon Dr., 760/778-8418, www.visitpalmsprings.com, 9am-5pm daily) was designed in 1965 by renowned architect Albert Frey as a gas station for the Palm Springs Aerial Tramway. The fully staffed visitors center has a wealth of books and maps about the historic city.

Other resources include the official **Palm Springs tourism website** (www.visitpalmsprings.com). For a gay tourism perspective, check out www.visitgaypalmsprings.com for recommended lodging, dining, and activities.

Getting Around

Palm Springs is swarming with **Uber** (www.uber.com) and **Lyft** (www.lyft.com) ride shares. There are also a few taxi services. **Desert City Cab** (760/328-3000, www.desertcitycab.com) offers 24-hour service to the entire Coachella Valley, including Palm Springs. **Yellow Cab of the Desert** (760/340-8294, www.yellowcabofthedesert.com) serves Palm Springs, Cathedral City, Rancho Mirage, La Quinta, Indio, and Indian Wells.

BIKE Palm Springs Bike Rentals (194 S. Indian Canyon, 760/832-8912, www.bikepsrentals.com, 8am-5pm daily Oct.-June, 8am-10am daily July-Sept.) rents premium cruisers ($25 for 4 hours, $35 per day), road bikes with carbon forks ($35 for up to 4 hours, $50 per day), full-suspension mountain bikes ($50 for up to 4 hours, $65 per day), tandems ($40 for 4 hours, $50 per day), and electric bikes ($44 for 4 hours, $60 per day), as well as child bikes and bike carriers ($15 for 4 hours, $20 per day). Rentals include free maps with touring routes, locks, and helmets.

Big Wheel Tours (760/779-1837, www.bwbtours.com) rents KHS and Benno brand bicycles. Cruisers, mountain bikes, hybrids, and road bikes are available by the hour ($12-18), half day ($25-40), full day ($35-60), and week ($90-195). Big Wheel Tours is based in Palm Desert, 15 miles (24 km) southeast of Palm Springs. Their bikes are available for delivery ($25-35; call to reserve). Big Wheel Tours also offers **bike tours** (4 hours, departs 8am and 1pm daily Oct.-May, 7am daily June-Sept., $105).

⚑ Side Trip: The San Jacinto Mountains

Follow Highway 243 or Highway 74 up from the desert floor and in under an hour you will find yourself in the much cooler San Jacinto Mountains. Tourism is the primary industry and most of the land surrounding Idyllwild is protected through the Mount San Jacinto State Park, Santa Rosa and San Jacinto Mountains National Monument, and San Bernardino National Forest.

Getting There

The two main jumping-off points into this destination are from the town of Idyllwild and the Palm Springs Aerial Tramway.

The **Palm Springs Aerial Tramway** (www.pstramway.com) allows visitors to reach the cool mountain air in about 10 minutes. The tramway leaves from Valley Station on the floor of Palm Springs and lifts visitors on a dizzying ride via suspended cable cars to traverse the length of rugged Chino Canyon, alighting in a crisp alpine climate at Mountain Station (elevation 8,516 feet) in Mount San Jacinto State Park. From Mountain Station, a network of trails (totaling 54 mi/87 km within the 14,000-acre wilderness) leads to pine forests, meadows, and striking views.

Stop at the **Long Valley Ranger Station** (0.25 mile west of Mountain Station) for maps and info. All trails (except the Long Valley Discovery Trail and Desert View Trail) require that you check in and complete a day-use permit.

When the tramway is shut down, day-hiking trails in the Long Valley Ranger Station vicinity of the Mount San Jacinto State Park are not accessible from the tramway's Mountain Station. As an alternative, visit Idyllwild and plan hikes in the network of trails around the mountain town.

★ Mount San Jacinto State Park and Wilderness

Subalpine forests, granite peaks, and mountain meadows quilt the 14,000-acre **Mount San Jacinto State Park and Wilderness** (www.parks.ca.gov and www.fs.usda.gov) in the heart of the San Jacinto Mountains. Craggy San Jacinto Peak, the highest peak in the park and the second highest in the San Jacinto Range (after Mount San Gorgonio) reaches nearly 11,000 feet and is snowcapped for much of the year. The steep mountain escarpments of the San Jacinto Range plunge 9,000 feet in less than four miles on the northeast side down to the desert floor.

Hiking trails offer sweeping views toward Palm Springs and more than 100 miles to the southeast and the Salton Sea. It's a destination for day hiking, backpacking, snowshoeing, and camping. The famous Pacific Crest Trail (PCT), a continuous 2,650-mile trail system that runs from Mexico to Canada, passes through the San Jacinto Mountains, and Idyllwild is a destination for PCT hikers.

Summer is the high season with visitors taking advantage of cooler temperatures, campgrounds, and hiking trails.

Hiking

Hiking trails are accessible from the town of Idyllwild and via the Palm Springs Aerial Tramway. A **wilderness permit** system is in place; everyone must obtain a wilderness permit prior to day hiking or overnight camping. Day-use permits are free and available at the Long Valley Ranger Station, the **Idyllwild Ranger Station** (54270 Pine Crest Ave., 909/382-2921, 8am-4pm Fri.-Tues.), and the entrance station for **Idyllwild Campground** (25905 Hwy. 243) in San Jacinto State Park.

The hiking season generally runs **April–November.** Keep in mind that temperatures may be very cold and trails may be impassable due to snow and ice. Expect a 30- to 40-degree temperature difference from the valley floor.

Desert View Trail

Slightly longer than the Long Valley Discovery Trail, the **Desert View Trail** (1.6 mi/3 km round-trip, 1 hour, 160 feet elevation gain, easy-moderate) starts from the Mountain Station (take a tram ride to the top). Enjoy the striking contrasts between this fresh alpine haven and the austere desert below via an easy to moderate loop trail that clocks in at less than two miles. The trail, which can be hiked clockwise or counterclockwise, undulates through rich pine forest, passing five rocky lookouts (notches) that give way to sweeping views of the Coachella Valley below. Each notch gives a different panoramic perspective and up-close views of colorful rock outcroppings.

To reach the trailhead at Upper Terminal Mountain Station via the Palm Springs Aerial Tramway, exit Mountain Station via the back entrance. The signed trail starts at the bottom of the walkway leading to trails, wilderness, and a ranger station.

Round Valley Loop to Wellman Divide

Hike the Round Valley Loop with lovely Round Valley and its luxuriant meadow

Mount San Jacinto Peak State Park and Wilderness

as your destination (4.5 mi/7 km round-trip, 3 hours) or tack on a steep addendum (6.5 mi/10.5 km round-trip, 4 hours) to see the spectacular views from Wellman Divide.

From the Long Valley Ranger Station follow the well-marked trail (**Low Trail** on maps) southeast toward Round Valley. The trail climbs steadily through pine forests. In early summer you may be crossing or traveling alongside bubbling seasonal snowmelt streams. At 1.8 miles (3 km) the trail splits. Continue right toward Round Valley and the meadow. You will reach **Round Valley** at 2.1 miles (3 km); it's a satisfying destination. Many people use it as an overnight spot, camping at the Round Valley **backcountry campground** or Tamarack Valley to the north.

Continuing from Round Valley the trail gets real, climbing 660 feet over a mile. The views from **Wellman Divide** make the short and steep trek worth it. They're spectacular, casting a visual net toward venerable Tahquitz Peak and deeper over the Santa Rosa Mountains. From here it's only 2.7 miles (5 km) to San Jacinto Peak.

Assuming you've had enough for the day (continuing on to San Jacinto Peak will add an additional 5.4 miles (9 km) round-trip, return 0.3 mile to a trail junction past Round Valley. Mix it up by taking the right loop (**High Trail** on maps). This will add a mere 0.3 mile to your hike but will vary your return scenery and give you unexpected views of Mountain Station as you descend the last mile to the ranger station.

To reach the trailhead, take the Palm Springs Aerial Tramway to the Upper Terminal Mountain Station. From Mountain Station the ranger station is 0.25 mile to the west. Check in and complete a day-use pass before beginning your hike.

San Jacinto Peak

San Jacinto Peak is the second-highest peak in the San Jacinto Mountains. The peak towers over Palm Springs to the west and the village of Idyllwild to the south. The vistas from the top are amazing, taking in the Coachella Valley, the Salton Sea, and looking north to the impressive San Bernardino Mountains and lofty Mount San Gorgonio.

There are several routes to **San Jacinto Peak** (12 mi/19 km round-trip, 6 hours, 2,300 feet elevation gain, strenuous) including from the town of Idyllwild. The most direct (and shortest) route begins from the top of the Palm Springs Aerial Tramway. From the Long Valley Ranger Station, follow the well-marked trail (**Low Trail** on maps) southeast toward Round Valley. The trail winds up steadily through pine forests. In early summer if there has been a good season of winter snowfall, you may come across lively seasonal streams. At 1.8 miles (3 km) the trail splits. Continue right toward Round Valley, reaching **Round Valley** at 2.1 miles (3 km). From

here the trail begins to ascend more seriously toward Wellman Divide, climbing 660 feet over the course of 1 mile. Take in the spectacular views from **Wellman Divide;** Tahquitz Peak and the Santa Rosa Mountains are in your sights. From here it's only 2.7 miles (4 km) to San Jacinto Peak. Follow the trail north toward San Jacinto Peak as it switchbacks steeply and the views grow increasingly sweeping. Just below the peak (0.3 mile) the trail splits again. Follow the steep trail up to the giant granite massif that is **San Jacinto Peak.** Soak in the views from the steep (and sometimes windy) pinnacle.

Return the way you came. After Round Valley you will reach a split with the Low and High Trails. Both return to the Long Valley Ranger Station. The **High Trail** (right split) adds a small amount of mileage (0.3 mile), but it takes you over ground you haven't covered. The good news: either way you're close to some well-earned food, drinks, and continued views (from the comfort of a chair) at Mountain Station.

To get there, take the Palm Springs Aerial Tramway to the upper terminal at Mountain Station. From Mountain Station the ranger station is 0.25 mile to the west. Check in and complete a day-use pass before beginning your hike.

Tahquitz Peak via Devil's Slide Trail

This striking, granite crag can be seen on the drive in from Highway 243. It stands sentinel over the town, and you'll catch glimpses of it from different vantage points. In addition to experiencing breathtaking views and a trip to a historic, furnished fire tower, if you kick off your time in Idyllwild with this spectacular hike to **Tahquitz Peak** (8.6 mi/12 km, 5 hours, 2,800 feet elevation gain, strenuous), you'll get to feel a sense of smug accomplishment every time you look up.

From the trailhead in Humber Park, follow the Devil's Slide Trail to Saddle Junction. From this junction, turn right onto the PCT heading south. You will

have a slight break from climbing before the trail ascends through pine forest. The climb continues along a ridge, the Desert Divide, with views into the Coachella Valley. After 1.3 miles (2 km) along the PCT, turn right onto an access trail and begin the final climb. When you come to a junction with the South Ridge Trail, stay to the right for the last rocky stretch before the lookout tower comes into view.

Climb the steps up to the deck of the lookout tower to get an eyeful. The tower was used historically as a fire lookout, positioned because of its 360-degree views. It has been preserved with historic furnishings, and volunteers maintain the space and greet hikers at the top on some weekends in season (May-Nov.). It adds an extra layer of richness to the experience to tap into some of the region's history and pick the volunteers' brains about trails and surrounding geography as well as enjoy the natural beauty. From the lookout tower deck, the Coachella Valley sprawls to the east, bounded by Joshua Tree National Park and the Little San Bernardino and Cottonwood Mountains. To the north, Marion Mountain looms, blocking views of San Jacinto Peak and the Palm Springs Aerial Tramway. To the southeast, the views extend as far as the Salton Sea.

To reach the trailhead from the Idyllwild Ranger Station, head northeast on Pine Crest Avenue for 0.6 mile. Turn left onto Fern Valley Road and continue for 1.8 miles (3 km) until you reach Humber Park. The trail begins on the upper level of the parking area.

Ernie Maxwell Scenic Trail

First off, here's a pro tip: Start the **Ernie Maxwell Scenic Trail** (5.3 mi/9 km round-trip, 2-3 hours, 550 feet elevation gain, easy) from the dirt road trailhead in Idyllwild. This way, you will gain elevation on the beginning stretch and have an easier return.

A gentle elevation gain through a mostly shaded, forested trail makes this a good choice for a leisurely but satisfying hike. (This is a good Sunday morning hike.) Starting from the **Tahquitz View Drive** trailhead, the path climbs gently through a mix of Jeffrey, ponderosa, and Coulter pines all the way to the **Humber Park** trailhead. The trail provides intermittent views toward Idyllwild and the southwest. The real highlight here is the immersive forest experience and the mellow grades. The trail is particularly nice in **September** and **October**. Once you reach the Humber Park trailhead, turn around and return the way you came.

From the Idyllwild Ranger Station (Hwy. 243 and Pine Crest Ave. in Idyllwild), head south on Highway 243 for 0.7 mile. Turn left onto Saunders Meadow Road just past the Mile High Café and before the Idyllwild School. Follow Saunders Meadow Road for 0.8 mile then turn left onto signed Pine Avenue. After 0.1 mile turn right onto the signed Tahquitz View Drive. The trailhead is in 0.6 mile. The pavement ends 0.2 mile into Tahquitz View Drive, and the road forks. Follow the left fork signed for the Ernie Maxwell Scenic Trail. The trailhead is signed on the right. Park along the dirt road.

Camping
Mount San Jacinto State Park (www.parks.ca.gov) operates two campgrounds near Idyllwild: Idyllwild Campground and Stone Creek Campground. Winter storms in 2019 closed both of these campgrounds indefinitely. Check for current conditions.

Idyllwild Campground (25905 Hwy. 243, 951/659-2607, www.reservecalifornia.com, year-round, $25) has 33 sites under a canopy of pine and dotted with manzanitas for tent camping, RVs, and trailers. Showers, flush toilets, water, picnic tables, and fire rings are onsite. The campground is walking distance to Idyllwild shops and restaurants.

Stone Creek Campground (Hwy. 243, www.reservecalifornia.com, May-Oct., $20) offers 50 sites for tent camping, as well as trailer and RV sites (no hookups or dump stations). Amenities include fire rings, picnic tables, water, and vault toilets. The campground is off Highway 243, about 6 miles (10 km) north of Idyllwild.

Getting Around
A **Forest Adventure Pass** is required to park at trailheads and day-use areas. Adventure Passes are available at the Idyllwild Ranger Station or at **Nomad Ventures** (54415 N. Circle Dr., 951/659-4853, www.nomadventures.com, 9am-5pm Thurs.-Mon.), as well as other ranger stations and retailers throughout the area.

Idyllwild
Idyllwild is a charming mountain town nestled in the San Jacinto Mountains. The artsy community is home to picturesque cabins with A-frame roofs hinting at snow, an exciting proposition in contrast with the sleekly flat mid-century desert dwellings below. Seasonal streams and hiking trails crisscross the hills. Inns with chainsaw-carved wildlife sculptures and fireplaces welcome visitors escaping the heat and traffic of the urban areas below.

The adjacent communities of Fern Valley, Pine Cove, and Idyllwild are generally grouped together and all considered "Idyllwild."

Getting There
The town of Idyllwild is in the San Jacinto Mountains above Palm Springs. To get here from Palm Springs, take North Palm Canyon Drive (Hwy. 111) north to I-10. Take I-10 west for 3 miles (5 km) to the town of Banning. At Banning, take Highway 243 and drive 25 twisting mountain miles (40 km) south to the town center. Note that Highway 243 may close due to snow or other inclement weather.

From the Coachella Valley, take Highway 74 west (from its intersection with Hwy. 111) and continue onto

Idyllwild

```
0                    0.5 mi
0          0.5 km
```

To Devil's Slide Trail

CHIPMUNK DR

TAHQUITZ RD
LODGE RD
DICKENSON RD
PALOMAR RD
RIMROCK RD

FERN VALLEY RD
SAN JACINTO RD
TAHQUITZ
PALOMAR RD
RIMROCK RD

JOHN MUIR RD

THE GRAND
IDYLLWILD LODGE

243

IDYLLWILD
BUNKHOUSE

JAMESON DR

FERN ST
BEST LN

PARKVIEW RD
IRIS RD

LA CASITA
RESTAURANT

PINE CREST AVE
CIRCLE DR
FIR ST
RIVER DR
ALDERWOOD RD

IDYLLWILD CAMPGROUND
(MT SAN JACINTO SP)

IDYLLWILD
RANGER
STATION

NOMAD
ADVENTURES

OAKWOOD ST

Strawberry Creek

SCENIC DR

TAHQUITZ RD

DARYLL RD

IDYLLWILD
VILLAGE MARKET

RED
KETTLE

PLANT FOOD
SUPPER CLUB

IDYLLWILD
REGIONAL PARK
CAMPGROUND

GASTROGNOME

VILLAGE CENTER DR

IDYLLWILD
INN

Idyllwild
County Park

IDYLLWILD
BREWPUB

CIRCLE DR

FERN DR

STRAWBERRY CREEK INN
BED & BREAKFAST

BICKNELL LN

LOOKOUT RD

MARIAN VIEW DR

ERNIE MAXWELL
SCENIC TRAIL

243

CIRCLE DR
TAHQUITZ TRAIL LN
STRAWBERRY VALLEY DR

CREST VIEW DR

CREST DR

CEDAR AVE
PINE AVE

TAHQUITZ VIEW DR

© MOON.COM

Highway 243 north to reach Idyllwild in 41 miles (66 km).

Shopping

The majority of the shops in Idyllwild are clustered in a three-block radius on North Circle Drive where it intersects with Highway 243. A website (http://idyllwildvisitorscenter.com) provides a town business directory of shopping, dining, and lodging.

Nomad Ventures (54415 N. Circle Dr., 951/659-4853, www.nomadventures.com, 9am-5pm Thurs.-Mon.) provides outdoor gear and equipment covering climbing, mountaineering, backpacking, hiking, trail running, and kayaking.

Wooley's (54274 N. Circle Dr., 951/659-0017, www.wooleys.com, 10:30am-5pm daily) offers sheepskin products, including sheepskin slippers, boots, and seat covers. They also stock clothing, cowboy hats, and winter hats—great if you're caught in the cooler temperatures of Idyllwild and need to make an emergency fashion purchase. Home furnishings include high-quality cowhide rugs, lambskin throws, and pillows.

Everitt's Minerals and Gallery (54300 N. Circle Dr., 951/659-7075, www. everittsminerals.com, 11am-5pm daily, hours vary) sells handmade jewelry and designs, exotic mineral specimens, rare fossils, and antique Japanese woodblock prints. Their gallery features 14 local and semi-local artists with fine art media including ceramics, sculpture, and painting.

Coyote Red's (54225 N. Circle Dr., 951/659-2305, 11am-4pm Mon.-Thurs., 11am-5pm Fri., 10am-5pm Sat., 10am-4pm Sun.) is a gourmet country store selling beef jerky and hot sauce. Their signature chipotle sauce rivals the best of them.

Remember When (54225 N. Circle Dr., 951/659-6456, 11am-4pm Sun.-Mon. and Thurs.-Fri., 10am-5pm Sat.) stocks nostalgic sweets, sodas, and toys. The almost 200 specialty sodas, throwback candies, and selection of simple toys are fun for the family.

Idyllwild Village Market (2600 Hwy. 243, 951/659-3800, www. idyllwildvillagemarket.com, 7am-10pm daily) is a gourmet goods shop with a full grocery plus deli, beer, liquor, and pizza.

Food

The **Red Kettle** (54220 N. Circle Dr., 951/659-4063, http://perrysredkettle. com, 7am-2pm daily, $8-11) is a great place to fuel up before a hike or to savor a casual weekend. They serve up classic American breakfasts like country ham and eggs and lunch specials like chili, burgers, soups, and salads in a quaint cottage setting.

Plant Food Supper Club (54241 Ridgeview Dr., 11am-8pm Wed.-Sat., 11am-4pm Sun.-Mon., $9-18) is the vegan brainchild of chef-owner Kelly Johnston-Gibson. She started this culinary adventure for small, select dinner parties on the back deck of her Idyllwild cabin and has since grown it into a bustling business with live music and a patio brunch in the town center. Both visitors and locals frequent her lovely A-frame location, established in 2016, which offers a full brunch, lunch, and dinner menu as well as organic wines, craft beers, fresh juices, smoothies, and tonics. Menu items range from banana pancakes and breakfast tacos to a grilled tempeh Reuben and sweet potato enchiladas verde.

★ **Idyllwild Brewpub** (54423 Village Center Dr., 951/659-0163, www. idyllwildbrewpub.com, noon-9pm Mon.-Thurs., noon-10pm Fri., 11am-10pm Sat., 11am-8pm Sun., $10-18) brought Idyllwild into the 21st century with the opening of this lively gastropub. They offer a full menu of competently brewed English, Belgian, U.S., and Canadian-style brews as well as a full bar. The menu offers hearty, shareable snacks like brisket nachos and buffalo wings and mains including burgers and fish-and-chips. The upstairs location has an indoor space with tables and a long bar and an outdoor patio with forest views. It is both family and party-friendly.

Take a 1970s ski lodge and spruce it up with design tips from *The Hobbit,* and you've got ★ **Gastrognome** (54381 Ridge View Dr., 951/659-5055, www. gastrognome.com, 10am-9pm Sun.-Thurs., 10am-9:30pm Fri.-Sat., winter hours vary, $10-34), the picturesque favorite of locals and visitors. A lengthy dinner menu features fish, chicken, lamb, steaks, and pasta dishes. The lunch menu is equally daunting with sandwiches, fish, seafood, pastas, vegetarian options, and steaks. When in doubt, the French onion soup is a solid choice. The charm of the restaurant might be its biggest selling point, but the food is generally well executed. Reservations are recommended for dinner on weekends.

In the Fern Valley neighborhood,

La Casita Mexican Restaurant (54650 N. Circle Dr., 951/659-6038, www. idyllwildlacasita.com, 11am-9pm daily summer, 11am-8pm daily winter, $10-20) anchors the other end of town with satisfying plates of Mexican food and margaritas served in a rustic, wood-paneled setting with a large patio. Located near the entrance to the hiking trails in Humber Park, the small restaurant can get packed.

Accommodations

The aesthetic here is rustic, and hotel accommodations range from boutique mountain lodges with elaborate amenities to frayed cabin motels with charming exteriors and interiors that have seen better days. Hotels and motels get you closer to town, while cabins make for a more secluded weekend. Make reservations in advance; Idyllwild can book completely on weekends.

Idyllwild Vacation Cabins (54380 N. Circle Dr., 951/663-0527, www. idyllwildvacationcabins.com, 7am-10pm Mon.-Fri.) is a local company with a large selection of rental cabins. You can search by price or preference: pet-friendly, with views, with hot tubs, on a creek, etc. Cabins are searchable and bookable on their website, but they also have an actual, physical location in Idyllwild's downtown and an actual, real live human in their office who can assist with booking. The office is convenient for last-minute bookings when your day trip turns into a weekend getaway. They also offer centralized management assistance.

The family-owned **Idyllwild Inn** (54300 Village Center Dr., 888/659-2552, www.idyllwildinn.com, $107-160) dates from 1904 and is a favorite of PCT hikers and repeat visitors. Set on five wooded acres in the center of town, it features cabins, suites, and theme rooms. Its 12 one- and two-bedroom rustic cabins are original with knotty pine paneling, fireplaces, and private decks. Cabin #9 is carved with historic graffiti dating to the 1950s. Eight new rustic cabins are family-friendly with queen beds and sleeper sofas. New rustic suites offer Jacuzzi tubs, queen beds, and sleeper sofas. Eight themed rooms are a relatively recent addition.

The ★ **Idyllwild Bunkhouse** (25525 Hwy. 243, 951/659-2201, www. idyllwildbunkhouse.com, $109-169) offers rustic, camp-themed rooms with knotty pine interiors with room configurations that appeal to couples or families. Queen bedrooms, two-room suites, queen plus twin bedrooms, and downstairs queen plus twin loft rooms all come with kitchenettes and private balconies with forest views. A continental breakfast is delivered to your door each morning. Amenities include DirecTV and Wi-Fi. The hotel is less than a mile north of town.

Nine rustic individually decorated rooms make up the **Strawberry Creek Inn** (26370 Hwy. 243, 951/659-3202, www.strawberrycreekinn.com, $197-207). The cozy rooms including courtyard, queen, and fireplace suites have Wi-Fi, private bathrooms, and TVs. Some also offer private decks, fireplaces, or canopy beds. A full, homemade breakfast is included. The two-story Strawberry Cottage on the property features a private entrance, full kitchen, and whirlpool tub. The inn is in the center of town.

Too much rustic got you down? **The Grand Idyllwild Lodge** (54820 Pinecrest Rd., 951/659-2383, www. grandidyllwildlodge.com, $265-315) might be the place for you. The Craftsman-style boutique lodge is situated at the top of the town in Fern Valley close to Aroma and Idyology restaurants and Humber Park hiking trails. They offer seven king suites and two queen guest rooms with private entrances, decks, gourmet breakfast, fireplaces, flat-screen smart TVs, a gym, Swedish-style sauna, and spa services.

Camping

Idyllwild Regional Park Campground
(54000 Riverside County Playground
Rd., 951/659-2656, www.rivcoparks.org,
$33) is less than a mile south of the state
park campground. Its 88 sites are situated
under shaded pine forest and are available year-round for tent, RV, and trailer
camping. Amenities include picnic tables, fire rings, flush toilets, and showers. Designated accessible sites are 1, 23,
and 39. Reservations are accepted April
through October; November to March,
the park has sites 1-6 available for first-
come, first-served camping. The park
also offers a nature center and interpretive trails.

Other seasonal campgrounds are open
in summer only; these are in the vicinity
of the Stone Creek Campground and are
operated by the **San Bernardino National
Forest** (909/382-2921, www.fs.usda.gov).

At **Fern Basin** (reserve at www.
recreation.gov, May-Sept., $10-34), about
6.5 miles (10.5 km) north of Idyllwild, 22
sites are set amid manzanitas, oaks, and
conifers at 6,400 feet. Amenities include
vault toilets, fire rings, and picnic tables,
but there is no drinking water.

Marion Mountain Campground (www.
recreation.gov, June-Nov., $10-34) has 24
campsites set in two loops amid a cedar
and ponderosa pine forest. Amenities
include vault toilets, fire rings, drinking
water, and picnic tables. It is about 7 miles
(11 km) north of Idyllwild.

Dark Canyon Campground (first-
come, first-served, May-Sept., $12) has
12 shaded tent-only campsites set next
to a seasonal creek at 5,900 feet elevation. Amenities include vault toilets, fire
rings, drinking water, and picnic tables.
Dark Canyon is 8 miles (13 km) north of
Idyllwild.

Getting Around

There is no public transportation available in Idyllwild—no buses, taxis, or ride
sharing services. Idyllwild is a small town
of less than 3 miles (5 km) from end to

end, and it is easy to get around by driving or walking. The town center has sidewalks and lighting, and if you are staying
directly in town, it is no problem to do
everything on foot.

Outside the town center the sidewalks
and lighting disappear. Both Highways
243 and 74 have steady traffic, and it can
be a little nerve-racking to be a pedestrian walking along the narrow shoulders of these dark roads at night. Carry
a flashlight so that you are visible to
drivers.

Desert Hot Springs

Situated along the San Andreas Fault,
Desert Hot Springs' claim to fame is
the abundance of hot natural mineral
springs that propelled the development
of the town's spas and resorts. The 1950s
were a heyday, and some of the operating
boutique hotels sport the clean lines and
neon signs of desert resort mid-century
architecture. Desert Hot Springs has
never achieved the popularity of nearby
Palm Springs. The town has seen growth
in recent years but much of it in the form
of newer residences. Desert Hot Springs'
spas are mixed amid the more recent
housing. The town attracts snowbirds
and other visitors looking for a more low-
key and affordable experience than Palm
Springs. Its spas range from retro-hip to
sleekly luxurious.

Getting There

Desert Hot Springs is north of Palm
Springs and I-10. To get here, follow
North Indian Canyon Drive north
from Palm Springs or take Highway 62
north from I-10 and turn east on Pierson
Boulevard.

Sights
Cabot's Pueblo Museum

Cabot Yerxa is the man responsible for
this fascinating Hopi-inspired 35-room
pueblo, an artistic masterpiece he built

Desert Hot Springs

MIRACLE SPRINGS
RESORT & SPA

DESERT HOT
SPRINGS
SPA HOTEL

SAN BRUNO RD
SAN ARDO RD
SAN REMO RD

SUNSET AVE

8TH ST
7TH ST
6TH ST
5TH ST

PALM DR

MESQUITE AVE

8TH ST
6TH ST

4TH ST
3RD ST
2ND ST

POMELO DR

EL
MOROCCO
INN

VISTA PL

AMBROSIO DR

SOUTH OF
THE BORDER

2ND ST
1ST ST

CASA
BLANCA

PIERSON BLVD

ACOMA AVE

BUENA VISTA AVE

CAHUILLA AVE

ESTRELLA AVE

POMELO DR
FOXDALE DR

VERBENA DR

FLORA AVE

TAMAR DR

SPRING RESORT
& DAY SPA

SAGEWATER SPA

CABOT'S
PUEBLO MUSEUM ★

DESERT VIEW AVE

ALTA LOMA

MAU WAY

ELISEO RD
REPOSO WAY

CLUB CIRCLE

HOPE
SPRINGS
RESORT

TUSCAN
SPRINGS

AMAPOLA

LIDO PALMS

PALM DR

OCOTILLO AVE

MESQUITE AVE

HACIENDA AVE

HACIENDA AVE

CACTUS DR
LA MESA DR
CALIENTE DR

OCOTILLO DR

MIRACLE HILL RD

CUANDO WAY

HIDALGO ST
HERMANO WAY
INAJA ST
QUINTA WAY

MOUNTAIN VIEW RD

EL CAJON DR

SARITA DR

MARK DR
NAHUM DR
LUIS DR

TWO BUNCH PALMS TRAIL

TWO BUNCH PALMS
RESORT & SPA

ESSENSE

PALM DR

PARK LN

VERBENA DR

CAMPANERO

VERXA RD

TARBUTTON RD

HOTEL LAUTNER

BRUNN LN

© MOON.COM

0   0.5 mi

0   0.5 km

---

entirely out of found materials between 1941 and 1950. **Cabot's Pueblo Museum** (67616 E. Desert View Ave., 760/329-7610, www.cabotsmuseum.org, 9am-4pm Tues.-Sun. Oct.-May, 9am-1pm Wed.-Sat. June-Sept., tours $13) offers guided tours of the home's interior, but you don't have to take the tour to visit the trading post and grounds, which include beautifully weathered outbuildings, a meditation garden, a well house, and *Waokiya,* a 43-foot-tall Native American sculpture carved from a fallen cedar. Tickets are available online and in-person and close one hour before tour start times.

Spas and Mineral Springs

The town of Desert Hot Springs, developed over natural hot and cold-water aquifers, is a haven for spa hounds who flock to the dozens of hotels that have tapped into these rich mineral aquifers to fill their swimming pools and hot tubs.

Desert Hot Springs Spa Hotel (11740 Mesquite Ave., 760/673-8689, www.dhsspa.com, 8am-10pm daily, $5-10 day pass) takes a quantity-over-quality approach. A day pass gets you access to the 1940s resort hotel's eight mineral pools in a large, palm-studded courtyard. The hotel also has an on-site café and sports bar. The hotel is well known as a party spot and has live music on weekends.

The charming Moroccan-themed **El Morocco Inn** (66810 4th St., 760/288-2527, www.elmoroccoinn.com, 9am-4pm daily, $50 pp, free with 1-hour spa) offers a huge, covered hot spa, outdoor mineral pool, sauna, and a range of spa services including massage, scrubs, masks, facials, and detoxifying treatments.

The **Miracle Springs Resort & Spa** (10625 Palm Dr., 760/251-6000, www.miraclesprings.com, 9am-6pm daily, age 21 and over only, $14) offers eight pools and spas for day use. They also have an on-site salon (manicures and pedicures) and a full-service spa. The on-site Capri restaurant serves breakfast, lunch, and dinner, and has a full bar and poolside lunch service.

At **The Spring Resort & Spa** (12699 Reposo Way, 760/251-6700, www.thespring.com, call for reservations 7:45am-8:45pm, with spa services only) guests receive timed use of the three mineral pools. They offer several different packages combining massages, scrubs, and wraps.

The quiet **Tuscan Springs Hotel & Spa** (68187 Club Cir., 760/251-0189, www.tuscansprings.com, $45 for four hours) offers day-use of their mineral pool (free with spa purchase).

The setting at family-friendly **Sam's Family Spa Hot Water Resort** (70875 Dillon Rd., 760/329-6457, www.samsfamilyspa.com, $18-25) includes a spring-fed swimming pool and a series of hot mineral pools tucked amid palm trees in a parklike setting.

The Spa at Desert Springs (JW Marriott Desert Springs Resort & Spa, 74-855 Country Club Dr., 760/341-1874, www.marriott.com, $45 per day) offers unlimited use of their heated outdoor saltwater pool, sauna, steam room, whirlpools, fitness equipment, and lounges (both co-ed and gender separated). Book a spa treatment ($80 and up) and use of amenities are included.

Food

There are dining options in Desert Hot Springs but few are destination-worthy. It's worth it to drive to Palm Springs 12 miles (19 km) south or take advantage of the kitchens and barbecues provided in some of the resorts.

Serving Mexican specialties and smoky salsa in a setting with colorful decor, **Casa Blanca** (66370 Pierson Blvd., 760/251-5922, www.casablancamenu.com, 7:30am-10pm daily, $6-18) is a popular choice for locals and visitors. Try the signature spinach enchiladas.

You can also enjoy the traditional Mexican plates and deep booths at **South of the Border** (11719 Palm Dr., 760/251-4000, 11am-9:30pm Sun.-Thurs., 11am-10pm Fri.-Sat., $9-12).

Essense (67425 Two Bunch Palms Trail, 760/329-8791, www.twobunchpalms.com, 7:30am-9pm Sun.-Thurs., 7:30am-10pm Fri.-Sat., $22-48) is the farm-to-table restaurant in the Two Bunch Palms Resort, offering brunch options from house-made granola to eggs Benedict. Dinner specialties include vegan lasagna and filet mignon with lump crab. Specialty cocktails, wines, local and organic beers, and snacks are served in the lounge.

Accommodations

Many hotels in Desert Hot Springs offer day-use services for non-hotel guests.

The Casablanca-inspired digs at ★ **El Morocco Inn** (66810 4th St., 760/288-2527, www.elmorroccoinn.com, from $180) walk the line between luxurious, kitschy, and chic. The hotel is strewn with extravagant Moroccan lamps, while rooms feature canopy beds. The hotel spoils guests with complimentary mint tea, snacks, breakfast, and a nightly Morocco-tini hour. There's also a desert garden with hammocks, a bocce ball court, a relaxation tent, and a movie and game library. The pool and gigantic covered spa are open 24 hours daily.

Lido Palms (12801 Tamar Dr., 760/329-6033, www.lidopalms.com, from $170) offers a chance to relax and rejuvenate. The nine-room mid-century retreat opens onto a neatly landscaped courtyard. Inside, slightly dated rooms feature tile floors, full kitchens, and fluffy robes. Amenities include a pool, a hot tub, and a spa that are open 24/7, plus a grill for guest use on-site. Children and pets are not permitted.

The upscale modernist **Sagewater Spa** (12689 Eliseo Rd., 760/220-1554, www.sagewaterspa.com, $219-349) offers a restful and serene experience. The seven guest rooms have views and full kitchens.

Spare mid-century style and desert chic meet over polished concrete floors at **Hope Springs Resort** (68075 Club Circle Dr., 760/329-4003, www.hopespringsresort.com, $200-250), which offers 10 rooms with king-size beds (four rooms include kitchens) that open onto a communal pool and spa. Guests take advantage of the continental breakfast, communal kitchen, and grill. Children and pets are not permitted.

Contemporary **The Spring Resort & Day Spa** (12699 Reposo Way, 760/251-6700, www.the-spring.com, $259-369) offers 12 understated guest rooms in view of the San Jacinto Mountains. Most rooms surround the courtyard pool and include rainfall showerheads and Egyptian cotton linens. Guests can look forward to a complimentary breakfast, a firepit, and three mineral pools.

Set on 77 lush acres, **Two Bunch Palms Resort & Spa** (67425 Two Bunch Palms Trail, 760/329-8791, www.

twobunchpalms.com, from $395) offers charm dating to 1930. Choose from the original "Grotto" rooms with king beds, or "Soulstice" rooms, which come in a range of layouts with either a king bed or two double beds; some rooms have patios or courtyards. Amenities include two mineral springs pools, a shaded grotto for soaking, and tennis courts, as well as the on-site restaurant **Essense.**

The **Hotel Lautner** (67710 San Antonio St., 760/832-5288, www.hotellautner.com, $295) was designed by John Lautner in 1947 and features concrete, redwood, lots of glass, and skylights. Four private vacation rental units with a boutique luxury feel offer private patios and share a communal space with a saltwater plunge pool, a firepit lounge, and a grilling area.

Joshua Tree National Park

Joshua Tree's surreal appeal draws casual day-trippers, spring wildflower hounds, serious hikers, and hard-core rock climbers in droves, all wanting to experience its beauty and strangeness. The park's location near major urban centers like Palm Springs and Los Angeles contributes to its popularity, as does its easy access for locals living in the gateway towns of Joshua Tree and Twentynine Palms. The tiny towns surrounding the park are filled with outsider art, alien-inspired feats of aeronautical engineering, and some of the best live music around.

Getting There

The West Entrance to Joshua Tree National Park is 40 miles (64 km) north of Palm Springs (about an hour's drive) and 145 miles east of Los Angeles (plan 3-4 hours for the drive from L.A., Friday afternoons can take up to 4-5 hours). The North Entrance near Twentynine Palms is 16 miles (26 km) farther east along Highway 62. The South Entrance is about 60 miles (97 km) east of Palm

Joshua Tree National Park

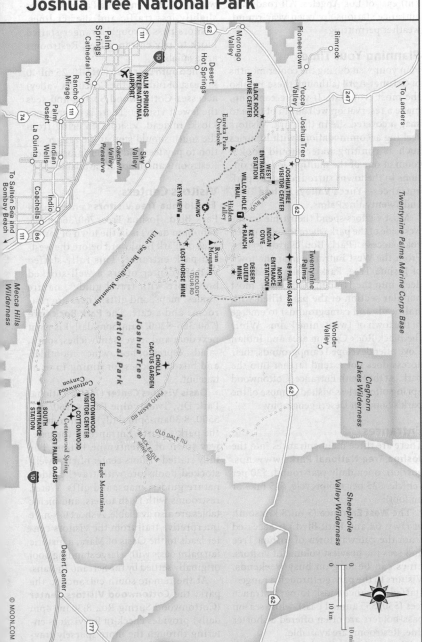

© MOON.COM

Springs along I-10 and 160 miles (260 km) east of Los Angeles. All roads and entrance stations are open year-round, weather permitting.

Planning Your Time

Plan your visit during the cooler months of **October-April** (although these are also the most crowded). If you're **camping,** make a reservation well ahead of time to snag a coveted site in the park. Visitors seeking accommodations with luxuries such as running water should book a room at one of the multiple lodging options in the towns surrounding the park entrances—**Yucca Valley, Joshua Tree,** and **Twentynine Palms.**

Most visitors spend their time on the west side of the park where the only paved road access (Park Boulevard) exists. From the West Entrance near the town of Joshua Tree, Park Boulevard delves deep into the Hidden Valley (the most popular section of the park filled with trailheads and campgrounds) to emerge in the town of Twentynine Palms. While the Black Rock Canyon area and Indian Cove offer developed campgrounds, their access does not extend farther into the park. At the South Entrance, Cottonwood Spring offers a less-visited glimpse of the park's Sonoran Desert geography.

Entrances

There are three main entrances into the **Joshua Tree National Park** (www.nps. gov/jotr, open daily year-round, $30 per vehicle, $25 per motorcycle, $15 bike or on foot):

The **West Entrance** (5 mi/8 km south of Hwy. 62 and Park Blvd.) is accessed from the gateway town of Joshua Tree and sees the heaviest volume of visitors. Lines can be long on busy weekends. Visitors to the park go through a ranger-staffed entrance kiosk to pay entrance fees ($30, $55 annual pass), while season pass-holders are often offered a shorter line. Restrooms are available.

The **North Entrance** (3 mi/5 km south of Hwy. 62 and Utah Trail) is in the gateway town of Twentynine Palms and sees slightly less traffic and shorter lines. Visitors pass through a ranger-staffed kiosk to pay entrance fees. Restrooms are available.

The **South Entrance** (off I-10, 25 mi/40 km east of Indio in the Coachella Valley) accesses Cottonwood Spring and sees the fewest visitors. There is no entrance kiosk; instead, visitors entering from the south should stop at the ranger station to pay fees and gather information. Restrooms and maps are available.

Visitors Centers

The **Joshua Tree Visitors Center** (6554 Park Blvd., Joshua Tree, 760/366-1855, 8am-5pm daily) is in the town of Joshua Tree on Park Boulevard before the western park entrance. This fully staffed visitors center offers a well-stocked bookstore with travel guides, nature guides, maps, and gifts. There are restrooms and a café. The **Park Rock Café** (760/366-8200, 8am-5pm daily) is right next door and serves sandwiches, soups, salads, espresso, beer, wine, smoothies, and boxed lunches for dining in or as takeout.

Oasis Visitors Center (74485 National Park Dr., Twentynine Palms, 760/367-5500, 8:30am-5pm daily) is en route to the park's North Entrance in the gateway town of Twentynine Palms. The fully staffed visitors center offers a well-stocked bookstore with travel guides, nature guides, maps, and gifts. Water, restrooms with flush toilets, and picnic tables are also available. A short 0.5-mile interpretive trail from the visitors center leads to the Oasis of Mara, a historic fan palm oasis with a large standing pool originally settled by the Serrano Indians.

At the remote south entrance to the park, the **Cottonwood Visitors Center** (Cottonwood Spring Rd., 8:30am-4pm daily) provides check-in for visitors entering through the more sparsely traveled southern entrance. The fully staffed visitors center offers a bookstore with travel guides, nature guides, maps, and gifts. Water, restrooms with flush toilets, and picnic tables are also available. A short botanical garden interpretive loop leaves from the visitors center. The visitors center is convenient to the Cottonwood Campground as well as Cottonwood Spring and the Hidden Palms Oasis hiking trail.

The **Black Rock Nature Center** (9800 Black Rock Canyon Rd., Yucca Valley, 760/367-3001, 8am-4pm Sat.-Thurs., 8am-8pm Fri. Oct.-May) is a small visitors center used primarily as a check-in for campers heading to the Black Rock Canyon Campground and other visitors to the Black Rock Canyon area. The ranger-staffed center has maps, books, and nature guides for purchase. Park entrance fees may also be paid here.

En route to the North Entrance, the **Twentynine Palms Visitors Center** (6847 Adobe Rd., Twentynine Palms, 760/361-1805, 10am-4pm daily fall-spring) welcomes you to the gateway town of Twentynine Palms and Joshua Tree National Park. The visitors center and gallery features maps, brochures, local books, Wi-Fi, a gift shop, electric car charging station, a community art gallery, and the Twentynine Palms Chamber of Commerce.

Information and Services

Services are more conspicuous in their absence. There is **no food** available inside the park. There are good dining options in the gateway towns along the edge of the park, including Yucca Valley, Joshua Tree, and Twentynine Palms. There are also full, chain grocery stores in the towns of Twentynine Palms and Yucca Valley.

Water is not widely available within the park; bring at least two gallons per person per day with you. Within the park, water may be available at the West Entrance ($0.25 fee), the Black Rock Campground, the Indian Cove Ranger Station, the Oasis Visitors Center in Twentynine Palms, and Cottonwood Campground at the south end of the park.

There is **limited cell service** in the park. Emergency phones are located at the Indian Cove Ranger Station and at the Hidden Valley Campground. In the event of an emergency, dial 911 or call 909/383-5651.

Sights
Black Rock Canyon

The Black Rock Canyon region is in the northwest corner of Joshua Tree, with a campground and several great hikes as well as easy access to the shops and restaurants of the Yucca Valley. The Black Rock area is characterized by craggy rolling peaks and piñons, juniper, and oak trees, giving it a different feel from the more popular Hidden Valley section of Joshua Tree. Though the Black Rock Canyon area is near the West Entrance, there is no direct access into the center of the park.

At 5,521 feet, **Eureka Peak Overlook** offers panoramic views of Joshua Tree and the surrounding valleys. Not only are the views spectacular, Eureka Peak is way less crowded than the very popular Keys View, a paved, drive-up viewpoint in the middle of the heavily visited central section of the park. From the summit, the Coachella Valley, Desert Hot Springs, and the San Jacinto Mountains (including the often snowcapped San Jacinto Peak) lie to the southwest, while views to the north take in the Morongo Valley. Look east into the park and you'll glimpse the Wonderland of Rocks.

Of course, there's a catch: Eureka Peak is not accessed via the park's main entrances. Instead, entry is via a graded dirt road from Yucca Valley (near the Black Rock Canyon Campground) that leads into Covington Flats, ending within a few hundred yards of the peak. It's also possible to hike to Eureka Peak via the trail from Covington Flats (8 mi/13 km

round-trip) or the Black Rock Canyon Campground (10 mi/16 km round-trip).

Getting There

From Highway 62 (29 Palms Hwy.) in the town of Yucca Valley, take La Contenta Road south. The road quickly becomes dirt and has some sandy places. In normal weather conditions, it should be passable for most two-wheel-drive cars. At 7.8 miles (13 km), turn right toward Eureka Peak. At 9.6 miles (15 km), turn right again toward Eureka Peak (signed). At 10.9 miles (18 km), you will reach a small parking area a few hundred yards below the peak.

Hidden Valley

From the park's West Entrance in Joshua Tree, Park Boulevard travels 25 miles (40 km) southeast, making a loop with the North Entrance in Twentynine Palms. This paved stretch is the most popular region of the park, with access to Queen Valley, Hidden Valley, Quail Springs, and the Wonderland of Rocks, as well as the majority of campgrounds and trailheads.

Keys Ranch

Colorful homesteader, rancher, and miner Bill Keys was an industrious and resourceful pack rat who fashioned a homestead and a life in the isolated desert. From 1917 to 1969, he and his family carved out a desert domain that included a ranch house, a schoolhouse, a store, and a workshop. Today, visitors can tour the well-preserved ruins of his Desert Queen Ranch, now listed on the National Register of Historic Places.

From October through May, park rangers lead 90-minute guided tours of **Keys Ranch** (by reservation only: call 760/367-5522, 9am-4:30pm daily, $10 over age 12, $5 children age 6-11, children under 6 free). This popular tour guides

Top to bottom: Sites in Joshua Tree National Park: Wonderland of Rocks; Cottonwood Spring; Cholla Cactus Garden.

you to a preserved historic homestead near the Hidden Valley Campground. The schedule varies, but tours are usually held once daily Friday-Sunday and offer your only peek at these historic remains.

Wonderland of Rocks
Dubbed the **Wonderland of Rocks,** for reasons that quickly become apparent, this region is characterized by a wildly eroded maze of striking granite rock formations studded with secret basins, gorgeous views, and history. The Wonderland of Rocks covers the area southeast of Indian Cove Campground and northeast of Hidden Valley Campground. Its compelling rock formations are visible to the east and north while driving along Park Boulevard, the main park road.

Indian Cove Campground and the parking area for the Barker Dam Nature Trail are the closest driving points into the belly of the beast. The area lures rock climbers and hikers. Four trails (Barker Dam Loop, Boy Scout Trail, Willow Hole, and Wonderland Wash) knife short distances into the Wonderland of Rocks. Rock climbing use trails are signed and established.

Ryan Ranch
Ryan Ranch was named after the Ryan brothers, Thomas and J. D. "Jep," who bought interest in the nearby Lost Horse Mine and set up camp at the Lost Horse Well at the base of Ryan Mountain. The homestead ruins date to 1896, but the region had been used by Native Americans prior to the mining era thanks to the availability of water. A short 0.5-mile stroll leads to remains of the ranch and its adobe bunkhouse, windmill, and outbuildings. A deeper search of the area reveals a pioneer cemetery and evidence of Native American habitation, including grinding stones. This interpretive site is accessed from a pullout on Park Boulevard between the Ryan Mountain trailhead and the turnoff for Ryan Campground.

Keys View
Impressive views spill from the lip of windswept **Keys View,** an observation point in the Little San Bernardino Mountains. Take in a panorama that stretches to the Salton Sea, Santa Rosa Mountains, San Andreas Fault, Palm Springs, San Jacinto Peak, and San Gorgonio Peak. The paved observation point is also wheelchair-accessible. Find it 7 miles (11 km) south of the Hidden Valley Campground, a 20-minute detour from Park Boulevard along Keys View Road.

Queen Valley
The **Queen Valley** is like a cross section of Joshua Tree's greatest hits with Joshua tree stands, mining ruins, Native American village sites, scenic hikes, and views! A series of short dirt roads crisscrosses the Queen Valley, chugging through one of the largest pockets of Joshua trees in the park. Mining ruins range from large gold operations, like the Desert Queen Mine, to way humbler affairs marked by the rusty remains of tent encampments. Evidence of Native American settlements dot the boulder-strewn landscape.

Established hiking trails follow a series of old mining roads to the **Desert Queen Mine, Lucky Boy Vista,** and the **Wall Street Mine.** To reach the Queen Valley area, follow the unpaved Queen Valley Road or Desert Queen Mine Road east to their terminus at Pine City.

Cottonwood Spring
Near the South Entrance to the park (off Pinto Basin Road, north of I-10), the Cottonwood region encompasses a visitors center, campground, and several trails. **Cottonwood Spring** itself is a fan palm oasis named for a surprising crop of native cottonwood trees that are mixed into the luxuriant vegetation surrounding the spring. Cottonwood Spring is on a paved road past the Cottonwood Campground in the vicinity of the Cottonwood Visitors Center.

Driving south through the endless landscape of the Pinto Basin, the **Cholla Cactus Garden** appears like an army of prickly planted teddy bears—their sheer numbers impress in this already surreal landscape. Though these cacti may look fuzzy, their multicolored arms are effective against predators. Urban legend-style photos show hapless visitors covered in cholla (aka jumping cactus), with segments that have attached themselves to those who got too close.

A small parking area allows visitors to stop and wander the 0.3-mile **interpretive trail** through a surreal crop of this strange flora. The trailhead for this nature walk is 20 miles (32 km) north of the Cottonwood Visitors Center on Pinto Basin Road.

★ Hiking

Joshua Tree offers fantastic hiking in an otherworldly landscape. The park has a range of hikes from easy nature trails to difficult cross-country adventures. Some of the longer trails lend themselves to backpacking (all backpackers overnighting in the backcountry must self-register for a free permit at any backcountry board).

Regardless of trail length, dehydration is the biggest factor to consider while hiking in Joshua Tree. Always carry at least **two gallons of water per day per person,** especially during strenuous activities, and plan your hike to coincide with cooler times of the day, such as early morning or late afternoon.

Black Rock Canyon
Hi-View Nature Trail
Distance: 1.3 mi/2 km round-trip
Duration: 0.5 hour
Elevation gain: 320 feet
Effort: Easy
Trailhead: near Black Rock Campground
Directions: Immediately before the entrance to Black Rock Campground, turn right onto a dirt road and drive 0.8 mile to a parking area.

For such a short trail, you'll be rewarded with panoramic views and desert knowledge. To hike the trail, follow the gentle grade clockwise. Take in the sweeping views of the Yucca Valley to the northeast, **Black Rock Canyon** and campground to the south, and the San Bernardino Mountains to the west. See if you can spot the highest peak in the San Bernardino Mountains: snowcapped San Gorgonio Mountain at 11,503 feet.

The trailhead can also be reached from a spur trail connecting from the **Black Rock Ranger Station,** where interpretive brochures are available.

Panorama Loop
Distance: 7.4 mi/12 km round-trip (8.6 mi/14 km round-trip to Warren Peak)
Duration: 4-5 hours
Elevation gain: 1,120 feet
Effort: Strenuous
Trailhead: Black Rock Canyon Backcountry Board
Directions: From Highway 62, turn south onto Avalon/Palomar Avenue for 2.9 miles (5 km). Turn left onto Joshua Lane for 0.9 mile. Turn right then left to follow San Marino Drive (Black Rock Canyon Rd.). Follow Black Rock Canyon Road 0.3 mile south. Look for a small dirt parking area and the Black Rock Canyon Backcountry Board.

Hike this crown of peaks—five in all— and you'll be rewarded with sweeping views extending from the Salton Sea to Mount San Jacinto and the Yucca Valley. Starting from the well-marked trailhead, travel south along a sandy trail that can feel like walking on a desert beach. The trail splits at 0.3 mile; head right to follow a sign pointing toward **Black Rock Canyon.** For the next 0.5 mile, you'll hike Black Rock Wash through open desert and a Joshua tree forest framed by a serrated landscape of ridges and peaks. The trail is easy to follow but splits into smaller washes and use trails at times. Pay attention to official trail markers (**PL** for Panorama Loop, **WP** for Warren Peak), as well as stone boundaries that mark the trail.

At just under 2 miles (3 km), you'll reach the base of the foothills and **Black**

Rock Spring. The spring usually does not have standing pools, but the ground may be damp. Oaks and other vegetation are abundant here (a good sign of water), and the area can be swarmed with flies, another giveaway. From Black Rock Spring, the trail narrows and cuts through the region's signature black rock formations.

At 2 miles (3km) the trail splits at a **signed intersection.** Stay right to reach the second loop entrance in 0.4 mile. From the **second intersection,** continue right to Warren Peak in 0.6 mile. (If you're up for it, I highly recommend this 1.2-mile round-trip detour to get the full eyeful and bragging rights. Six peaks in a day? Sure!) If you're only following the Panorama Loop, this will be a **left turn** at the intersection.

The **Panorama Loop** (3 mi/5 km) begins by climbing a steady grade through the foothills, following the remains of an old road. The grade tops out at a sharp ridge with spectacular views to the southeast across the Coachella Valley—you can see all the way to the Salton Sea on a clear day. Across the valley to the southwest are the impressive San Jacinto Mountains and Mount San Jacinto. At 5,154 feet, this ridge marks the highest point in the hike (including Warren Peak).

From here the trail continues to be one big reward as you wind your way along four more peaks on an open ridge that gives you an eyeful far across the Yucca Valley. Once you've made your way back down to the canyon floor (6.6 mi/10.5 km), turn right to follow the Black Rock Canyon wash the final 2 miles (3 km) to the trailhead.

Warren Peak

Distance: 6 mi/10 km round-trip
Duration: 3-4 hours
Elevation gain: 1,070 feet
Effort: Strenuous
Trailhead: Black Rock Canyon Backcountry Board
Directions: From Highway 62, turn south onto Avalon /Palomar Avenue for 2.9 miles (5 km). Turn left onto Joshua Lane for 0.9 mile. Turn right then left

to follow San Marino Drive (Black Rock Canyon Rd.). Take Black Rock Canyon Road 0.3 mile south. Look for a small dirt parking area and the Black Rock Canyon Backcountry Board.

At 5,103 feet, Warren Peak is the 10th-highest peak in the park. Considering that the highest peak, Quail Mountain, clocks in only 713 feet higher at 5,814 feet, Warren Peak's ranking is more impressive than it might sound at first. The trail to Warren Peak manages to be a moderate hike with a huge view payoff.

Starting from the well-marked trailhead, follow the trail for the **Panorama Loop** to the second intersection where it junctions with the trail to Warren Peak (WP). Stay right to continue to **Warren Peak.** At the next intersection at 2.4 miles (4 km), stay straight (right). You're only 0.6 mile from Warren Peak, and it comes into clear view. The trail climbs steeply up to the knobby peak where you're rewarded with panoramic views—the San Jacinto Mountains, Coachella Valley, Yucca Valley, and toward Hidden Valley and the Wonderland of Rocks in the heart of Joshua Tree. When you're done basking in the views, return the way you came. A use trail exiting the peak dead-ends at a ridge; pay attention to where you entered the peak.

Hidden Valley

This is the most popular area of the park, as it includes access to Queen Valley, Hidden Valley, Quail Springs, and the Wonderland of Rocks. Expect filled parking lots and plenty of company on the trails.

North View Maze Loop

Distance: 6.4 mi/10 km round-trip
Duration: 4 hours
Elevation gain: 400 feet
Effort: Moderate
Trailhead: Drive 1.7 miles (3 km) south from the West Entrance. The trailhead is a small, dirt parking area on your left.

This hike combines the North View and Maze Loop for a spectacular loop trail through fantastical boulder formations, Joshua tree forest, craggy viewpoints, desert wash, and past a window rock. It is also lightly traveled compared to more popular hikes so add solitude to the mix of reasons to hike here. The trail starts out in a wash heading north toward low hills and a signed intersection. Head left/north to follow the **North View Trail.** The trail leaves the wash to wind into the hills, and you are quickly transported to a secluded rock amphitheater, surrounded on all sides by towering formations. A few dips in the cracked rock walls allow for glimpses of the desert below. Two spur trails (Copper Mountain View and West Hills) at about 1.7 miles (3 km) allow you to catch more views both north and into the park.

The trail winds down to a deep wash at 2.5 miles (3.5 km). Cross it and be on the lookout for a signed intersection at 2.7 miles (3.7 km). Here, head right toward the **Loop Trail.** The next section continues generally south until it reaches the maze. Here the trail cuts directly through rectangular slabs of rock to emerge on flat desert floor on the other side.

Your next landmark will be **Window Rock,** a prominent peak in front of you as you continue south. Keep looking up, and you will see the eagle-shaped hole in the mountain, only visible from a distance. At an intersection, turn right to head west and continue the loop back to the parking area. (Continuing straight adds 1.9 mi/3 km as it loops around Window Rock.) The remaining stretch is an enjoyable, flat walk through sparse Joshua tree desert.

Quail Springs Trail

Distance: 6 mi/10 km round-trip
Duration: 3 hours
Elevation gain: 243 feet
Effort: Moderate
Trailhead: Quail Springs Basin Picnic area; look for an unmarked, eroded trail on the west side of the paved parking area.

Quail Springs Historic Trail, as it is named on some topo maps, strikes out

through peaceful open desert, intersecting with historic routes like the Johnny Lang Canyon (original claim-holder for the Lost Horse Mine) and connecting with a network of trails that extend to the western park entrance. It is also used to access **Quail Mountain,** the highest peak in Joshua Tree National Park at 5,814 feet.

The first 3 miles (5 km) of the trail to the base of Quail Mountain are peaceful and open, crossing what looks like a grassy plain that doesn't necessarily fit into our ideas of boulder-strewn Joshua Tree. The silvery husks of downed Joshua trees further add to the prehistoric savanna feel. The silence is punctuated by the occasional sound of a bird or a car along Park Boulevard, the main road within distant sight for most of the hike, making this place feel that much more secret.

From the picnic area the trail is clearly defined. One mile in, the route splits with **Quail Springs wash,** and footprints are visible in both forks. Although the wash (right) will take you in generally the same direction as the trail (due west), the going is easier on the trail. Take the left fork to continue. At 2 miles (3 km), the trail crosses the access route to **Johnny Lang Canyon,** veering off to the south (left). Continue straight.

At 2.9 miles (5 km) you will reach signs indicating that the area used to be **private property.** An out-of-place weathered parking curb as well as sun-silvered timber and metal odds and ends are strewn about. A pile of boulders a few hundred yards to the north marks the site of the 1920s **homestead of John Samuelson,** a Swedish immigrant who was ultimately denied his homestead claim in 1928 by the U.S. land office because of his Swedish heritage. His house burned down in the 1930s.

This is a good turnaround point, or you can continue to Quail Mountain or to eventually intersect with Park Boulevard near the West Entrance. (Note: To continue along the Quail Springs Trail requires maps, planning, and possibly a car shuttle at the other end.)

Lost Horse Mine

Distance: 4-7.4 mi/6-12 km round-trip

Duration: 2-4 hours

Elevation gain: 450-570 feet

Effort: Moderate to strenuous (very steep, rocky grades climbing Lost Horse Mountain)

Trailhead: Far end of the dirt parking area at the end of Lost Horse Mine Road

Directions: From Park Boulevard take Keys View Road south for 2.4 miles (4 km). Turn left onto the signed Lost Horse Mine Road and follow it for 0.9 mile to the parking area.

One of the **best preserved mining sites** in Joshua Tree National Park, the beautifully weathered stamp mill at the Lost Horse Mine was in operation from 1894 to 1931. The mill's breadth and sturdy construction are a testament to the mine's success as one of the highest producing in Joshua Tree history. The first person to file a claim was Johnny Lang of local lore who, in Wild West campfire tale fashion, had recently had his horses stolen by a gang of local cattle rustlers. The mill and surrounding ruins (look for rock house foundations, equipment, and mining tunnels) are the highlight of the out-and-back hike, but the loop offers more surprises and history.

The signed loop trail is located in the middle of the parking lot and directs hikers counterclockwise. The trail climbs (gradually then steeper at 2.5 mi/4 km) around the flank of stark **Lost Horse Mountain** through a mix of Joshua trees, yucca, and juniper, following an old mining road. On the way it crosses paths with the **Optimist Mine;** only a picturesque stone chimney and scattered artifacts remain. Beyond these ruins the trail climbs precipitously, giving way to sweeping views toward the northeast, Wonderland of Rocks, and Queen Valley. At 4.7 miles (8 km) the rocky trail hits the ridge below the Lost Horse Mountain Summit, and the **Lost Horse Mine** comes into view below. Take time to check out the area.

Although the mill and tunnels are fenced off, remains of rock houses and artifacts make this an interesting place to explore. You've done the hard work—the way back is mostly downhill with pleasant views looking toward Lost Horse Valley. Keep an eye out for additional rock structure remains and mining artifacts.

Willow Hole Trail

Distance: 7 mi/11 km round-trip

Duration: 3-4 hours

Elevation gain: Negligible

Effort: Moderate

Trailhead: Parking area for Boy Scout Trail

The Willow Hole Trail strikes into the heart of the Wonderland of Rocks. The flat, sandy track and lack of elevation gain mean that your main job is to admire the spectacular scenery. At 1.2 miles (2 km), the trail splits at a signed intersection. The left fork continues as the **Boy Scout Trail,** ending at the **Indian Cove Campground** in another 6.4 miles (12 km). Most people hike the Boy Scout Trail as a shuttle hike with a car at either end. To continue on the **Willow Hole Trail,** stay to the right. The trail officially ends unceremoniously in 3.5 miles (5.5 km) in a sandy, boulder-filled wash at so-named **Willow Hole.** As you may have guessed, Willow Hole itself is marked by a stand of willow trees. Depending on seasonal rains, the area can be filled with ephemeral pools of water.

Boy Scout Trail

Distance: 8 mi/13 km one-way (with car shuttle at one end)

Duration: 4-5 hours

Elevation gain: 1,265 feet (mostly downhill)

Effort: Moderate

South Trailhead: South Keys West Backcountry Board 0.7 mile east of the Quail Springs picnic area

North Trailhead: Indian Cove Backcountry Board, near the Indian Cove Ranger Station

This scenic eight-mile trail skirts the western edge of the Wonderland of Rocks before it winds through sharp mountains and rocky canyons to end in open desert

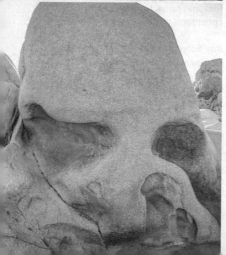

at the Indian Cove Backcountry Board. With the shifting landscape and elevation along the Boy Scout Trail, the plant zones transition so that you have the chance to move through classic Joshua tree forest and mesquite, piñon, and oak at the higher elevations, then yucca and boulder gardens, and creosote and cholla at the lower altitudes. This hike is the **most popular overnight backpacking hike** in the park. The Wonderland of Rocks to the east is a day-use area only: campsites must be west of the Boy Scout Trail. Sections of the trail are indistinguishable or unmarked, especially through washes. Carry a topo map.

The trail begins as a pleasant stroll through a Joshua tree forest along a well-defined sandy track on the western edge of the Wonderland of Rocks. At 1.3 miles (2 km) the trail splits with the **Willow Hole Trail.** Follow the signed junction to the left.

From here the trail climbs slightly before leveling on a high plateau, and the vegetation transforms with piñon, juniper, oak, and cholla cactus. At 3.8 miles (6 km) the trail continues into an open wash marked by a **signpost.** For the next half a mile the trail can be hard to follow through a series of washes. You'll pass a split with the **Big Pine Trail** on your left at 4 miles (6 km). Beyond the split, look out for an old cement cattle trough as a landmark.

The trail exits the wash on the left at 4.4 miles (7 km) and winds to the head of a deep canyon with austere desert views. From here the trail descends steeply to the canyon floor then heads right into the wash. Follow the rugged canyon for a mile, heading northeast. Yucca and barrel cactus line your way.

Exit the canyon at 6.2 miles (10 km), bearing right at a signpost. The trail spills into an open *bajada*. The final leg of the trail crosses open desert to end at the **Indian Cove Backcountry Board.**

Top to bottom: Mojave Desert views from Warren Peak; ruins at Lost Horse Mine; Skull Rock.

Hidden Valley

Distance: 1 mi/2 km round-trip
Duration: 0.5 hour
Elevation gain: 20 feet
Effort: Easy
Trailhead: Hidden Valley Campground

This one-mile loop passes through granite boulders to emerge in scenic **Hidden Valley,** once wetter, grassier, and used for cattle grazing during the ranching halcyon of the early-mid 1900s. The well-signed trail circles the small, enclosed valley, delving into the monzogranite **boulder piles** with tempting bouldering opportunities.

Barker Dam

Distance: 1.3 mi/2 km round-trip
Duration: 0.5 hour
Elevation gain: Negligible
Effort: Easy
Trailhead: Paved parking area and signed trailhead off of Hidden Valley Road

On the southern edge of the Wonderland of Rocks, the popular 1.3-mile loop trail winds through closely lined boulders to a small pond that can be dry at certain times of year. Ranchers dammed the natural pond for cattle, taking advantage of a site used by Native Americans for centuries. The well-marked trail is easy to follow.

The watering hole is now a stop for migrating birds, bighorn sheep, and other wildlife. This area is also home to the **Disney petroglyphs.** During shooting for a film in the 1960s, a film crew painted over existing Native American petroglyphs to make them more dramatic for the shoot, possibly adding some of their own—a cultural travesty.

Wall Street Mill

Distance: 3 mi/5 km round-trip
Duration: 1.5 hours
Elevation gain: 23 feet
Effort: Easy
Trailhead: Barker Dam parking area; the trailhead for the Wall Street Mill is clearly signed.

When local rancher **Bill Keys** wanted to build a mill for processing ores from local mines, he scrounged an existing one and relocated it, tapping into the time-honored desert tradition of moving defunct mining cabins and structures to new, profitable locations. The mill was originally located at Pinyon Well and had been in operation since 1891. Keys rebuilt the mill and employed it from 1932 to 1942 to mill ore for different miners in the area. The mill was used briefly in 1949 and again as late as 1966. When Keys died, the National Park Service took over the mill site and has done an excellent job of preserving it. In addition to the mill, you'll find **abandoned cars** and other equipment and **artifacts.** The site also used to have a bunkhouse, now gone.

To get to the mill, begin at the marked trailhead for the Wall Street Mill in the Barker Dam parking area. The trail veers east, clearly marked with stone trail boundaries and occasional arrows. In 0.3 mile the trail hits a second, smaller parking lot then picks up again on the left. At 0.5 mile an unexpected psychedelic pink marks the remains of the **Wonderland Ranch,** tempting exploration. A short side trip will lead you to the foundations, crumbling walls, and scattered artifacts of the ranch.

Another historic bonus awaits in the form of the **Desert Queen Well** ruins one mile into the hike. A tall windmill, once used to pump water, still stands over piles of weathered timbers and an old tank.

The **Wall Street Mill** is definitely the highlight. Leave time to admire the well and poke around the area.

Wonderland Wash

Distance: 2 mi/3 km round-trip
Duration: 1 hour
Elevation gain: 75 feet
Effort: Moderate
Trailhead: Barker Dam parking area. Begin at the signed trailhead for the Wall Street Mill.

A use trail past the Wonderland Ranch cuts into the Wonderland of Rocks via a secluded wash to end at the Astro Domes, an impressive pair of granite monoliths popular with rock climbers. Begin at the signed trailhead for the Wall Street Mill. At 0.5 mile, an unexpected crumbling pink structure marks the scattered remains and crumbling walls of the Wonderland Ranch. To the left of the ruins, an unmaintained trail heads east through low boulders into the wash. On the other side, the trail follows the wash northeast. Although the trail dries up at times, follow the wash. You will occasionally have to pick your way. At 0.3 mile into the wash cross the remains of a stone dam used by cattle ranchers. Continuing up the wash, you are surrounded by thriving desert vegetation and the striking rock formations of the Wonderland of Rocks. At 1 mile, look for the giant dome of white tank granite, outstanding for its monolithic, uncracked state in this maze of jumbled boulder piles. The trail dwindles beyond this, but it is possible to continue deeper into the Wonderland of Rocks. Otherwise, return the way you came.

Pine City Site

Distance: 3-4 mi/5-6 km round-trip
Duration: 2 hours
Elevation gain: 150 feet
Effort: Moderate
Trailhead: Parking area for Desert Queen Mine

"Site" not "city" is the operative word here. Pine City is long gone, marked by piñons and a few scattered mining tunnels. The highlights of this hike are the easy, open trail winding through classic Mojave Desert flora, picturesque boulders, and its location off the beaten path of Park Boulevard.

The trail starts at the end of the graded, dirt Queen Valley Road, and although the trailhead is less than a mile from Park Boulevard, it offers more **solitude** than some of the more popular nearby hikes. The trail gains slight elevation as it heads toward the **Pine City site** (1.5 mi/2.5 km) or the **Pine Canyon overlook** (2 mi/3 km). The slight elevation makes this an easy desert trek but

Willow Hole

also gives rise to shifts in desert vegetation along the way. Hearty desert creosote gives way to yuccas and Joshua trees and eventually junipers and piñons. Cholla and barrel cacti spike the landscape. At 1.3 miles (2 km) you'll see your first pine trees interspersed in a picturesque bay of stacked monzonite boulders. The "city" itself is also marked by these pines at 1.5 miles (2 km). Here the trail splits slightly with the left (main) fork continuing another 0.5 mile to an overlook on the edge of Pine Canyon. The trail down into the canyon is unmaintained beyond the overlook. The right fork continues the extra few hundred yards to Pine City proper.

Desert Queen Mine and Wash

Distance: 1-7 mi/2-11 km round-trip
Duration: 1-5 hours
Elevation gain: 160-660 feet
Effort: Easy to strenuous
Trailhead: Pine City/Desert Queen Mine

This steep, rugged wash in the Queen Valley saw a lot of mining action from the 1890s until the 1960s. A short trek to the Desert Queen Mine reveals the rust-varnished equipment, mining tunnels, and massive tailings of a successful California gold mine. Continuing down the wash turns up more scattered mining debris and, eventually, scant remains of other, meaner mining camps, never as rich as the Desert Queen, hinting at a harsh life for miners scraping out a living.

To reach the Desert Queen Mine, take the **unsigned trail** from the Pine City parking area. At 0.3 mile you will see the picturesque remains of a **miner's stone cabin** on your right. Continuing straight, you will soon reach an overlook. This is a great stop or a destination. From the overlook, you can see across the wash to the mines on the hillside and the old road snaking along the rocky embankment. Tailings, the huge piles of silvery rock excavated from the mining tunnels, are mounded monuments to mining on the wash floor.

To get a closer look at the **Desert Queen Mine's** equipment and tunnels, backtrack to the stone house and follow the road down into the wash then back up to the mining site.

If this didn't satisfy your itch for exploration, a rugged hike through the wash brings you to a much smaller mining site. From the top of the Desert Queen Mine, return to the wash and turn right (north) to continue exploring the wash. After a few hundred yards, the canyon jogs and the hike trends generally east. The sandy-floored canyon is wild and scenic with steep walls, clusters of boulders, and scattered mining debris, testament to the power of desert floods. **Two boulder jams** block your way, but they are passable by use trails. After the second boulder jam, the wash widens and you'll see tailings from the **Gold Hill Mine.** The miners' small tent community of John's Camp was located on a long, low shelf on the right side 3 miles (5 km) from your starting point in the wash below the Desert Queen Mine. Return the way you came.

Lucky Boy Vista

Distance: 3.6 mi/6 km round-trip
Duration: 2 hours
Elevation gain: 150 feet
Effort: Moderate
Trailhead: Pine City/Desert Queen Mine parking area. Trailhead is unsigned at the south end of the parking area (on the right just past parking entrance).

What makes the Lucky Boy Vista such a nice hike is its combination of views, Native American history, mining history, solitude, and the pleasant walk through boulder-strewn desert piñon and yucca gardens. Heads up: there are a number of use trails, old mining roads, and washes crossing this area near the Desert Queen Mine, so it is easy to veer off your route if you're not paying attention. Carry a map and compass and know how to use them.

Start from the Pine City/Desert Queen Mine parking area. The sandy trail is clearly defined but unmarked. It starts by heading south then curves through a series of washes lined with striking stacked rock formations. Look for signs of the Native American village that once inhabited this site in the form of a pair of *morteros* along this stretch. At 0.8 mile, the trail forks. The left (north) trail heads toward the Desert Queen Mine and Wash. Rock scrambling is required. To reach the Lucky Boy Vista, turn right (south) and follow the trail. Continue south/southeast over the next mile. You will pass through a **gate,** a holdover from the era of mines and private property. Beyond the gate, the trail forks and begins to climb slightly. Take the left fork to follow the old mining road. The **Elton Mine site** is easily identifiable from its shuttered mining tunnels at about 1.5 miles (2 km). The trail continues past the mine site to pause on a lofty plateau with views of Split Rock—the **Lucky Boy Vista.** Follow the return trail.

At 2.6 miles (4 km) the trail forks at an easy-to-miss **No Camping post.** Stay straight (west) to complete the loop. Turning right will take you back to where you started the trail. At 3.1 miles (5 km) you will reach the **Desert Queen Mine Road.** Turn right for the last half mile to complete the loop.

Skull Rock

Distance: 1.7 mi/2.7 km round-trip
Duration: 0.5-1 hour
Elevation gain: 157 feet
Effort: Easy
Trailhead: Parking for Skull Rock and the nature trail is located on Park Boulevard near the Jumbo Rocks Campground entrance. The trail begins to the right of the landmark Skull Rock.

Skull Rock, anthropomorphically named for its gaunt eye socket-like depressions, is a popular rock formation along Park Boulevard. The concave hollows, called *tafoni,* originally began as small pits. Over time they cyclically filled with rainwater and eroded. After your photo op at the skull, follow the 1.7-mile nature trail as it winds through the scenic boulder and plant-strewn landscape. From the right side of the skull, the trail hooks over to **Jumbo Rocks Campground,** passing interpretive signs on desert ecology along the way. Turn right when you reach the campground. The trail follows the campground road until it intersects with Park Boulevard. It crosses the road to wind back through more boulders with views of the surrounding desert before it completes the loop at Skull Rock.

Arch Rock Nature Trail

Distance: 0.5 mile round-trip
Duration: 0.5 hour
Elevation gain: 30 feet
Effort: Easy
Trailhead: White Tank Campground across from site 9

The highlight of this trail is a delicately eroded arch, tucked into a boulder pile formation in the first third of the loop. The rest of the trail winds through **carved rock formations** to return to the starting point at **White Tank Campground.** Though the trail is short, several social trails split off from the official trail and can make it hard to follow. Pay attention to where you're going.

Split Rock Loop

Distance: 2 mi/3 km round-trip
Duration: 1 hour
Elevation gain: 133 feet
Effort: Easy
Trailhead: From the northern park entrance in Twentynine Palms, head south for 6.7 miles (10.7 km). Turn right into the signed Split Rock picnic area and park in the parking and picnic area at the end of the road. The trail begins next to a giant split rock at the north (far) end of the parking lot.

The family-friendly Split Rock Loop Trail allows you to immerse yourself in the details of the landscape. The hike starts from a small picnic area and winds for 2 miles (3 km) through boulders and desert flora. Yucca, paddle cactus, and mesquite are interspersed with the boulders lining your pathway. Look for lizards sunning themselves on the sunbaked rocks.

Indian Cove
49 Palms Oasis

Distance: 3 mi/5 km round-trip
Duration: 2-3 hours
Elevation gain: 360 feet
Effort: Moderate
Trailhead: The trailhead is accessed from a parking area at the end of Canyon Road, about 1.7 miles (2 km) east of Indian Cove Road, off of Hwy. 62.
Directions: From Hwy. 62, turn right onto Canyon Road, signed for 49 Palms Oasis. (Note: It is only signed heading east.) A small animal hospital on Hwy. 62 is a good landmark. Follow Canyon Road (signed for 49 Palms Oasis) for 1.7 miles (2 km) to the trailhead.

This natural oasis surrounded by **native fan palms** secluded in a rocky canyon is a striking destination. From the trailhead, the trail climbs up over a ridge and then winds down through arid hills. The trail is easy to follow, passing through a flinty landscape that gives no indication of its secret oasis until you are close. You'll see the oasis from a distance, nestled

against the jagged hills, before you reach it. There are only 158 fan palm oases in North America, and five in Joshua Tree; this is clearly a special place, used historically by Cahuilla Indians and offering precious habitat for bighorn sheep, quail, and coyotes. Tread lightly in this fragile ecosystem.

Cottonwood Spring
Mastodon Peak

Distance: 3 mi/5 km round-trip
Duration: 1.5-2 hours
Elevation gain: 375 feet
Effort: Moderate
Trailhead: The path begins at a nature trail a few yards east of the Cottonwood Spring sign and staircase; campers follow a signed trail from the eastern end of Loop A.
Directions: From the Cottonwood Visitors Center continue 1.2 miles (2 km) southeast on the Cottonwood Campground road until it dead-ends at Cottonwood Spring.

Mastodon's rocky peak crowns this loop hike and affords dramatic desert views stretching toward the Eagle Mountains, San Jacinto Mountains, and as far as the Salton Sea. On the way, the preserved remains of the Mastodon Mine add some historical spice to the trail. The peak was named by miners for its resemblance to the prehistoric creature. If you spend enough time in the desert sun, it's possible you'll start to see dubious shapes in the rocks, too.

The Mastodon Peak loop is very well-signed and clearly established. It begins on a nature trail that leaves from the parking area and heads northwest to a junction at 0.5 mile. Turn right (left leads to the campground) to continue toward the base of the foothills. Just past the junction, concrete foundations mark the site of the old **Winona Mill.** From the base of the mountains, the trail climbs toward the peak and the remains of the **Mastodon Mine,** clinging to the hillside below the peak at 1.4 miles (2 km). From the mine there are sweeping views toward the west and the Cottonwood

Mountains. George Hulsey operated the gold mine from 1919 to 1932. He was also responsible for building the Winona Mill, used to process ore from the Mastodon Mine and other claims to the north in the Dale Mining District. Continue the loop down the mountain. At the base of the hills the trail forks. To complete the loop, turn right. (A left turn will take you to the Lost Palms Oasis in approximately 3 mi/5 km.) The loop has a strong finish at scenic **Cottonwood Spring.** From the spring, follow the staircase up to the parking lot.

For a longer hike, combine a trip to the Lost Palms Oasis for a spectacular 9.5-mile trek.

Lost Palms Oasis

Distance: 7.5 mi/12 km round-trip
Duration: 4-5 hours
Elevation gain: 460 feet
Effort: Moderate
Trailhead: The trail begins at a staircase leading down to Cottonwood Spring; campers follow a signed trail from the eastern end of Loop A.
Directions: From the Cottonwood Visitors Center continue 1.2 miles (2 km) southeast on the Cottonwood Campground road until it dead-ends at Cottonwood Spring.

This trail undulates through striking desert scenery before dropping down to a secluded canyon and the largest collection of fan palms in the park.

The trail is straightforward, making a beeline to the southeast along a well-signed route. It starts from scenic **Cottonwood Spring** and ripples over an up-and-down landscape dominated by a series of ridges and washes. The trail is almost completely exposed, flanked by interesting desert gardens including barrel cacti, ocotillo, and desert willows.

The trail edges into the foothills of the Eagle Mountains before emerging to overlook a steep canyon and the Lost Palms Oasis, tucked on a rugged canyon hillside. The name makes sense in this remote place. The **Lost Palms Oasis** is a watering hole for bighorn sheep and

other wildlife. A steep trail continues to the boulder- and palm-strewn canyon floor. Shaded and peaceful, this is a great place to take a break before your return. If you're still feeling like exploring, continue to follow the trail down the canyon. One mile of picking your way and rock scrambling will bring you to another fan palm stand—the **Victory Palms.**

For a longer hike, add the loop to Mastodon Peak and the Mastodon Mine (adds 2 mi/3 km) for a total 9.5-mile (15-km) hike.

Biking

Biking within Joshua Tree National Park is confined to roads that are open to vehicles, but there are some good rides along the park's paved and backcountry roads. For road biking, **Park Boulevard** offers a great route through the park's most spectacular scenery. The paved road runs 25 miles (40 km) from the West Entrance in Joshua Tree to the North Entrance in Twentynine Palms, with many opportunities for shorter stretches in between. **Pinto Basin Road,** the other main park road, cuts through the Pinto Basin's open desert with scenery that's less rewarding than Park Boulevard, but also more lightly traveled. It runs 30 miles (48 km) from its start four miles south of the North Entrance.

For mountain biking, the short series of dirt roads crossing the **Queen Valley** (the Hidden Valley area between Barker Dam and the Pine City Backcountry Board) totals 13.4 miles (21 km) and offers scenic rides through large stands of Joshua trees. The **Geology Tour Road** stretches slightly downhill for its first 5.4 miles (9 km) to Squaw Tank; beyond this, it loops 6 miles (10 km) through Pleasant Valley. Be cautious as the road is sandy and rutted at points.

There are no bike rentals available in Joshua Tree National Park. Near the West Entrance in the town of Joshua Tree, **Joshua Tree Bicycle Shop** (6416 Hallee Rd., Joshua Tree, 760/366-3377, www.

joshuatreebicycleshop.com, 10am-6pm Mon.-Sat., $20 per hour, $65 per day) is a full-service bike shop that rents bikes and offers repairs and ride recommendations.

Rock Climbing

From rock stars to beginners, climbers of all levels are drawn to the park's traditional-style crack, slab, and steep-face climbing and its vast array of climbs. More than 400 climbing formations and more than 8,000 recognized climbs make it a world-class destination.

To keep an ear to the ground about closed routes and any other climbing info, **Climber's Coffee** (Hidden Valley Campground, 8am-10am Sat.-Sun. mid-Oct.-Apr.) offers the opportunity to meet Joshua Tree's climbing ranger and share information with other climbers.

There are many great rock climbing guides sold in the park's visitors centers, as well as outfitters outside the park. Classic guides include *The Trad Guide to Joshua Tree* by Charlie and Diane Winger and a number of guides by rock climber and author Randy Vogel (*Rock Climbing Joshua Tree, Rock Climbing Joshua Tree West*). More recent books on the market include *Joshua Tree Rock Climbs* by Robert Miramontes and Bob Gaines's *Best Climbs Joshua Tree National Park.*

Here are a few spots where you can watch the action (or get in on it):

- The **Quail Springs** picnic area has another, more adventurous side. While families picnic at this scenic spot, rock climbers tackle popular formations like Trashcan Rock, Hound Rocks, and the White Cliffs of Dover.

- **Intersection Rock** at the turnoff to Hidden Valley Campground is a classic with over two dozen routes established by a handful of pioneering climbers in the 1960s.

- **Hidden Valley Campground** has a high concentration of quality routes, meaning you don't have to leave your

campsite to experience some of Joshua Tree's finest.

- A use trail along the scenic Wonderland Wash in the **Wonderland of Rocks** region leads to the **Astro Domes,** a destination heavy on solitude and a scenic journey to reach the dual granite monoliths.

- **Cap Rock** has a lot going for it: a place in rock-and-roll history (Gram Parsons), a good selection of routes for beginning climbers, a great boulder circuit, and some of the most classic boulder problems in Joshua Tree.

- There are many classic climbing routes at the **Jumbo Rocks Campground,** but **Conan's Corridor,** a short walk northwest from the end of the loop presents some interesting challenges.

- While you can't climb the official Split Rock itself, the **Split Rock** region offers many routes next to an easy-to-access picnic area and loop trail.

Climbing Guides

To get in on the action as a first-timer or experienced climber looking to hone your skills, you may want to take a group class or a private guided climb through one of several outfitters in the area. The park website has a full list of permitted guides. **Joshua Tree Rock Climbing School** (760/366-4745, www.joshuatreerockclimbing.com) offers year-round rock climbing classes and private guided outings. **Cliffhanger Guides** (6551 Park Blvd., 209/743-8363, www.cliffhangerguides.com, 8am-6pm daily) maintains a brick-and-mortar presence on Park Boulevard to help book your custom guided rock climbing adventures with half-day and full-day rates for up to 10 people. **Vertical Adventures** (800/514-8785, www.vertical-adventures.com) is available for one- to multiday courses, as well as private instruction and guided climbing in Joshua Tree National Park and

Idyllwild's Tahquitz and Suicide Rocks from May to September. **Climbing Life Guides** (760/780-8868, www.joshuatreeclimbinglifeguides.com) are available for guiding rock climbing and technical climbing instruction for up to six people. **Joshua Tree Guides** (www.joshuatreeguides.com) offers private guided climbs for beginners through advanced climbers for half and full days, as well as guided weekend trips.

Outfitters and Gear

To gear up for your rock climbing (or other) adventures, check out one of the three outfits located on the main drag in Joshua Tree close to the intersection of Park Boulevard and Highway 62.

Nomad Ventures (61795 Twentynine Palms Hwy., Joshua Tree, 760/366-4684, www.nomadventures.com, 8am-6pm Sun.-Thurs., 8am-8pm Fri.-Sun., summer hours vary) is the most extensively stocked of the Joshua Tree outfitters, with a huge selection of climbing gear, an assortment of camping and hiking gear, and a wide selection of guidebooks (including rock climbing guides).

Coyote Corner (6535 Park Blvd., Joshua Tree, 760/366-9683, www.joshuatreevillage.com, 9am-6pm Sun.-Thurs., 9am-7pm Fri.-Sat.) is eclectically stocked with gifts and gear ranging from T-shirts, jewelry, novelty items, and books to camping, hiking, and rock climbing gear. The best part? Showers! For about $5, you can buy a hot shower, quite a bonus considering none of Joshua Tree's campgrounds have showers.

Joshua Tree Outfitters (61707 Twentynine Palms Hwy., Joshua Tree, 760/366-1848, 9am-5pm daily) mainly specializes in camping gear rentals, including tents, sleeping bags, coolers, camp stoves, water containers, and lanterns. They also rent rock climbing guides and bouldering pads and offer

Top to bottom: crows perched in Joshua Tree; rock climbers; a park campground.

gear repair. Their retail space is sparsely stocked, but it has a few high-quality clothing items and miscellaneous gear, maps, and books.

Horseback Riding

With more than 250 miles of equestrian trails and trail corridors, horseback riding is a great way to experience Joshua Tree National Park if you bring your own horse. Two campgrounds offer equestrian camping with overnight areas for stock animals: **Ryan Campground** (760/367-5545, $15, no water, closed in summer), in centrally located Hidden Valley, and **Black Rock Canyon** (877/444-6777, www.recreation.gov, $20, water available) in Joshua Tree's northwest corner. Reservations are required.

Both campgrounds lie along the continuous 36-mile **California Riding and Hiking Trail** that extends through Joshua tree forests, washes, canyons, and open lands from northwestern Black Rock Canyon east to the North Entrance. Popular areas for equestrian users include trails near the West Entrance and Black Rock Canyon. Horse trail maps are available for download from the park website. Special **permits** (760/367-5545) are required for camping with stock in the backcountry.

If you're not bringing your own horse, **Joshua Tree Ranch** (760/366-5357, www.joshuatreevillage.com, $35 per hour pp) offers guided private and group trail rides from their ranch, located less than 2 miles (3 km) from the park's West Entrance.

Camping

There are no hotels or lodges inside the park boundaries. The closest lodgings are just outside the park in the gateway towns of Joshua Tree, Yucca Valley (both via the West Entrance), and Twentynine Palms (at the North Entrance).

Inside the Park

There are seven NPS campgrounds within the park boundaries, two of which—**Black Rock Campground** (99 sites) and **Indian Cove Campground** (101 sites, first-come, first-served June-Sept.)—accept seasonal **reservations** (877/444-6777, www.recreation.gov, $20) October through May. The other five campgrounds are first-come, first-served year-round. Campgrounds in Joshua Tree start to fill up on Thursday mornings most weekends October through May, beginning with the more popular and centrally located campsites like **Hidden Valley** (44 sites, first-come, first-served year-round, $15), ★ **Jumbo Rocks** (124 sites, reservation-only Oct.-May, first-come, first-served June-Sept., $15), and **Ryan Campground** (31 sites, first-come, first-served year-round, $15), which have sites tucked in among Joshua Tree's famous boulders and Joshua trees. By Thursday evening, your options are limited. If you can't make it into the park by Thursday afternoon, and you don't have a reservation, better have a contingency plan. Fortunately, there is overflow camping and private camping available outside the park boundaries. In summer, all campgrounds are first-come, first-served.

Only three campgrounds—Black Rock, Indian Cove, and Cottonwood—have **drinking water.** Even if you are staying at one of these campgrounds, it is wise to bring at least two gallons of water (per person per day) with you into the park.

There are no RV hookups at any of the park campgrounds. Black Rock and Cottonwood Campgrounds have RV-accessible potable water and dump stations, and there are spaces that can accommodate trailers under 25 feet at Hidden Valley and White Tank Campgrounds.

Sheep Pass Group Camp (6 sites, 877/444-6777, www.recreation.gov, $35-50) is a tent-only group campground centrally located off of Park Boulevard in between Ryan and Jumbo Rocks Campgrounds. Amenities include vault toilets, fire rings, and picnic tables. There is no drinking water.

Belle Campground (18 sites, first-come, first-served Oct.-May, $15) is a small, low-key campground with cozy sites tucked amid a pile of rock formations. Amenities include vault toilets, fire rings, and picnic tables. There is no drinking water and reservations are not accepted.

The smallest campground in the park, **White Tank** (15 sites, first-come, first-served year-round, $15) is a laid-back campground with sites tucked in amid scattered rock formations. Sites can accommodate trailers and RVs (under 25 feet). Amenities include vault toilets, fire rings, and picnic tables. There is no drinking water and reservations are not accepted.

Cottonwood Campground (62 sites, reservation only Oct.-May, first-come, first-served June-Sept., $20) is much more lightly visited, which makes finding a site here slightly less competitive. The campsites are scattered across an open desert dotted with creosote. Though there is little to divide them, the sites are nicely spaced and offer some privacy. The nearby Cottonwood Visitors Center is a fully stocked visitors center and bookstore, while hiking trails to scenic Lost Palms Oasis and Mastodon Peak depart directly from the campground. There are also trailer and RV sites with water fill-up and a dump station. The **Cottonwood Group Campground** (3 sites, 877/444-6777, www.recreation.gov, $35-40) provides tent-only sites by reservation. Amenities include flush toilets, fire rings, picnic tables, and drinking water.

Outside the Park

Campgrounds in the park fill quickly October through May. Outside the park, options include backcountry camping on BLM land or at a privately owned RV park in Joshua Tree.

Joshua Tree Lake RV and Campground (2601 Sunfair Rd., Joshua Tree, 760/366-1213, www.joshuatreelake.com, first-come, first-served, $10 pp tent sites, $4 children 12 and under; $25-40 RV sites, reservations accepted) is 14 miles (23 km) north of the West Entrance. The well-maintained property offers tent and RV camping in open desert. Sites include picnic tables and firepits. The campground has a small fishing lake, a store with firewood and basic supplies, RV hookups, hot showers, flush toilets, and a playground.

Overflow camping is available on **Bureau of Land Management** (BLM, www.nps.gov/jotr) land both north and south of the park. Note that BLM camping includes no amenities (toilets, water, firepits, or drinking water). Fires are allowed in self-contained metal firepits (provide your own) in the overflow camping south of the park, but are not allowed on BLM camping north of the park. Bring your own firewood.

Getting Around

For exploring Joshua Tree National Park, it is vital to **have your own vehicle;** there is limited seasonal transportation inside the park. To reach the **West Entrance** from I-10 near Palm Springs, head north on Highway 62 for about 30 miles (48 km) to the town of Joshua Tree. Turn south on Park Boulevard and follow the road into the park. To reach the **North Entrance** near Twentynine Palms, continue east on Highway 62 for 16 more miles (26 km) and turn south on Utah Trail. To reach the **South Entrance,** follow I-10 east for 60 miles (97 km) to Cottonwood Spring Road and turn north.

Several major car rental agencies are available in nearby Palm Springs. Car rentals in Yucca Valley are available from **Enterprise** (57250 29 Palms Hwy., 760/369-0515, www.enterprise.com, 8am-noon, 1pm-6pm Mon.-Fri., 9am-noon Sat.).

Yucca Valley is also the best place to fuel up before entering the park. Within the park, there are frequent, free parking areas near sights and major trailheads.

Shuttle

The **Roadrunner Shuttle** (8am-5pm daily, free) leaves from the town of Twentynine Palms from two locations (Twentynine Palms Transit Center, Adobe and Cactus; Oasis Visitors Center) beginning at 8am daily. Routes travel west along Park Boulevard, the park's main thoroughfare. The shuttle stops at popular sights, hikes, and rock climbing destinations including Ryan Mountain, Barker Dam, and the Quail Springs Picnic Area. Campground stops include Jumbo Rocks and Hidden Valley. Parking can be busy on weekends in fall and spring.

Yucca Valley

The town of Yucca Valley, 13 miles (21 km) west of the park's main West Entrance, is the largest in this area. Funky boutiques and vintage stores compete with big-box stores, grocery stores, and chain hotels for the character of the place. These reminders of 21st-century suburban living feel strangely out of place against the timeless beauty of the desert. However, if you need services, Yucca Valley will likely have what you need. Its proximity to Pappy & Harriet's makes it a magnet for artists and musicians.

Getting There

The town of Yucca Valley is at the junction of Highways 63 and 247, approximately 28 miles (45 km) north of Palm Springs. From I-10, take Highway 62 north for 20 miles (32 km). Access to the Black Rock Canyon area of Joshua Tree National Park is via Joshua Lane south (about 5 mi/8 km).

Sights

Pioneertown

Created as a Wild West movie set in 1946, **Pioneertown** (Pioneertown Rd.) was founded by Hollywood investors as a frontier town that served as a backdrop for Western movies. Some of the big names that helped establish Pioneertown included Roy Rogers, Gene Autry, Russell Hayden, and the Sons of the Pioneers (which gave Pioneertown its name). The 1940s and 1950s saw Pioneertown as a popular filming destination, with more than 50 films and television shows featuring the stables, saloons, jails, and shops of the main street. As part of the setup, a functioning motel provided quarters for the Hollywood set who were there for filming. When not filming, Pioneertown did double duty as a roadside attraction and tourist spot. Visitors came for the ice cream parlor, the bowling alley, and the motel.

The adjacent **Pappy & Harriet's Pioneertown Palace** (53688 Pioneertown Rd., 760/365-5956, www.pappyandharriets.com) was originally part of the set as a dusty cantina facade. It was eventually turned into a functioning cantina that served as a biker burrito bar from 1972 to 1982. In 1982, the cantina debuted as Pappy & Harriet's Pioneertown Palace.

Today Pioneertown continues as a family-friendly attraction. Visitors can wander the main street, taking in the frontier buildings. The original soundstage has been restored and now features live music some weekend afternoons. Visitors can also browse a handful of **retail shops** (open weekends) that feature gifts, soap, and pottery. And of course, no Wild West town would be complete without a staged **gunfight,** available on Mane Street most weekends.

Getting There

Pioneertown is 4 miles (6 km) north of Yucca Valley. From the intersection of Highway 62 and Pioneertown Road, turn left to head north for 4 miles (6 km). Pioneertown's Mane Street is located adjacent to Pappy & Harriet's Pioneertown Palace, and the two share parking.

The Integratron

George Van Tassel (1910-1978) held respectable jobs as an aeronautical engineer for Lockheed Douglas Aircraft and as a test pilot for Hughes Aviation, but arguably his real life's work was as an inventor and UFO advocate.

Van Tassel was the engineer behind **The Integratron** (2477 Belfield Blvd., Landers, 760/364-3126, www.integratron. com, $35-40 by appointment only, private $300-1,300), a spherical, all-wood dome originally intended as an electrostatic generator to promote cellular rejuvenation and time travel. An avowed alien contactee, Van Tassel claimed that extraterrestrials from Venus gave him the formula to build the structure. The building's ship-tight wood construction and dome shape imbued it with an amazing sound resonance.

The current owners of The Integratron haven't yet figured out how to tap into the structure's time travel aspects, but they are intent on rejuvenation (at least for the soul). The only way to visit The Integratron is by reserving a private or "pop-up" **sound bath** (by appointment only). Sound baths last one hour and include 25 minutes of crystal bowl harmonies followed by recorded music for relaxation and meditation. Reserving a sound bath also gives you access to the structure's grounds and a display about the history of The Integratron.

Giant Rock

Tens of thousands of people attended George Van Tassel's annual Spacecraft Conventions held at **Giant Rock** (3 mi/5 km north of The Integratron), the largest freestanding boulder in the world coming in at seven stories high and covering 5,800 square feet of ground. The

Pappy & Harriet's Pioneertown Palace

spiritually powerful place was a sacred Native American site and meeting place for local tribes until the 1900s.

Van Tassel used to hold weekly meditations in rooms underneath Giant Rock that had originally been dug by a local prospector. From the 1950s to the 1970s, Van Tassel used these meditations to try to attract UFOs. He was eventually successful (according to him) in 1953, when a saucer from the planet Venus landed and he was invited onto the ship and given the formula for The Integratron. Sadly, a visit to Giant Rock today shows a sad disrespect for nature and history: broken glass litters the ground and graffiti detracts from the impressive landmark.

Getting There

The Integratron is in Landers, north of the town of Yucca Valley. From the intersection of Highways 62 and 246 (Old Woman Springs Rd.), turn left onto Highway 247 and head north for 10.6 miles (15 km). Turn right (west) onto

Reche Road and continue 2.3 miles (3 km). Turn left (north) onto Belfield Boulevard and continue 2 miles (3 km) to The Integratron.

Food

The location of the sushi restaurant **Kimi Grill** (54850 29 Palms Hwy., 760/369-1122, lunch 11:30pm-2:30pm Mon.-Fri., noon-3pm Sat., dinner 5pm-9:30 Mon.-Sat., $11-20) inside the Travelodge Inn and Suites in the desert town of Yucca Valley does not inspire confidence. However, their sushi is pretty good. They serve all the standards plus some creative rolls, tempura, teriyaki, bento boxes, and poke bowls as well as beer and sake.

Locals' favorite **C&S Coffee Shop** (55795 29 Palms Hwy., 760/365-9946, 5:30am-7:30pm Mon.-Sat., 6am-7:30pm Sun., $6-11) offers hearty breakfast and brunch in an old-school diner setting. The heaping plates and early opening set you up for a power breakfast before your morning hike in Joshua Tree. Lunch and dinner add classic diner sandwiches and hearty home-cooked daily specials like meatloaf and fish-and-chips.

Gourmet coffee shop **Frontier Café** (55844 29 Palms Hwy., 760/820-1360, www.cafefrontier.com, 7am-7pm Fri.-Wed., 7am-10pm Thurs., $3-11) serves breakfast sandwiches, oatmeal, and yogurt alongside coffee, espresso, and tea. Lunch includes specialty sandwiches and salads including vegan options as well as a small but selective beer and wine list in the eclectic, artsy space with a small patio.

★ **Pappy & Harriet's Pioneertown Palace** (53688 Pioneertown Rd., Pioneertown, 760/365-5956, www.pappyandharriets.com, 5pm-2am Mon., 11am-2am Thurs.-Sun., lunch and dinner until 9:30pm, $7-30) was originally built in the 1940s as part of the Pioneertown Wild West film set. The barbecue restaurant and saloon, which also triples as a music venue, packs in die-hard fans and first-timers every night. The food (burgers, sandwiches, salads, Tex-Mex, steaks, chili, and veggie options) is legitimately good, far surpassing run-of-the-mill bar food. Reservations for dinner are highly recommended two weeks in advance (seatings: 5pm-5:30pm and 7pm). Wait times without a reservation can be staggering (2-3 hours). Lunches are mellower and the back patio is a great place for a weekend brunch.

Joshua Tree

The town of **Joshua Tree** is a small artsy outpost that welcomes visitors through the park's main West Entrance, which is 5 miles (8 km) south. A cluster of charming restaurants (and a saloon) as well as outfitters, gift shops, and hotels offer a picturesque getaway with a laid-back desert vibe.

Getting There

The town of **Joshua Tree** lies 7 miles (11 km) east of Yucca Valley along Highway 62. To enter the park through the West Entrance, follow Quail Springs Road as it heads south, becoming Park Boulevard at the park boundary. The sights of Hidden Valley can be reached in 14 miles (23 km).

Sights
Noah Purifoy Outdoor Desert Art Museum

TOP EXPERIENCE

Artist Noah Purifoy (1917-2004) used found items to create assemblage sculptures that were dubbed Junk Dada. The title feels dead-on. In the surreal **Noah Purifoy Outdoor Desert Art Museum** (63030 Blair Ln., www.noahpurifoy.com, sunrise-sunset daily, free but donations appreciated), metal, plywood, porcelain, paper, cotton, and glass are twisted and stacked into sculptures spread across 10 acres of an otherworldly artscape.

The sculptures are whimsical, political, and comical with broken pieces and discarded junk mended into recognizable shapes. Made from cheap plywood and gaudy paint, the interior of the brightly colored *Carousel* is jammed with computer monitors, discarded office machinery, and analog artifacts. Other sculptures, such as *Shelter* and *Theater,* are reminiscent of abandoned mining camps and Wild West towns, resuscitated once again into a cobbled together reminder of the American Dream scattered across rocky desert.

Getting There

From Highway 62 in the town of Joshua Tree, turn north onto Yucca Mesa Road and drive 4 miles (6 km) to Aberdeen Drive. Turn right (east) and continue another 4 miles (6 km) to Center Street. Turn left (north) onto Center Street, and make the next right onto Blair Lane (dirt road).

Food

The burgers are hot and the beers are cold at the ★ **Joshua Tree Saloon** (61835 29 Palms Hwy., 760/366-2250, www. thejoshuatreesaloon.com, 7am-midnight Sun.-Thurs., 7am-2am Fri.-Sat., $8-22). The saloon does a good job of obliging a steady stream of hungry tourists and locals with consistently good food and service amid weathered Wild West decor. The bar and grill dishes out well-executed burgers, salads, sandwiches, and solid veggie options and has a full bar. The Yard, the outdoor patio, is open weekends (weather permitting) for barbecue, cocktails, and live music. Pets are allowed and it's a good spot for kids. The inside saloon and outdoor patio are all ages.

Crossroads Café (61715 29 Palms Hwy., 760/366-5414, www.crossroadscafejtree. com, 7am-9pm daily, $8-12) offers reimagined diner fare with a Southwest bent and lots of vegetarian options. Knotty pine walls and reclaimed wood touches bring warmth to the small contemporary diner space, which bustles with hungry hikers as well as locals. Breakfast and lunch are the most popular times, but they have a simple dinner menu as well. Beer and wine are served.

The tiny **Natural Sisters Café** (61695 29 Palms Hwy., 760/366-3600, www. thenaturalsisterscafe.com, 7am-7pm daily, $6-14) serves organic, vegan, and vegetarian breakfast and lunch, coffee, smoothies, and made-to-order fresh juices. They also offer tempting pies and pastries. Lines can get long on busy weekends in the park.

JT Country Kitchen (61768 29 Palms Hwy., 760/366-8988, 6am-3:30pm daily, $8-10 cash only) is a down-home café serving tasty American diner-style breakfast and lunch. Try the sausage breakfast burrito or pancakes.

The **Joshua Tree Coffee Company** (61738 29 Palms Hwy., 760/974-9272,

Noah Purifoy Outdoor Desert Art Museum

www.jtcoffeeco.com, 7am-6pm daily) serves organic locally roasted coffee in a hip space tucked behind Pie for the People.

Pie for the People (61740 29 Palms Hwy., 760/366-0400, www. pieforthepeople.net, 11am-9pm Sun.-Thurs., 11am-10pm Fri.-Sat., $10-26) tosses very respectable thin-crust New York-style pizzas with a myriad of toppings as well as specialty pizzas. Dine in their casual contemporary space or call for delivery.

Sam's Indian Restaurant (61380 29 Palms Hwy., 760/366-9511, www. samsindianfood.com, 11am-9pm Mon.-Sat., 3pm-8pm Sun., $10-15) serves heaping plates of authentic Indian classics. They also appropriate their fluffy naan into pizza and subs, making for a diverse menu. Situated in a strip mall, the casual and cozy space serves satisfying food and beer that hits the spot after a day in the park. Their menu is also available for takeout.

Accommodations

The 1950s hacienda-style ★ **Joshua Tree Inn** (61259 29 Palms Hwy., 760/366-1188, www.joshuatreeinn.com, office open 3pm-8pm daily, from $115) offers funky courtyard rooms and rock-and-roll history. With eclectic furniture, Spanish tile floors, and outdoor patios in its 11 rooms, as well as a huge seasonal pool, landscaped courtyard, and firepit, they've tapped into a formula that keeps a dedicated following coming back.

Safari Motor Inn (61959 29 Palms Hwy., 760/366-1113, www. joshuatreemotel.com, $74-88) is a good base camp for exploring Joshua Tree. This basic budget motel has rooms with single king, single queen, or two queen beds, coffeemakers, minifridges, and a swimming pool on the property. It's the closest motel to the western entrance of the national park and walking distance to food and drinks.

The ★ **Mojave Sands** (62121 29 Palms Hwy., 760/550-8063, www. mojavesandsatjoshuatree.com, $135-300) is an impeccably renovated, industrial-chic desert modern retreat with an emphasis on the *treat*. Its five rooms and suites faced with glass and steel beams look over common grounds brought to life with a reflecting pool, reclaimed wood, and metal. The rooms feature polished concrete floors, open showers, locally made bath products, vintage turntables, and mini record collections. The two suites add kitchens and living areas. Suite 5 has an outdoor clawfoot tub and shower.

The romantic **Sacred Sands B&B** (63155 Quail Springs Rd., 760/424-6407, www.sacredsands.com, $330-360) is a luxury retreat poised on a hill with sweeping desert views 1.3 miles (2 km) from the park's West Entrance. Each of the two serene guest rooms offers an indoor shower with river-rock floors, and an outdoor shower, a private terrace with hot tub, and a meditation platform round out the amenities. Stays require a two-night minimum and include a complimentary gourmet breakfast.

Both secluded and colorful, **Spin and Margie's Desert Hide-A-Way** (64491 29 Palms Hwy., www.deserthideaway.com, $150-195) is a Southwestern-themed inn with Americana road trip-inspired grounds tucked away on the outskirts of Joshua Tree. Four suites and a cabin feature tile floors, fully equipped kitchens or kitchenettes, dining areas, outdoor courtyard and lounge areas, and flat-screen televisions.

The **Desert Lily Bed and Breakfast** (8523 Star Ln., 310/849-7290, http:// thedesertlily.com, $175-248) is a rustic yet romantic place near the west entrance of Joshua Tree National Park. The property offers four self-catering cabins (available year-round) plus a bed-and-breakfast (closed July-Aug.) in a main house with gourmet breakfast.

Twentynine Palms

The town of Twentynine Palms gives passage to Joshua Tree National Park's quieter North Entrance. The historic 29 Palms Inn anchors the tourism experience here. The small town is scattered across open desert. It's home to a military base and a few functional businesses, including inexpensive motels, a grocery store, and gas stations.

Getting There

The town of Twentynine Palms sits 15 miles (24 km) east of Joshua Tree along Highway 62 in a remote section of the valley. The **Oasis Visitors Center** (74485 National Park Dr., Twentynine Palms, 760/367-5500, 8:30am-5pm daily) and the North Entrance to the park are accessed by heading south on Utah Trail, which becomes Park Boulevard in about 4 miles (6 km).

Food and Accommodations

The ★ **29 Palms Inn** (73950 Inn Ave., 760/367-3505, www.29palmsinn.com, lunch 11am-2pm Mon.-Sat., 9am-2pm Sun., $7-16, dinner 5pm-9pm Sun.-Thurs., 5pm-9:30pm Fri.-Sat., $15-32) is the charming center of the desert inn's 70-acre universe, offering dining room and poolside dining for lunch and dinner daily. The eclectic menu pulls off classic steaks, seafood, and pastas with a fresh touch. Acoustic music accompanies dinner nightly. The eclectic **lodge** ($140-230) includes nine 1930s adobe bungalows with tile floors, fireplaces, and private sun patios, eight wood frame cabins with private decks, and seven two-bedroom guesthouses. A charming swimming pool allows for poolside dining and lounging.

The **Harmony Motel**'s (71161 29 Palms Hwy., 760/367-3351, www.harmonymotel.com, $75-95) claim to fame is that U2 stayed here when making their iconic album *Joshua Tree*. The colorful 1950s motel is set on a hilltop above Twentynine Palms, 6 miles (10 km) from the northern park entrance. The grounds have a pool, hot tub, and nice views of the Little San Bernardino Mountains. The hotel offers seven cheerful, homey rooms and one cabin. Some rooms have kitchenettes, and a common dining room with coffee is available to guests.

Getting to Route 66

From Twentynine Palms, it's possible to connect north to Route 66. From Highway 62, head east for 7 miles (11 km). Turn left onto Godwin Road, drive 3 miles (5 km) and then turn right on Amboy Road. You'll reach the "town" of Amboy on Route 66 in about 40 miles (64 km).

Route
66

Route 66

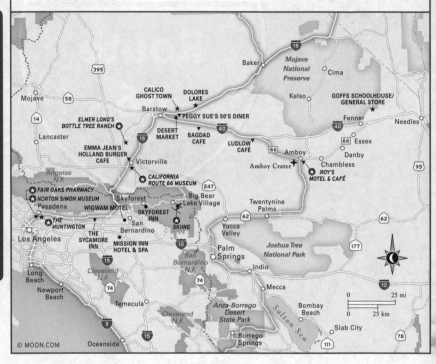

© MOON.COM

Subject of song and TV, Route 66 is where the lore of the American road trip was born.

Originally established in 1926 as a continuous route between Chicago and Los Angeles, the Mother Road—as it was called by John Steinbeck in *The Grapes of Wrath*—was the route Great Depression farmers took to flee the Dust Bowl and seek out new lives in the blossoming city of Los Angeles. With the rising stature of car and motorcycle culture in the 1950s, nothing said freedom and adventure like the open road.

By the 1980s, most of Route 66 had been replaced by modern interstate freeways, and its remote desert portions fell into disuse as newer, faster routes took over. Small roadside towns that had cropped up to offer gas, food, and lodging to Route 66 drivers suddenly found themselves far removed from the main highway and withered into modern ghost towns.

In Southern California, historic Route 66 snakes west along either side of I-40, peppered with (mostly abandoned) gas stations, train stations, motels, and attractions. From Amboy to Barstow, these mid-20th-century time capsules create a roadside museum spaced out against the starkness of the Mojave Desert.

At the transportation hub of Barstow, Route 66 leaves I-40 to dogleg south parallel with I-15 over a mountain pass into the Inland Empire east of Los Angeles. Unlike the abandoned desert stretches,

Highlights

★ **Roy's Motel and Café, Amboy:** This abandoned motel In a remote ghost town remains an architectural treasure (page 244).

★ **Elmer Long's Bottle Tree Ranch, Oro Grande:** Folk artist Elmer Long created a veritable forest of glass and light in his front yard with 200 installations of "trees" comprising antique bottles and found-art objects, pictured above (page 251).

★ **California Route 66 Museum, Victorville:** Iconic emblems of the Mother Road live on at this comprehensive museum (page 252).

★ **Skiing in Big Bear:** Within a two-hour drive of Southern California's strong winter surf sits Southern California's best skiing (page 255).

★ **Fair Oaks Pharmacy, Pasadena:** In operation since 1915, this old-school soda fountain, pharmacy, and restaurant is a neighborhood staple (page 261).

★ **The Huntington, San Marino:** This gorgeous research library is set on beautiful grounds that invite further exploration (page 261).

★ **Norton Simon Museum, Pasadena:** Visit one of the best private art collections, now shared with the public (page 261).

Best Restaurants

★ **Ludlow Café, Ludlow:** This desert gem offers a hearty breakfast and lunch (page 248).

★ **Emma Jean's Holland Burger, Victorville:** This classic Route 66 diner serves big sandwiches and even bigger burgers (page 252).

★ **Sycamore Inn, Rancho Cucamonga:** This old-school steak house on Historic Route 66 actually predates the Mother Road (page 258).

★ **La Grande Orange Café, Pasadena:** Hyperlocal ingredients shine at this café housed in the historic 1934 Del Mar Station (page 262).

★ **Lunasia Dim Sum House, Pasadena:** For the best dim sum in greater Los Angeles, try this local mainstay (page 262).

---

this portion of Route 66 is a business thoroughfare as it continues west through a parade of residential communities nestled into the rolling foothills.

As Route 66 moves into the San Gabriel Valley, road-trippers can enjoy their first glimpse of the historic city of Pasadena, arguably the most charming destination along this route.

Getting There

Route 66 stretches west from the town of Needles at the California state border all the way to the coast at Santa Monica. This stretch of the road trip picks up Route 66 at Amboy near I-40 and continues west to Barstow before turning south into the Inland Empire east of Los Angeles. It finishes following Route 66 in Pasadena, although it's possible (but difficult) to follow it all the way to the coast at Santa Monica.

While Route 66 follows the National Trails Highway from Amboy west to Barstow, the road is closed to through traffic from Kelbaker Road east to Essex Road. An eastern portion of Route 66, through Fenner and Goffs, is accessible heading north from I-40 at the Essex Road exit.

From Barstow, Route 66 turns south,

following the National Trails Highway as it parallels I-15 through Victorville into San Bernardino and the Inland Empire. A good stretch of Route 66 through the Inland Empire is along Foothill Boulevard. West of Foothill Boulevard is where you will begin to encounter L.A.'s infamous traffic.

For a contiguous road-trip loop, follow driving directions from the town of Joshua Tree at the northern border of Joshua Tree National Park. If arriving from the east via Las Vegas and Death Valley, start the route from the town of Baker on I-15.

From Joshua Tree
65 mi/105 km, 1 hr
From the town of **Joshua Tree**, take CA-62 east to the town of Twentynine Palms. Turn left at Adobe Road and drive 2 miles (3 km) north to Amboy Road. Turn right on Amboy Road and follow it for 60 miles (97 km) as it veers east then north to **Amboy.** The drive should take about an hour.

From Las Vegas
177 mi/280km, 3 hr
Road-trippers from the eastern gateway of Las Vegas will skip some Route 66 sights during the long drive on I-15 to Barstow, where they pick up the Mother

Best Accommodations

★ **Sky Forest Inn:** Sitting atop an abrupt forest slope, this small hotel offers some of the most striking views in Southern California (page 256).

★ **Wigwam Motel, San Bernardino:** Freestanding, tepee-shaped rooms make this a wonderfully kitschy stop (page 259).

★ **Mission Inn Hotel & Spa, Riverside:** Born during Southern California's citrus boom of the late 19th century, this opulent hotel is the largest Mission Revival structure in California (page 260).

★ **The Langham Huntington, Pasadena:** This elegant hotel dates from the early 20th century and aptly captures Pasadena's old-school charm (page 262).

Road south into the Inland Empire. Fortunately, a few roadside attractions are worth pulling over for.

Stop in the town of **Baker** for gas and then drive 47 miles (76 km) west on I-15, pulling off onto the frontage road to gaze at **Lake Dolores Waterpark,** an abandoned water park covered in colorful graffiti. Back on I-15, continue 12 miles (19 km) west to **Yermo** for a milkshake at **Peggy Sue's Diner,** a retro diner stuck in the 1950s. In 12 miles (19 km), you'll come to **Barstow** and head south on I-15 into the Inland Empire.

Stopping in Baker

The small town of Baker is 95 miles (153 km) west of Las Vegas and 177 miles (280 km) east of Los Angeles on I-15. It offers a quick stop between the two cities for fast food, expensive gas, and the **world's largest thermometer,** with access into either Mojave National Preserve (via Kelbaker Rd. south) or Death Valley National Park (via Hwy. 127 north).

From Baker, Kelbaker Road heads 68 miles (109 km) south through the **Mojave National Preserve,** passing the Kelso Depot and the Kelso Dunes. Kelbaker Road exits the preserve south, crossing I-40, to end on Route 66, 5 miles (8 km) east of **Amboy.**

Air or Train

The closest airport to the Inland Empire is the **Ontario International Airport** (N. Archibald Ave. and E. Airport Dr., 909/544-5300, www.flyontario.com), roughly 67 miles (108 km) west of Palm Springs on I-10. A curious assortment of flights service the smaller **Palm Springs International Airport** (3400 E. Tahquitz Canyon Way, 760/318-3800, www.palmspringsca.gov).

Both **Los Angeles International Airport** (LAX, 1 World Way, Los Angeles, 855/463-5252, www.flylax.com) and **Hollywood Burbank Airport** (BUR, 2627 N. Hollywood Way, Burbank, 818/840-8840, https://hollywoodburbankairport.com) are within easy driving distance.

The **McCarran International Airport** (LAS, 5757 Wayne Newton Blvd., Las Vegas, NV, 702/261-5211, www.mccarran.com) is within a two-hour drive of the towns of Baker and Amboy.

Car rentals are available at all airports. **Amtrak**'s (www.amtrak.com) *Southwest Chief* stops in Barstow (685 N. 1st Ave.) at the historic Casa del Desierto, a former Harvey House, and in Victorville (16858 S. D. St.). However, there are no services at these stations. You'll need to arrange a car rental in advance to continue the route.

Getting Around

Before embarking onto Route 66, make sure you have a full tank of **gas;** you'll be driving through the Mojave Desert, where fuel is scarce and prohibitively expensive. Also make sure that your car is in good working order—there is spotty cell phone service along much of this drive, and high daytime temperatures can pose a serious health risk if you get stranded on a remote road. Pack plenty of drinking water in your car; at least one gallon (3.7 liters) per person per day; even on relatively mild days the desert air is arid enough to rapidly dehydrate you.

Most stretches of Historic Route 66 east of Amboy and west of Fenner are closed to through traffic due to bridges that have been washed out by storms and left in disrepair.

Amboy

TOP EXPERIENCE

If you make one stop driving along Historic Route 66, make it Amboy, home of the architecturally splendid Roy's Café and the Amboy Crater. As you drive along the route, appreciate the Route 66 road badges painted on the highway, and notice how many people have spelled out their names with stones along the slope of berm below the still-functioning railroad tracks.

Getting There

From Joshua Tree, head east on Highway 62 for 22 miles (35 km). At the junction with Godwin Road, turn left and drive 2 miles. Turn right on Amboy Road and drive north for 40 miles (64 km) to Amboy at the junction with National Trails Highway. To join Route 66, continue driving west.

To go straight to Amboy from Barstow, follow I-40 east for 80 miles (129 km) then exit on Kelbaker Road south for 11 miles (18 km) to meet with Route 66 east of Amboy. To follow Route 66 east the whole way from Barstow to Amboy, exit Barstow on East Main Street. The road turns into Joseph L. Boll Avenue, then National Trails Highway, which parallels I-40 until it crosses the freeway heading south at Newberry Springs. Route 66 continues to Amboy. The drive from Barstow to Amboy takes about 1.5 hours without stops.

★ Roy's Motel and Café

On the north side of the National Trails Highway (Route 66) is the dusty town of Amboy, home to the iconic **Roy's Motel and Café** (87520 National Trails Hwy., 760/733/1066, 7am-8pm daily). The quintessential mid-century highway stop, when Roy's opened in 1938, this blip of a desert town had only 65 residents. Nevertheless, Roy's was built to attract road-trippers' attention, designed in the futuristic Googie style of architecture, influenced by car culture and inspired by the dawning of the space age. Stopping to get a picture in front of the Roy's sign is a Route 66 rite of passage.

Though the motel is closed, gas is available, and the café sells soft drinks. Restrooms are located outside in the back of the building.

Amboy Crater

About 3 miles (5 km) west of Roy's, on the south side of National Trails Highway, is **Amboy Crater** (BLM Needles Field Office, 1303 S. U.S. 95, Needles, 760/326-7000, www.blm.gov, dawn-dusk daily, free). The 250-foot crater, a volcanic cinder cone, formed roughly 6,000 years ago; a moderate hiking trail (1.7 mi/2.7 km) leads to the top. Hiking to the rim is not recommended during summer or in windy conditions. Avoid pathways where people tried to drive ATVs up to the crater; these are not trails and can be dangerous.

The Lost Towns of Route 66

Driving east, the former railroad water stations and towns along California's eastern stretch of Route 66 were named in alphabetical order—Amboy, Bristol, Chambless, Danby, Essex, Fenner, and Goffs. Unfortunately, only Amboy, Fenner, and Goffs remain open to through traffic. Now a part of the National Trails Highway, Route 66 is closed from Kelbaker Road east to I-40, making the defunct towns of **Chambless, Danby,** and **Essex** inaccessible by car. This was once a happening strip with cafés, auto garages, and other roadside amenities. Today, they're just dilapidated buildings cooking under the desert sun.

Route 66

However, one old alignment of Route 66 remains open heading northeast from the Essex Road exit off I-40, traveling on to **Fenner** and **Goffs,** which, ironically, were written off the Route 66 route by a 1931 realignment.

Fenner was originally established in 1883, when the town operated as a watering station for steam trains. Today, it's best known for its vintage gas station sign, which once again became visible to drivers when I-40 replaced Route 66, thanks to individual, building-high red letters spelling out "G A S" in silhouette. If you're low on **gas,** get it here because the next service station is 55 miles (89 km) away.

Originally, **Goffs** was home to employees of the Santa Fe Railway and a popular stop on Route 66 until 1931, when the Mother Road was realigned to follow a more direct route from Needles to Essex. As you enter Goffs today, look for the abandoned **General Store** on the north side of the highway. In better condition is the Spanish Mission-style **Goffs Schoolhouse** (37198 Lanfair Rd., 9am-4pm Sat.-Mon. Oct.-June, free) built in 1914. Sitting unused for decades, by 1982 it was in ruins; the **Mojave Desert Heritage and Cultural Association** (www.mdhca.org) restored it to its original condition.

Mojave National Preserve

At more than 2,500 square miles (5,475 sq. km), **Mojave Desert National Preserve** (90942 Kelso Cima Rd., www.nps.com, free) is the third-largest national park in the contiguous United States. With Death Valley National Park competing to the north and Joshua Tree National Park to the south, this multifaceted park receives less attention than it deserves. Its vast landscapes rise and fall from mountain peaks to desert valleys and feature a Joshua tree forest larger and denser than that of the tree's namesake park. Depending where you look in the Mojave Preserve, you'll find volcanic rock formations, scenic sand dunes, abandoned mines, or a historic train depot. View it as a scenic day trip, or as a camping stopover to break up the drive between Death Valley and Joshua Tree or along Route 66.

Getting There

Mojave National Preserve fits entirely between I-15 and I-40 and is immediately accessible from either freeway. From Barstow, head 89.6 miles (144.2 km) north on I-15 to Cima Road south into the park or 79.8 miles (129 km) east on I-40 to Kelbaker Road north. These two roads connect to one another in the center of the park via Kelso-Cima Road.

Note that Kelbaker Road also connects to I-15 at Baker, where it joins up with CA-127 North for 101 miles (163 km) to Death Valley National Park. From I-40, Kelbaker Road continues south 66.7 miles (107.3 km) to Historic Route 66.

From Las Vegas, take I-15 south 67.5 miles (108.6 km) to Cima Road.

Sights
Cima Dome

More than 80 million years ago, seismic activity created a subterranean magma buildup that resulted not in a volcano, but the **Cima Dome & Volcanic Field National Natural Landmark** (Cima Rd.). Much of the magma crystallized into granite below the surface, which eventually pushed its way above the ground to form a jagged mountain that has subsequently eroded into a symmetrical dome rising 1,500 feet and covering 70 square miles (181 sq. km). The large smooth dome is visible from I-15 north of Baker, but driving through it along Cima Road sends you right into the captivating Joshua tree woodland covering its slopes. It's the largest Joshua tree forest in the world, covering around 150 square miles (388 sq. km), with over a million trees, some of which are 1,000 years old and up to 30 feet in height. To the west of the dome, look for dozens of cinder cones that formed as volcanic vents, as well as rocky black lava fields from lava flows that likewise spouted from below the surface.

Kelso Depot Visitor Center

Part informative center, part museum, the **Kelso Depot Visitor Center** (90942 Kelso Cima Rd., 760/252-6108, www.nps. gov, 10am-5pm Thurs.-Mon., free) dates to 1924 when it served as a remote train station, telegraph office, and dormitory for rail employees. The old structure has been preserved and is now the park's visitors center. Exhibition rooms detail its railroad history, the area's natural history and geography, and also host a desert art gallery. Upstairs, recreated dorm rooms provide a peek at the life and housing of former railroad workers. Restrooms and drinking water are available in a separate building.

Mitchell Caverns

Once a roadside attraction in the Providence Mountains, **Mitchell Caverns** (38200 Essex Rd., 760/928-2586, www. parks.ca.gov, tours at 10am and 2pm Fri.-Sun., 10am only Jun.-Aug., $10 adult, $5 children under 16, $10 per vehicle) re-opened for public tours following five years of infrastructure upgrades. The sequence of caves feature fish fossils (a remnant of when this desert was underwater) and limestone rock formations such as stalactites, stalagmites, and unusual cave shields. To take the tour, visitors must be fit enough to complete the strenuous 1.6-mile hike. Reservations are required (call 760/928-2586, 8am-5pm Mon.).

Hiking

Dozens of hiking opportunities present themselves throughout the Mojave, showing off different aspects of the park. On the north side of the park, a 3-mile round-trip through Joshua trees takes you to **Teutonia Peak** (12 mi/19 km south of I-15 on Cima Rd.), which offers impressive Cima Dome views.

South of Cima Dome, **Rock Spring Loop Trail** (5 mi/8 km east of Black Canyon Rd. on Cedar Canyon Rd.) offers a glimpse of the Mojave's human history, starting with the small stone cottage called the Rock House, originally occupied by a World War I veteran who moved to the desert to mitigate the effects of a poison gas attack. Farther along, the trail reaches a mill used by miners of gold, silver, and copper in the region, before reaching Rock Spring, a life-giving water source used by a military post and indigenous Mojave people before that. The trail passes over a scenic ridge before concluding the 1-mile loop.

At higher elevations in the center of the park, the **Hole-in-the-Wall Information Center** (1 Black Canyon Rd., closed) offers two trailheads. The **Hole-in-the-Wall Nature Trail** (0.5 mile) is a scenic hike offering informative signs about desert flora. The more rigorous **Rings Trail** (1.5 mi/2.4 km, round-trip) gets its name from the iron rings that help you ascend or descend the steep portions of narrow Banshee Canyon, a pockmarked formation with literal holes in its walls. Note that this hike requires more upper body strength.

To the southwest, the **Kelso Dunes Trail** (3 mi/5 km round-trip, 1 hour) offers a rigorous hike around sandy dunes that light up at sunrise and sunset. At the top of the dunes, agitate the sands and listen to the boom as it rolls down the sides—but mind your footing! The trailhead is 8 miles south of Kelso Depot and 3 miles west of Kelbaker Road on Kelso Dunes Road. There are parking and bathrooms at the trailhead.

Note: The roads leading to these trailheads are often potted and degraded. Drive with caution to avoid structural damage to your vehicle. Many areas experience extreme heat; pack plenty of water and wear sunscreen and protective clothing.

Camping

Surrounded by cinder cones and other lava formations, the **Hole-in-the-Wall Campground** (1 Black Canyon Rd., year-round, $12) offers 35 first-come, first-served campsites with picnic tables, fire rings, trash receptacles, pit toilets, and potable water. The campground is at a 4,400-foot elevation. To get there from I-40, take the exit for Essex Road north

Top to bottom: Amboy Crater; on the Teutonia Peak Trail in the Mojave Desert; Ludlow Café.

and drive 9.5 miles (13 km). Veer right onto Black Canyon Road and drive north for 10 miles (16 km) to the campground. It's also possible to get here from the north via Kelso Cima Road and Cedar Canyon Road, but the washboard road is rough and potholed.

At 5,600 feet, the **Mid Hills Campground** (Wild Horse Canyon Rd., year-round, $12) offers cooler temperatures and similar amenities, but no potable water. The 26 campsites are first-come, first-served; those in the far loop are shaded by piñons and junipers. Check fire restrictions and plan to bring your own firewood for use in the firepits. Mid Hills is 7 miles (11 km) north of Hole-in-the-Wall Campground on the rough Black Canyon Road. Turn west and continue 2 miles (3 km) to the campground. Trailers and RVs are not advised.

Ludlow

TOP EXPERIENCE

In 1882, Ludlow was a regular water stop for the Atlantic and Pacific Railroad. It was also a prosperous mining town after ore was discovered in the nearby hills.

In the 1940s, Ludlow boasted a motor court (still in operation today), cabins, and the ★ **Ludlow Café** (68315 National Trails Hwy., 760/733-4501, 6am-6pm daily, $6-12). The gabled-roof building showcases a modernist facade, and the no-frills menu has everything you'd want in a classic roadside diner experience: fluffy pancakes, hearty biscuits and gravy, and all-day breakfast. Plus, they have frothy malts, friendly and fast service, and a photo-worthy Route 66 mural painted on the exterior of the building. Walk off your meal by wandering over to see the vintage trucks on display next door.

Getting There

From Amboy, drive 5 miles (8 km) west to the eerily silent town of Bagdad. Continue west on National Trails Highway (Rte. 66) for 20 miles (32 km) to the town of Ludlow. If you need **gas,** there is a 76 station where Route 66/National Trails Highway crosses I-40 on Crucero Road.

Newberry Springs

Bagdad Café

Bagdad was once a bustling place, considering it's in the middle of the desert. After Route 66 was rerouted in 1973, the town floundered. By 1991, the remaining buildings were razed, leaving little more than rusted-out cars and creosote. The **Bagdad Café** (46548 National Trails Hwy., 760/257-3101, 7am-7pm daily, $6-12), which inspired the Academy Award-nominated 1987 German film of the same name, was originally located in Bagdad (about 50 mi/81 km east), but the actual filming took place here in Newberry Springs. The food is hit-or-miss, but the ambience and film history make it a worthwhile stop for a cold drink on a 120°F (49°C) day.

Getting There

From Ludlow, drive west on Route 66/I-40 for 28 miles (45 km) to Newberry Springs.

◈ Side Trip on I-15

Not all of the roadside attractions are along I-40. Take this side trip north to I-15 to discover a few hidden gems.

Lake Dolores Waterpark

There's nothing creepier—or cooler—than an abandoned water park. **Lake Dolores Waterpark** (which also operated under the names Rock-a-Hoola and Discover Waterpark) sits crumbling under the desert sun about 20 minutes north of Newberry Springs.

Lake Dolores Waterpark opened in the late 1950s as a playground and campground with a 273-acre artificial lake. Dwindling attendance in the 1980s caused the park to close in 1990. After a renovation and reopening in 1998, the park was forced to close for good in 2004.

Calico Ghost Town

Despite the "No Trespassing" signs, the park is easy to access and a worthy stop for adventurous urban explorers.

Getting There

From Newberry Springs, take Newberry Road north for 6 miles (10 km), turning east as it becomes Palma Vista Road. In 1 mile (1.6 km), turn left (north) on Harvard Road. Follow Harvard Road north for 3 miles (5 km) to I-15 and turn west onto Hacienda Road. Drive 2.5 miles (4 km) west on Hacienda Road to the water park on the north side of the road.

Yermo

Peggy Sue's Diner (35654 W. Yermo Rd., 760/254-3370, www.peggysuesdiner.com, 6am-9pm daily, $9-14) is a Hollywood version of the 1950s, with black-and-white checkered floors, pictures of Marilyn and Elvis on the walls, and a life-size sculpture of Betty Boop dressed as a waitress. Skip the food and go straight for a cherry, strawberry, or chocolate milkshake.

Calico Ghost Town (36600 Ghost Town Rd., 800/862-2542, http://cms.sbcounty.gov, 9am-5pm daily, $8 adults, $5 children 4-11) haunts the former site of Calico, a mining town that sprang up in 1881 as part of the California silver rush. Its old-timey buildings were restored in the 1950s, and the place now serves as a tourist attraction.

Getting There

From Yermo, drive south on Hacienda Road for about 2.5 miles (4 km). Turn right onto Yermo Road and drive 5.5 miles (8.9 km) west. At a T junction, turn left (west) to continue on East Yermo Road and the town of Yermo.

To return to Route 66, head west on Yermo Road and turn left (south) on Dagget-Yermo Road. In 2.5 miles (4 km), turn right (west) on National Trails Highway (Route 66).

Daggett

Daggett was named after California Lieutenant Governor John Daggett. In the late 1800s, the town was a supply center that accommodated the nearby silver mines in Calico. It took teams of mules to haul water and ore from Daggett to Calico. By 1902, Daggett was supported by three borax mines; more than $90 million worth of silver was removed from the Calico Hills. Daggett was also the California inspection station mentioned in Steinbeck's *Grapes of Wrath*. Some of the buildings still standing date back more than 100 years.

If you want to stock up on soda and snacks, stop by **Desert Market** (35596 Santa Fe Ave., 760/254-2774, 8am-8pm Mon.-Sat., 9am-6pm Sun.), a family-owned convenience store and local gathering spot.

Getting There

To get there from Route 66 (National Trails Hwy.), turn right (north) on Daggett-Yermo Road. Cross the tracks and take the first right (east) on Santa Fe Street. The market is two blocks on the north side, across the street from an old garage that used to repair mining equipment.

Barstow

As the mining boom busted in nearby Calico and Daggett, Barstow became an important railway hub and stopping point for travelers entering California via Route 66. In the 1950s, car transportation became more prevalent, and Barstow's main drag turned into a popular place to stop along the Mother Road.

Getting There

From Daggett, drive west on National Trails Highway for 2.5 miles (4 km). Turn left (south) on Nebo Street and take the next right to join I-40 west. Continue 2.5 miles (4 km) on I-40 to take Exit 2. Turn left, go under I-40, and then turn right to take the South Frontage Road for about 1 mile (2 km). Turn right (north) to follow East Main Street into Barstow.

Casa del Desierto Harvey House

Casa del Desierto Harvey House (681 N. 1st Ave., 760/818-4400, www. barstowharveyhouse.com, 8:30am-5pm Mon.-Fri., 10am-2pm Sat., free) was built in 1885 as a restaurant and hotel for Santa Fe Railway passengers. After it burned down in 1908, famed architect Mary Colter rebuilt it in 1913 in a style that fuses 16th-century Spanish and Classical Revival architecture. In 1999, the city of Barstow renovated and reopened Casa del Desierto. Today, it houses the **Route 66 Mother Road Museum** (760/255-1890, www.route66museum.org, 10am-4pm Fri.-Sun., free) and the **Western America**

Railroad Museum (685 N. 1st Ave., 760/256-9276, www.barstowrailmuseum. org, 11am-3pm Fri., 11am-4pm Sat.-Sun., free).

From Route 66, turn right (north) onto 1st Avenue. Drive 0.4 mile and the road will curve to the right (east). Casa del Desierto Harvey House is on the right.

Food and Accommodations
Unfortunately, decent food and lodging options in Barstow are limited. **Lola's Kitchen** (1244 E. Main St., 760/255-1007, 4am-7:30pm Mon.-Fri., 4am-4:30pm Sat., $5-12) is hidden away in a strip mall. It's easy to miss, but if you want good Mexican food, make a point to visit—the chile relleno is near perfection.

The 1922 **Route 66 Motel** (195 W. Main St., 760/256-7866, www. route66motelbarstow.com, $50-60) offers an acceptable choice, with a retro neon sign and vintage cars parked out front, plus funky Route 66 memorabilia throughout the property. Guest rooms

don't offer much in the way of amenities or style, but the price is cheap.

◆ Side Trip: Oro Grande

★ Elmer Long's Bottle Tree Ranch
Passing through Helendale, keep an eye out for **Elmer Long's Bottle Tree Ranch** (24266 National Trails Hwy., 760/684-2601, dawn-dusk daily, free). You don't want to skip this place.

Ever since he was a kid camping with his father in the 1950s, Elmer Long has collected treasures from trash heaps in the desert. They found stuff from as far back as the 1800s. Elmer's father started collecting glass bottles from these father-son treasure hunts, and after he died, Elmer inherited the collection. To memorialize his father—and show off the astounding and odd collection of found

Elmer Long's Bottle Tree Ranch

objects—Elmer turned "one man's trash, another man's treasure" into an art installation of nearly 200 bottle trees. When the sun shines through them, they glimmer in hues of amber, sapphire, and emerald. Wander the "forest" of glass trees, and you'll come across other sculptures made from antique signs, vintage gas pumps, old cars, toys, wind chimes, wheel wells, teapots, and more. If you leave a donation, you can take a piece of glass as a souvenir.

Getting There

From Barstow, drive west on Main Street (Route 66/National Trails Hwy.) for 23 miles (37 km) past Hinkley Road, then through Helendale. Look for Oro Grande in less than 2 miles (3 km).

Victorville

Mormons made their way to Victorville in the 1860s and established a telegraph station here. When Route 66 arrived in 1926, it passed through the center of what is today considered "Old Town" Victorville. During the peak of Route 66, Victorville's dude ranches and apple orchards were the perfect locations for movie producers to film several Hollywood B films, including *It Came from Outer Space*. In 1940, Herman J. Mankiewicz penned the first two drafts of *Citizen Kane* at the Green Spot Motel on Route 66.

Getting There

From Oro Grande, head south on National Trails Highway for 4 miles (6 km). Crossing under the I-15 overpass brings you into Victorville. Continue 1 mile (1.6 km) south on D Street.

★ California Route 66 Museum

To see the Green Spot Motel's green neon sign, as well as other iconic Route 66 memorabilia, visit the **California Route 66 Museum** (16825 S. D St., 760/951-0436, http://califrt66museum. org, 10am-4pm Mon. and Thurs.-Sat., 11am-3pm Sun., free). Explore more than 4,500 square feet of photographs, artifacts from now-defunct Route 66 businesses, antique radios, and a Ford Model T from 1917. Be sure to ask questions of the friendly, knowledgeable staff.

Food

Juicy burgers and crispy chicken-fried steak come with a side of history and fame at ★ **Emma Jean's Holland Burger** (17143 N. D St., 760/243-9938, www. hollandburger.com, 5am-3pm Mon.-Fri., 6am-12:30pm Sat., cash only, $6-10). Inside these mint-green walls, Emma Jean's has been serving Route 66ers since 1947. In fact, it has been around longer than any other restaurant in the area. It was also the restaurant Uma Thurman walked into after being buried alive in Quentin Tarantino's cult classic *Kill Bill 2*. The milkshakes are the big winners here, as are the burgers. The Brian Burger comes topped with Ortega chili and melted swiss cheese and sits between slices of thick, parmesan-crusted garlic bread. The portions are huge, so split a sandwich or leave your diet outside where it belongs.

Cajon Pass

South of Victorville, Route 66 has been subsumed by I-15 all the way to San Bernardino—except for a 6.4-mile stretch of old highway coming out of the Cajon Pass, a mountain pass between the San Bernardino and San Gabriel Mountains; the rift was formed by the shifting of the San Andreas Fault. Popular among trainspotters, Cajon Pass is often photographed and featured in books and magazines.

Getting There

From Victorville, take I-15 south for about 20 miles (32 km) to Cleghorn Road (Exit 129). Exit and turn right onto Cajon Boulevard. The historic route continues 15.8 miles (26 km) to Virgil Avenue in San Bernardino, with options to rejoin I-15 at Kenwood Avenue or jump on the US-215 south at Devore Avenue. Note that the pass can close due to snow in inclement weather.

◈ Side Trip: Big Bear

TOP EXPERIENCE

It's a point of Southern California pride that you can ski and surf in the same day, and that's mostly thanks to Sugarloaf Mountain, home to the ski runs of Big Bear Lake (pop. 5,242). Within a three-hour drive of the coast, this lakeside resort town is a popular weekend destination year-round, but especially in winter. In warm seasons, mild weather and green forest scenery attract hikers and bikers to the lake's southern shore, where the ski runs are converted in summer into mountain bike trails.

The drive to Big Bear means taking the aptly named **Rim of the World Scenic Byway,** a winding road cut into the mountainside that offers views of the coast on a clear day—admittedly smog makes those rare, but the vistas prove stunning regardless, especially at sunset. Along the road, you'll come across the residential community of Lake Arrowhead and nearby Sky Forest, which sits on a slope so steep you really feel like you're floating above the valley.

Getting There

Big Bear is 104 miles (167 km) south of Barstow; the drive will take 2-2.5 hours depending on road and weather conditions. From Barstow, take I-15 south for about 50 miles (80 km) to Cajon Pass. At Cajon Junction, take CA-138 east for 24.5 miles (39.4 km) to the junction with CA-18. Turn left to head east on CA-18 toward Big Bear Lake. You're now on the Rim of the World Scenic Byway, which travels past Lake Arrowhead and Sky Forest before reaching Big Bear Lake in 30.5 miles (49 km).

Note that this route may close due to snow and tire chains may be required. For updated road conditions, contact **CalTrans** (800/427-7623, www.dot.ca.gov).

Scenic Drive

The road carved into the mountainside to Big Bear Lake has earned the name of the **Rim of the World Scenic Byway** (Hwys. 138, 18, and 38, www.fs.usda.gov), but really it only goes as far as the rim of the San Bernardino Mountains between Cajon Pass and San Gorgonio Pass, 110 miles (177 km) in all. At times, though, it does feel as if the whole world stretches before you. The narrow, steep, and winding two-way highway skirts the edge of the mountains with little between the cars and the steep drops below, so it can (and should) be slow going. But it can also be quite pretty; even the smoggy Inland Empire can look dreamy from this vantage point. The best times to enjoy the drive are at sundown and a day or two following a rainstorm, when clear skies open up visibility all the way to the Pacific Ocean.

Though the road is open year-round, it may close due to snow, and tire chains may be required. For road conditions, contact **CalTrans** (800/427-7623, www.dot.ca.gov).

Sights
Big Bear Lake Village

All the expected amenities may be found at **Big Bear Lake Village** (Pine Knot Ave. at CA-18), including bars, restaurants, a movie theater, and a music venue. Wood carvings of bears are common throughout the community's tree-lined streets, a particularly quaint sight when leaves change color in the fall and when snow frosts the rustic buildings in winter. Though sleepy during the week in the off-season, the village stays surprisingly crowded on weekends and during ski season.

Alpine Zoo

There are many wild animals in Big Bear Lake, but you may not encounter them at a convenient time or place. For a safe viewing, spend a little time at **Alpine Zoo** (Moonridge Rd. at Clubview Dr., 909/584-1299, www.bigbearzoo.org, $12 adults, $9 children age 3-10). The zoo provides a home for animals indigenous to the area—wolves, bobcats, and bears—that have been injured, orphaned, or imprinted on humans and cannot be safely released into the wild. A few, such as a pair of majestic, one-eyed Himalayan snow leopards, hail from similar mountain environments around the world.

Lake Arrowhead

Charming **Lake Arrowhead** (off Hwy. 18, www.lakearrowhead.com) is a worthy stopping point on the Rim of the World Scenic Byway. The private lake offers public access to its waterfront through a shopping center in downtown **Lake Arrowhead Village** (CA-173, 1.8 mi/2.9 km north of CA-18) where visitors can enjoy a lakeside meal or board the **Arrowhead Queen Tour Boat** (909/336-6992, http://lakearrowheadqueen.com, 11am-5pm daily, $18.50 adult, $14

children 12 and under) for a steamboat ride around the lake.

Uphill from the lake is the picturesque **Tudor House** (800 Arrowhead Villa Rd., 909/336-5000, www.tudorhouseentertainment.villas), which operated as a casino and brothel during Prohibition and was patronized by L.A. mobster Bugsy Siegel. Today the pretty building is a community center and performance venue.

Sky Forest

As scenic as it sounds, **Sky Forest** (CA-18 at Kuffel Canyon Rd.) sits above Lake Arrowhead on the Rim of the World Scenic Byway where it offers dazzling views from a sheer, cliffside forest location. For a convenient viewpoint, stop at **Switzer Park Picnic Area** (28527 CA-18, 909/382-2790, www.fs.usda.gov, 6am-10pm daily). Nearby is **SkyPark at Santa's Village** (28950 CA-18, 909/744-9373, www.skyparksantasvillage.com, 9am-5pm Thurs.-Sun., day pass $42 adults,

$32 children 4-12, $10 parking), a multi-faceted entertainment and activities complex with an ice-skating rink, mountain bike park, zip-line tours, climbing walls, bungee jumps, and the park's original attraction, Santa's Village.

★ Skiing

In the winter months, Southern California's best skiing takes place at a pair of sister resorts: **Big Bear Mountain** (43101 Goldmine Dr., 844/462-2327, www.bigbearmountainresort.com, 9am-4pm Mon.-Fri., 8:30am-4pm Sat.-Sun., lift tickets $79-109/day) and **Snow Summit** (880 Summit Blvd.). Some days, the resorts offer half day (10 percent off full price) and night session tickets ($59), so watch for announcements. In summer months, the ski runs are converted to a series of mountain bike tracks; ski lift racks carry bike and biker up the mountain, and they roll down over jumps and berms. Or, just ride one of the lifts to enjoy the view of the lake below. Bike, ski, and snowboard rentals are available, but pricey.

Food and Accommodations

Breakfast in Big Bear Lake means there's a line waiting for a host of hearty, country-style dishes at **Grizzly Manor Cafe** (41268 Big Bear Blvd., 909/866-6226, www.grizzlymanorcafe.com, 6am-2pm daily, $8-15). In Big Bear Lake Village, **Saucy Mama's** (618 Pine Knot Ave., 909/878-0165, 11am-9:30pm daily, $8-20) offers the town's favorite pizza, pasta, and Italian subs. Enjoy the view of Sky Forest over a tasty slice at **LouEddies Pizza** (28561 CA-18, 909/336-4931, www.loueddiespizza.com, 11:30am-8pm Sun.-Thurs., 11:30am-8:30pm Fri.-Sat., $15-18).

Most Big Bear visitors rent one of thousands of rustic cabins scattered around the south shore, booking directly online through web services **Big Bear Vacations** (www.bigbearvacations.com) or **Big Bear Cool Cabins** (www.bigbearcoolcabins.

Big Bear in winter

com). For affordable lodging within Big Bear Village, try **Robinhood Resort** (www.robinhoodresorts.com) or go closer to the lake with the cabin-like hotel experience of **Big Bear Frontier** (40472 Big Bear Blvd., 800/457-6401, www.big-bear-cabins.com, from $110).

For a unique and memorable lodging experience a little ways down the mountain, check into the ★ **Sky Forest Inn** (28717 CA-18, 909/744-8822, www.skyforestinn.com, from $180). It's nestled against the mountainside, so make sure to reserve a suite with the magnificent Sky Forest view.

Information and Services
Conveniently located within Big Bear Village, **Big Bear Visitors Center** (630 Bartlett Rd., 909/866-7000, www.bigbear.com, 9am-5pm daily) has information regarding a wide range of tourist activities in and around the lake area.

San Bernardino and the Inland Empire

Exiting the mountains over Cajon Pass, Historic Route 66 picks up again in the sprawling suburbia of Los Angeles collectively known as the Inland Empire. Unlike the Mojave portions of the old route, this stretch passes through towns that never died, making it a slow ride with plenty of stoplights and congested commercial districts.

Beginning with **San Bernardino,** the depressed crossroads best known as the birthplace of McDonald's, this section of Route 66 follows Foothill Boulevard through Rialto, Fontana, Rancho Cucamonga, Upland, Claremont, and La Verne, with each town growing more affluent as you near Los Angeles. You'll encounter the occasional historic building or restaurant, but unless you're a serious Route 66 enthusiast, it's not terribly exciting and is easy to bypass on the freeway.

At the town of **San Dimas,** Route 66 passes into the San Gabriel Valley as it makes its finishing push into **Pasadena.** The quaint bedroom communities of Glendora, Azusa, Duarte, Monrovia, and Arcadia offer little more than a concrete slice of suburbia and a gateway to the sprawling metropolis of Los Angeles.

Getting There
From the Cajon Pass, Route 66 runs parallel to I-15. In less than 2 miles (3 km), turn left on Kenwood Avenue and join I-15 south. Immediately after entering the freeway, get into the middle/left lanes toward Riverside/San Bernardino I-215. Bear left to follow I-215. Drive 3.5 miles (5.6 km) to Exit 50 and turn right. In about 1,000 feet (305 meters), cross the railroad tracks and take an immediate left (south) on Cajon Boulevard. Drive 4.5 miles (7.2 km) to 21st Street. Make a right (west) and then an immediate left to follow North Mt. Vernon Avenue as it heads south into San Bernardino. In 1.5 miles (2.4 km), turn right (west) on West 5th Street, which soon turns into Foothill Boulevard.

From Los Angeles, I-10 heads east for 60 miles (97 km) straight into San Bernardino. Optional I-210, parallel to the north, more closely follows Route 66 through this area, connecting to and from Pasadena. Both freeways experience heavy traffic during most daytime hours. The drive takes one hour when conditions are clear, more than two hours when not. Alternately, driving off freeway on Historic Route 66 between San Bernardino and Pasadena takes 2 or 2.5 hours, without stops.

Following Route 66
To stay on Historic Route 66 all the way to Pasadena, you can drive a mostly straight line, but there are a few key turns and street changes. Out of San Bernardino, Route 66 continues west on Foothill Boulevard about 30.7 miles (49 km) through the Inland Empire to San Dimas. At Amelia Avenue, Foothill

Boulevard doglegs to the north, and the name of the road changes to Historic Route 66. After 0.8 mile (1.3 km), keep left at the fork to stay on Route 66.

Continue another 3.8 miles (6 km) to the San Gabriel Valley community of Azusa, where Historic Route 66 skews right to rejoin Foothill Boulevard. After the merge, the route continues west for 2.2 miles (3.5 km) to Irwindale Avenue, where the road name changes to Huntington Drive. Stay on Huntington Drive 6.4 miles (10 km) until it reaches a fork at the Santa Anita Park horse track. Take the fork right onto Colorado Place, which continues 0.5 mile before turning into Colorado Boulevard and entering Pasadena.

Sights

The **Aztec Hotel** (305 W. Foothill Blvd., Monrovia) is one of the few remaining examples of Mayan Revival architecture in the entire country. In 1925, architect Robert Stacy-Judd merged art deco sensibilities with Mayan script, known as glyphs. Though closed while undergoing renovations, this rare historical landmark is worth a photo-op.

San Bernardino History and Railroad Museum

Built in 1918, the Santa Fe Depot is an architectural beauty that sports Mission Revival, Moorish Revival, and Spanish colonial styles. It's also home to the **San Bernardino History and Railroad Museum** (1170 W. 3rd St., 909/888-3634, www.sbdepotmuseum.com, 9am-noon Wed., 10am-3pm Sat., free), a museum of automobile and train artifacts, including 19th-century horse-drawn buggies. A former Harvey House, the depot is listed on the National Register of Historic Places. Today, it functions as the San Bernardino Amtrak station.

Top to bottom: Cucamonga Service Station; Moonlight Forest Festival lanterns at the Los Angeles County Arboretum; Wigwam Motel.

Original McDonald's Site and Museum

San Bernardino hasn't experienced its best years of late, and I don't advise dwelling there. However, fast-food fans may stop to appreciate the site of the first ever McDonald's restaurant, where today stands the **Original McDonald's Site and Museum** (1398 N. E St., 909/885-6324, 9am-5pm Mon.-Fri., 10am-5pm Sat.-Sun., free). It's not the original building, unfortunately (that was torn down in 1972), but it does house a collection of McDonald's artifacts dating to the 1940s, including Happy Meal toys and vintage packaging including the first Happy Meal boxes.

Cucamonga Service Station

At the intersection of Archibald Avenue, in the berg of Rancho Cucamonga, sits the lemon yellow vintage gas station, **Cucamonga Service Station** (9670 E. Foothill Blvd., Rancho Cucamonga, 909/271-1024, www.route66ieca.org, 10am-3pm Thurs.-Sat., noon-3pm Sun., free). Lovingly restored to its original 1915 condition, the landmark conjures a sense of the architecture Route 66 drivers witnessed when they passed through here in the 1920s and '30s. Once a Richfield Oil service station, the photogenic sight now bills itself as a museum, though it's mainly a great place to pick up Route 66 souvenirs.

Santa Anita Park

Los Angeles area horse races have been run at this Arcadia location of **Santa Anita Park** (285 Huntington Dr., Arcadia, 626/574-7223, www.santaanita.com, race days Sept.-June, $5 adults, free children under 18, $4 parking) since 1934. At one time, its annual Santa Anita Handicap offered the biggest purse in all of horse racing, and there's a statue out front of its most famous winner, Seabiscuit. The Breeder's Cup venue was briefly suspended during its 2018-2019 racing season and the park's long-term future is uncertain.

Los Angeles County Arboretum

Natural springs feed a lake, brook, and a waterfall, in addition to 127 acres of tree groves and botanical gardens, at the **Los Angeles County Arboretum** (301N N. Baldwin Ave., Arcadia, 626/821-3222, www.arboretum.org, 9am-4:30pm daily, $9 adults, $4 children 5-12). Part of the original Rancho Santa Anita, the plot was once owned by 19th-century developer Elias Jackson "Lucky" Baldwin, founder of Santa Anita Park, and on the shores of his namesake Baldwin Lake is the historic Queen Anne Cottage, built in 1885 for his fourth wife. The arboretum's other attractions include aquatic gardens, an herb garden, a tropical greenhouse, and a rose garden. Its large botanical collection includes 180 species of aloe, 70 types of plumeria, an Engelmann oak grove boasting 250 trees, and more than 60 cultivars of magnolias, which bloom from February into early March. Each year it hosts the colorful **Moonlight Forest Festival** (Nov.), a nighttime festival featuring illuminated dragons and dazzling lantern designs.

Food and Accommodations

Even if you don't love doughnuts (but really, who doesn't love doughnuts?), make it a point to stop at **The Donut Man** (915 E. Route 66, Glendora, 626/335-9111, www.thedonutmanca.com, 24 hours daily). Since 1972, people have been flocking to this place for its delectable morsels of fried dough. Try one of the famous fresh peach- and strawberry-stuffed doughnuts, then order a maple-frosted cruller for the road.

The historic 1848 ★ **Sycamore Inn** (8318 Foothill Blvd., Rancho Cucamonga, 909/982-1104, www.thesycamoreinn. com, 5pm-9pm Mon.-Thurs., 5pm-10pm Fri.-Sat., 4pm-8:30pm Sun., $13-60) opened almost 70 years before Route 66 came through. The restaurant serves old-school fine dining fare like buttery prime rib, creamy mashed potatoes, and stuffed mushrooms capped with blue cheese.

Whether it ever reopens remains a mystery, but it's fun to at least spot **Bono's Historic Orange** (15395 E. Foothill Blvd., Fontana), the 1936 roadside orange juice stand shaped like a giant orange.

The ★ **Wigwam Motel** (2728 E. Foothill Blvd., Rialto, 909/875-3005, www.wigwammotel.com, $75-90) is all fun roadside kitsch. At this 1949 motor court, each guest room takes the shape of a 20-foot-tall (6-m) tepee (not a wigwam, despite the property's name). The tepees are roomy enough to fit a comfy bed, flat-screen TV, and a minifridge. When you're not in your tepee, enjoy the motel's amenities, such as free Wi-Fi, an outdoor firepit, swimming pool, and gift shop.

Pasadena

Said to be named for the Chippewa term meaning "of the valley," Pasadena (pop. 142,647) was actually populated by the Hahamog-na tribe of the Tongva Nation prior to the Spanish founding of the San Gabriel Mission. But as California changed hands from Spain to Mexico to the United States, the city's enviable Mediterranean climate made it a popular settling ground for East Coasters and Midwesterners, who took to calling it "the crown of the valley" and ultimately named it in the language of a Midwest tribe. It was settled as a citrus grove and later a resort town, and the architecture of historic Old Pasadena still reflects its turn-of-the-20th-century heyday, offering an elegant backdrop for its famous Tournament of Roses Parade. The importance of the city as a SoCal cultural hub is evidenced by the fact that the nation's first modern freeway, I-110, was built to connect Pasadena to downtown Los Angeles.

Top to bottom: cherry blossoms in Old Town Pasadena; Fair Oaks Pharmacy; Pavilion of the Three Friends in The Huntington's Chinese garden.

The Mission Inn Hotel & Spa

Mission Inn

Fine hotels are few and far between along this leg of Historic Route 66, but if you head about 10 miles (16 km) south of where the route picks up in San Bernardino, you'll find a gorgeous hotel that's a destination all by itself: The ★ **Mission Inn Hotel & Spa** (3649 Mission Inn Ave., Riverside, 951/784-0300, www.missioninn.com, from $199). A National Historic Landmark, the Riverside hotel is the largest example of Mission Revival architecture in the United States. For road-trippers looking to dust off and break up the drive out of SoCal's deserts, Mission Inn and its spa amenities offer a picturesque break from your touring agenda.

Riverside was once the birthplace of California's booming citrus industry, attracting fortune seekers and investors from around the world. In 1903, Riverside local Frank Augustus Miller saw the need for luxury accommodations and began expanding the site of the adobe boardinghouse his father had established in 1876. As plans for the property grew ever more ambitious, construction continued over the next three decades until the hotel covered an entire city block. The original Mission Revival style was embellished by other global influences and the resulting estate offers a delightful and diverse maze of towers, domes, archways, flying buttresses, lush gardens, and a 13th-century church bell. Miller returned from his European travels with artwork and furniture to decorate the property, which hosted presidents, celebrities, and historic aviators who are honored by 140 copper wings mounted on the Inn's **Famous Fliers Wall**.

As Riverside's heyday came and went, the hotel fell into disuse and disrepair prior to a detailed restoration in the late 1980s. Mission Inn has since reclaimed its status as an upscale destination lodging, earning a Four Diamond rating. In addition to four restaurants, the hotel offer the European-style spa services of **Kelly's Spa** (800/440-5910) and an on-site **museum** with 75-minute, docent-led **tours** (951/788-9556, $13 adults, children under 12 free).

Getting There

From San Bernardino, take Highway 210 west for 56 miles (90 km) into Pasadena, or follow Historic Route 66 (described above). From downtown Los Angeles, take I-110 north for roughly 10 miles (16 km).

Sights

You'll find stonemasonry and brick facades in short supply in Southern California, which makes historic **Old Pasadena** (Fair Oaks Ave. and Colorado Blvd., www.oldpasadena.org) an interesting place to explore. The city came of age in the early 20th century and it looks it, with stately old buildings and tree-lined streets providing a scenic venue for shopping and dining.

★ Fair Oaks Pharmacy

Fair Oaks Pharmacy (1526 Mission St., South Pasadena, 626/799-1414, www.fairoakspharmacy.net, 9am-9pm Mon.-Thurs., 9am-10pm Fri.-Sat., 10am-8pm Sun.) is a 1915 corner drugstore where soda jerks pour floats, egg creams, and lime rickeys. The soda fountain has a menu of melts, burgers, hot dogs, and sandwiches. While you wait for your meal, walk around the store to admire the collection of antique toys, rare and classic candies, vintage advertisements, and Route 66 memorabilia. There's also a fully functional pharmacy where you can consult with a clinical pharmacist about anything that ails you.

★ The Huntington

With a library housing nearly a half-million rare books, an impressive art museum featuring European and American works, and 120 acres of botanical gardens, **The Huntington** (1151 Oxford Rd., San Marino, 626/405-2100, www.huntington.org, 10am-5pm Wed.-Mon., $25 weekdays or $29 weekends adults, $13 children 4-11) offers many hours of fascinating exploration. It's been a full century since Henry and Arabella Huntington

entrusted their estate to "the advancement of learning," and each year thousands of scholars visit its research library, while 750,000 other guests come for the cultural artifacts and beautiful grounds, including a Japanese garden, lily pond, rose garden, and Shakespeare garden.

★ Norton Simon Museum

Thanks to its namesake's startling personal art collection, the **Norton Simon Museum** (411 W. Colorado Blvd., 626/449-6840, www.nortonsimon.org, noon-5pm Mon., Wed., Thurs., 11am-8pm Fri.-Sat., 11am-5pm Sun., $18 adults, free children 18 and under) has thousands of art pieces available to fill its galleries and sculpture garden, including works by Rembrandt, Degas, Renoir, and Picasso. Roughly 1,000 pieces are on view at any given time, including great European works from the Renaissance to the 20th century, and more than two thousand years' worth of art from South and Southeast Asia.

Shopping

If you're a book lover, don't leave Pasadena without visiting the long-standing institution **Vroman's Bookstore** (695 E. Colorado Blvd., 626/449-5320, www.vromansbookstore.com, 9am-9pm Mon.-Thurs., 9am-10pm Fri.-Sat., 10am-9pm Sun.). In addition to a fine assortment of books, Southern California's oldest and largest independent book store, founded in 1894, routinely plays host to top author events.

Festivals and Events

Rose Parade

The annual **Tournament of Roses Parade** (Colorado Blvd., www.tournamentofroses.com, Jan., $50-100 bleacher seats) has taken place every New Year's Day since 1890. On January 1st, more than 40 rose-covered floats parade down Colorado Boulevard accompanied by marching bands and equestrian teams, and followed by the Rose Queen and her court. The spectacular event is watched by hundreds of thousands of spectators and is broadcast nationwide. Bleacher seats are expensive, so it's not unusual to see people camping out overnight for free curbside seating. If that doesn't sound appealing, try to find a sidewalk spot east of Lake Avenue early in the morning.

Food

★ **La Grande Orange Café** (260 S. Raymond Ave., 626/356-4444, www. lgostationcafe.com, 11am-10pm Mon.-Thurs., 11am-11pm Fri., 10am-11pm Sat., 9am-9pm Sun., $13-29) is a spunky little spot in the restored 1934 Del Mar railroad station. Regional and seasonal American dishes grace the menu, and LGO (as it's colloquially called) offers daily specials such as "Neighborhood Nights" on Monday and Tuesday (buy one entrée, get one for $5) and "Wine Wednesdays" (with discounted bottles of vino).

The egg salad sandwich at **Euro Pane Bakery** (950 E. Colorado Blvd., 626/577-1828, http://europanebakery.juisyfood. com, 7am-4:30pm Mon.-Sat., 7am-3pm Sun., $4-8) is a local fave. But it's the sweets that bring the crowds to this neighborhood bakery. Try to choose just one type of macaron from seven flavors: blackberry, hazelnut, mocha, passion fruit, pistachio, raspberry, and sea salt caramel. There are also pound cakes (pear spice, orange) and tarts (lemon, brown butter, custard) to tempt you.

San Gabriel Valley is notably home to some of the most acclaimed dim sum in the United States, so your best bet is to eat at ★ **Lunasia Dim Sum House** (239 E. Colorado Blvd., 626/793-8822, www. lunasiadimsum.com, 11am-9:30pm Mon.-Fri., 10am-9:30pm Sat.-Sun., $15-50).

For the city's best-loved hamburger since 1963, check out **Pie'n Burger** (913 E. California Blvd., 626/795-1123, www. pienburger.com, 7am-9pm Sun.-Thurs., 7am-10pm Fri.-Sat., $11-15), an old-school American food counter that does, in fact, serve a wide variety of pies.

Accommodations

Right on the Rose Parade route, the **Saga Motor Hotel** (1633 E. Colorado Blvd., 626/795-0431, www.thesagamotorhotel. com, from $79) offers guests free breakfast, free Wi-Fi, pet-friendly rooms, and a heated pool. It's a clean and affordable option in a great location. For a better-appointed urban stay, upgrade to the **Hotel Constance Pasadena** (928 E. Colorado Blvd., 626/898-7900, www. hotelconstance.com, from $178), a cosmopolitan hotel in downtown Pasadena that boasts a stylish bar and rooftop pool.

Nestled in among the beautiful neighborhoods of South Pasadena, the converted Arts & Crafts home of **The Bissell House Bed & Breakfast** (201 Orange Grove Ave., 626/441-3535, www. bissellhouse.com, from $180) offers five distinct rooms with en suite bathrooms. Amenities include in-room breakfast and a swimming pool.

For a high-end stay near the Huntington Library, ★ **The Langham Huntington** (1401 S. Oak Knoll Ave., 626/568-3900, www.langhamhotels.com, from $247) fits right into the posh neighborhood, with manicured green lawns, elegant public spaces, and a beautiful lap-length swimming pool ideal for lounging. Elegant rooms in beige and caramel tones feature king or queen beds with views of the mountains or gardens. Amenities include marble baths, flat-screen TVs, and high-speed Internet. Guests have a wide choice of dining options on the property, as well as luxury spa services.

Route 66 to Santa Monica

the terminus of Route 66 at the Santa Monica Pier

To follow the original Route 66 from Pasadena to where it ended in Los Angeles, drive south on Fair Oaks Avenue to where it dead-ends at Huntington Drive. Turn right (west) and drive 3.5 miles (5.6 km) on Huntington Drive. Continue on North Mission Road for about 0.3 mile (0.5 km), then take a right (west) onto North Broadway. In 1.5 miles (2.4 km), stay right (don't follow Spring St.) to continue on Broadway. Drive 2.5 miles (4 km) down Broadway to 7th Street and you've done it! This is the **first end point** of the original Route 66, from 1926 to 1936!

Later, the route was extended farther west to conclude at the coast, specifically Santa Monica at the intersection of Olympic and Lincoln Boulevards. To follow that route, backtrack on Broadway toward Chinatown, and head west on Cesar Chavez Avenue. After 0.4 mile, Chavez becomes Sunset Boulevard. Follow Sunset 3.1 miles (5 km), then turn left on Santa Monica Boulevard, also known as Route 2. Santa Monica travels 14.2 miles (23 km) through Hollywood, West Hollywood, and Beverly Hills before ultimately reaching the city of Santa Monica. Turn left on Lincoln Boulevard to find the terminus at Olympic Boulevard, or continue to the 2009 terminus at Santa Monica Pier, where the Mother Road ends within steps of the vast Pacific Ocean. This drive from Pasadena to Santa Monica should take 90 minutes when traffic is clear; most of the time expect it to take 2-3 hours.

Death
Valley and
Las Vegas

Death Valley and Las Vegas

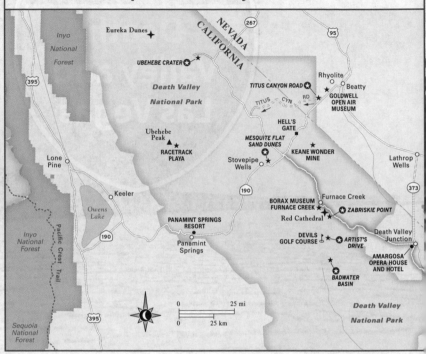

Inyo National Forest

Eureka Dunes

UBEHEBE CRATER

Death Valley National Park

Ubehebe Peak

RACETRACK PLAYA

Lone Pine

Keeler

Owens Lake

Inyo National Forest

PANAMINT SPRINGS RESORT

Panamint Springs

NEVADA
CALIFORNIA

267
95

Rhyolite
TITUS CANYON ROAD   Beatty
GOLDWELL OPEN AIR MUSEUM
TITUS CYN RD

HELL'S GATE

MESQUITE FLAT SAND DUNES
Stovepipe Wells   KEANE WONDER MINE

Lathrop Wells

190

373

BORAX MUSEUM   Furnace Creek
FURNACE CREEK
Red Cathedral   ZABRISKIE POINT

DEVILS   Death Valley Junction
GOLF COURSE   ARTIST'S DRIVE

AMARGOSA OPERA HOUSE AND HOTEL

BADWATER BASIN

Death Valley National Park

Pacific Crest Trail

Sequoia National Forest

395

190

395

0   25 mi
0   25 km

Widely recognized thanks to its ominous name, Death Valley is known for its extremes.

The national park is home to Badwater Basin, the lowest elevation in North America, and has registered temperatures as high as 134.1°F (56.7 °C). In more hospitable weather, Death Valley provides some enthralling road-trip scenery. The sprawling park lies in the northern Mojave Desert, shaped by steep mountains that rise in stark contrast to the low valley floors they encircle. During your roller-coaster descent into the park, breathtaking and panoramic expanses of unspoiled desert terrain are broken only by the occasional straight lane of asphalt.

A mere two hours east, Las Vegas, Nevada, provides a convenient, neon-lit base for travelers. With a long day of driving, you can squeeze in a handful of iconic Death Valley sights and still make it back in time to catch dinner and a show before hitting the casinos. Sin City also makes for an easy launch point to cruise along Route 66.

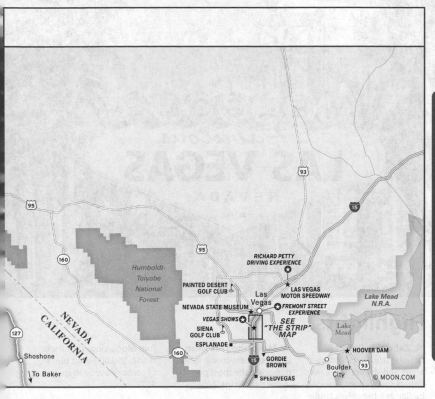

Getting There

Death Valley is an enormous national park surrounded by hundreds of miles of desert and best accessed by car. That said, it's a long drive from anywhere: five hours from Los Angeles and more than two from Las Vegas, the nearest major airport.

Las Vegas does provide a convenient hub for this region, with easier flight access than LAX and plentiful hotels and restaurants in a region otherwise bereft of either.

Getting to Death Valley
From Los Angeles
290 mi/467 km, 5 hr
From Los Angeles, follow I-10 east out of the city and into the Inland Empire.

Mileage and drive times for this stretch may vary, but the 60-mile (97-km) trip can take up to 2-3 hours in the congested traffic that is typical of the area.

East of Ontario, I-10 meets I-15. Turn north onto I-15 and drive 200 miles (320 km) north to **Baker,** passing through Barstow en route. **Barstow** offers your last convenient stop for affordable gas and services.

From Barstow, it's 65 miles (105 km) to Baker. In Baker, exit north for Highway 127 into **Death Valley National Park.** (Note that I-15 continues east into Las Vegas in 95 miles (153 km) and Kelbaker Road exits south to enter Mojave National Preserve.)

Follow CA-127 north for 83 miles (134 km) to Death Valley Junction where you'll turn west on CA-190 and drive 18 miles (29 km) to the park's southern

Highlights

★ **Zabriskie Point:** A popular stop for photographers and visitors, this vantage point overlooks eroded badlands—the colors kindle at sunrise and sunset (page 274).

★ **Artist's Drive:** Named for its palette of brightly colored rock, this special drive owes its splashy scenery to oxidized metal concentrations within the volcanic rock (page 275).

★ **Badwater Basin:** The lowest point in North America at 282 feet below sea level, these vast salt flats encapsulate the mesmerizing yet unforgiving landscape of Death Valley (page 276).

★ **Mesquite Flat Sand Dunes:** These iconic sand dunes are the most popular in the park (page 276).

★ **Titus Canyon Road:** This one-way road winds past rugged rock formations, sweeping canyon views, petroglyphs, and even a ghost town, before ending at the valley floor (page 278).

★ **Ubehebe Crater:** A powerful volcanic explosion created this impressive crater, where an easy trail allows hikers into its colorful depths (page 279).

★ **Fremont Street Experience:** Part music video, part history lesson, this "experience" lights up downtown Las Vegas in a

four-block-long, 12-million-diode, 550,000-watt burst of sensory overload (page 307).

★ **Vegas Shows:** Las Vegas shows are the stuff of legends. From pop star residencies to Blue Man Group to the epic artistry of Cirque du Soleil, there's a show here that you won't want to miss (page 309).

★ **Richard Petty Driving Experience:** If all this time on the open road has you hankerin' to truly drive fast, don your NASCAR cap and kick into high gear on a professional raceway (page 314).

entrance. **Furnace Creek,** the park hub, is another 12.4 miles (20 km).

From Las Vegas
142 mi/229 km, 2.5 hr
From Las Vegas, follow I-95 north for 87 miles (140 km) to the **Amargosa Valley.** Drop south on Highway 373, crossing the state line, to arrive in Death Valley Junction in 23.6 miles (38 km). From Death Valley Junction, drive 18 miles (29 km) west on CA-190 to the park's southern entrance. **Furnace Creek**, the park hub, is another 12.4 miles (20 km).

Detour to Rhyolite
An alternate route passes through **Beatty, Nevada,** and the ghost town of **Rhyolite.** From Amargosa Valley, continue north on I-95 for 29.4 miles (47 km) to Beatty, Nevada. Turn south on Highway 374 for 19.3 miles (31 km) to the east entrance of the park, colloquially known as Hell's Gate. Rhyolite is 6 miles (10 km) west of Beatty; drive 4 miles (6 km) on Highway 374, then turn right (north) onto Rhyolite Road to explore the town.

From Rhyolite it's about 24 miles (39 km) south to Scotty's Castle Road and Highway 190 near Stovepipe Wells.

Getting to Las Vegas
Las Vegas makes a good base or a stopover for a Southern California road trip, with relative proximity to Death Valley, Route 66, and the Mojave National Preserve.

From Los Angeles
287 mi/462 km, 5-6 hr
From Los Angeles, it is a 287-mile drive east to Las Vegas. Plan at least five hours for the long drive. From Los Angeles, drive east on I-10 for about 40 miles (64 km). Near the city of Ontario, I-10 meets the junction with I-15. Head north on I-15 for the next 230 miles (370 km) into Las Vegas. This route can be heavily congested on weekdays during rush hour and on the weekend.

The town of **Baker** sits where I-15 meets CA-127. If you're in need of food or gas, get it here; it will be the last you see of either for quite some time.

Air
Los Angeles International Airport (LAX, 1 World Way, Los Angeles, 855/463-5252, www.flylax.com) offers direct flights from around the world, but with constant traffic congestion and long lines from check-in to security, you must arrive two hours ahead of departure time; three for international or holiday flights. Car rentals are available at the airport.

More than 900 planes arrive or depart **McCarran International Airport** (LAS, 5757 Wayne Newton Blvd., Las Vegas, NV, 702/261-5211, www.mccarran.com) every day. Terminal 1 hosts domestic flights, while Terminal 3 has domestic and international flights. Car rentals are available at the airport.

Death Valley National Park

Death Valley is the largest national park in the Lower 48 states, with terrain ranging from 282 feet below sea level to more than 10,000 feet above. The park's many natural attractions are scattered hundreds of miles apart; distances are far and seeing the sights requires a lot of driving. Death Valley is best as an overnight trip, which allows time to stop in between to explore painted mountain ridges, old mining camps, ghost towns, waterfalls, petroglyphs, and other sacred spots of the valley's indigenous peoples.

First-time visitors should prioritize their time near Furnace Creek, which is within close proximity of key attractions such as **Badwater Basin, Artist's Drive, Zabriskie Point**, and **Dante's Peak**. The main park hub is furnished with twin

Best Restaurants

★ **The Last Kind Words Saloon:** This is the Old West atmosphere you came to the California desert to find, manifesting in a modern bar and steak house (page 284).

★ **The Egg & I:** You can order something other than eggs at this Vegas favorite—but why would you (page 316)?

★ **Mon Ami Gabi:** Order the baked gruyère and a baguette and channel your inner Hemingway for a traditional French bistro experience (page 316).

★ **RM Seafood:** Soft lines and brushed metal accents evoke a glittering sea, while the menu reflects chef Rick Moonen's advocacy of sustainable fishing practices (page 317).

★ **Rose. Rabbit. Lie.:** Order six or eight small plates per couple and let the sultry torch singers and rousing dancers play on as you nosh the night away (page 317).

★ **Phat Phrank's:** The no-frills presentation keeps the focus on the food: California- and New Mexico-inspired variations of traditional Mexican fare (page 318).

★ **Le Thai:** The best of Las Vegas's impressive roster of Thai restaurants boasts playful interpretations of traditional cuisine in a trendy yet unpretentious atmosphere (page 318).

hotels, campgrounds, general stores, restaurants, and gas.

Geographically central, the park hub of **Stovepipe Wells** offers camping, dining, lodging, and gas. The touring outpost dates to 1926 and sits on the original toll road (now Hwy. 190) that officially kicked off the tourism era in Death Valley. It's close to **Mesquite Flat Dunes**, **Scotty's Castle,** and **Rhyolite**.

In the park's remote northwest section, **Panamint Springs** sits below the summit of 11,049-foot Telescope Peak, the highest point in the park. Panamint Springs offers the closest access to the **Wildrose Kilns. The area's high elevation means that some roads may only be accessible March-November.**

Visiting the Park

Temperate much of the year, Death Valley becomes an inferno in summer with oppressive daytime temperatures soaring to well over 100°F (38°C) from **mid-May to early October**. Most services remain open in summer, but some business hours may fluctuate off-season. It's a good idea to call ahead if you're traveling in the summer.

Spring is peak season, with daytime temperatures pleasantly warm and moderate at night. Most businesses are open, and there may be wildflowers during wetter years.

Fall has equally lovely temperatures and is generally less crowded. **Winter** can be a great time to visit the lower elevations around Furnace Creek; however, some park roads may close due to snow. Always be prepared for the temperature to drop as much as 40 degrees at night.

Entrances

Death Valley National Park ($30 per passenger vehicle, $25 per motorcycle, $15 per person on bike or foot, good for seven days) is bisected by Highway 190 from east to west. Furnace Creek, accessed via Highway 190, serves as the main park entrance station. The most direct route from the east (near Las Vegas) is via Pahrump and Highway 190. South of the park, I-15 passes through Baker where

Best Hotels

★ **Ranch at Death Valley:** Furnace Creek's budget-conscious hotel offers tidy rooms and a refreshing pool 190 feet below sea level (page 285).

★ **Stovepipe Wells Hotel:** Its position near the center of Death Valley makes this affordable lodging a worthy base of operations for multiday adventurers (page 285).

★ **Harrah's:** It may seem middle-of-the-road, but its location puts it in the middle of the Vegas action (page 295).

★ **Bellagio:** All the romance of Italy manifests through dancing fountains, botanical gardens, intimate bistros, and—in case the spirit moves you—a wedding chapel (page 298).

★ **Cosmopolitan:** Part Museum of Modern Art, part *Cabaret* Kit Kat Klub, this center-Strip resort blends visual overload with sensuous swank (page 300).

★ **Mandalay Bay:** Let the conscientious staff and serene elegance of this end-of-the-Strip hotel take you away from Vegas's pounding hip-hop and clanging slot machines (page 303).

★ **Golden Nugget:** A Strip-style resort in the otherwise staid downtown district, the Nugget features a waterslide surrounded by a shark-filled aquarium (page 306).

Highway 127 travels north to Death Valley Junction and Highway 190.

Park passes are available from a cash or card kiosk outside the visitors center as well as at the **Stovepipe Wells Ranger Station** (CA-190 at Stovepipe Wells, 760/786-2342, limited hours daily). Park notifications and payment kiosks may also be found at park entrances, including **Hell's Gate** (Hwy. 374) and **Ryan Kiosk** (Hwy. 190).

Visitors Centers

The **Furnace Creek Visitor Center** (Hwy. 190, 760/786-3200, www.nps.gov/deva, 8am-5pm daily) is within the Western-themed village of Furnace Creek and provides information on park sights, activities, and programs, as well as camping and hiking. Interpretive displays offer an overview of the park's natural and cultural history. Park passes, permits, and information are available.

Reservations

Spring, fall, and **holiday weekends** can be competitive times for lodging. Make reservations a few weeks to several months in advance if you want to stay inside the park. If all park lodging is booked, your next option is in one of the gateway towns such as Lone Pine, California, or Beatty, Nevada.

Furnace Creek Campground (Furnace Creek, 877/444-6777, www.recreation. gov, year-round) is the only park campground that accepts reservations (Oct. 15-Apr. 15).

Information and Services

There are **limited services** within Death Valley. Stock up on water, food, and any necessary supplies before entering the park. Gas, ice, and limited food and supplies are available at Furnace Creek, Stovepipe Wells, and Panamint Springs.

Death Valley National Park

DIRT ROAD DESIGNATIONS

Graded
Dirt Road

Dirt Road
High Clearance

Rough Dirt Road
4WD

Extremely
Rough Road
Short Wheelbase
4WD

NEVADA
CALIFORNIA

Deep Springs

266

95

Death Valley
National Park

267

UBEHEBE CRATER

MESQUITE
SPRING

TITUS CANYON
ROAD

Palm Spring

TITUS CYN.

RD

374

BEATTY
AIRPORT

TEAKETTLE
JUNCTION

LOST BURRO MINE

95

RACETRACK
PLAYA

Lathrop
Wells

Mexican Spring

JACKASS
AEROPARK

136

Keeler

Stovepipe
Wells

Owens
Lake

STOVEPIPE WELLS
HOTEL

BEATTY
JUNCTION

190

MESQUITE FLAT
SAND DUNES

FURNACE
CREEK

Furnace
Creek

PANAMINT SPRINGS
RESORT

SKIDOO

Indian
Village

ZABRISKIE POINT

Panamint
Springs

AGUEREBERRY
CAMP

RANCH AT
DEATH VALLEY

190

Wildrose
Peak

ARTIST'S
DRIVE

Death Valley
Junction

WILDROSE
CHARCOAL
KILNS

BADWATER
BASIN

DANTES
VIEW

PANAMINT VALLEY RD.

Telescope
Peak

395

BALLARAT
GHOST TOWN

Shoshone

TRONA WILDROSE RD.

127

Indian
Wells

Trona

Death Valley
National Park

TRONA
AIRPORT

178

Inyokern

14

Ridgecrest

395

TRONA
PINNACLES

To Baker

0   10 mi

0   10 km

© MOON.COM

Two Days in Death Valley

Day 1

Enter the park from the east via Highway 127 and make a beeline to the Furnace Creek area, home to most of the park's iconic sights. Turning west onto Highway 190 into the park, stop at **Zabriskie Point** to admire the badland's banded colors (the hills light up at sunset).

You can't say you've been to Death Valley until you've seen **Badwater Basin.** You'll know you've gone too far when you stop going downhill, because this is the lowest point in North America: 282 feet below sea level. White salt crystals form a flat lake bed that remains bone dry most of the time. Badwater's pale salt flats strike an unforgettable contrast to the mountains rising high above.

Detour onto **Artist's Drive,** a one-way driving tour of the painted badlands within the valley. Lining the side of the road, oxidized metals within the volcanic rock formations reflect bright splashes of color: green, red, purple, and more. Plan an hour for the drive, with more time to stop and take photos. Then park the car and stretch your legs for the hike into **Golden Canyon.**

With few hotels to choose from, opt to overnight at **Ranch at Death Valley.** It's close to the many memorable sights and offers a fun place to mingle at night. Enjoy dinner and drinks at **Last Kind Words Saloon.** If it's a clear night, head out on a stargazing excursion. **Harmony Borax Works** usually has a clear view of the sky and is close to Furnace Creek, but most sites will work.

Day 2

Rise early and drive to **Dante's Peak** for an unparalleled view of the desert valley as the sunrise brings it to life. Stop for breakfast at the hotel, then pack a lunch for a day of driving. Follow Highway 374 north, briefly exiting the park to explore the ghost town of **Rhyolite.** Reenter Death Valley National Park with an off-road adventure down **Titus Canyon Road,** which deposits you back on Scotty's Castle Road. If there's time, drive north to hike to the rim of **Ubehebe Crater.**

Returning south, plan to arrive at **Mesquite Flat Sand Dunes** before sundown so you may experience the shifting dunes in all their golden-hour glory. From Stovepipe Wells, you can exit the park west via Highway 190 or east via Highway 127.

Sights

Borax Museum

The **Borax Museum** (760/786-2345, 9am-9pm daily, donation) at Furnace Creek between the restaurants and golf course is housed in the oldest building in Death Valley. Built in 1883, it was once the assay office for the Monte Blanco Mine in what is now the Twenty Mule Team Canyon. It was moved to Furnace Creek, where it packs in exhibits on Native Americans in Death Valley as well as mining history and the history of borax, the "white gold" of the valley. The outdoor exhibits include a 60-ton oil-burning locomotive that hauled borate, which gives some idea of the brute force it took to tackle mining in the harsh environment.

Harmony Borax Works

A short paved path leads to the site of the **Harmony Borax Works** (1 mi north of Furnace Creek). A 20-mule-team wagon, the remains of a borax refinery, and interpretive signs tell the textbook history of the site as a base of operations for borax mining and processing from 1883 to 1888. The deeper history may well be in the harsh, exposed salt flats that extend in a white glare north and west. It was here that mostly Chinese laborers

The Hottest Place on Earth

It was in Furnace Creek that, on July 10, 1913, the air temperature reached 134.1°F (56.7°C) degrees, the hottest temperature ever recorded on the planet. Not by coincidence, the world's hottest ground temperature was also recorded here, a sole-melting 201°F (93.9°C) on July 15, 1972. Death Valley earns its name most in July, but dangerous daytime temperatures are the norm May-September. If you visit during these months, bring plenty of drinking water and avoid becoming stranded in the dry heat. You'll be rewarded with the experience of a lifetime in one of Southern California's greatest natural treasures.

lived in tent communities, harvesting borate, which they raked into mounded "haystacks" for processing. Mercifully, the temperatures were too hot in Furnace Creek for the operations to continue in summer.

It is possible to see the faint eroded remains of some of the **borax haystacks** on a 1.5-mile walk across the salt pan. From the parking area, drive the graded road as it begins to veer right into Mustard Canyon. Park here and walk 1.5 miles (2.5 km) west across exposed open desert, passing strange salt formations and eventually hitting the rows of haystacks, which run north and south. The salt flats form a shallow seasonal lake, making this walk impossible at times. Even when it is passable, mud can make the passage difficult, and footprints can remain for years. Do not walk through the haystacks; instead, enjoy them from a safe distance. Do not attempt this in summer due to the extreme heat or after a rain.

★ Zabriskie Point

The iconic banded ridges of **Zabriskie Point** are a popular stop for photographers and visitors, especially when colors kindle at sunrise and sunset. **Manly Beacon,** a rock outcropping to the north, commemorates William L. Manly, a guide who rescued California gold rush pioneers attempting an 1849 valley crossing. The darker ridgelines are formed by lava. Zabriskie Point may be viewed from a scenic overlook just off Highway 190, 7 miles (11 km) south of Furnace Creek;

look for the parking and follow the short but steep path to the top of the bluff.

Dante's View

As the name suggests, **Dante's View** provides spectacular panoramic views of Death Valley. The Panamint Mountains rise dramatically from the stiflingly low Badwater Basin salt flats at 282 feet below sea level to Telescope Peak, snowcapped much of the year and the highest point in the park at 11,049 feet. On a clear day, you can see all the way to Mount Whitney, the

highest point in the contiguous 48 states. The Owlshead Mountains to the south, the Funeral Mountains to the north, and the Greenwater Mountains to the east make this a good place to get your bearings and be dazzled at the same time. Visit at sunrise to see the whole valley suffused with morning light. Some people bring telescopes out at night for unparalleled **stargazing.**

To get there from Furnace Creek, drive south to the intersection of Highway 190 and Badwater Basin Road. Follow Highway 190 east for 10.7 miles (17 km), then turn right onto Furnace Creek Wash Road. At 7.5 miles (12 km), continue onto Dante's View Road. Drive 5.5 miles (9 km) to the parking area and overlook. The total drive from Furnace Creek is about 24 miles (39 km).

★ Artist's Drive

Wild bursts of color appear to paint volcanic rock formations scaling the sides of the Black Mountains, and gentle **Artist's Drive** offers a convenient way to experience the chaotic jumble of hues from your car. Differing concentrations of oxidized metals splash the mountainside with green, rose, yellow, purple, and red hues. The paved 9-mile (14-km) scenic loop is a one-way road starting on Badwater Road, 5 miles (8 km) south of Furnace Creek. There are plenty of places to pull over for the many pictures you will want to take.

As with many good things in Death Valley, they get even better once you step out of your car. It's possible to explore **one short, colorful canyon** 3.5 miles (5.5 km) in, at the second dip in the road. There is a small turnout at the top of the rise on the right side where you can park. Hike up the wash at the bottom of the dip about 50 yards, where a pink fall marks the entrance to the canyon. Look for mud drippings and slickensides (rocks polished smooth by movement along a fault) and enjoy the scramble over several boulder jams.

Zabriskie Point

A popular stop is the **Artist's Palette,** a scenic viewpoint 4.5 miles (7 km) into the drive. The low hills right next to a small parking area show heavy signs of use from visitors walking out onto them. Note: this doesn't actually offer a better view of the hills, but does damage to the fragile hillsides.

Devil's Golf Course

You'll want to put your camera on the macro setting to capture the controlled chaos of the **Devil's Golf Course** (Badwater Rd., 11 mi/18 km south of Furnace Creek). On the northern end of the eerie, stark salt flats of Badwater Basin, Devil's Golf Course is filled with spiky salt crystals that you have to see close-up to appreciate. Groundwater seeps up to the surface, forming the jagged pinnacles.

It's extremely difficult to walk out here. Take the graded dirt road to a small parking lot, where you can see the formations at closer range. If you step out into them, place your feet carefully between the pinnacles. A few awkward steps into the frenetic landscape will reveal tiny salt crystals, sprouting wildly in the barbed ground.

TOP EXPERIENCE

★ Badwater Basin

Badwater Basin (Badwater Rd., 16 mi/26 km south of Furnace Creek) is a Death Valley classic. If you're going to visit one place in Death Valley, this is it. This is the lowest point in North America at 282 feet below sea level, and if you look up at the bluffs rising above the small parking lot, you'll notice a marker indicating how far up it is to zero. Walk a wide, mile-long path out onto the salt flats to examine the delicate salt-crystal formations on their surface and marvel at the contrast between the flat, white basin and the steep rise of mountain ranges

encircling it. Bring your camera, because there are photo ops aplenty, and bring water, because a mile in this arid, sunbaked place can dehydrate you right quick!

★ Mesquite Flat Sand Dunes

The **Mesquite Flat Sand Dunes** (Hwy. 190, 2 mi/3 km east of Stovepipe Wells) are iconic to Death Valley and are the most popular sight in the park. In order to form, dunes require wind, sand, and a place for the sand to collect. These three things exist in spades in this austere section of the park, just east of the village of Stovepipe Wells. The sculpted dunes are visible from Stovepipe Wells and beyond, rising out of the desert floor to catch the light of the sky in smooth, unbroken crests and lines. Such is the power of the dunes that they seem to draw people from miles around, so expect to find yourself among scores of other visitors scrambling their slopes for a more photogenic view of their wind-groomed ridges.

Rhyolite

A minor gold rush sparked the birth of **Rhyolite** (www.nps.gov) in 1904, when prospectors Shorty Harris and E. L. Cross found gold in the Bullfrog Hills, named for their green-spotted rocks. The first post office opened in 1905, and by 1908 the population numbered in the thousands. The town boasted an ice cream parlor, a school, an ice plant, and a train station. But the town's fortunes quickly turned: by 1911 the mine had closed, and by 1920 only 14 people remained.

Today, the main road through the **ghost town** leads past crumbling banks once bursting with gold. Some ruins are two stories tall, towering like era monuments. The beautiful Mission-style **train station** remains intact and looks like it could open tomorrow. Side roads lead to the red-light district, **cemetery,** and mine ruins.

Rhyolite might be most famous for its **bottle house,** built by enterprising miner Tom Kelly out of a plentiful material on hand—beer and liquor bottles. It took more than 50,000 bottles to make this structure, which was restored by Paramount Pictures in 1925, as Rhyolite began to be used as a filming location.

The **Goldwell Open Air Museum** (1 Golden St., 702/870-9946, www.goldwellmuseum.org, year-round, free) is a sculpture installation and art park next to Rhyolite, sharing the land and the desert backdrop. Belgian artists began the museum in the 1980s using the surreal location to showcase larger-than-life sculptures. A tiny **visitors center** (10am-4pm most days) sits centrally among the sculptures, with T-shirts and museum gifts for sale; there are no services.

Rhyolite makes an interesting stop when driving between Death Valley and Las Vegas. From Stovepipe Wells, Rhyolite is about 30 miles (48 km) northeast, a 40-minute drive. Head east on Highway 190 to Daylight Pass Road. A well-marked entrance on the left indicates the 2-mile road to Rhyolite. Plan to

Badwater Basin

spend an hour or two strolling among the crumbling buildings and art.

Scotty's Castle

One of the most popular destinations in the park, 1920s mansion **Scotty's Castle** is scheduled to reopen in 2020, following years of repair after flash floods in October 2015 severely damaged the historic structures and grounds. Scotty's Castle Road/Highway 267 between the Grapevine Ranger Station and I-95 to the east also remained closed. For the latest information, call 760/786-3200 or check online.

The history of Scotty's Castle is as unlikely as the sight of the turreted castle against the rocky hills. Walter Edward Scott, better known as **Death Valley Scotty,** was an infamous Death Valley swindler. Beginning in 1902 he convinced would-be investor after investor that he had found a rich gold deposit somewhere in Death Valley. To keep investors interested, he produced good-quality ore from other mines, but delayed actual visits to the mine with wild tales of armed gangs, ambushes, and other perils of the scorching valley.

Scotty's attempt to swindle Chicago millionaires Albert and Bessie Johnson yielded an unlikely lifelong friendship. Scotty's colorful personality dampened Albert Johnson's initial anger over the fraudulent claims, and in 1922, Scotty convinced his rich benefactors to build a mansion here instead. Designed in the Mission Revival and Spanish colonial style that was fashionable at the time, the estate's structures boast picturesque adobe archways, terra-cotta roof tiles, and several towers. When the stock market crashed in 1929, the Johnsons lost money and slowed construction on the house. Some sections, including a large swimming pool, were never fully finished.

The interior is fully furnished with the Johnson's original possessions, including 1920s period furnishings, rich tapestries, mosaic tile work, arched doorways, and a spiral staircase. Underground tours reveal the inner workings of the house and thousands of tiles intended for the never completed pool.

Although Death Valley Scotty always claimed that the property was his, he lived in a humble cabin nearby. He is buried on a hill on the property and his grave can be reached by a short hike.

Scotty's Castle is within easy reach of both Furnace Creek and Stovepipe Wells, about an hour's drive along paved park roads.

★ Titus Canyon Road

If you're looking to make a dramatic entrance into Death Valley, drive **Titus Canyon Road.** The **27-mile one-way dirt road** sweeps through rugged rock formations, hangs over canyon views, skirts past **petroglyphs,** and even rolls through a **ghost town,** eventually passing through what is arguably the grand finale: the canyon narrows. The narrows tower overhead, barely letting cars squeeze through before they open wide to reveal the barren Death Valley floor.

The one-way Titus Canyon Road starts from Highway 374 (Daylight Pass Rd.), 6 miles (10 km) south of Beatty, Nevada. Plan to spend **three hours** driving Titus Canyon Road to its terminus at Scotty's Castle Road. It's a slow drive on a one-lane dirt road that can be rutted or rocky, and it hugs the canyon wall at points. The National Park Service officially recommends a two-wheel drive **high-clearance** vehicle (an urban SUV is usually fine) but cautions that a 4WD vehicle may be needed in inclement weather.

Early morning and the golden evening hour are lovely times to capture the light, but if you choose to drive this road in the evening, give yourself enough time to reach the valley floor before dark. The National Park Service does not recommend this drive in summer; the area is lightly patrolled, and any breakdown can be dangerous due to the heat.

★ Ubehebe Crater

With the 2020 reopening of Scotty's Castle Road, park visitors will once again have direct access to the **Ubehebe Crater.** Perhaps 300 years ago, a powerful volcanic explosion created this colorful crater that measures 600 feet deep and a half mile across. Ubehebe Crater is actually part of a cluster of volcanic craters that includes the **Little Hebe Crater,** a smaller and younger crater just to the west.

An easy 1.5-mile round-trip **hike** around the edge of Ubehebe Crater allows you to peer down into the colorful depths of Ubehebe Crater, Little Hebe Crater, and other smaller craters. Known as maar volcanoes, the craters at Ubehebe were created through steam and gas explosions, which occurred when hot magma reached groundwater. It may be tempting to hike down to the bottom of the craters, and some people do, but it's quite hard to get back out.

From Stovepipe Wells, head east on Highway 190 for 7 miles (11 km), then turn left on Scotty's Castle Road. Continue north for 33.4 miles (53.8 km) to the fork at the Grapevine Ranger Station. At the fork, continue left on Highway 190 for 5.4 miles (9 km) to the signed parking area for Ubehebe Crater. The drive takes about one hour.

Keane Wonder Mine

Keane Wonder Mine was one of the most successful gold mines in Death Valley. And with its well-preserved aerial tramway, it's one of the best historical examples of a gold-mining operation in the park. Gold was discovered on the site in 1904, and serious mining efforts began in 1907 when the 20-stamp mill and tramway were installed. The mine's glory days ended in 1912, and they sputtered on and off until operations ended for good after 1940. The aerial tramway left behind is a one-mile-long feat of engineering,

Top to bottom: the Harmony Borax Works; Artist's Drive; Ubehebe Crater at sunset.

designed to haul ore from 1,500 feet up the steep Funeral Mountains, across a 500-foot-deep canyon to an extensive milling complex below.

From Stovepipe Wells, take Highway 190 13.7 miles (23 km) east to the signed Beatty Cutoff Road. Turn left and travel 5.7 (10 km) miles north to the signed road for Keane Wonder Mine. Drive 2.8 miles (5 km) to a parking area. From here stroll around the site where the camp and mill were located. For views of the lower tram terminal and first few tram towers, take the short trail at the end of the road. To reach the upper tramway terminal and Keane Wonder Mine, follow the old mining road for 1.4 miles (2.5 km) and a 1,500-foot ascent.

Wildrose Charcoal Kilns

Once used to make charcoal for the mining efforts in the area, the **Wildrose Charcoal Kilns** now stand as works of hand-engineered beauty. The kilns are made of cut limestone, quarried locally and cemented with gravel, lime, and sand. They stand approximately 25 feet tall, their walls curving gracefully inward to form a beehive shape. The Modock Consolidated Mining Company built them in 1877 to fuel the smelters of lead-silver mines in the Argus range to the west. The structures were designed to reflect as much interior heat as possible, and they reflect sound waves just as well. Walk through the arches into the interior of the kilns to experience echoes.

The kilns are in the Panamint Springs section of the park. From the park hub of Panamint Springs (Hwy. 190), drive 16 miles (26 km) east on Highway 190 to Emigrant Canyon Road. Turn right onto Emigrant Canyon Road and drive 21 miles (34 km) south to the road's end. The kilns are 7 miles (11 km) past Wildrose Campground. The road is paved most of the way; the last 2 miles (3 km) of gravel are slightly rough but should be suitable for most cars.

Natural Bridge

Recreation
Hiking

Hiking in Death Valley is no joke. Be prepared with a map, sunscreen and sun protection, and at least two liters of water per person.

Badlands Loop

Distance: 2.7-7.8 mi/4-12 km round-trip
Duration: 1.5-4.5 hours
Elevation gain: 875 feet
Effort: Moderate
Access: Passenger vehicles
Trailhead: Badwater Basin Road at the Golden Canyon turnoff, 2 miles (3 km) south of the Badwater Road junction. Take the signed, graded dirt road on the east (left) side of the road to the parking area.

This hike is a Death Valley classic that leads through eroded badlands, old mining claims, shifting canyons, and the spectacular scenery from Zabriskie Point, which offers views of Manly Beacon, a lava cap in stark contrast to the eroded landscape.

The **full loop** begins at the Golden Canyon Parking area, continues to Red Cathedral, winds through badlands to iconic Zabriskie Point, and returns to the Golden Canyon Parking area off Badwater Road via Gower Gulch. It can also be broken into **shorter hikes:** Golden Canyon to Red Cathedral (3 mi/5 km round-trip), Gower Gulch loop (4.3-mi/7 km loop, 5.3 mi/8 km with spur to Red Cathedral), and the Badlands Loop (2.7-mi/5 km loop starting from Zabriskie Point). The trailhead from Golden Canyon is very popular and can be crowded along the first mile.

Begin the hike on the interpretive trail in Golden Canyon. Pamphlets, available at the trailhead, draw your attention to the canyon's geologic features. The **Golden Canyon Trail** leads up a gravel wash for about 1 mile toward the huge **Red Cathedral** formation. Look for the signed junction for **Red Cathedral** or **Zabriskie Point.** The trail to Zabriskie Point continues up Golden Canyon for another 1.9 miles (3 km). For Zabriskie Point, head east.

To return from Zabriskie Point via Gower Gulch, retrace your steps (0.5 mile from the trailhead) to a signed intersection to Golden Canyon or Gower Gulch. Head left into **Gower Gulch** and follow the wash for 3 miles (5 km) back to the parking area. As the canyon walls narrow, look for colorful mineral deposits. You'll also pass some old borax mines; signs warn to stay away. Once you emerge from the gulch, you're on the home stretch back to the Golden Canyon trailhead. Another 0.8 mile west across exposed desert brings you to the trailhead.

Natural Bridge

Distance: 0.7-1.4 mi/2-3 km round-trip
Duration: 30-45 minutes
Elevation gain: 180-470 feet
Effort: Easy
Access: Passenger vehicles
Trailhead: Badwater Road, 13.1 miles (21 km) south of Highway 190. Take the signed and graded dirt road east for 1.8 miles (3 km) to a small parking lot.

Death Valley Side Trips

A couple of Death Valley road-trip destinations are so remote, they require their own day trips. Top off the gas tank before embarking to these locations you can truly only get to on purpose.

Eureka Dunes

The **Eureka Dunes** are the northernmost sight in the park, and getting to them requires a special trip outside the park and back in after a 150-mile loop through Nevada. The Eureka Dunes cover an area 3 miles wide and 1 mile long; they are the tallest sand dunes in California, towering more than 680 feet from the enclosed valley floor. To justify the seven-hour round-trip, you can easily spend a night or two to soak in this special place. **The Eureka Dunes Dry Camp,** at the base of the dunes, has primitive camping spots with firepits, picnic tables, and one pit toilet.

The Racetrack

Despite being at least three hours from anywhere, **The Racetrack** can be a big draw. Many visitors make the long and difficult drive to this eerie expanse of dry lake bed scattered with the faint trails of rocks that have skated across its surface. Access is via Racetrack Valley Road, 26 miles (42 km) of rutted, rocky washboard. Many people stay in Furnace Creek or Stovepipe Wells and turn the adventurous, three- to four-hour drive into a long day trip, but outdoor adventurers could manage several days here in mild weather. Set up camp at primitive **Homestake Dry Camp** and explore **Ubehebe Peak;** hidden mining camps like **Ubehebe Mine, Lost Burro Mine, Lippincott Mine,** and the **Goldbelt Mining District;** and the occasional canyon.

Natural Bridge is one of the few natural bridges in the park, and it's definitely the biggest. This easy hike is popular, so be prepared to share it. Just 0.7 mile in from the trailhead, Natural Bridge spans a red-wall canyon that contrasts with the bright sky above. Look back toward Badwater Basin to see Telescope Peak in the distance.

Most people turn around at the bridge, but the canyon continues another 0.7 mile. Shortly past the arch, check out the polished conglomerate falls on the right and look for mud formations that resemble candle drippings high up on the canyon walls. There are two places where you will have to scramble up a few small rock falls, but nothing that is a hike-stopper. The trail effectively ends at a vertical 15-foot fall another 0.7 mile in. Turn around and retrace your steps to the trailhead.

Sidewinder Canyon

Distance: 2-4 mi/3-6 km round-trip
Duration: 2-4 hours
Elevation gain: 600-800 feet
Effort: Easy
Access: All vehicles
Trailhead: Dirt road and large parking area near old gravel pit 31.4 miles (51 km) south of Furnace Creek (on left).

The unassuming hills at the base of Smith Mountain do not hold any particular draw from the road, but delving in quickly brings you to a sinewy maze of slot canyons, some of the deepest in Death Valley, with hidden natural bridges and sculpted alcoves. This hike is not a straightforward out and back with one defining destination. A series of slot canyons intersect the main canyon and give you the fun of discovery in the twisting arches and hollows that leave only a glimpse of sky at times as some passages narrow to less than arm's length.

The hike begins on the right (south) side of the parking area. A faint but well-traveled trail heads toward the dark opening of Sidewinder Canyon, which begins as a low gravel trench. There are three main slots (some hiking literature counts six, although some of these dead-end quickly). The first slot canyon is 1 mile in from the trailhead on your right. Over the next 0.5 mile you will come across two more. This is a fun hike for making your own discoveries, literally around each new turn.

Mosaic Canyon

Distance: 2.8 mi/4 km round-trip
Duration: 1 hour
Elevation gain: 730 feet
Effort: Easy
Access: Passenger vehicles
Trailhead: Mosaic Canyon Road on the western edge of Stovepipe Wells Village. Turn left (south) onto Mosaic Canyon Road and drive 2.4 miles (4 km) along a graded dirt road to a small parking area with restrooms at the end.

Mosaic Canyon is a great introduction to the Cottonwood Mountain canyons. It's accessible but lovely, with a chance to wander through polished marble, colorful mosaic stone, and satisfying narrows. It's an easy drive to the trailhead just outside Stovepipe Wells. The hike can generally be made by anyone as it follows the gravel canyon floor. It does require a few easy rock scrambles over polished bedrock along the way.

The hike begins at the signed **trailhead** in the parking area and immediately enters a **broad wash,** which is the mouth of the canyon. The straightforward trail continues **south** into the canyon; ignore any side trails. The **first narrows**—pretty but shallow—begin almost immediately and wind between walls of polished marble and mosaics. These are a preview of the **second narrows,** which start behind a boulder jam at 1.1 miles (2 km). Bypass the boulders with an easy scramble and follow

the trail on the left. The scenic second narrows twist through polished bedrock and rich mosaics, earning the canyon its name. The second narrows end too soon in 0.3 mile at an **18-foot wall.**

Stargazing

TOP EXPERIENCE

Death Valley is a designated **Gold Tier Dark Sky Park,** which means that it experiences extremely low levels of light pollution. Clear nights provide world-class stargazing, particularly around the new moon. To make the most of the dark skies, bring a chair and warm clothes to the destination of your choice about an hour or more after sunset; your eyes will need at least 30 minutes to adjust. Once they do, you should be able to see nebulae and the Milky Way. Binoculars, telescopes, and cameras with slow shutters can make the experience extra special. A red flashlight will help preserve your night vision.

For guided stargazing, plan your visit to coordinate with the **Death Valley Dark Sky Festival** (www.nps.gov/deva, Mar.), which organizes free stargazing events including guided hikes and night-sky photography programs. Events are usually held around the new moon each spring.

Golf

If vacation means golf to you, you're in luck. The **Furnace Creek Golf Course** (Hwy. 190, 760/786-2301, www.furnacecreekresort.com, 6am-6pm daily, greens fees $30-74) claims to be the lowest-elevation golf course in the world. At 214 feet below sea level, it's hard to dispute. This 18-hole golf course doesn't let you forget that it's on an oasis; it's lined with palm and tamarisk trees and dotted with water. Temperatures soar in summer, but the resort takes a tongue-in-cheek approach, hosting the Heatstroke tournament every June.

Food

Furnace Creek

Most of the restaurants in Furnace Creek are connected to the hotels, the majority of which are at the **Ranch at Death Valley** (Hwy. 190, 760/786-2345, www.oasisatdeathvalley.com).

Just off the golf course, **The 19th Hole** (11am-5:30pm Wed.-Sun. mid-Oct.-mid-May, $7-17) offers the cheapest fare, mostly burgers and sandwiches, with a full bar and cold beer in casual outdoor dining. For all-you-can-eat diners, **The Ranch 1849 Buffet** (hours vary daily, $30 pp) offers a wide variety of serve-yourself dishes.

The star of the bunch is ★ **The Last Kind Words Saloon** (hours vary, generally 11am-9pm daily, $15-95). Named after a Larry McMurtry novel, the Western-styled saloon is all steer skulls, wagon wheels, and polished wood. It features a full bar with cocktails and draft beer and a menu of steaks, ribs, seafood, and more. Make reservations for a large party, as the wait can be long.

An assortment of snacks, frozen food, drinks, and fresh produce are for purchase at Furnace Creek Ranch's **General Store** (Hwy. 190, 7am-9pm daily).

At the posh **Inn at Death Valley** (Hwy. 190, 760/786-2345, www.oasisatdeathvalley.com) the menu steers in a more upscale direction. The **Inn Dining Room** (760/786-3385, 7:30am-10:30am and 11:30am-2:30pm daily year-round; dinner 5pm-9pm daily Oct.-Apr., 6pm-10pm daily May-Sept.) uses organic and prime ingredients in its menu offerings, served in a classic lodge-style dining room with a view. At sunset, the west-facing bank of windows frames the sun's fiery drop behind the rugged Panamint Mountains. The dining room is open for breakfast ($12-21), lunch ($10-14), and dinner ($27-68).

Stop in the elegant **lounge** (2:30pm-10pm) for a cocktail or appetizer before dinner. The menu at the **Pool Café** (11am-5pm daily, $12-14) offers light fare. The inn caters to lodge guests and those staying at The Ranch; a light dress code (no tank tops or T-shirts) is expected.

Outside of the Furnace Creek hotels, head to Indian Village to try Indian fry bread and fry-bread tacos at **Timbisha Tacos** (900 Indian Village Rd., 760/258-7858, www.timbishatacos.com, 10am-6pm Mon.-Sat., 11am-3pm Sun., $8-14). The flat-bread tacos are filled with ground beef and provide a tasty, casual treat, plus the opportunity to meet friendly locals.

Stovepipe Wells

Hotels and restaurants go together in Stovepipe Wells. The **Stovepipe Wells Hotel** (Hwy. 190, 760/786-2387, www.deathvalleyhotels.com) offers the **Toll Road Restaurant** (760/786-7090, 7am-10am and 5:30pm-9pm daily), which has a buffet breakfast ($7-13) as well as dinner ($12-20). The **Badwater Saloon** (11:30am-9pm daily year-round) serves lunch (11:30am-5pm daily, $8-15), snacks (5pm-9pm daily), and, of course, drinks.

The invitingly named **General Store** (7am-10pm daily year-round) is actually a glorified convenience store and gift shop selling souvenirs like specialty candy and T-shirts, plus a few basics like cold sodas, beer, ice, coffee, aspirin, and sunscreen. Don't expect to find any next-level camping supplies.

Panamint Springs

The restaurant at **Panamint Springs Resort** (40440 Hwy. 190, 775/482-7680, www.panamintsprings.com, 7am-9:30pm daily, $10-30) serves a pared-down breakfast buffet (7am-11am), plus appetizers, burgers, pizzas, and salads for lunch and dinner. The **bar** serves wine and more than 150 beers.

Accommodations

Any lodging available outside the park requires a 30- to 60-minute drive, so staying at park-operated hotels inside one of the three park hubs makes the most sense for visitors.

Furnace Creek

The ★ **Ranch at Death Valley** (Hwy. 190, 760/786-2345, reservations 800/236-7916, www.oasisatdeathvalley.com, year-round, $215-370) is the less-formal lodging option in Furnace Creek, but it still offers a comfortable and enjoyable stay. Casual and family-friendly accommodations are set in a sprawling wood complex of cabins, two-story standard rooms, and deluxe motel-style rooms. **Deluxe rooms** are housed in single-story buildings and usually include two queen beds; patios feature French doors overlooking a manicured lawn dotted with social firepits and palm trees leading to the pool. The **wood cabins** are single-story duplexes that give a nod to Furnace Creek's historic status, furnished with two double beds or one queen. **Standard rooms** are located in four two-story buildings and have two queens (rollaway beds are permitted). All rooms feature French doors with small patios or balconies affording views of the surrounding desert and mountains, as well as air-conditioning, hair dryers, in-room coffeemakers, a minifridge, TV, and telephones. Standard and Deluxe rooms include full private baths, while cabins include a private bath with a shower but no tub.

On the high end, **Inn at Death Valley** (Hwy. 190, 760/786-2345, reservations 800/236-7916, www.oasisatdeathvalley. com, year-round, $400-550) provides the ultimate contrast to the austerity of the valley floor, with manicured grounds and luxury accommodations. The inn offers a variety of rooms, as well as one pool bungalow and 11 two-room casitas newly added in 2018. **Standard rooms** include either a king bed or a double with a twin and have a private bath, with views of the gardens, desert, or mountains. **Deluxe rooms** are slightly bigger than standard rooms and feature either a king bed or a double with a twin and have a full bath. **Luxury Spa rooms,** located in the North Wing, are larger still and offer a king or two double beds, with garden or desert views and spa tubs. Double rooms add a shared deck or terrace. **Standard Hillside rooms** do not have views but offer an intimate setting with a king bed and a private bath. Suites feature a king and a pullout sofa in an adjoining parlor. The **Pool Bungalow** is a stand-alone building with a queen bed, a full bath, and easy access to the pool. In addition, 11 **two-room casitas** are interspersed around the pool and oasis gardens.

The resort boasts a spring-fed swimming pool with cabanas and a poolside bar, a wellness center with treatment rooms, and an on-site restaurant and lounge all set amid lush oasis gardens.

Stovepipe Wells

All things being relative, ★ **Stovepipe Wells Hotel** (760/786-2387, www. deathvalleyhotels.com, $144-216) is centrally located. The hotel has 83 basic rooms that are substantially cheaper than those at Furnace Creek, making it a good place to set up base camp to explore the Nevada Triangle as well as to make forays into other regions of the park. **Deluxe rooms** include two queen beds or one king and have views of the Mesquite Flat Sand Dunes. **Standard rooms** have either two queens or one king. **Patio rooms** are original to the hotel and can accommodate one or two people (no cribs or rollaways). All rooms have air-conditioning, TVs, minifridges, coffeemakers, and private baths with showers, and access to the swimming pool is included. Rooms do not have phones; Wi-Fi is available in the hotel lobby.

Panamint Springs

Panamint Springs Resort (40440 Hwy. 190, 775/482-7680, www. panamintsprings.com, 7am-9:30pm daily year-round) offers the only accommodations, food, supplies, and gas within the park boundaries on the west side of the park. The rustic resort opened in 1937, when the first toll road across the

Panamint Valley was built from Stovepipe Wells. The resort ($74-220) has affordable motel rooms, a cottage, cabins, tent cabins, RV spaces, and tent sites. The 14 basic **motel rooms** ($74-150) vary only by bed type: one queen; one king; one queen and one double; or one queen and two doubles. All rooms have evaporative cooling systems with vents in the ceiling and a private bath with a shower. Rooms with three beds include air-conditioning units.

A two-bedroom **cottage** ($149-169), situated behind the resort's restaurant, comes with a queen bed, one bunk bed (double on bottom and single on top), a living area, satellite TV, air-conditioning, and a private bath with a full tub and shower. Nine **cabins** ($89-$154) are the newest lodging addition. These stand-alone hand-built structures offer a simple one-room design with knotty pine interiors, air-conditioning, small bathrooms with showers, and a covered outdoor sitting area. They vary by bed type: one king, one queen, one full, or a bunk cabin with one full and a twin bunk bed.

There are no phones in any rooms, and Panamint Springs does not have a landline. Cell phones will not work. There is a general store with basic supplies, gas, and an ATM. Wireless Internet is available on request for sending basic messages (no streaming).

Outside the Park

Should you prefer to stay outside the park, head to Death Valley Junction and the **Amargosa Opera House and Hotel** (Hwy. 127, Death Valley Junction, 760/852-4441, www.amargosa-opera-house.com, 7am-10:30pm daily, from $90, $5 tours) is a functioning hotel originally constructed by the Pacific Coast Borax Company. The hotel has a reputation for being haunted and has been featured on ghost-hunter TV shows like the Travel Channel's *Ghost Adventures*. Hotel rooms are small and simple. A **café** (760/852-4432, 8am-3pm Fri.-Mon., $8-14) offers breakfast and lunch as well as coffee and espresso.

Camping

All of the park campgrounds experience high winds, especially at night, regardless of the time of year or the temperature. If you are tent camping, make sure to have your tent properly staked and secure anything that could blow away (camp chairs love to catch air when you're not watching). If you're relying on RV electrical hookups, plan for electricity surges.

If you will be camping in Death Valley in summer, choose a campground at higher elevations in the park.

Furnace Creek

There are four campgrounds clustered around Furnace Creek, all with their pros and cons. While conveniently located, they get oppressively hot in the summer. Take advantage of **day passes** ($5) available to access the nearby Ranch at Death Valley's pool and showers. (The pool and shower passes are available to anyone, not just campground guests.)

Furnace Creek Campground (877/444-6777, www.recreation.gov, year-round, $22, $36 with hookups) has 136 tent and RV sites. It's the only park campground that accepts **reservations** (Oct. 15-Apr. 15), which makes it a good option for travelers who like to have a set itinerary. Sites book months in advance during busy weekends in spring, winter, and on holidays. From mid-April to mid-October, sites are first-come, first-served; reservations are not accepted.

Sunset Campground (first-come, first-served, Nov.-May, $14) is across the road from Furnace Creek Campground. With 270 sites, it caters mainly to RVs and is peaceful but spare. Amenities include water, flush toilets, and a dump station.

Texas Spring (first-come, first-served, mid-Nov.-May, $16) shares an entrance with Sunset Campground, but it is a little more scenic, tucked farther into the hills with tamarisks offering shade at a few of the sites. This is the most popular campground in the area, and its 92 tent and RV sites fill quickly. Amenities include water, picnic tables, firepits, flush toilets, and a dump station. Site passes for Sunset and Texas Spring are sold at automated kiosks that accept major credit cards and cash. Passes are for general overnight admission but are not site-specific.

The privately run **Fiddlers' Campground** (Ranch at Death Valley, 760/786-2345 or 800/236-7916, www. oasisatdeathvalley.com, $18) offers RV sites (no hookups, back-in only) with one tent allowed per site. While not the place for those seeking desert solitude, it does include amenities such as wireless Internet and access to Ranch at Death Valley's pool, showers, and sports facilities. Communal picnic tables and firepits are available within the campground but not at individual sites. Sites can be reserved year-round through Oasis at Death Valley.

Stovepipe Wells

Stovepipe Wells Campground (190 sites, first-come, first-served, mid-Sept.-early May, $14) has a central location for exploring a big swath of Death Valley. Aside from the prime location, the campground resembles a parking lot, although the surrounding desert and Cottonwood Mountains are lovely. The tent sites and RV sites (with hookups) are completely exposed, which means it can be blazingly hot, and there is no privacy. Amenities include picnic tables, potable water, and flush toilets. There is access to the Stovepipe Wells Hotel pool and showers ($4 per day).

Within Stovepipe Wells Campground, the **Stovepipe Wells RV Park** (14 sites, year-round, $37) has sites next to the General Store. Fees include access to the swimming pool and to Wi-Fi in the hotel lobby.

Scotty's Castle

Mesquite Spring (30 sites, first-come, first-served, year-round, $14) is the only developed campground in the area around Scotty's Castle, north of Furnace

Creek. The pretty campground is dotted with mesquite bushes and set along low hills at an elevation of 1,800 feet. The temperature is bearable most of the year, except in summer. Sites are exposed, but are spaced far enough apart that you get some privacy. Reservations aren't accepted, but it's likely you'll get a spot even in the busy spring season. Payment is via an automated kiosk, which accepts credit cards and cash; put your receipt on the site marker. Amenities include picnic tables, firepits, and access to flush toilets and water; there are no RV hookups, but there is a dump station.

Panamint Springs

The **Panamint Springs Resort campground** (40440 Hwy. 190, 775/482-7680, www.panamintsprings.com, 7am-9:30pm daily year-round, $10-65) has a total of 76 accommodations, including **tent cabins** (1-5 people, $35-65), **RV sites** (30- and 50-amp hookups, $20-35), **tent sites** (1 tent, 1 vehicle, $10), and one group site. All sites have firepits; most have picnic tables. Amenities include drinking water and flush toilets. Best of all, they have **hot showers** (free with a site, fee for nonguests), a rarity in Death Valley. (Furnace Creek, on the other side of the park, is the only other campground with showers.) Campsites fill quickly, so reserve in advance. There is a surcharge of $5 for pets in RV and tent sites.

Emigrant Campground (10 sites, first-come, first-served, year-round, free) is a tiny tent-only campground at the junction of Highway 190 and Emigrant Canyon Road. It's a pretty spot that more closely resembles a day-use area. Sites are small, close together, and exposed to the open desert. At 2,100 feet elevation and with no shade, it can be uncomfortably hot in summer. Amenities include picnic tables, drinking water, and restrooms with flush toilets. Emigrant is directly off paved Highway 190, approximately 21 miles (34 km) east of Panamint Springs.

Cheerful and sunny **Wildrose Campground** (Wildrose Rd., 23 sites, first-come, first-served, year-round, free) is tucked away at the lower end of Wildrose Canyon. At 4,100 feet elevation, the camp sits at a good midlevel point and avoids the scorching temperatures of the valley floor. Wildrose is open year-round and rarely fills. The level sites don't offer privacy or shade, but the peaceful campground is in a quiet and lovely section of the park. Amenities include picnic tables, firepits, potable water, and pit toilets; the campground is accessible to small trailers.

To get here from Highway 190, turn south at Emigrant Campground and take Emigrant Canyon Road south for approximately 21 miles (34 km), to the end of Emigrant Canyon Road. The campground will be after the left turn.

Las Vegas

The chance at fortune has lured vacationers into the southern Nevada desert ever since the Silver State legalized gambling in 1931.

At first, the "sawdust joints"—named for the stuff spread on the floor to sop up spilled beer (and perhaps a few tears)—that popped up along downtown's Fremont Street were the center of the action, but they soon faced competition from a resort corridor blooming to the south on Highway 91. The burgeoning entertainment district reminded Los Angeles nightclub owner Billy Wilkerson of Sunset Boulevard in Hollywood, so he dubbed it "The Strip," and together with Bugsy Siegel built the Flamingo, the first upscale alternative to frontier gambling halls. Their vision left a legacy that came to define Las Vegas hotel-casinos. Las Vegas has gone through many reinventions in the decades since—from city of sleaze to Mafia haven, family destination, and upscale resort town. Today, Las Vegas is known for its fine restaurants,

music festivals, and people-watching as much as its slot machines and craps tables.

Getting There

With its relative proximity to Death Valley, Route 66, and the Mojave National Preserve, Las Vegas makes a good base or a stopover for a Southern California road trip.

From Los Angeles

From Los Angeles, it is a 270-mile (435-km) drive east to reach Las Vegas. From L.A., take I-10 east for about 40 miles (64 km). At the junction with I-15 near Ontario, head north on I-15 for the next 230 miles (370 km). This route can be heavily congested weekdays during rush hour and at any time on the weekend.

Stopping in Baker

Whether driving to Las Vegas or Death Valley, you will pass near the small crossroads town of Baker where I-15 meets CA-127. If you're in need of food or gas, get them here; it will be the last you see of either for quite some time.

By Air, Train, or Bus

More than 900 planes arrive or depart **McCarran International Airport** (LAS, 5757 Wayne Newton Blvd., 702/261-5211, www.mccarran.com) every day, making it the sixth busiest in the country and 19th in the world. Terminal 1 hosts domestic flights, while Terminal 3 has domestic and international flights.

McCarran Airport provides easy transfers to the Las Vegas Strip using **shuttle vans, buses,** and **rental cars.** Limousines are available curbside for larger groups. Dedicated McCarran shuttles leave the main terminal from outside exit doors 10 and 11 about every five minutes bound for the Rent-A-Car Center. International airlines and a few domestic flights arrive at Terminal 3. Here, the shuttle picks up outside doors 51 through 58. Taxicabs are also available at the center.

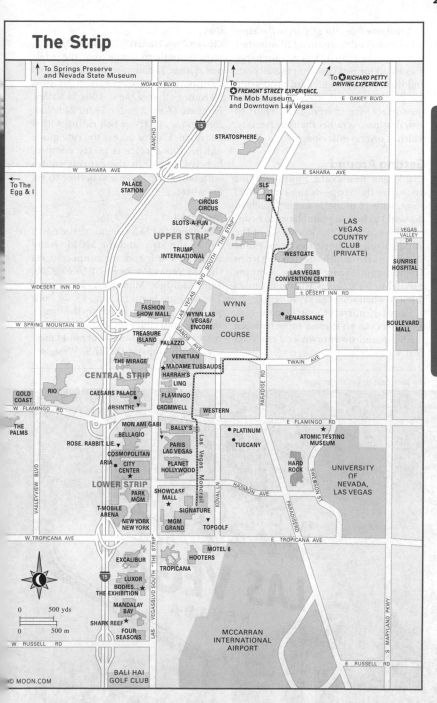

A **taxi ride** from the airport to the Strip (15 minutes) or downtown (20 minutes) runs no more than $25. A $2 surcharge is assessed for pickups from the airport, and there is a $3 credit card processing fee. It's cheaper and often faster to take the surface streets from the airport to your destination rather than the freeway, which is several miles longer.

Getting Around

Las Vegas Boulevard South—better known as the Strip—is the city's focal point, with 14 of the 25 largest hotels in the world welcoming gamblers and hedonists from around the world. Six of the world's 10 biggest hostelries line a 4-mile (6-km) north-south stretch between Tropicana and Sahara Avenues. Running parallel to I-15, this is what most folks think of when someone says "Vegas."

Since I-15 mirrors the Strip to the east, it can serve as an express route between the Strip and **downtown** and the Arts District.

Bus

Citizen Area Transit (CAT, 702/228-7433, www.rtcsouthernnevada.com), the public bus system, is managed by the Regional Transportation Commission. CAT runs 39 routes all over the Las Vegas Valley. Fares are $6 for 2 hours, $8 for 24 hours, free under age five when riding with a guardian. Call or access the ride guide online. Bus service is pretty comprehensive, but even the express routes with fewer stops take a long time to get anywhere.

Monorail

The site of the SLS Casino on the north end of the Strip and the MGM Grand near the south end are connected via the **Las Vegas Monorail** (702/699-8200, 7am-midnight Mon., 7am-2am Tues.-Thurs., 7am-3am Fri.-Sun., $5, 24-hour pass $12). Reaching speeds up to 50 mph, the monorail glides above traffic to cover the 4-mile (6-km) route in about 14 minutes, with stops at the SLS, Westgate,

the Welcome to Las Vegas sign

Convention Center, Harrah's/The Linq, Flamingo/Caesars Palace, Bally's/Paris, and MGM Grand. More than 30 major resorts are now within easy reach along the Strip without a car or taxi. Tickets are available at vending machines at each station as well as at station properties.

Casinos
Upper Strip

Ranging from Spring Mountain Road to the Stratosphere, the Upper Strip is known for its throwback swagger, but has something for everyone. Visitors can opt for world-class art, celebrity chef creations, midway games, stand-up comedy—and friendly rates at old standby casinos.

Stratosphere Casino, Hotel, and Tower

Restaurants: Top of the World, McCalls, Nunzio's Pizzeria, Fellini's, Crafted Buffet, Roxy's Diner, Tower Creamery, Starbucks, McDonald's, El Nopal Mexican Grill, Wok Vegas, Chicago Food House

Entertainment: *MJ Live*, L.A. Comedy Club

Attractions: SkyJump, Top of the Tower thrill rides, Elation Pool, Radius Pool, Observation Deck, Roni Josef Spa, Tower Shops, Fitness Center

Nightlife: Sin City Hops, Air Bar, CBar, 107 Sky Lounge

It's altitude with attitude at this 1,149-foot-tall (350-m) exclamation point on the north end of the Strip. The **Stratosphere Tower** (2000 Las Vegas Blvd. S., 702/380-7777, www.stratospherehotel. com, $103-146) is the brainchild of entrepreneur, politician, and professional poker player Bob Stupak. Daredevils will delight in the 40-mph quasi-freefall at SkyJump, along with the other vertigo-inducing thrill rides on the tower's observation deck. The more faint of heart may want to steer clear not only of the rides but also of the resort's double-decker elevators, which launch guests to the top of the tower at 1,400 feet per minute. But even acrophobes should conquer their fears long enough to enjoy the views from the restaurant and bars more than 100 floors up, where the **Chapel in the Clouds** can also ensure a heavenly beginning to married life.

If the thrill rides on the observation deck aren't your style, get a rush of gambling action on the nearly 100,000-square-foot (9,290-sq-m) ground-floor casino. Or perhaps the two swimming pools (one is tops-optional) and the dozen bars and restaurants are more your speed.

Spot-on impersonators and elaborate choreography make the Stratosphere's two tribute shows among the best in town. Each night, one of two Michael Jackson impersonators takes the stage at *MJ Live* (daily 7pm, $61-90), backed by a full cast of dancers, a live band, and a dazzling array of lighting effects in the Stratosphere Theater.

Roxy's Diner (daily 24 hours, $10-15) is a trip back to the malt shop for comfort food, red vinyl booths, checkered floors, and wisecracking waitstaff.

SLS

Restaurants: Katsuya, Bazaar Meat, Cleo, Umami Burger, 800 Degrees, Northside Café & Chinese Kitchen, The Perq
Entertainment: The Foundry, Sayers Club
Attractions: Foxtail Pool
Nightlife: Center Bar, Monkey Bar, W Living Room

On the site of the legendary Sahara Casino, **SLS** (2535 Las Vegas Blvd. S., 702/761-7000, www.slslasvegas.com, $139-249) draws 21st-century Frank and Sammy wannabes and the rest of the swanky sophisticate set. It's Rat Pack cool, filtered through modern hipsterism.

Two towers offer standard rooms of 325-360 square feet, with suites measuring up to a spacious 730 square feet. All standard accommodations boast televisions, minibars and snacks at no extra charge, soft pastel accents, and 310-thread-count sheets atop BeautyRest mattresses. A third tower is the independent **W Hotel,** where guests in the European-accented rooms enjoy their own entrance, pool, and spa.

Chef José Andrés doesn't want guests at **Bazaar Meat** (5:30pm-10pm Sun.-Thurs., 5:30pm-11pm Fri.-Sat., $65-140) ordering a huge bone-in rib eye, rack of lamb, or inch-thick tuna steak. He wants you to try them all. His Spanish-influenced meat-centric dishes are meant to be shared. The restaurant's decor reinforces that aim with long communal tables, open cooking stations, and a small gaming area.

Sayers Club (10pm-2am Thurs.-Sat.) bills itself as a live music venue. There's plenty of live indie pop, folk, and psychobilly bands on weekends, but with lots of open space and an industrial-warehouse feel, it's a natural environment for DJs. The go-go cages, platforms, and poles seem imported en masse from the Sayers' original location on L.A.'s Hollywood Boulevard.

Wynn Las Vegas/Encore

Restaurants: Andrea's, Costa Di Mare, Country Club, Lakeside Seafood, Mizumi, Sinatra, SW Steakhouse, Tableau, Wing Lei, The Buffet, Allegro, La Cave, The Café, Jardin, Red 8 Asian Bistro, Wazuzu, Terrace Point Café, Goodies on Demand, Charlie's Bar & Grill
Entertainment: *Le Rêve,* Encore Theater
Attractions: Lake of Dreams, Esplanade shopping, Wynn Salon and Spa, Encore Salon and Spa, fitness center, pools
Nightlife: XS, Intrigue, Encore Beach Club, Eastside Lounge, Lobby Bar, Players Bar, Parasol Up, Parasol Down, Tower Suite Bar

An eponymous monument to indulgence, ★ **Wynn** (3131 Las Vegas Blvd. S., 702/770-7000 or 888/320-9966, www.wynnlasvegas.com, $200-450) is mogul Steve Wynn's $2.5 billion invitation to wallow in the good life. Gaze at Wynn's art, one of the best and most valuable private collections in the world. The appropriately named **Encore** is next door. The twins' opulence is matched with casino areas awash in red—carpet, tapestries, and neon. Although guests come to explore the privileges of wealth, they can also experience the wonders of nature without the inconvenience of bugs and dirt. Lush plants, waterfalls, lakes, and mountains dominate the pristine landscape. Plans call for further growth with the construction of **Paradise Park,** a sandy lagoon and waterfront entertainment complex. The lake will be big enough for waterskiing and nonmotorized boating, while bars, boutiques, ice cream stands, and nightly fireworks will tempt beachcombers.

In addition to the gourmet offerings, don't miss the dim sum and Hong Kong barbecue at **Red 8 Asian Bistro** (11:30am-midnight Sun.-Thurs., 11:30am-1am Fri.-Sat., $20-40). Then party to excess at **XS** ($20-50) where Skrillex, David Guetta, or some other world-class DJ is likely to be spinning this weekend.

The formal sophistication belies the hotels' location on the site of the old Desert Inn, with the unself-conscious swagger Frank, Dino, and Sammy brought to the joint. Both towers boast some of the biggest guest rooms and suites on the Strip, with the usual (although better-quality) amenities, including TVs, and a few extra touches, like remote-controlled drapes, lights, and air-conditioning. Wynn's guest rooms are appointed in wheat, honey, and other creatively named shades of beige. Encore's all-suite accommodations are more colorful, with the scheme running toward dark chocolate and cream.

Center Strip

On the Center Strip (between Harmon Ave. and Spring Mountain Rd.), the casinos are packed in tight. Though the sidewalks can become masses of humanity on weekend nights, all the temptations are within walking distance.

The Venetian

Restaurants: AquaKnox, Factory Kitchen, Bouchon, Bouchon Bakery, Black Tap Burgers and Beer, CR Creat, Chica, Delmonico Steakhouse, Mercato della Pescheria, Grand Lux Café, Juice Farm, Noodle Asia, Public House, Sugarcane, Canyon Ranch Café, Yardbird, Zio Gelato, Buddy V's Ristorante, Canaletto, Canonita, Carlo's Bakery, Casanova, Cocolini, Lobster ME, Tao Asian Bistro, Coffee Bean and Tea Leaf, Trattoria Reggiano, Food Court

Entertainment: *Human Nature Juke Box*

Attractions: Madame Tussauds Las Vegas, gondola rides, Streetmosphere, Grand Canal Shoppes, Tao Beach

Nightlife: Tao Nightclub, Rosina, Bellini Bar, The Dorsey, Sin City Brewing Co., Rockhouse, Fat Tuesday, Gondola Bar

The Venetian (3355 Las Vegas Blvd. S., 702/414-1000 or 866/659-9643, www.venetian.com, $209-349) comes close to capturing the elegance of Venice. An elaborate faux-Renaissance ceiling fresco greets visitors in the hotel lobby, and the sensual treats just keep coming. A life-size streetscape—with replicas of the Bridge of Sighs, Doge's Palace, the Grand Canal, and other treasures—gives the impression that the best of the Queen of the Adriatic has been transplanted in toto.

Top to bottom: take a gondola ride at The Venetian; the Palazzo; Forum shops at Caesar's Palace.

Tranquil rides in authentic **gondolas** with serenading pilots are perfect for relaxing after a hectic session in the casino. Canal-side, buskers entertain the guests in the **Streetmosphere** (St. Mark's Square, noon-6pm daily on the hour, free), and the **Grand Canal Shoppes** (10am-11pm Sun.-Thurs., 10am-midnight Fri.-Sat.) entice strollers, window-shoppers, and serious spenders.

World-class DJs, A-list celebrities, and wall-to-wall hardbodies pack **Tao Nightclub** (10:30pm-5am Thurs.-Sat.) at the end of each week to groove to thumping house and hip-hop. Reservations and advance tickets are recommended, as this is one of the hottest party spots in town, with a powerful light and sound system, two dance rooms, and open architecture. Scattered throughout, bathing beauties luxuriate, covered (more or less) only by rose petals.

After you've shopped till you're ready to drop, **Madame Tussauds Las Vegas** (10am-8pm Sun.-Thurs., 10am-9pm Fri.-Sat., $30 adults, $20 ages 4-12, free under age 4) invites stargazers for hands-on experiences with their favorite entertainers, superheroes, and athletes.

Fine dining options abound. Try the lobster ravioli or traditional pizza and pasta dishes in the bistro setting of **Trattoria Reggiano** (10am-midnight daily, $20-30). Or step away from the Italian theme and go French at Thomas Keller's **Bouchon** (702/414-6200, 7am-1pm and 5pm-10pm Mon.-Thurs., 7am-2pm and 5pm-10pm Sat.-Sun., $30-65). Try the sensational croque madame sandwich with its rich Mornay sauce, or climb a tower of french fries to recover from a night in Sin City. The luxe setting features high ceilings, wood columns, and tile floors.

The Venetian spares no expense in the hotel department. Its 4,027 suites are tastefully appointed with plum accents and Italian (of course) marble, and at 650 square feet, they're big. They include sunken living rooms and Roman tubs.

The Palazzo

Restaurants: Coffee Bean and Tea Leaf, Cut, Grand Lux Café, Once, Hong Kong Café, Espressamente Illy, Juice Farm, Lagasse's Stadium, Lavo, Morels Steakhouse & Bistro, Grimaldi's Pizzeria, Sushisamba, Solaro, Canyon Ranch Grill
Attractions: Grand Canal Shoppes, Atrium Waterfall
Nightlife: Fusion Latin Mixology Bar, Laguna Champagne Bar, Lavo Lounge, Double Helix Wine and Whiskey Bar

A domed skylight illuminates a faux-ice sculpture, bronze columns, and lush landscaping surrounding the lobby at **The Palazzo** (3325 Las Vegas Blvd. S., 702/607-7777 or 866/263-3001, www.palazzo.com, $239-349). Motel 6 this ain't. A big chunk of the casino is smoke-free, embodying the casino's efforts toward energy efficiency and environmentally friendly design.

The Palazzo is a gourmand's dream, with a handful of four-star establishments dominated, as you would expect, by Italian influences.

Accommodations are all suites, measuring even larger than The Venetian's, with Roman tubs, sunken living rooms, and sumptuous beds that would make it tough to leave the room if not for the lure of the Strip.

The Mirage

Restaurants: Tom Colicchio's Heritage Steak, Otoro, Cravings Buffet, Carnegie Delicatessen, Paradise Café, Pantry, LVB Burger, Osteria Costa, Stack, Paradise Café, California Pizza Kitchen, Blizz Frozen Yogurt, The Roasted Bean
Entertainment: *LOVE*, Terry Fator, Aces of Comedy, Matt Goss
Attractions: Secret Garden and Dolphin Habitat, Aquarium, Mirage Volcano, Atrium
Nightlife: 1 Oak, Rhumbar, The Still, The Sports Bar, Lobby Bar, Center Bar, Parlor Cocktail Lounge, Heritage Steak Lounge, Stack Lounge, Otoro Lounge

The Mirage (3400 Las Vegas Blvd. S., 702/791-7111 or 800/627-6667, www.mirage.com, $140-300) was the first "understated" megaresort, starting a trend that brought Vegas full circle to the mature pursuits it was built on—gourmet dining, lavish production shows, hip music, and hard liquor. This Bali Hai-themed paradise lets guests bask in the wonders of nature alongside the sophistication and pampering of resort life. More an oasis than a mirage, the hotel greets visitors with exotic bamboo, orchids, banana trees, secluded grottoes, and peaceful lagoons. Dolphins, white tigers, stingrays, sharks, and a volcano provide livelier sights.

The Mirage's guest rooms have tasteful appointments and some of the most comfortable, down-comforter beds in town. The standard rooms emit a modern and relaxing feel in golds, blacks, and splashes of tangerine, mauve, and ruby.

Bump and grind at **1 Oak** (10:30pm-4am Wed., Fri., Sat.), an urban space with lots of hip-hop and gritty, socially aware artwork. Two separate rooms have bars, DJs, and crowded dance floors. With dark walls and sparse lighting, it's a sinful, sexy venue for the beautiful people to congregate.

The Mirage commands performances by the world's top headliners, but Cirque du Soleil's Beatles show *LOVE* packs them in every night for a celebration of the Fab Four's music.

Harrah's

Restaurants: Ruth's Chris Steak House, Flavors the Buffet, Oyster Bar, Ben & Jerry's, Toby Keith's I Love This Bar & Grill, Fulton Street Food Hall, Starbucks
Entertainment: *Tenors of Rock, Menopause the Musical,* Mac King Comedy Magic, Tape Face, Big Elvis, The Comedy Lineup, *X Country*
Nightlife: Carnaval Court, Numb Bar, Piano Bar, Signature Bar

Adjacent to the happening Linq, ★ **Harrah's** (3475 Las Vegas Blvd. S., 800/214-9110, www.caesars.com/harrahs-las-vegas, $115-201) suddenly finds itself on the cutting edge of the Las Vegas party scene. The venerable property has taken a few baby steps toward hipsterism, booking the topless *X Country* revue and the raunchy *Menopause the Musical*. Still,

conservative habits are hard to break, and **Mac King's** family-friendly comedy magic show remains one of the best afternoon offerings in town.

Carnaval Court, outside on the Strip's sidewalk, capitalizes on the street-party atmosphere with live bands and juggling bartenders. Just inside, Vegas icon **Big Elvis** (2pm, 3:30pm, and 5pm Mon., Wed., and Fri., free) performs in the **Piano Bar,** which invites aspiring singers to the karaoke stage Monday through Wednesday evenings, and dueling twin sister keyboardists take over each night at 9pm. The country superstar lends his name and unapologetic patriotism to **Toby Keith's I Love This Bar & Grill** (11:30am-2am Sun.-Thurs., 11:30am-3am Fri.-Sat., $15-25). Try the fried bologna sandwich.

For the best experience, book a room in the renamed Valley Tower. Its 600 rooms and 72 suites feature subtle blues and grays along with traditional Harrah's purple in geometric designs and artwork throughout. Backlighted vanities, big windows, and modern lights and fixtures add to the sleek design.

Caesars Palace

Restaurants: Bacchanal Buffet, Gordon Ramsay Hell's Kitchen, Gordon Ramsay Pub & Grill, Restaurant Guy Savoy, Brioche by Guy Savoy, Pronto by Giada, Beijing Noodle No. 9, Mesa Grill, Old Homestead Steakhouse, Rao's, Mr. Chow, Searsucker, Nobu, Café Americano, Forum Food Court (Smashburger, The Halal Guys, Earl of Sandwich, Crepes and More, La Gloria, Difara Pizza, Tiger Wok and Ramen), Starbucks
Entertainment: *Absinthe*
Attractions: Fall of Atlantis, aquarium, Appian Way Shops, Forum Shops
Nightlife: Omnia, Fizz, Cleopatra's Barge, Spanish Steps, Numb Bar, Alto Bar, Lobby Bar, Vista Lounge, Montecristo Cigar Bar

The Roman Empire probably would look a lot like Las Vegas had it survived this long. ★ **Caesars Palace** (3570 Las Vegas Blvd. S., 866/227-5938, www.caesars.com, $175-300) has incorporated all of ancient Rome's decadence while adding a few thousand slot machines. Caesars opened with great fanfare in 1966 and has ruled the Strip ever since. Like the empire, it continues to expand and innovate, now boasting 3,348 guest rooms in six towers and 140,000 square feet of gaming space accented with marble, fountains, gilding, and royal reds. Wander the grounds searching for reproductions of some of the world's most famous statuary, including Michelangelo's *David*.

Cleopatra's Barge (7pm-2am Tues.-Wed., 8pm-3am Thurs.-Sat.), a floating lounge, attracts the full spectrum of the 21-and-over crowd for late-night bacchanalia. Local rockers and pop-choral fusionists are the current house bands, with occasional forays from touring groups taking the stage for acoustic performances in the intimate, 170-seat venue.

Guests luxuriate in the **Garden of the Gods Pool Oasis**, with each of several distinct water-and-sun shrines catering to a different proclivity. Gamblers can play at a swim-up blackjack table at Fortuna; beach bunnies can flaunt it toplessly at Venus; tanners can roast in peace at Apollo; kids can frolic at Temple; and the wealthy can splurge on cabanas at Bacchus. What, no aqueduct?

All roads lead to the **Forum Shops** (10am-11pm Sun.-Thurs., 10am-midnight Fri.-Sat.), a collection of famous designer stores, specialty boutiques, and restaurants. An hour here can do some serious damage to your bankroll. You'll also find the *Fall of Atlantis* show (hourly 11am-11pm Sun.-Thurs., 11am-11pm Fri.-Sat., free), a multisensory, multimedia depiction of the gods' wrath.

Caesars is the center of the world for celebrity chefs, with culinary all-stars lending their names to multiple eateries. Epicureans enjoy beef Wellington or eggs in purgatory at **Gordon Ramsay Hell's Kitchen.** More casual guests can get their British on at **Gordon Ramsay Pub & Grill** (11am-11pm Sun.-Thurs., 11am-midnight Fri.-Sat., $25-40). Sip a Guinness while munching on shepherd's pie, bangers and mash, and fish-and-chips among the iconic red London-style phone booths.

With so many guest rooms in six towers, it seems Caesars is always renovating somewhere. Most newer guest rooms are done in tan, wood, and marble. Ask for a south-facing room in the Augustus or Octavius tower to get commanding vistas of both the Bellagio fountains and the Strip.

The Linq

Restaurants: Guy Fieri's Vegas Kitchen and Bar, Chayo Mexican Kitchen & Tequila Bar, Hash House a Go Go, Nook Café, Off the Strip
Entertainment: Mat Franco's *Magic Reinvented*
Attractions: High Roller, Fly Linq Zipline, VR Adventures, Auto Collection, Club Tattoo, Influence pool, Brooklyn Bowl, Silver Sky Chapel
Nightlife: 3535, Catalyst, O'Shea's, Tag Lounge and Bar

Rooms at **The Linq** (3535 Las Vegas Blvd. S., 800/634-6441, www.caesars.com/linq, $99-249) are sleek, stylish, and smallish, at 250-350 square feet. Pewter and chrome are accented with eggplant, orange, or aqua murals depicting vintage Vegas in all its neon glory. Other amenities include marble countertops, flat-screen TVs, and iPod docks. But the hotel is really just a way to stay close to all the Gen X-focused boutiques, bars, and restaurants in the adjacent outdoor promenade.

The high point of this pedestrian-friendly plaza is the **High Roller** (adult $22-32, age 4-12 $9-19), the highest observation wheel in the world, but there's plenty more to warrant a stop. **Brooklyn Bowl** (5pm-1am Sat.-Thurs., 5pm-2am Fri., $15-25) has you covered on eat, drink, and be merry, combining ten-pin excitement with dozens of beer taps, delectable finger foods, and live entertainment. The spicy diablo shrimp highlights the modern fare at **Chayo Mexican Kitchen & Tequila Bar** (9am-midnight Sun.-Thurs., 9am-3am Fri.-Sat., $16-28), but the menu takes a backseat to the tequila-fueled party. There's a mechanical bull in the middle of the dining room, for goodness' sake. Patio seating puts diners and drinkers in prime people-watching territory. Vegas icon and local favorite **O'Shea's** (24 hours daily) brings back the lowbrow frivolity of the kegger party with cheap drafts, heated beer pong matches, and a rockin' jam band that keeps the festivities raging well into the wee hours.

Flamingo

Restaurants: Center Cut Steakhouse, Paradise Garden Buffet, Jimmy Buffett's Margaritaville, Carlos N Charlie's, Beach Club Bar & Grill, Club Cappuccino, Café Express Food Court (Bonanno's Pizza, Johnny Rockets, L.A. Subs, Pan Asian Express)

Entertainment: Donny and Marie, Piff the Magic Dragon, *Legends in Concert*, *X Burlesque*

Attractions: Wildlife Habitat

Nightlife: It's 5 O'Clock Somewhere Bar, Garden Bar, Bugsy's Bar

Named for Virginia "Flamingo" Hill, the girlfriend of Benjamin "don't call me Bugsy" Siegel, the **Flamingo** (3555 Las Vegas Blvd. S., 702/733-3111, www.caesars.com/flamingo-las-vegas, $109-219) has at turns embraced and shunned its gangster ties, which stretch back to the 1960s. After Bugsy's (sorry, Mr. Siegel's) Flamingo business practices ran afoul of the Cosa Nostra and led to his untimely end, Meyer Lansky took over. Mob ties continued to dog the property until Hilton Hotels bought the Flamingo in 1970, giving the joint the legitimacy it needed. Today, its art deco architecture and pink-and-orange neon conjure images of aging mafiosi lounging by the pool in a Vegas where the mob era is remembered almost fondly. At the **Flamingo Wildlife Habitat** (8am-dusk daily, free), ibis, pelicans, turtles, koi fish, and, of course, Chilean flamingos luxuriate amid riparian plants and meandering streams.

Guests can search for their lost shaker of salt at **Jimmy Buffett's Margaritaville** (702/733-3302, 8am-1am Sun.-Thurs., 8am-2am Fri.-Sat., $20-30).

Piff the Magic Dragon (8pm, days vary, $69) performs mind-boggling card tricks with deadpan delivery and the help of adorable Chihuahua Mr. Piffles. Most of the humor is family-friendly, but the venue recommends audience members be age 13 and over.

The Flamingo transformed many of its guest rooms into Fab Rooms in 2012, but the older Go Rooms are actually more modern, dressed in swanky mahogany and white. The rooms are only 350 square feet, but boast high-end entertainment systems and TVs, vintage art prints, padded leather headboards, and all the other Vegas-sational accoutrements. Fab Rooms are more boldly decorated, incorporating swatches of hot pink.

Rio

Restaurants: VooDoo Steakhouse, Carnival World & Seafood Buffets, Royal India Bistro, Wine Cellar & Tasting Room, KJ Dim Sum & Seafood, All-American Bar & Grille, Hash House a Go Go, Pho Da Nang Vietnamese Kitchen, Guy Fieri's El Burro Borracho, Sports Deli, Smashburger, Starbucks

Entertainment: Penn & Teller, Comedy Cellar, Chippendales, *X Rocks*

Attractions: VooDoo Beach, VooDoo Zip Line, KISS by Monster Mini Golf, Masquerade Village, Count's Tattoo Company, Rio Las Vegas Spa and Salon

Nightlife: VooDoo Rooftop Nightclub & Lounge, IBar, Flirt Lounge, Masquerade Bar, Purple Zebra Daiquiri Bar

This Carnival-inspired resort of more than 2,500 all-suite accommodations just off the Strip keeps the party going with terrific buffets, beautiful people-magnet bars, and steamy shows. "Bevertainers" at the **Rio** (3700 W. Flamingo Rd., 866/983-4279, www.caesars.com/rio-las-vegas, $99-199) take breaks from schlepping cocktails by jumping on mini-stages scattered throughout the casino to belt out tunes or shimmy to the music. Dancers and other performers may materialize at your slot machine to take your mind off your losses.

Rio suites measure about 600 square feet. The hotel's center-Strip location and room-tall windows provide middle-of-the-action sights. A dressing area separate from the bathroom makes night-on-the-town preparations easy.

VooDoo Beach is a complex comprising four pools, a maze of waterfalls, cabanas, and more. Kids are welcome everywhere but Voo Pool, which attracts the over-21 crowd with a bar, spa treatment tables, and topless bathing.

Lower Strip

The Lower Strip—roughly between the "Welcome to Fabulous Las Vegas" sign and Harmon Avenue—is a living city timeline. The Tropicana is here, providing a link to the mobbed-up city of the 1960s and 1970s. Camelot-themed Excalibur, completed in 1990, and the Egyptian-inspired Luxor, which opened in 1993, serve as prime examples from the city's hesitant foray into becoming a "family" destination in the early 1990s. Across from the Tropicana, the emerald-tinted MGM Grand opened in 1993 as a salute to *The Wizard of Oz*. City Center puts the mega in megaresort—condos, boutique hotels, trendy shopping, a huge casino, and a sprawling dining and entertainment district—and cemented the city's biggest-is-best trend. The Lower Strip seems made for budget-conscious families. Rooms are often cheaper than mid-Strip, and there are plenty of kid-friendly attractions (even a roller coaster).

The Palms

Restaurants: Scotch 80 Prime, Laguna, Send Noodles, A.Y.C.E. Buffet, Lucky Penny, The Eatery food court

Entertainment: Pearl Theater, Brendan Theater

Nightlife: Rojo, Tonic, Unknown Bar, Apex Social Club, Camden Cocktail Lounge

Station Casinos spent nearly $1 billion to buy and renovate **The Palms** (4321 W. Flamingo Rd., 866/942-7777, www.palms.com, $110-175), where rock star excess was just another Tuesday night when it opened in 1999 to penthouse views, uninhibited pool parties, lavish theme suites, and several televised parties. The 2,500-seat **Pearl Concert Theater** still regularly hosts

rock concerts, and the Fantasy Tower still lets guest splurge on rooms with bowling lanes, basketball courts, curated art, and more. The original Ivory Tower offers large guest rooms. They're sleek, with geometric shapes and custom artwork, but their best features are the feathery beds and luxurious comforters. The rejuvenating shower and "spa-inspired" stone, glass, and chrome bathrooms help get the day started. The newest tower, Palms Place, has 599 studios and one-bedrooms with suite views, gourmet kitchens, and a nearby restaurant, spa, and pool.

Bellagio

Restaurants: Lago, Yellowtail, Spago, Harvest by Roy Ellamar, Jasmine, Fix, Michael Mina, Picasso, Prime Steakhouse, Le Cirque, Noodles, The Buffet, Bellagio Patisserie, Starbucks, Café Bellagio, Pool Café, Juice Press

Entertainment: Cirque du Soleil's O

Attractions: Fountains at Bellagio, Bellagio Conservatory & Botanical Garden, Bellagio Gallery of Fine Art, public art

Nightlife: Hyde, Lily Bar & Lounge, Petrossian Bar, Baccarat Bar, Pool Bar, Sports Bar Lounge

With nearly 4,000 guest rooms and suites, ★ **Bellagio** (3600 Las Vegas Blvd. S., 702/693-7111 or 888/987-6667, www. bellagio.com, $199-349) boasts a population larger than the village perched on Lake Como from which it borrows its name. To keep pace with its Italian namesake, Bellagio created a lake between the hotel and Las Vegas Boulevard. The views of the lake and its **Fountains at Bellagio** (3pm-midnight Mon.-Fri., noon-midnight Sat., 11am-midnight Sun.) are free, as is the 80,000-flower aromatic fantasy at **Bellagio Conservatory & Botanical Garden** (24 hours daily). The **Bellagio Gallery of Fine Art** (10am-8pm daily, $18) would be a bargain at twice the price—you can spend an edifying day at one of the world's priciest resorts (including a cocktail and lunch) for less than $50. Even if you don't spring for gallery admission, art demands your attention throughout the hotel and casino.

The 2,000 glass flower petals in Dale Chihuly's *Fiori di Como* sculpture bloom from the lobby ceiling, foreshadowing the opulent experiences to come. Masatoshi Izumi's *A Gift from the Earth*, comprising four massive basalt sculptures representing wind, fire, water, and land, dominates the hotel's main entrance.

The display of artistry continues but the bargains end at **Via Bellagio** (10am-midnight daily), the resort's shopping district, including heavyweight retailers Armani, Prada, Chanel, Gucci, and their ilk.

Befitting Bellagio's world-class status, intriguing and expensive restaurants abound. **Michael Mina** (5:30pm-10pm Mon.-Sat., $70-100) is worth the price. Restrained decor adds to the simple elegance of the cuisine, which is mostly seafood with European and Asian influences.

Bellagio's tower rooms are the epitome of luxury, with Italian marble, oversize bathtubs, remote-controlled drapes,

the view from the Bellagio

Egyptian-cotton sheets, and 510 square feet in which to spread out. The sage-plum and indigo-silver color schemes are refreshing changes from the goes-with-everything beige and the camouflages-all-stains paisley often found on the Strip.

Paris Las Vegas

Restaurants: Burger Brasserie, Mon Ami Gabi, Hexx, Martoranos, Gordon Ramsay Steak, Eiffel Tower Restaurant, JJ's Boulangerie, Beef Park, Café Belle Madeleine, Sekushi, La Creperie, Le Café Ile St. Louis, Le Village Buffet, Yong Kang Street

Entertainment: *Sex Tips for Straight Women from a Gay Man, Marilyn! The New Musical,* Anthony Cools, I Love the '90s, Jeff Civillico – Comedy In Action

Attractions: Eiffel Tower

Nightlife: Napoleon's Lounge, Alexxa's Bar, Le Cabaret, Le Central, Le Bar du Sport, Gustav's, Chateau Nightclub & Rooftop

Designers used Gustav Eiffel's original drawings to ensure that the half-size tower that anchors **Paris Las Vegas** (3655 Las Vegas Blvd. S., 877/242-6753, www. caesars.com/paris-las-vegas, $149-276) conformed—down to the last cosmetic rivet—to the original. That attention to detail prevails throughout this property, which works hard to evoke the City of Light, from large-scale reproductions of the Arc de Triomphe, Champs-Élysées, and Louvre to more than half a dozen French restaurants. The tower is perhaps the most romantic spot in town to view the Strip; you'll catch your breath as the elevator whisks you to the observation deck 460 feet up, then have it taken away again by the lights from one of the most famous skylines in the world. Back at street level, the cobblestone lanes and brass streetlights of **Le Boulevard** (8am-2am daily) invite shoppers into quaint shops and patisseries. The casino offers its own attractions, not the least of which is the view of the Eiffel Tower's base jutting through the ceiling. Paris is one of the first casinos to test "skill-based" gaming, which combines video poker with video games. It also offers a variation of fantasy football during the NFL season.

Entertainment veers toward the bawdy, with **Anthony Cools—The Uncensored Hypnotist** (9pm Tues. and Thurs.-Sun., $49-82) cajoling mesmerized subjects through very adult simulations. The same venue hosts the Broadway export *Sex Tips for Straight Women from a Gay Man* (7pm Sun., Tues., Thurs., Fri., 9pm Mon., 7pm and 11pm Sat., $52-92), in which the audience and flamboyant Dan help uptight Robyn shed her bedroom inhibitions. Hip-hop, R&B, and pop artists take viewers back to the "golden age" in **I Love the '90s** (9pm Thurs.-Mon., $70-135).

You'll be wishing you had packed your beret when you order a beignet and cappuccino at **Le Café Ile St. Louis** (6pm-11pm Sun.-Thurs., 6am-midnight Fri.-Sat., $12-20). While the checkered tablecloths and streetlights scream French sidewalk café, the menu tends toward American comfort food.

Standard guest rooms in the 33-story tower are decorated in a rich earth-tone palette and have marble baths. There's nothing Left Bank bohemian about them, however. The guest rooms exude little flair or personality, but the simple, quality furnishings make it a moderately priced option. Book a Red Room if modern decor is important to you.

Cosmopolitan

Restaurants: Scarpetta, Rose. Rabbit. Lie., E by José Andrés, STK, Beauty & Exxex, Blue Ribbon, China Poblano, Zuma, Secret Pizza, Eggslut, Estiatorio Milos, The Henry, Holsteins, Jaleo, The Juice Standard, Milk Bar, Momofuku, Overlook Grill, Starbucks, Va Bene, Wicked Spoon

Attractions: public art

Nightlife: Marquee, Bond, The Chandelier, Clique, The Study, Vesper Bar

Modern art, marble bath floors, and big soaking tubs in 460-square-foot rooms evoke urban penthouse living at ★ **Cosmopolitan** (3708 Las Vegas Blvd. S., 702/698-7000, www. cosmopolitanlasvegas.com, $220-4,380). The hefty rates do nothing to harsh the

NYC vibe. Because it's too cool to host production shows, the resort's entertainment schedule mixes DJs of the moment with the coolest headliners.

That nouveau riche attitude carries through to the dining and nightlife. **Rose. Rabbit. Lie.** (6pm-midnight Wed.-Sat., $70-125) is equal parts supper club, nightclub, and jazz club. Bluesy, jazzy torch singers, magicians, tap and hip-hop dancers, and a rocking sound system keep the joint jumping. If you go for dinner, order 5-6 small plates per couple. **Vesper Bar** (24 hours daily), named for James Bond's favorite martini, prides itself on serving hipster versions of classic cocktails. Possibly the best day club in town, **Marquee** (11am-sunset daily Apr.-Oct.), on the roof, brings in the beautiful people with DJs and sweet bungalow lofts. When darkness falls, the day club becomes an extension of the pulsating Marquee nightclub (10:30pm-5am Mon. and Fri.-Sat.).

Aria

Restaurants: Bardot, Sage, Catch, Herringbone, Blossom, Jean Georges Steakhouse, Carbone, Aria Patisserie Javier's, Lemongrass, The Buffet, Julian Serrano Tapas, Aria Café, Five50 Pizza Bar, The Pub, Bobby's Burger Bar, Burger Lounge, Starbucks, Pressed Juicery, Pinkberry
Entertainment: Cirque du Soleil's Zarkana
Attractions: public art, Crystals
Nightlife: Jewel, Alibi, Baccarat Lounge, High Limit Lounge, Lift Bar, Lobby Bar, Pool Bar, Sports Bar

All glass and steel, ultramodern ★ **Aria** (3730 Las Vegas Blvd. S., 702/590-7757, www.aria.com, $210-379) would look more at home in Manhattan than Las Vegas. Touch pads control the drapes, the lighting, the music, and the climate in Aria's fern- or grape-paletted guest rooms. Program the "wake up scene" before bedtime, and the room will gradually summon you from peaceful slumber at the appointed time. A traditional hotel casino, Aria shares the City Center umbrella with **Vdara,** a Euro-chic boutique hotel with no gaming.

Guests are invited to browse an extensive public art collection, with works by Maya Lin, Jenny Holzer, and Richard Long, among others. **Crystals,** a 500,000-square-foot mall, lets you splurge among hanging gardens. Restaurants fronted by Julian Serrano and Michael Mina take the place of Sbarro's and Cinnabon.

Park MGM

Restaurants: Primrose, Bavette's Steakhouse, Eataly, Roy Choi, Starbucks
Entertainment: Park Theater
Nightlife: Double Barrel Roadhouse, Moneyline Sports Bar & Book, On the Road, Juniper Cocktail Lounge

The former Monte Carlo has gotten the MGM glam treatment, and now, as **Park MGM** (3770 Las Vegas Blvd. S., 702/730-7777, www.parkmgm.com, $99-179), it pulls the big names (Cher, Bruno Mars, etc.) into its bustling Park Theater. Rooms in the middle-of-the-action hotel weigh in at over 400 square feet. They are decorated in hunter green, and the alcove bed and blackout curtains screen guests, even when they choose the Strip-view accommodations. Curated art makes each room unique.

Hard Rock

Restaurants: MB Steak, Culinary Dropout, Fu Asian Kitchen, Mr. Lucky's, Nobu, Pink Taco, Oyster Bar, Fuel Café, Goose Island Pub, Pizza Forte, Juice Bar, Dunkin' Donuts
Entertainment: Magic Mike Live, The Joint, Raiding the Rock Vault, Vinyl, Soundwaves
Nightlife: Rehab Pool Party, Smashbar, Vanity, Center Bar, Sidebet Draft Bar, Luxe Bar, Midway Bar

Young stars and the media-savvy 20-somethings who idolize them contribute to the frat party mojo at the **Hard Rock** (4455 Paradise Rd., 800/473-7625, www.hardrockhotel.com, $129-275). While the casino is shaped like an LP, if your music collection dates back to wax records, this probably isn't the place for you. The gaming tables and machines are located in the "record label," and the shops and restaurants are in the "grooves."

Contemporary and classic rockers regularly grace the stage at **The Joint** and party with their fans at **Rehab Pool Parties** (11am-dusk Fri.-Sat.). The provocatively named **Pink Taco** (11am-10pm Sun.-Thurs., 11am-2am Fri.-Sat., $15-25) dishes up Mexican and Caribbean specialties.

The 1,500 sleek guest rooms include stocked minibars, Bose CD sound systems, and 55-inch plasma TVs, a fitting crib for wannabe rock stars.

New York New York

Restaurants: Tom's Urban, Il Fornaio, Nine Fine Irishmen, Gallagher's Steakhouse, America, New York Pizzeria, Chin Chin Café & Sushi Bar, Broadway Burger Bar & Grill, Gonzalez y Gonzalez, Shake Shack, 48th and Crepe, Greenberg's Deli, Fulton's Fish Frye, Village Bakery, Times Square to Go, Nathan's Famous, Starbucks
Entertainment: Cirque du Soleil's *Zumanity*, Brooklyn Bridge buskers, dueling pianos, The Park
Attractions: Hershey's Chocolate World, Big Apple Coaster & Arcade, T-Mobile Arena
Nightlife: Coyote Ugly, The Bar at Times Square, Center Bar, Pour 24, Big Chill, High Limit Bar, Lobby Bar, Chocolate Bar

One look at this loving tribute to the city that never sleeps and you won't be able to fuhgedaboutit. From the city skyline outside (the skyscrapers contain the resort's hotel rooms) to laundry hanging between crowded faux brownstones indoors, **New York New York** (3790 Las Vegas Blvd. S., 702/740-6969 or 866/815-4365, www.newyorknewyork.com, $130-255) will have even grizzled Gothamites feeling like they've come home again.

The **Big Apple Coaster** (11am-11pm Sun.-Thurs., 10:30am-midnight Fri.-Sat., $15, all-day pass $26) winds its way around the resort, an experience almost as hair-raising as a New York City cab ride, which the coaster cars are painted to resemble.

Dueling pianists keep **The Bar at Times Square** (1pm-2:30am Mon.-Thurs.,

11am-2:30am Fri.-Sun.) rocking into the wee hours, and the sexy bar staff at **Coyote Ugly** (6pm-3am daily) defy its name.

The Park takes dining, drinking, and strolling to new heights. The plaza surrounding T-Mobile Arena, where the NHL's Vegas Golden Knights and the hottest musical acts play, incorporates responsible landscaping and artistic, if artificial, shade structures.

New York New York's 2,023 guest rooms are standard size, 350-400 square feet. The roller coaster zooms around the towers, so you might want to ask for a room out of earshot.

MGM Grand

Restaurants: Morimoto, Joël Robuchon, Tom Colicchio's Craftsteak, Michael Mina Pub 1842, Emeril's New Orleans Fish House, L'Atelier de Joël Robuchon, Wolfgang Puck Bar & Grill, Hakkasan, Hecho En Vegas, Crush, MGM Grand Buffet, Fiamma Italian Kitchen, Tap Sports Bar, Dapper Doughnut, Blizz, Pieology, Avenue Café, Cabana Grill, Corner Cakes, Starbucks, Subway, Pan Asian Express, Bonanno's New York Pizzeria, Sports Deli, China Tang, Häagen-Dazs, Nathan's Famous, Original Chicken Tender, Tacos N 'Ritas, Johnny Rockets
Entertainment: Cirque du Soleil's *Kà*, David Copperfield, Virtual Reality, Jabbawockeez, Brad Garrett's Comedy Club, MGM Garden Arena
Attractions: Topgolf, Level Up, CSI: The Experience, CBS Television City Research Center
Nightlife: Wet Republic, Hakkasan, Level Up, Whiskey Bar, Losers Bar, Centrifuge, Lobby Bar

Gamblers enter **MGM Grand** (3799 Las Vegas Blvd. S., 888/646-1203, www.mgmgrand.com, $130-250) through portals guarded by MGM's mascot, the 45-foot-tall king of the jungle. The uninitiated may feel like a gazelle on the savanna, swallowed by the 171,000-square-foot casino floor, the largest in Las Vegas. But the watering hole, MGM's pool complex, is relatively predator-free. MGM capitalizes on the movie studio's greatest hits. Even the hotel's emerald facade evokes the magical city in *The Wizard of Oz*.

Boob tube fans can volunteer for studies at the **CBS Television City Research Center** (10am-8:30pm daily, free), where they can screen pilots for shows under consideration. If your favorite show happens to revolve around solving crimes, don some rubber gloves and search for clues at **CSI: The Experience** (9am-8pm daily, age 12 and up $32, not recommended for children under 12). Three crime scenes keep the experience fresh.

MGM Grand houses enough top restaurants for a week of gourmet dinners. You can take your pick of celebrity chef establishments, but **L'Atelier de Joël Robuchon** (5pm-10pm daily, $75-200) offers the most bang for the buck. Counter service overlooks kitchen preparations, adding to the anticipation.

Standard guest rooms in the Grand Tower are filled with the quality furnishings you'd expect. The West Tower guest rooms are smaller, at 350 square feet, but exude swinging style with high-tech gizmos; the 450-square-foot rooms in the Grand Tower are more traditional.

Tropicana

Restaurants: Bacio, Fresh Mix, Robert Irvine's Public House, Oakville Steakhouse, Red Lotus Asian Kitchen, Savor Buffet

Attractions: Xposed!

Entertainment: David Goldrake Imaginarium, Purple Reign, the Prince Tribute, Rich Little, Laugh Factory

Nightlife: Tropicana Lounge, Lucky's Sports Bar, Coconut Grove Bar

When it opened in 1959, the **Tropicana** (3801 Las Vegas Blvd. S., 702/739-2222, www.troplv.com, $140-200) was the most luxurious, most expensive resort on the Strip. It has survived several boom-and-bust cycles since then, and its decor reflects the willy-nilly expansion and refurbishment efforts through the years. Today, the rooms have bright, airy South Beach themes with plantation shutters, light wood, 42-inch plasma TVs, and garden views.

The beach chic atmosphere includes a large pool complex with reclining deck chairs and swim-up blackjack. After a slow start, Las Vegas is now quite LGBTQ-friendly. On summer Saturdays (noon-7pm) the pool deck hosts **Xposed!,** a gay-friendly pool party with sand volleyball, go-go dancers, and trendy DJs.

Luxor

Restaurants: Tender Steak & Seafood, Rice & Company, Public House, T&T Tacos & Tequila, The Buffet, Pyramid Café, Backstage Deli, Blizz, Burger Bar, Ri Ra Irish Pub, Slice of Vegas, Hussong's Cantina, Bonanno's Pizzeria, Johnny Rockets, LA Subs, Nathan's Famous, Original Chicken Tender, Starbucks

Entertainment: Carrot Top, Blue Man Group, Fantasy

Attractions: Bodies…the Exhibition, Titanic artifacts, Temptation Sunday

Nightlife: Centra, Aurora, Flight, High Bar, PlayBar

Other than its pyramid shape and name, not much remains of the Egyptian theme at the **Luxor** (3900 Las Vegas Blvd. S., 702/262-4000, www.luxor.com, $99-220). In its place are upscale and decidedly post-pharaoh nightclubs, restaurants, and shops. Many are located in the **Shoppes at Mandalay Place,** on the sky bridge between Luxor and Mandalay Bay. The huge base of the pyramid houses a cavernous casino, while the slanted walls and twin 22-story towers contain 4,400 guest rooms. Luxor also has the largest atrium in the world, an intense light beam that is visible from space, and inclinators—elevators that move along the building's oblique angles.

Staying in the pyramid makes for interesting room features, such as a slanted exterior wall. Stay on higher floors for panoramic views of the atrium below. Tower rooms are newer and more traditional in their shape, decor, and amenities.

Mandalay Bay

Restaurants: Aureole, Red Square, Lupo by Wolfgang Puck, Charlie Palmer Steak, Fleur by Hubert Keller, Rick Moonen's RM Seafood, Kumi, Stripsteak, Libertine Social, Border Grill, Rx Boiler Room, Rivea, Ri

Ra Irish Pub, BBQ Mexicana, Della's Kitchen, Hussong's Cantina, Citizens Kitchen & Bar, Slice of Vegas, Seabreeze Café, Burger Bar, Bayside Buffet, Noodle Shop, Bonanno's Pizzeria, Nathan's Famous, Pan Asian Express, Johnny Rockets, Subway, Mizuya Sushi/Sake, Sports Book Grill, Starbucks, Yogurt In

Entertainment: House of Blues, *Michael Jackson One*, Nashville Unplugged

Attractions: Shark Reef, Mandalay Place

Nightlife: Foundation Room, Light, Daylight Beach Club, Skyfall, Minus 5 Ice Bar, Rhythm & Riffs, Eyecandy Sound Lounge, Orchid Lounge, Evening Call, Fat Tuesday, Bikini Bar, Verandah Lounge, 1923 Bourbon Bar

The South Pacific behemoth ★ **Mandalay Bay** (3950 Las Vegas Blvd. S., 877/632-7800, www.mandalaybay.com, $150-300) has one of the largest casino floors in the world at 135,000 square feet. The paradise comprises eight pools, including a lazy river, a 1.6-million-gallon wave pool complete with a real beach made of five million pounds of sand, an adults-only dipping pool, and tops-optional sunbathing deck. You could spend your entire vacation in the pool area, gambling at the beach's three-level casino, eating at its restaurant, and loading up on sandals and bikinis at the nearby Pearl Moon boutique. The beach hosts a concert series during summer.

House of Blues (hours vary by event) hosts live blues, rock, and acoustic sets and a surprisingly good restaurant. It's the site of the Sunday **Gospel Brunch** (702/632-7600, 10am and 1pm Sun., $55), where a gospel choir serenades guests with contemporary spirituals as they dine on Southern delicacies like chicken and waffles, biscuits and gravy, brisket, and more.

Mandalay Place (10am-11pm daily), on the sky bridge between Mandalay Bay and the Luxor, is smaller and less hectic than other casino malls. It features unusual shops, such as the Guinness Store, celebrating the favorite Irish stout, and Cariloha, with clothes, accessories, and housewares made of bamboo. The shops share space with eateries and

Mandalay Bay

high-concept bars like **Minus 5 Ice Bar** (11am-3am daily), where barflies don parkas before entering the below-freezing (23°F/-5°C) establishment. The glasses aren't just frosted; they're fashioned completely out of ice.

An urban hip-hop worldview and the King of Pop's unmatched talent guide the vignettes in *Michael Jackson One* (7pm and 9:30pm Fri.-Tues., $69-170). Michael's musical innovation and the Cirque du Soleil trademark aerial and acrobatic acts pay homage to the human spirit.

Sheathed in Indian artifacts and crafts, the **Foundation Room** (5pm-3am daily) is just as dark and mysterious as the subcontinent, with private rooms piled with overstuffed furniture, fireplaces, and thick carpets; a dining room; and several bars catering to various musical tastes.

Vegas pays tribute to Paris, Rome, New York, and Venice, so why not Moscow? Round up your comrades for caviar and vodka as well as continental favorites

at **Red Square** (5pm-10pm Sun.-Thurs., 5pm-11pm Fri.-Sat., $35-50). Look for the headless Lenin statue at the entrance.

Standard guest rooms are chic and roomy, with warm fabrics and plush bedding. Get a north-facing room and put the floor-to-ceiling windows to use gazing the full length of the Strip. The guest rooms are big, but nothing special visually; the baths are fit for royalty, with huge tubs and glass-walled showers. To go upscale, check out the Delano boutique hotel or book at the Four Seasons—both are part of the same complex.

Downtown
Binion's

Restaurants: Top of Binion's Steakhouse, Binion's Deli, Binion's Café, Benny's Smokin BBQ & Brews

Entertainment: Hypnosis Unleashed

Nightlife: Cowgirl Up Cantina, Whiskey Licker

Before Vegas became a resort city, it catered to inveterate gamblers, hard drinkers, and others on the fringes of society. Ah, the good old days! A gambler himself, Benny Binion put his place in the middle of downtown, a magnet for the serious player, offering high limits and few frills. **Binion's** (128 Fremont St., 702/382-1600, www.binions.com) now attracts players with occasional $1 blackjack tables and a poker room frequented by grizzled veterans. This is where the World Series of Poker began, and the quaint room still stages some wild action on its 10 tables. Players can earn $2 per hour in comps—about double what they can pull down in most rooms. A $4 maximum rake and big-screen TV add to the attraction. The little den on Fremont Street still retains the flavor of Old Vegas.

The hotel at Binion's closed in 2009, but the restaurants remain open, including the **Top of Binion's Steakhouse** (5pm-10pm daily, $40-55), famous for its Fremont Street views, aged steaks, and chicken-fried lobster appetizer.

Golden Nugget

Restaurants: Vic & Anthony's, Chart House, Grotto, Lillie's Asian Cuisine, Red Sushi, Cadillac Mexican Kitchen, Buffet, The Grille, Claim Jumper, Starbucks
Entertainment: 52 Fridays
Attractions: Hand of Faith, shark tank
Nightlife: Rush Lounge, Troy Liquor Bar, H2O Bar at the Tank, Claude's Bar, Ice Bar, Bar 46, Cadillac Tequila Bar, Stage Bar

The ★ **Golden Nugget** (129 E. Fremont St., 702/385-7111, www.goldennugget. com, $129-249) beckons diners and gamblers with gold leaf and a 61-pound gold nugget in the lobby. Landry's, the restaurant chain and Nugget owner since 2005, has maintained and restored the hotel's opulence, investing $300 million for casino expansion, more restaurants, and a newer 500-room hotel tower. Rooms are appointed in dark wood and warm autumn hues.

If you don't feel like swimming with the sharks in the poker room, you can get up close and personal with their finned namesakes at the **Golden Nugget Pool** (9am-6pm daily, free), an outdoor pool with a three-story waterslide that takes riders through the hotel's huge aquarium, home to sharks, rays, and other exotic marinelife. Bathers can also swim up to the aquarium for a face-to-face with the aquatic predators. Waterfalls and lush landscaping help make this one of the world's best hotel pools.

Sights
Gondola Rides

When in a facsimile of Venice do as the Venetians do, and let a gondolier serenade you in the **indoor gondolas** (Venetian, 3355 Las Vegas Blvd. S., 702/607-3982, www.venetian.com, 10am-11pm Sun.-Thurs., 10am-midnight Fri.-Sat., $29) that skirt the Grand Canal Shoppes inside The Venetian under the mall's painted-sky ceiling fresco for a half mile; **outdoor gondolas** (11am-10pm daily, weather permitting, $29) skim The Venetian's 31,000-square-foot lagoon for 12 minutes, giving riders a unique perspective

on the Las Vegas Strip. Plying the waters at regular intervals, the realistic-looking gondolas seat four, but couples who don't want to share a boat can pay double.

Secret Garden and Dolphin Habitat

It's no mirage—those really are pure-white tigers lounging in their own plush resort on The Mirage casino floor. Legendary Las Vegas magicians Siegfried and Roy, who have dedicated much of their lives to preserving big cats, opened the **Secret Garden** (Mirage, 3400 Las Vegas Blvd. S., 702/791-7188, www.miragehabitat.com, 10am-6pm daily, $22 adults, $17 age 4-12, free under 4) in 1990. In addition to the milky-furred tigers, the garden is home to blue-eyed, black-striped white tigers as well as black panthers, lions, and leopards. Although caretakers don't "perform" with the animals, if your visit is well-timed you could see the cats playing, wrestling, and even swimming in their pristine waterfall-fed pools.

Visit the Atlantic bottlenoses at the **Dolphin Habitat** right next door, also in the middle of The Mirage's palm trees and jungle foliage. The aquatic mammals don't perform on cue either, but they're natural hams and often interact with their visitors, nodding their heads in response to trainer questions, turning aerial somersaults, and "walking" on their tails across the water. An underwater viewing area provides an unusual perspective into the dolphins' world.

High Roller

The dazzling view from 50 stories up is unparalleled on jumbo Ferris wheel the **High Roller** (Linq, 3545 Las Vegas Blvd. S., 702/777-2782 or 866/574-3851, www.caesars.com/linq/high-roller, 11:30am-2:30am daily, adult $22-32, youth $9-19). Ride at night for a perfect panorama of the famous Strip skyline. Ride at dusk for inspiring glimpses of the desert sun setting over the mountains. Forty passengers fit in each of the High Roller's 28 compartments, lessening wait time for the half-hour ride circuit. With **Happy Half Hour** tickets (noon-1am daily, age 21 and up, $52) passengers can board special bar cars and enjoy unlimited cocktails during the ride. Book online to save on tickets.

★ Fremont Street Experience

With the rise of the Las Vegas Strip in the last quarter of the 20th century, downtown Las Vegas was all but forgotten. That changed in 1995 with the opening of the **Fremont Street Experience** (702/678-5600, www.vegasexperience.com), an ambitious plan to transform downtown and its tacky "Glitter Gulch" reputation into a pedestrian-friendly enclave. Highlighted by a four-block-long canopy festooned with 12 million light-emitting diodes 90 feet in the air, the Fremont Street Experience is downtown's answer to the Strip's erupting volcanoes and fantastic dancing fountains. The canopy, dubbed Viva Vision, runs atop Fremont Street between North Main Street and North 4th Street.

Once an hour between dusk and 1am, the promenade goes dark and all heads lift toward the canopy, supported by massive concrete pillars. For six minutes, visitors are enthralled by the multimedia shows that chronicle Western history, span the careers of classic rock bands, or transport viewers to fantasy worlds. Viva Vision runs several different shows daily.

Before and after the light shows, strolling buskers sing for their supper, artists create five-minute masterpieces, caricaturists airbrush souvenir portraits, and (sometimes scantily) costumed characters pose for photos. Tipping is all but mandatory ($2-5 is fair). Fremont Street hosts top musical acts, including some A-listers during big Las Vegas weekends such as National Finals Rodeo, NASCAR

Top to bottom: the Fremont Street Experience; the Neon Museum and Boneyard; Las Vegas Springs Preserve.

races, and New Year's. The adjacent Fremont East Entertainment District houses quirky eateries, clubs, and art galleries.

Neon Museum and Boneyard

Book a one-hour guided tour of the **Neon Museum and Boneyard** (770 Las Vegas Blvd. N., 702/387-6366, www.neonmuseum.org, 8:30am-10pm daily, $19-26 adults, $15-22 students, seniors, and veterans) and take a trip to Las Vegas's more recent past. The boneyard displays 200 old neon signs that were used to advertise casinos, restaurants, bars, and even a flower shop and a dry cleaner. Several have been restored to their former glory and are illuminated during the more costly nighttime tours. The boneyard is not open for self-guided exploration, but the **visitors center,** housed in the scallop-shaped lobby of the historical La Concha Motel, offers a prime example of Googie architecture and can serve as a base for a do-it-yourself tour of restored neon displayed as public art. A word of caution: The neighborhood surrounding the museum and public neon signs is a bit sketchy after dark.

Mob Museum

The **Museum of Organized Crime and Law Enforcement** (300 Stewart Ave., 702/229-2734, http://themobmuseum.org, 9am-9pm daily, $24, seniors, military, law enforcement, and teachers $18, age 11-17 $14, under age 11 free) chronicles Las Vegas's Mafia past and the cops and agents who finally ran the wiseguys out of town. The museum is inside the city's downtown post office and courthouse, appropriately the site of the 1951 Kefauver Hearing investigating organized crime.

Displays include the barber chair where Albert Anastasia was gunned down while getting a haircut, as well as an examination of the violence, ceremony, and hidden meanings behind Mafia "hits," all against a grisly background—the wall from Chicago's St. Valentine's Day Massacre that spelled the end of six members of Bugs Moran's crew and one hanger-on.

Downtown Arts District

Centered at South Main Street and East Charleston Boulevard, the district gives art lovers a concentration of galleries to suit any taste, plus an eclectic mix of shops, eateries, and other surprises. The **Arts Factory** (107 E. Charleston Blvd., 702/383-3133, www.theartsfactory.com), a two-story redbrick industrial building, is the district's birthplace. It hosts exhibitions, drawing classes, and poetry readings. Tenants include a toy shop, a yoga studio, a roller-skate store, and studios belonging to artists working in every medium and genre imaginable. One downstairs space, **Jana's RedRoom** (11am-7pm Wed.-Sun. and by appointment), displays and sells canvases by local artists.

Virtually all the galleries and other paeans to urban pop culture in the district participate in Las Vegas's **First Friday** (https://ffflv.org, 5pm-11pm 1st Fri. each month) event, which includes wine receptions, pub crawls, art lessons, and plenty of exhibits.

Las Vegas Springs Preserve

The **Las Vegas Springs Preserve** (333 S. Valley View Blvd., 702/822-7700, www.springspreserve.org, 10am-6pm daily, $19 adults, $17 students and over age 64, $11 ages 5-17, free under age 5) is where Las Vegas began, at least from a Eurocentric viewpoint. More than 100 years ago, the first nonnatives in the Las Vegas Valley—Mormon missionaries from Salt Lake City—stumbled on this clear artesian spring. Of course, the native Paiute and Pueblo people knew about the springs and exploited them millennia before the Mormons arrived. You can see examples of their tools, pottery, and houses at the site, now a monument to environmental stewardship, historical preservation, and geographic discovery. The preserve is home to lizards, rabbits, foxes, scorpions, bats, and more. The nature-minded will love the cactus, rose, and sage gardens, and there's even an occasional cooking demonstration using the desert-friendly fruits, vegetables, and herbs grown here.

Nevada State Museum
Visitors can spend hours studying Mojave and Spring Mountains ecology, southern Nevada wildlife (both contemporary and prehistoric), and local mining and railroad history at the **Nevada State Museum** (309 S. Valley View Blvd., 702/486-5205, http://nvculture.org, 9am-5pm Tues.-Sun., $19 adults, included in admission to the Springs Preserve, $17 college students and ages 65 and over, $11 ages 5-17, free under 5). Permanent exhibits describe southern Nevada's role in warfare, mining, and atomic weaponry and include skeletons of a Columbian mammoth, which roamed the Nevada deserts 20,000 years ago, and the ichthyosaur, a whalelike remnant of the Triassic period. The *Nevada from Dusk to Dawn* exhibit explores the nocturnal lives of the area's animal species. Other exhibits trace the contributions of Las Vegas's gaming, marketing, and business communities.

Atomic Testing Museum
Members of the "duck and cover" generation will find plenty to spark Cold War memories at the **Atomic Testing Museum** (755 E. Flamingo Rd., 702/794-5151, www.nationalatomictestingmuseum.org, 10am-5pm Mon.-Sat., noon-5pm Sun., $22). Las Vegas embraced its role as ground zero in the development of the nation's atomic and nuclear deterrents after World War II. Business leaders welcomed defense contractors to town, and casinos hosted bomb-watching parties as nukes were detonated at the Nevada Test Site, a huge swath of desert 65 miles (105 km) away. One ingenious marketer promoted the Miss Atomic Bomb beauty pageant in an era when patriotism overcame concerns about radiation.

The museum presents atomic history without bias, walking a fine line between appreciation of the work of nuclear scientists, politicians, and the military and the catastrophic consequences their activities and decisions could have wrought. The museum's best permanent feature is a short video in the Ground Zero Theatre, a multimedia simulation of an actual atomic explosion. The theater, a replica of an observation bunker, is rigged for motion, sound, and rushing air.

One gallery helps visitors put atomic energy milestones in historical perspective, along with the age's impact on 1950s and 1960s pop culture. Another permanent exhibit explains the effects of radiation and how it is tracked and measured. Just as relevant today are the lectures and traveling exhibits that the museum hosts. Computer simulators, high-speed photographs, Geiger counters, and other testing and safety equipment, along with first-person accounts, add to the museum's visit-worthiness.

Nightlife and Entertainment
★ Shows
Whatever kind of live entertainment you've ever wanted to experience, chances are you can find it in Vegas, where shows may feature music, dancing, comedy, magic, circus acrobats, burlesque pageantry, and in all statistical likelihood, all of the above. Las Vegas is one of the best places in the world to find a spectacle. Pick your poison.

Cirque du Soleil
Cirque du Soleil's surreal brand of artsy acrobatic spectacle has so thrived in Las Vegas there are six distinct productions to choose from. The first Cirque show in Las Vegas, *Mystère* (Treasure Island, 3300 Las Vegas Blvd. S., 702/894-7722 or 800/392-1999, www.cirquedusoleil.com/mystere, 7pm and 9:30pm Sat.-Wed., $76-149) most resembles a traditional circus, with trapeze artists, feats of strength, and clowns.

Two Cirque productions feature water acrobatics. Perfectly sculpted specimens of human athleticism and beauty flip, swim, dive, and show off their muscles. *O* (Bellagio, 3600 Las Vegas Blvd. S., 866/983-4279, www.cirquedusoleil.com/O, 7:30pm and 9:30pm Wed.-Sun., $107-187) gets its title from the French word for water, *eau,* pronounced like the letter O in English. The huge production features a $90 million set, and a 1.5-million-gallon (5.7-million-l) pool of water. Aquatic stream-of-unconsciousness *Le Rêve* (Wynn, 3131 Las Vegas Blvd. S., 702/770-9966, www.wynnlasvegas.com, 7pm and 9:30pm Fri.-Tues., $115-175) depicts a romantically conflicted woman's fevered dream (*rêve* in French). There's not a bad seat in this the theater in the round; those in the first couple of rows are in the "splash zone" of clowns and acrobats.

Martial arts, acrobatics, puppetry, and flashy pyrotechnics highlight *Kà* (MGM Grand, 3799 Las Vegas Blvd. S., 702/531-3826, www.mgmgrand.com, 7pm and 9:30pm Sat.-Wed., $75-209), which tells the story of separated twins seeking their fate via battle scenes played out on floating, rotating platforms. The show's title was inspired by the ancient Egyptian belief of *ka,* in which every human has a spiritual duplicate.

The cabaret-style *Zumanity* (New York New York, 3790 Las Vegas Blvd. S., 866/983-4279, www.cirquedusoleil.com/zumanity, 7pm and 9:30pm Fri.-Tues., $75-145) show makes no pretense of story line, but instead takes audience members through a succession of sexual and topless fantasies ranging from teasing to torrid—cellmates, sexual awakening, bathing beauties, ménage à trois, and more for the uninhibited over-18 crowd.

Finally, the breathtaking visual artistry of Cirque du Soleil is performed to Beatles music in *LOVE* (Mirage, 3400 Las Vegas Blvd. S., 866/983-4279, www.cirquedusoleil.com/love, 7pm and 9:30pm Tues.-Sat., $86-196). Dancers, aerial acrobats, and other performers interpret the Fab Four's lyrics and recordings, playing off a custom soundscape made from original master tapes from Abbey Road Studios.

Blue Man Group

In a category of its own since debuting in Vegas in 2000, the **Blue Man Group** (Luxor, 3900 Las Vegas Blvd. S., 702/262-4400 or 877/386-4658, www.blueman.com, 7pm and 9:30pm daily, $69-128) famously features a group of bald men, painted blue, and banging on instruments made of PVC tubes. It continues to wow audiences with its thought-provoking, quirkily hilarious gags and percussion performances.

Live Music

Rather than tour, high-wattage stars from Sinatra to Elvis have long made a habit of taking **musical residencies** in a Vegas venue and letting the fans come to them. Generational music icons often

commit to long stays in Sin City, typically performing shows on weekends for weeks, months, and occasionally years. Recent stars have included Gwen Stefani, Bruno Mars, Mariah Carey, Billy Idol, Lady Gaga, James Taylor, Drake, Cher, Aerosmith, and Boyz II Men.

Check these venues to see who's in town during your visit: **Park Theater at MGM Grand** (3770 Las Vegas Blvd. S., www.parkmgm.com), **Zappos Theater at Planet Hollywood** (3667 Las Vegas Blvd. S., www.caesars.com), and **The Coliseum at Caesar's Palace** (3570 Las Vegas Blvd. S., www.caesars.com).

Interactive Shows

Fans of comic books, sci-fi, fantasy, and movies may pick from a growing list of immersive, interactive experiences. One virtual reality experience immerses teams of four (10 years and older) in a full-body, multimedia *Star Wars* adventure at **Secrets of the Empire** in the **Grand Canal Shoppes** (Venetian, 3377 Las Vegas Blvd. S., 385/323-0090 10am-11pm Sun.-Thurs., 10am-midnight Fri.-Sat., $32-37). Gear up to go undercover as Imperial Stormtroopers, solving puzzles and escaping traps, on a mission to steal plans vital to the rebel cause.

Train to become a Marvel Avenger at the Scientific Training and Tactical Intelligence Operative Network center, otherwise known as **Avengers S.T.A.T.I.O.N.** (Treasure Island, 3300 Las Vegas Blvd. S., 702/894-7722, www.stationattraction.com, 10am-10pm daily, $34, age 4-11 $24). You get to see lots of to-scale Iron Man suits and do things like see how your hands measure up to the Hulk's.

If Las Vegas strikes you as a proper place to train for the zombie apocalypse, brave the Fremont Street Experience attraction **Fear the Walking Dead** (425 Fremont St., 702/947-8342, www.vegasexperience.com, 1pm-1am Sun.-Thurs., 1pm-2am Fri.-Sat., $30). The 20-minute walk-through attraction is

Cirque du Soleil's "O"

part haunted house, part escape room, part video game.

Pound on the table with your goblet and let loose a hearty "huzzah!" to cheer your king to victory at the **Tournament of Kings** (Excalibur, 3580 Las Vegas Blvd. S., 702/597-7600, www.excalibur.com, 6pm and 8:30pm Sat.-Sun. and Wed.-Thurs., 6 pm Fri. and Mon., $76). Pledge your banners and back your hero as he participates in jousts, swordfights, and riding contests at this festival hosted by King Arthur and Merlin. This one's a dinner show, with a medieval feast eaten by hand, while Arthur and Merlin are called upon to save the day. It's one of the best family shows in Las Vegas.

Lounge Acts

The Vegas lounge act is the butt of a few jokes and more than one satire, but they offer some of the best values in town— a night's entertainment for the price of a few drinks and a small cover charge. Every hotel in Las Vegas worth its salt has a lounge. These acts are listed in the free entertainment magazines and the *Las Vegas Review-Journal*'s helpful website, but unless you're familiar with the performers, it's the luck of the draw: They list only the entertainer's name, venue, and showtimes.

For reliable shows with that Old Vegas feel, try crooner **Matt Goss** (Mirage, 3400 Las Vegas Blvd. S., 702/791-7111, www.mirage.com, 7:30pm Tues., Fri.-Sun., $18-88), a worthy and dapper heir to Darin, Damone, and Sinatra. Or there is the thinking person's singing impressionist, **Gordie Brown** (Hooters, 115 E. Tropicana Ave., 702/739-9000, www.gordiebrown.com, 7pm Wed.-Thurs. and Sat.-Mon., $59-80) who pokes fun at Vegas legends while honoring them with his considerable song skills.

To relive the golden era when Frank, Dean, Sammy, and Joey ruled the Strip, hit **The Rat Pack Is Back** (Tuscany, 255 E. Flamingo Rd., 702/947-5981, www.ratpackisback.com, 7:30pm Mon.-Sat.,

$60-66), but if you bow to the King, **All Shook Up** (Planet Hollywood, 3667 Las Vegas Blvd. S., 702/260-7200, www.vtheaterboxoffice.com, 6pm daily, $60-70) is the only all-Elvis impersonator show on the Strip, surveying Elvis's hits from rock-and-roll pioneer to his time as a movie idol. The intimate 300-seat showroom makes every seat a good one.

Adult Revues

A sleazy, foulmouthed ringmaster leads a cast of world-class performers singing, dancing, and committing wild feats of acrobatics, magic, and striptease in **Absinthe** (Caesars Palace, 3570 Las Vegas Blvd. S., 855/234-7469, www.absinthevegas.com, 8pm and 10pm daily, $99-159). Check your inhibitions at the door, lest you find yourself the target of raunchy jokes. The in-the-round audience configuration assures there's not a bad seat in the house, but with VIP tickets, the performers are, sometimes literally, right in your lap.

From the producers of *Absinthe*, **Opium** (Cosmopolitan, 3708 Las Vegas Blvd. S., 702/698-7000, www.cosmopolitanlasvegas.com, 8pm and 10pm Wed.-Sun., 8pm Mon. and Thurs., $79-129) invites you to stowaway on an interstellar burlesque show of R-rated joke, singers, and specialty acts that you will never see on *America's Got Talent*.

Based on the wildly popular movies, **Magic Mike Live** (Hard Rock, 4455 Paradise Rd., 800/745-3000, www.magicmikelivelasvegas.com, 7pm and 10pm Wed.-Sun., $55-165) puts men front and center, starring baby oil-slathered hunks in tight jeans, tear-away T-shirts, and less, strutting around a facsimile of Club Domina.

Comedy

Nearly gone are the days of top-name comedians as resident headliners. However, A-listers like Ron White, George Lopez, Jerry Seinfeld, Wayne Brady, and others still make regular appearances as part of the **Aces of Comedy** (Mirage, 3400 Las Vegas Blvd. S., 702/791-7111, www.mirage.com, 7:30pm-10pm Fri.-Sat., $50-60).

The journeymen and up-and-coming have half a dozen places to land gigs when they're in town. Among the best are the **Comedy Cellar** (Rio, 3700 W. Flamingo Rd., 702/777-2782, www.comedycellar.com/las-vegas, 7pm and 9pm Tues.-Sun.), **Brad Garrett's Comedy Club** (3799 Las Vegas Blvd. S., 866/740-7711, www.bradgarrettcomedy.com, 8pm daily, $43-65, plus $22 when Garrett performs) at the MGM Grand, **L.A. Comedy Club** (Stratosphere, 2000 Las Vegas Blvd. S., 702/380-7777 or 800/998-6937, www.thelacomedyclub.com, 8pm daily, 6pm and 10pm shows some nights, $47-64), and **Laugh Factory** (Tropicana, 3801 Las Vegas Blvd. S., 702/739-2222, www.laughfactory.com, 8:30pm and 10:30pm daily, $38-55).

Magic Shows
Magic shows are nearly as ubiquitous as comedy, with the more accomplished, such as **Penn & Teller** (Rio, 3700 W. Flamingo Rd., 702/777-2782, www.pennandteller.com, 9pm Sat.-Wed., $77-97), **Criss Angel** (Planet Hollywood, 3667 Las Vegas Blvd. S., 702/785-5555, https://crissangel.com/planet-hollywood-mindfreak, 7pm, Wed.-Sun., 9:30pm Sat., $69-139), and **David Copperfield** (MGM Grand, 3799 Las Vegas Blvd. S., 866/740-7711, www.davidcopperfield.com, 7pm and 9:30pm Sun.-Fri., 4pm, 7pm, and 9:30pm Sat., $78-123), playing long-term gigs in their own showrooms.

The best smaller-scale magicians also have the distinction of being kid-friendly. With a plaid suit, good manners, and a silly grin, **Mac King** (Harrah's, 3475 Las Vegas Blvd. S., 866/983-4279, www.mackingshow.com, 1pm and 3pm Tues.-Sat., $36-47) has tricks and banter skewed enough to make even the most jaded teenager laugh. Two *America's Got Talent* alumni have taken up residency at Planet Hollywood. **Nathan Burton Comedy Magic** (Planet Hollywood, 3667 Las Vegas Blvd. S., 866/919-7472, www.nathanburton.com, 4pm daily, $50-60) serves up epic disappearing acts, while **Murray the Magician** (Planet Hollywood, 3667 Las Vegas Blvd. S., 866/919-7472, www.murraymagic.com, 4pm Sat.-Mon. and Thurs., $60-80) mixes comedy banter with his sleight of hand.

Rides and Games
Daredevils will delight in the vertigo-inducing thrill rides on the observation deck at the **Stratosphere Tower** (2000 Las Vegas Blvd. S., 702/383-5210, www.stratospherehotel.com, 10am-1am Sun.-Thurs., 10am-2am Fri.-Sat., $15-120). The newest ride, SkyJump Las Vegas ($120), invites the daring to plunge into space for a 15-second free fall culminating in a gentle landing. A handful of similarly thrilling attractions are $25 each, including the elevator ride to the top of the tower.

For an up-close, high-speed view of the Fremont Street Experience canopy and iconic casino signs, take a zoom on **SlotZilla** (425 Fremont St., 702/678-5780, www.vegasexperience.com, 1pm-1am Sun.-Thurs., 1pm-2am Fri.-Sat., $25-45), a 1,750-foot-long (533.4-m) zip line that takes off from the world's largest slot machine (only in Vegas, right?). A lower, slower version is also available. Fly before 6pm to save $5 per ride.

Exotics Racing (6925 Speedway Blvd., Ste. C-105, 702/802-5662, www.exoticsracing.com, 7am-8pm Mon.-Fri., 8am-7pm Sat.-Sun., $300-500 for five laps), **Dream Racing** (7000 Las Vegas Blvd. N., 702/599-5199, www.dreamracing.com, $199-500 for five laps), and **Speed Vegas** (14200 Las Vegas Blvd. S., 888/341-7133, www.speedvegas.com, $39-99 per lap) offer similar pedal-to-the-metal thrills in Porsches, Ferraris, Lamborghinis, and more. All offer add-ons such as videos of your drive, passenger rates, and ride-alongs with professional drivers.

★ **Richard Petty Driving Experience**
Okay road-tripper, if you're ready to take the wheel of a 600-hp stock car, check out the **Richard Petty Driving Experience** (Las Vegas Motor Speedway, 7000 Las Vegas Blvd. N., 800/237-3889, www.drivepetty.com, days and times vary, $109-3,200). The Rookie Experience ($499) lets NASCAR wannabes put the stock car through its paces for eight laps around the 1.5-mile (2.4-km) tri-oval after extensive safety training. To feel the thrill without the responsibility, opt for the three-lap ride-along ($109) in a two-seat stock car with a professional driver at the wheel.

Spectator Sports

Legal sportsbooks and an innate talent for spectacle have long made Las Vegas a professional sports mecca, but the arrival of the NFL in 2020 will be the feather in the gambling city's cap. That's pending completion of $2 billion retractable-roof stadium built to house the **Las Vegas Raiders** (www.raiders.com), the hallowed franchise moving here from Oakland.

The city has already gone gaga over the **Vegas Golden Knights** (T-Mobile Arena, 3780 Las Vegas Blvd. S., 702/645-4259, www.nhl.com/goldenknights), Sin City's first major-league franchise, with the NHL. The team advanced to the Stanley Cup finals in its first ever season, making it the most successful expansion franchise in the history of forever. Tickets are hard to come by: check the resale sites, if you're willing to pay a premium.

But the sport that put Las Vegas on the map is prizefighting. Las Vegas retains the title as heavyweight boxing champion of the world, and mixed martial arts has come on doubly strong. Nevada's legalized sports betting, its history, and the facilities at the **MGM Grand Garden Arena** (3799 Las Vegas Blvd. S., www.mgmresorts.com), **Mandalay Bay Events Center** (3950 Las Vegas Blvd. S., www.mandalaybay.com), **T-Mobile Arena** (3780 Las Vegas Blvd. S., http://

www.t-mobilearena.com), and other locations make it a natural for the biggest matches. For the megafights, expect to dole out big bucks to get inside the premier venues. Check the venues' websites for tickets.

For a fight experience without the bling, fans can find a lower card pretty much every month from March to October at the Hard Rock, Sam's Town, Sunset Station, Palms, or another midsize arena or showroom. The fighters are hungry, the matches are entertaining, and the cost is low, with tickets priced $15-100.

Regular **NASCAR** races go down at **Las Vegas Motor Speedway** (7000 Las Vegas Blvd. N., 702/644-4444, www.lvms.com), which boasts a 1.5-mile (2.4-km) tri-oval for NASCAR races, bolstered by the Neon Garage interactive fan experience in the speedway's infield, bringing fans up close with their favorite drivers and their crews. The racing omniplex also features a quarter-mile (0.4-km) strip for dragsters; a paved oval for modifieds, late models, bandoleros, legends, and bombers; and a half mile (0.8-km) clay oval for off-roaders. There's also a motocross track and a road course.

Golf

A world-class golfing destination, Las Vegas is chock-full of picturesque courses. The only course open to the public on the Strip is **Bali Hai** (5160 Las Vegas Blvd. S., 888/427-6678, www.balihaigolfclub.com, $149-189), next to Mandalay Bay on the south end of casino row. The South Pacific theme includes lots of lush green tropical foliage, deep azure ponds, and black volcanic outcroppings. There's plenty of water to contend with at **Siena Golf Club** (10575 Siena Monte Ave., 702/341-9200, www.sienagolfclub.com, $85). Six small lakes, deep fairway bunkers, and desert scrub provide significant challenges off the tee. The first Las Vegas course to adopt an ecofriendly xeriscape design, **Painted Desert** (5555 Painted Mirage

Side Trip to Hoover Dam

The 1,400-mile (2,253-km) Colorado River has been carving and gouging great canyons and valleys with red sediment-laden waters for 10 million years. For 10,000 years Native Americans, the Spanish, and Mormon settlers coexisted with the fitful river, rebuilding after spring floods and withstanding the droughts that often reduced the mighty waterway to a muddy trickle in fall. But a 1905 flood convinced the Bureau of Reclamation to "reclaim" the West, primarily by building dams and canals. The most ambitious of these was Hoover Dam: 40 million cubic yards (30.5 million cubic m) of reinforced concrete, turbines, and transmission lines.

Hoover Dam remains an engineering marvel, attracting millions of visitors each year. It makes an interesting half-day escape from the glitter of Las Vegas, only 30 miles (48 km) to the north. The one-hour **Dam Tour** (every 30 minutes, 9:30am-3:30pm daily, $30 age 8 and over) offers a guided exploration of its power plant and walkways, along with admission to the visitors center. The two-hour **Power Plant Tour** ($15 adults, $12 seniors, children, and military, uniformed military and children under 4 free) focuses on the dam's construction and engineering through multimedia presentations, exhibits, docent talks, and a power plant tour.

Getting There

The bypass bridge diverts traffic away from Hoover Dam, saving time and headaches for both drivers and dam visitors. Still, the 35-mile (56-km) drive from central Las Vegas to a parking lot at the dam will take 45 minutes or more. From the Strip, I-15 South connects with I-215 southeast of the airport, and I-215 East takes drivers to US-93 in Henderson. Remember that US-93 shares the roadway with US-95 and I-515 till well past Henderson. Going south on US-93, exit at NV-172 to the dam. Note that this route is closed on the Arizona side; drivers continuing on to the Grand Canyon must retrace NV-172 to US-93 and cross the bypass bridge. A parking garage ($10) is convenient to the visitors center and dam tours, but free parking is available at turnouts on both sides of the dam for those willing to walk.

Rd., 702/645-2570, www.painteddesertgc.com, $45-90) uses cacti, mesquite, and other desert plants to separate its links-style fairways. The 6,323-yard (5,782-m), par 72 course isn't especially challenging. All are eminently playable and fair, although the dry heat makes the greens fast and the city's valley location can make for some havoc-wreaking winds in the spring.

Shopping

Unless you're looking for a specific item or brand, you can't go wrong browsing the shopping center in your casino/hotel. However, Vegas never fails to offer a few uniquely wondrous, lavish, or creative shopping experiences.

Caesars Palace initiated the concept of spectacle shopping in 1992 when it unveiled the **Forum Shops** (3570 Las Vegas Blvd. S., 702/893-3807, www.caesars.com, 10am-11pm Sun.-Thurs., 10am-midnight Fri.-Sat.). Top-brand luxury stores coexist with fashionable hipster boutiques amid some of the best people-watching on the Strip. There's an hourly show, you'll find one of only two spiral escalators in the United States, and you can check out the feeding of the fish in the big saltwater aquarium twice daily.

Even browsing, you'll get a memorable experience at The Venetian's **Grand Canal Shoppes** (Venetian, 3377 Las Vegas Blvd. S., 702/414-4525, www.grandcanalshoppes.com, 10am-11pm Sun.-Thurs., 10am-midnight Fri.-Sat.) reproducing the feel of Venice right down to the gondolas. Its "Streetmosphere" includes strolling minstrels and specialty acts, and many of these entertainers find their way to St. Mark's Square for seemingly impromptu performances.

To go really high end, Hermès, Prada, Rolex, and Loro Piana count themselves among the tenants at Steve Wynn's **Esplanade** (Wynn/Encore, 3131 Las Vegas Blvd. S., 702/770-7000, www.wynnlasvegas.com, 10am-11pm Sun.-Thurs., 10am-midnight Fri.-Sat.). Wide, curved skylights, fragrant flowers, and delicate artwork create a pleasant window-shopping experience.

Perfectly situated in the flourishing urban arts district, the **Downtown Container Park** (707 E. Fremont St., 702/359-9982, www.downtowncontainerpark.com, 11am-9pm Mon.-Thurs., 11am-10pm Fri.-Sat., 11am-8pm Sun.) packs 40 boutiques, galleries, bars, and bistros into their own shipping containers.

Food

As with most things, casinos lead the way in the Las Vegas dining scene. Check casino coverage for ideas on which types of food may be available in your vicinity. Below are a few non-casino options worth checking out, as well as a handful of can't-miss dining destinations that best represent the classic Vegas excursion.

Upper Strip

If you're going to make an effort to go to breakfast, make it ★ **The Egg & I** (4533 W. Sahara Ave., Ste. 5, 702/364-9686, http://theeggworks.com, 6am-3pm daily, $10-20). The local institution offers stuff like banana muffins and stuffed French toast in addition to eggs, but if you don't order one of the huge omelets, you're just being stubborn.

All-you-can-eat buffets are a timeless Vegas tradition, but they're not made for bargain hunters anymore. For the most decadent start to your day, head over to Bally's **Sterling Brunch Buffet** (3645 Las Vegas Blvd. S., 702/967-7258, www.caesars.com, 9:30am-2:30pm Sun.,

$95-125), the only fine dining buffet in town for the likes of lobster-tail, rack of lamb, caviar, truffle potatoes, Belgian waffles, and Perrier-Jouet champagne.

For upscale dining with a view, the 360-seat and 360-degree **Top of the World** (Stratosphere, 2000 Las Vegas Blvd. S., 702/380-7711 or 800/998-6937, www.topoftheworldlv.com, 11am-11pm daily, $50-80), on the 106th floor of Stratosphere Tower, makes a complete revolution once every 80 minutes, giving you the full city panorama from more than 800 feet above the Strip. Order the seafood fettuccine or surf-and-turf gnocchi with lobster and beef short rib.

Long a hangout for the Rat Pack, athletes, presidents, and certain Sicilian "businessmen," **Piero's** (355 Convention Center Dr., 702/369-2305, http://pieroscuisine.com, 5:30pm-10pm daily, $40-60) still attracts the celebrity set with leather booths, stone fireplace, stellar service, and assurance they won't be bothered by autograph hounds. The menu hasn't changed much since the goodfellas started coming here in the early 1980s; its Italian cuisine is heavy (and we do mean "heavy") on the veal, breading, cheese, and sauce.

Center Strip

At the Caesars Palace **Bacchanal Buffet** (3570 Las Vegas Blvd. S., 702/731-7928, www.caesars.com, 7:30am-10pm Mon.-Fri., 8am-10pm Sat.-Sun., $30-60, $15 wine, beer, and mimosa supplement), specialty dishes range from gourmet (smoked pork belly) to pub grub (Bacchanal sliders) and include plenty of international delicacies such as curry, dim sum, crepes, and more, prepared in bustling show kitchens and with many presented small-plate style.

Lower Strip

The steaks and seafood at ★ **Mon Ami Gabi** (Paris, 3655 Las Vegas Blvd. S., 702/944-4224, www.monamigabi.com, 7am-11pm daily, $35-55) are comparable to those at any fine Strip establishment—at about half the price. It's a French bistro, so you know the crepes and other lunch specials are terrific, but you're better off coming for dinner. Try the baked goat cheese appetizer.

Paris casino's **Eiffel Tower Restaurant** (Paris, 3655 Las Vegas Blvd. S., 702/948-6937, http://eiffeltowerrestaurant.com, 11:30am-3pm and 4:30pm-10:30pm Mon.-Thurs., 11:30am-3pm and 4:30pm-11pm Fri., 10am-3pm and 4:30pm-11pm Sat., 10am-3pm and 4:30pm-10:30pm Sun., $60-100) hovers an elegant 100 feet above the Strip. Order the soufflé, have a glass of wine, and bask in the romantic piano strains as the bilingual culinary staff perform delicate French culinary feats with Bellagio's fountains as a backdrop.

If you're really hankering for fish, chef Rick Moonen is to be commended for his advocacy of sustainable seafood harvesting practices, and his ★ **RM Seafood** (Mandalay Bay, 3950 Las Vegas Blvd. S., 702/632-9300, http://rmseafood.com, 11:30am-11pm daily, $45-90) practices what he preaches. You can almost hear the tide-rigging whir and the mahogany creak in the yacht-club restaurant setting.

If you're looking for beer and comfort food, try one of the city's better gastropubs. Chef Shawn McClain blurs the lines between avant-garde and comfort food at **Libertine Social** (Mandalay Bay, 3950 Las Vegas Blvd. S., 702/632-7558, www.mandalaybay.com, 5pm-10:30pm daily, $35-55). The best dishes revolve around cured meats. Start with the crab and spinach dip, then pick one cured meat and pair it with roasted cauliflower.

For a more modern take on a steak house, check Tom Colicchio's **Craftsteak** (MGM Grand, 3799 Las Vegas Blvd. S., 702/891-7318, www.craftsteaklasvegas.com, 5pm-10pm Sun.-Thurs., 5pm-10:30pm Fri.-Sat., $50-75). The care used by the small farms from which it buys ingredients is evident in the full flavor of the excellently seasoned steaks and chops. Spacious with gold, umber, and light woodwork, Craftsteak's decor is conducive to good times and neither overbearing nor intimidating.

Michael Mina Pub 1842 (MGM Grand, 3799 Las Vegas Blvd. S., 702/891-3922, www.michaelmina.net, 11:30am-10pm Thurs.-Mon., $20-35) delivers tasty burgers and barbecue. Better yet, order appetizers and sides, then share the joy of smoked salmon dip, soft pretzels and beer cheese, and oniony mac-and-cheese.

For the most Vegas of dining experiences, set time aside for the Cosmopolitan's reinvention of the social club. Equal parts supper club, nightclub, and jazz club, ★ **Rose. Rabbit. Lie.** (Cosmopolitan, 3708 Las Vegas Blvd. S., 702/698-7440, www.cosmopolitanlasvegas.com, 6pm-midnight Wed.-Sat., $70-125) serves a mostly tapas-style menu. Sharing is encouraged, with about four small plates per person satisfying most appetites, especially if you splurge on the chocolate terrarium for dessert. The supper club experience includes varied entertainment throughout the evening (mostly singers, but sometimes magicians and acrobats), but no one will blame you for focusing on the food and cocktails.

Downtown

Downtown's **The Buffet** (Golden Nugget, 129 E. Fremont St., 702/385-8152, www.goldennugget.com, 7am-10pm daily, breakfast $15, lunch $16, dinner $21-28, weekend brunch $22) leaves nothing to be desired, with extras like an omelet station, calzone, and a fine banana cake putting it a cut above the ordinary buffet.

On the affordable side, the **Garden Court Buffet** (Main Street Station, 200 N. Main St., 702/387-1896, www.mainstreetcasino.com, 7am-3pm and 4pm-9pm Mon.-Thurs., 7am-3pm and 4pm-10pm Fri.-Sun., breakfast $8, lunch $9, dinner $12-15, Fri. seafood $23-26) will satisfy your taste buds and your bank account. The fare is mostly standard, with some specialties designed to appeal to the casino's Asian and Pacific Islander target market.

Restaurant holdovers from Old Vegas add plenty of historical character to the city's dining options. Fronted by ex-mob mouthpiece and former Las Vegas mayor Oscar Goodman, **Oscar's** (Plaza, 1 S. Main St., 702/386-7227, www.oscarslv.com, 4pm-10pm daily, $40-70) is dedicated to hizzoner's favorite things in life—beef, booze, and broads. With dishes named, apparently, for former wiseguy clients—Fat Herbie, Crazy Phil, Joe Pig, etc., you're in for an Old Vegas treat, full of the scents of leather, cigars, and broiling steaks.

Off Strip

The perfectly cooked steaks and attentive service that once attracted Frank Sinatra, Nat "King" Cole, Natalie Wood, and Elvis are still trademarks at **Golden Steer** (308 W. Sahara Ave., 702/384-4470, www.goldensteerlasvegas.com, 4:30pm-10:30pm daily, $45-65). A gold rush motif and 1960s swankiness still abide here, along with classics like crab cakes, big hunks of beef, and Caesar salad prepared tableside.

For more casual meals, leave the Strip to find ★ **Phat Phrank's** (4850 W. Sunset Rd., http://phatphranks.com, 702/247-6528, 7am-7pm Mon.-Fri., 9am-4pm Sat., $10-15) where the atmosphere is light and the fish tacos crispy and delicious. Try all three of the house salsas; they're all great complements to the offerings, especially the flavorful pork burrito and *adobada torta*.

In the budding bohemia of East Fremont Street, ★ **Le Thai** (523 E. Fremont St., 702/778-0888, www.lethaivegas.com, 11am-11pm Mon.-Thurs., 11am-midnight Fri.-Sat., 4pm-10pm Sun., $10-25) attracts a diverse clientele ranging from ex-yuppies to body-art lovers. Most come for the three-color curry, and you should too. There's nothing especially daring on the menu,

but the *pad prik, ga pow,* and garlic fried rice are better than what's found at many Strip restaurants that charge twice as much. Choose your spice level wisely; Le Thai does not mess around.

Accommodations

Casino accommodations offer the closest thing to a sure bet as you will find in Vegas (see the *Casinos* section for information). If you don't want to expose yourself or your kids to the smoke or vices on display at casinos, or need proximity to the airport, you will find plenty of choices. Note: most Strip hotels charge **resort fees** of $20-40 per night, on top of the quoted room rate.

At the high end, feel like royalty at City Center's **Waldorf Astoria** (City Center, 3752 Las Vegas Blvd. S., 800/925-3673, $205-425), the former Mandarin Oriental. Renovations are ongoing, though the City View rooms still maintain many Mandarin motifs. A master control panel in each of the room allows guests to set the lighting, temperature, and music preference.

Catering to families and vacationers seeking a more "residential" stay, **Platinum** (211 E. Flamingo Rd., 702/365-5000 or 877/211-9211, www.theplatinumhotel.com, $113-194) uses the latest technology to reduce its carbon footprint. Standard suites are an expansive 910 square feet of muted designer furnishings and accents, and they include all modern conveniences, such as high-speed Internet, high-fidelity sound systems, full kitchens, and oversize tubs.

There are several low-cost independent motels north of the Strip resorts and downtown, scattered along Las Vegas Boulevard and east of downtown along Boulder Highway. Just steps from the Fremont Street Experience, the **Downtowner** (129 N. 8th St., 702/384-1441, www.downtownerlv.com, $34-58) offers minimalist rooms in white with red, gray, and black accents. The pool and lounge areas are luxuries in this neighborhood at this price range, though you have to cross the street to get to the pool.

A reasonable choice east of the Strip, the three-story **Mardi Gras** (3500 Paradise Rd., 702/731-2020, www.mardigrasinn. com, $89-162) boasts the largest-in-class rooms, free airport shuttle, and on-site slot casino. Similarly, **Fortune Hotel & Suites** (325 E. Flamingo Rd., 703/732-9100, www.fortunelasvegas.com, $55-90) offers a free ride to and from the airport and a clean pool. Rooms are 300 square feet.

Motels along the Lower Strip are priced lower than at the resorts but higher than those to the north, reflecting premium real estate costs. Still a good bet is **Hotel Galaxy** (5201 Dean Martin Dr., 702/778-7600, www.hotelgalaxyvegas.com, $69-129), off Flamingo and convenient to the Strip and the airport. The pool is clean, and rooms come with a microwave and minifridge.

The closest hostel to the Strip, **Hostel Cat** (1236 Las Vegas Blvd. S., 702/380-6902, http://hostelcat.com, $23-40) puts the focus on group activities, organizing pub crawls, beer pong and video game tournaments, movie nights, and more. There's even a 24-hour party table where there are always interesting fellow travelers to talk to.

Six blocks east of the downtown resorts, **Las Vegas Hostel** (1322 Fremont St., 702/385-1150 or 800/550-8958, http://lasvegashostel.net, $16-41) has a swimming pool and a hot tub. The rates include a make-your-own pancake breakfast, a billiards and TV room, and wireless Internet. The hostel also arranges day trips and offers loaner bikes to explore the area on your own.

Information and Services

The **Las Vegas Convention and Visitors Authority** (3150 Paradise Rd., 702/892-0711 or 877/847-4858, www.lvcva.com, 8am-5pm daily) maintains a website of special hotel deals, show tickets, and other offers at www.lasvegas.com. One of LVCVA's priorities is filling hotel rooms. You can also call the same number for convention schedules and entertainment offerings. The **Las Vegas Chamber of Commerce** (575 Symphony Park Ave., Ste. 100, 702/641-5822, www. lvchamber.com) has a bunch of travel resources and fact sheets on its website. For-profit **Vegas.com** is a good resource for up-to-the-minute show schedules and reviews.

Santa
Barbara

Santa Barbara

Solvang

RANCHO SAN MARCOS
GOLF COURSE

154

Los Padres

National Forest

CHUMASH
PAINTED CAVE

COLD SPRING
TAVERN

OLD MISSION
SANTA BARBARA

SANTA BARBARA
BOTANIC GARDEN

Gaviota
State Park

TWIN LAKES
GOLF COURSE

SANTA
BARBARA

LOTUSLAND

Santa
Barbara

Refugio
State Beach

El Capitán
State Beach

101

SANTA BARBARA
AIRPORT

HIDDEN OAKS
GOLF COURSE

Arroyo Burro
Beach County Park

STEARNS WHARF

SEE
"DOWNTOWN
SANTA BARBARA"
MAP

PACIFIC

OCEAN

0   10 mi

0   10 km

Channel Islands
National Park

© MOON.COM

The scenic central coastline marries the sparkle of Southern California beaches with the rolling green hills and towering forests of the north.

Santa Barbara (pop. 92,101) draws frequent comparisons to Mediterranean beach resorts, and a comparable climate, architecture, and epicurean lifestyle earn its nickname: the American Riviera. Nestled against the lush slopes of a small mountain range, the tourist-friendly town benefits from sunny southern exposure, its white-sand beaches fronting the Pacific Ocean looking south.

Though a small city, strong tourism and the presence of the University of California, Santa Barbara, mean sophisticated amenities, attracting artists and exhibitions of global interest to its cultural venues. The unique combination of cultural cachet and natural beauty helps the region thrive as a getaway destination for other Southern California residents, from casual weekenders arriving by train to Hollywood elite who make the exclusive hillside community of Montecito a second home. Many visitors come seeking another fruit of Santa Barbara's similarity to southern Europe: the coastal hillsides provide ideal growing

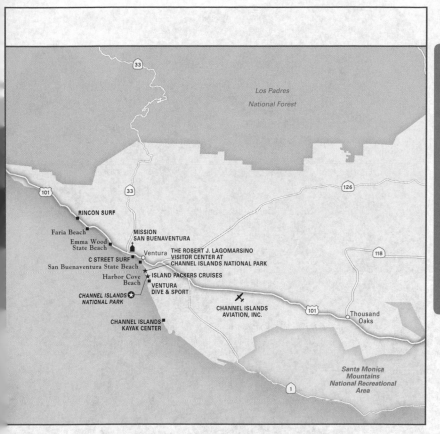

conditions for grapes. This has become one of California's top wine regions, best known for its pinot noirs.

Getting There

Gas stations are easy to find within Santa Barbara, though it's advisable to check fuel and tire levels before driving to mountainous sites on CA-154.

From Los Angeles
95 mi/153 km, 2.5 hr

Santa Barbara is accessed via US-101, approximately 95 miles (153 km) north of Los Angeles and the same distance south of San Luis Obispo. From US-101 in Santa Barbara, take the Garden Street exit to reach downtown; take the Cabrillo Boulevard exit to access local beaches.

From downtown Los Angeles, the drive can take about two hours in clear conditions. However, freeway conditions are rarely clear when leaving Los Angeles, which often seems in a perpetual rush hour. When possible, avoid departing during rush hour (8am-9am and 4pm-6pm) on weekdays.

Scenic Route

The scenic drive along the Pacific Coast Highway (CA-1) passes through **Malibu**; be aware that the ocean on your left actually sits to your south. Take I-10 West until it ends at the Santa Monica coast

Highlights

★ **Old Mission Santa Barbara:** It's known as the queen of the missions for its beauty and lush setting (page 326).

★ **Stearns Wharf:** A great pier topped by tourist attractions offers views of both the ocean and the city, backdropped by mountains (page 326).

★ **Lotusland:** In posh Montecito, this sprawling garden estate features thousands of exotic plants (page 331).

★ **Chumash Painted Cave:** A small section of Chumash culture is preserved in these cryptic cave paintings (page 332).

★ **Channel Islands National Park:** Raw island wilderness is just a quick ferry ride from Ventura (page 341).

Best Restaurants and Accommodations

★ **Dawn Patrol:** This breakfast favorite is the best place to start your day (page 336).

★ **La Super-Rica Taqueria:** A favorite of legendary chef Julia Child, this taco shop's secret is its hand-made tortillas (page 337).

★ **Stella Mare's:** French country dining and amazing desserts are on the menu in this historical Santa Barbara home (page 337).

★ **Black Sheep Restaurant:** Seasonal ingredients and diverse cultural influences result in haute cuisine that's the best in the city (page 338).

★ **Cold Springs Tavern:** Getting to this former stagecoach stop is half the fun—and the excellent BBQ is worth the drive (page 338).

★ **Simpson House Inn:** Opulent rooms, a formal English garden, and evening wine-tastings are features of this Santa Barbara B&B (page 338).

then merge onto CA-1 north for 47 miles (76 km). CA-1 merges with US-101 about 40 miles (64 km) southeast of Santa Barbara.

Along the way, stop to experience the old-world opulence of the **Getty Villa** (17985 CA-1, Pacific Palisades, 310/440-7300, www.getty.edu, reservations required), enjoy seafood with a view at Malibu's most famous fish shack **Neptune's Net,** (42505 CA-1, 310/457-3095, www.neptunesnet.com), or appreciate one of Malibu's impressive beaches.

From San Diego

From San Diego, it's approximately 220 miles (354 km) north to Santa Barbara, with the caveat that any route you take involves passing through Orange County and Los Angeles. Freeway traffic in either location may turn your four-hour drive into a five- or six-hour trek.

Stopping in Los Angeles

From downtown San Diego, take I-5 north for 116 miles (187 km) to US-101. Stay on US-101 out of Los Angeles, which will take you past **Disneyland, downtown L.A.,** and **Hollywood,** giving you a chance to stop and explore top sights like The Broad museum, Griffith Park, or the Hollywood Walk of Fame, or grab quick eats at Grand Central Market, Tommy's Original Burger, or Zankou Chicken.

Stopping in Santa Monica

For an alternative route, take I-5 north from San Diego for 76 miles (122 km). Merge onto I-405 north and drive 63 miles (101 km) north to meet US-101 en route to Santa Barbara. This itinerary takes the same amount of time (adjusting for traffic), but travels past Santa Monica, affording an easy stop at **The Getty Center** museum, or a longer sojourn checking out **Venice Beach** or the **Santa Monica Pier.**

Bypass some of the Orange County traffic on this route by taking the cashless toll road CA-73 west from I-5 at **Laguna Niguel** ($7.48 toll, enforced by license plate photos, payable at www.thetollroads.com). This then connects to I-405, where the only way to avoid traffic is to take the slower coastal route. When I-405 north reaches Santa Monica, take I-10 west to the coast and follow the scenic route from Los Angeles.

Air, Train, or Bus

The nearest international airport is **Los Angeles International Airport** (LAX, 1 World Way, 855/463-5252, www.flylax.com), and flights into **Hollywood Burbank Airport** (BUR, 2627 N. Hollywood Way, Burbank, 818/840-8840, https://hollywoodburbankairport.com) get you almost as close.

Santa Barbara Municipal Airport (500 Fowler Rd., 805/683-4011, www.santabarbaraca.gov) is the gateway for visitors via air travel with daily flights from Los Angeles (LAX), San Francisco, Las Vegas, Phoenix, Denver, and other starting points. Car rentals are available from all major service providers.

The Santa Barbara **Amtrak** station (209 State St., 800/872-7245, www.amtrak.com) is housed in a historical landmark building. Routes provide service from San Luis Obispo to San Diego on the *Pacific Surfliner,* and from Seattle to Los Angeles on the *Coast Starlight.*

The **Greyhound station** (224 Chapala St., 800/752-4841, www.greyhound.com) is adjacent to the train station, providing service several times a day from Santa Barbara and Carpinteria to LAX, as well as other options. Car rental service providers are conveniently located near the Amtrak and Greyhound stations.

Sights

★ Old Mission Santa Barbara

Old Mission Santa Barbara (2201 Laguna St., 805/682-4713, www.santabarbaramission.org, self-guided tours 9am-4:15pm daily, $12 adults, $7 children 5-17), with its coral pink facade, is considered the prettiest of all the California missions, albeit one of the least authentic. A self-guided tour takes you through the interior courtyard, where a center fountain is encircled by palm trees, and the cemetery where a beautiful Moreton Bay fig tree planted around 1890 still stands. From there it is a few steps into the church. It has the most decorated of the mission interiors, with lots of vibrant stenciling surrounding the doors and altar and a complete painted wainscoting. Large paintings flank both walls. Near the formal entrance, a small gated room houses the only original altar and tabernacle in the California mission chain, dating from 1786.

After leaving the church, you'll enter the museum section, which houses old photographs and artifacts from the early services. The on-site **Serra Shop** (9am-5pm daily) sells gifts and souvenirs. One-hour docent tours are also available daily.

★ Stearns Wharf

Santa Barbara's most visited landmark, **Stearns Wharf** (intersection of State St. and Cabrillo Blvd., www.stearnswharf.org) was built in 1871 to allow ships to off-load supplies for a burgeoning town with no natural harbor. Today, it's covered with ocean view restaurants and souvenir shops peddling seashells, personalized tchotchkes, and other ubiquitous tourist gifts. But it also boasts impressive views of the beach, city, and sailboats embarking from the adjacent Santa Barbara Harbor. Cars may drive and park on the wharf, and there are no railings at some sections, so keep an eye on little ones.

One destination on the wharf is the **Ty Warner Sea Center** (211 Stearns Wharf, 805/962-2526, www.sbnature.org, 10am-5pm daily, $8.50 adults, $7.50 children 13-17, $6 children 2-12). A branch of the Santa Barbara Museum of Natural History, this two-story building specializes in local ocean life, offering aquariums and touch tanks that get you closer to sharks, jellyfish, sea cucumbers, and starfish.

The Funk Zone

About a dozen square blocks are squeezed between Stearns Wharf and US-101, bisected by train tracks. The urban neighborhood is affectionately known as **The**

Funk Zone (east of State St., north of Cabrillo Blvd.), a cluster of converted warehouse spaces that include wine-tasting rooms, boutiques and antiques shops, and hip restaurants, all of which provide a gritty alternative to the almost antiseptic facade of downtown.

State Street
Santa Barbara's main drag, central to all of its urban life, radiates off of **State Street** (between E. Anapamu St. and E. Haley St.), which runs north to south from the city center to the coast. Most of the shops, restaurants, bars, and cultural venues lining block after block employ the charm of the city's Mediterranean influence, creating a gorgeous walking district of whitewashed stucco, blue ceramic tiles, terra-cotta rooftops, and matching redbrick sidewalks. High-end retailers provide tremendous window-shopping, while the sidewalks offer an endless supply of people-watching.

MOXI, The Wolf Museum of Exploration + Innovation
Loaded with hands-on exhibits and technology tools that illustrate scientific principles, **MOXI, The Wolf Museum of Exploration + Innovation** (125 State St., 805/770-5000, www.moxi.org, 10am-5pm daily, $15 adults, $10 children 3-12) thrills kids, but also provides an entertaining education for curious adults as well. Whether it's plucking the strings of a giant guitar, creating movie sound effects, or setting an elaborate Rube Goldberg device into action, there's always something to be learned amid the fun.

El Presidio de Santa Bárbara State Historic Park
The Spanish colony of Santa Barbara was established April 21, 1782, on the site of **El Presidio de Santa Bárbara State Historic**

Top to bottom: Old Mission Santa Barbara; Stearns Wharf; Santa Barbara County Courthouse.

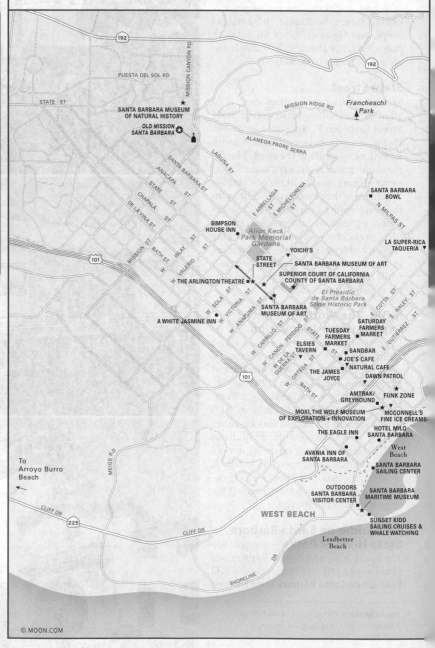

Downtown Santa Barbara

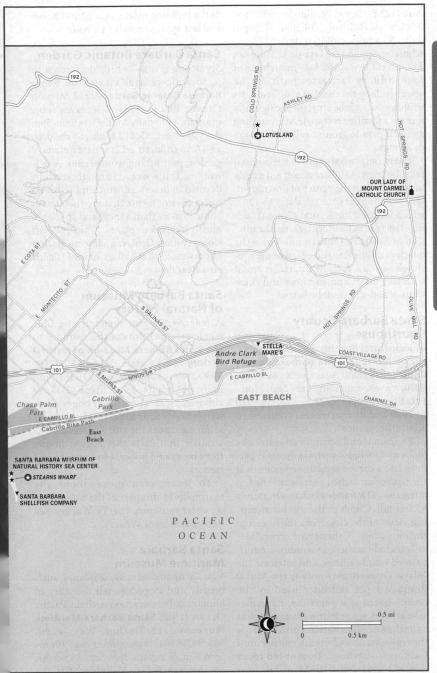

Park (123 E. Canon Perdido St., 805/965-0093, www.sbthp.org, 10:30am-4:30pm daily, $5 adults, children under 17 free, admission includes Casa de la Guerra). The presidio was the last in a chain of four military fortresses built by the Spanish along the coast of California. Its whitewashed adobe structures originally formed a fortified rectangle, surrounding an open parade ground called the Plaza de Armas.

Today, only two sections of the original presidio remain and are preserved as this historic park in the center of downtown. One building, El Cuartel, dates to 1782, which makes it the second-oldest standing structure in California (after the mission at San Juan Capistrano). Once the quarters assigned to the guard of the presidio's western gate, El Cuartel is small with tiny doors and windows and thick walls of sun-dried adobe brick.

Santa Barbara County Courthouse

Modeled after Spanish-Moorish palaces, the picturesque Santa Barbara County Courthouse (1100 Anacapa St., 805/568-3070, www.sbcourts.org, 8am-5pm Mon.-Fri., 10am-4:30pm Sat.-Sun., free) opened in 1929 and its courtrooms continue to administer justice.

The compound occupies an entire city block and includes vast, landscaped gardens and a carved sandstone fountain at the base of an arched entryway. The top attraction, El Mirador clock tower, stands 85 feet tall. Climb to the top for sweeping views of the city, from the ocean to the mountains. Other architectural details include arabesque windows, hand-painted wood ceilings, and intricate tile inlays. Of particular note is the Mural Room, a large hall once used by the county board of supervisors. Its namesake artwork spans four walls and depicts a timeline of Santa Barbara history, from the region's native Chumash culture until California statehood. Docent-led tours (805/962-6464, 2pm daily Mon.-Sat., free)

of the building meet in the Mural Room and last approximately one hour.

Santa Barbara Botanic Garden

Sprawling across 78 hillside acres with panoramic coastal views, the Santa Barbara Botanic Garden (1212 Mission Canyon Rd., 805/682-4726, www.sbbg.org, 9am-6pm daily Mar.-Oct., 9am-5pm daily Nov.-Feb. 15, $12 adults, $8 children 13-17, $6 children 2-12) is part botanical garden, part hiking wonderland. A network of trails weave through sections devoted to desert, canyon, and redwood forest environments that are themselves home to more than a thousand species of mostly indigenous plants. At the Pritzlaff Conservation Center, a viewing station offers scenic vistas to the Channel Islands on a clear day.

Santa Barbara Museum of Natural History

A massive, 74-foot skeleton of a blue whale greets visitors at the entrance to the Santa Barbara Museum of Natural History (2559 Puesta Del Sol, 805/969-9990, www.sbnature.org, 10am-5pm daily, $12 adults, $8 children 13-17, $7 children 2-12). The whale's bones alone weigh nearly four tons. Inside, the museum continues the story of the diverse wildlife that calls this region home, from bears and bobcats to seabirds and raptors.

To learn even more about the marinelife in this part of the world, visit its sister museum, the Ty Warner Sea Center at Stearns Wharf.

Santa Barbara Maritime Museum

Vintage diving helmets, seaplanes, surfboards, and torpedoes tell the story of humankind's interaction with the Pacific Ocean at the Santa Barbara Maritime Museum (113 Harbor Way, #190, 805/962-8404, www.sbmm.org, 10am-5pm Sun.-Fri., 9am-3pm Sat., $8 adults, $5 children 6-17). A highlight is the

Chumash *tomols*—a long, narrow boat used by the region's indigenous people.

The literal star attraction is a 12-foot-tall prismatic dome that used to be the lens of the Point Conception Lighthouse. Built in Paris and originally installed in 1855, the lens's rainbow light refractions have been on display here since 2013.

Santa Barbara Museum of Art

The **Santa Barbara Museum of Art** (1130 State St., 805/963-4364, www.sbmuseart. org, 11am-5pm Tues.-Sun., $10 adults, $6 children 6-17, free admission Thurs. nights 5pm-8pm) has impressive art and antiquities collections for a city of this size, showcasing photography and acclaimed modern painters of North America and Europe. Not to be missed are the museum's ancient Egyptian artifacts, Roman marble sculptures, and a 2,600-piece collection of Asian art spanning four thousand years, notably 18th-century Japanese woodblock prints and embroidered costumes from the Qing dynasty of China.

★ Lotusland

Polish-born opera singer and bon vivant Madame Ganna Walska had a flair for attracting wealthy husbands. She was on her sixth when she bought this lush, 37-acre garden estate in 1941. When that marriage ended, she devoted the rest of her life—and a considerable fortune—to amassing more than 3,200 exotic plants from around the globe to design one of the world's grandest private gardens, which she named **Lotusland** (Cold Spring Rd., Montecito, 805/969-9990, www. lotusland.org, tours at 10am and 1:30pm Wed.-Sat. Feb. 16-Nov. 15, $50 adults, $25 children 3-17).

Walska wanted her life's work to be shared with the public, and she bequeathed the estate to the Ganna Walska

---

Top to bottom: blue whale skeleton outside the Santa Barbara Natural History Museum; cactus garden at Lotusland; Chumash Painted Cave.

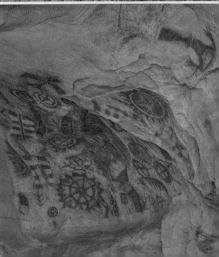

Lotusland Foundation for that purpose. After some significant legal wrangling with the neighborhood residents, the botanical gardens opened in 1993 on a restricted, tour-only basis.

Book a spot on the tour well ahead of time for a chance to view the breathtaking property. The botanical collection boasts rare agaves, orchids, and dragon trees, and the grounds are divided into dedicated orchards and gardens, including a Japanese Garden, Water Garden, Topiary Garden, Cactus Garden, and the famous Blue Garden, where the plants range in hue from silver to blue.

★ Chumash Painted Cave

It only takes a few minutes to experience the sandstone cave paintings at **Chumash Painted Cave State Historic Park** (CA-154, 805/733-3713, www.parks.ca.gov, dawn-sunset, free), but it takes a mountain adventure to get there. The cave was discovered in the 1870s; its artistry is known to be of Chumash origin, but the subjects depicted in the rock art are open to interpretation. The petroglyphs were created using mineral pigments and depict what is believed to be Chumash cosmology, possibly representing a 17th-century solar eclipse. Some images are thought to date back 1,000 years or more.

The cave is about 11 miles (18 km) northwest of Santa Barbara off CA-154. To get there from Santa Barbara, you'll follow some very windy and very narrow roads. From CA-154, turn right on Painted Cave Road, which narrows to one lane. In 2 miles, keep an eye out on the left for an obscure crag of rock with a small interpretive sign and a scrape of driveway beside it. You'll need to climb a steep path to reach the cave, and should you and your car be hale enough to muster the journey, you'll find an iron gate barring its entrance, placed there more than a century ago to preserve artwork so delicate that flash photography is prohibited.

Recreation

Beaches

Long, flat **Leadbetter Beach** (Shoreline Dr. at Loma Alta Dr., 805/564-5418, www.santabarbaraca.gov, 24 hours) is the best in Santa Barbara. Sheer cliffs rise from the sand, trees dot the point, and the beach is protected by the harbor's breakwater, making it ideal for swimming.

Named for its location relative to Stearns Wharf, **East Beach** (Cabrillo Blvd. at S. Milpas St., sunrise-10pm daily) is all soft sand, with a dozen volleyball nets, a snack bar, a children's play area, and the Cabrillo Bike Path. Corresponding **West Beach** (Cabrillo Blvd. at State St., sunrise-10pm daily) offers a small stretch of sand and volleyball nets right beside the wharf.

Known locally as Hendry's Beach, dog-friendly **Arroyo Burro Beach** (Cliff Dr. and Las Positas Rd., sunrise-10pm daily)

is a popular spot for surfers and kayakers. It's far enough removed from downtown to win favor with locals.

Biking

The Cabrillo Bike Path is a flat bike route alongside the coast that leads more than four miles from Leadbetter Beach through Butterfly Beach in Montecito. The car-free section of the **Cabrillo Bike Path** (Cabrillo Blvd. from Bath St. to Milpas St.) runs a leisurely 1.3 miles past the sands of West Beach and East Beach.

Santa Barbara's relatively flat landscape around downtown and the beaches makes for a bike-friendly place to pedal around. **Wheel Fun Rentals** (24 E. Mason St., 805/966-2282, www.wheelfunrentalssb.com, 8am-6pm daily, $8-20/hr) rents beach cruisers and tandem or electric bikes. For higher-caliber road bikes, seek out **Santa Barbara Bikes To-Go** (736 Carpinteria St., 805/628-2444, www.sbbikestogo.com, 9am-5pm daily, $65-105/day).

Boating and Water Sports

Santa Barbara's coast provides many different ways to play in the Pacific Ocean. Sailboats and yachts embark daily from a very active Santa Barbara Harbor, just west of Stearns Wharf. The simplest way to get in on the action is to book a cruise or whale-watching excursion with **Sunset Kidd Sailing Cruises** (125 Harbor Way, #13, 805/962-8222, www.sunsetkidd.com, tours 10am-4pm daily, $40 adult, $25 children age 4-10).

For a more hands-on experience, the **Santa Barbara Sailing Center** (805/962-2826, www.sbsail.com, cruises $40-50, rentals $35-65/hr or $120-260/day, charters from $295/day) offers sailing lessons, boat charters, and harbor cruises and rents small boats.

Both outfits offer whale-watching cruises (Feb. 15-May 15). With a little luck you may spot a migrating blue whale, the world's largest mammal.

To get out in the ocean, visit **Paddle Sports Center** (117 Harbor Way,

kayaks on a Santa Barbara beach

Wine-Tasting in Santa Barbara

Catering to the affections of crushed-grape aficionados, the **Santa Barbara Urban Wine Trail** (www.urbanwinetrailsb.com) leads to about 25 premium tasting rooms, all within blocks of downtown and the beach. Most are open 10am-6pm, with some last pours offered as late as 8pm. Most belong to the Santa Barbara County Vintners' Association, whose membership is made up of only licensed growers with a winery facility in Santa Barbara County and at least 75 percent annual production in Santa Barbara County. Seventeen tasting rooms are in Santa Barbara's up-and-coming **Funk Zone neighborhood** (www.funkzone.net), which offers plenty to see and do beyond wine, including galleries and shops.

805/617-3425, www.paddlesportsca.com, 8am-4:30pm daily, rentals from $12/hr, classes $55-95 pp, tours $60-200 pp). They rent kayaks, surfboards, and SUPs and support kayaking tours, surf lessons, and combo SUP and yoga classes.

Golf

Santa Barbara is home to public and private golf courses of varying quality. For an affordable nine-hole course, look to **Hidden Oaks** (4760 Calle Camarada, 805/967-3493, www.hiddenoaksgolfcoursesb.weebly.com, 8:30am-8pm daily, $13) and **Twin Lakes** (6034 Hollister Ave., 805/964-1414, www.twinlakesgolf.com, 7am-7pm daily, $15). For 18 holes, try **Santa Barbara Golf Club** (3500 McCaw Ave., 805/687-7087, www.santabarbaraca.gov, 6am-8:30pm daily, $53) or the world-class **Rancho San Marcos** (4600 CA-154, 805/683-6334, www.rsm1804.com, 7am-5:30pm daily, $70 Mon.-Fri., $89 Sat.-Sun.).

Entertainment and Events

Nightlife

Many of the bars and nightclubs are on or around the main drag of State Street, much of which caters to college students from the nearby university.

Bars with strong, cheap drinks include **Joe's Cafe** (536 State St.,

805/966-4638, www.joescafesb.com, 7:30am-10pm Sun.-Thurs., 7:30am-midnight Fri.-Sat.), which packs a pretty potent punch. Voted the "best" Santa Barbara happy hour, **Sandbar Mexican Restaurant and Tequila Bar** (514 State St., 805/966-1388, www.sandbarsb.com, 11am-2am daily, 3pm-7pm happy hour Sun.-Fri.) features superb drinks, half-off appetizers, and a lively outdoor patio.

Well-known pubs are **The James Joyce** (513 State St., 805/962-2688, www.sbjamesjoyce.com, 11am-2am daily), a traditional Irish watering hole with weekend bands, and **Dargan's Irish Pub & Restaurant** (18 E. Ortega St., 805/568-0702, www.dargans.com, 11:30am-2am daily), which serves some good Irish stew, Guinness, and Irish music.

Play a few rounds of pool or sit back with a beer or glass of wine and listen to rock bands at **Elsie's Tavern** (117 De La Guerra, 805/963-4503, noon-2am Mon.-Fri., 4pm-2am Sat.-Sun.). Jazz and soul bills are mixed in at **SOhO Restaurant and Music Club** (1221 State St., 805/962-7776, www.sohosb.com, restaurant 6pm-1am daily, $10 and up).

For a night of dancing, **Wildcat Lounge** (15 W. Ortega St., 805/962-7970, www.wildcatlounge.com, 4pm-2am daily) is "the" dance club in Santa Barbara and offers a full bar. **MR8X** (409 State St., 805/957-4111, www.m8rxsb.com, 6pm-10pm Wed.-Fri., plus noon-8pm Sun. during NFL season) packs a nightclub into a historic landmark building dating back to 1889.

Wine fans may want to explore the Urban Wine Trail, but after the tasting rooms close **Les Marchands Wine Bar & Merchant** (131 Anacapa St., Ste. B, 805/284-0380, www.lesmarchandswine. com, 11am-9pm Sun.-Thurs., 11am-10pm Fri.-Sat.) still offers a vast selection of wine by the glass and excellent international beer and cider. Craft beer fans have ever more to look forward to with the arrival of **Figueroa Mountain Brewing Co.** (137 Anacapa St., F, 805/694-2252, 11am-11pm Sun.-Thurs., 11am-midnight Fri.-Sat.), **Modern Times Beer** (418 State St., 805/566-9194, www.moderntimesbeer. com, 11am-11pm Mon.-Thurs., 11am-midnight Fri.-Sun.), and **Draughtsmen Aleworks** (1131 State St., 805/387-2577, www.draughtsmenaleworks.com, 11:30am-9pm daily) tasting rooms.

Live Music
Legendary bands and musicians perform in a relatively intimate outdoor amphitheater, **Santa Barbara Bowl** (1122 N. Milpas St., 805/962-7411, www.sbbowl. com); recent headliners include Willie Nelson, Brian Wilson, John Legend, and Radiohead.

The Arts
A couple of the vintage theaters along State Street host musical and theatrical events and also shows films. Nearly a century old, the 1924 **Granada Theatre** (1214 State St., 805/899-2222, www.granadasb. org) showcases touring Broadway shows, stand-up comedy, world music, dance, and more. The **Arlington Theatre** (1317 State St., 805/963-4408, www. thearlingtontheatre.com) features the Santa Barbara International Film Festival as well as big-name performers. It's worth the price of admission to admire its 1931 Spanish colonial and Mission Revival architecture, which features a covered courtyard with a fountain. Elaborate Spanish balconies, staircases, and houses are built out from the walls, creating the illusion of a Spanish colonial town.

Catch a fabulous musical comedy, theatrical play, or musical performance by the **Ensemble Theatre Company** at **The New Vic Theater** (33 W. Victoria St., 805/965-5400, www.etcsb.org, $25 and up).

Exclusively filled with original works, the Santa Barbara Art Association's **Gallery 113** (1114 State St., #8, 805/965-6611, www.gallery113sb.com, 11am-5pm Mon.-Sat., 1pm-5pm Sun.) hosts numerous exhibitions.

Festivals and Events
The biggest event of the year, **Fiesta** or **Old Spanish Days** (downtown Santa Barbara, 805/962-8101, www. oldspanishdays-fiesta.org, late July or early Aug., tickets: Carriage Museum, 129 Castillo St., $25) is a weeklong celebration of the city's Spanish, Mexican, and Native American history. Events feature *folklórico,* flamenco, Aztec music and dance, fantastic foods, and the amazing El Desfile Histórico (Historical Parade).

The Santa Ynez Band of Chumash Indians hosts the annual **Intertribal Pow-Wow** (Live Oak Camp, 4600 CA-154, Los Padres National Forest, 805/686-5097, www.santaynezchumash.org, late Sept./ early Oct.), where hundreds of tribes gather in honor of culture and heritage, with drummers from the United States and Canada, a variety of foods, and authentic handmade native crafts.

Hollywood notables gather for the annual **Santa Barbara International Film Festival** (805/963-0023, www.sbiff.org, $75 tickets), which includes tributes, movie screenings, and a gala.

The first Thursday of each month, the Santa Barbara Arts Collaborative curates the **First Thursday Art Crawl** (Del La Guerra St. and Anacapa St., www. sbartscollaborative.org, 5:30pm first Thurs. of the month, free), focusing on the best of the local art scene.

Shopping

The six blocks of State Street (between Cota St. and Anapuma St.) are effectively a shopping mall, with many of the usual national retail and designer chain stores. At the Anapuma Street end, **La Arcada** (1114 State St., 805/966-6634, www.laarcadasantabarbara.com, 9am-11pm Mon.-Sat.) offers unique local boutiques, galleries, and specialty shops.

Treasures abound at **Santa Barbara Arts** (1114 State St., 805/884-1938, www.sbarts.net, 11am-5:30pm daily), with an eclectic mix of artist-made creations from handmade jewelry to ceramics to paintings. You'll find fine oil paintings and sculptures in the **Waterhouse Gallery** (1114 State St., 805/962-8885, www.waterhousegallery.com, 11am-5pm daily). Look for French handmade chocolates at **Chocolats du CaliBressan** (1114 State St., #25, 805/568-1313, www.chococalibressan.com, 10am-7pm Mon.-Fri., 11am-6pm Sat., noon-5pm Sun.).

The Italian Pottery Outlet (929 State St., 805/564-7655, www.italianpottery.com, 10am-6:30pm daily) carries the biggest collection of Italian pottery and ceramics at affordable prices.

Mystique Sonique (1103 State St., 805/568-0473, www.mystiquesonique.com, 10am-7pm daily) has a great selection of all things vintage, hip, and chic for both men and women. **Fuzion Gallery & Boutique** (1115 State St., 805/687-6401, www.fuzionglass.com, 11am-7pm Sun.-Thurs., 11am-8pm Fri.-Sat.) stocks cutting-edge clothing from around the world, as well as from local start-ups. Hidden gem **Lovebird Boutique & Jewelry Bar** (535 State St., 805/560-9900, www.lovebirdsb.com, 9am-7pm Mon.-Fri., 9am-9pm Sat.-Sun.) has beautiful unique adornments.

This close to one of the nation's most productive agricultural regions, you'll find a nearly endless assortment of locally grown nuts and produce at the **Santa Barbara Farmers Market** (www.sbfarmersmarket.org). Two weekly markets take place downtown: an evening market (State St. and Ortega St., 3pm-6:30pm Tues.) and another on the weekend (Santa Barbara St. and Cota St., 8:30am-1pm Sat.).

Food

There are pancakes and other breakfast standards, but a build-your-own-hash option makes breakfast a favorite of ★ **Dawn Patrol** (324 State St., 805/962-2889, www.dawnpatrolsb.com, 7:30am-2pm daily, $8-15), which sources mostly local ingredients.

For coffee or a quick bite, take your pick of food vendors populating the **Santa Barbara Public Market** (38 W. Victoria St., 805/770-7702, www.sbpublicmarket.com, 7:30am-10pm Mon.-Wed., 7:30am-11pm Thurs.-Fri., 8am-11pm Sat., 8am-10pm

Sun., $6-16). Choose from pizza, tacos, noodles, and even cupcakes.

Vegans and vegetarians will find happiness and smoothies at **The Natural Café** (508 State St., 805/962-9494, www.thenaturalcafe.com, 11am-9pm Sun.-Thurs., 11am-9:30pm Fri.-Sat., $8-16), which also sources regional ingredients for their menu items.

People line up daily to see why culinary icon Julia Child frequented ★ **La Super-Rica Taqueria** (622 N. Milpas St., 805/963-4940, 11am-9pm Thurs., Sun., and Mon., 11am-9:30pm Fri.-Sat., $4-10 cash only). Order at the kitchen window and watch soft corn tortillas being made by hand: they're the vessels for a long list of street tacos.

Expect a wait at **Arigato Sushi** (1225 State St., 805/965-6074, 5:30pm-10pm Sun.-Thurs., 5:30pm-10:30pm Fri.-Sat., $20-40), the city's favorite sushi spot. For a more varied Japanese dining experience, reserve seats for the exquisite prix fixe menus of **Yoichi's** (230 E. Victoria St.,

805/962-6627, www.yoichis.com, 5pm-9pm Tues.-Sun., seven courses $100 pp, four courses $65 pp Tues.-Thurs.). The restaurant was opened by a Japanese master chef who moved here after falling in love with Santa Barbara while on vacation with his wife.

Touting fresh, wild-caught, and sustainable menu options for more than four decades, **Enterprise Fish Company** (225 State St., 805/962-3313, 11:30am-10pm Sun.-Thurs., 11:30am-11pm Fri.-Sat., $17-65) is a local institution near the train station. At Stearns Wharf, go for seafood with a view at the **Santa Barbara Shellfish Company** (230 Stearns Wharf, 805/966-6676, 11am-9pm daily, $14-24).

A Funk Zone favorite, **The Lark** (131 Anacapa St., 805/284-0370, www.thelarksb.com, 5pm-10pm Tues.-Sun., $16-50) wows Instagramming foodies with trending ingredients and boatloads of creativity. An upscale establishment inside a historic 1872 house, ★ **Stella Mare's** (50 Los Patos Way, 805/969-6705,

Cold Springs Tavern

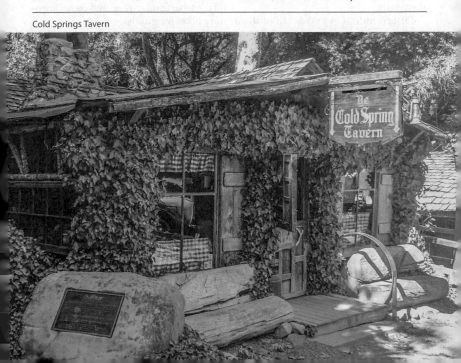

www.stellamares.com, 11:30am-9pm Tues.-Thurs., 11:30am-10pm Fri., 10am-10pm Sat., 10am-9pm Sun., $12-32) offers romantic, French country-style dining, rounded out by desserts like chocolate ganache cream puffs and lavender vanilla crème brûlée.

A welcoming bar and restaurant with a haute cuisine chef, ★ **Black Sheep Restaurant** (26 E. Ortega St., 805/965-1113, www.blacksheepsb.com, 5pm-10pm Tues.-Sat., 5pm-9pm Sun., $18-30, $60 pp tasting menu) might sneakily serve the best food in the city. A mix of high- and lowbrow dishes reveals refined cooking techniques and diverse Asian, South American, and European influences that are often inspired by seasonal produce acquired at the farmers market a block away.

Locally beloved **McConnell's Fine Ice Creams** (728 State St., 805/324-4402, www.mcconnells.com, 11:30am-10pm Sun.-Thurs., 11:30am-11pm Fri.-Sat., $5-12) scoops out creative rotating flavors two at a time, to get you closer to trying them all.

Fifteen miles (24 km) north of town sits the San Marcos Pass, a popular 19th-century stagecoach route for travelers between Los Angeles and Northern California. The wooden stagecoach stop that was built there in 1860 still stands, now providing victuals to travelers along the modern-day highway, CA-154. Inside this 150-year-old time capsule is the ★ **Cold Springs Tavern** (5995 Stagecoach Rd., 805/967-0066, www.coldspringtavern.com, 11am-9pm Mon.-Fri., 8am-9pm Sat.-Sun., $10-30), famous for its tri-tip, sandwiches, chili, burgers, steaks, and ribs.

Accommodations

Santa Barbara is an expensive place to stay, regardless of time of year, weather, or even economic downturns. Most properties require a two-night minimum during the summer.

In the Funk Zone, **The Wayfarer** (12 E. Montecito St., 805/845-1000, www.wayfarersb.com, $50-90 dorms, $150-350 private rooms) offers both dorm beds and private rooms, along with bikes, a communal kitchen, summer pool parties, and musical instruments for impromptu jam sessions in the lobby lounge.

The **Avania Inn** of Santa Barbara (128 Castillo St., 805/963-4471, $109-300) features pillow-top beds, a complimentary hot breakfast, free parking, and a steamy redwood sauna.

In a quiet part of West Beach sits **The Eagle Inn** (232 Natoma Ave., 805/965-3586, www.theeagleinn.com, $120-480), which features a central lodge and adjacent cottages. Varying amenities may include a whirlpool tub or fireplace.

For beachfront stays, the dog-friendly **Hotel Milo** (202 W. Cabrillo Blvd., 805/965-4577, www.hotelmilosantabarbara.com, $150-360) features beautiful outdoor gardens, views of the wharf and harbor, and complimentary bikes for guests.

The nicest B&B for the price is **A White Jasmine Inn** (1327 Bath St., 805/966-0589, www.whitejasmineinnsantabarbara.com, $170-350), composed of three cottages, with richly decorated rooms and fragrant surrounding gardens.

The ★ **Simpson House Inn** (121 E. Arrellaga, 805/963-7067, www.simpsonhouseinn.com, from $280) features opulent rooms on an 1874 estate with a well-manicured and formal English garden. A vegetarian breakfast starts the morning, afternoon tea and desserts are available at midday, and there's wine-tasting in the evening. It's a short walk to State Street.

One block from the wharf, the Spanish-Moorish architecture of **Hotel Californian** (36 State St., 805/870-9427, www.thehotelcalifornian.com, from $400) looks like it could have been there a hundred years—but it hasn't. The gorgeous (and relatively new) hotel features rooms with modern amenities and a rooftop pool with 360-degree views.

Information and Services

The staff at **Santa Barbara Visitors Center** (1 Garden St., 805/965-3021, www.santabarbaraca.com, 9am-5pm Mon.-Sat., 10am-5pm Sun. Feb.-Oct., 9am-4pm Mon.-Sat., 10am-4pm Sun. Nov.-Jan.) are available to assist visitors by answering questions and providing local area and service information. The center is centrally located in downtown inside a traditional adobe building.

The **Outdoors Santa Barbara Visitor Center** (113 Harbor Way, 4th Fl., 805/884-1475, www.outdoorsb.sbmm. org, 11am-5pm Sun.-Fri., 9am-3pm Sat.) offers visitors exhibits and information about offshore destinations including Channel Islands National Park and Channel Islands National Marine Sanctuary.

Getting Around

Gridded streets around the vicinity of downtown are easy to navigate by car, with one-way passages and parking restrictions well marked. Roads become much windier and unpredictable driving into the hillsides above town. Car sharing services **Uber** (www.uber.com) and **Lyft** (www.lyft.com) offer affordable rides in the compact downtown area.

The **Santa Barbara Metropolitan Transit District** (805/963-3364, www.sbmtd.gov) runs buses throughout the city, including the neighboring cities of Goleta and Montecito. SBMTD's route 11 bus links the airport with downtown Santa Barbara. A **shuttle bus** (9am-6pm daily fall-spring, 9am-10pm daily summer, $0.50) runs every 15 minutes along State Street between downtown, Sola Street, and along the waterfront. Bus route 22 goes right to the Museum of Art, Old Mission Santa Barbara, and more.

Ventura

Roughly 80 miles (129 km) northwest of Los Angeles, the coastal town of **Ventura** (pop. 110,790) is a beachy, surfer-friendly community with a cheerful, beer-and-tacos mentality. Its walkable Main Street, just three blocks from the beach, features eclectic small businesses and architecture, with art deco facades next to turn-of-the-20th-century structures next to polished tile-and-glass designs.

Getting There

Ventura is 27.5 miles (44 km) south of Santa Barbara on US 101.

Mission San Buenaventura

At the west end of Main Street, **Mission San Buenaventura** (211 E. Main St., 805/643-4318, www.sanbuenaventuramission.org, 10am-5pm Sun.-Fri., 9am-5pm Sat., $5 adults, $2 children 5-17) was the ninth mission in California, established in 1782. It is one of the few missions to still have wooden bells on display. From the gift shop, where the self-guided tour begins, the door opens to the courtyard, a beautifully landscaped area with a fountain in the center, surrounded by a few benches and interlocking short pathways. Across the courtyard, the church itself is long and narrow, a neoclassical-looking arch over the altar giving a more modern feel to the interior. The area behind the church is part of the original brick reservoir.

Recreation
Beaches
Whatever your taste, Ventura has the beach for you. **San Buenaventura State Beach** (901 San Pedro St., 805/968-1033, www.parks.ca.gov, dawn-dusk daily) offers two miles of sea and sand for swimming, surfing, and picnicking. Accessed

off Main Street, **Emma Wood State Beach** (W. Main St. and Park Access Rd., 805/968-1033, www.parks.ca.gov, www.reservecalifornia.com, dawn-dusk daily, $10 per vehicle) can be rocky but makes a great spot for windsurfing or camping. Families flock to **Harbor Cove Beach** (1900 Spinnaker Dr., dawn-dusk daily), where the harbor's breakwaters provide relative safety from the ocean currents. Food and other amenities can be found across the street at Ventura Harbor Village. Farther north, **Faria Beach** (4350 W. US-101, at State Beach exit, 805/654-3951, www.ventura.org, dawn-dusk daily) is available for tent camping and has 15 RV hookups.

Surfing

Ventura is also known for **surfing,** with **The Rincon** (Bates Rd. and US-101) its most famous landmark. Located between Santa Barbara and Ventura, The Rincon is a small cliffside cove between US-101 and the ocean. The intense swells make it a surfer's dream. Near the pier, **C-Street** is the nickname for another popular surfing spot, a mile-long stretch of sand at the end of California Street. Spectators gather along the concrete boardwalk to see wave-riders in action. For surf rentals, **Ventura Surf Shop** (88 E. Thompson Blvd., 805/643-1062, www.venturasurfshop.com, 9am-6pm Mon.-Sat., 9am-5pm Sun., $15-30/day) has been serving the area more than 50 years.

Whale-Watching

Between the coast and the Channel Islands sits the Santa Barbara Channel, the seasonal migratory path of gray whales, humpback whales, and massive blue whales. Popular whale-watching tours depart from Ventura with **Island Packers** (1691 Spinnaker Dr., Ventura, 805/642-1393, www.islandpackers.com, $38 adults, $28 children 3-12). Depending on the season, you may also spot several species of dolphin as well as orca pods.

Mission San Buenaventura

Food and Accommodations

If the margaritas and Mexican cuisine don't impress at **Limon y Sal** (589 E. Main St., 805/628-3868, 11am-11pm daily, $10-16), the decor will—the vast restaurant occupies a gorgeous 1928 bank building.

For seafood fans, **Spencer Makenzie's Fish Company** (806 E. Thompson Blvd., 805/643-8226, www.spencermakenzies. com, 11am-9pm Sun.-Thurs., 10:30am-9pm Fri.-Sat., $8-12) has a reputation for great fish tacos and fish-and-chips.

Ventura is full of chain hotels and motels. For something different, downtown's **Bella Maggiore Inn** (67 S. California St., 805/652-0277 or 800/523-8479, www. bellamaggioreinn.com, $95-180) has a definite European feel. Just three blocks from the beach, the 32 rooms in this charmingly peculiar spot are all configured differently, and the inn almost feels more like a large bed-and-breakfast than a hotel.

You can also stay in the cozy rooms of a converted Victorian church,

complete with stained-glass windows, at the **Victorian Rose Bed & Breakfast** (896 E. Main St., 805/641-1888, www. victorianroseventura.com, $99-179).

★ Channel Islands National Park

Channel Islands National Park is made up of eight islands, though only five (Anacapa, Santa Cruz, Santa Rosa, San Miguel, and Santa Barbara) are within sight of the mainland. These areas have been federally protected since 1980. Long before they were tourist spots, they were ranchlands. And even longer before that, some 13,000 years ago, archaeological evidence suggests that they were inhabited by indigenous people. Today, they're one of the last remaining wilderness spots in California.

Visiting the Park

Channel Islands National Park (805/658-5730, www.nps.gov/chis, no entrance fee) is one of the least-visited national parks in the United States, which works to its benefit: receiving fewer visitors preserves its unspoiled wilderness. With an abundance of sea caves, picturesque arches, and unique wildlife, the islands offer memorable backpacking, camping, scuba diving, kayaking, and surfing adventures.

The National Park Service restricts access to the Channel Islands. While a number of boating operations bring divers to explore the waters surrounding the five islands, only a handful of permitted concessionaires may provide passengers access to the islands themselves.

Getting There and Around

To access the islands by boat, the only ferry service leaves Ventura from **Island Packers** (1691 Spinnaker Dr., Ventura, 805/642-1393, www.islandpackers.com), including day ($59-105 adults, $41-84 children) and overnight trips ($79-147 adults, $57-126 children). It offers transportation to five of the islands, including Channel Island whale-watching cruises and kayaking trips. Anacapa and Santa Cruz are about an hour each way by boat. The outer islands—Santa Rosa, Santa Barbara, and San Miguel—cost more to reach and take over two hours each way.

For groups, air travel is possible by charter from Camarillo Airport via **Channel Islands Aviation** (305 Durley Ave., Camarillo, 805/987-1301, $1,200 day trip up to 8 passengers, $1,760 camping up to 7 passengers) to Santa Rosa Island only.

Plan to walk or kayak your way around. There's no public transportation on any of the islands, and biking is not allowed.

Seasons

Temperatures average in the mid-60s to the low 50s year-round, but this is the coast, so be prepared for high winds and fog. The outer islands of Santa Rosa and San Miguel experience more frequent high winds, at times up to 30 knots. Other islands have more moderate winds. However, during the late spring and summer months, fog thickens, challenging visibility.

Park Entrances

Boaters must access Santa Barbara Island via the landing cove; dock access is limited. Access to Santa Rosa Island is permitted via coastline or beaches with piers available at Bechers Bay. Access to San Miguel Island is through Cuyler Harbor (beach only) or Tyler Bight. Access to Anacapa Island is at East Anacapa or Frenchy's Cove; however, a permit is required at Middle Anacapa, and visitors must be accompanied by a park ranger (no access is allowed for West Anacapa). Access to Santa Cruz Island is available via the pier at Scorpion Anchorage or Prisoners Harbor.

Channel Islands

Visitors Centers

Robert J. Lagomarsino Visitor Center (1901 Spinnaker Dr., Ventura, 805/658-5730, www.nps.gov/chis, 8:30am-5pm daily) is in Ventura and provides interpretive programs, tidepool displays, a bookstore, and island exhibits.

The small visitor contact stations on Anacapa and Santa Barbara Islands include resource displays and information on each island. Scorpion Ranch on Santa Cruz Island also houses information.

Information and Services

In addition to the visitors centers, information about travel to the Channel Islands may be found through **The Nature Conservancy** (800/628-6860, www.nature.org), including details on landing private watercraft. Private boaters must receive permission to land on certain islands, including Santa Cruz Island.

A permit is required for camping and backcountry camping. Camping

reservations (888/448-1474, www.recreation.gov, $15 permits) can be made online up to five months in advance.

For weather reports, check the **Channel Islands Internet Weather Kiosk** (www.channelislands.noaa.gov/news/kiosk.html).

Sights and Recreation

All the islands offer hiking, water activities, and camping. Trails range from relatively flat to steep, rugged, mountainous paths. It is important to remember to stay within park boundaries and not hike on The Nature Conservancy property, which is clearly marked by a fence line.

Personal kayaks may be brought on the ferry, while rentals are available from **Channel Island Kayak Center** (3600 S. Harbor Dr. Ste. 2-108, Oxnard, 805/984-5995, www.cikayak.com, noon-5pm Mon.-Fri., 10am-5pm Sat.-Sun., rentals from $12.50/hr, $35/day). For snorkel and scuba rentals, try **Ventura Dive & Sport** (1559 Spinnaker Dr., #108, 805/650-6500, www.venturadive.com, 10am-6pm Mon.-Fri., 8am-6pm Sat., 8am-5pm Sun., $10-50 snorkel, $45-65 scuba).

On **Santa Cruz Island,** Scorpion Beach offers some of the best areas for water sports, with easy beach access and nearby sea caves for adventure exploration. Prisoners Harbor and Smugglers Cove also provide beach access; however, snorkeling and diving are not allowed. To access kelp beds, snorkelers and divers should explore near the pier and at the bay's eastern end. Kayaking at Scorpion Beach and sea caves is offered exclusively by **Channel Islands Adventure Company** (805/884-9283, www.sbadventureco.com, $119 pp, plus ferry costs).

Santa Rosa Island offers sandy beaches, with easy access, and great opportunities for surfing. The north shore is best in winter and spring, and the south shore is best in summer and fall.

Aggressive winds at **San Miguel Island** make water activities dangerous for the inexperienced. However, overnight stays offer time enough for an exceptional 16-mile ranger-guided hike to Point Bennett, where you can see one of the largest ensembles of wildlife.

Santa Barbara Island is a great place to see seals and sea lions from Landing Cove and from the overlook points of Sea Lion Rookery and Elephant Seal Cove. There are incredible stands of native vegetation and wildflowers. Kayakers can explore Sea Lion Rookery to the south, which offers a wonderland of wildlife, sea caves, and ocean arches.

The Landing Cove on **Anacapa Island** provides excellent swimming, diving, and snorkeling, but remember there are no lifeguards. Kayakers can head east toward Arch Rock or west toward Cathedral Cove for marinelife- and wildlife-viewing and sea caves. Hiking is limited on the island to only about two miles of trail.

There is no fishing on any of the islands, and visitors are asked to stay on the trails and not disturb the flora or fauna. Visitors are also asked to avoid animal nesting areas and to stay out of caves if not professionally guided. The park website contains a detailed list of restrictions.

Camping

Camping is available by **reservation only.** Campsites are primitive, with basic picnic tables and pit toilets. Trash containers are not provided; campers are expected to pack out their own garbage. Campsites are all close together, so don't expect a lot of privacy during high season. **Water** is available at the Scorpion Anchorage on Santa Cruz, at the Santa Rosa campground, and nowhere else. Due to the wind, San Miguel and Santa Rosa campgrounds have **windbreaks** for each campsite.

There are **no food venues, stores, or restaurants** on the islands. Plan accordingly and bring your own food and water.

Fires are not permitted except on eastern Santa Cruz Island, where fire pits and wood are provided.

Camping on Santa Rosa Island beaches is for experienced kayakers and boaters on a seasonal basis, and a permit is required ($10-15/night).

A **40-pound weight limit** restriction is imposed by the boat concessionaire. Bring the necessities, keeping in mind what is available on-site. Campgrounds are a half mile from the landings, except for Santa Rosa and San Miguel, where the campgrounds are 1-1.5 miles away. The eastern Santa Cruz site is an easy flat walk, while San Miguel and Santa Barbara require an uphill trek. Anacapa is uphill as well and includes stairs—a lot of stairs (approximately 156).

The Gaviota Coast

El Capitán State Beach

The first of three state beaches west of Santa Barbara, **El Capitán State Beach** (off US-101, 805/968-1033, www.parks.ca.gov, dawn-sunset daily, $10) offers visitors a sandy shoreline, rocky tidepools, and stands of sycamore and oak trees along El Capitán Creek. It's a perfect setting for swimming, fishing, surfing, picnicking, and camping. A stairway provides access from the bluffs to the beach area. Amenities include RV sites with hookups, pay showers, restrooms, hiking and bike trails, a fabulous beach, a seasonal general store, and an outdoor arena. Many of the camping sites offer an ocean view.

Getting There

From downtown Santa Barbara, take US-101 North for 17 miles (27 km) and look for El Capitán signs. Take Exit 117 and, at the bottom of the exit, turn left and drive under the bridge. The road will take you right into the park.

Refugio State Beach

Refugio State Beach (10 Refugio Beach Rd., Goleta, 805/968-1033, www.parks.ca.gov, dawn-sunset daily, $10) is a small strip of grass that abuts the water. It offers excellent coastal fishing, snorkeling, and scuba diving, as well as hiking, biking trails, and picnic sites, with 1.5 miles of flat shoreline. Palm trees planted near Refugio Creek give a distinctive look to the beach and camping area.

Getting There
Refugio is 20 miles (32 km) west of Santa Barbara and 3 miles (5 km) west of El Capitán on US-101 at Refugio Road.

Gaviota State Park
Gaviota State Park (US-101, 805/968-1033, www.parks.ca.gov, 7am-sunset daily, $10) offers a beach, hiking trails, and hot springs. The trailhead to **Gaviota Peak** (6 mi/10 km round-trip) is at the parking area. The route is mostly rugged and wide leading upward, and the views of the ocean and the Channel Islands are fantastic. The trail that leads to the hot springs is shorter, only a mile, but there are still some beautiful scenic views along the way. Surfers and kayakers use a boat hoist on the west end of the beach to access the Santa Barbara Channel waters. At Gaviota Beach, US-101 turns east, hugging the coastline.

Getting There
Gaviota State Park is 33 miles (53 km) west of Santa Barbara on US-101 and 6 miles (10 km) west of Refugio State Beach.

Top to bottom: stairway to El Capitán State Beach; Refugio State Beach; Gaviota State Park beach.

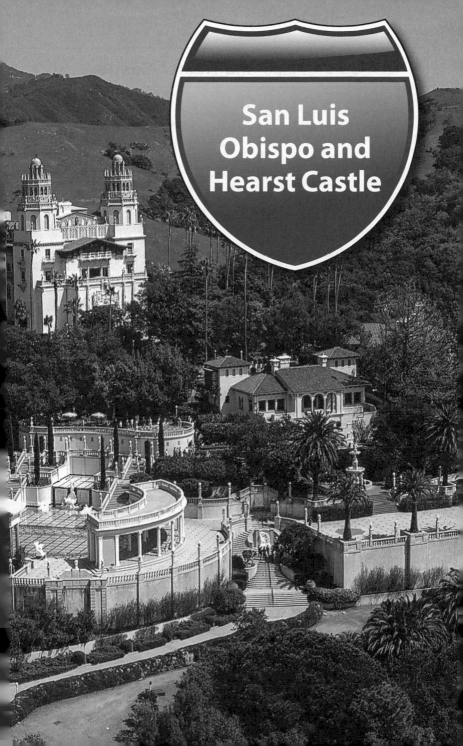

San Luis
Obispo and
Hearst Castle

San Luis Obispo and Hearst Castle

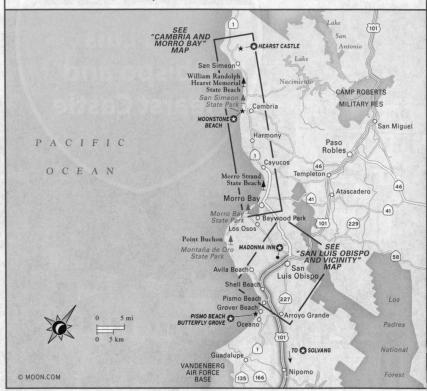

SEE "CAMBRIA AND MORRO BAY" MAP

★ HEARST CASTLE

Lake San Antonio

San Simeon

William Randolph Hearst Memorial State Beach

San Simeon State Park

Lake Nacimiento

CAMP ROBERTS MILITARY RES

Cambria

San Miguel

MOONSTONE BEACH

Harmony

Paso Robles

Cayucos

Templeton

Atascadero

Morro Strand State Beach

Morro Bay

Morro Bay State Park

Baywood Park

Los Osos

Point Buchon

Montaña de Oro State Park

MADONNA INN

SEE "SAN LUIS OBISPO AND VICINITY" MAP

Avila Beach

San Luis Obispo

Shell Beach

Pismo Beach

Grover Beach

Arroyo Grande

PISMO BEACH BUTTERFLY GROVE

Oceano

Guadalupe

TO ★ SOLVANG

VANDENBERG AIR FORCE BASE

Nipomo

Los Padres National Forest

PACIFIC OCEAN

0   5 mi
0   5 km

© MOON.COM

North of Santa Barbara, southern beach culture rolls into the agrarian sprawl of California's Central Coast, rich in ocean vistas and watched over by a castle.

This scenic stretch of highway offers a mix of beach resorts, wine country, small-town life, and ranch-style barbecue. As US-101 continues north of Santa Barbara, the road splits into parallel routes for 60 miles. CA-1 follows the coast past Vandenburg Air Force Base, while US-101 travels inland for 94 miles to rejoin CA-1 as it passes through the resort town of Pismo Beach and enters the endearing college town San Luis Obispo.

The charming creekside village serves as the cultural hub for the area and is home to California Polytechnic State University, flourishing strawberry, nut, and avocado farms, and a burgeoning wine-growing region.

Heading out of San Luis Obispo, CA-1 splits west from US-101 to roughly follow a line of ancient volcanic hills known as the Nine Sisters. The road leads to the coast where the Sisters culminate in the unmistakable coastal landmark of Morro Rock in the town of Morro Bay. Here begins a remote stretch of

Highlights

★ **Solvang:** The Danish-style town charms travelers with windmills, cobblestone streets, and a Hans Christian Andersen museum (page 350).

★ **Pismo Beach Butterfly Grove:** November-February, tens of thousands of butterflies congregate in one of the largest of the gathering spots

for monarchs in California (page 353).

★ **Madonna Inn:** The famed road-trip stopover is kitschy, over the top, and excessively pink (page 355).

★ **Moonstone Beach:** For breathtaking ocean views, tidepools brimming with life, and a possible precious stone

or two, stroll this boardwalk along the Central Coast (page 362).

★ **Hearst Castle:** No visit to the California coast is complete without a tour of this grand mansion on a hill, conceived and built by publishing magnate William Randolph Hearst (page 365).

coast highway that boasts views so dazzling, they inspired publishing magnate William Randolph Hearst to build the opulent, no-expense-spared Hearst Castle high in the hills of San Simeon.

Getting There

From Santa Barbara
100 mi/161 km, 1.5-2 hr
From Santa Barbara, two scenic routes travel to San Luis Obispo: the coastal route or the mountain route. Surprisingly, the mountain route will be quickest in clear traffic (90 minutes).

Mountain Route
From Santa Barbara, take CA-154 North, driving the steep and windy highway through the Santa Ynez Mountains before joining US-101 at Los Olivos in 37 miles (60 km). CA-154 offers the added benefit of passing the **Chumash Painted Cave** (Painted Cave Rd. at 5.5-mile mark). Should you be hungry, stop at the historic **Cold Springs Tavern** (Stagecoach Rd. at 9.2 miles), a rustic wooden cabin that dates to 1886 and serves delicious barbecue.

Coastal Route
From Santa Barbara, take CA-1/US-101 North, which heads west along the Pacific Ocean before turning north in 32 miles (52 km) at **Gaviota State Park** on the Gaviota Coast. Past Gaviota, the two highways diverge, each traveling inland. CA-1 takes longer (90 minutes) and is only recommended if you plan to stop at **La Purisma Mission,** 55 miles (89 km) north of Santa Barbara.

By contrast, US-101 takes 65 minutes and passes near **Los Olivos** (52 mi/84 km) and **Solvang** (east on CA-246 at 43 mi/69 km). The best reason to continue north on US-101 past Los Olivos is because it passes the census-designated place of Nipomo, noteworthy for the oak-fired

rib eye of its regionally beloved **Jocko's Famous Steakhouse** (Teft St. exit).

From Santa Barbara, continue north on either route as they reconvene in 82 miles (132 km) at **Pismo Beach.**

Air, Train, or Bus
San Luis Obispo County Regional Airport (901 Airport Dr., 805/781-5205) is a commercial airport with flights to Los Angeles, San Francisco, and Phoenix. Car rentals are available.

The downtown **Amtrak** (1011 Railroad Ave., 800/872-7245, www.amtrak.com) station offers service from Seattle to Los Angeles via the *Coast Starlight* route and to San Diego on the *Pacific Surfliner.*

Buellton and Solvang

The town of Buellton holds one of California's classic roadside landmarks, **Andersen's Pea Soup Restaurant** (376 Ave. of the Flags, 805/688-5581, www.peasoupandersens.net, 7am-10pm daily, $10-14), advertised up and down the coast. The **Hitching Post** (406 CA-246 E., 805/688-0676, www.hitchingpost2.com, 4pm-9:30pm Mon.-Fri., 3pm-9:30pm Sat.-Sun., $25-50) restaurant gained fame in the wine-loving road-trip movie *Sideways.*

Getting There
Buellton is a block west of US-101 at the Solvang exit. From Santa Barbara, drive 45 miles (72 km) north on US-101. Turn west on CA-246 to enter the town of Solvang in 3.5 miles (6 km).

★ Solvang
East of Buellton and US-101 is one of the country's most famous mock-European tourist traps, the Danish-style town of **Solvang** (pop. 5,385). Set up by a group of Danish immigrants in 1911 as a cooperative agricultural community, Solvang found its calling catering to passing

travelers. The compact blocks of wind-mills, cobblestone streets, and old-world architecture charm road-trippers and busloads of tourists with the **Hans Christian Andersen Museum** (1680 Mission Dr., 805/688-2052, 10am-5pm daily), a Little Mermaid statue, and, more recently, regional winery tasting rooms. **The Elverhoj Museum of Art & History** (1624 Elverhoy Way, 805/686-1211, www.elverhoj.org, 11am-4pm Wed.-Sun., $5 suggested donation) chronicles the cultural influence of the Danish people.

Old Mission Santa Inés

East of Solvang's windmills and gables, the brooding hulk of **Old Mission Santa Inés** (1760 Mission Dr., 805/688-4815, 9am-5pm daily, $5 guided tours) stands as a sober reminder of the region's Spanish colonial past. Built in 1804, it was once among the more prosperous of the California missions, but now it is worth a visit mainly for the gift shop selling all manner of devotional ornaments.

Pop singer Michael Jackson's Neverland Ranch lies in the foothills of the Santa Ynez Valley, southeast of Solvang via the truly scenic CA-254, which loops inland and continues south to Santa Barbara.

Allow 2-4 hours to wander the area, depending on whether you stop in one of Solvang's tourist trap restaurants for Danish puffed pancakes, called Æbleskivers.

La Purisima Mission

Mission La Purisima Concepcion de Maria Santisima (2295 Purisima Rd., Lompoc, 805/733-3713, www.lapurisimamission.org, self-guided tours 9am-5pm daily, free one-hour guided tours daily at 1pm, $6 per vehicle) is one of the best of the 21 California missions to visit. Its extensive restoration and wide grounds evoke the

Top to bottom: Danish architecture in Solvang; Old Mission Santa Inés; La Purisima Mission.

Wine-Tasting in the Santa Maria Valley

After CA-1 splits off from US-101 in Pismo Beach, the drive south along either highway is largely inland until it reaches Gaviota near Santa Barbara. Since you won't be missing any coastal scenery, you could take a detour even farther inland to the Santa Maria Valley to sample wines in the region made famous by the movie *Sideways*. Running roughly parallel to US-101, **Foxen Canyon Road** is a back road hugging the foothills, with multiple wineries along the way.

From the north on US-101, take the East Betteravia Road exit and head east about 3 miles (5 km) until it turns into Foxen Canyon Road. From this point, Tepusquet Road, where Kenneth Volk Vineyards is located, is about 10 miles (16 km) away. From the south, take the Alisos Canyon Road turnoff from US-101, about 25 miles (40 km) north of the CA-1/US-101 split in Gaviota. Follow Alisos Canyon Road 6.5 miles (11 km) and turn left onto Foxen Canyon Road. Foxen Canyon Road eventually turns into East Betteravia Road and connects back to US-101.

On a little road off Foxen Canyon Road, award-winning **Kenneth Volk Vineyards** (5230 Tepusquet Rd., 805/938-7896, www.volkwines.com, 10:30am-4:30pm Thurs.-Mon.) offers all the strange wines you've never tried. In addition to the standard offerings like chardonnay and cabernet sauvignon, Kenneth Volk is a champion of heirloom varieties like cabernet pfeiffer, négrette, verdelho, and aglianico. You won't regret the long trek to get to the tranquil 12-acre property along the Tepusquet Creek, surrounded by oak and sycamore trees.

Set in an old barn, **Rancho Sisquoc** (6600 Foxen Canyon Rd., 805/934-4332, www.ranchosisquoc.com, 10am-4pm Mon.-Thurs., 10am-5pm Fri.-Sun.) makes a beautiful spot for a picnic. The wood-sided tasting room is rustic but comfortable, and the surrounding setting—a vast field with low hills in the distance—is perfect for some quiet wine-enhanced relaxation.

Foxen Winery (7600 Foxen Canyon Rd., 805/937-4251, www.foxenwinery.com, 11am-4pm daily) is known for its rustic wood tasting room: It looks like a run-down shed. But the wines are a far cry from rustic. In addition to the usual suspects, the winery is one of the few to produce the underappreciated chenin blanc. Foxen's long-standing reputation goes back six generations, and its 10 acres are the only dry-farmed vineyard in the area, meaning that irrigation is not used.

remoteness of the landscape during the mission period.

The mission was founded on December 8, 1787, but was destroyed by an earthquake in 1812. The fathers then rebuilt the mission in a different spot, and it is that mission that a quarter of a million visitors enjoy today as a state historic park. Sitting inside 2,000 acres are trails for simple hikes and walks, and when you visit, you can examine the five-acre garden that shows native and domestic plants typical of a mission garden, including fig and olive trees and a wide variety of plants like sage and Spanish dagger. Animals typical of the times, such as burros, horses, longhorn cattle, sheep, goats, and turkeys are displayed in a corral in the main compound.

Wandering through the sleeping quarters, weaving shop, candle-making room, chapel, and many other rooms on display, you can get a feel for daily life in the mission. You can also see few conical Chumash huts. This is one of the few missions that do not have church services, since it's now a state park.

La Purisima is easily accessible from CA-1: In Lompoc, take Purisima Road east to the mission.

Pismo Beach

After diverging inland for nearly 80 miles north of Santa Barbara, US-101 and CA-1 rejoin the Pacific coast at Pismo Beach (pop. 8,237). The happy-go-lucky resort captures a vintage postcard version of a beach town, with loads of hotels, restaurants, and surf radiating out from a central pier at the end of Pomeroy Avenue, the main drag. Thanks to miles of accessible coastline, Pismo stays popular from one long California summer to the next, rousing back to life any sunny weekend in between.

Getting There

From Santa Barbara, follow US-101 North for 95 miles (153 km) to Pismo Beach. From San Luis Obispo, Pismo Beach is 14 miles (23 km) south via US-101.

★ Pismo Beach Butterfly Grove

Pismo Beach Butterfly Grove (CA-1 just south of North Pismo State Beach Campground, 805/773-7170, www.monarchbutterfly.org, docents available 10am-4pm daily Nov.-Feb., free) sees the return of monarch butterflies each November-February. The butterflies migrate 2,000 miles to this small grove of eucalyptus trees near the beach to mate, though fewer have made the journey in recent years. Docents give talks about the butterflies and their unique but short lives and potential endangerment.

Beaches

All the surf, sun, and family fun takes place on the beach north and south of **Pismo Beach Pier** (west of end of Pomeroy Ave.). A metered parking lot fronts the beach, which has restroom and shower facilities. A long boardwalk heads in either direction and offers ocean views

Top to bottom: monarch butterflies at Pismo Beach Butterfly Grove; sunset at Pismo Beach Pier; Splash Cafe.

from above the sand. The pier also provides a great vantage point for watching the surfers below.

At the south end of the city beach, Pismo Creek marks the beginning of the 17-mile **Pismo State Beach** (399 S. Dolliver St.). The undeveloped beach is accessible from the North Beach Campground, where you can park in the lot ($5 day use). The beach access trail can also be reached along the sand from the Pismo City Beach (west end of Pomeroy Ave.) and from the Pismo Beach Butterfly Grove (CA-1 south of North Pismo State Beach Campground). While walking along the beach, stick to the north side of Grand Avenue; south of the beach off-road vehicles are permitted.

Recreation

The waves off Pismo pier are suitable for beginner surfers and can be fun for intermediate riders much of the year. For surfboard rentals, try **Pismo Beach Surf Shop** (470 Price St., Pismo Beach, 805/773-2089, www.pismobeachsurf-shop.com, $15 half day). For surf lessons or to attend a surf camp, book a session with **Sandbar Surf School** (110 Park Ave., Pismo Beach, 805/835-7873, www.sand-barsurf.com, $70 pp).

Vehicles are permitted onto the relatively flat sands at **Oceano Dunes** (Pier Ave. west of CA-1, Oceano, 805/773-7170, http://ohv.parks.ca.gov, $5 day use per vehicle), which covers the entire half of Pismo State Beach south of Grover Avenue. Drive at your own risk. Only true off-road vehicles and ATVs should tackle the dune-heavy **State Recreational Vehicle Area** (south of Pier Ave.). Vehicle rental agencies cluster near the park entrance, led by **Steve's ATV Rentals** (332 Pier Ave., Oceano, 805/481-2597, www.stevesatvrentals.com, $40-275 per hour).

Nightlife

Things can get loud and lively behind the neon lights of **Harry's Night Club & Beach Bar** (690 Cypress St., 805/773-1010, www.harryspismobeach.com, hours and cover varies), which hosts live music or DJs playing popular dance hits. For a more laid-back scene, enjoy darts and craft beer at the surfer bar **The Board Room** (160 Hinds Ave., #101, 805/295-6222, www.theboardroompismobeach.com, 2pm-10pm Mon.-Wed., noon-10pm Thurs. and Sun., noon-midnight Fri.-Sat.).

Food

If there's a restaurant worth the driving, it's ★ **Jocko's Famous Steakhouse** (125 N. Thompson Ave., Nipomo, 805/929-3686, http://jockossteakhouse.com, 8am-10pm Sun.-Thurs., 8am-11pm Fri.-Sat., $15-34), which is 12 miles (19 km) south of Pismo Beach. The casual steak house fires fine cuts of California beef over red oak and serves it for a song—dinner reservations are a must. Or drop in around lunchtime for the "small steak sandwich," 10 ounces of grilled rib eye atop two thick slices of garlic bread. The side of piquito beans is a regional favorite.

In town, local institution **Splash Cafe** (197 Pomeroy, 805/773-4653, www.splashcafe.com, 8am-8:30pm Sun.-Thurs., 8am-9pm Fri.-Sat., $7-12) is best known for its clam chowder. The beachy counter shop deals primarily in fried seafood, fish sandwiches, burgers, and tacos. Thick shakes further entice beachgoers.

For a more involved seafood experience, strap on a bib at the **Cracked Crab** (751 Price St., 805/773-2722, www.crackedcrab.com, 11am-9pm Sun.-Thurs., 11am-10pm Fri.-Sat., $20-50), where diners crack into a mountain of shellfish, including Maine lobster or five varieties of crab such as the local Dungeness.

Oyster Loft (101 Pomeroy Ave., 805/295-5104, www.oysterloft.com, 4pm-9pm Mon.-Thurs., 5pm-10pm Fri.-Sat., 5pm-9pm Sun., $20-50) serves upscale seafood on an outdoor patio overlooking Pismo Beach. Shellfish is the specialty here, with a raw oyster bar and fresh oysters at happy hour (4pm-5pm Mon.-Thurs.).

Enjoy creative Latin American cuisine with gorgeous ocean views at the cliffside **Ventana Grill** (2575 Price St., 805/773-0000, http://ventanagrill.com, 11am-9pm Mon.-Sat., 10am-9pm Sun., $20-40). It's worth the visit for the margarita selection alone.

Casual diners in search of Mexican food should look for **Papi's Grill** (1090 Price St., 805/295-6660, 11am-9pm Mon.-Sat., 10am-9pm Sun., $4-10), where handmade corn tortillas and tasty salsas add depth to the beach town's best tacos.

Accommodations

A few lower-priced chain hotels dot Pismo Beach and the surrounding communities of Avila Beach and Grover Beach. Close to town, yet still perched above sea level, **Kon Tiki Inn** (1621 Price St., 888/566-8454, http://www.kontiki-inn.com, from $150) makes oceanfront rooms decent and affordable, while also offering stairs to the beach.

Overshadowed by a spate of newer oceanfront hotels a few steps closer to the pier, the **Sea Venture Beach Hotel** (100 Ocean View Ave., 805/773-4994, www.seaventure.com, from $170) typically offers rooms at a relative bargain, with options for fireplaces and balcony Jacuzzis.

For a splurge, the **Dolphin Bay Resort and Spa** (2727 Shell Beach Rd., 800/516-0112, www.thedolphinbay.com, from $340) has one of the best locations on the Central Coast, perched just yards from cliffs that drop dramatically down to the Pacific Ocean. At nearly 1,000 square feet, the one-bedroom suites have full kitchens, fireplaces, and flat-screen plasma TVs. Bikes are provided for all guests.

Campsites are available at the **North Beach Campground** (800/444-72705, www.reservecalifornia.com, $35) at Pismo State Beach (399 S Dolliver St., Pismo Beach).

San Luis Obispo

San Luis Obispo (pop. 47,571), known as SLO to locals, is a sleepy community that often lives up to its nickname. It's also a university town—home to the California Polytechnic State University, San Luis Obispo (Cal Poly)—which enlivens the community when classes are in session. Most of the town's action takes place in a compact downtown district along Higuera Street, where restaurants and bars feature back patios along the banks of the charming, tree-lined San Luis Obispo Creek.

Sights
★ Madonna Inn

West of US-101, at the foot of town, the **Madonna Inn** (100 Madonna Rd., 805/543-3000, www.madonnainn.com) is a remarkable example of what architecturally minded academic types like to call vernacular kitsch. Created by local contractor Alex Madonna, who died in 2004, the Madonna Inn offers over 100 unique rooms, each decorated in a wild barrage of fantasy motifs. Bright pink honeymoon suites are known as "Just Heaven" and "Love Nest." The "Safari Room" is covered in fake zebra skins above a jungle-green shag carpet. The name of the "Cave Man Room" speaks for itself (Yabba dabba doo!). *Roadside America* rates the Madonna Inn as "the best place to spend a vacation night in America." Even if you can't stay the night (rooms from $200), browse postcards in the gift shop, or dine in its lavishly over-the-top Gold Rush Steak House. Guys should head down to the men's room, where the urinal trough is flushed by a waterfall.

Mission San Luis Obispo de Tolosa

Built in 1772, **Mission San Luis Obispo de Tolosa** (751 Palm St., 805/781-8220, www.missionsanluisobispo.org, 9am-5pm daily summer, 9am-4pm daily winter, $2 donation) is the fifth California mission founded by Junípero Serra and the only L-shaped mission in the state. An adjacent museum chronicles the daily lives of the Chumash tribal and Spanish colonial periods. Today, the mission church operates as a parish church of the Diocese of Monterey.

San Luis Obispo Museum of Art
Set alongside the creek, San Luis Obispo Museum of Art (1010 Broad St., 805/543-8562, www.sloma.org, 11am-5pm Wed.-Mon. year-round, 11am-5pm daily July 5-Labor Day, free) is a small gallery that showcases the work of local painters, sculptors, fine-art photographers, and special exhibitions.

Nightlife
Pub life thrives in SLO, including the creekside patio and live entertainment of The Frog & Peach Pub (728 Higuera St., 805/595-3764, www.frogandpeachpub. com, noon-2am daily). Also nestled creekside, SLO Brew (736 Higuera St., 805/543-1843, www.slobrew.com, 11:30am-2am Tues.-Fri., 10am-midnight Sat. 10am-6pm Sun.) pairs its house-brewed beer with rock, country, blues, funk, and cover band concerts most nights.

Exceptional imported beers are the focus at Spike's Pub (570 Higuera St., 805/544-7157, www.spikespub.com, 3pm-1am daily). Morro Bay wild-ale producer The Libertine (1234 Broad St., 805/548-2337, www.libertinebrewing. com, 11am-10pm Mon.-Wed., 11am-11pm Thurs.-Sat., 10am-10pm Sun.) serves all kinds of brews out of its downtown SLO beer and wine pub.

Luis Wine Bar (1021 Higuera St., 805/762-4747, www.luiswinebar.com, 3pm-11pm Sun.-Thurs., 3pm-midnight Fri.-Sat.) has a relaxing atmosphere and an extensive wine list from San Luis Obispo County and the entire Central Coast.

Creekside wine bar Luna Red (1023 Chorro St., 805/540-5243, www.

lunaredslo.com, 11:30am-9pm Mon.-Thurs., 11:30am-midnight Fri., 9am-midnight Sat., 9am-9pm Sun.) is a trendy place in a Spanish-style building with fine wines, cocktails, and tapas.

As with most things SLO, nightlife also includes the Madonna Inn and its Silver Bar Cocktail Lounge (100 Madonna Rd., 805/784-2432, www.madonnainn. com, 10am-midnight Mon.-Sat., 9am-11pm Sun.), decorated with Alice in Wonderland wingback chairs, retro pink barstools, and a blooming fuchsia carpet.

Shopping
A mix of local and national retailers populates the five blocks comprising downtown, primarily along Monterey and Marsh Streets, and the main drag on Higuera. Cool, hip clothing is at Ambiance (737 Higuera St., 805/540-3380, www.shopambiance.com, 10am-8pm Mon.-Sat., 11am-7pm Sun.), with jewelry and accessories for every occasion. HepKat Clothing & Beauty Parlor (785 Higuera St., 805/547-0777, www. hepkatclothing.com, 10am-8pm daily) is a fashion-forward boutique that doubles as a beauty salon.

An open-air market, Avila Valley Barn (560 Avila Beach Dr., 805/595-2816, www. avilavalleybarn.com, 9am-6pm daily) provides another opportunity for gift shopping, gourmet foods, and even hay-rides. Stop by The Secret Garden Herb Shop (740 Higuera St., Ste. A, 805/544-4372, www.organicherbshop.com, 11am-6pm daily) and choose from rows and rows of fragrant organic teas.

Taste California olive oils and balsamic vinegars, available for sale by the ounce, at We Olive (958 Higuera St., 805/595-1376, www.weolive.com, 10am-5:30pm Mon.-Sat., 10am-5pm Sun.). Assorted local goods are found at The Crushed Grape (491 Madonna Rd., #1, 805/544-4449, www.crushedgrape.com, 9:30am-5:30pm Mon.-Fri., 9:30am-4pm Sat.), including a host of gourmet foods, gift baskets, and wines.

San Luis Obispo and Vicinity

To Morro Bay

EL CHORRO REGIONAL PARK

CAMP SAN LUIS OBISPO

Los Padres

National

Forest

BISHOPS PEAK

Bishop Peak

W FOOTHILL BLVD

CERRO SAN LUIS

Cerro San Luis Obispo

Laguna Lake

SYCAMORE CANYON RD

MADONNA INN

Cal Poly San Luis Obispo

MISSION SAN LUIS OBISPO DE TOLOSA

LA CUESTA INN/APPLE FARM/PEACH TREE INN

JAFFA CAFÉ

SAN LUIS OBISPO MUSEUM OF ART

AMTRAK

AVENUE INN DOWNTOWN

SOUTH ST

San Luis Obispo

CRUSHED GRAPE GIFTS

WALLY'S BICYCLE WORKS

S HIGUERA ST

TANK FARM RD

SAN LUIS OBISPO COUNTY REGIONAL AIRPORT

BUCKLEY RD

EL CAMINO REAL

ORCUTT RD

BAILEYANA, TANGENT & TRUE MYTH TASTING ROOM

BIDDLE RANCH RD

SEXTANT WINES

TIFFANY RANCH RD

ORCUTT RD

CORBETT CANYON RD

PRICE CANYON RD

AVILA BEACH DR

AVILA VALLEY BARN

Avila Beach

San Luis Obispo Bay

DOLPHIN BAY RESORT & SPA

VENTANA GRILL

Shell Beach

KON TIKI INN

PAPI'S GRILL

CRACKED CRAB

PISMO BEACH SURF SHOP

Pismo Beach

PISMO BEACH PIER

PACIFIC OCEAN

Grover Beach

PISMO BEACH BUTTERFLY GROVE

To Solvang

Arroyo Grande

LOPEZ DR

HUASNA RD

0   2 mi

0   2 km

© MOON.COM

Wine-Tasting in Edna Valley

Vineyards sprawl across San Luis Obispo's **Edna Valley,** embracing cool, coastal conditions that prove ideal for growing favorite oenophile varietals such as pinot noir and chardonnay. Around 30 wineries operate throughout the valley, mostly around CA-227.

Standout wineries in the valley include the century-old yellow schoolhouse tasting room surrounded by vineyards at **Baileyana** (5828 Orcutt Rd., 805/269-8200, www.baileyana.com, 10am-5pm daily), which offers wines including pinot noir rosé and alternative whites. **Sextant Wines** (1653 Old Price Canyon Rd., 805/542-0133, www.sextantwines.com, 10am-4pm Mon.-Fri., 10am-5pm Sat.-Sun.), housed in the old mercantile building of the Township of Old Edna, offers a conceptual and sometimes literal blend of fruit grown in SLO and farther north in the warmer climate around Paso Robles.

Getting There

The Edna Valley is accessed off CA-227, which splits from US-101 south of San Luis Obispo around the Madonna Inn. It rejoins US-101 south in Arroyo Grande, near Pismo Beach.

The SLO community comes out Thursday evenings for the idyllic **Downtown SLO Farmers Market** (Higuera St. between Osos and Nipomo, 805/541-0286 www.downtownslo.com/farmers-market, 6pm-9pm Thurs.) to literally enjoy the fruits (and vegetables and nuts) of the region's year-round growing season. You'll also find terrific local barbecue, activities for children, and quirky live music. While you're in the area, take a moment to add fresh gum to **Bubblegum Alley** (733 Higuera St.), where millions of pieces of chewed gum have been applied to its walls since the 1950s.

Recreation

Hiking

San Luis Obispo has several hiking and biking areas. Probably the most well-known is **Bishop Peak** (4 mi/6 km round-trip), the highest of the Nine Sisters (or Morros), a chain of volcanic peaks in the Santa Lucia Mountains that stretch east from Morro Bay. Several switchbacks climb through open oak woodlands, and up the west and east summits of the peak. There are plenty of oak trees, California blackberry, sage scrub, chaparral, monkey flower, and poison oak, which you'll want to avoid. The peak can be accessed from two trailheads, from either Patricia Drive or Highland Drive.

Biking

Bicycles are welcome at **Cerro San Luis Obispo,** a member of the Nine Sisters, and the mountain has multiple biking trails. The best trails are accessed via Marsh Street or Carriage Road.

In the heart of downtown, **Wally's Bicycle Works** (209 Bonetti Dr., 805/544-4116, www.wallysbikes.com, 10am-6pm Mon.-Fri., 10am-5pm Sat., $35-40/day) offers bike and gear rentals at good prices.

Food

House-roasted coffee goes with café breakfasts, salads, and sandwiches at **Kreuzberg Coffee** (685 Higuera St., 805/439-2060, www.kreuzbergcalifornia.com, 7:30am-10pm daily, $5-10), the sort of large, central coffee shop that doubles as a community hub. After 6pm, light pub-style fare is served, along with wine and beer, often accompanied by live entertainment in the shop and/or a small performance space in the back.

The Central Coast takes pride in its contribution to American barbecue: the ranch hand cut of sirloin known as tri-tip. Fans flock from every direction for the tri-tip sandwiches at **Firestone Grill** (1001 Higuera St., 805/783-1001, 11am-10pm Sun.-Wed., 11am-11pm Thurs.-Sat., $6-13), which serves chewy rolls topped by thin slices of tender, slow-cooked beef and barbecue sauce.

You'll find a full ranch and barbecue experience at **F.McLintock Saloon & Dining** (686 Higuera St., 805/541-0686, 7am-9pm Sun.-Thurs., 7am-9:30pm Fri.-Sat., $20-45), particularly during the Thursday Farmers Market, when long lines form for the variety of barbecued meats cooked by whooping grill masters on the sidewalk.

A popular stop, **Jaffa Café** (1308 Monterey St., 805/543-2449, www.jaffacafe.us, 10:30am-9pm Mon.-Fri., 11am-9pm Sat.-Sun., $8-14) whips up phenomenal Mediterranean dishes, including gyros, falafels, kebabs, and excellent hummus.

A pioneer of farm-to-table cuisine in the area, **Big Sky Café** (1121 Broad St., 805/545-5401, 7am-9pm Mon.-Thurs., 7am-10pm Fri., 8am 10pm Sat., 8am-9pm Sun., $15-25) takes advantage of its proximity to farming, ranching, and fishing to provide vegetarian, pescatarian, and meat dishes.

A hot spot for locals and an iconic dining experience, **Novo Restaurant and Lounge** (726 Higuera St., 805/543-3986, www.novorestaurant.com, 11am-9pm Mon.-Thurs., 11am-1am Fri.-Sat., 10am-9pm Sun., $18-36) features a riverside patio, a flavorful array of international dishes, an endless selection of wine, and a full bar.

Inside the Madonna Inn, the **Gold Rush Steak House** (100 Madonna Rd., 805/543-3000, www.madonnainn.com, 5pm-10pm daily, $30-70) offers by far the most ornate decor of any restaurant in

Top to bottom: the caveman room at the Madonna Inn; the Gold Rush Steak House at the Madonna Inn; Bishop Peak.

the region. It's a traditional mid-century steak house . . . except for the hot pink leather booths, an oak-pit grill, and a giant tree adorned with light fixtures in the center of the dining room.

Accommodations

San Luis has a number of good places to stay, with reasonable rates that drop considerably after the summertime peak season. First on the list is the famed ★ **Madonna Inn** (100 Madonna Rd., 805/543-3000, www.madonnainn. com, from $220), a whimsical hotel with kitschy vibes, eccentric taste, and an excessively "pink" café. Every room is uniquely and memorably decorated, to the point that they're featured on postcards in the gift shop.

On the more affordable side, you can share a dorm room at **Hosteling International San Luis Obispo** (1617 Santa Rosa St., 805/544-4678, from $35), which is close to the train station as well as downtown. The hostel offers a fireplace lounge, a grill-equipped patio, a kitchen, and musical instruments available for guests to play. A shaded porch and tree swing highlight the pleasantly budget-friendly **Peach Tree Inn** (2001 Monterey St., 805/543-3170, www.peachtreeinn. com, from $75).

Avenue Inn Downtown San Luis Obispo (345 Marsh St., 805/543-6443, from $100) also offers affordable rates and is in walking distance to downtown restaurants and shopping. **La Cuesta Inn** (2074 Monterey St., 805/543-2777, from $150) has large rooms, free continental breakfast, and free DVD rentals, a steal for the price.

Several hotels offer charming accommodations for a bit more cash. **Apple Farm** (2015 Monterey St., 805/544-2040, www.applefarm.com, from $180) is an upscale country hotel with rooms that are smaller than average but cozy and tastefully decorated. The **Petit Soleil Bed & Breakfast** (1473 Monterey St., 805/549-0321, www.petitsoleilslo.com, $180-300), a lovely European-style bed-and-breakfast, offers elegant morning meals and complimentary evening wine-tasting.

Live like a rock star at the **SLO Brew Lofts** (738 Higuera St., 805/543-1843, www.slobrew.com/the-lofts, from $300). In the center of downtown, the brick wall lofts above the SLO Brew beer and music venue trade the quiet life for kitchens and amenities like vinyl records, musical instruments, and MTV-like decor.

Information and Services

San Luis Obispo Visitor Center (895 Monterey St., 805/781-2777, www.slo-chamber.org, 9:30am-5pm Sun.-Wed., 9:30am-6pm Thurs.-Sat.) is a good resource for brochures and maps. They also provide information on available discounts for restaurants and events.

Getting Around

Most everything in SLO's downtown area is within walking distance, and in cases where walking is not preferred, county bus lines run consistently throughout town. **San Luis Obispo Regional Transit Authority** (179 Cross St., 805/781-4833, www.slorta.org, $1.50 one-way) operates bus routes throughout the region, including to Paso Robles, San Simeon, Cambria, Morro Bay, and Pismo Beach.

◈ Side Trip: Morro Bay and Cayucos

Morro Bay

Morro Bay (pop. 10,648) is part of a coastal California that seems to be vanishing. It's not fancy or pretentious here, and hasn't been overbuilt with trendy shops and hotels. The atmosphere is languid; visitors can stroll along the Embarcadero to the call of sea lions, browsing the small shops and snacking on saltwater taffy. You're just as likely to see veteran fisherfolk walking around town as tourists.

The defining geographical feature of Morro Bay is the impressive ancient volcanic and sacred Chumash site called **Morro Rock,** an unmistakable round formation rising out of the bay. You cannot climb on it since it's home to endangered peregrine falcons. The **Museum of Natural History** (20 State Park Rd., 805/772-2694, 10am-5pm daily, $3 adults, children under 17 free) has a great location in the back bay, near the marina, with a view of the rock. It's a small, kid-friendly museum, with touch exhibits about sand, waves, and animals and a good assortment of stuffed birds, like the peregrine falcon, and a massive albatross dangling from the ceiling. There's also a full-size skeleton of a minke whale on the outside deck overlooking the bay.

Shopping

Morro Bay is a good place to shop for vintage finds, thanks to a high concentration of antiques shops. Most are found along Morro Bay Boulevard, east of Main Street, or head north on Main Street to explore the charming art deco structure housing **Morro Bay Antiques** (1612 Main St., 805/225-1620, www.morrobayantiques.info, 10am-5pm daily).

Food

Frankie and Lola's (1154 Front St., 805/771-9306, www.frankieandlolas.com, 6:30am-2pm daily, $8-14) serves breakfast and lunch in a small, deliberately low-key space. It is one of the few places to open early, should you need breakfast before you leave town. You can see the rock while you enjoy the creative food, like French toast that is dipped in crème brûlée and mixed with whole nuts.

Local favorite ★ **Taco Temple** (2680 N. Main St., 805/772-4965, www.tacotemple.com, 11am-9pm daily, $14-30) serves the largest tacos you've ever seen. Order the fresh local catch and split it with a friend—do not try to tackle a burrito on your own!

Accommodations

Morro Bay is a relaxing place to spend the night. The **Sundown Inn** (640 Main St., 805-772-7381, www.sundownmotel.com, $75-100) is a budget choice, with few amenities except for a coffeemaker in the room and a Wi-Fi signal. The rooms are standard size and minimally decorated, but clean and comfortable. The conveniently located **Estero Inn** (501 Embarcadero, 805/772-1500, www.esteroinn.com, $140-200) also has eight well-appointed rooms.

Cayucos

The little resort town of **Cayucos** (pop. 2,592) revolves around its beach: swimming, surfing, kayaking, and skin diving are popular, and there's a pier for rock fishing and surf fishing year-round at Estero Bay.

Food and Accommodations

Most of the restaurants are along Ocean Avenue. **Schooners** (171 N. Ocean Ave., 805/995-3883, www.schoonerswharf.com, 11am-9pm Sun.-Thurs., 11am-10pm Fri.-Sat., $12-26) is a great spot for seafood. Just in front of the beach, **Ruddell's Smokehouse** (101 D St., 805/995-5028, www.smokerjim.com, 11am-6pm daily, $6-10) offers smoked fish in sandwiches, salads, or stuffed into spongy flour tortillas for delicious, quick eats.

Private vacation rentals abound in Cayucos, but more traditional accommodations include the central, beachfront, and pet-friendly **Shoreline Inn** (1 N. Ocean Ave., 805/995-3681, www.cayucosshorelineinn.com, $125-200) and the charming **On the Beach Bed & Breakfast** (181 N. Ocean Ave., 805/995-3200, http://californiaonthebeach.com, $150-250), with ocean views and easy access to the beach.

Getting There

From San Luis Obispo, drive 13 miles (21 km) north on US-101 to Morro Bay. From Morro Bay, continue 6 miles (10 km) north on US-101 to Cayucos.

Cambria

Located roughly 10 miles (16 km) south of Hearst Castle, **Cambria** (pop. 6,032) owes much of its prosperity to that giant attraction. But this small beach town becomes surprisingly spacious when you start exploring it. Plenty of visitors come here to ply Moonstone Beach, peruse the charming downtown area, and just drink in the laid-back, art-town feel.

Getting There

Cambria sits 9.3 miles (15 km) south of San Simeon on CA-1. About 4 miles (6 km) south of Cambria, CA-46 west connects 22 miles (35 km) inland to US-101.

Sights
★ Moonstone Beach

For breathtaking views of seascapes, wildlife, and tidepools, stroll the board-walk at **Moonstone Beach** (Moonstone Beach Dr.). Follow along the cliffs to find the way down to the beach. Although you won't find moonstone here, you will find plenty of agates, and possibly jasper and California jade. On the northern end of Moonstone Beach, **Leffingwell Landing** (San Simeon-Monterey Creek Rd.) offers spectacular views for the amateur or professional photographer and is a wonderful area to explore tidepools and marinelife.

Nitt Witt Ridge

While William Randolph Hearst built one of the most expensive homes ever seen in California, local eccentric Arthur Harold Beal (aka Captain Nit Wit or Der Tinkerpaw) got busy constructing the cheapest "castle" he could. **Nitt Witt Ridge** (881 Hillcrest Dr., 805/927-2690, $10, by appointment only) is the result of five decades of scavenging trash and

From top to bottom: Morro Rock; Moonstone Beach; young elephant seals at Piedras Blancas.

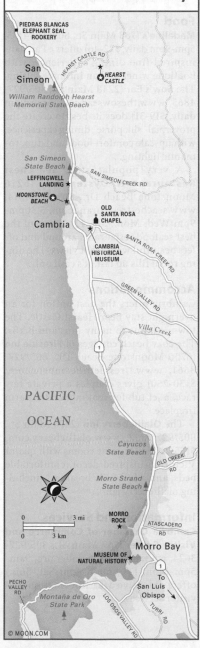

Cambria and Morro Bay

PIEDRAS BLANCAS
ELEPHANT SEAL
ROOKERY

San
Simeon

HEARST CASTLE RD

HEARST
CASTLE

*William Randolph Hearst
Memorial State Beach*

*San Simeon
State Beach*

LEFFINGWELL
LANDING ★

MOONSTONE
BEACH

SAN SIMEON CREEK RD

OLD
SANTA ROSA
CHAPEL

Cambria

CAMBRIA
HISTORICAL
MUSEUM

SANTA ROSA CREEK RD

GREEN VALLEY RD

Villa Creek

PACIFIC

OCEAN

*Cayucos
State Beach*

OLD CREEK RD

*Morro Strand
State Beach*

0   3 mi
0   3 km

MORRO
ROCK
★

ATASCADERO
RD

Morro Bay

MUSEUM OF
NATURAL HISTORY ★

To
San Luis
Obispo

PECHO
VALLEY
RD

*Montaña de Oro
State Park*

LOS OSOS VALLEY RD

TURRI RD

© MOON.COM

using it as building supplies to create a multistory home like no other on the coast. Today, you can make an appointment with owners Michael and Stacey O'Malley to take a tour of the property. (Please don't just drop in.)

Cambria Historical Museum

One of Cambria's oldest homes, the Guthrie-Bianchini House is the site of the **Cambria Historical Museum** (2251 Center St., 805/927-2891, http://cambriahistoricalsociety.com/museum.html, 1pm-4pm Fri.-Sun., 10am-1pm Mon., free). Built in 1870, the house was later sold to Benjamin Franklin, rumored to be a relative of the Benjamin Franklin who helped draft the Declaration of Independence and the U.S. Constitution, among a number of other historic acts. Today, it preserves exhibits on Cambria's treasures of the past, including an oar from the lifeboat of the SS *Montebello,* which sank off the coast of Cambria on December 23, 1941.

The Old Santa Rosa Chapel

A National Historic Registry Landmark, **The Old Santa Rosa Chapel** (2353 Main St., 805/927-1175, www.santarosachapel. com, 10am-3pm Fri.-Mon., free) is one of the oldest churches in the county. It rests on a hilltop among a pine and oak forest near an old pioneer cemetery. Although the chapel's final mass was in 1963, this pristine white church built of pine draws couples for wedding ceremonies, families for special celebrations, and curious visitors interested in the town's early settlement roots.

Recreation

Fiscalini Ranch Preserve (CA-1 to Windsor, past Shamel Park, 805/927-2856, www.ffrpcambria.org) offers one of the most popular trails, **Bluff Trail,** which is a continuation of the California Coastal Trail and offers awe-inspiring ocean views from almost every direction.

It is a fairly easy walk, including both a paved pathway and boardwalk. Bikes are allowed on specified trails only, and pets must be leashed.

Entertainment

Enjoy draft beer, pool, and $3 hot dogs at **Mozzi's Saloon** (2262 Main St., 805/927-4767, www.mozzissaloon.com, 1pm-close Mon.-Fri., 11m-close Sat., noon-close Sun.), in a historical building reminiscent of the cowboy days. For a good cocktail or specialty drink, go to **Moonstone Beach Bar & Grill** (6550 Moonstone Beach Dr., 805/927-3859, www.moonstonebeach.com, 11am-3pm and 5pm-9pm Mon.-Sat., 10:30am-3pm and 5pm-9pm Sun.), or for a full bar and one of the best Bloody Marys around, drop by **West End Bar and Grill** (774 Main St., 805/927-5521, www.west-endcambria.com, 10am-2am Mon.-Fri., 8am-2am Sat.-Sun.), a hub for meeting up with friends for a drink or watching a game on one of four TVs.

For music and $1 pints, **The Cambria Pub & Steakhouse** (4090 Burton Dr., 805/927-0782, 11am-9pm Sun.-Thurs., 11am-10pm Fri.-Sat.) brings in a good-size happy hour crowd. For eclectic entertainment, **Cambria Pines Lodge** (2905 Burton Dr., 805/927-4200, www.cambriapineslodge.com, 5pm-9pm daily) offers music including folk, rock, jazz, and even karaoke in its lounge.

Shopping

Filled with vintage treasures from more than 30 dealers, **Rich Man Poor Man Antique Mall** (2110 Main St., 805/203-5350, www.richmanpoormanantiques.com, 10am-5pm daily) features furniture, glassware, rugs, tapestries, art, and jewelry, all within a unique two-floor, loft building. At **Antiques on Main** (2338 Main St., 805/927-4292, 10am-5pm daily), you're bound to find something

to take home after browsing more than 10,000 square feet of goods.

Food

Madeline's (788 Main St., 805/927-4175, 5pm-9pm daily, $22-46) offers a Parisian-inspired fine dining experience, with boutique wines and an intimate setting. The **Sow's Ear** (2248 Main St., 805/927-4865, www.thesowsear.com, 5pm-9pm daily, $19-31) does its best to create the proverbial "silk purse" dining experience, with upscale comfort foods and dim, romantic lighting.

A very popular stop, **Sea Chest Restaurant & Oyster Bar** (6216 Moonstone Beach Dr., 805/927-4514, www.seachestrestaurant.com, 5:30pm-9pm Wed.-Mon., $18-42) is one of the best seafood restaurants around and offers beautiful waterfront views. The dining room fills up fast. It's cash only.

Accommodations

Cambria offers the best option for an overnight stay near Hearst Castle. The town is home to many inns and B&Bs. The cozy beach cottages of **Fireside Inn** (6700 Moonstone Beach Dr., 805/927-8661, www.firesideinncambria.com, $130-250) gives couples a private terrace, a jet tub for soaking, and a warm fireplace.

The **Olallieberry Inn** (2476 Main St., 805/927-3222, www.olallieberry.com, $155-210) offers nine rooms with quaint Victorian-inspired decor, comfortable beds, and a full daily breakfast (including olallieberry jam).

Information and Services

Cambria Chamber of Commerce and Visitor Center (767 Main St., 805/927-3624, www.cambriachamber.org, 9am-5pm Mon.-Fri., noon-4pm Sat.-Sun.) offers extensive area information and visitor services.

San Simeon

As the coastal highway skirts the Pacific Ocean north of San Luis Obispo, it passes a smattering of Central Coast beach retreats, eventually rising to the breathtaking wooded cliffs of Big Sur, leaving Southern California in the rearview mirror. But before it does, there's San Simeon (pop. 462), home to California's most opulent state park: Hearst Castle, the preserved country getaway that once hosted Hollywood's elite.

The tiny town of San Simeon was originally founded to support the construction of the century-old estate on the hill; its dock received material shipments and eventually the priceless global art, antiques, and furniture that decorate the castle. Today, the descendants of zebras once kept in Hearst's private zoo graze alongside cattle in pastures fronting the highway. Across the road, the ocean continues to provide the gorgeous vistas that inspired the famous tycoon to build his American palace. It can be convenient to stay in San Simeon or nearby Cambria, but Hearst Castle also makes a great day trip from San Luis Obispo or Pismo Beach.

Getting There

San Simeon is 10 miles (16 km) north of Cambria on CA-1.

Sights
★ Hearst Castle

TOP EXPERIENCE

In 1919, inspired by a lifetime of European travels, silver-mining heir and newspaper magnate William Randolph Hearst decided to "build a little something" on the hilltop campsite of his family's 250-thousand-acre cattle ranch. Even after divesting vast property holdings after the Great Depression, Hearst remained devoted to his San Simeon country home, which was under construction

for three decades. Hearst notoriously changed his mind about details large and small; architect Julia Morgan gamely managed revisions to produce an architectural marvel that overlooks one of the most magnificent coastal views in the state.

The result is **Hearst Castle** (750 Hearst Castle Rd., 800/444-4445, www.hearst-castle.org, 9am-4pm daily, $25 adults, $12 children 5-12), a lavish estate that boasts three luxurious guest cottages, several swimming pools, a private zoo, and gardens ornamented by ancient Greek, Roman, and Egyptian sculptures. At its center sits Casa Grande, a mansion with domed towers modeled after the Moorish palaces of Spain and filled with European medieval and Renaissance antiquities.

Hearst hosted hundreds of guests for weekend-long fêtes, including world leaders and other luminaries of the time, such as Winston Churchill, Cary Grant, and Charlie Chaplin (known to play on the property's tennis courts with Wimbledon champion Fred Perry). Following Hearst's death, the 127-acre property was donated to the state of California, and it has operated as a museum ever since.

Tours

Several distinct guided **tours** (from 9am daily) explore the grounds, residences, and the great rooms of the house. Purchase tour tickets at the visitors center or online (www.reservecalifornia.com) up to 60 days in advance.

A variety of tour options explore select parts of the house; most tours last 1-2 hours. At the end of each tour, guests are welcome to stroll the grounds, which include access to its glorious terraces, manicured gardens, and famed swimming pools: the Neptune Pool, where turquoise waters shimmer with the reflections of the Greek columns and statuary surrounding it, and the ornate Roman Pool, an indoor spectacle boasting vaulted arch ceilings beset with blue and gold-infused mosaic tiles.

Guest are not permitted to drive to the castle. Instead, buses continually shuttle tour groups from the visitors center, which provides food vendors, restrooms, and copious free parking. Return shuttles board outside the Roman Pool every 15 minutes. Plan on spending a minimum of 3-4 hours here, not including drive time.

William Randolph Hearst Memorial State Beach

The **William Randolph Hearst Memorial State Beach** (750 Hearst Castle Rd., 805/927-2020, www.parks.ca.gov, dawn-dusk daily) is just across from the entrance to Hearst Castle and offers beautiful coastline views off a 1,000-foot wooden pier, surrounded by sandy beaches. Fishing is permitted off the pier without a license, but limits are enforced. There are plenty of picnic areas and hiking and kayaking opportunities. The park also encompasses the **Coastal Discovery Center** (805/927-6575, www.

montereybay.noaa.gov, 11am-5pm Fri.-Sun. and holidays, free), which offers educational and interactive exhibits detailing coastal geography and history.

Piedras Blancas

First illuminated in 1875 to guide mariners along the rocky California coast, the **Piedras Blancas Light Station** (15950 CA-1, 805/927-7361, www.piedrasblancas.org, tours: 9:45am Tues., Thurs., and Sat., $10 adults, $5 children 6-17) now serves as a national monument and wildlife sanctuary. Lighthouse tours are offered three mornings per week and provide a more detailed glimpse of the region's cultural and natural history.

About 2 miles (3 km) south of the lighthouse, the **Northern Elephant Seal Rookery** (CA-1, 805/924-1628, www.elephantseal.org) has been a gathering spot for elephant seals since the 1990s. In winter months, the seals come here to breed, and by summer, they molt. Winter is the

Hearst Castle's indoor Roman Pool

best time to view the males, females, and newborn pups. At the large, dirt parking area, plaques detail facts about the elephant seal. A **visitor center** (Plaza del Cavalier, 250 San Simeon Ave., 805/924-1628) is located south of the viewing areas.

Accommodations

The closest lodging to Hearst Castle is a cluster of affordable motels in San Simeon. There are a few uninspiring eats in San Simeon, but Cambria will be the best bet for decent food. The **San Simeon Lodge** (9520 Castillo Dr., 805/927-4601, www.sansimeonlodge.net, from $49) is a 60-unit motel close to the beach.

For a step up, try **Cavalier Oceanfront Resort** (9415 Hearst Dr., 805/927-4688, www.cavalierresort.com, from $150), a pet-friendly 50-year-old hotel with heated pools, a fitness center, and options including in-room fireplaces and ocean views.

Essentials

Getting There

Air

The following airports offer the best access to Southern California.

Los Angeles International Airport (LAX, 1 World Way, 855/463-5252, www.flylax.com) is Southern California's biggest and one of the world's busiest airports.

Hollywood Burbank Airport (BUR, 2627 N. Hollywood Way, Burbank, 818/840-8840, https://hollywoodburbankairport.com), 35 miles (56 km) from LAX, is much closer to Hollywood.

John Wayne Airport (SNA, 18601 Airport Way, Santa Ana, 949/252-5200, www.ocair.com), about 15 miles (24 km) from Disneyland in Southern California's Orange County, connects to all the major West Coast cities.

San Diego International Airport (SAN, 3225 N. Harbor Dr., 619/400-2404, www.san.org) is a regional, single-runway commercial airport with domestic flights and limited international providers.

A valid photo ID (driver's license or passport) and boarding pass are required to pass through airport security checkpoints. Depending on the time of year and time of day, security wait times can take 30 minutes or more, and checked bags must be processed at least 45 minutes prior to getscheduled departure time to ensure timely arrival at your destination. Plan to arrive two hours early for all LAX flights. Consult your airline to monitor flight delays, cancellations, and other changes.

All airports provide assistance to the elderly and individuals with disabilities. Food, restrooms, rental car companies, and taxi and shuttle services are on-site.

Train

Expedient train travel is available between San Diego, Orange County, Los Angeles, and Santa Barbara, with bus service connecting mid-size and major cities. Service to remote areas is spotty at best.

Amtrak (800/872-7245, www.amtrak.com) offers service between coastal cities in Southern California on the *Pacific Surfliner* line, which runs from San Luis Obispo to Santa Barbara, Los Angeles, and San Diego. Trains arrive and depart from **San Luis Obispo** (1011 Railroad Ave.); **Santa Barbara** (209 State St.); Los Angeles's **Union Station** (800 N. Alameda St.); and San Diego's **Santa Fe Depot** (1050 Kettner Blvd.).

Bus

Greyhound Lines (800/231-2222, www.greyhound.com) serves major cities in Southern California, with nationwide connections. Buses travel main interstates going both north and south (US-101, I-5), stopping in many small towns, including points along the coast. Buses do not stop in state or national parks or at tourist attractions.

Urban bus stations are often in areas where it may not be safe to walk to or from the station. Small towns don't always have dedicated bus stations, so contact the provider to locate a curbside bus stop.

Tickets may be purchased online with a credit card or at a station ticket window when available, using credit, debit, travelers checks, or cash. Be sure to bring photo ID. Smartphone users may download Greyhound's mobile app to manage trips, search schedules, and find terminal locations.

Car Rental and Ride Share

Major international rental car companies are easily found at major airports, and most allow you to pick up a car in one location (Los Angeles, for example) and drop it off in another (like San Diego). Rentals require a valid credit card and driver's license for all registered drivers, with a minimum age requirement of 21. Expect to pay around $30 per day and up, plus taxes, fees, and insurance (optional), as well as additional fees for drivers under the age of 25. If you are in the military or a member of AAA, AARP, or Costco, discounts may apply. For higher fees, most rental companies offer optional upgrades including alternative fuel and all-wheel-drive vehicles.

Rental car companies include:

- **Avis** (800/331-1212, www.avis.com)

- **Budget** (800/218-7992, www.budget.com)

- **Dollar** (800/800-3665, www.dollar.com)

- **Enterprise** (800/261-7331, www.enterprise.com)

- **Hertz** (800/654-3131, www.hertz.com)

- **National** (877/222-9058, www.nationalcar.com)

- **Thrifty** (800/847-4389, www.thrifty.com)

In addition to traditional car rental agencies, Internet-based car-sharing services offer short-term on-demand rentals for driving within some cities. **Zipcar** (866/494-7227, www.zipcar.com) rents vehicles by the hour, with cars picked up and dropped off at designated parking lot locations. Zipcar serves the following Southern California cities: Burbank, Claremont, Los Angeles, Malibu, Pasadena, San Diego, San Luis Obispo, Santa Barbara, Santa Monica, and West Hollywood. Service requires advanced online member registration—including proof of driver's license—and should be completed a week or two prior to use.

Smartphone car-sharing services provide taxi alternatives, with on-demand door-to-door rides between specific destinations within a city. **Uber** (www.uber.com) is available in most large and mid-size Southern California cities, as well as a few smaller coastal towns, while **Lyft** (www.lyft.com) is primarily available in large cities. Both require credit card payment and downloading an app to your phone.

Driving Directions

The freeway was invented in Los Angeles, and most destinations along this road trip connect with the City of Angels via major freeways. **Highway 101** (CA-101) extends northwest from Los Angeles to Santa Barbara and San Luis Obispo. **I-5** travels from Los Angeles south through Anaheim to San Diego and all the way to the border with Mexico. **I-10** starts on the coast in Santa Monica and stretches east through Los Angeles to Palm Springs and Joshua Tree. Southern Californians often refer to freeways by their number, using the word *the* (*the* 10, *the* 5, and *the* 101).

East of L.A. and before reaching Palm Springs, I-10 intersects with a third major route. **I-15** is an inland freeway that extends north to Las Vegas and south to San Diego. Though it's no longer a major highway, **Route 66** runs parallel to I-10 before it turns north along I-15 through the Cajon Pass. At Barstow, Route 66 heads east into the Mojave Desert, parallel to **I-40**. The historic Route 66 barely exists in some sections, while other stretches have to be bypassed, making the scenic route slow and hard to follow.

The iconic Pacific Coast Highway (**CA-1**) trades great scenery for occasional red lights and gaps in continuity. CA-1 follows the coast from San Diego north, weaving in and out of I-5 through the beach cities of Orange County. In southern Los Angeles, CA-1 picks up in Santa Monica and continues north through Malibu where it merges with US-101 north. CA-1 splits off from US-101 in San Luis Obispo, skirting the coast north to Hearst Castle.

Southern California's mountains and deserts are connected by smaller state highways and often provide alternate routes that can prove faster or more interesting options than the major interstates.

Road Rules

Drivers and all passengers are required by law to wear a seat belt. All motorcyclists must wear a helmet. Infant and child safety seats are required for children under 4 feet 9 inches (145 centimeters) and/or under the age of 8. It is illegal to operate a vehicle and a handheld device at the same time. There are severe penalties ($1,000 or more) for throwing litter or garbage of any kind from a vehicle. Drinking and driving is illegal; driving while intoxicated is extremely dangerous and subject to heavy fines and jail time. Always abide by posted speed limits and other road signs to avoid pricey traffic tickets, parking tickets, or tows.

Highway Safety

Roads in Southern California may feature sharp curves and steep ledges with no shoulders or guardrails. Drive as slowly as road conditions demand, even if that's slower than the posted speed limit. Routes with appealing views often offer periodic Vista Points, small pullouts or parking lots where drivers can get off the road and park. Watch the road for inattentive drivers trying to sneak long peeks at the scenery while behind the wheel.

In case of an emergency, always carry flares, a spare tire, and a jack and wrench. Though on some parts of the road you may not receive cell phone service, carry a phone with you. Only pull over when absolutely necessary! Otherwise, wait until you reach a pullout or other safe area. When pulling over, get as far onto the shoulder as you can.

To receive reports on **road conditions,** call **511.** If your phone carrier does not support 511, call toll-free at 800/427-7623. For **emergency assistance** and services, call **911.**

Road and Weather Conditions

Road and weather conditions in Southern California are usually pretty safe

road in Death Valley

year-round. The most hazardous condition you are likely to encounter in the coastal regions is fog. When visibility is opaque, use the pullouts as needed and wait until the roadway clears; otherwise, use low beams and drive *very* slowly.

In winter, snow may be a factor in mountain areas and at high elevation. Tire chains may be required on some roads, and drivers should be prepared to install them. In inclement weather, some highways may be closed indefinitely making routes impassable.

Following heavy precipitation, mudslides and rockslides may close coastal roads and even freeways for extended stretches. Always check traffic conditions following a period of heavy rain or snowfall.

California deserts present a different hazard: extreme heat and aridity. Drivers should keep at least a gallon of water per person in their vehicles for emergencies. Dehydration can happen quickly when stranded in the desert.

The biggest emergencies often involve natural disasters. The increasing frequency of wildfires in California has cost lives as well as destroyed cherished landmarks and landscapes. Malibu is still recovering from the 2018 Woolsey Fire, which wiped out most of its coastal forest. The risk of wildfire only gets higher in the summer months, when extreme temperatures and dry conditions threaten inland forests and deserts. Monitor news and weather channels before hitting the road to your next destination, and never ignore public evacuation orders.

Check road condition updates when planning your route and again before hitting the road each day, and be prepared to take alternate routes in the event of a road closure. To check for road closures and conditions, consult the **California Department of Transportation** (www.quickmap.dot.ca.gov) or dial 511.

Wildlife on the Road

On rural or remote drives, coyotes, deer, and bears can run onto the road without warning. Closer to urban areas, coyotes, raccoons, possums, and other small animals are common. Warning signs are usually posted in areas with a high instance of animal crossings. If you do come upon wildlife standing in the road, slow your vehicle and honk your horn—do not get out of the vehicle or attempt to pass and never feed wildlife. Wait until the road is clear, then continue on your way.

Road Etiquette

Some portions of this road trip are on two-lane highways, which means there are few opportunities for faster vehicles to pass slower traffic. California state law requires that slower vehicles use turnouts or safely pull over when five or more cars line up behind them. If another driver makes it clear they want to pass, then let them; hopefully slower drivers will do the same for you. Avoid jeopardizing your safety by trying to navigate a winding, unfamiliar highway at an uncomfortable speed. It is imperative to always leave at least one car length between your vehicle and the one ahead of you (especially motorcyclists and bicyclists!).

Traffic can get pretty congested in Southern California, especially around the larger cities. Avoid driving during rush hour (usually 7am-9am and 3pm-6pm) when possible and check traffic conditions in advance online. If navigating around road construction or an accident, alternate one car from each lane to merge at a time.

Parking

Most attractions, museums, parks, and beaches offer on-site parking, though many require a fee. When booking a hotel, ask if there is a secured parking garage or an open lot, and if there is a daily fee (parking fees can be up to $40 per day in cities). Some hotels offer free parking.

Fuel

While gas stations are plentiful near urban areas, they can be few and far between in remote parts of the southern desert, particularly around Death Valley, the Mojave Desert, along Route 66, and at the Salton Sea. There will be long stretches where you may not see a gas station for miles. When driving through these stretches, be aware of your vehicle's miles per gallon and fuel up whenever the opportunity appears. Gas prices in the desert are higher than in cities and suburbs, so even topping off half a tank can be worthwhile. The GasBuddy app and website (www.gasbuddy.com) guides users to fueling stations and sometimes highlights the cheapest rates.

Motorcycles

If Southern California offers an amazing road trip, you better believe this goes for motorcycles as well. When driving on the road, be mindful of motorcycle riders; it's recommended to keep at least three car lengths between your vehicle and a motorcycle. Motorcycle helmets are required by law. Riders should never use the shoulder (or fog line) to pass another vehicle. Use pullouts when necessary and watch for wildlife darting across the road. Windstorms and rains can create difficult road conditions for riders, including fallen tree branches, debris, and standing water.

Visas and Officialdom

Passports and Visas

Whether coming to the United States from abroad, or planning to cross into Mexico, you'll need a **passport.** Depending on your country of origin, visiting Southern California may also require a **visa.**

Visitors with current passports from one of the following countries qualify for the **visa waiver program:** Andorra, Australia, Austria, Belgium, Brunei, Chile, Czech Republic, Denmark, Estonia, Finland, France, Germany, Greece, Hungary, Iceland, Ireland, Italy, Japan, Latvia, Liechtenstein, Lithuania, Luxembourg, Malta, Monaco, the Netherlands, New Zealand, Norway, Portugal, San Marino, Singapore, Slovakia, Slovenia, South Korea, Spain, Sweden, Switzerland, Taiwan, and the United Kingdom. They must apply online with the Electronic System for Travel Authorization at www.cbp.gov and hold a **return plane ticket** to their home countries within 90 days from their time of entry. Holders of **Canadian passports** don't need visas or waivers. In most countries, the local U.S. embassy can provide a **tourist visa.** Plan for at least two weeks for visa processing, longer during the busy summer season (June-Aug.). More information is available online: www.travel.state.gov.

Customs

Foreigners and U.S. citizens age 21 or older may import (free of duty) the following: one liter of alcohol (33.8 fluid ounces), 200 cigarettes (one carton), 100 cigars, and $800 worth of gifts.

International travelers must declare amounts that exceed $10,000 in cash (U.S. or foreign), travelers checks, or money orders. Meat products, fruits, and vegetables are prohibited due to health and safety regulations.

Drivers entering California stop at **Agricultural Inspection Stations.** They don't need to present a passport, visa, or even a driver's license but should be prepared to present fruits and vegetables, even those purchased within neighboring states just over the border. If you've got produce, it could be infected by a known problem pest or disease; expect it to be confiscated on the spot.

International Driving Permits

International visitors need to secure an **International Driving Permit** from their home countries before coming to the United States and are expected to be familiar with the driving regulations of the states they will visit. They should also bring the government-issued driver's license from their home countries. More information is available online: www.usa.gov/visitors-driving.

Travel Tips

Conduct and Customs

The legal **drinking age** in the United States is 21. Expect to have your ID checked not only in bars and clubs, but also before you purchase alcohol in restaurants, wineries, and markets. **Recreational marijuana** is legal to possess in amounts up to one ounce in California, but may only be purchased by adults 21 and over at licensed, dedicated retailers. Smoking marijuana in public is prohibited by law and not allowed at most hotels.

Smoking cigarettes is banned in many places. Don't expect to find a smoking section in restaurants or an ashtray in bars. Some establishments allow smoking on outdoor patios. Many hotels, motels, and inns are also nonsmoking. Smokers should request a smoking room when making reservations. Note that in California, it's illegal to sell cigarettes to anyone under 21.

Money

The currency is the **U.S. dollar ($).** Most businesses accept the **major credit cards** Visa, MasterCard, Discover, and American Express—either with magnetic strip or chip technology. ATM and debit cards work at many stores and restaurants, and ATMs are available throughout the region. You can **change currency** at any international airport or bank. Currency exchange may be easier in large cities and more difficult in rural and wilderness areas.

Banking hours tend to be 8am-5pm Monday-Friday, 9am-noon Saturday. Never count on a bank being open on Sunday. There are **24-hour ATMs** not only at banks but at many markets, bars, and hotels. A **convenience fee** of $2-4 per transaction may apply.

Internet Access

While many hotels and B&Bs offer free Wi-Fi, some charge a fee of $6-12 per hour. Free Wi-Fi is becoming more and more available at cafés and public libraries. Do not expect to find Internet-friendly locations within rural areas, parks, or campgrounds. Likewise, cellular data transmissions may be unavailable at remote locations.

Cell Phones

Several spots along the winding Pacific Coast Highway are dead zones. Cell service is simply unreliable even from the best carrier. Check your phone and make your calls on arrival or before leaving a travel hub or large town along the route.

Hotel and Motel Chains

Hotel and motel chains like **Best Western** (800/780-7234, www.bestwestern.com), **Motel 6** (800/557-3435, www.motel6.com), **Days Inn** (800/225-3297, www.daysinn.com), and **Super 8** (800/454-3213, www.super8.com) are easy to find. Many offer discount rates (depending on season) and reasonable amenities. Expect higher rates during the summer (July-Sept.) on the coast, from fall through spring (Oct.-May) in the desert, and during winter (Dec.-Feb.) in the mountain areas.

If you plan on spending the summer at the beach, make hotel or campground reservations in advance. If you prefer to wing it, you might find some good lodging deals as a walk-in guest. Shop for deals and use discount cards or auto-membership discounts that offer lower rates at participating hotels and motels. Local visitors centers often have complimentary magazines with hotel and motel discount coupons; you may also find these at restaurants, convenience stores, and local businesses.

Midweek rates are often cheaper unless a special event is taking place. Be sure to ask if the quoted rate includes tax, as this can add 10 percent or more to your final bill. If you find yourself without accommodations, many online travel apps, including www.hoteltonight.com, www.hotwire.com, and www.priceline.com, offer last-minute bookings.

Traveling with Children

Children will enjoy aquariums, amusement parks, and, perhaps most of all, the beach. Many beaches and parks are equipped with bathrooms. You'll also find several good family-friendly restaurant and hotel options. Generally hotels allow up to four in a room, so be sure to inquire about a suite if necessary.

The main concerns when traveling the highway with children are that the long drive can make them antsy and the twists and turns can cause nausea, even for moms and dads. Estimated drive times throughout this book may take longer with children, owing to restroom breaks and other stops. Bring plenty of car-fun activities to keep your kids busy, like books and travel games.

Parents should be wary of their children's activities, primarily at scenic lookout points and on trails. Many scenic pullouts do not have guardrails; it can be extremely unsafe to stand close to any cliff's edge, as loose earth can make it easy to slip and fall, and erosion may cause the ground to disappear beneath your feet.

Senior Travelers

If you are over 60 years of age, ask about potential discounts. Nearly all attractions, amusement parks, theaters, and museums offer discount benefits to seniors. Be sure to have some form of valid identification on hand or you'll end up having to pay full price. A driver's license or current passport will do.

Accessibility

Most public areas are equipped to accommodate travelers with disabilities, including hotels, restaurants, museums, public transportation, and several state and national parks where you'll find paved trails. That said, there are still some attractions that will pose challenges, such as certain historic sights and wildlife areas.

Those with permanent disabilities, including visual impairments, should inquire about a free **Access Pass** (888/275-8747, ext. 3, www.store.usgs.gov/accesspass) from the National Park Service. It is offered as part of the America the Beautiful—National Park and Federal Recreational Lands Pass Series. You can obtain an Access Pass in person at any federal recreation site or by submitting a completed application by mail ($10 processing fee). The pass does not provide benefits for special recreation permits or concessionaire fees.

Environmental Concerns

California has environmental concerns that involve water pollution, disruption of fish and wildlife habitats, and emissions. The state has poured resources into conservation and preservation efforts and has moved forward with renewable energy, recycling, and composting campaigns.

You can do your part as a visitor and protect the natural environment through the following: Stay on trails and do not step on plantlife; utilize pet waste receptacles in pet-friendly campgrounds; protect water sources by camping at least 150 feet (46 m) from lakes and streams; leave rocks and plants as you find them; light fires only where permitted and use only established firepits; pack it in, pack it out—check your campsite for garbage and properly dispose of it or take it with you.

Health and Safety

If immediate help is needed, always **dial 911;** otherwise, go to the nearest 24-hour hospital emergency room.

Carry your **medical card** and a list of any **medications** you are taking. Keep a **first-aid kit** in your car or luggage, and take it with you when hiking. A good kit should include sterile gauze pads, butterfly bandages, adhesive tape, antibiotic ointment, alcohol wipes, pain relievers for both adults and children, and a multipurpose pocketknife.

Do not ignore **health or safety warnings!** Some beaches within California have health warning signs posted due to potential bacteria in the water. If you see such a sign, stay out of the water or risk getting sick.

Ocean dangers can include strong undercurrents, stingrays, jellyfish, sharks, sharp underwater hazards, extreme cold, and massive rogue waves in the winter. Inexperienced swimmers, and especially children, should only enter the water when a lifeguard is on duty. Experienced swimmers should take caution as well; changing tides and rip currents may prove an unseen yet life-threatening risk at beaches.

Whether you're in a large city, resort area, small town, or even a wilderness area, take precautions against **theft.** Don't leave any valuables in the car. If you must, keep them out of sight in the trunk or a compartment with a lock. Keep wallets, purses, cameras, mobile phones, and other small electronics on your person when possible.

Crime is more prevalent in large cities. Be alert to your surroundings, just as you would in any unfamiliar place. Avoid using ATMs at night or walking alone after dark. Carry your car keys in your hand when walking out to your car. Certain **urban neighborhoods** are best avoided at night. Call a taxi to avoid walking too far to get to your car or waiting for public transportation.

Keep a safe distance from **wildlife.** Stay at least 300 feet (91 m) away. Bring binoculars if you want an up-close view. If you encounter a bear or cougar, do not run or turn your back! Try to appear larger and bring pepper spray and a walking stick to use in defense. Stay in a group when hiking, as these animals typically target lone prey. Keep children close and where you can see them.

Be cautious at **viewpoints,** especially along coastal cliffs. Losing your footing in loose earth can be fatal, and erosion may cause cliff edges to drop away beneath your feet. Keep children from sitting on or climbing over railings.

Resources

Tourist information

California Association of Boutique & Breakfast Inns (www.cabbi.com): The state's only association of member B&Bs and boutique lodging.

Discover Los Angeles (www.discoverlosangeles.com): The official guide to the Los Angeles area, where you can learn about the city's neighborhoods, culture, attractions, restaurants, events, and nightlife.

San Diego (www.sandiego.org): The city's web-based travel guide, where local area information and special offers on area attractions and activities are provided, including trip planners.

Visit California (www.visitcalifornia.com): This California Tourism Industry-run site offers detailed information on Southern California travel offerings.

Visit Las Vegas (www.visitlasvegas.com): This site keeps track of the many casinos, shows, restaurants, and accommodations in tourist mecca Las Vegas.

Visit Palm Springs (www.visitpalmsprings.com): Get updated recommendations on how to bide your leisure time in the desert oasis.

Visit Pasadena (www.visitpasadena.com): Tourism authority for the historic town of Pasadena.

Visit Santa Barbara (www.santabarbaraca.com): Find info on Santa Barbara, including history, food and shopping guides, events, and lodging.

Newspapers and Magazines

Desert Sun (www.independent.com): Packed with information on visual arts, galleries, theater, food venues, and hotels.

LA Weekly (www.laweekly.com): Los Angeles's key alt-weekly news source and guide to local culture and events.

Las Vegas Weekly (www.lasvegasweekly.com): A weekly guide to food and culture in Las Vegas.

Los Angeles Times (www.latimes.com): A long-standing news publication with a fantastic Arts & Culture section.

San Diego CityBeat (www.sdcitybeat.com): A weekly guide to San Diego's eclectic mix of food, music, art, and culture.

San Diego Reader (www.sandiegoreader.com): This free alt-weekly magazine provides insights into local food, theater, and events.

San Diego Union-Tribune (www.utsandiego.com): This is the daily newspaper for the San Diego metro area.

Santa Barbara Independent (www.independent.com): Packed with information on visual arts, galleries, theater, food venues, and hotels.

Travel Guidebooks

Anderson, Ian. *Moon San Diego.* Avalon Travel, 2018. America's Finest City is rich with cultural heritage and military history, but mostly people visit for beaches, beer, and tacos.

Blough, Jenna. *Moon Death Valley National Park.* Avalon Travel, 2019. A deep dive into the geography and natural wonders of North America's lowest national park.

379

Blough, Jenna. *Moon Palm Springs & Joshua Tree.* Avalon Travel, 2019. A detailed exploration of two of Southern California's popular desert destinations.

Faulkner, Halli Jastaran. *Moon Los Angeles.* Avalon Travel, 2018. A focused look at greater Los Angeles, from beaches to cultural centers.

Stienstra, Tom. *Moon California Camping.* Avalon Travel, 2018. A thorough compendium on finding the right place to camp wherever you go in California.

Stienstra, Tom, and Ann Marie Brown. *Moon California Hiking.* Avalon Travel, 2016. The complete guide to 1,000 of the best hikes in the Golden State.

Thornton, Stuart. *Moon Santa Barbara & the Central Coast.* Avalon Travel, 2014. Agriculture, beach culture, wine country, and California history meet in California's Central Coast. A definitive guide.

History and Culture
Estrada, William D. *Los Angeles' Olvera Street.* Arcadia Publishing, 2006. A historical look at El Pueblo de la Reina de Los Angeles where the city was born in 1781—and its evolution.

Krim, Arthur. *Route 66: Iconography of the American Highway.* George F. Thompson Publishing, 2014. Comprehensive history of Route 66 and its cultural significance.

Rothman, Hal, and Char Miller. *Death Valley National Park: A History.* University of Nevada Press, 2013. A natural and cultural history of Death Valley and its development as a national park.

Scheffler Innis, Jack. *San Diego Legends: Events, People, and Places That Made History.* Sunbelt Publications, 2004. Everything you'd want to know about San Diego—a fantastic historical account of the rise of the seaside city, including stories about the infamous "nudist invasion" of the 1935 California-Pacific Exposition, the murder of the first mayor, and more.

Outdoor Recreation
California Department of Parks & Recreation (www.parks.ca.gov): Provides camping, off-highway-vehicle, and boating information, including fees and regulations.

National Park Service (www.nps.gov): Provides detailed information for all national parks on the West Coast, which includes fees, hours, trails, fishing regulations, and more.

Recreation.gov (www.recreation.gov): Provides national parks and forests campground information with options to reserve campsites.

Reserve California (www.reservecalifornia.com): Offers online reservations for California state parks and campgrounds.

Surfline (www.surfline.com): A fantastic website that provides current surfing conditions along the entire coast.

Trail Link (www.traillink.com): A national database of hiking and biking trails.

Spectator Sports

Anaheim Ducks (www.nhl.com/ducks): The official site for Anaheim's NHL pro hockey team.

Los Angeles Angels of Anaheim (www.mlb.com/angels): The official site for Anaheim's Major League Baseball team.

Los Angeles Chargers (www.chargers.com): The official website of the pro football team in greater Los Angeles.

Los Angeles Clippers (www.nba.com/clippers): The official website for Los Angeles's second NBA team.

Los Angeles Dodgers (www.mlb.com/dodgers): The official website of the six-time World Series Champion Major League Baseball team.

Los Angeles FC (www.lafc.com): The official website for the Major League Soccer team playing in Los Angeles.

Los Angeles Galaxy (www.lagalaxy.com): The official website for U.S. Major League Soccer's five-time champions.

Los Angeles Kings (www.nhl.com/kings): The official website for the NHL pro hockey team playing in Los Angeles.

Los Angeles Lakers (www.nba.com/lakers): The official website of the 16-time NBA champions.

Los Angeles Rams (www.therams.com): The official website of the NFL pro football team in Los Angeles.

Los Angeles Sparks (http://sparks.wnba.com): Official website of the professional women's basketball team representing Los Angeles in the WNBA.

San Diego Padres (www.mlb.com/padres): The official website for San Diego's Major League Baseball team offers schedules and tickets.

INDEX

LIST OF MAPS

PHOTO CREDITS

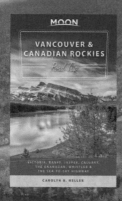

Road Trip USA

Covering more than 35,000 miles of blacktop stretching from east to west and north to south, *Road Trip USA* takes you deep into the heart of America.

This colorful guide covers the top road trips including historic Route 66 and is packed with maps, photos, illustrations, mile-by-mile highlights, and more!

MOON TRAVEL GUIDES TO EUROPE

MOON
AMALFI COAST
With Capri, Naples & Pompeii
LAURA THAYER

MOON
BARCELONA & MADRID
JESSICA JONES

MOON
CROATIA & SLOVENIA
SHANN FOUNTAIN ALIPOUR

MOON
EDINBURGH, GLASGOW & THE ISLE OF SKYE
SALLY COFFEY

MOON
FRENCH RIVIERA: NICE, CANNES, MONACO & ST-TROPEZ
JON BRYANT

MOON
ICELAND
JENNA GOTTLIEB

MOON
IRELAND
CAMILLE DeANGELIS

MOON
NORMANDY & BRITTANY
With Mont Saint-Michel
CHRIS NEWENS

MOON
NORWAY
DAVID NIKEL

MOON
PORTUGAL
CARRIE-MARIE BRATLEY

MOON
PRAGUE, VIENNA & BUDAPEST
JENNIFER D. WALKER
AUSTIN SCALLON

MOON
ROME, FLORENCE & VENICE
ALEXEI J. COHEN

GO BIG AND GO BEYOND...

These savvy city guides include strategies to help you see the top sights *and* find adventure beyond the tourist crowds.

...OR TAKE THINGS ONE STEP AT A TIME

MOON

TRIP OF A LIFETIME

ANGKOR WAT

MOON

TRIP OF A LIFETIME

GALÁPAGOS ISLANDS

MOON

JAPAN

JONATHAN DEHART

MOON

TRIP OF A LIFETIME

MACHU PICCHU

MOON

MOROCCO

MOON

NORWAY

MOON

TRIP OF A LIFETIME

PATAGONIA

WAYNE BERNHARDSON

MOON

ROME, FLORENCE & VENICE

ALEXEI J. COHEN

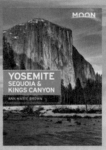

MOON

YOSEMITE SEQUOIA & KINGS CANYON

ANN MARIE BROWN

MOON

Drive & Hike

APPALACHIAN TRAIL

THE BEST TRAIL TOWNS, DAY HIKES, AND ROAD TRIPS IN BETWEEN

TIMOTHY MALCOLM

MOON

CAMINO DE SANTIAGO

SACRED SITES, HISTORIC VILLAGES, LOCAL FOOD & WINE

BEEBE BAHRAMI

MOON

USA NATIONAL PARKS

THE COMPLETE GUIDE TO ALL 59 PARKS

BECKY LOMAX

MOON.COM
@MOONGUIDES

MAP SYMBOLS

▬▬▬ Expressway	○ City/Town	✈ Airport	⚲ Golf Course
▬▬ Primary Road	◉ State Capital	✗ Airfield	🅿 Parking Area
▬▬ Secondary Road	⊛ National Capital	▲ Mountain	Archaeological Site
┄┄┄ Unpaved Road	★ Point of Interest	✛ Unique Natural Feature	⛪ Church
▬ Feature Trail	• Accommodation	🌴 Waterfall	Gas Station
- - - - Other Trail	▼ Restaurant/Bar	▲ Park	Glacier
⋯⋯⋯ Ferry	■ Other Location	🚩 Trailhead	Mangrove
▬▬ Pedestrian Walkway	△ Campground	⛷ Skiing Area	Reef
▭▭▭ Stairs			Swamp

CONVERSION TABLES

°C = (°F - 32) / 1.8
°F = (°C x 1.8) + 32
1 inch = 2.54 centimeters (cm)
1 foot = 0.304 meters (m)
1 yard = 0.914 meters
1 mile = 1.6093 kilometers (km)
1 km = 0.6214 miles
1 fathom = 1.8288 m
1 chain = 20.1168 m
1 furlong = 201.168 m
1 acre = 0.4047 hectares
1 sq km = 100 hectares
1 sq mile = 2.59 square km
1 ounce = 28.35 grams
1 pound = 0.4536 kilograms
1 short ton = 0.90718 metric ton
1 short ton = 2,000 pounds
1 long ton = 1.016 metric tons
1 long ton = 2,240 pounds
1 metric ton = 1,000 kilograms
1 quart = 0.94635 liters
1 US gallon = 3.7854 liters
1 Imperial gallon = 4.5459 liters
1 nautical mile = 1.852 km

°FAHRENHEIT	°CELSIUS	
230	110	
220		
210	100	WATER BOILS
200		
190	90	
180	80	
170		
160	70	
150		
140	60	
130		
120	50	
110		
100	40	
90	30	
80		
70	20	
60		
50	10	
40		
30	0	WATER FREEZES
20		
10	-10	
0		
-10	-20	
-20		
-30	-30	
-40	-40	

MOON SOUTHERN CALIFORNIA ROAD TRIPS

Avalon Travel
Hachette Book Group
1700 Fourth Street
Berkeley, CA 94710, USA
www.moon.com

Editor and Series Manager: Sabrina Young
Acquiring Editor: Nikki Ioakimedes
Copy Editor: Ashley Benning
Production and Graphics Coordinator: Ravina Schneider
Cover Design: Erin Seaward-Hiatt
Interior Design: Darren Alessi
Moon Logo: Tim McGrath
Map Editor: Kat Bennett
Cartographers: Albert Angulo, Lohnes + Wright, John Culp, Kat Bennett
Proofreader: Caroline Trefler
Indexer: Greg Jewett

ISBN-13: 978-1-64049-126-7

Printing History
1st Edition — January 2020
5 4 3 2 1

Front cover photo: San Diego © Created by MaryAnne Nelson / Getty Images

Printed in China by R. R. Donnelley